DELUXE EDITION

VITA AYALA | RAÚL ALLÉN | PATRICIA MARTÍN | KANO | TANA FORD

CONTENTS

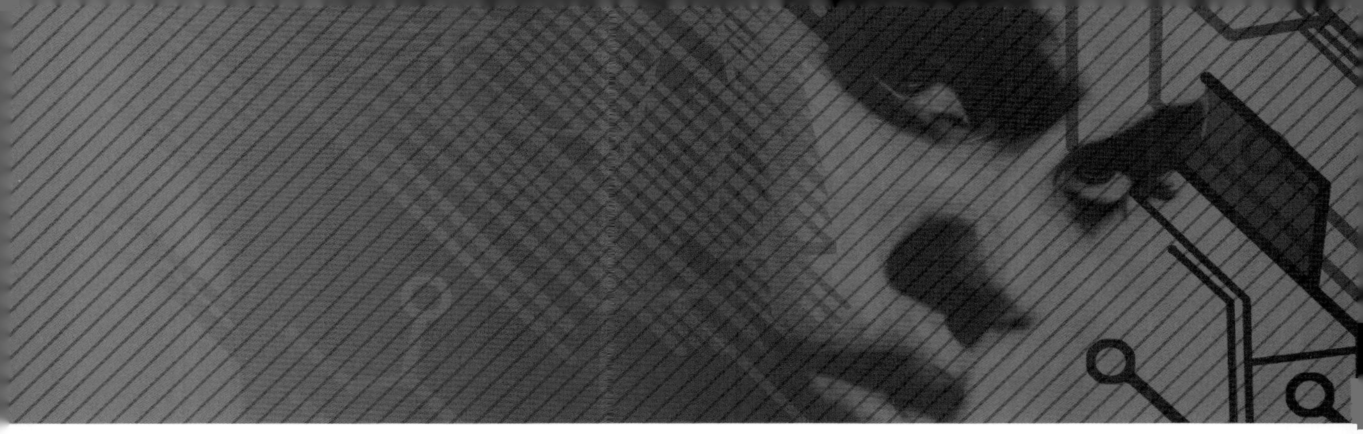

CHAMPION

LIVEWIRE #9-12

Writer: Vita Ayala
Artists: Tana Ford (#9-12) and Bruno Oliveira (#12)
Color Artists: Kelly Fitzpatrick (#9-12)
and Ruth Redmond (#12)
Letterer: Saida Temofonte
Cover Artist: Stacey Lee
Associate Editor: David Menchel
Editor: Heather Antos

GALLERY

Raúl Allén
Kris Anka
Vita Ayala
CAFU
Helen Chen
Katie Cook
Tana Ford
Megan Hutchison
Kano
Irene Koh
Lewis LaRosa
Stacey Lee
Patricia Martín
Harvey Tolibao
Koi Turnbull
Kevin Wada
Annie Wu

Collection Cover Art: Stacey Lee

Dan Mintz
Chairman

Fred Pierce
Publisher

Walter Black
VP Operations

Travis Escarfullery
Director of Design
& Production

Peter Stern
Director of International Publishing
& Merchandising

Lysa Hawkins
Heather Antos
David Wohl
Senior Editors

Jeff Walker
Production & Design Manager

John Petrie
Senior Manager
Sales & Merchandising

Danielle Ward
Sales Manager

Gregg Katzman
Marketing & Publicity Manager

Ivan Cohen
Collection Editor

Steve Blackwell
Collection Designer

Russ Brown
President, Consumer Products,
Promotions & Ad Sales

FUGITIVE

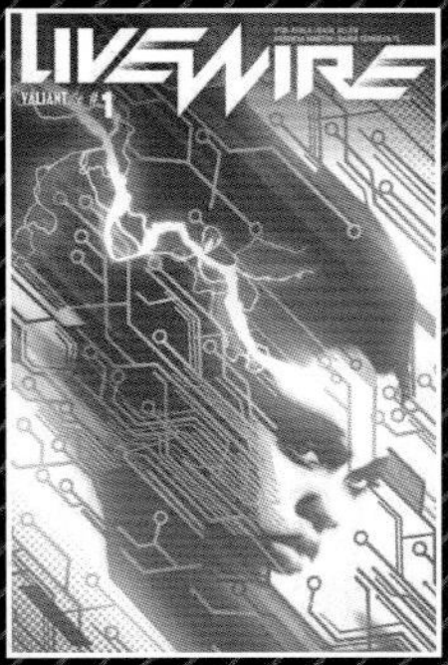
LIVEWIRE
VALIANT #1

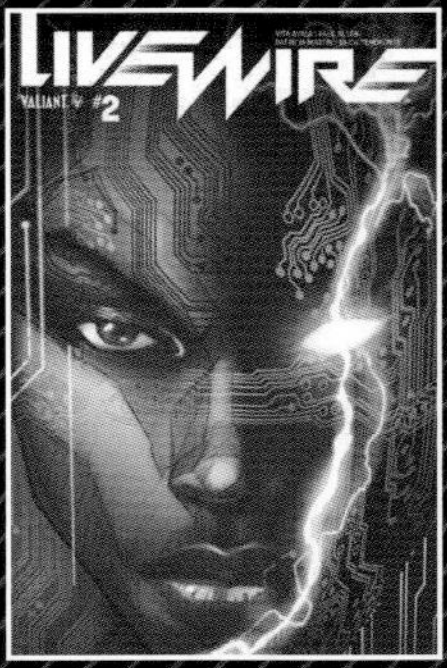
LIVEWIRE
VALIANT #2

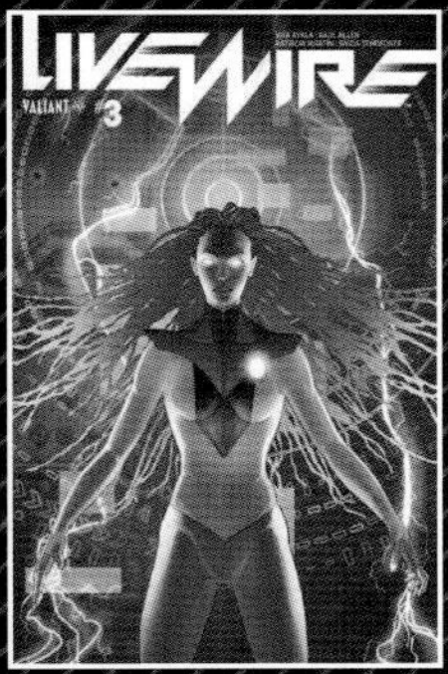
LIVEWIRE
VALIANT #3

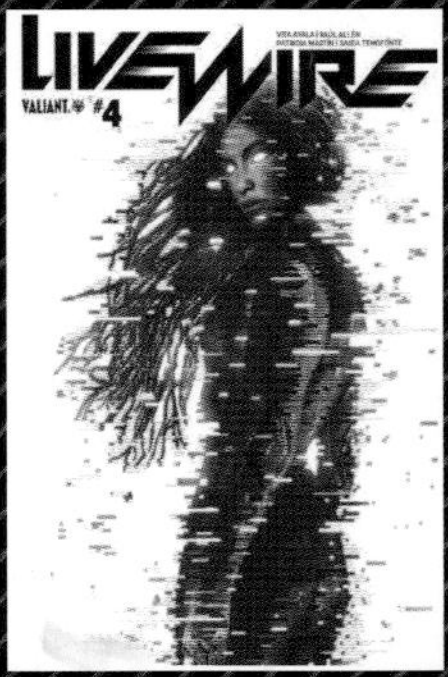
LIVEWIRE
VALIANT #4

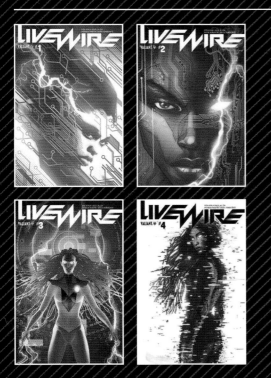

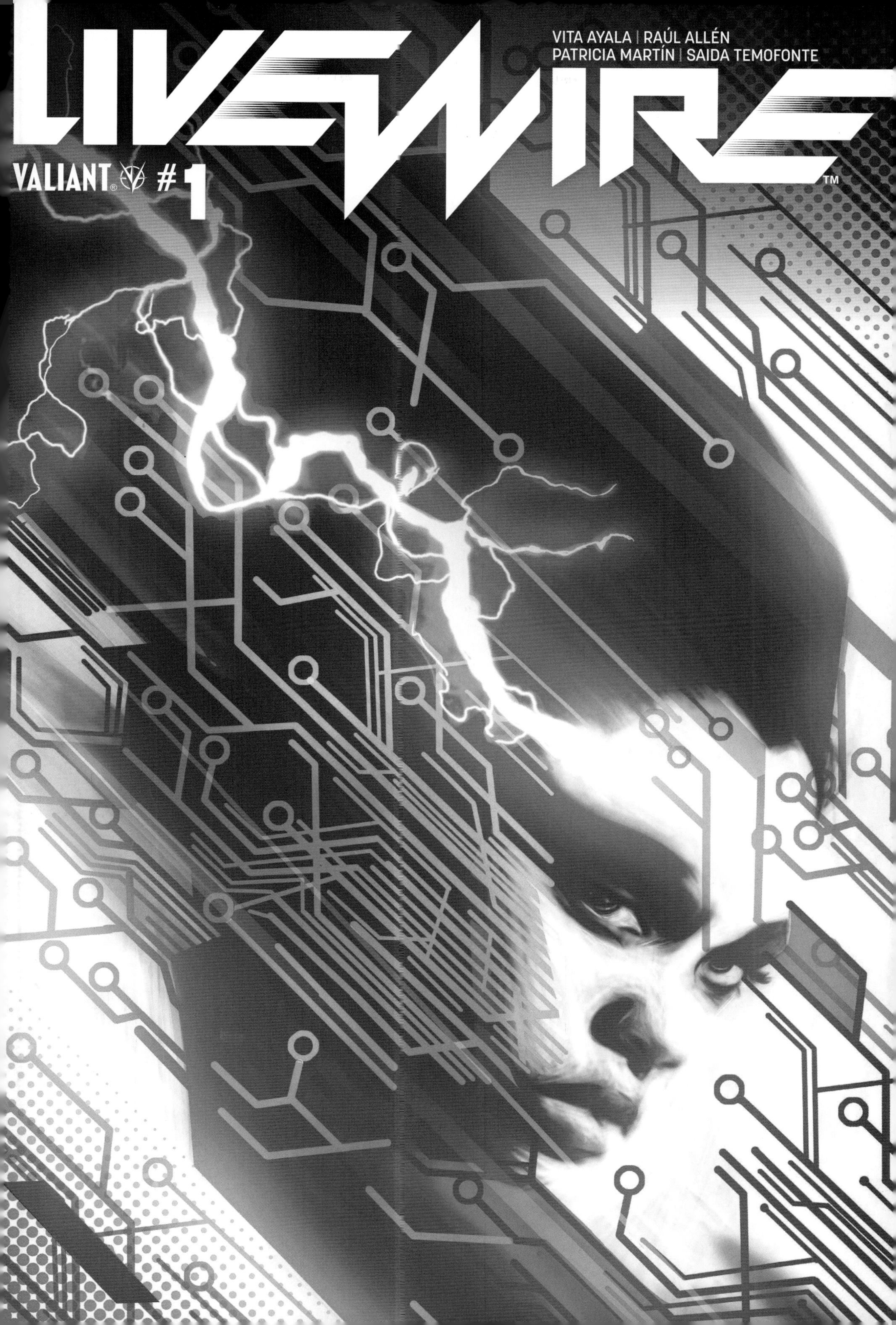
LIVEWIRE™
VITA AYALA | RAÚL ALLÉN
PATRICIA MARTÍN | SAIDA TEMOFONTE
VALIANT®
#1

LIVEWIRE ™

Guardian. Warrior. Fugitive.

Meet Amanda McKee, the superpowered psiot known as Livewire. With her incredible teletechnopathic abilities, Amanda has unrestricted access to the digital world that keeps our own afloat, able to control anything from a social media account to the satellites in the atmosphere. But Amanda was never interested in control, only helping those in need - a hero, until the United States Government betrayed her and her fellow psiots, forcing her to take extreme actions to ensure her own survival.

Now, Amanda is picking up the pieces, one digital fractal at a time...

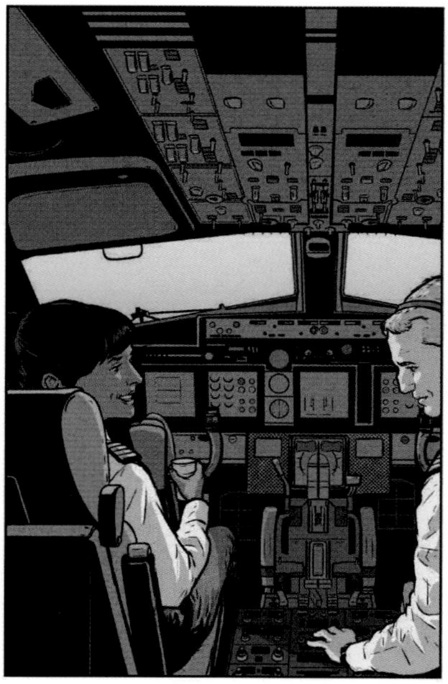
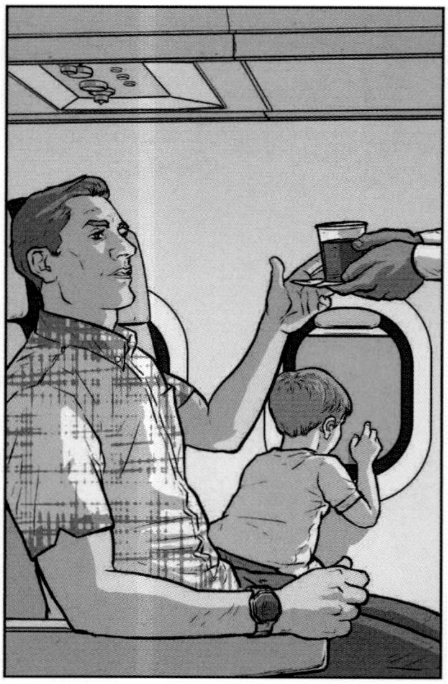
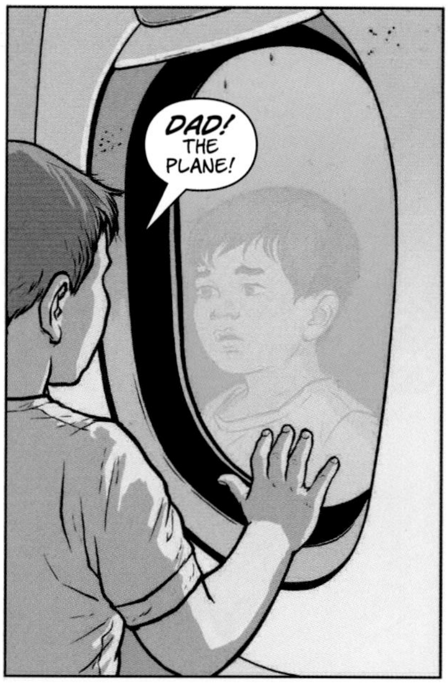
DAD! THE PLANE!
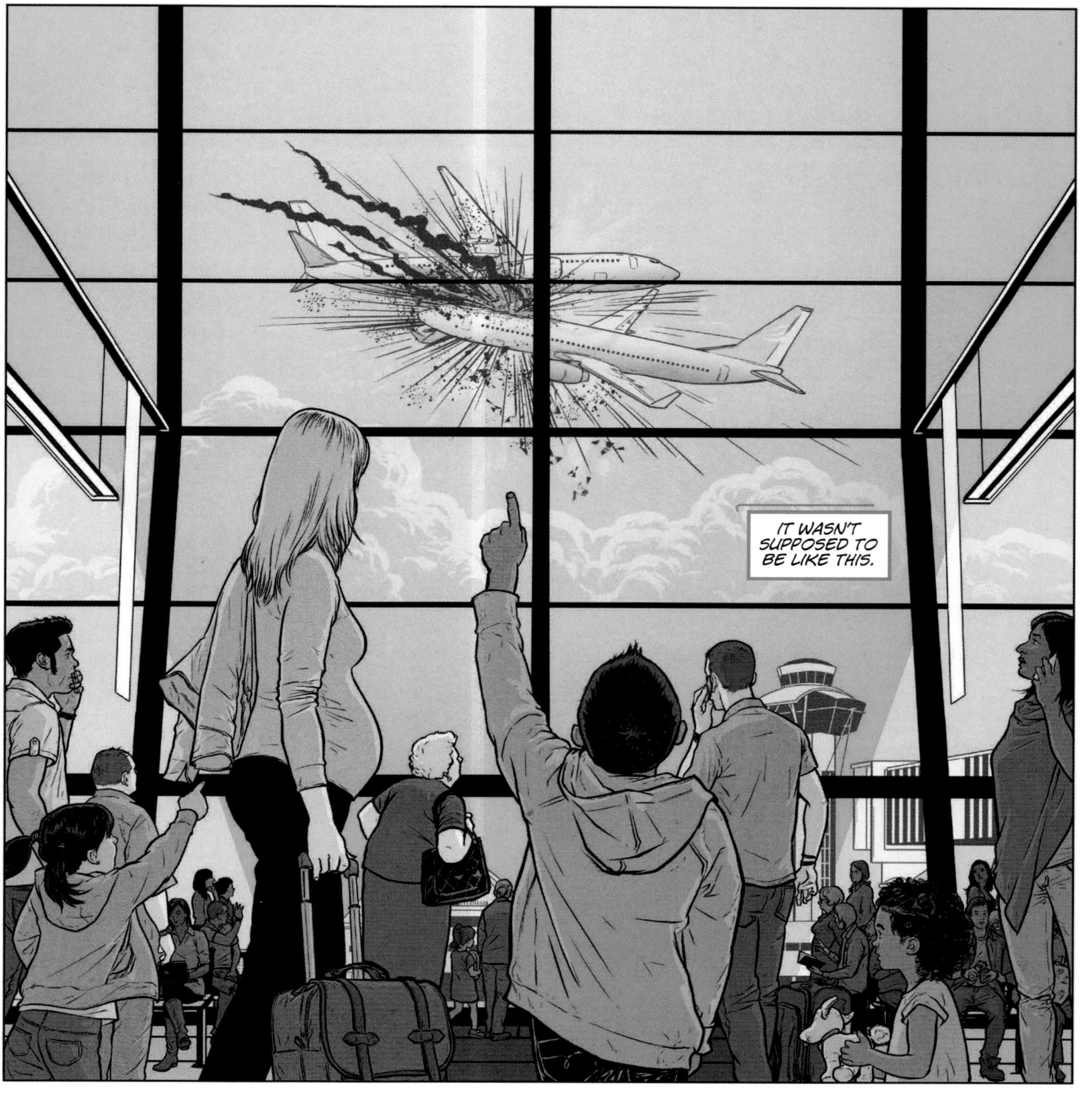
IT WASN'T SUPPOSED TO BE LIKE THIS.

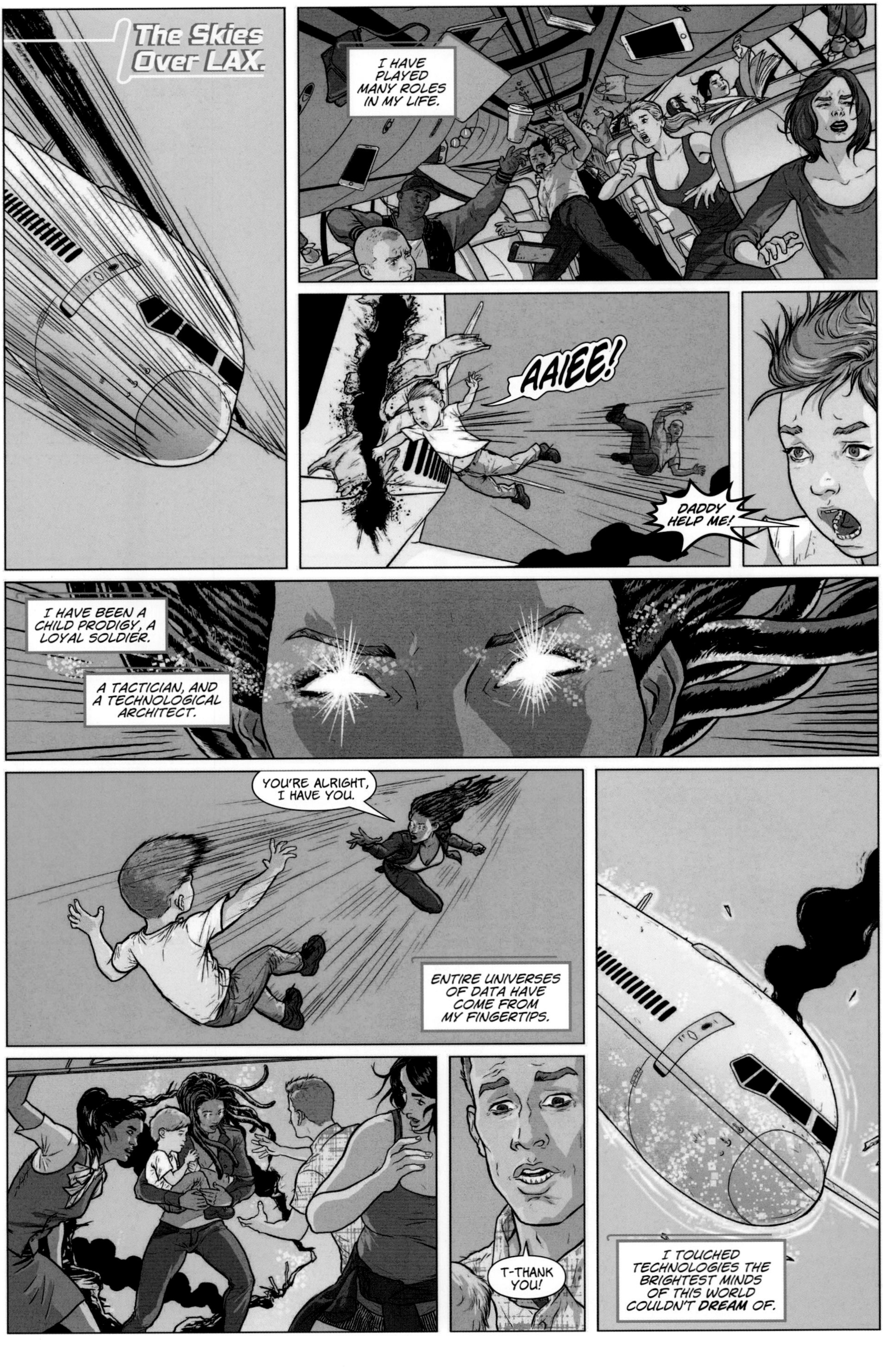
The Skies Over LAX.
I HAVE PLAYED MANY ROLES IN MY LIFE.
AAIEE!
DADDY HELP ME!
I HAVE BEEN A CHILD PRODIGY, A LOYAL SOLDIER.
A TACTICIAN, AND A TECHNOLOGICAL ARCHITECT.
YOU'RE ALRIGHT, I HAVE YOU.
ENTIRE UNIVERSES OF DATA HAVE COME FROM MY FINGERTIPS.
T-THANK YOU!
I TOUCHED TECHNOLOGIES THE BRIGHTEST MINDS OF THIS WORLD COULDN'T **DREAM** OF.

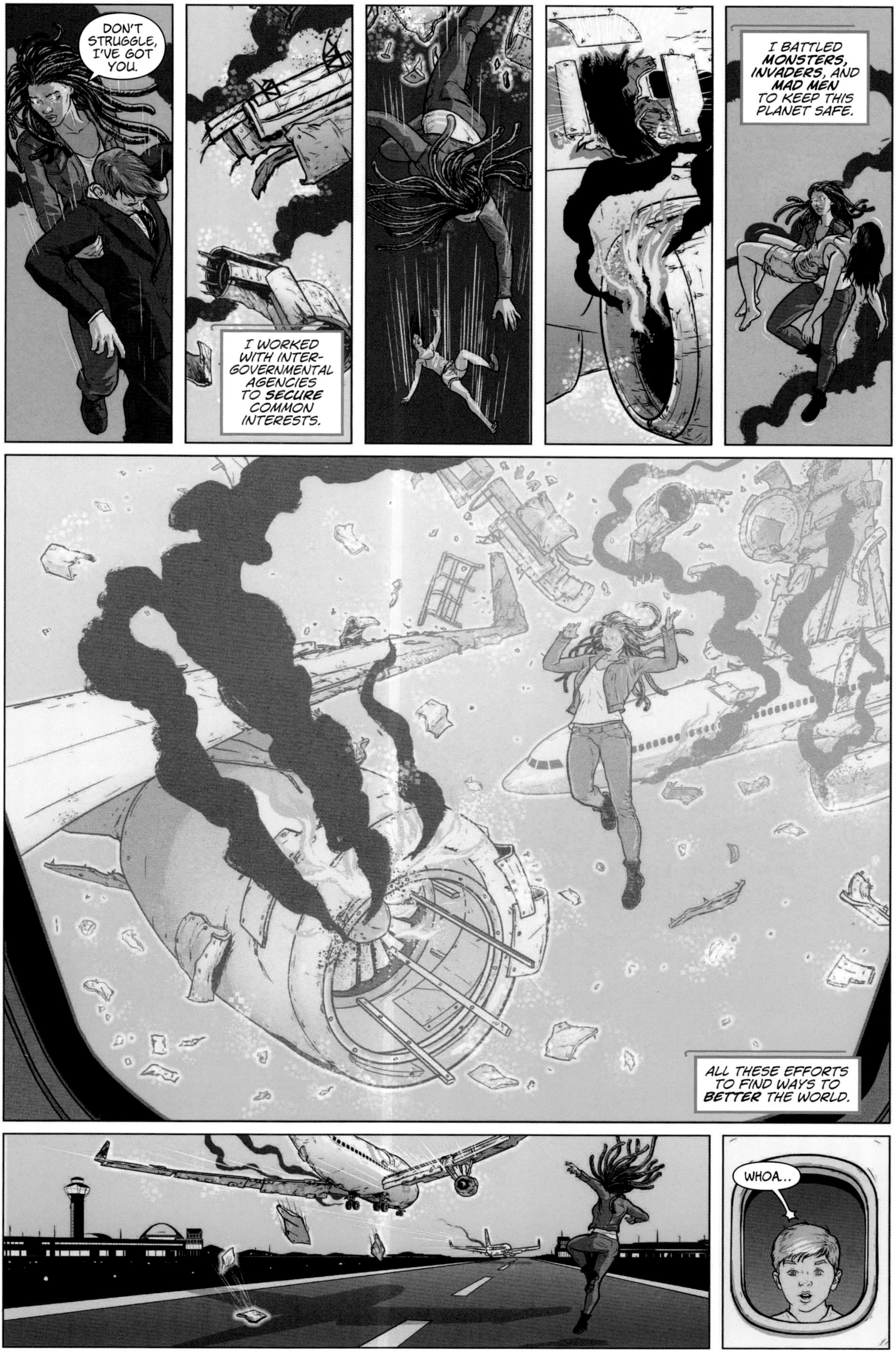
DON'T STRUGGLE, I'VE GOT YOU.
I WORKED WITH INTER-GOVERNMENTAL AGENCIES TO SECURE COMMON INTERESTS.
I BATTLED MONSTERS, INVADERS, AND MAD MEN TO KEEP THIS PLANET SAFE.
ALL THESE EFFORTS TO FIND WAYS TO BETTER THE WORLD.
WHOA...

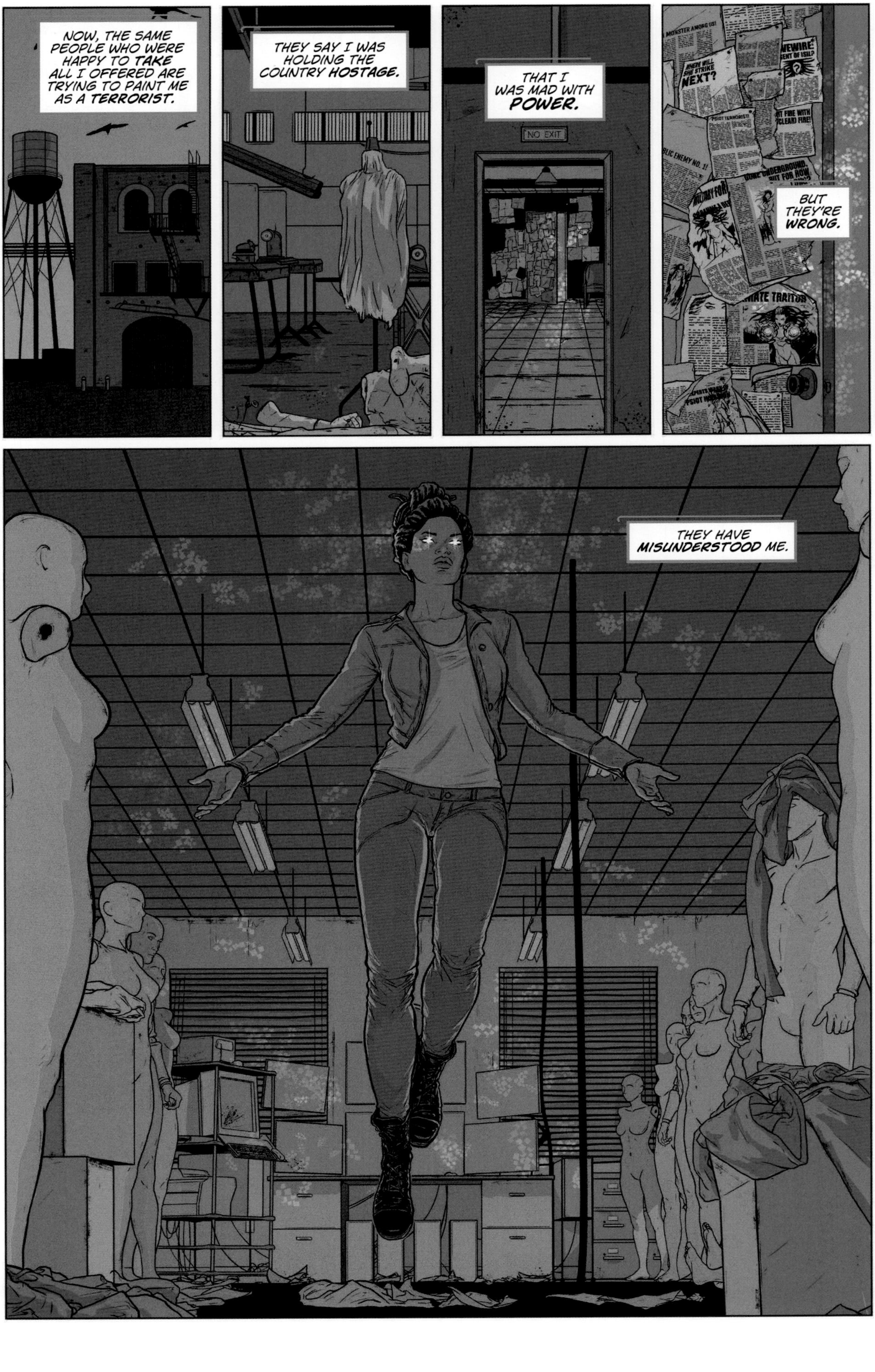
NOW, THE SAME PEOPLE WHO WERE HAPPY TO TAKE ALL I OFFERED ARE TRYING TO PAINT ME AS A TERRORIST.
THEY SAY I WAS HOLDING THE COUNTRY HOSTAGE.
THAT I WAS MAD WITH POWER.
NO EXIT
BUT THEY'RE WRONG.
THEY HAVE MISUNDERSTOOD ME.

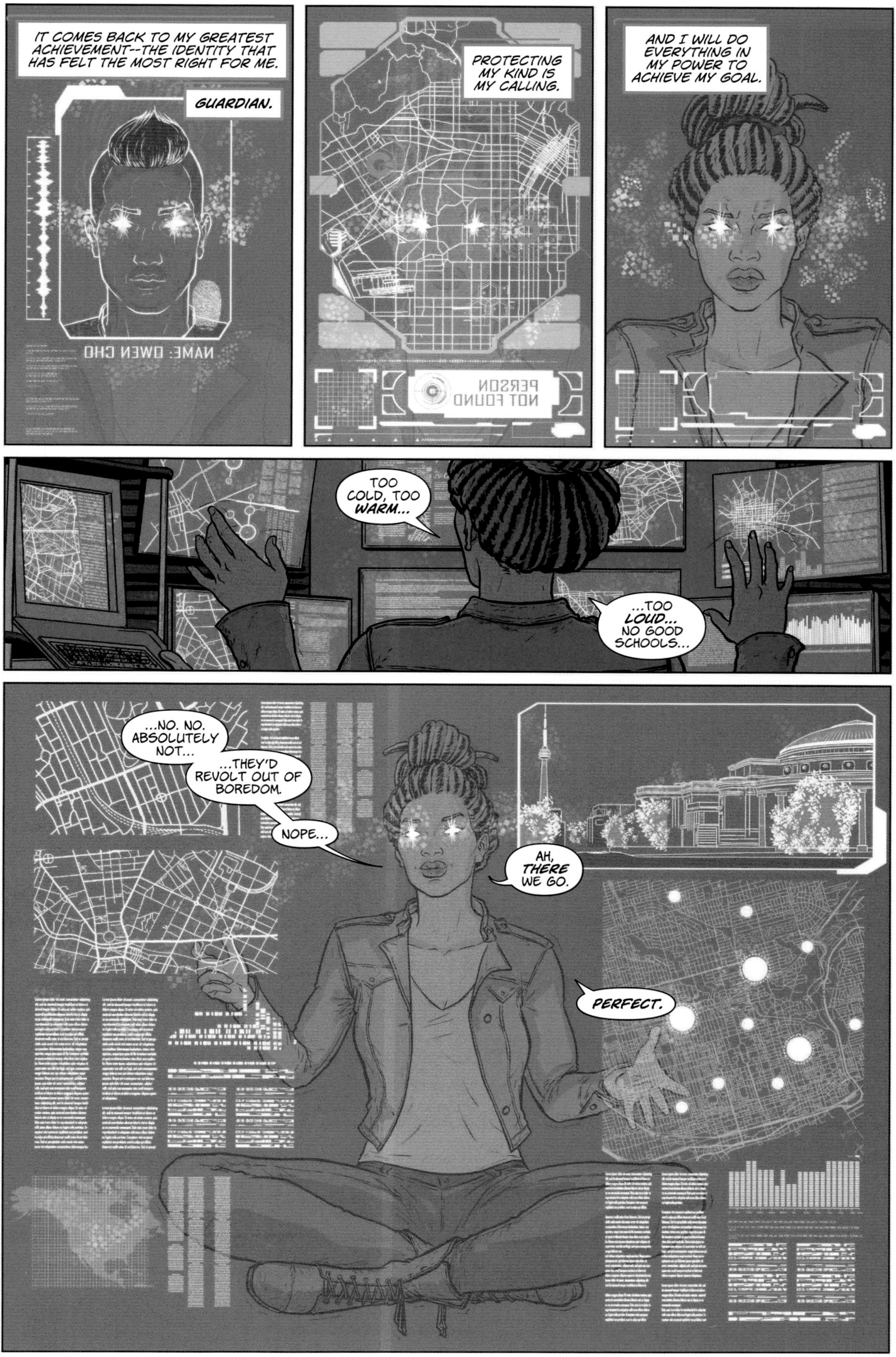
IT COMES BACK TO MY GREATEST ACHIEVEMENT--THE IDENTITY THAT HAS FELT THE MOST RIGHT FOR ME.
GUARDIAN.
NAME: OWEN CHO
PROTECTING MY KIND IS MY CALLING.
PERSON NOT FOUND
AND I WILL DO EVERYTHING IN MY POWER TO ACHIEVE MY GOAL.
TOO COLD, TOO WARM...
...TOO LOUD... NO GOOD SCHOOLS...
...NO. NO. ABSOLUTELY NOT...
...THEY'D REVOLT OUT OF BOREDOM.
NOPE...
AH, THERE WE GO.
PERFECT.

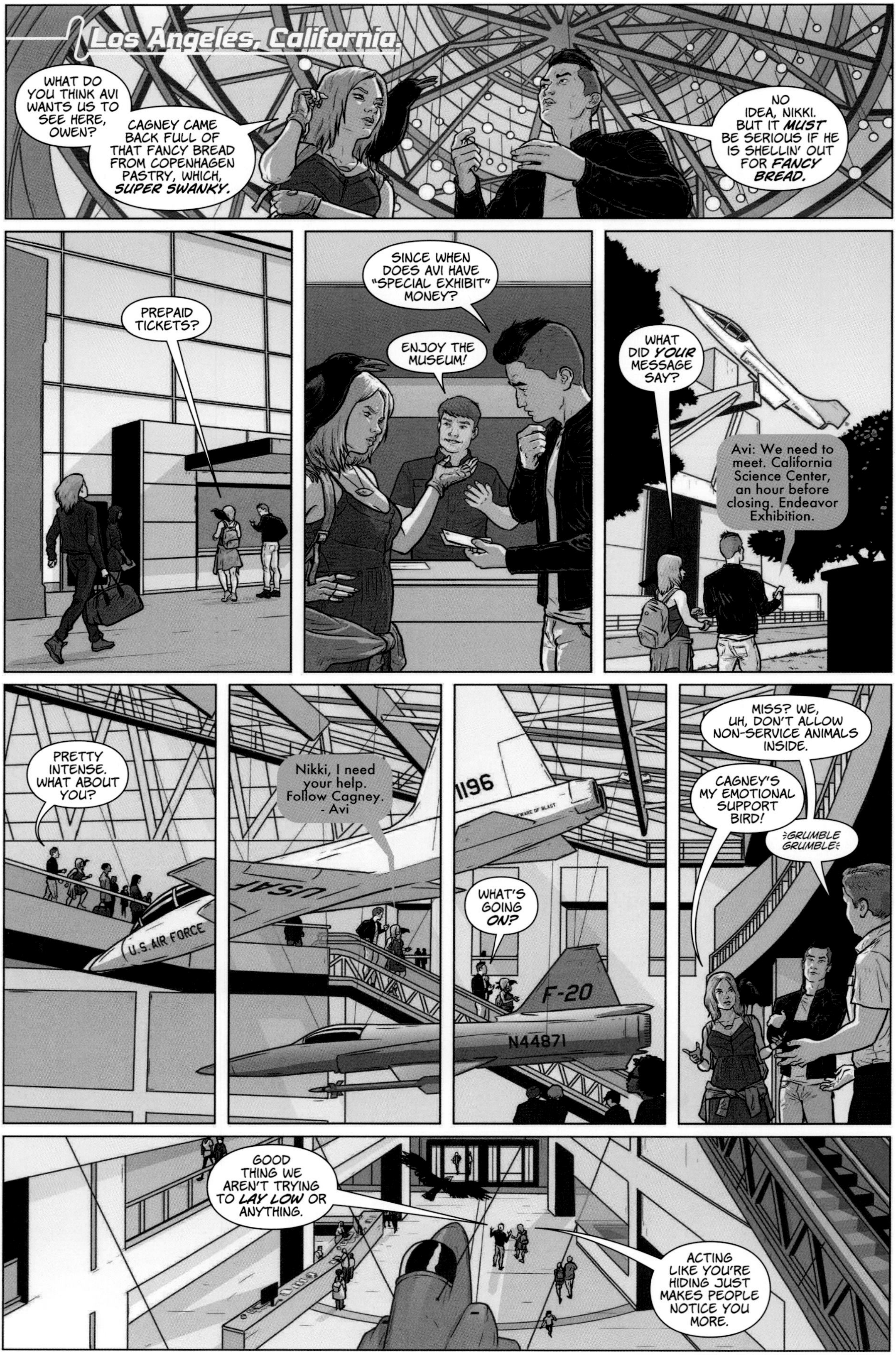
Los Angeles, California.
WHAT DO YOU THINK AVI WANTS US TO SEE HERE, OWEN?
CAGNEY CAME BACK FULL OF THAT FANCY BREAD FROM COPENHAGEN PASTRY, WHICH, SUPER SWANKY.
NO IDEA, NIKKI. BUT IT MUST BE SERIOUS IF HE IS SHELLIN' OUT FOR FANCY BREAD.
PREPAID TICKETS?
SINCE WHEN DOES AVI HAVE "SPECIAL EXHIBIT" MONEY?
ENJOY THE MUSEUM!
WHAT DID YOUR MESSAGE SAY?
Avi: We need to meet. California Science Center, an hour before closing. Endeavor Exhibition.
PRETTY INTENSE. WHAT ABOUT YOU?
U.S. AIR FORCE
USAF
Nikki, I need your help. Follow Cagney. - Avi
1196
WHAT'S GOING ON?
F-20
N44871
MISS? WE, UH, DON'T ALLOW NON-SERVICE ANIMALS INSIDE.
CAGNEY'S MY EMOTIONAL SUPPORT BIRD!
GRUMBLE GRUMBLE
GOOD THING WE AREN'T TRYING TO LAY LOW OR ANYTHING.
ACTING LIKE YOU'RE HIDING JUST MAKES PEOPLE NOTICE YOU MORE.

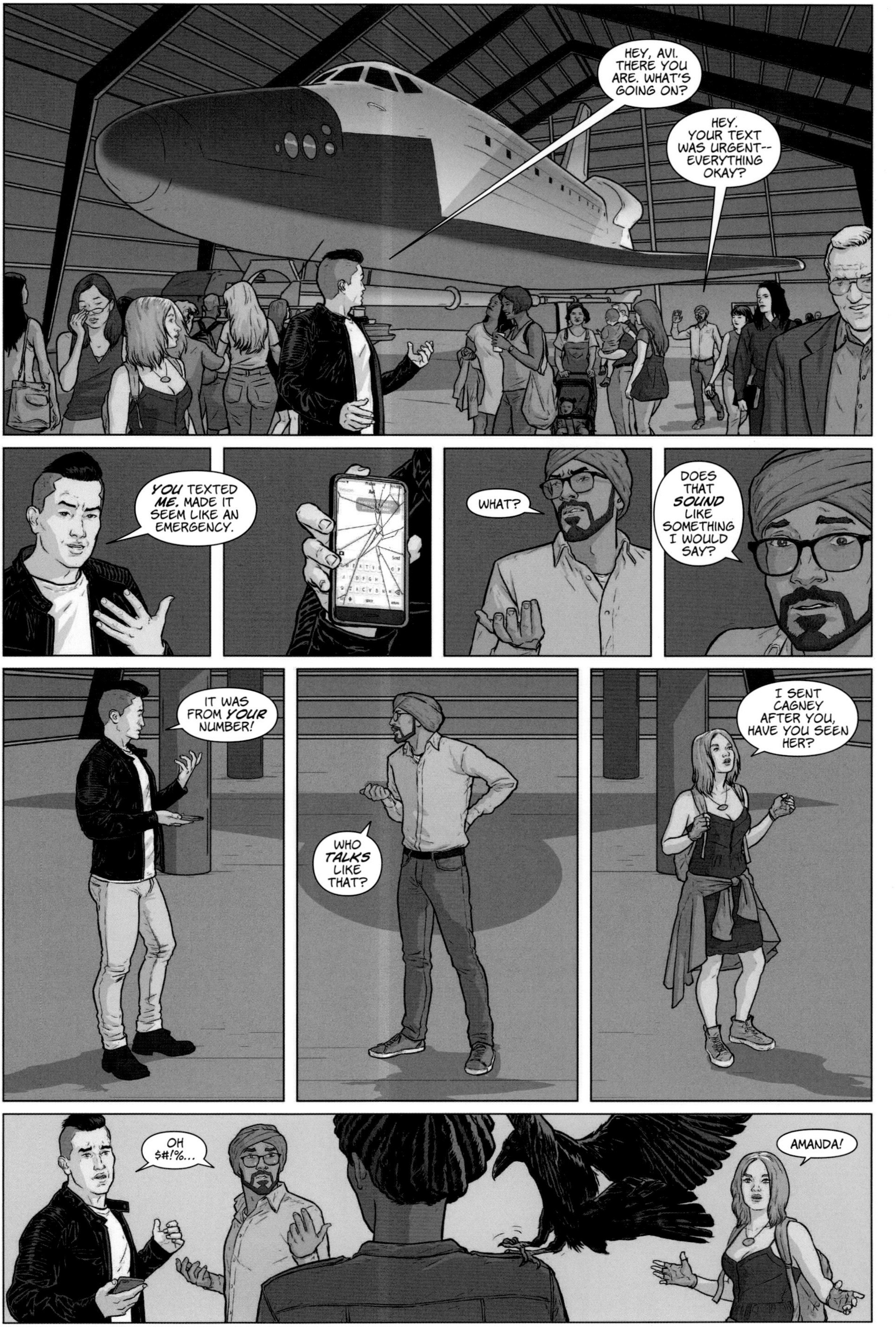
HEY, AVI. THERE YOU ARE. WHAT'S GOING ON?
HEY. YOUR TEXT WAS URGENT-- EVERYTHING OKAY?
YOU TEXTED ME. MADE IT SEEM LIKE AN EMERGENCY.
WHAT?
DOES THAT SOUND LIKE SOMETHING I WOULD SAY?
IT WAS FROM YOUR NUMBER!
WHO TALKS LIKE THAT?
I SENT CAGNEY AFTER YOU, HAVE YOU SEEN HER?
OH $#!%...
AMANDA!

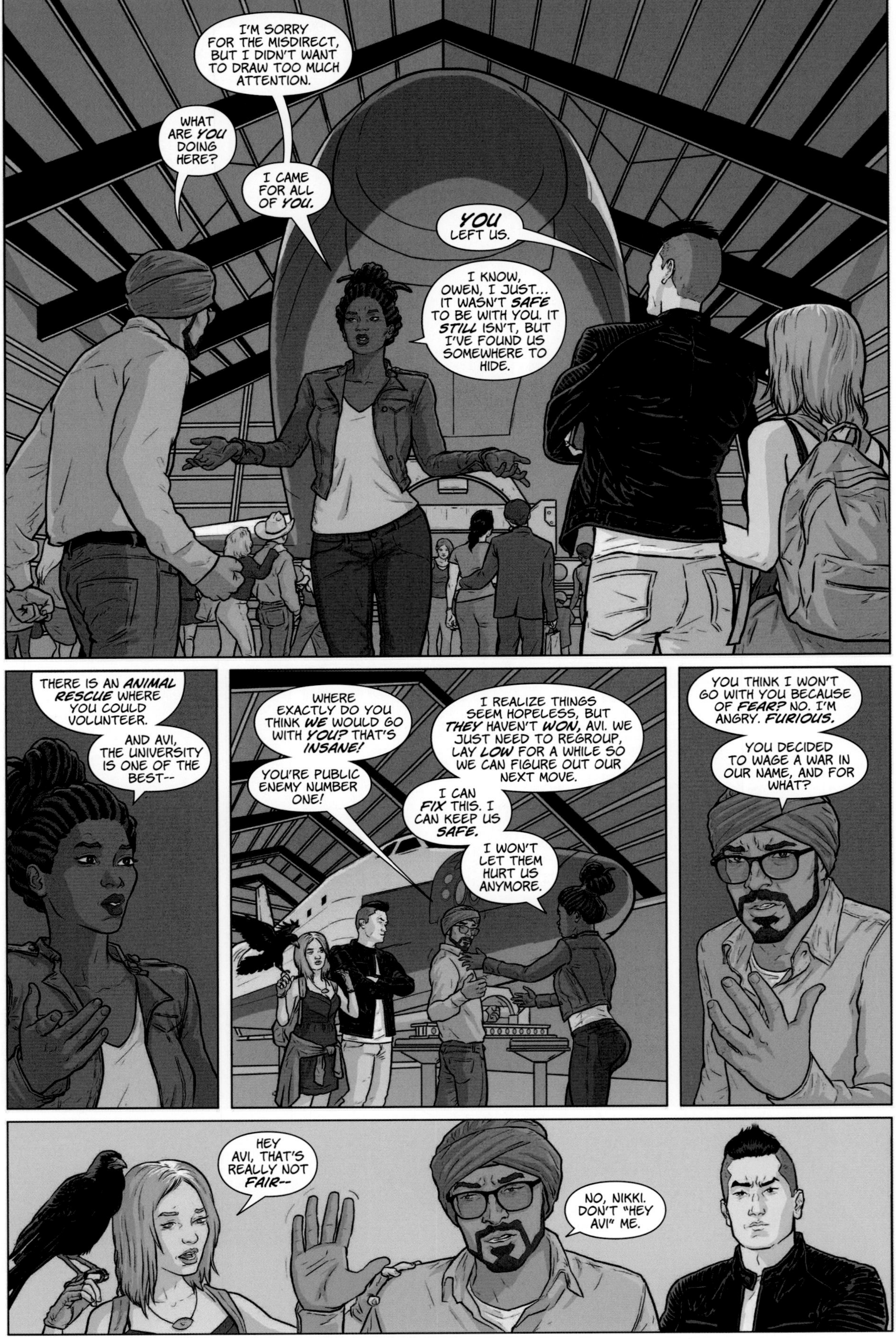
I'M SORRY FOR THE MISDIRECT, BUT I DIDN'T WANT TO DRAW TOO MUCH ATTENTION.
WHAT ARE YOU DOING HERE?
I CAME FOR ALL OF YOU.
YOU LEFT US.
I KNOW, OWEN, I JUST... IT WASN'T SAFE TO BE WITH YOU. IT STILL ISN'T, BUT I'VE FOUND US SOMEWHERE TO HIDE.
THERE IS AN ANIMAL RESCUE WHERE YOU COULD VOLUNTEER.
AND AVI, THE UNIVERSITY IS ONE OF THE BEST--
WHERE EXACTLY DO YOU THINK WE WOULD GO WITH YOU? THAT'S INSANE!
YOU'RE PUBLIC ENEMY NUMBER ONE!
I REALIZE THINGS SEEM HOPELESS, BUT THEY HAVEN'T WON, AVI. WE JUST NEED TO REGROUP, LAY LOW FOR A WHILE SO WE CAN FIGURE OUT OUR NEXT MOVE.
I CAN FIX THIS. I CAN KEEP US SAFE.
I WON'T LET THEM HURT US ANYMORE.
YOU THINK I WON'T GO WITH YOU BECAUSE OF FEAR? NO. I'M ANGRY. FURIOUS.
YOU DECIDED TO WAGE A WAR IN OUR NAME, AND FOR WHAT?
HEY AVI, THAT'S REALLY NOT FAIR--
NO, NIKKI. DON'T "HEY AVI" ME.

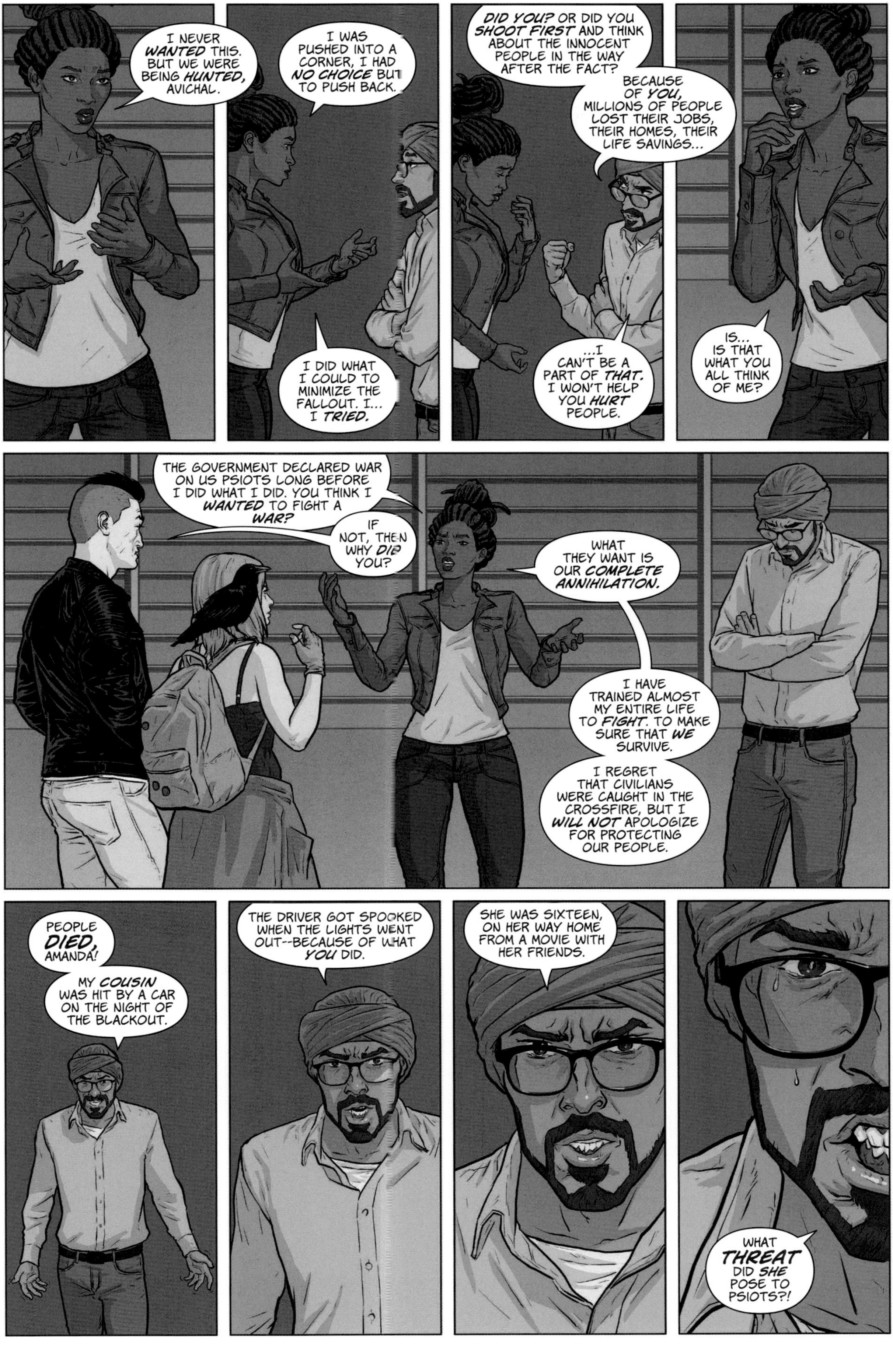
I NEVER WANTED THIS. BUT WE WERE BEING HUNTED, AVICHAL.
I WAS PUSHED INTO A CORNER, I HAD NO CHOICE BUT TO PUSH BACK.
I DID WHAT I COULD TO MINIMIZE THE FALLOUT. I... I TRIED.
DID YOU? OR DID YOU SHOOT FIRST AND THINK ABOUT THE INNOCENT PEOPLE IN THE WAY AFTER THE FACT?
BECAUSE OF YOU, MILLIONS OF PEOPLE LOST THEIR JOBS, THEIR HOMES, THEIR LIFE SAVINGS...
...I CAN'T BE A PART OF THAT. I WON'T HELP YOU HURT PEOPLE.
IS... IS THAT WHAT YOU ALL THINK OF ME?
THE GOVERNMENT DECLARED WAR ON US PSIOTS LONG BEFORE I DID WHAT I DID. YOU THINK I WANTED TO FIGHT A WAR?
IF NOT, THEN WHY DID YOU?
WHAT THEY WANT IS OUR COMPLETE ANNIHILATION.
I HAVE TRAINED ALMOST MY ENTIRE LIFE TO FIGHT. TO MAKE SURE THAT WE SURVIVE.
I REGRET THAT CIVILIANS WERE CAUGHT IN THE CROSSFIRE, BUT I WILL NOT APOLOGIZE FOR PROTECTING OUR PEOPLE.
PEOPLE DIED, AMANDA!
MY COUSIN WAS HIT BY A CAR ON THE NIGHT OF THE BLACKOUT.
THE DRIVER GOT SPOOKED WHEN THE LIGHTS WENT OUT--BECAUSE OF WHAT YOU DID.
SHE WAS SIXTEEN, ON HER WAY HOME FROM A MOVIE WITH HER FRIENDS.
WHAT THREAT DID SHE POSE TO PSIOTS?!

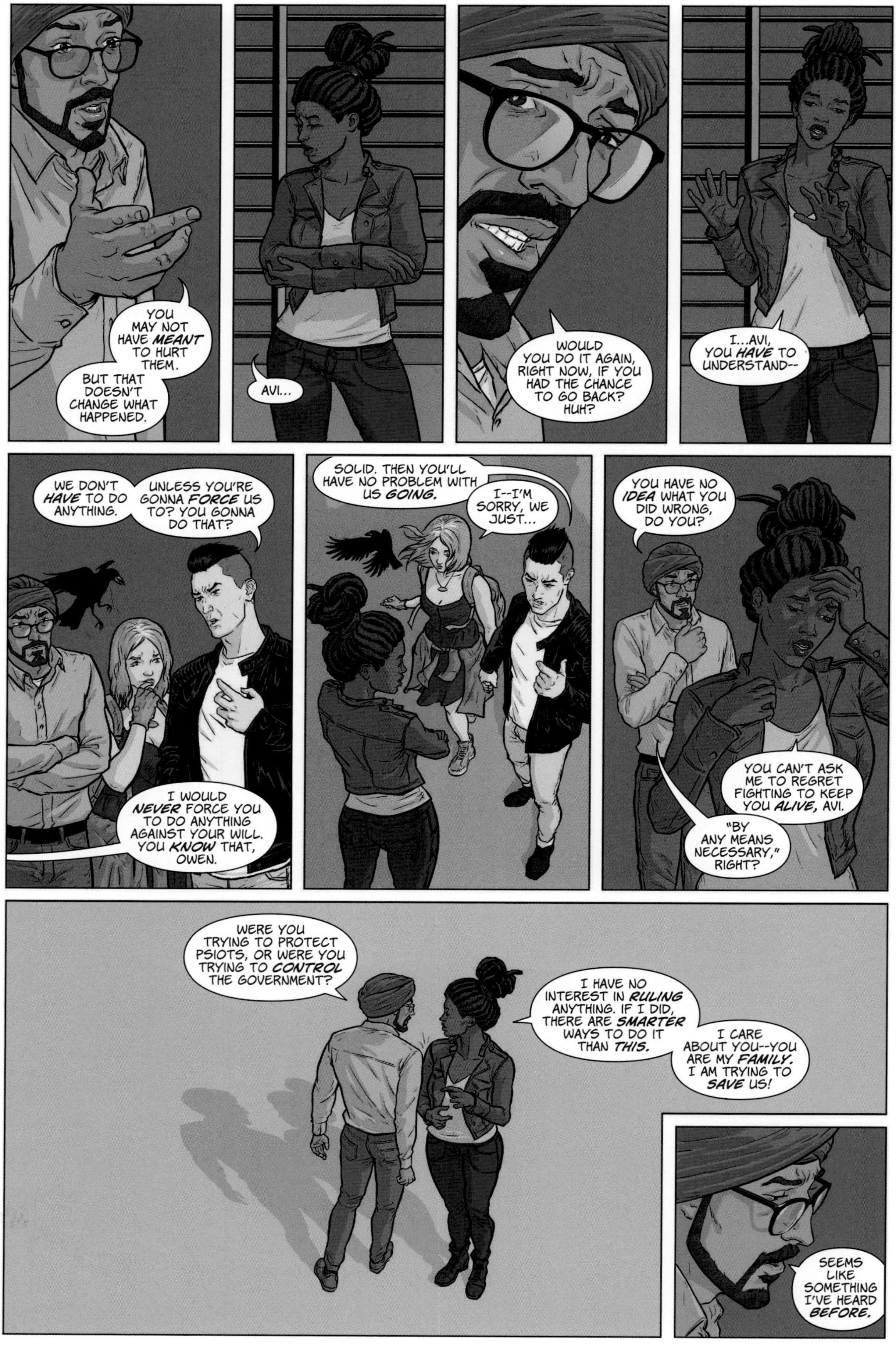
YOU MAY NOT HAVE MEANT TO HURT THEM.
BUT THAT DOESN'T CHANGE WHAT HAPPENED.
AVI...
WOULD YOU DO IT AGAIN, RIGHT NOW, IF YOU HAD THE CHANCE TO GO BACK? HUH?
I...AVI, YOU HAVE TO UNDERSTAND--
WE DON'T HAVE TO DO ANYTHING.
UNLESS YOU'RE GONNA FORCE US TO? YOU GONNA DO THAT?
I WOULD NEVER FORCE YOU TO DO ANYTHING AGAINST YOUR WILL. YOU KNOW THAT, OWEN.
SOLID. THEN YOU'LL HAVE NO PROBLEM WITH US GOING.
I--I'M SORRY, WE JUST...
YOU HAVE NO IDEA WHAT YOU DID WRONG, DO YOU?
YOU CAN'T ASK ME TO REGRET FIGHTING TO KEEP YOU ALIVE, AVI.
"BY ANY MEANS NECESSARY," RIGHT?
WERE YOU TRYING TO PROTECT PSIOTS, OR WERE YOU TRYING TO CONTROL THE GOVERNMENT?
I HAVE NO INTEREST IN RULING ANYTHING. IF I DID, THERE ARE SMARTER WAYS TO DO IT THAN THIS.
I CARE ABOUT YOU--YOU ARE MY FAMILY. I AM TRYING TO SAVE US!
SEEMS LIKE SOMETHING I'VE HEARD BEFORE.

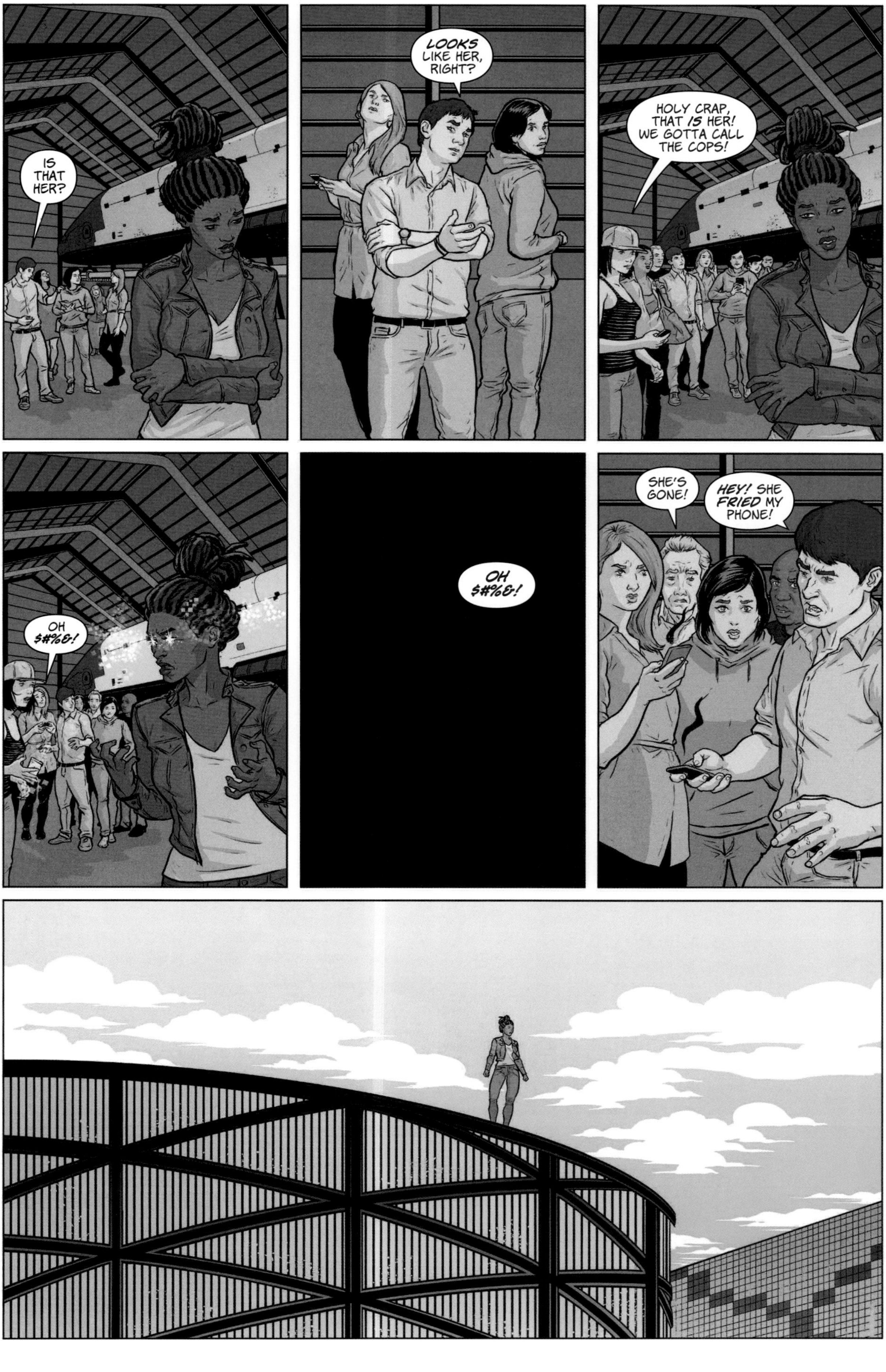
IS THAT HER?
LOOKS LIKE HER, RIGHT?
HOLY CRAP, THAT IS HER! WE GOTTA CALL THE COPS!
OH $#%&!
OH $#%&!
SHE'S GONE!
HEY! SHE FRIED MY PHONE!

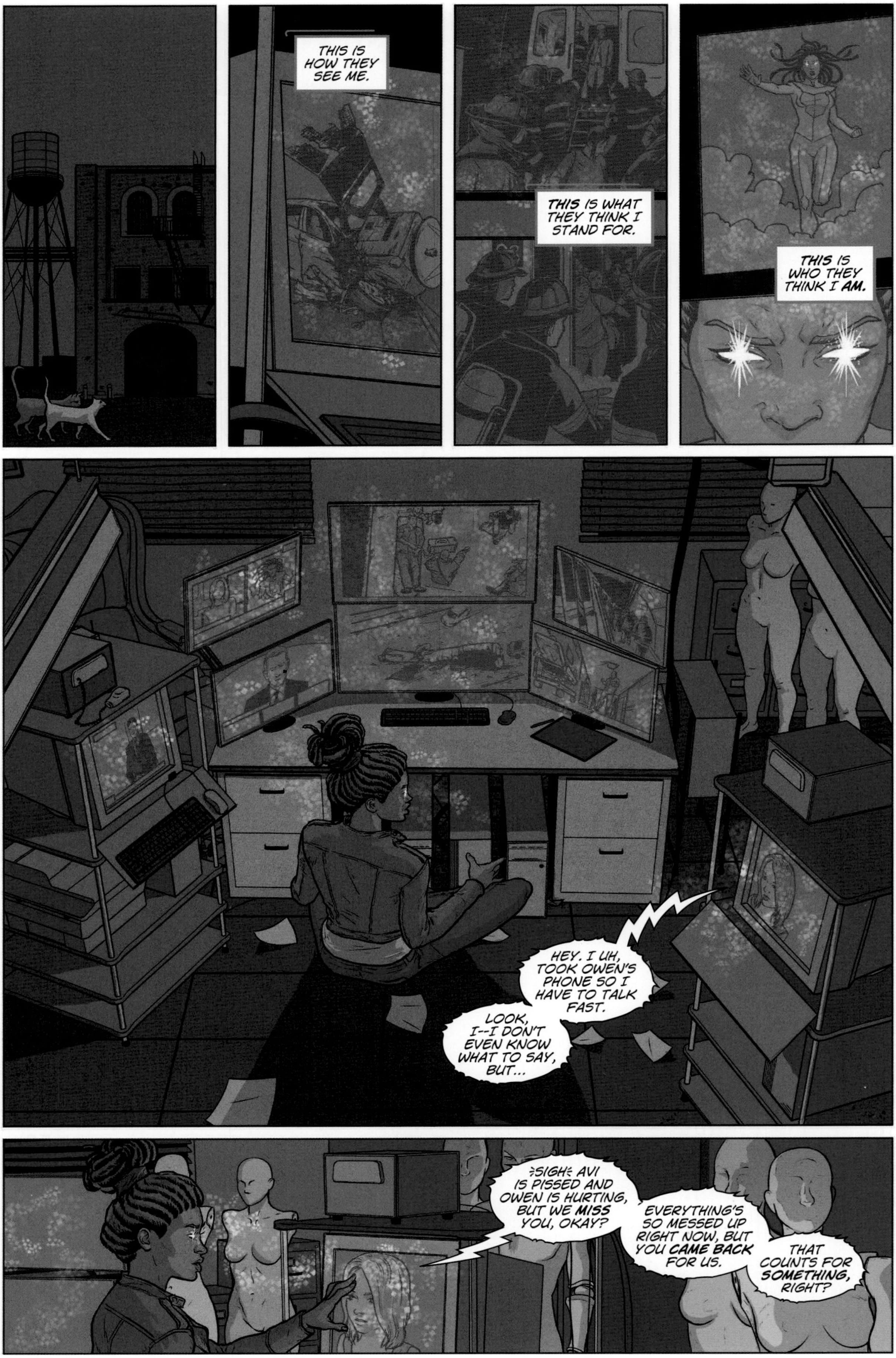
THIS IS HOW THEY SEE ME.
THIS IS WHAT THEY THINK I STAND FOR.
THIS IS WHO THEY THINK I AM.
HEY. I UH, TOOK OWEN'S PHONE SO I HAVE TO TALK FAST.
LOOK, I--I DON'T EVEN KNOW WHAT TO SAY, BUT...
⁼SIGH⁼ AVI IS PISSED AND OWEN IS HURTING, BUT WE MISS YOU, OKAY?
EVERYTHING'S SO MESSED UP RIGHT NOW, BUT YOU CAME BACK FOR US.
THAT COUNTS FOR SOMETHING, RIGHT?

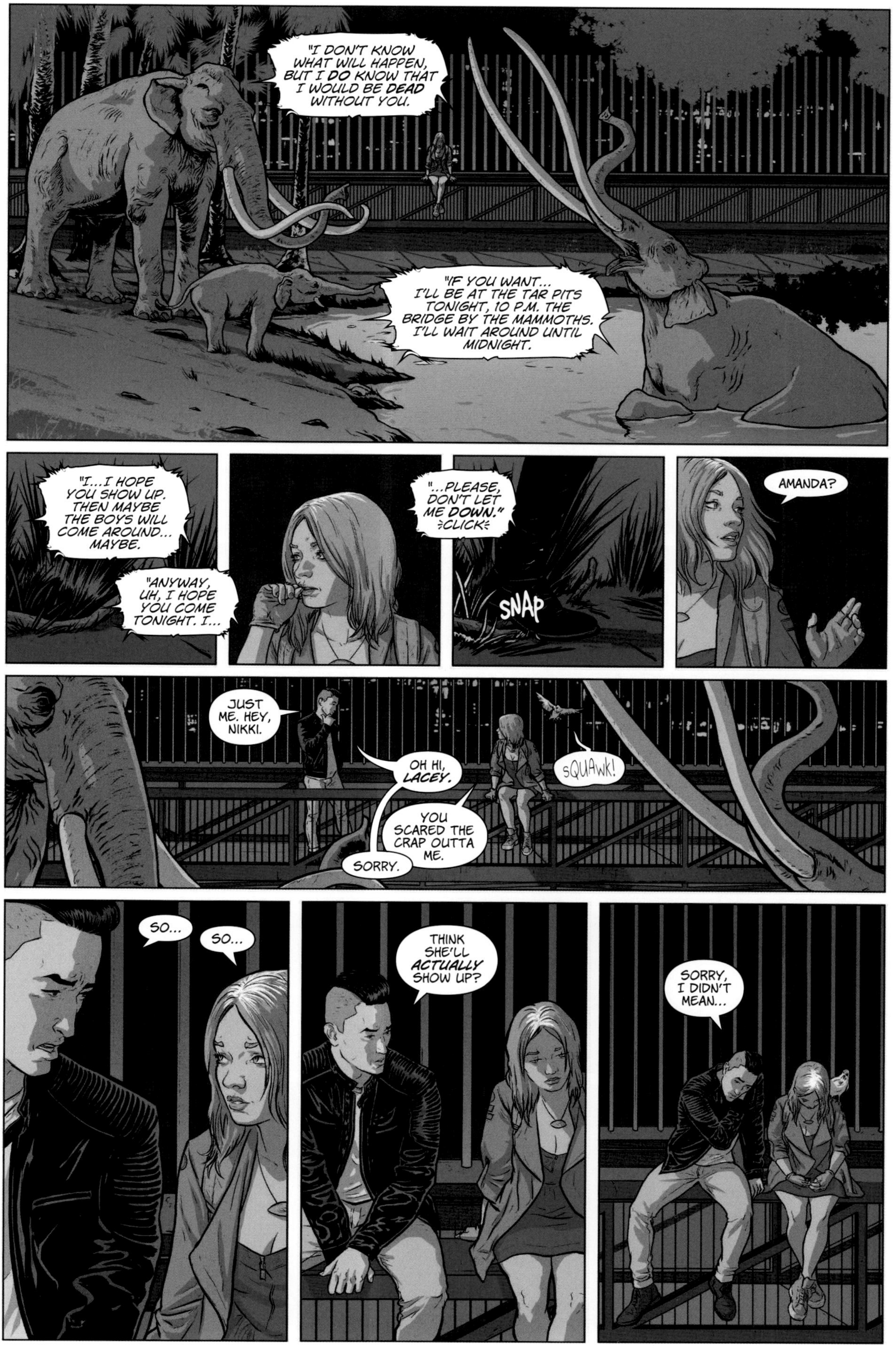
"I DON'T KNOW WHAT WILL HAPPEN, BUT I DO KNOW THAT I WOULD BE DEAD WITHOUT YOU.
"IF YOU WANT... I'LL BE AT THE TAR PITS TONIGHT, 10 P.M. THE BRIDGE BY THE MAMMOTHS. I'LL WAIT AROUND UNTIL MIDNIGHT.
"I...I HOPE YOU SHOW UP. THEN MAYBE THE BOYS WILL COME AROUND... MAYBE.
"ANYWAY, UH, I HOPE YOU COME TONIGHT. I...
"...PLEASE, DON'T LET ME DOWN." CLICK
SNAP
AMANDA?
JUST ME. HEY, NIKKI.
OH HI, LACEY.
YOU SCARED THE CRAP OUTTA ME.
SORRY.
SQUAWK!
SO...
SO...
THINK SHE'LL ACTUALLY SHOW UP?
SORRY, I DIDN'T MEAN...

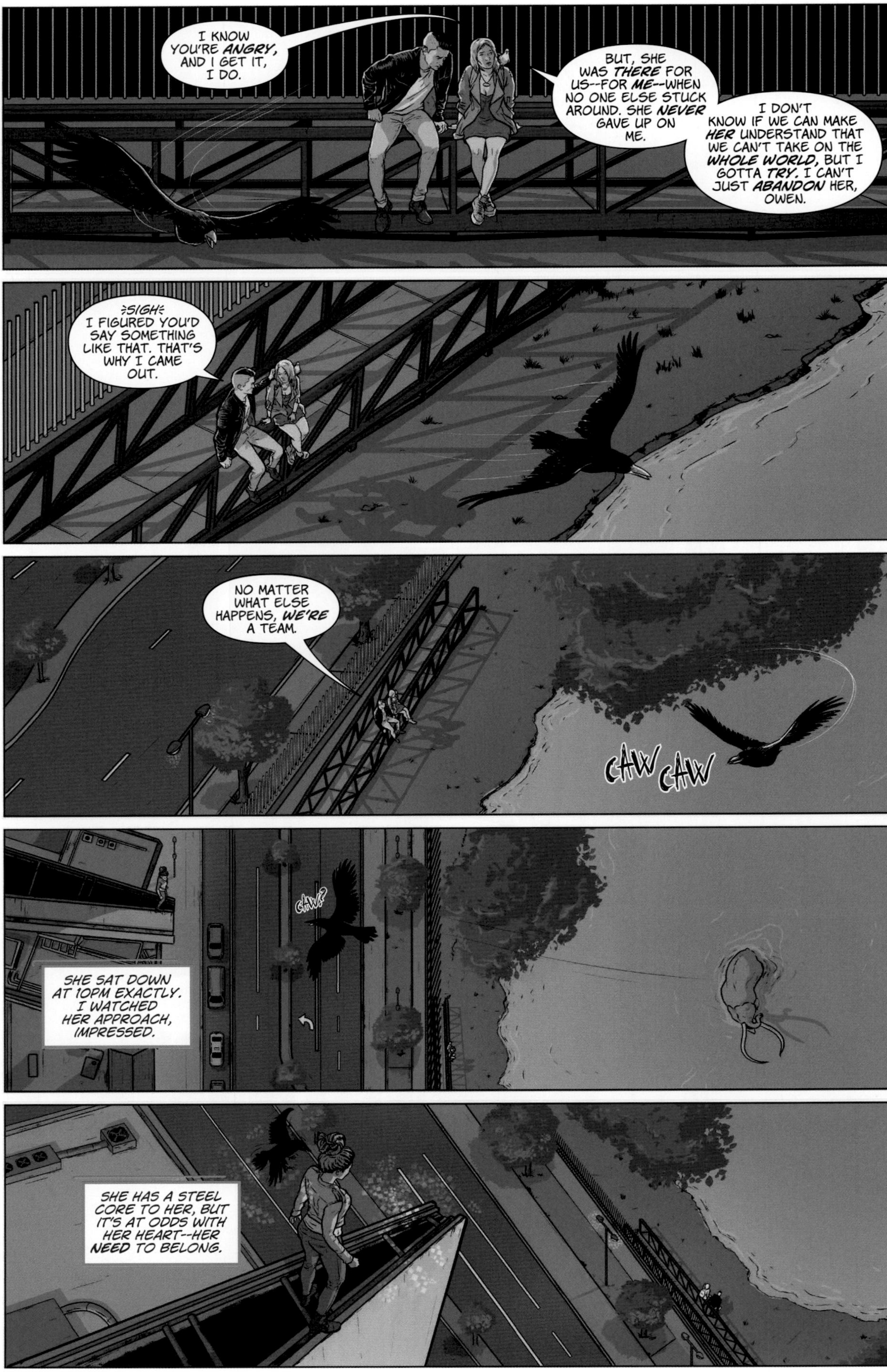
I KNOW YOU'RE ANGRY, AND I GET IT, I DO.
BUT, SHE WAS THERE FOR US--FOR ME--WHEN NO ONE ELSE STUCK AROUND. SHE NEVER GAVE UP ON ME.
I DON'T KNOW IF WE CAN MAKE HER UNDERSTAND THAT WE CAN'T TAKE ON THE WHOLE WORLD, BUT I GOTTA TRY. I CAN'T JUST ABANDON HER, OWEN.
⊰SIGH⊱ I FIGURED YOU'D SAY SOMETHING LIKE THAT. THAT'S WHY I CAME OUT.
NO MATTER WHAT ELSE HAPPENS, WE'RE A TEAM.
CAW CAW
CAW?
SHE SAT DOWN AT 10PM EXACTLY. I WATCHED HER APPROACH, IMPRESSED.
SHE HAS A STEEL CORE TO HER, BUT IT'S AT ODDS WITH HER HEART--HER NEED TO BELONG.

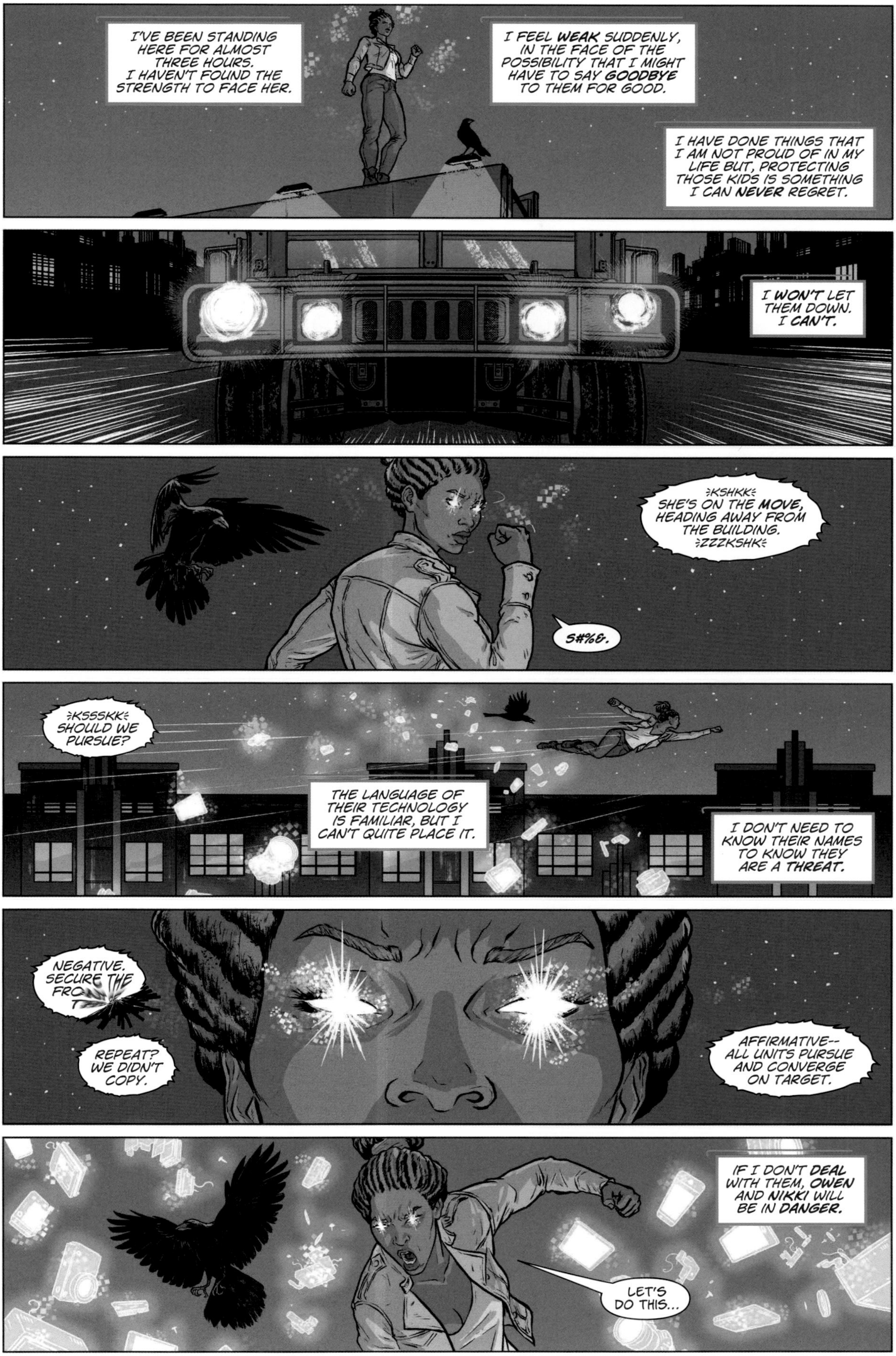
I'VE BEEN STANDING HERE FOR ALMOST THREE HOURS. I HAVEN'T FOUND THE STRENGTH TO FACE HER.
I FEEL WEAK SUDDENLY, IN THE FACE OF THE POSSIBILITY THAT I MIGHT HAVE TO SAY GOODBYE TO THEM FOR GOOD.
I HAVE DONE THINGS THAT I AM NOT PROUD OF IN MY LIFE BUT, PROTECTING THOSE KIDS IS SOMETHING I CAN NEVER REGRET.
I WON'T LET THEM DOWN. I CAN'T.
KSHKK SHE'S ON THE MOVE, HEADING AWAY FROM THE BUILDING. ZZZKSHK
S#%&.
KSSSKK SHOULD WE PURSUE?
THE LANGUAGE OF THEIR TECHNOLOGY IS FAMILIAR, BUT I CAN'T QUITE PLACE IT.
I DON'T NEED TO KNOW THEIR NAMES TO KNOW THEY ARE A THREAT.
NEGATIVE. SECURE THE FRO
REPEAT? WE DIDN'T COPY.
AFFIRMATIVE-- ALL UNITS PURSUE AND CONVERGE ON TARGET.
IF I DON'T DEAL WITH THEM, OWEN AND NIKKI WILL BE IN DANGER.
LET'S DO THIS...

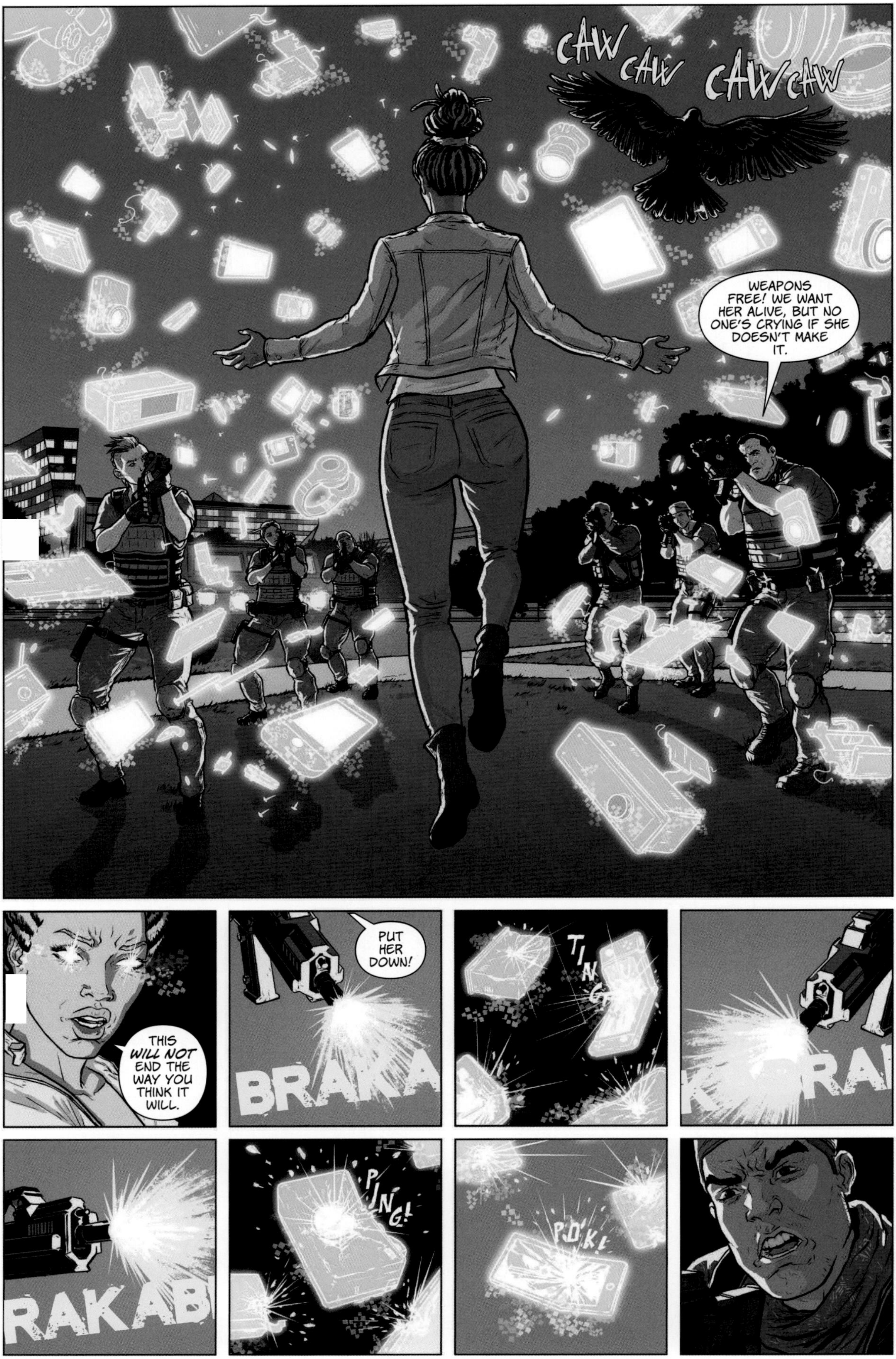
CAW CAW CAW CAW
WEAPONS FREE! WE WANT HER ALIVE, BUT NO ONE'S CRYING IF SHE DOESN'T MAKE IT.
THIS *WILL NOT* END THE WAY YOU THINK IT WILL.
PUT HER DOWN!
BRAKA
TING
RAKAB
PING!
POK!

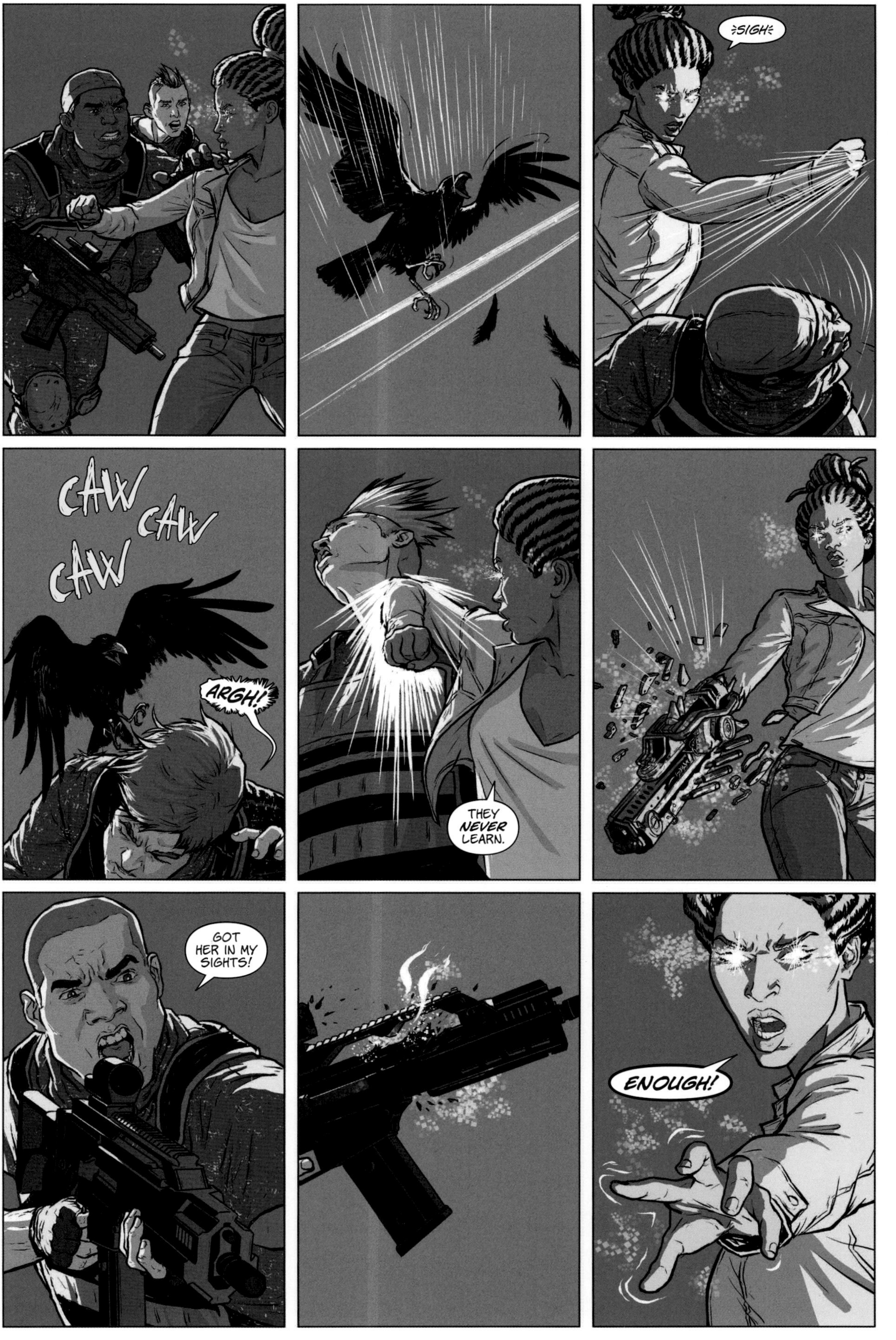
SIGH
CAW CAW CAW
ARGH!
THEY NEVER LEARN.
GOT HER IN MY SIGHTS!
ENOUGH!

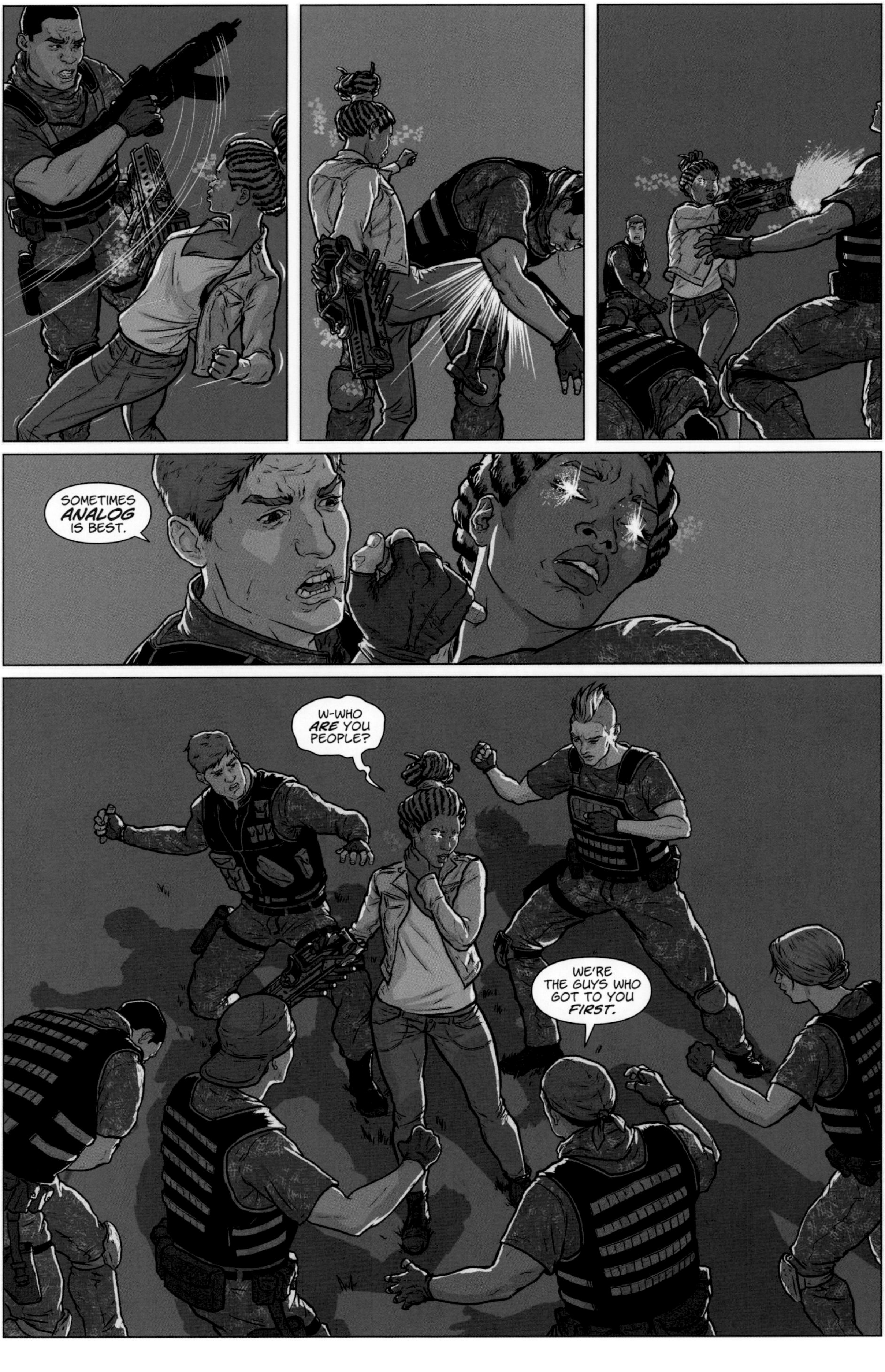
SOMETIMES ANALOG IS BEST.
W-WHO ARE YOU PEOPLE?
WE'RE THE GUYS WHO GOT TO YOU FIRST.

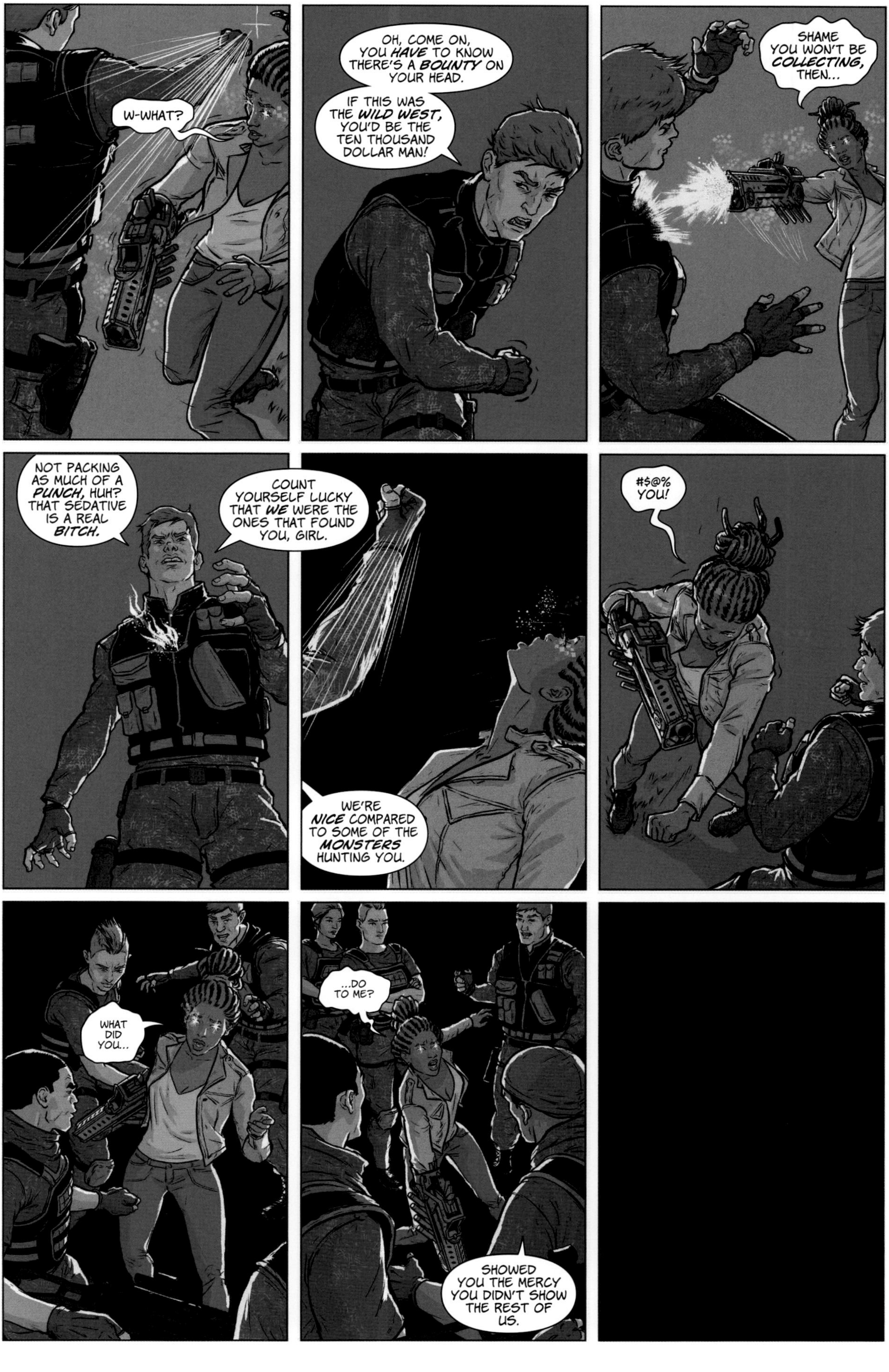
W-WHAT?
OH, COME ON, YOU HAVE TO KNOW THERE'S A BOUNTY ON YOUR HEAD.
IF THIS WAS THE WILD WEST, YOU'D BE THE TEN THOUSAND DOLLAR MAN!
SHAME YOU WON'T BE COLLECTING, THEN...
NOT PACKING AS MUCH OF A PUNCH, HUH? THAT SEDATIVE IS A REAL BITCH.
COUNT YOURSELF LUCKY THAT WE WERE THE ONES THAT FOUND YOU, GIRL.
WE'RE NICE COMPARED TO SOME OF THE MONSTERS HUNTING YOU.
#$@% YOU!
WHAT DID YOU...
...DO TO ME?
SHOWED YOU THE MERCY YOU DIDN'T SHOW THE REST OF US.

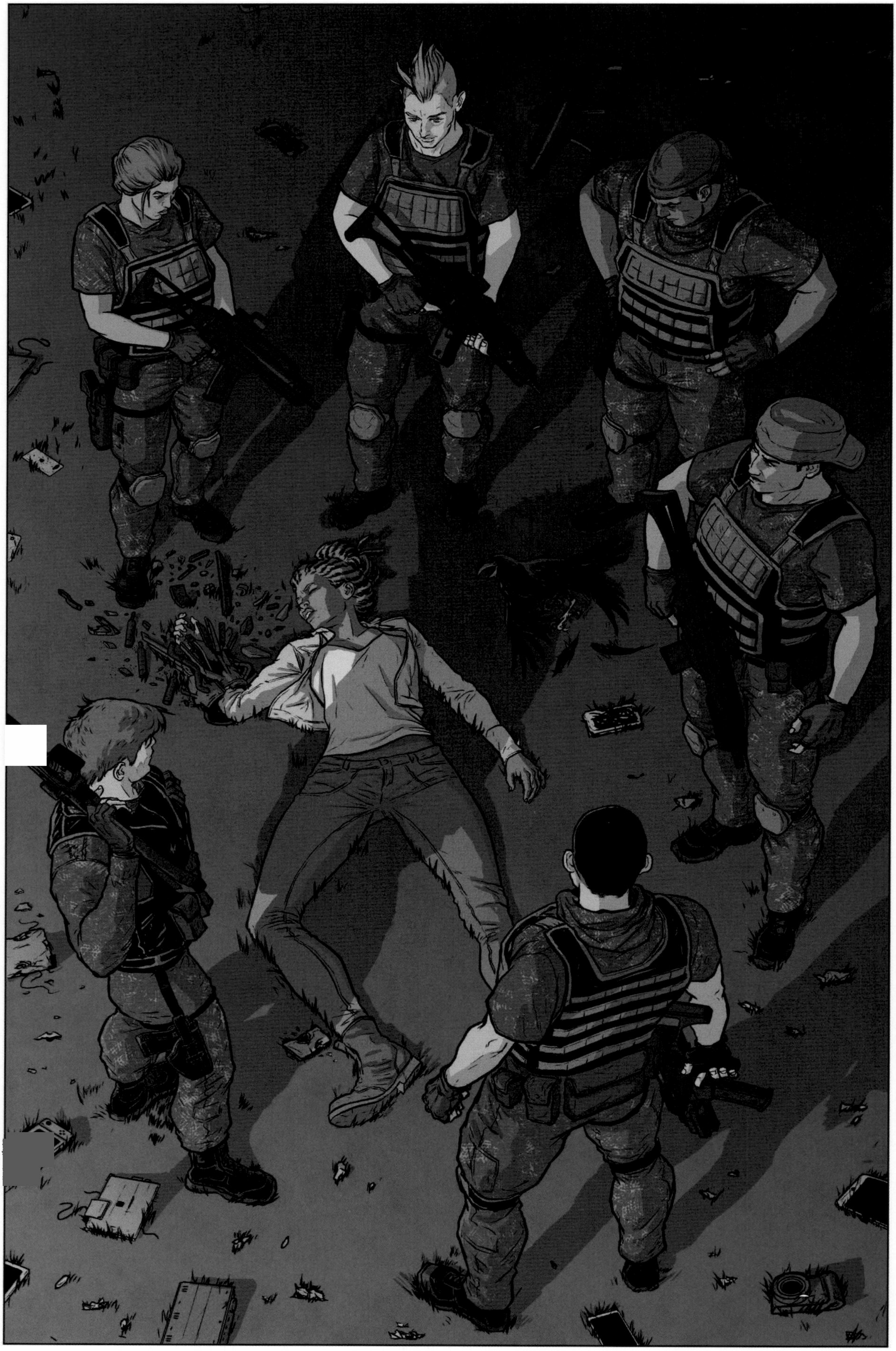

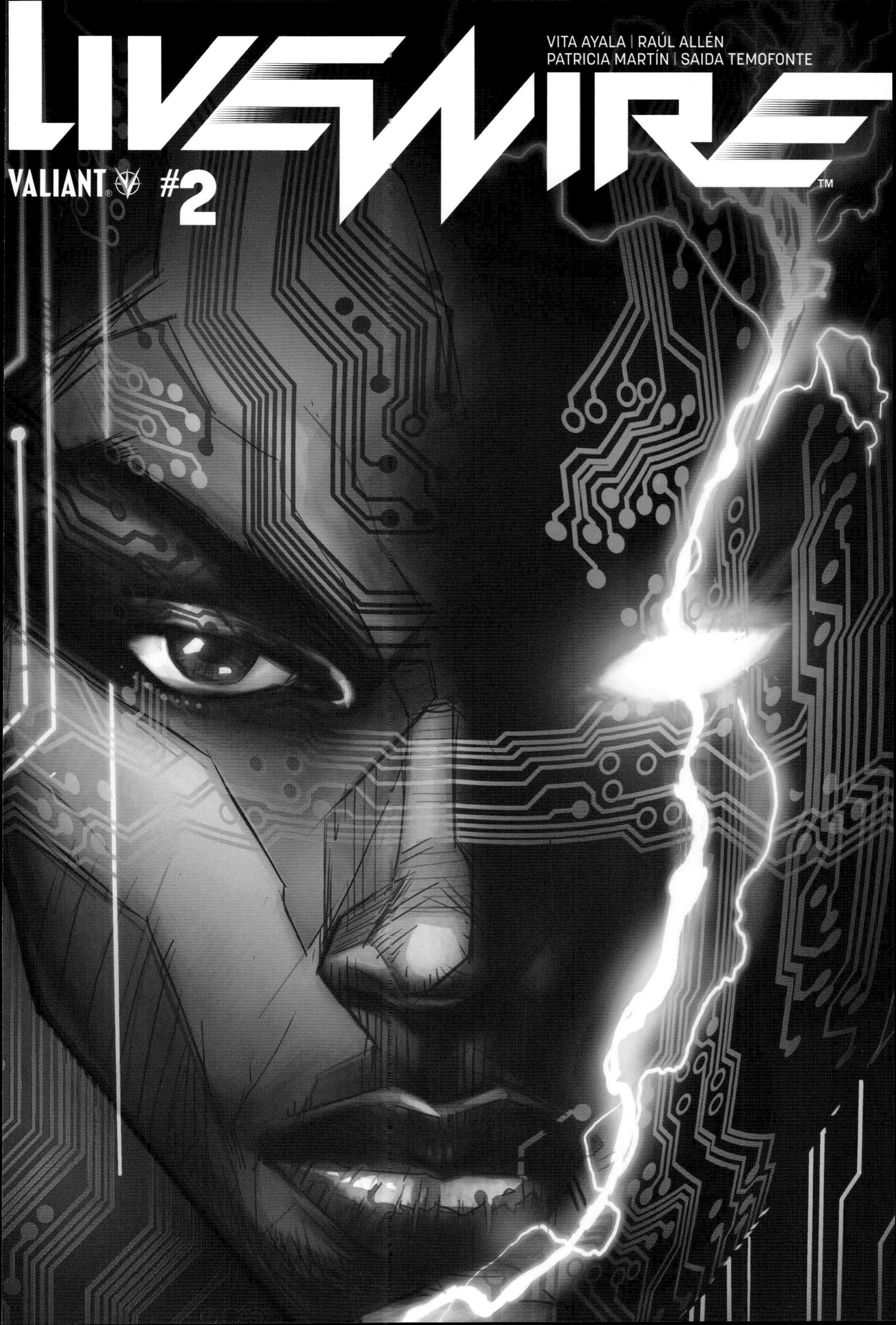
LIVEWIRE™
VITA AYALA | RAÚL ALLÉN
PATRICIA MARTÍN | SAIDA TEMOFONTE
VALIANT®
#2

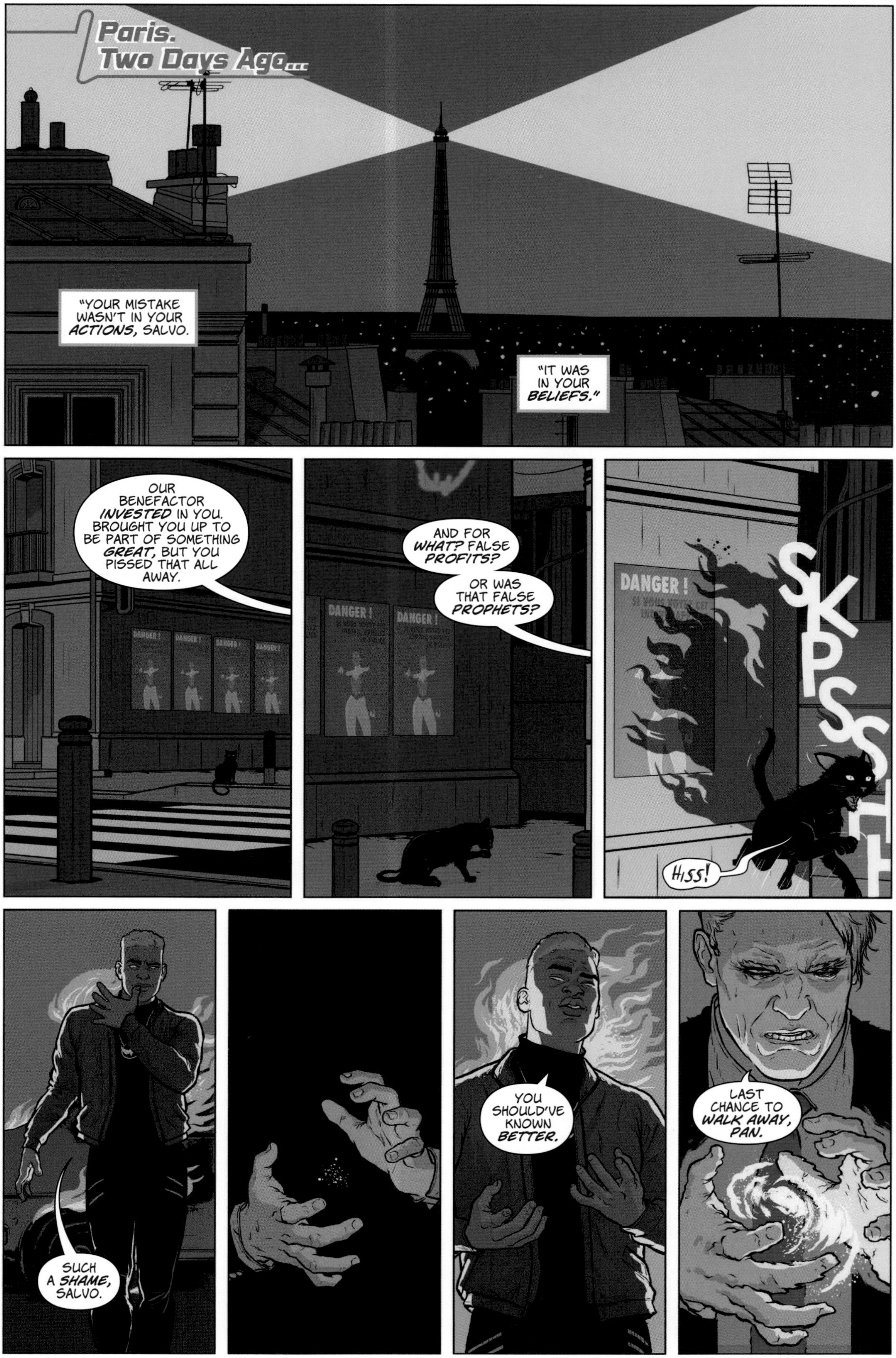
Paris. Two Days Ago...
"YOUR MISTAKE WASN'T IN YOUR ACTIONS, SALVO.
"IT WAS IN YOUR BELIEFS."
OUR BENEFACTOR INVESTED IN YOU. BROUGHT YOU UP TO BE PART OF SOMETHING GREAT, BUT YOU PISSED THAT ALL AWAY.
DANGER !
AND FOR WHAT? FALSE PROFITS?
OR WAS THAT FALSE PROPHETS?
DANGER !
DANGER !
SKPSSH
HISS!
SUCH A SHAME, SALVO.
YOU SHOULD'VE KNOWN BETTER.
LAST CHANCE TO WALK AWAY, PAN.

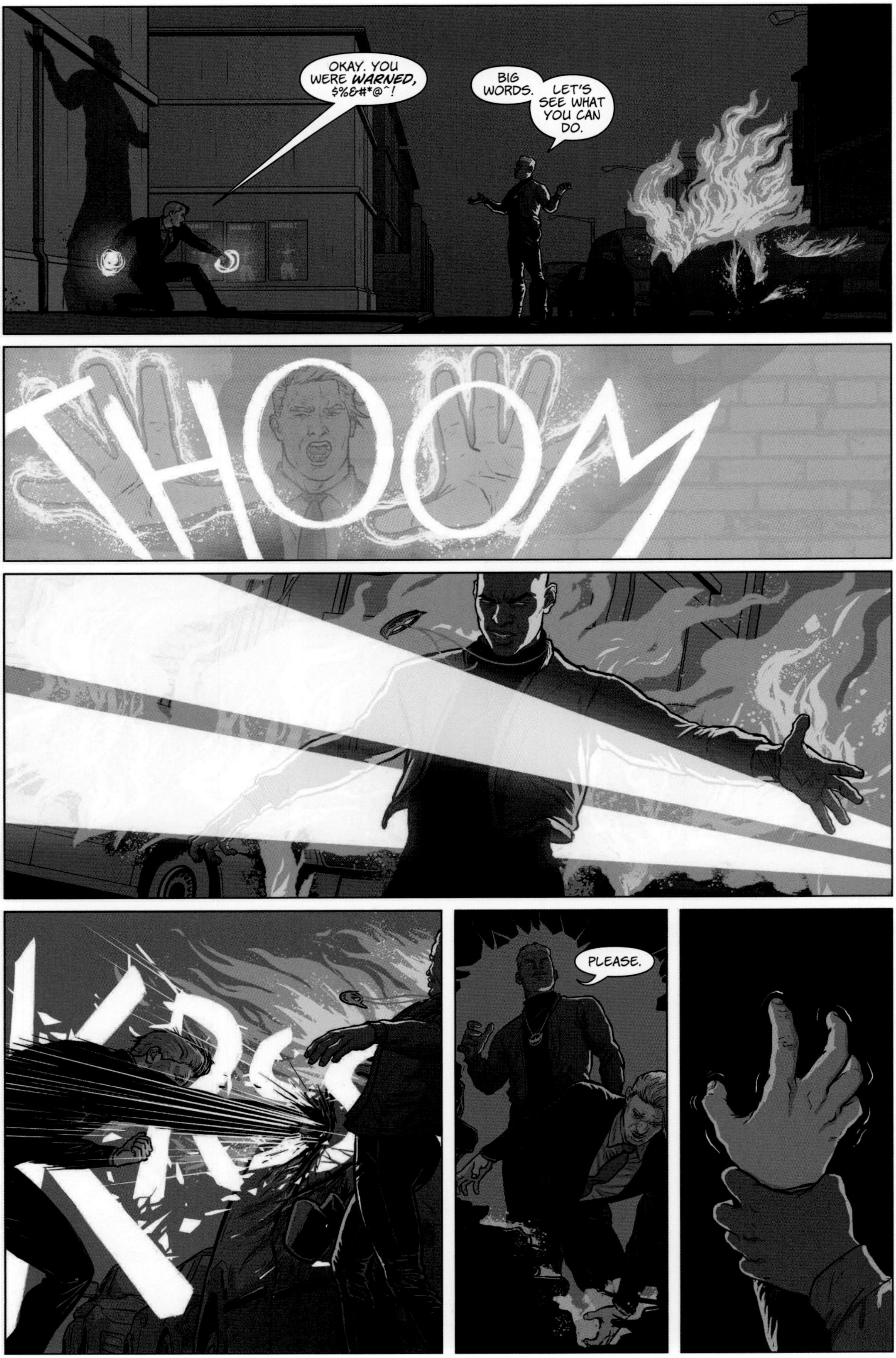
OKAY. YOU WERE WARNED, $%&#*@^!
BIG WORDS.
LET'S SEE WHAT YOU CAN DO.
THOOM
PLEASE.

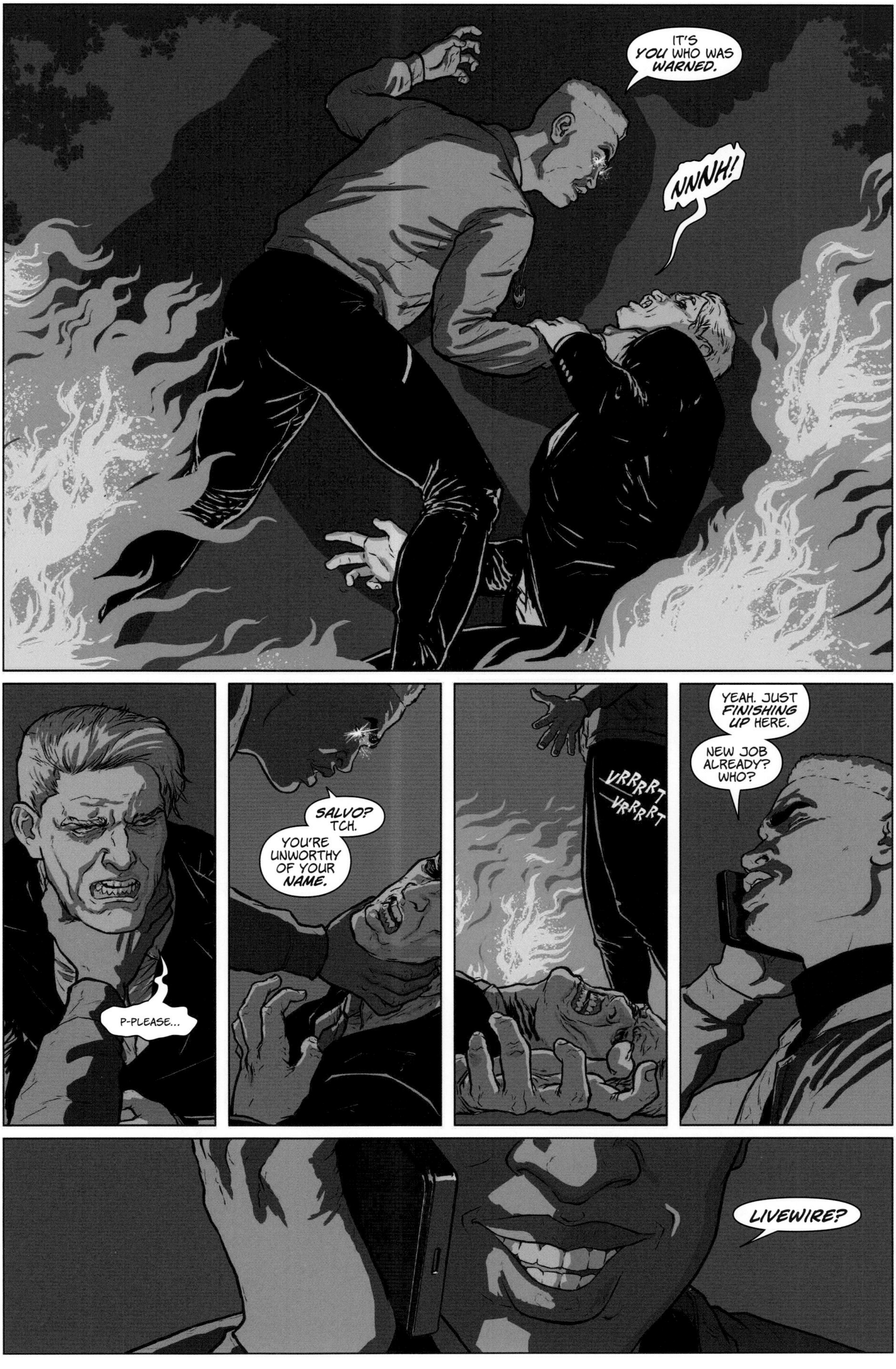
IT'S YOU WHO WAS WARNED.
NNNH!
P-PLEASE...
SALVO? TCH.
YOU'RE UNWORTHY OF YOUR NAME.
VRRRRT VRRRRT
YEAH. JUST FINISHING UP HERE.
NEW JOB ALREADY? WHO?
LIVEWIRE?

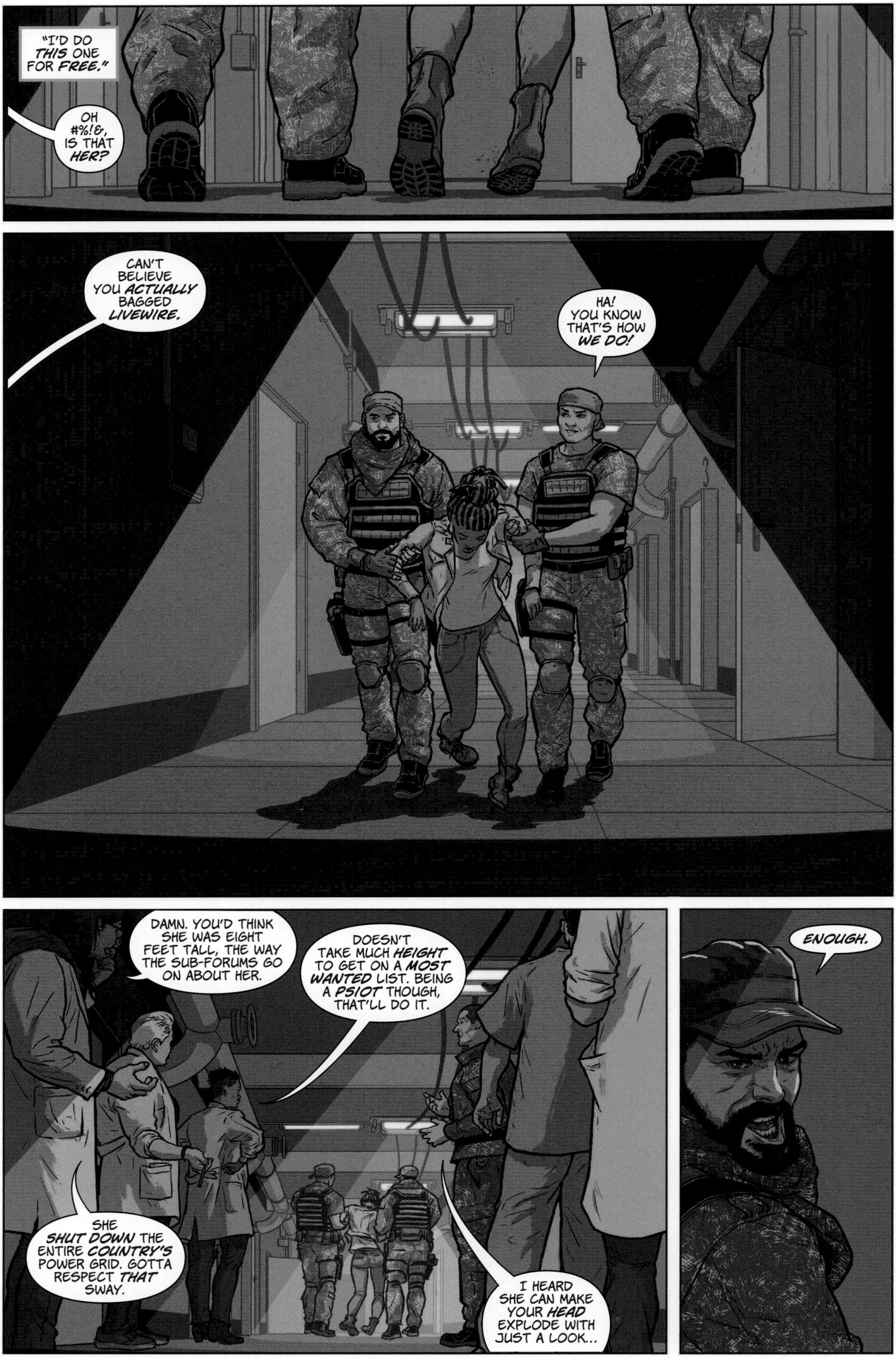
"I'D DO THIS ONE FOR FREE."
OH #%!&, IS THAT HER?
CAN'T BELIEVE YOU ACTUALLY BAGGED LIVEWIRE.
HA! YOU KNOW THAT'S HOW WE DO!
DAMN. YOU'D THINK SHE WAS EIGHT FEET TALL, THE WAY THE SUB-FORUMS GO ON ABOUT HER.
DOESN'T TAKE MUCH HEIGHT TO GET ON A MOST WANTED LIST. BEING A PSIOT THOUGH, THAT'LL DO IT.
SHE SHUT DOWN THE ENTIRE COUNTRY'S POWER GRID. GOTTA RESPECT THAT SWAY.
I HEARD SHE CAN MAKE YOUR HEAD EXPLODE WITH JUST A LOOK...
ENOUGH.

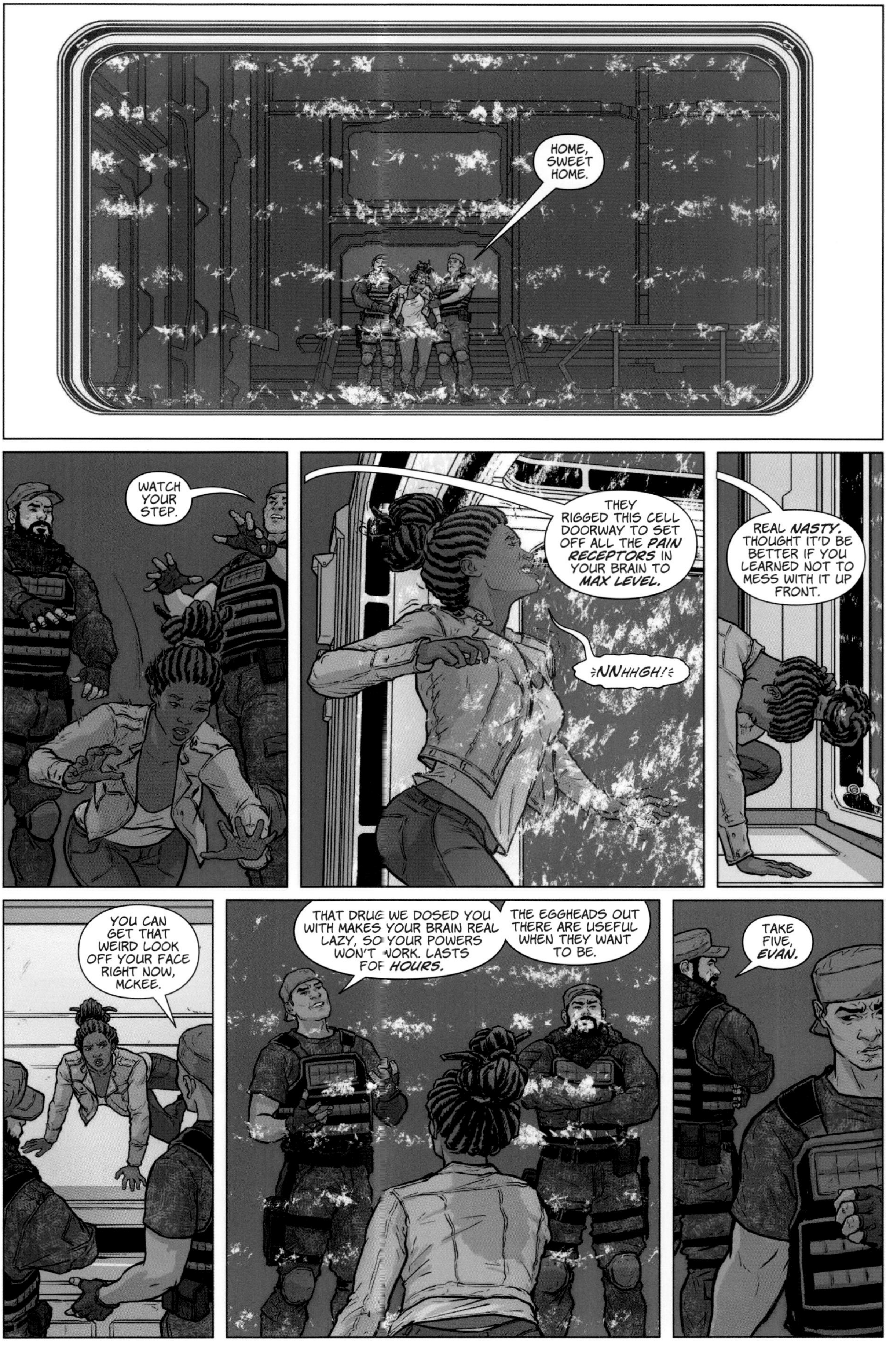
HOME, SWEET HOME.
WATCH YOUR STEP.
THEY RIGGED THIS CELL DOORWAY TO SET OFF ALL THE PAIN RECEPTORS IN YOUR BRAIN TO MAX LEVEL.
NNHHGH!
REAL NASTY. THOUGHT IT'D BE BETTER IF YOU LEARNED NOT TO MESS WITH IT UP FRONT.
YOU CAN GET THAT WEIRD LOOK OFF YOUR FACE RIGHT NOW, MCKEE.
THAT DRUG WE DOSED YOU WITH MAKES YOUR BRAIN REAL LAZY, SO YOUR POWERS WON'T WORK. LASTS FOR HOURS.
THE EGGHEADS OUT THERE ARE USEFUL WHEN THEY WANT TO BE.
TAKE FIVE, EVAN.

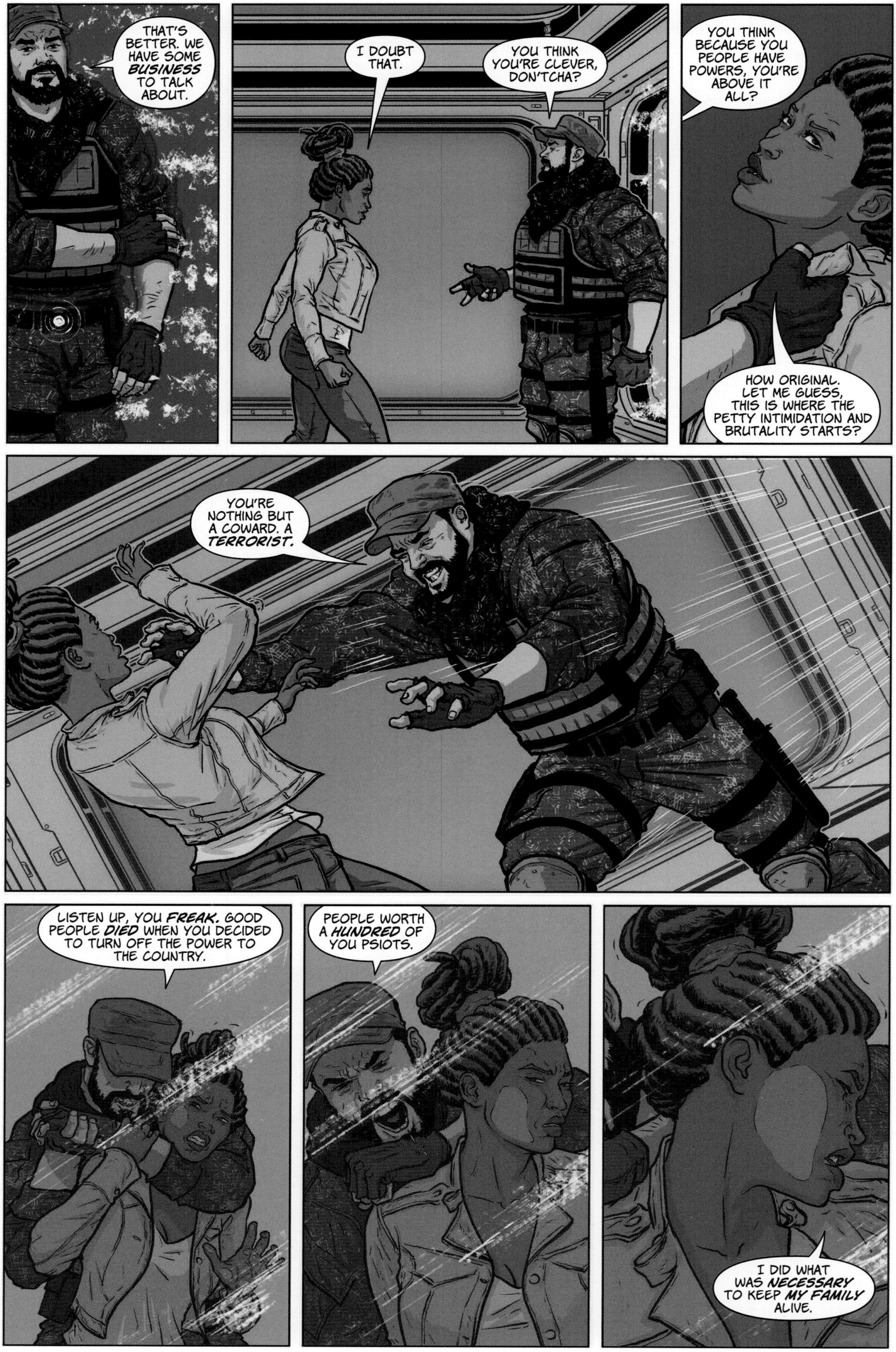
THAT'S BETTER. WE HAVE SOME BUSINESS TO TALK ABOUT.
I DOUBT THAT.
YOU THINK YOU'RE CLEVER, DON'TCHA?
YOU THINK BECAUSE YOU PEOPLE HAVE POWERS, YOU'RE ABOVE IT ALL?
HOW ORIGINAL. LET ME GUESS, THIS IS WHERE THE PETTY INTIMIDATION AND BRUTALITY STARTS?
YOU'RE NOTHING BUT A COWARD. A TERRORIST.
LISTEN UP, YOU FREAK. GOOD PEOPLE DIED WHEN YOU DECIDED TO TURN OFF THE POWER TO THE COUNTRY.
PEOPLE WORTH A HUNDRED OF YOU PSIOTS.
I DID WHAT WAS NECESSARY TO KEEP MY FAMILY ALIVE.

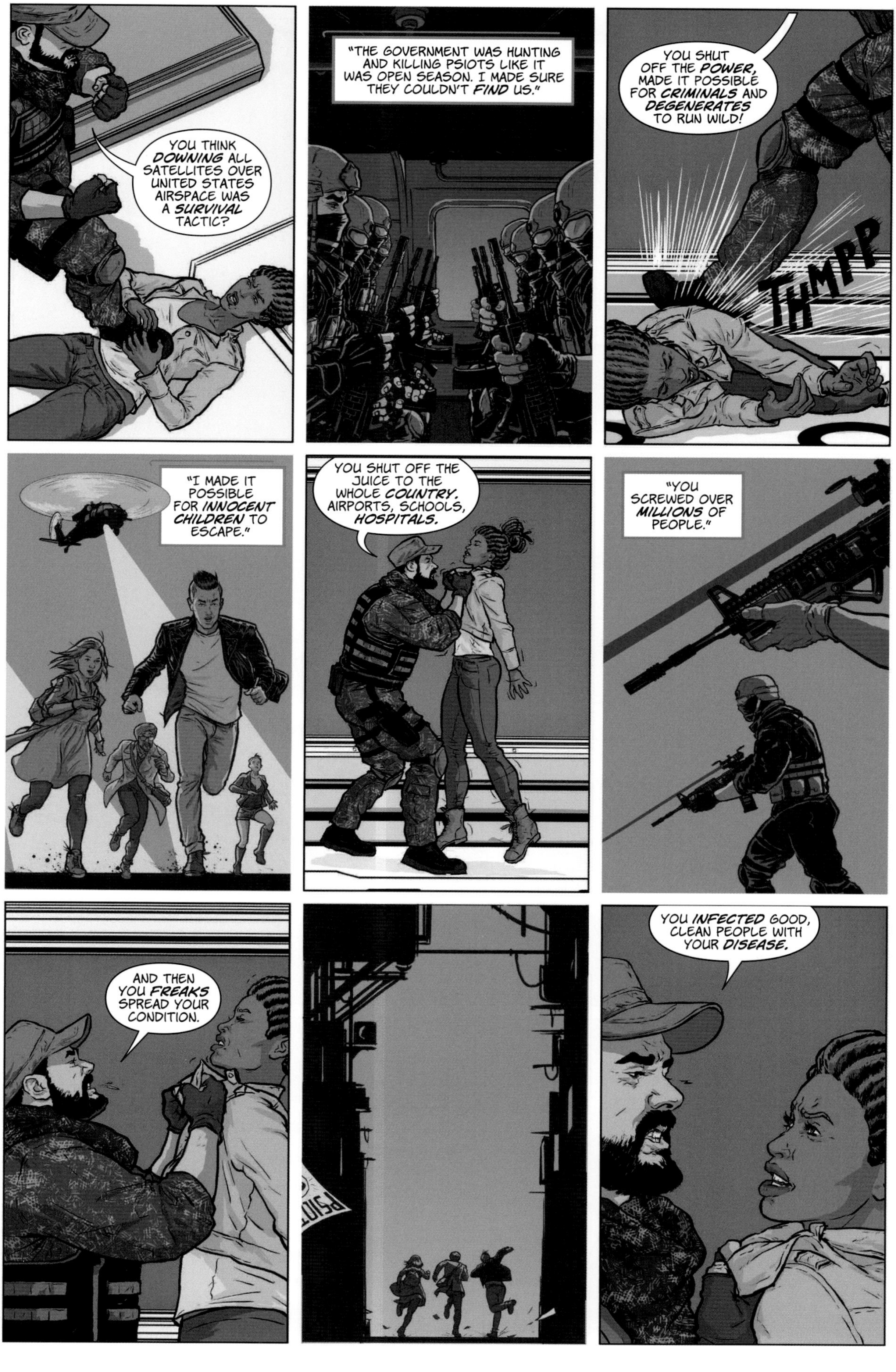
YOU THINK DOWNING ALL SATELLITES OVER UNITED STATES AIRSPACE WAS A SURVIVAL TACTIC?
"THE GOVERNMENT WAS HUNTING AND KILLING PSIOTS LIKE IT WAS OPEN SEASON. I MADE SURE THEY COULDN'T FIND US."
YOU SHUT OFF THE POWER, MADE IT POSSIBLE FOR CRIMINALS AND DEGENERATES TO RUN WILD!
THMPP
"I MADE IT POSSIBLE FOR INNOCENT CHILDREN TO ESCAPE."
YOU SHUT OFF THE JUICE TO THE WHOLE COUNTRY. AIRPORTS, SCHOOLS, HOSPITALS.
"YOU SCREWED OVER MILLIONS OF PEOPLE."
AND THEN YOU FREAKS SPREAD YOUR CONDITION.
YOU INFECTED GOOD, CLEAN PEOPLE WITH YOUR DISEASE.

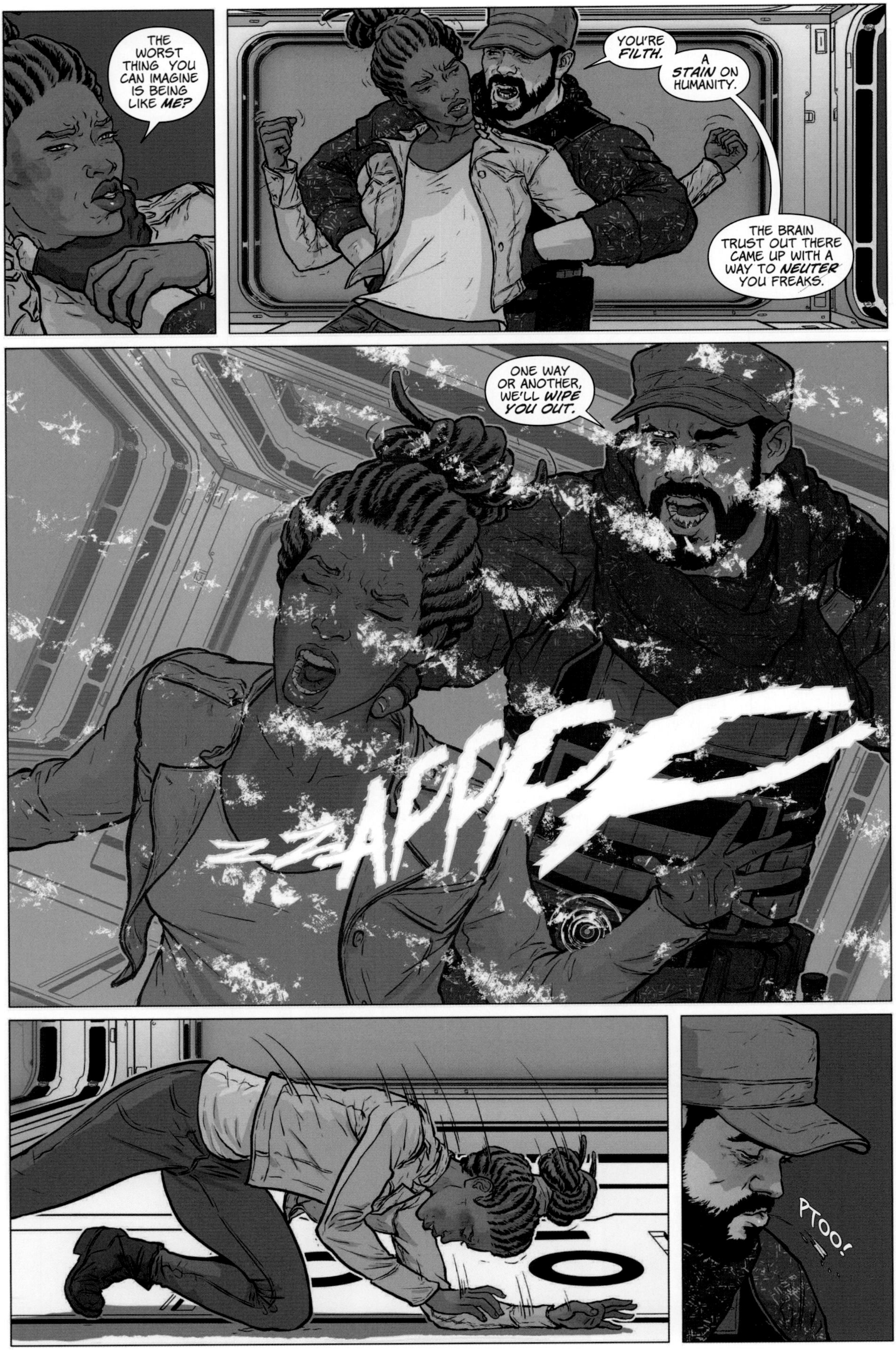
THE WORST THING YOU CAN IMAGINE IS BEING LIKE *ME?*
YOU'RE *FILTH.*
A *STAIN* ON HUMANITY.
THE BRAIN TRUST OUT THERE CAME UP WITH A WAY TO *NEUTER* YOU FREAKS.
ONE WAY OR ANOTHER, WE'LL *WIPE YOU OUT.*
ZZZAPPFF
PTOO!

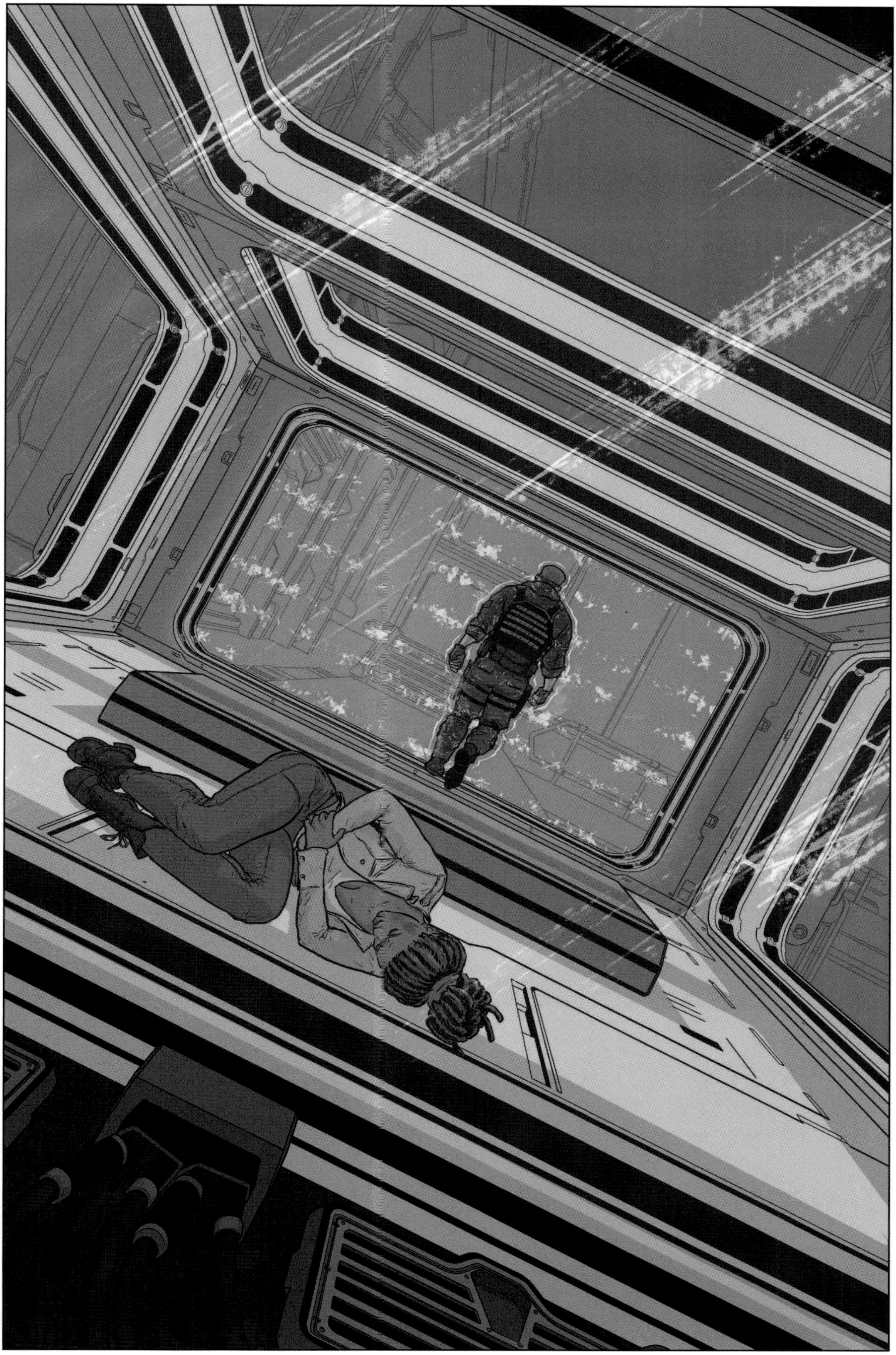

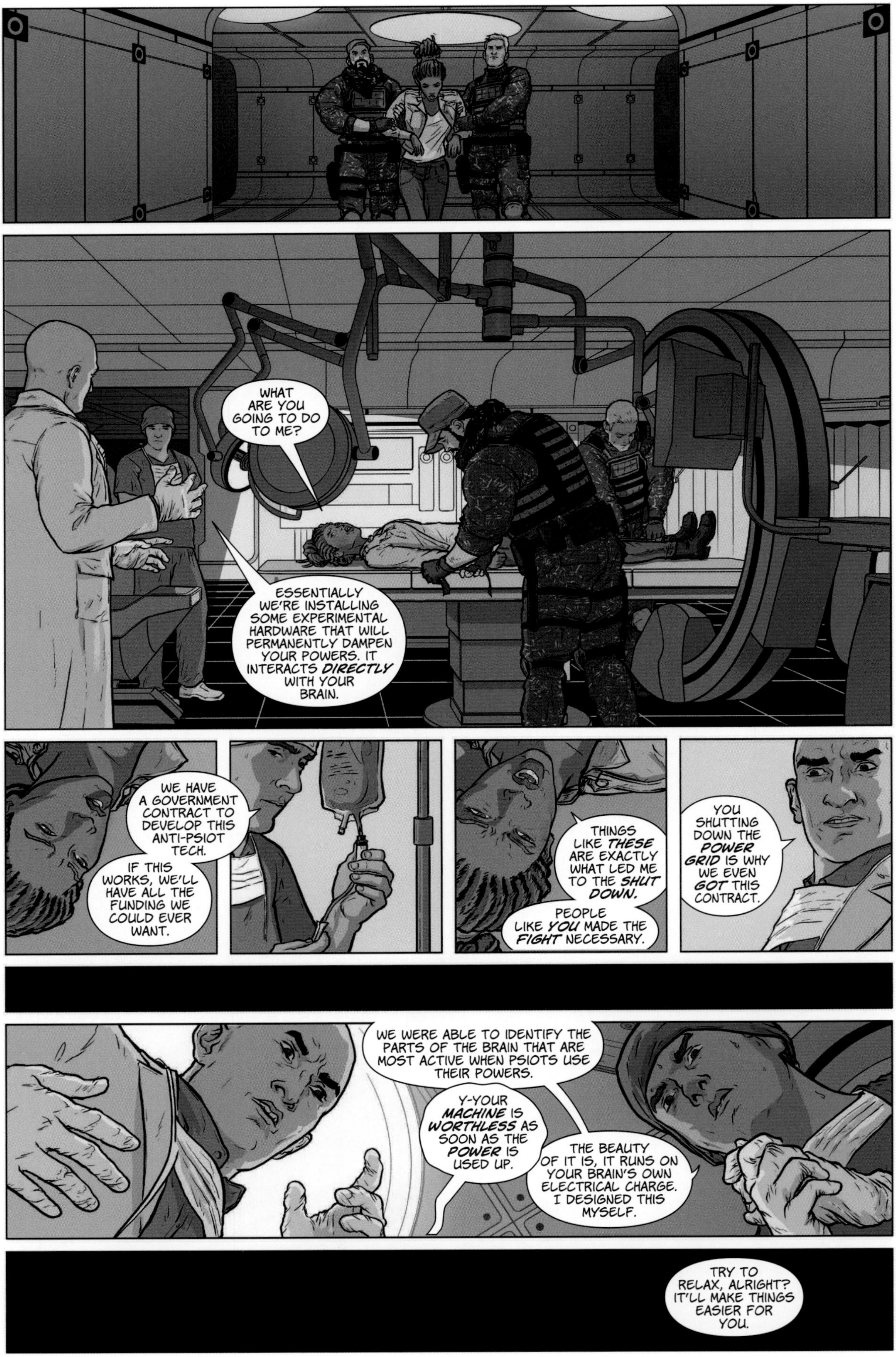
WHAT ARE YOU GOING TO DO TO ME?
ESSENTIALLY WE'RE INSTALLING SOME EXPERIMENTAL HARDWARE THAT WILL PERMANENTLY DAMPEN YOUR POWERS. IT INTERACTS DIRECTLY WITH YOUR BRAIN.
WE HAVE A GOVERNMENT CONTRACT TO DEVELOP THIS ANTI-PSIOT TECH.
IF THIS WORKS, WE'LL HAVE ALL THE FUNDING WE COULD EVER WANT.
THINGS LIKE THESE ARE EXACTLY WHAT LED ME TO THE SHUT DOWN.
PEOPLE LIKE YOU MADE THE FIGHT NECESSARY.
YOU SHUTTING DOWN THE POWER GRID IS WHY WE EVEN GOT THIS CONTRACT.
WE WERE ABLE TO IDENTIFY THE PARTS OF THE BRAIN THAT ARE MOST ACTIVE WHEN PSIOTS USE THEIR POWERS.
Y-YOUR MACHINE IS WORTHLESS AS SOON AS THE POWER IS USED UP.
THE BEAUTY OF IT IS, IT RUNS ON YOUR BRAIN'S OWN ELECTRICAL CHARGE. I DESIGNED THIS MYSELF.
TRY TO RELAX, ALRIGHT? IT'LL MAKE THINGS EASIER FOR YOU.

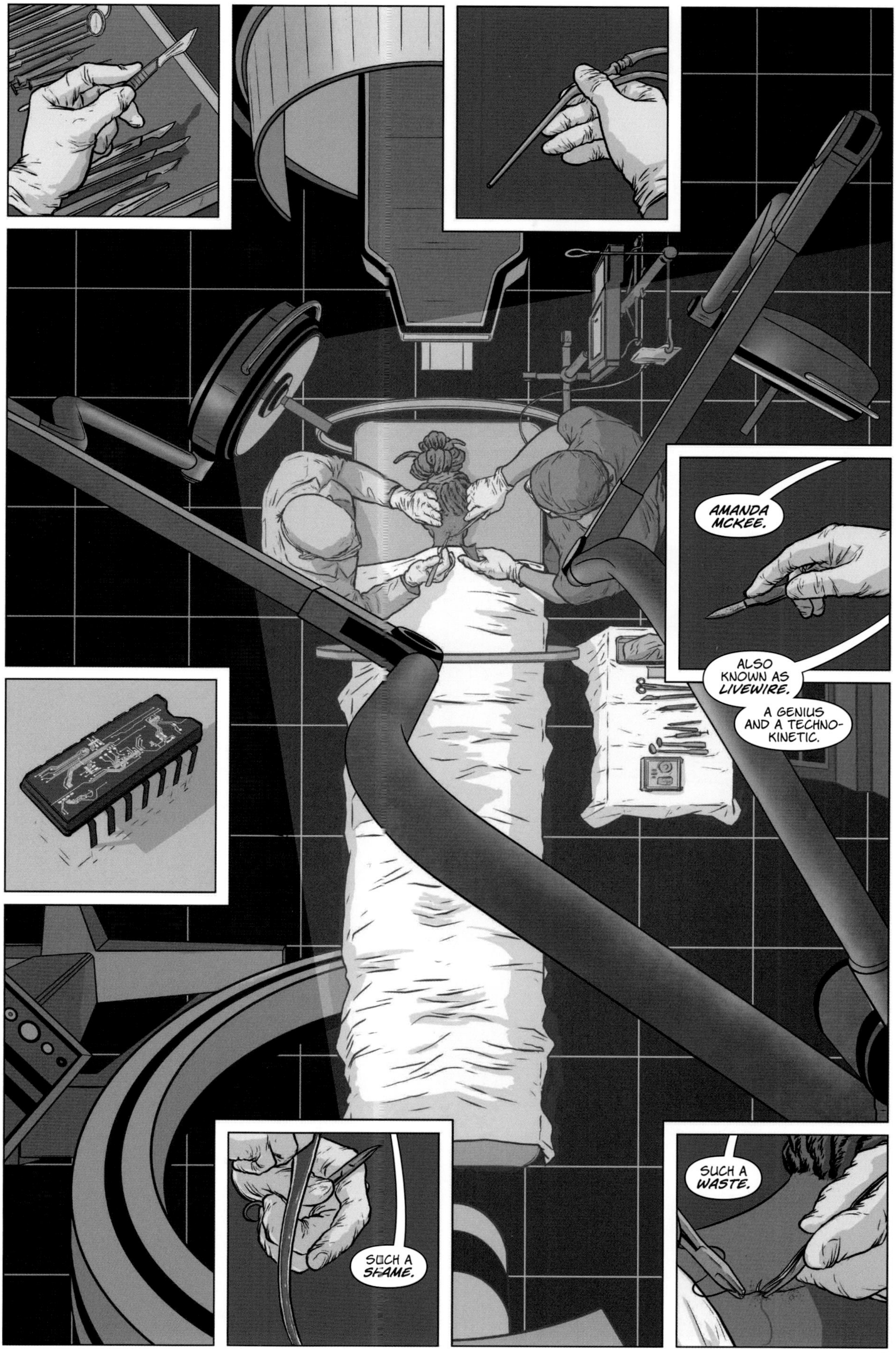
AMANDA MCKEE.
ALSO KNOWN AS LIVEWIRE.
A GENIUS AND A TECHNO-KINETIC.
SUCH A SHAME.
SUCH A WASTE.

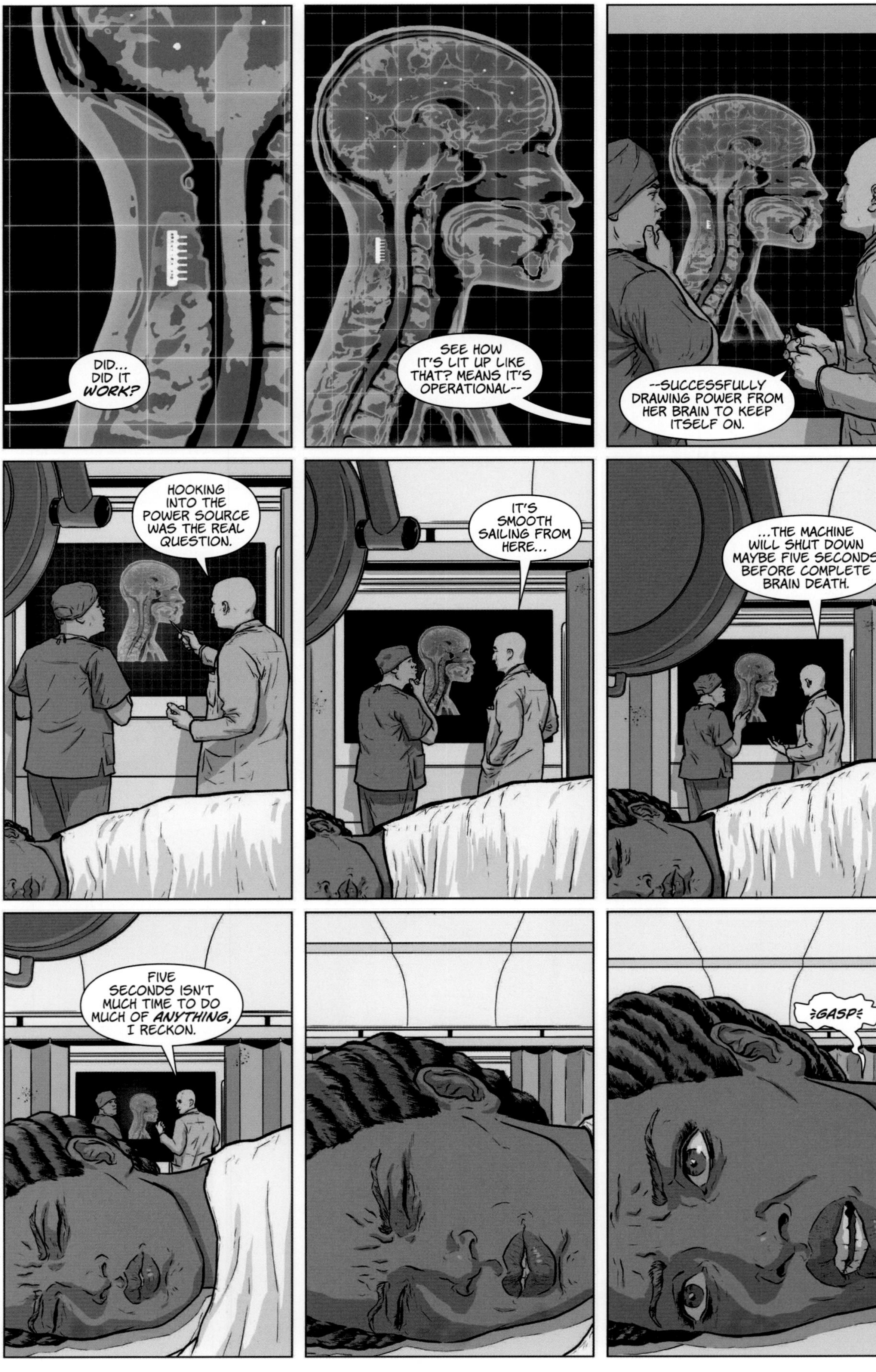
DID... DID IT *WORK?*
SEE HOW IT'S LIT UP LIKE THAT? MEANS IT'S OPERATIONAL--
--SUCCESSFULLY DRAWING POWER FROM HER BRAIN TO KEEP ITSELF ON.
HOOKING INTO THE POWER SOURCE WAS THE REAL QUESTION.
IT'S SMOOTH SAILING FROM HERE...
...THE MACHINE WILL SHUT DOWN MAYBE FIVE SECONDS BEFORE COMPLETE BRAIN DEATH.
FIVE SECONDS ISN'T MUCH TIME TO DO MUCH OF *ANYTHING,* I RECKON.
GASP

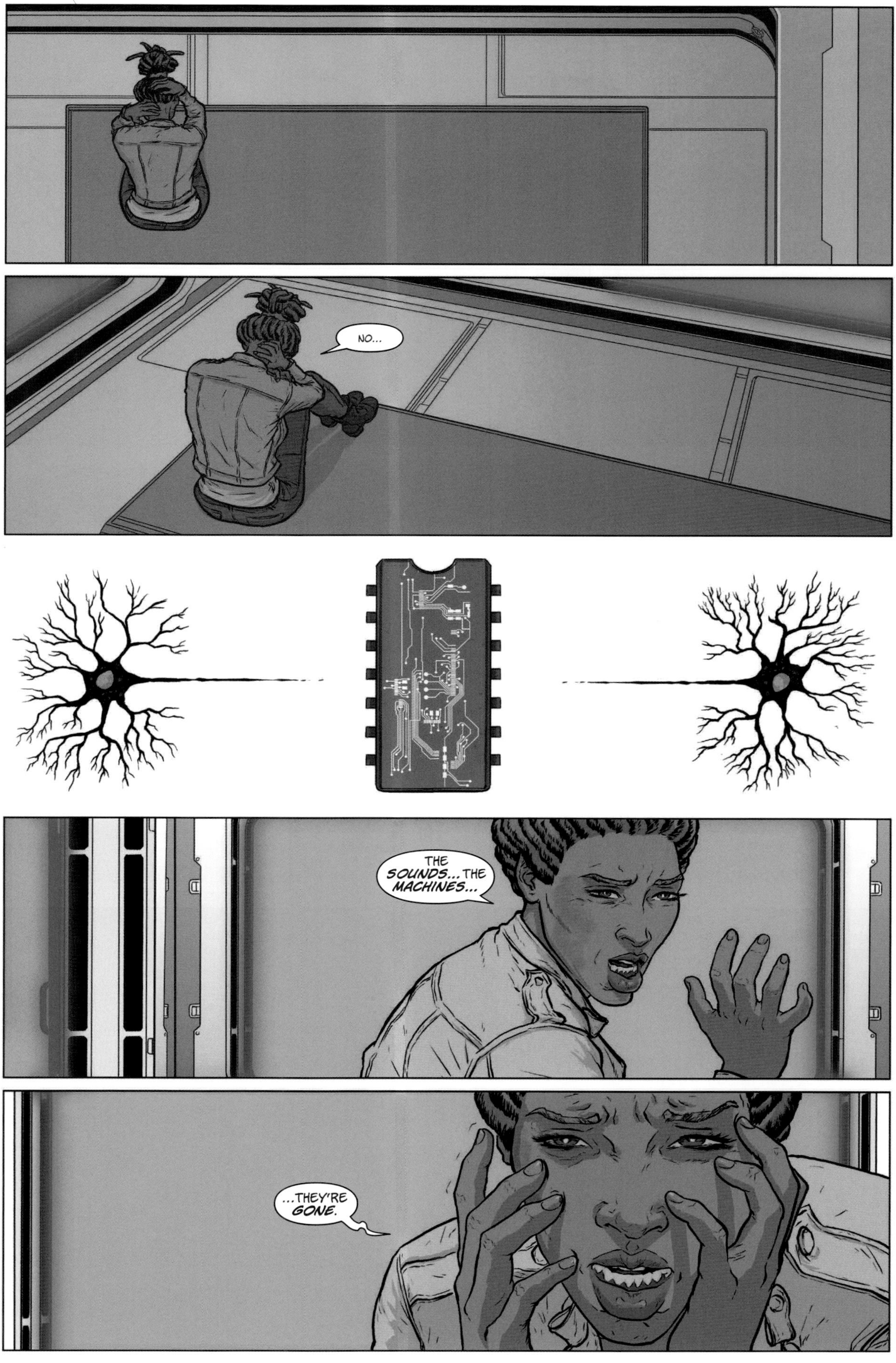
NO...
THE SOUNDS... THE MACHINES...
...THEY'RE GONE.

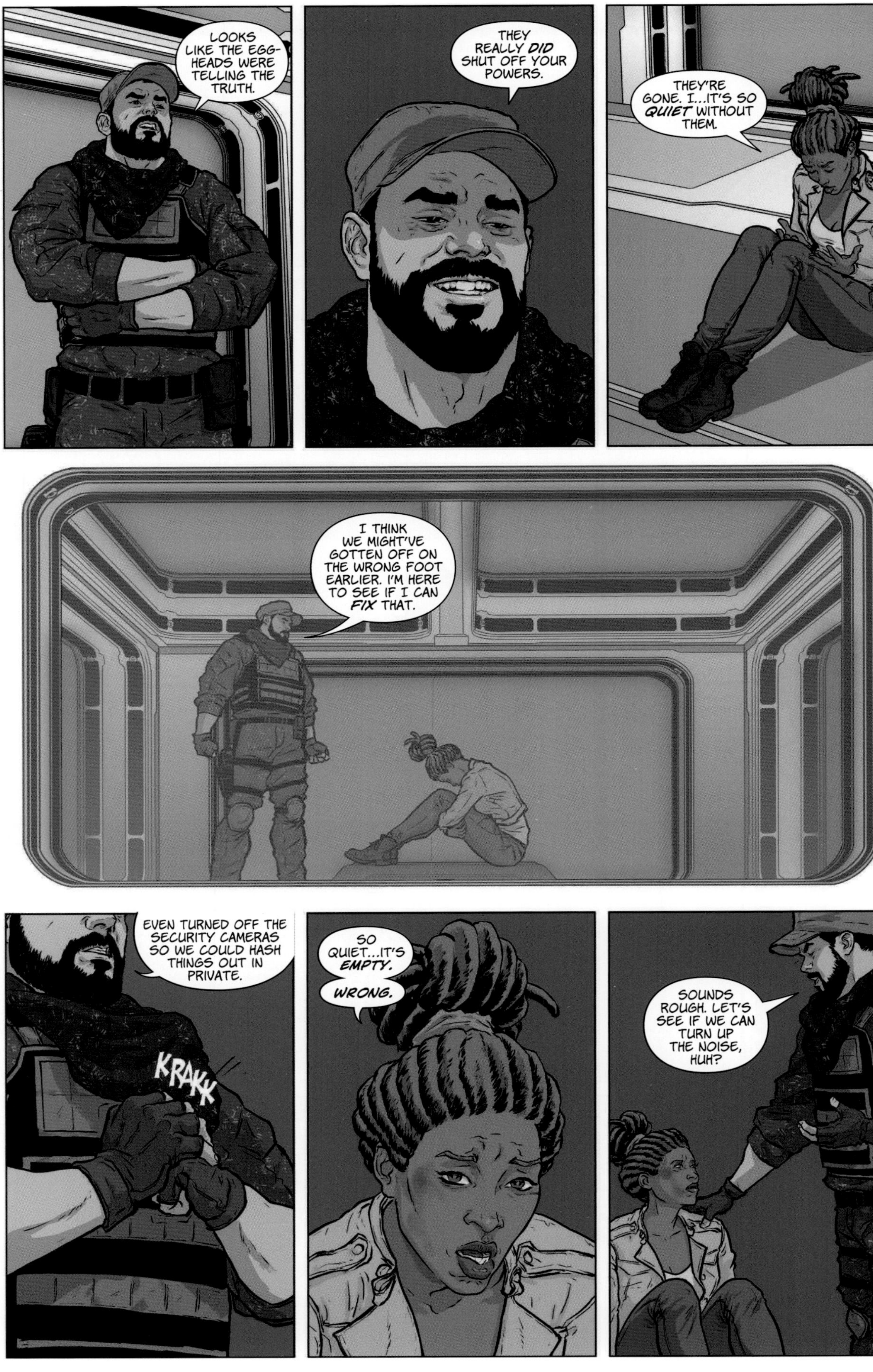
LOOKS LIKE THE EGG-HEADS WERE TELLING THE TRUTH.
THEY REALLY *DID* SHUT OFF YOUR POWERS.
THEY'RE GONE. I...IT'S SO *QUIET* WITHOUT THEM.
I THINK WE MIGHT'VE GOTTEN OFF ON THE WRONG FOOT EARLIER. I'M HERE TO SEE IF I CAN *FIX* THAT.
EVEN TURNED OFF THE SECURITY CAMERAS SO WE COULD HASH THINGS OUT IN PRIVATE.
KRAKK
SO QUIET...IT'S *EMPTY.*
WRONG.
SOUNDS ROUGH. LET'S SEE IF WE CAN TURN UP THE NOISE, HUH?

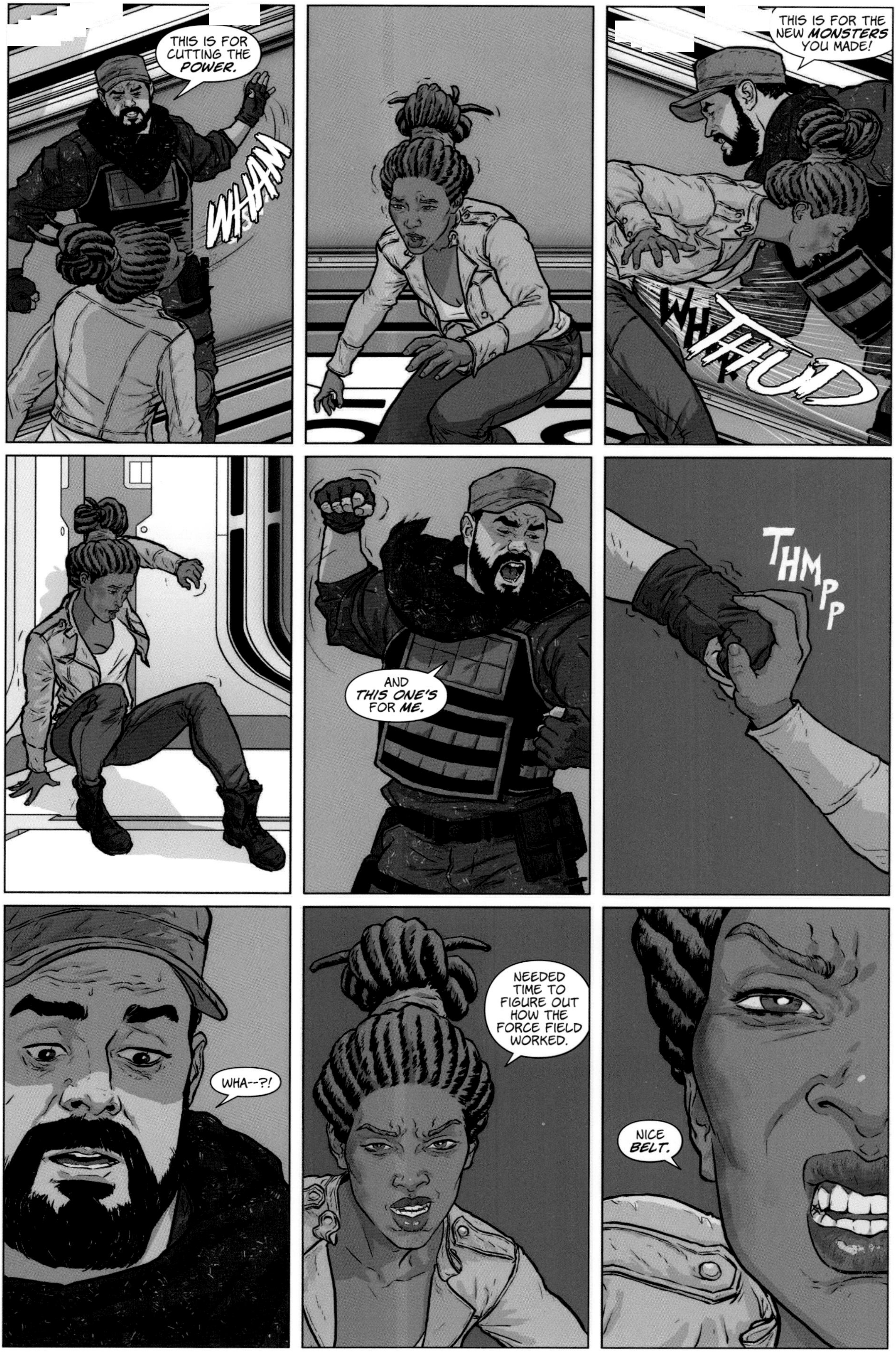
THIS IS FOR CUTTING THE POWER.
WHAM
THIS IS FOR THE NEW MONSTERS YOU MADE!
THUD
AND THIS ONE'S FOR ME.
THMPP
WHA--?!
NEEDED TIME TO FIGURE OUT HOW THE FORCE FIELD WORKED.
NICE BELT.

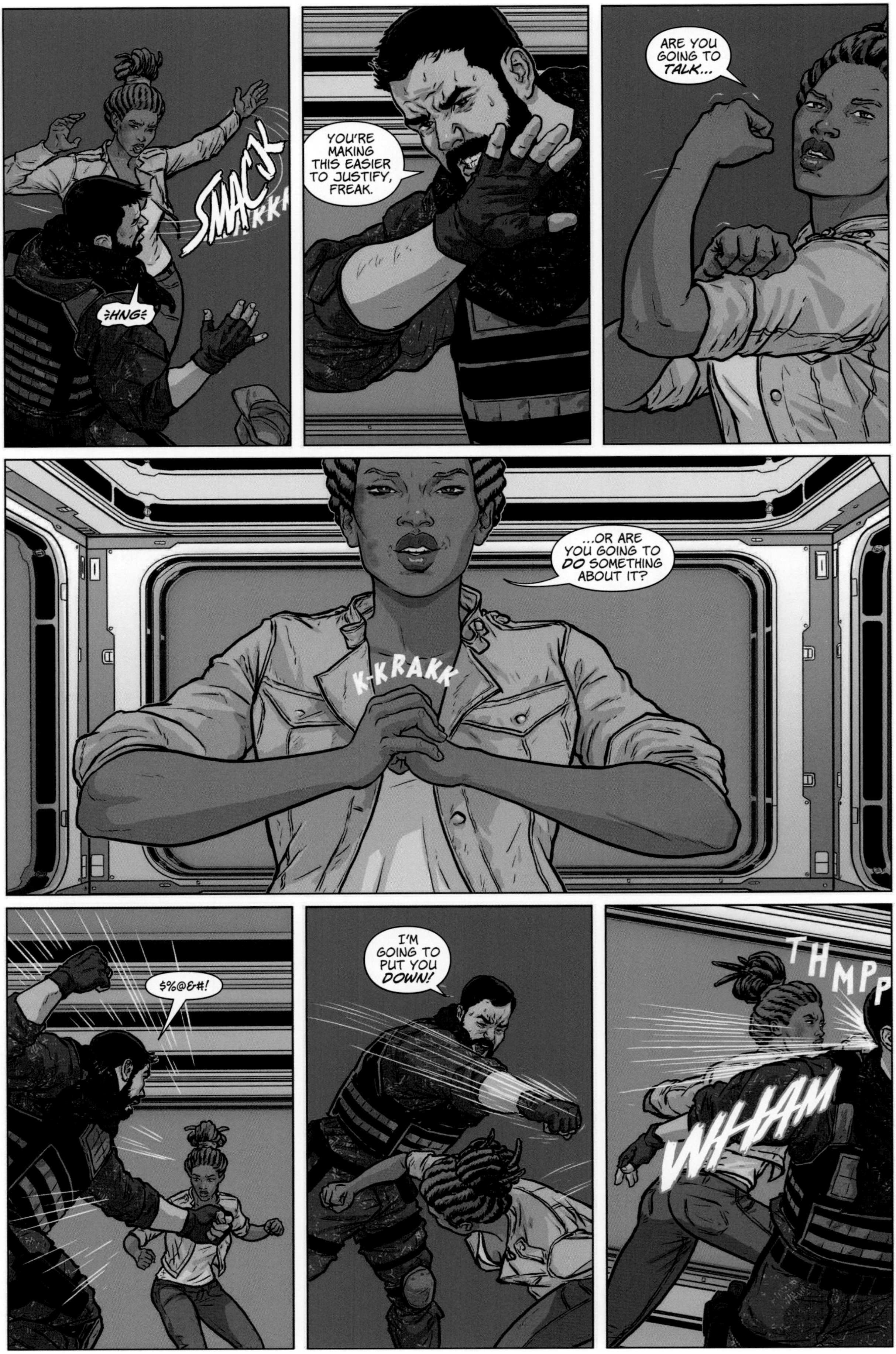
SMACK
HNG
YOU'RE MAKING THIS EASIER TO JUSTIFY, FREAK.
ARE YOU GOING TO TALK...
...OR ARE YOU GOING TO DO SOMETHING ABOUT IT?
K-KRAKK
$%@&#!
I'M GOING TO PUT YOU DOWN!
THMPP
WHAM

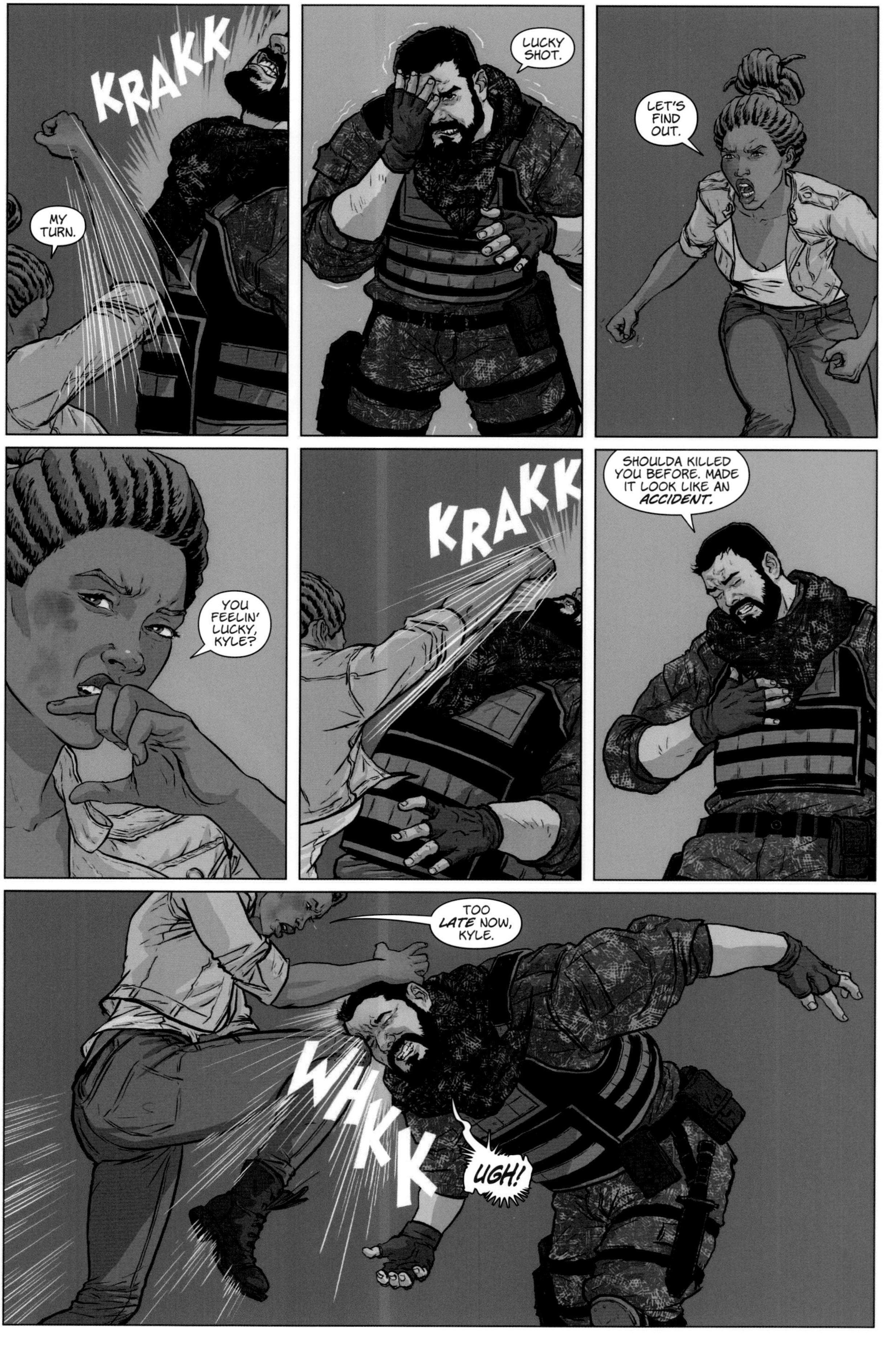
KRAKK
MY TURN.
LUCKY SHOT.
LET'S FIND OUT.
YOU FEELIN' LUCKY, KYLE?
KRAKK
SHOULDA KILLED YOU BEFORE. MADE IT LOOK LIKE AN *ACCIDENT.*
TOO *LATE* NOW, KYLE.
WHKK
UGH!

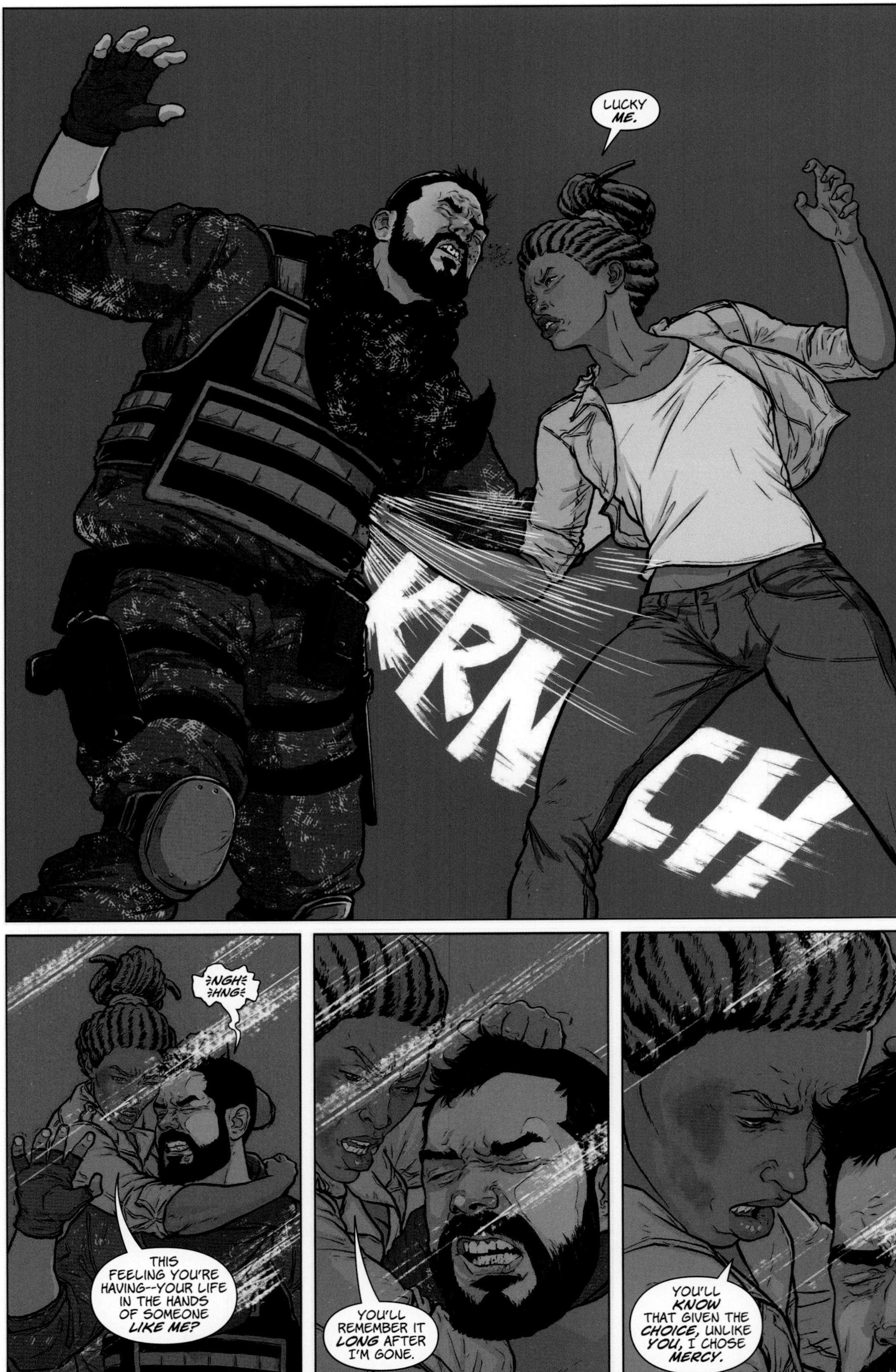
LUCKY ME.
KRNCH
NGH HNG
THIS FEELING YOU'RE HAVING--YOUR LIFE IN THE HANDS OF SOMEONE LIKE ME?
YOU'LL REMEMBER IT LONG AFTER I'M GONE.
YOU'LL KNOW THAT GIVEN THE CHOICE, UNLIKE YOU, I CHOSE MERCY.

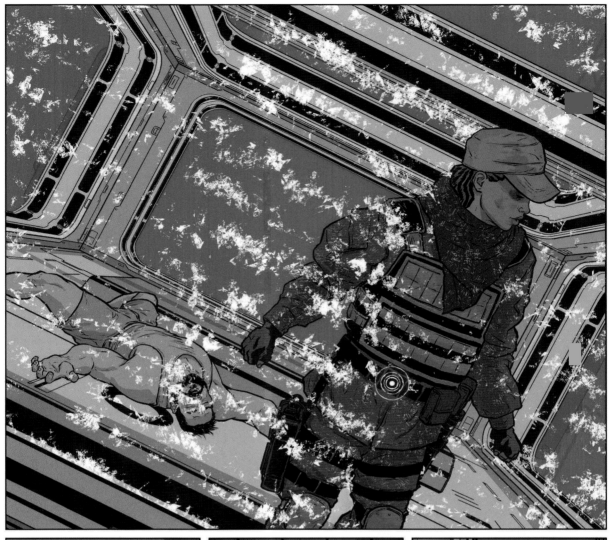

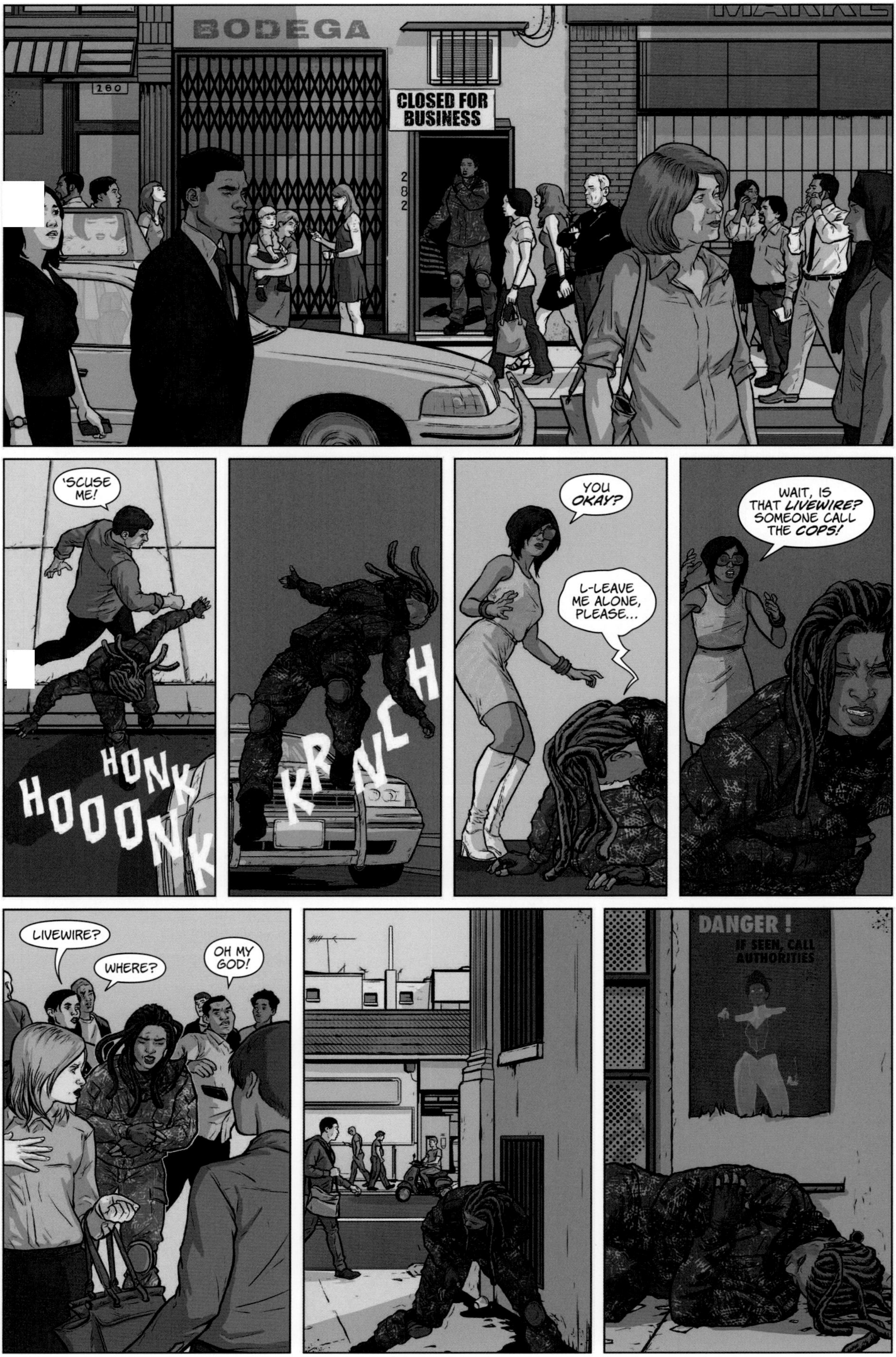
BODEGA
260
CLOSED FOR BUSINESS
282
'SCUSE ME!
HONK
HOOONK
KRNCH
YOU OKAY?
L-LEAVE ME ALONE, PLEASE...
WAIT, IS THAT LIVEWIRE? SOMEONE CALL THE COPS!
LIVEWIRE?
WHERE?
OH MY GOD!
DANGER !
IF SEEN, CALL AUTHORITIES

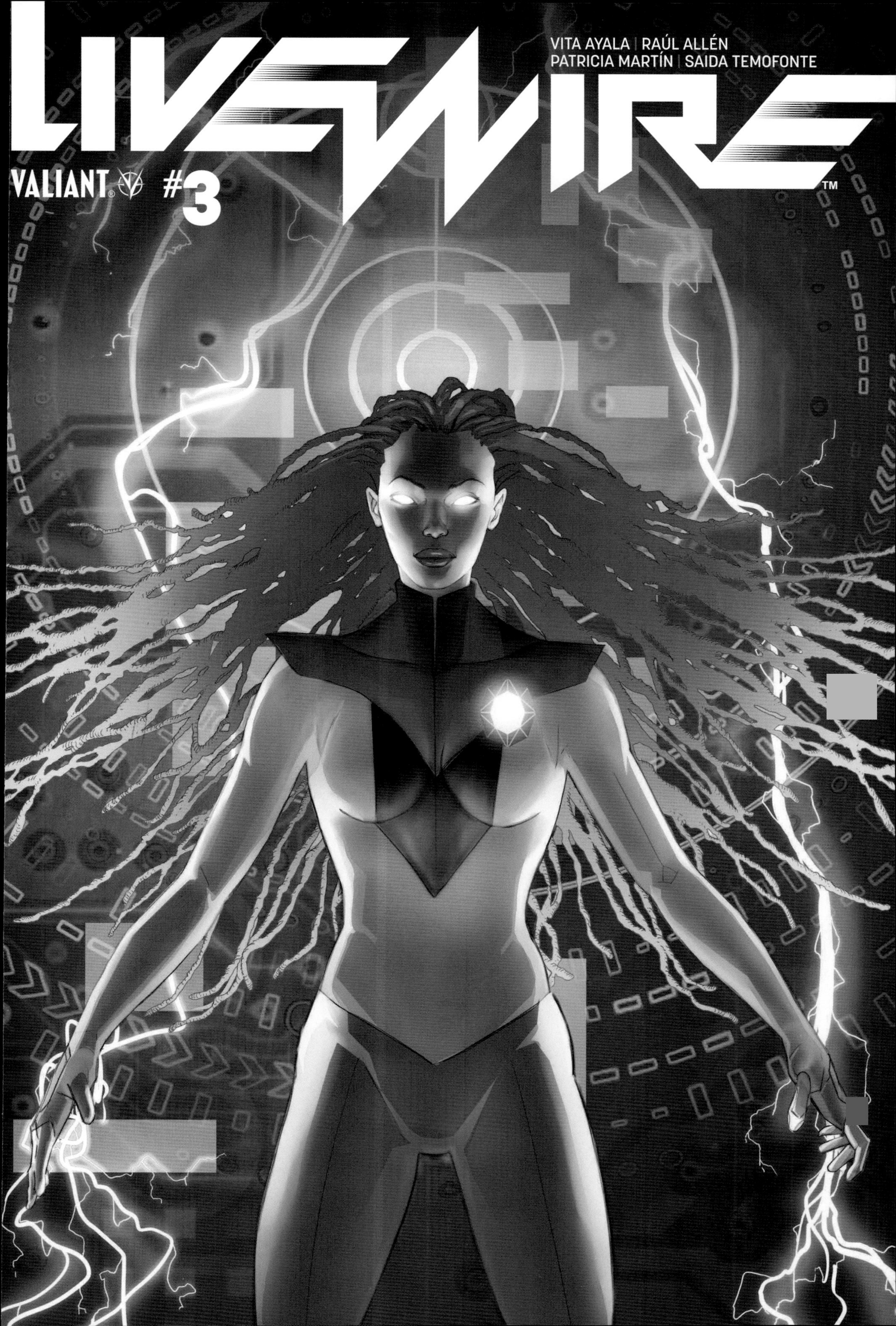
LIVEWIRE
VITA AYALA | RAÚL ALLÉN
PATRICIA MARTÍN | SAIDA TEMOFONTE
VALIANT
#3
TM

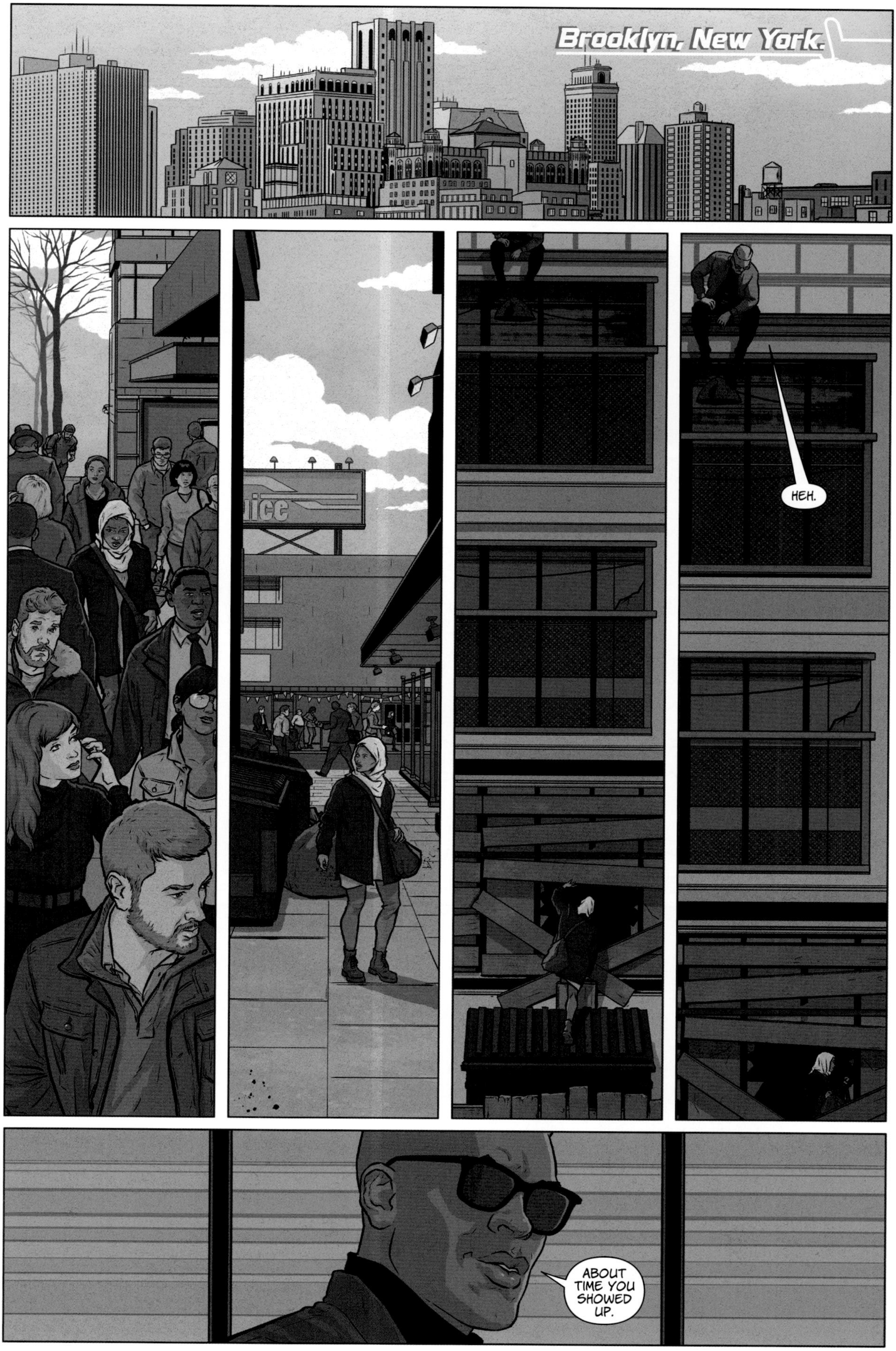
Brooklyn, New York.
HEH.
ABOUT TIME YOU SHOWED UP.

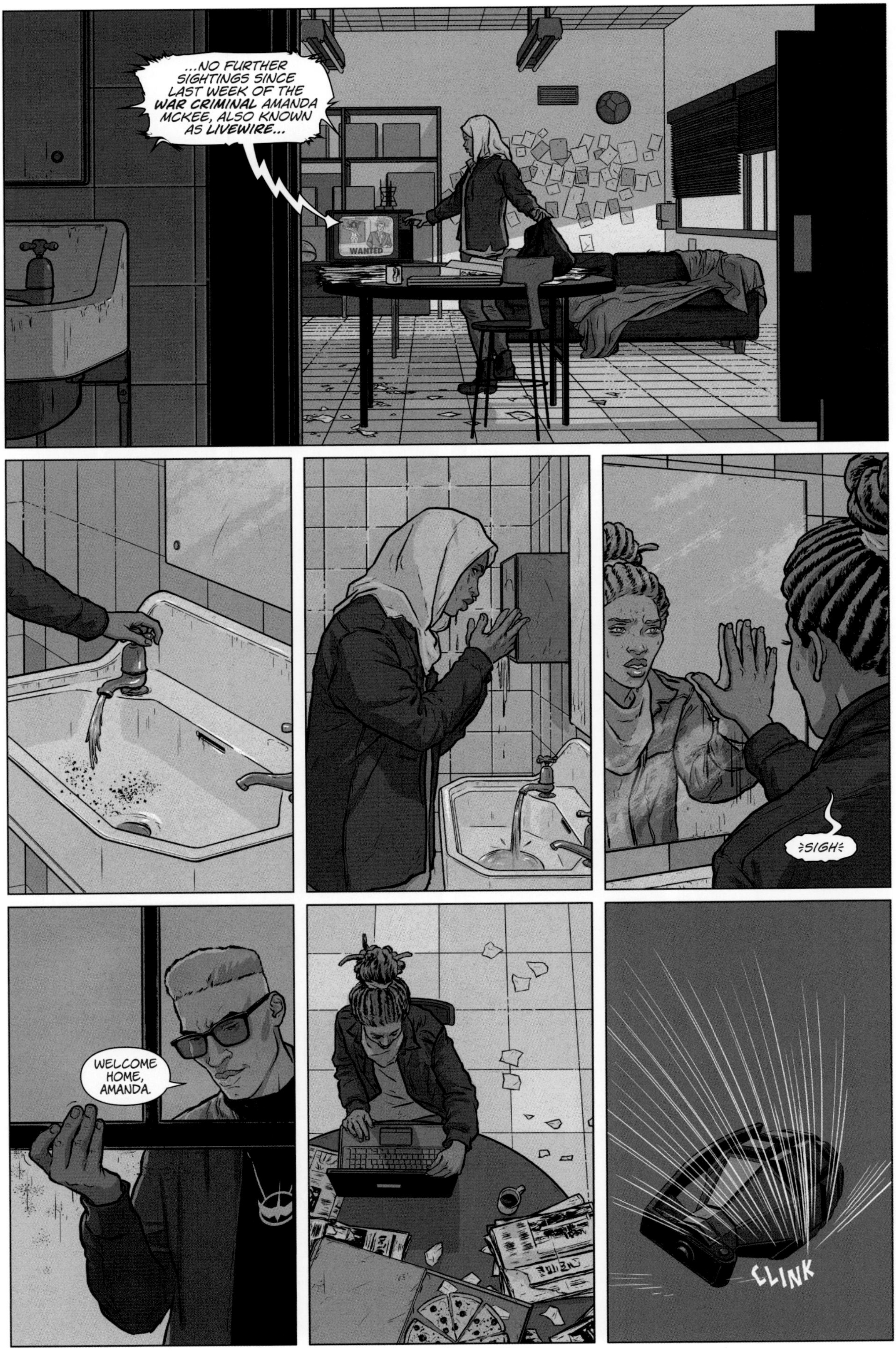
...NO FURTHER SIGHTINGS SINCE LAST WEEK OF THE WAR CRIMINAL AMANDA MCKEE, ALSO KNOWN AS LIVEWIRE...
WANTED
SIGH
WELCOME HOME, AMANDA.
CLINK

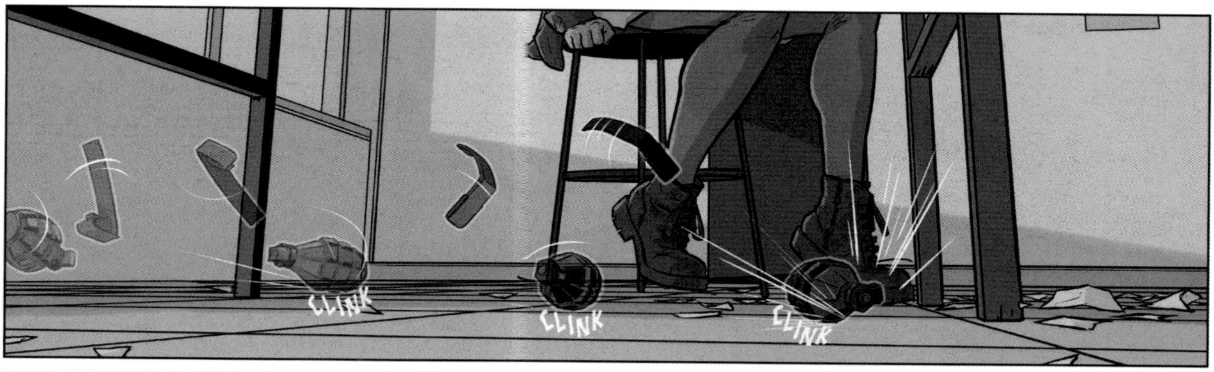
CLINK
CLINK
CLINK
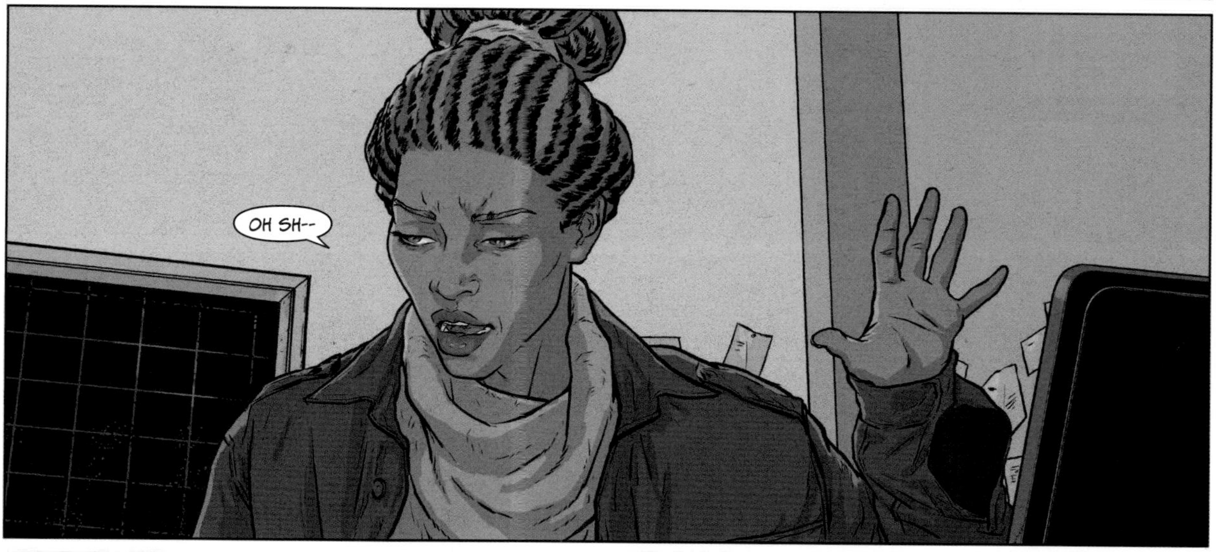
OH SH--
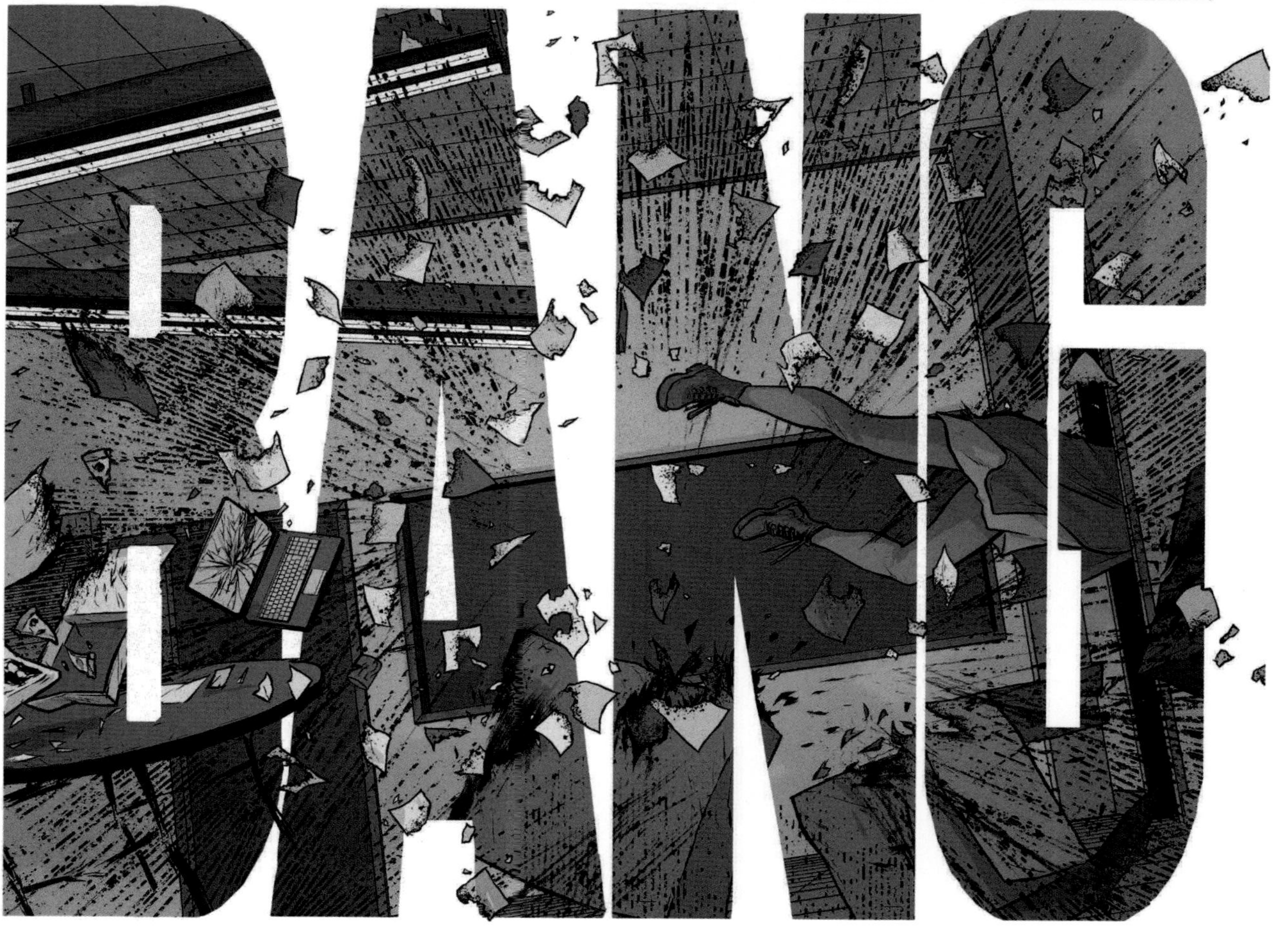
BANG

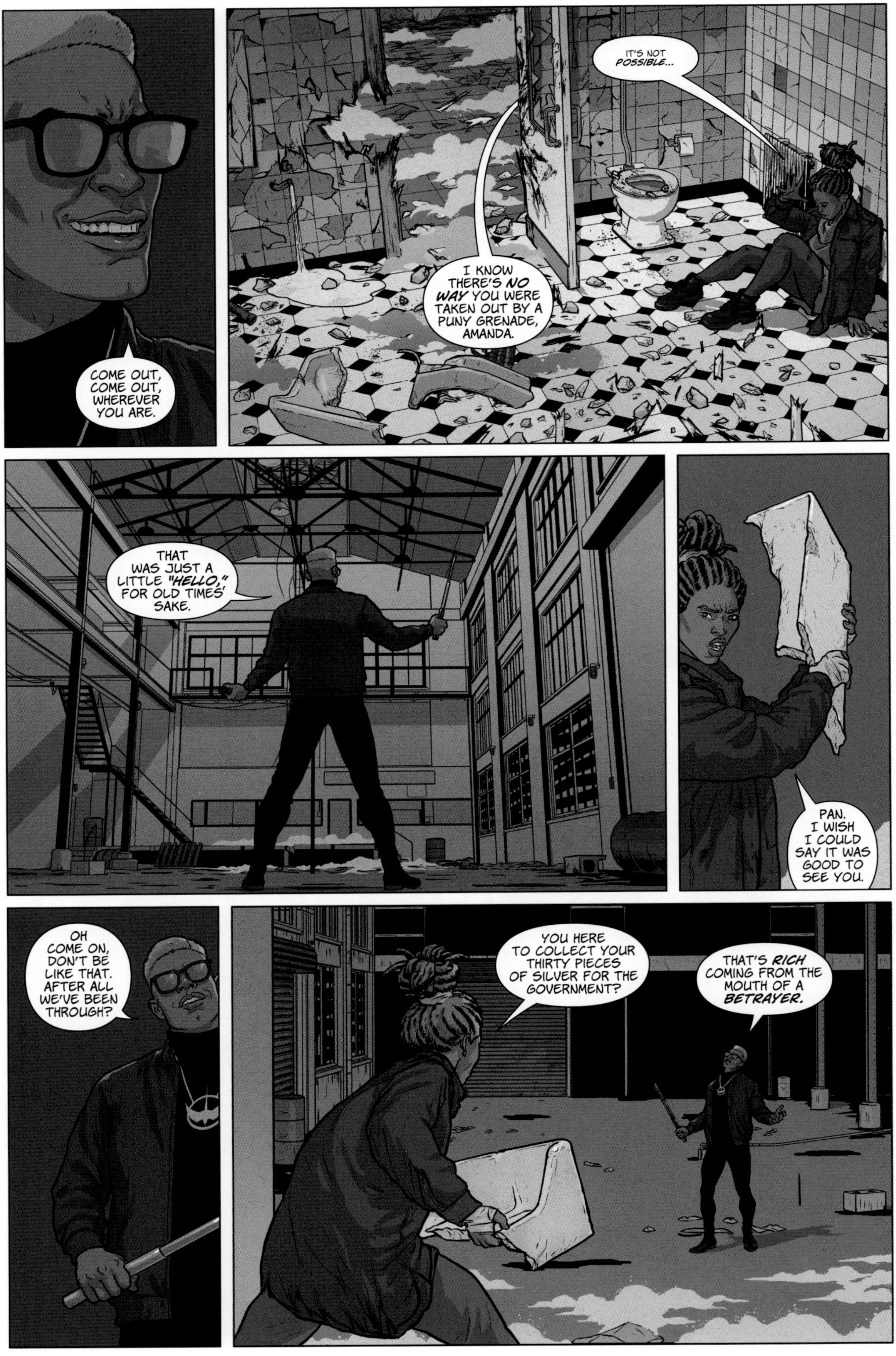
COME OUT, COME OUT, WHEREVER YOU ARE.
IT'S NOT POSSIBLE...
I KNOW THERE'S NO WAY YOU WERE TAKEN OUT BY A PUNY GRENADE, AMANDA.
THAT WAS JUST A LITTLE "HELLO," FOR OLD TIMES' SAKE.
PAN. I WISH I COULD SAY IT WAS GOOD TO SEE YOU.
OH COME ON, DON'T BE LIKE THAT. AFTER ALL WE'VE BEEN THROUGH?
YOU HERE TO COLLECT YOUR THIRTY PIECES OF SILVER FOR THE GOVERNMENT?
THAT'S RICH COMING FROM THE MOUTH OF A BETRAYER.

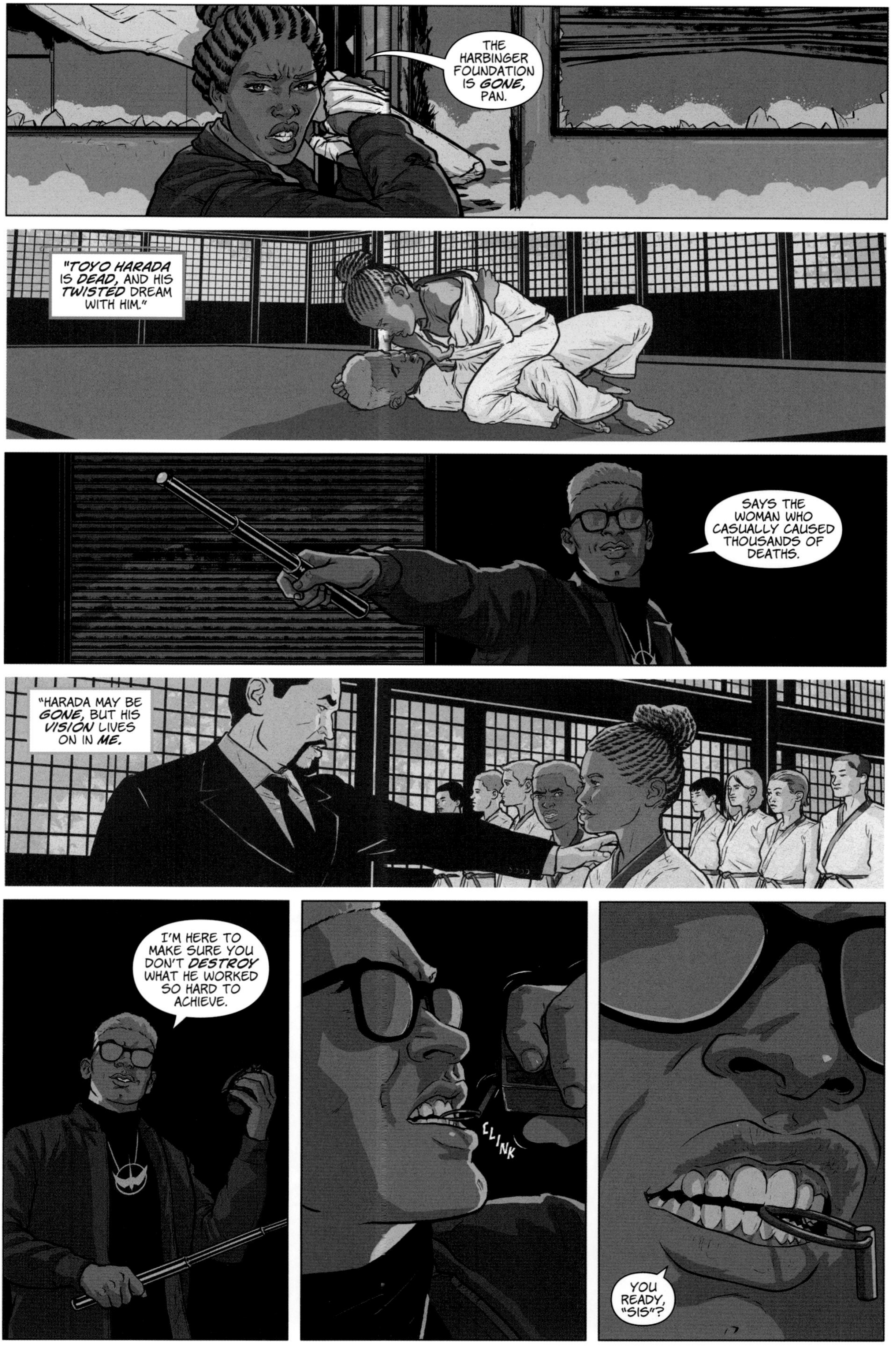
THE HARBINGER FOUNDATION IS GONE, PAN.
"TOYO HARADA IS DEAD, AND HIS TWISTED DREAM WITH HIM."
SAYS THE WOMAN WHO CASUALLY CAUSED THOUSANDS OF DEATHS.
"HARADA MAY BE GONE, BUT HIS VISION LIVES ON IN ME.
I'M HERE TO MAKE SURE YOU DON'T DESTROY WHAT HE WORKED SO HARD TO ACHIEVE.
CLINK
YOU READY, "SIS"?

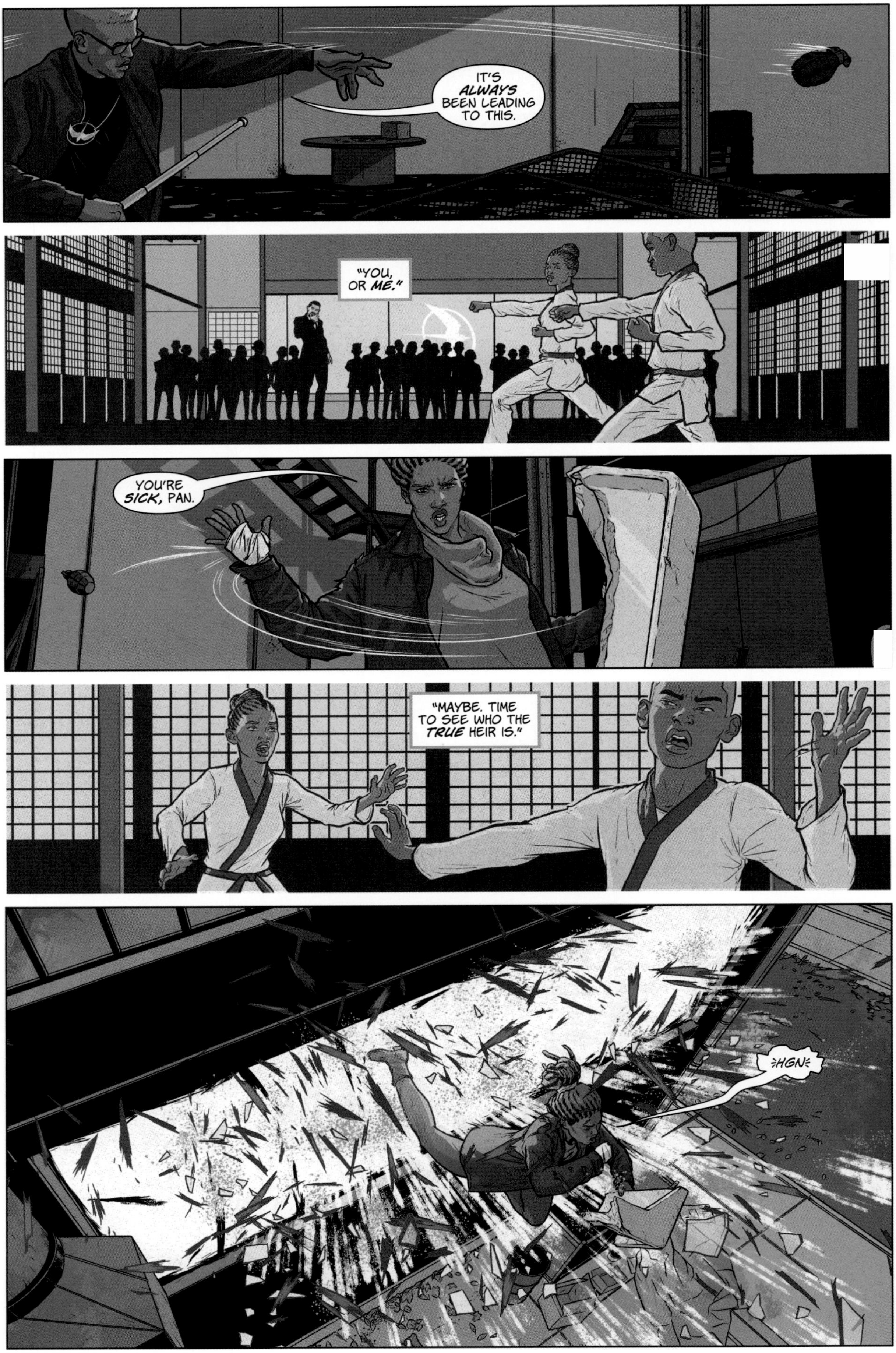
IT'S ALWAYS BEEN LEADING TO THIS.
"YOU, OR ME."
YOU'RE SICK, PAN.
"MAYBE. TIME TO SEE WHO THE TRUE HEIR IS."
HGN

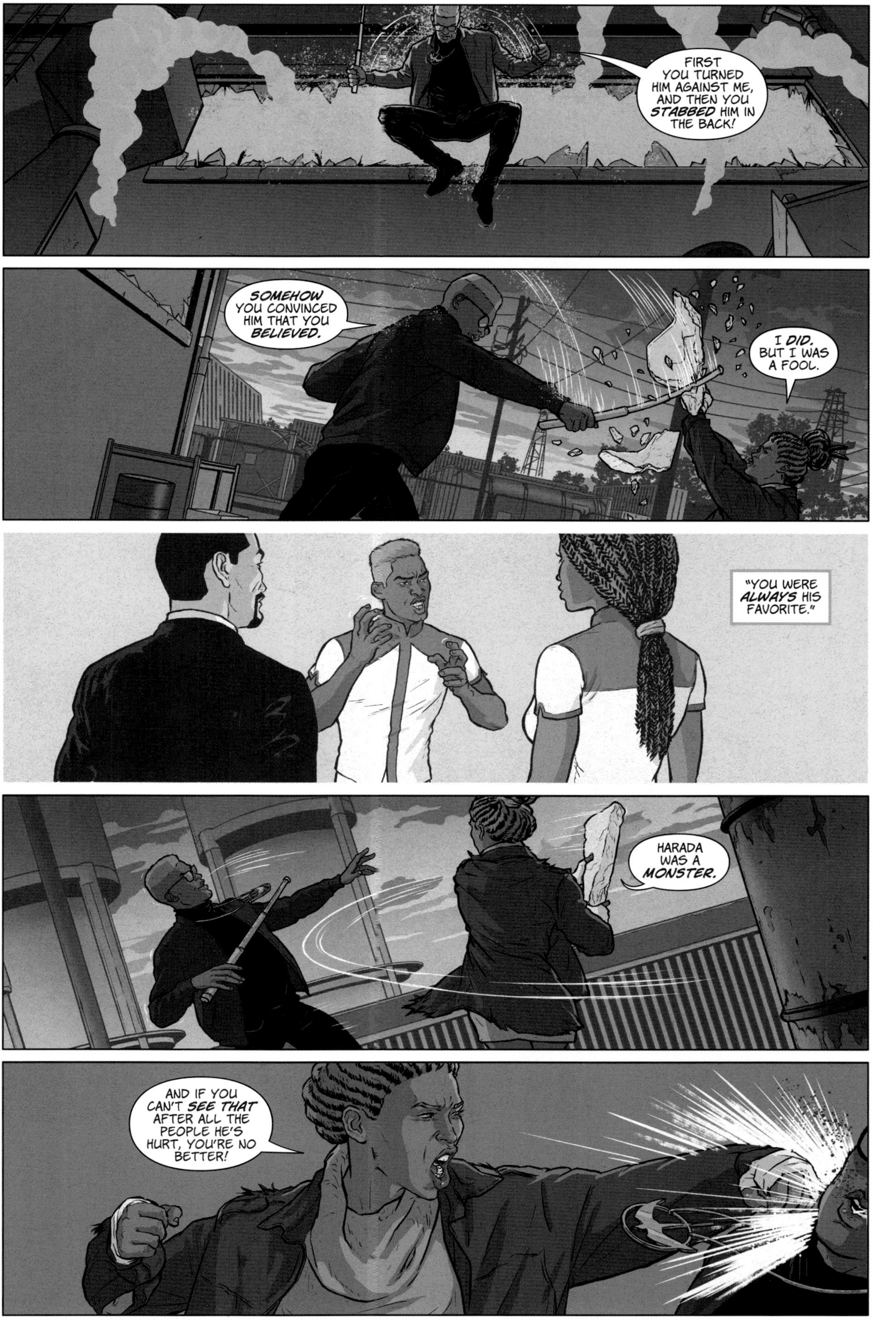
FIRST YOU TURNED HIM AGAINST ME, AND THEN YOU STABBED HIM IN THE BACK!
SOMEHOW YOU CONVINCED HIM THAT YOU BELIEVED.
I DID. BUT I WAS A FOOL.
"YOU WERE ALWAYS HIS FAVORITE."
HARADA WAS A MONSTER.
AND IF YOU CAN'T SEE THAT AFTER ALL THE PEOPLE HE'S HURT, YOU'RE NO BETTER!

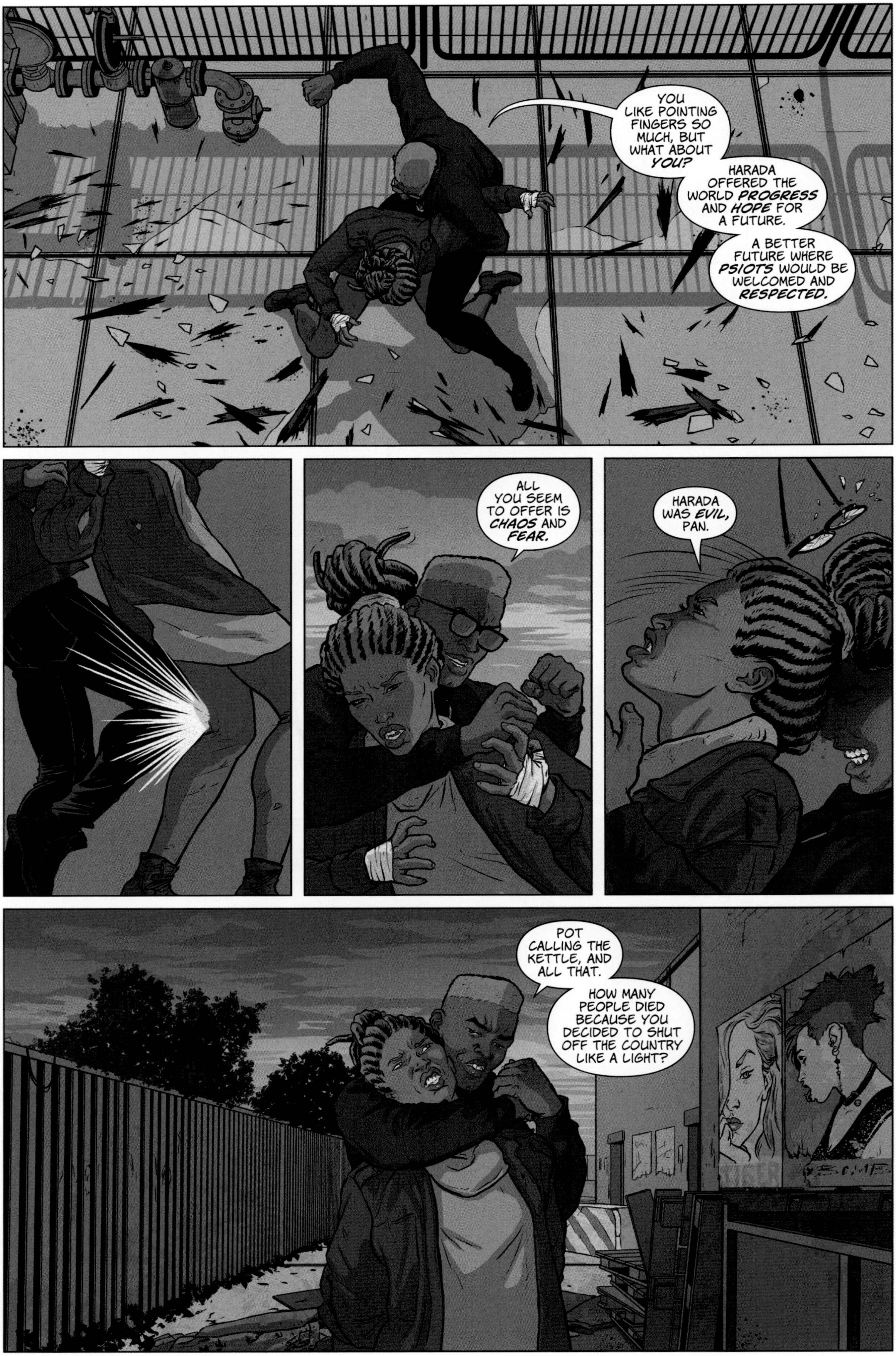
YOU LIKE POINTING FINGERS SO MUCH, BUT WHAT ABOUT YOU?
HARADA OFFERED THE WORLD PROGRESS AND HOPE FOR A FUTURE.
A BETTER FUTURE WHERE PSIOTS WOULD BE WELCOMED AND RESPECTED.
ALL YOU SEEM TO OFFER IS CHAOS AND FEAR.
HARADA WAS EVIL, PAN.
POT CALLING THE KETTLE, AND ALL THAT.
HOW MANY PEOPLE DIED BECAUSE YOU DECIDED TO SHUT OFF THE COUNTRY LIKE A LIGHT?

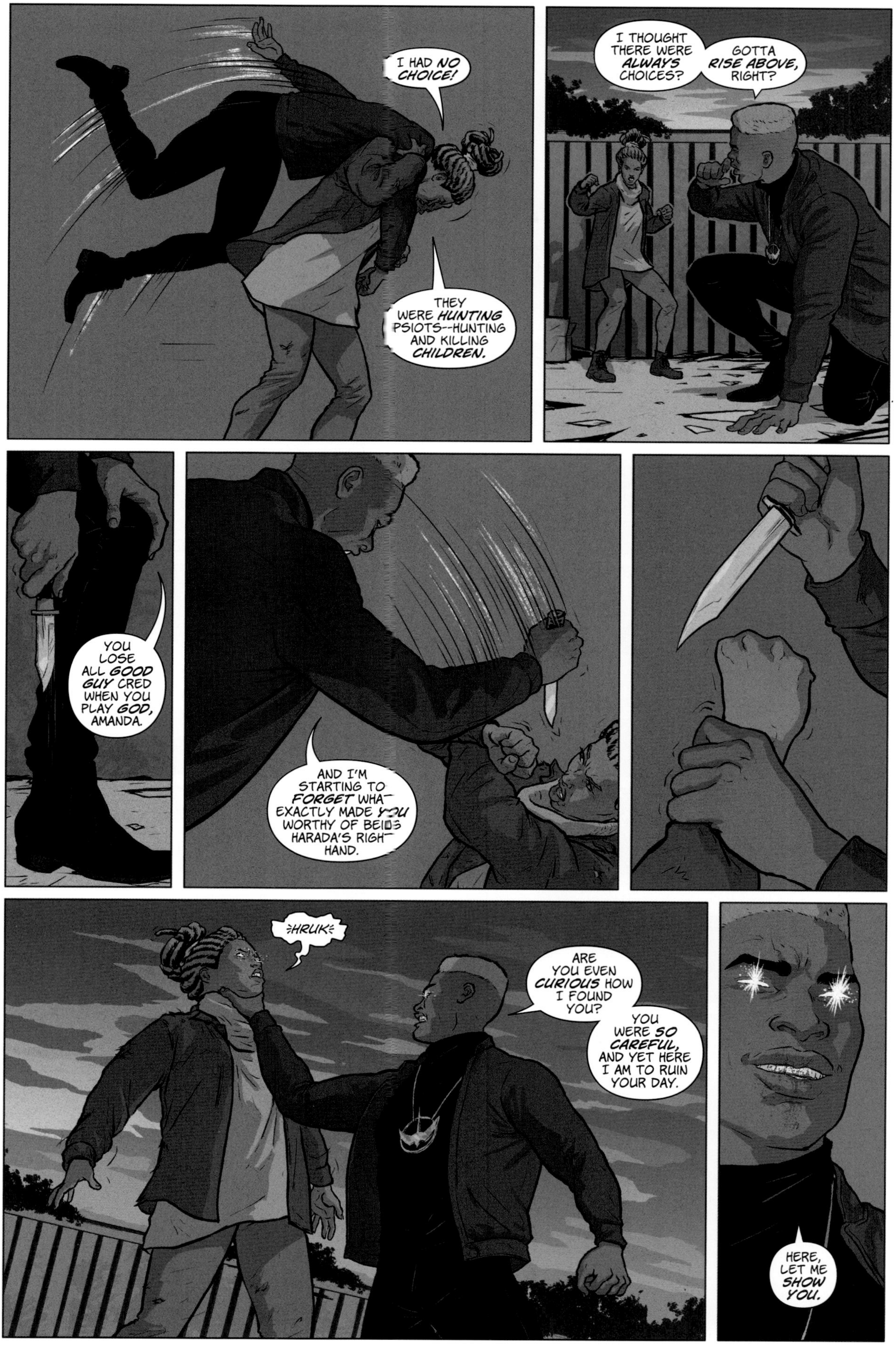
I HAD **NO CHOICE!**
THEY WERE **HUNTING** PSIOTS--HUNTING AND KILLING **CHILDREN.**
I THOUGHT THERE WERE **ALWAYS** CHOICES?
GOTTA **RISE ABOVE,** RIGHT?
YOU LOSE ALL **GOOD GUY** CRED WHEN YOU PLAY **GOD,** AMANDA.
AND I'M STARTING TO **FORGET** WHAT EXACTLY MADE **YOU** WORTHY OF BEING HARADA'S RIGHT HAND.
HRUK
ARE YOU EVEN **CURIOUS** HOW I FOUND YOU?
YOU WERE **SO CAREFUL,** AND YET HERE I AM TO RUIN YOUR DAY.
HERE, LET ME **SHOW YOU.**

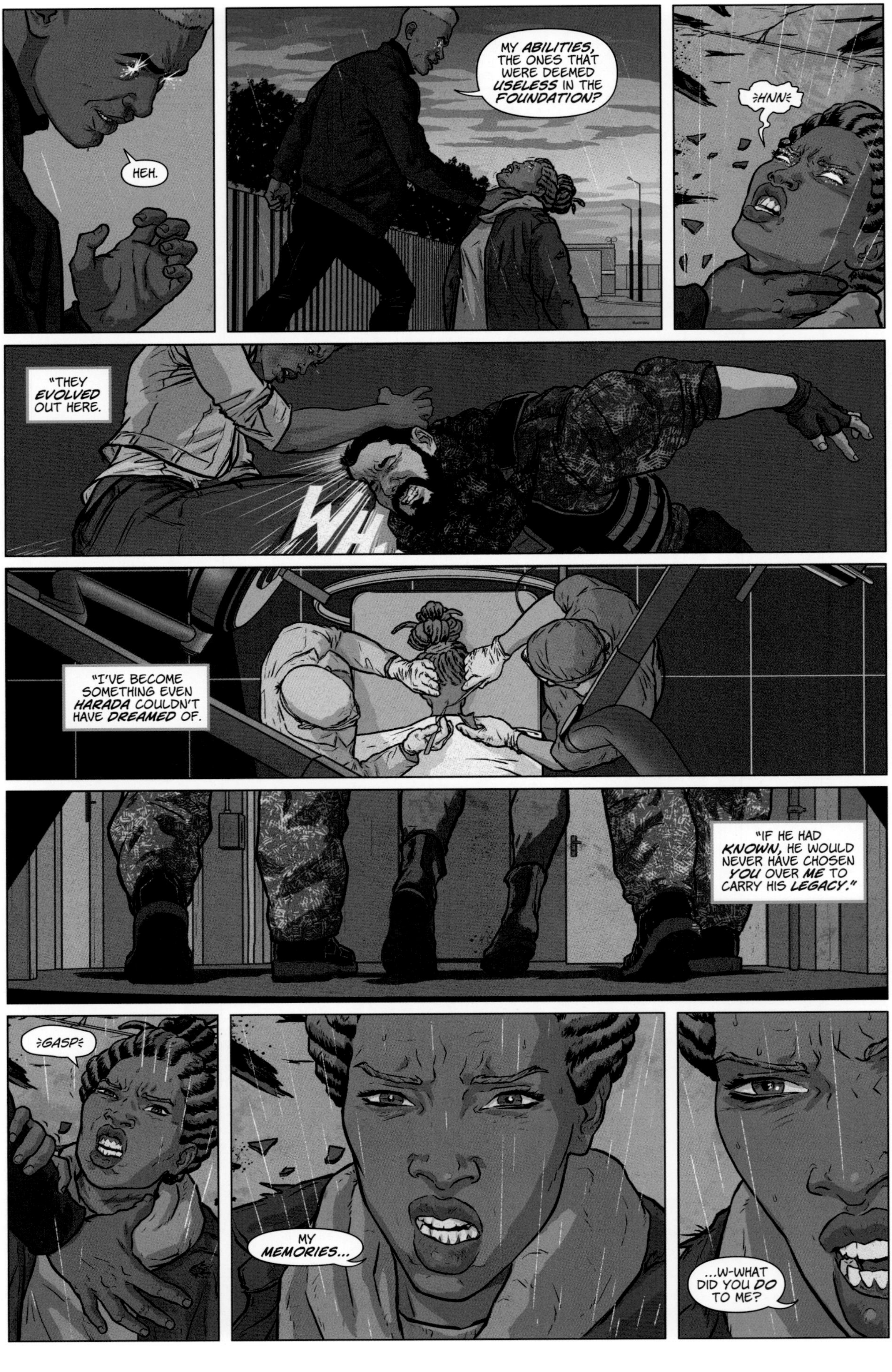
HEH.
MY ABILITIES, THE ONES THAT WERE DEEMED USELESS IN THE FOUNDATION?
HNN
"THEY EVOLVED OUT HERE.
WH
"I'VE BECOME SOMETHING EVEN HARADA COULDN'T HAVE DREAMED OF.
"IF HE HAD KNOWN, HE WOULD NEVER HAVE CHOSEN YOU OVER ME TO CARRY HIS LEGACY."
GASP
MY MEMORIES...
...W-WHAT DID YOU DO TO ME?

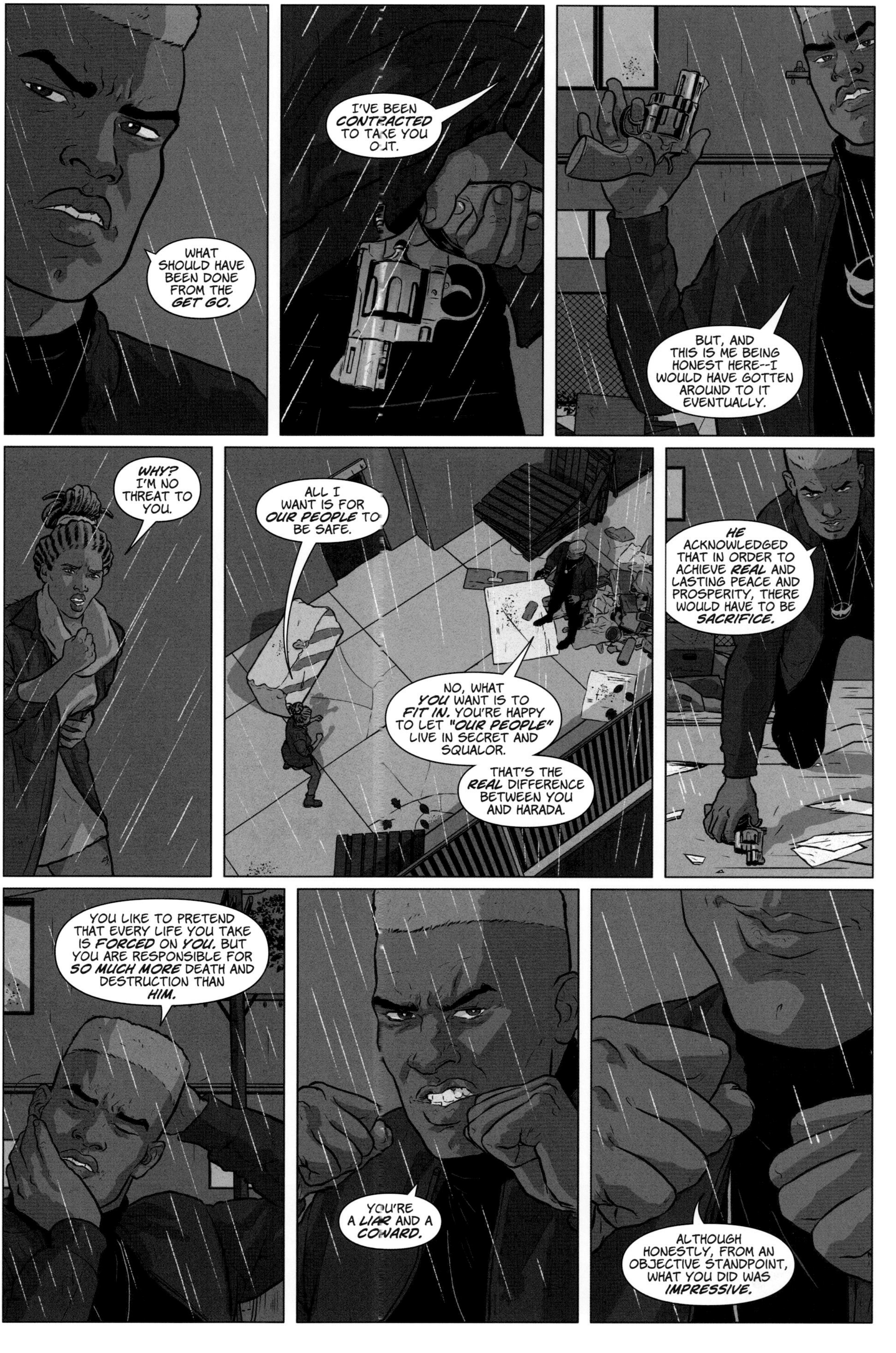
WHAT SHOULD HAVE BEEN DONE FROM THE *GET GO.*
I'VE BEEN *CONTRACTED* TO TAKE YOU OUT.
BUT, AND THIS IS ME BEING HONEST HERE--I WOULD HAVE GOTTEN AROUND TO IT EVENTUALLY.
WHY? I'M NO THREAT TO YOU.
ALL I WANT IS FOR *OUR PEOPLE* TO BE SAFE.
NO, WHAT *YOU* WANT IS TO *FIT IN.* YOU'RE HAPPY TO LET *"OUR PEOPLE"* LIVE IN SECRET AND SQUALOR.
THAT'S THE *REAL* DIFFERENCE BETWEEN YOU AND HARADA.
HE ACKNOWLEDGED THAT IN ORDER TO ACHIEVE *REAL* AND LASTING PEACE AND PROSPERITY, THERE WOULD HAVE TO BE *SACRIFICE.*
YOU LIKE TO PRETEND THAT EVERY LIFE YOU TAKE IS *FORCED ON YOU.* BUT YOU ARE RESPONSIBLE FOR *SO MUCH MORE* DEATH AND DESTRUCTION THAN *HIM.*
YOU'RE A *LIAR* AND A *COWARD.*
ALTHOUGH HONESTLY, FROM AN OBJECTIVE STANDPOINT, WHAT YOU DID WAS *IMPRESSIVE.*

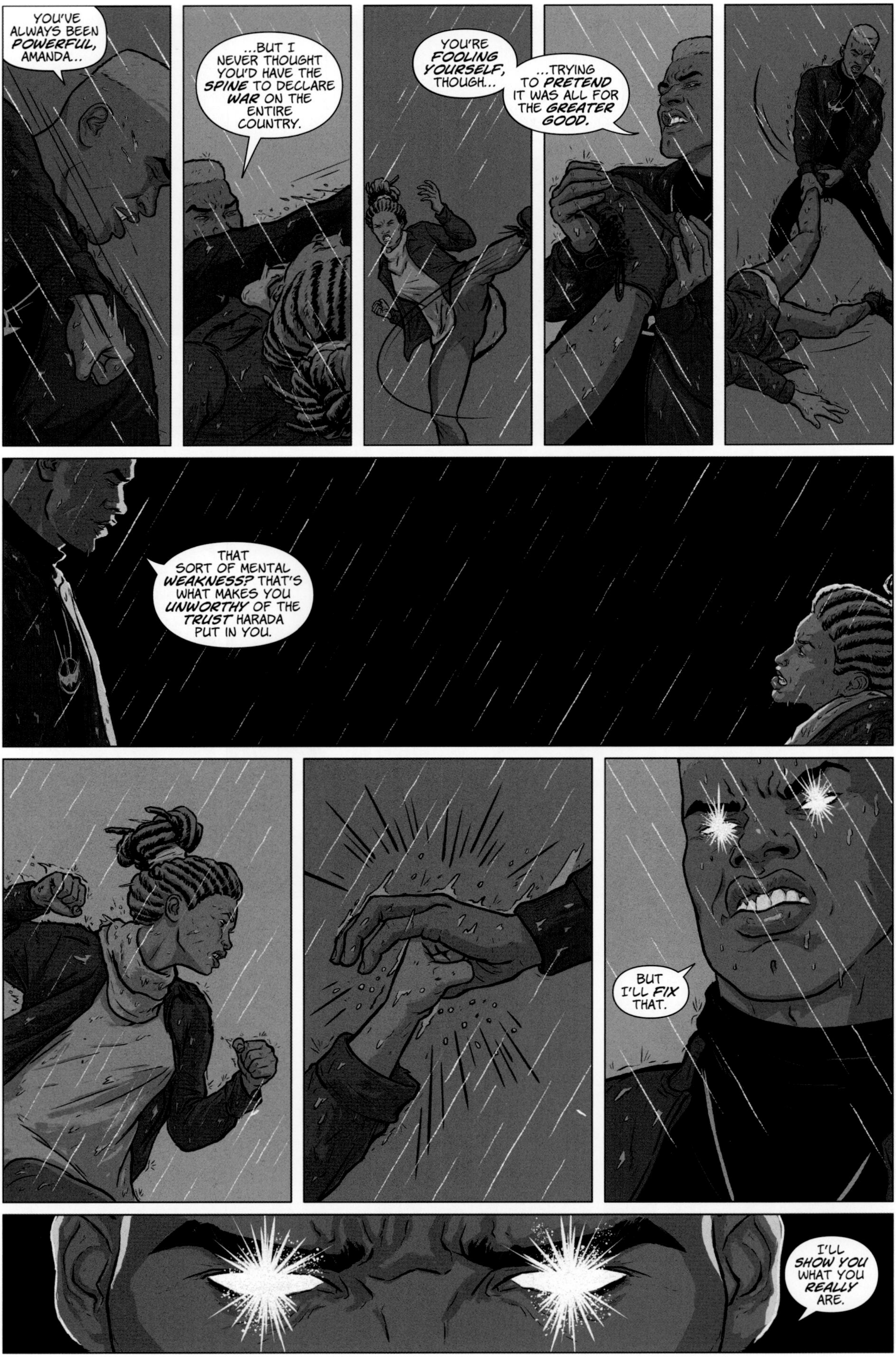
YOU'VE ALWAYS BEEN POWERFUL, AMANDA...
...BUT I NEVER THOUGHT YOU'D HAVE THE SPINE TO DECLARE WAR ON THE ENTIRE COUNTRY.
YOU'RE FOOLING YOURSELF, THOUGH...
...TRYING TO PRETEND IT WAS ALL FOR THE GREATER GOOD.
THAT SORT OF MENTAL WEAKNESS? THAT'S WHAT MAKES YOU UNWORTHY OF THE TRUST HARADA PUT IN YOU.
BUT I'LL FIX THAT.
I'LL SHOW YOU WHAT YOU REALLY ARE.

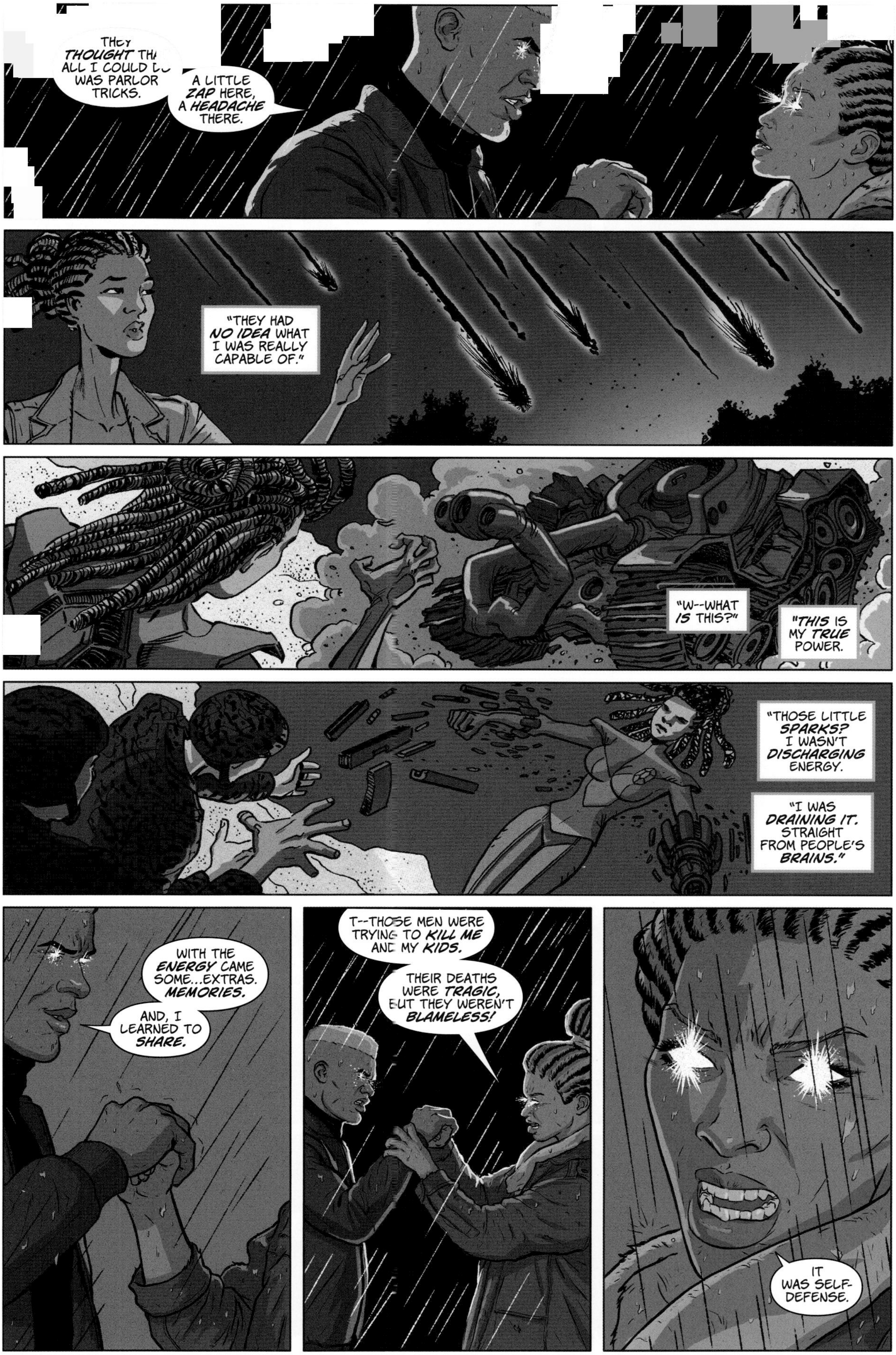
THEY THOUGHT THA ALL I COULD DO WAS PARLOR TRICKS.
A LITTLE ZAP HERE, A HEADACHE THERE.
"THEY HAD NO IDEA WHAT I WAS REALLY CAPABLE OF."
"W--WHAT IS THIS?"
"THIS IS MY TRUE POWER.
"THOSE LITTLE SPARKS? I WASN'T DISCHARGING ENERGY.
"I WAS DRAINING IT. STRAIGHT FROM PEOPLE'S BRAINS."
WITH THE ENERGY CAME SOME...EXTRAS. MEMORIES.
AND, I LEARNED TO SHARE.
T--THOSE MEN WERE TRYING TO KILL ME AND MY KIDS.
THEIR DEATHS WERE TRAGIC, BUT THEY WEREN'T BLAMELESS!
IT WAS SELF-DEFENSE.

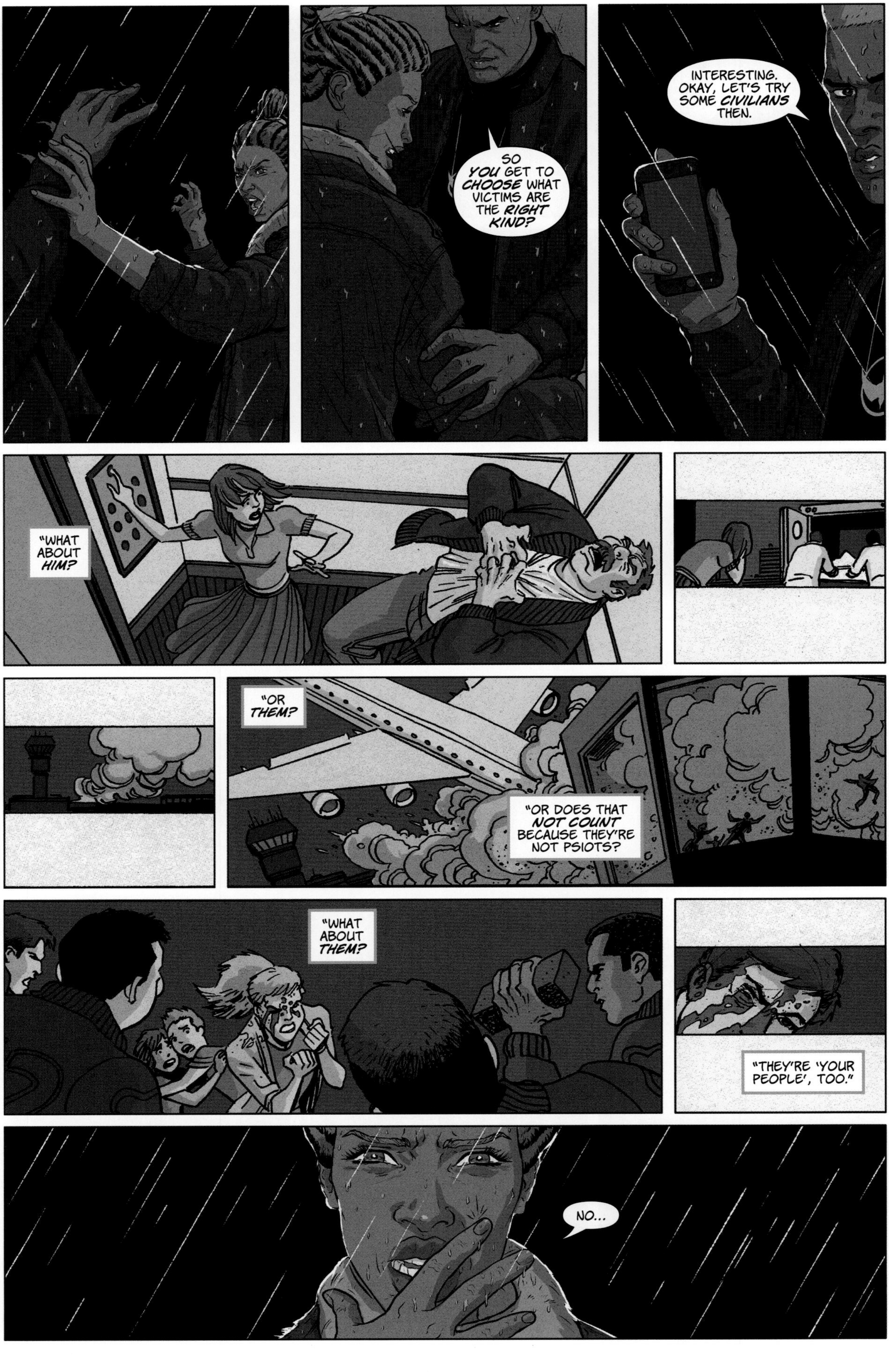
SO YOU GET TO CHOOSE WHAT VICTIMS ARE THE RIGHT KIND?
INTERESTING. OKAY, LET'S TRY SOME CIVILIANS THEN.
"WHAT ABOUT HIM?
"OR THEM?
"OR DOES THAT NOT COUNT BECAUSE THEY'RE NOT PSIOTS?
"WHAT ABOUT THEM?
"THEY'RE 'YOUR PEOPLE', TOO."
NO...

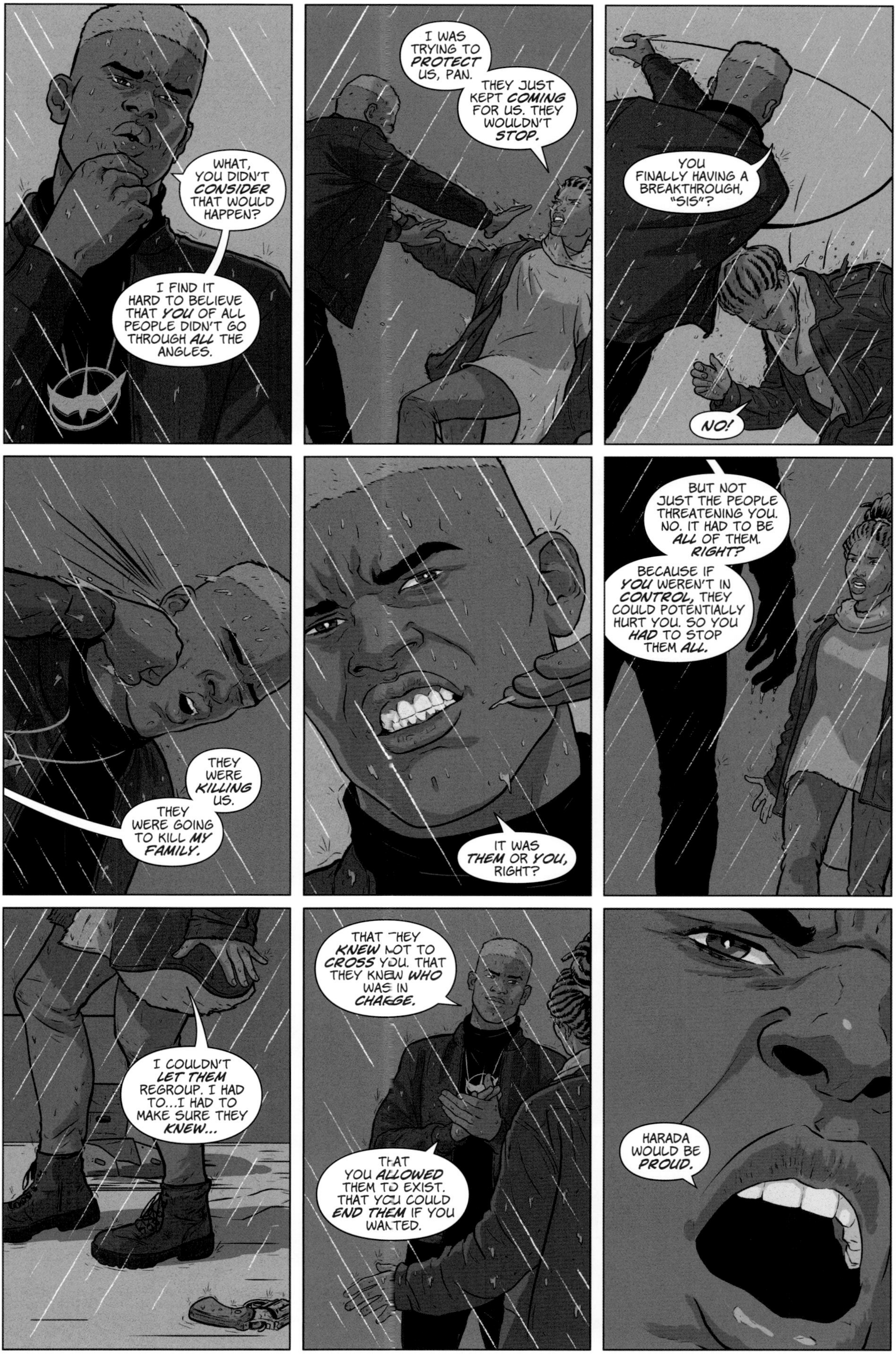
WHAT, YOU DIDN'T CONSIDER THAT WOULD HAPPEN?
I FIND IT HARD TO BELIEVE THAT YOU OF ALL PEOPLE DIDN'T GO THROUGH ALL THE ANGLES.
I WAS TRYING TO PROTECT US, PAN.
THEY JUST KEPT COMING FOR US. THEY WOULDN'T STOP.
YOU FINALLY HAVING A BREAKTHROUGH, "SIS"?
NO!
THEY WERE KILLING US.
THEY WERE GOING TO KILL MY FAMILY.
IT WAS THEM OR YOU, RIGHT?
BUT NOT JUST THE PEOPLE THREATENING YOU. NO. IT HAD TO BE ALL OF THEM. RIGHT?
BECAUSE IF YOU WEREN'T IN CONTROL, THEY COULD POTENTIALLY HURT YOU. SO YOU HAD TO STOP THEM ALL.
I COULDN'T LET THEM REGROUP. I HAD TO...I HAD TO MAKE SURE THEY KNEW...
THAT THEY KNEW NOT TO CROSS YOU. THAT THEY KNEW WHO WAS IN CHARGE.
THAT YOU ALLOWED THEM TO EXIST. THAT YOU COULD END THEM IF YOU WANTED.
HARADA WOULD BE PROUD.

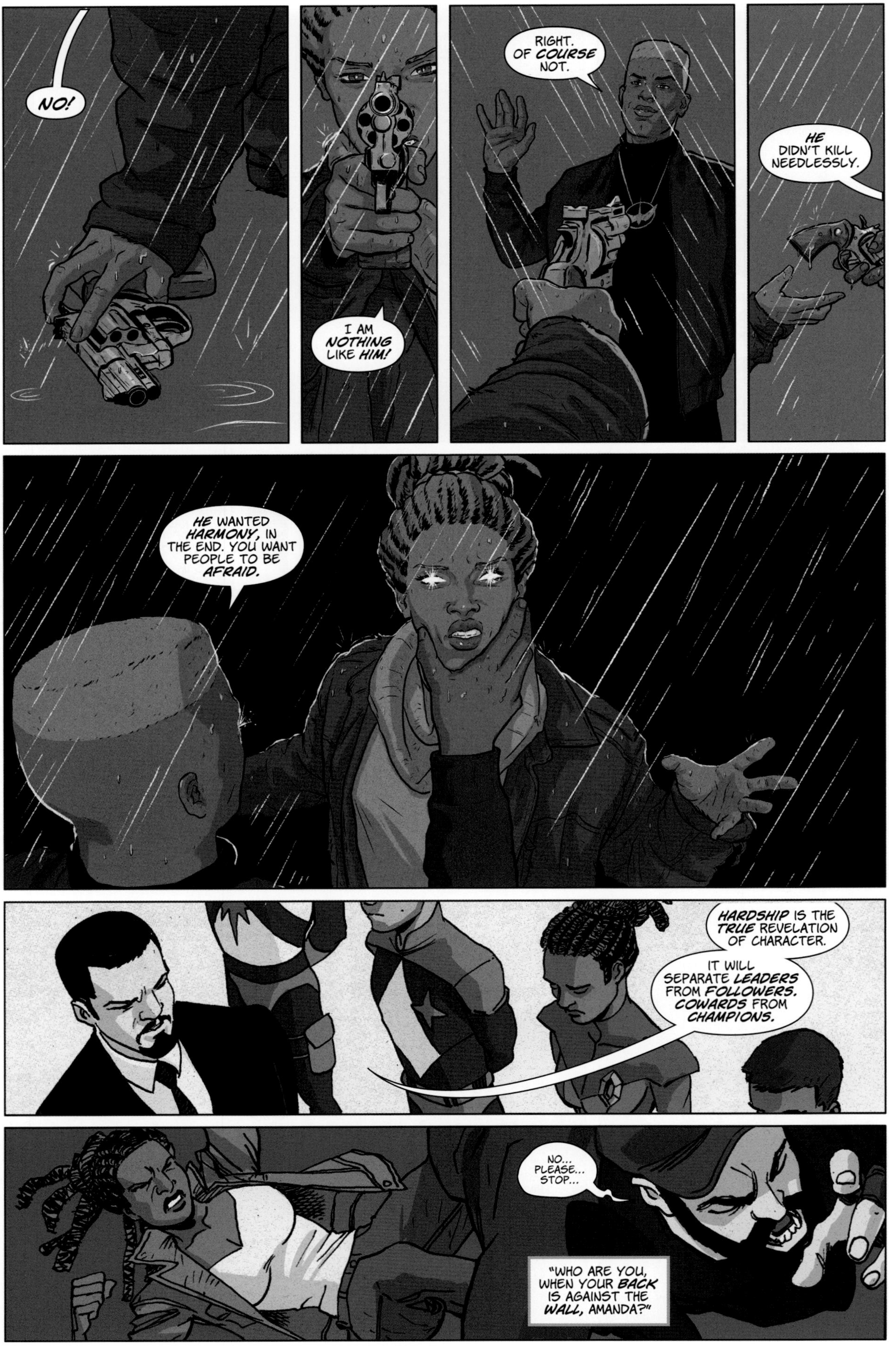
NO!
I AM NOTHING LIKE HIM!
RIGHT. OF COURSE NOT.
HE DIDN'T KILL NEEDLESSLY.
HE WANTED HARMONY, IN THE END. YOU WANT PEOPLE TO BE AFRAID.
HARDSHIP IS THE TRUE REVELATION OF CHARACTER.
IT WILL SEPARATE LEADERS FROM FOLLOWERS. COWARDS FROM CHAMPIONS.
NO... PLEASE... STOP...
"WHO ARE YOU, WHEN YOUR BACK IS AGAINST THE WALL, AMANDA?"

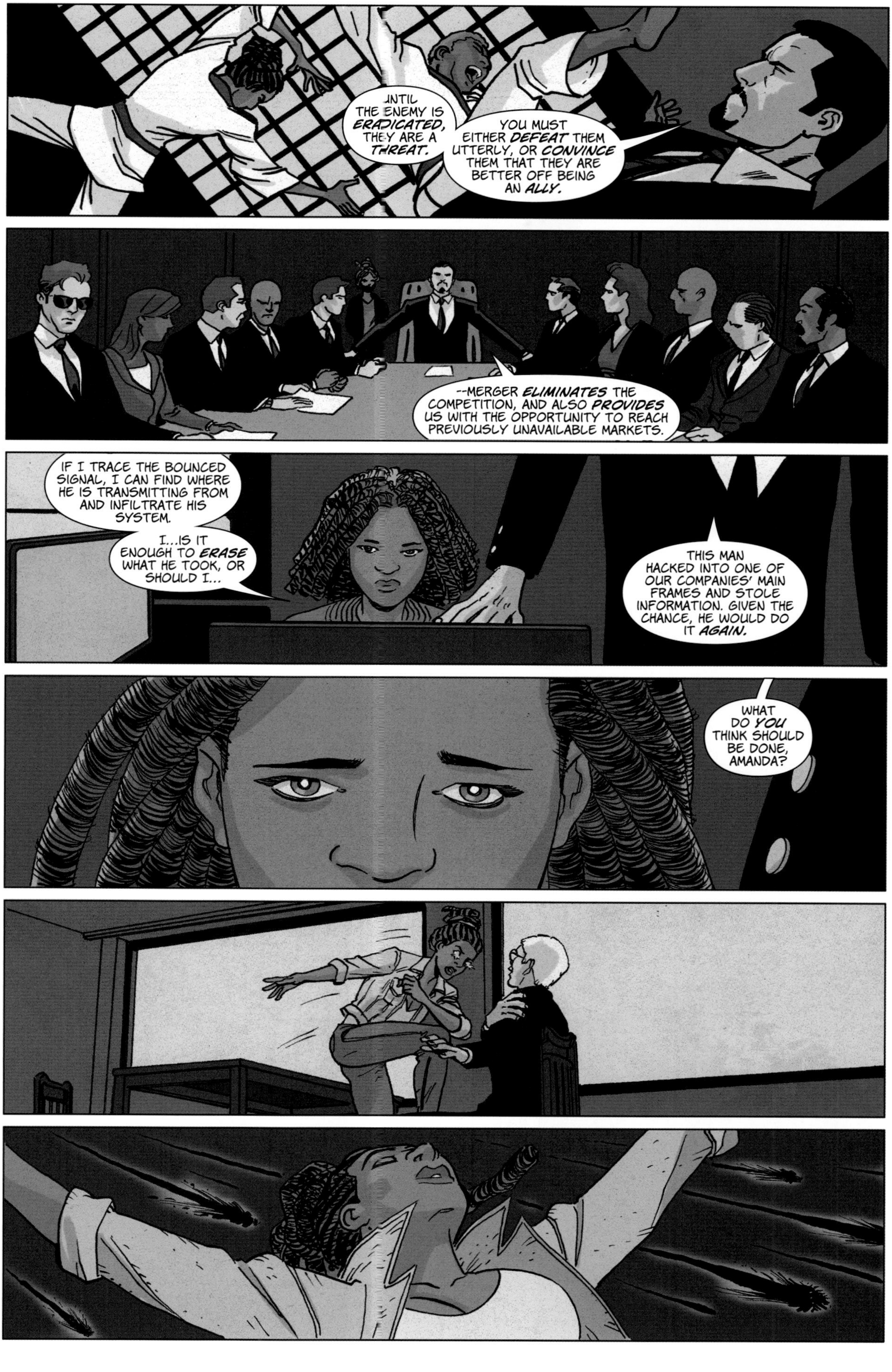
UNTIL THE ENEMY IS ERADICATED, THEY ARE A THREAT.
YOU MUST EITHER DEFEAT THEM UTTERLY, OR CONVINCE THEM THAT THEY ARE BETTER OFF BEING AN ALLY.
--MERGER ELIMINATES THE COMPETITION, AND ALSO PROVIDES US WITH THE OPPORTUNITY TO REACH PREVIOUSLY UNAVAILABLE MARKETS.
IF I TRACE THE BOUNCED SIGNAL, I CAN FIND WHERE HE IS TRANSMITTING FROM AND INFILTRATE HIS SYSTEM.
I...IS IT ENOUGH TO ERASE WHAT HE TOOK, OR SHOULD I...
THIS MAN HACKED INTO ONE OF OUR COMPANIES' MAIN FRAMES AND STOLE INFORMATION. GIVEN THE CHANCE, HE WOULD DO IT AGAIN.
WHAT DO YOU THINK SHOULD BE DONE, AMANDA?

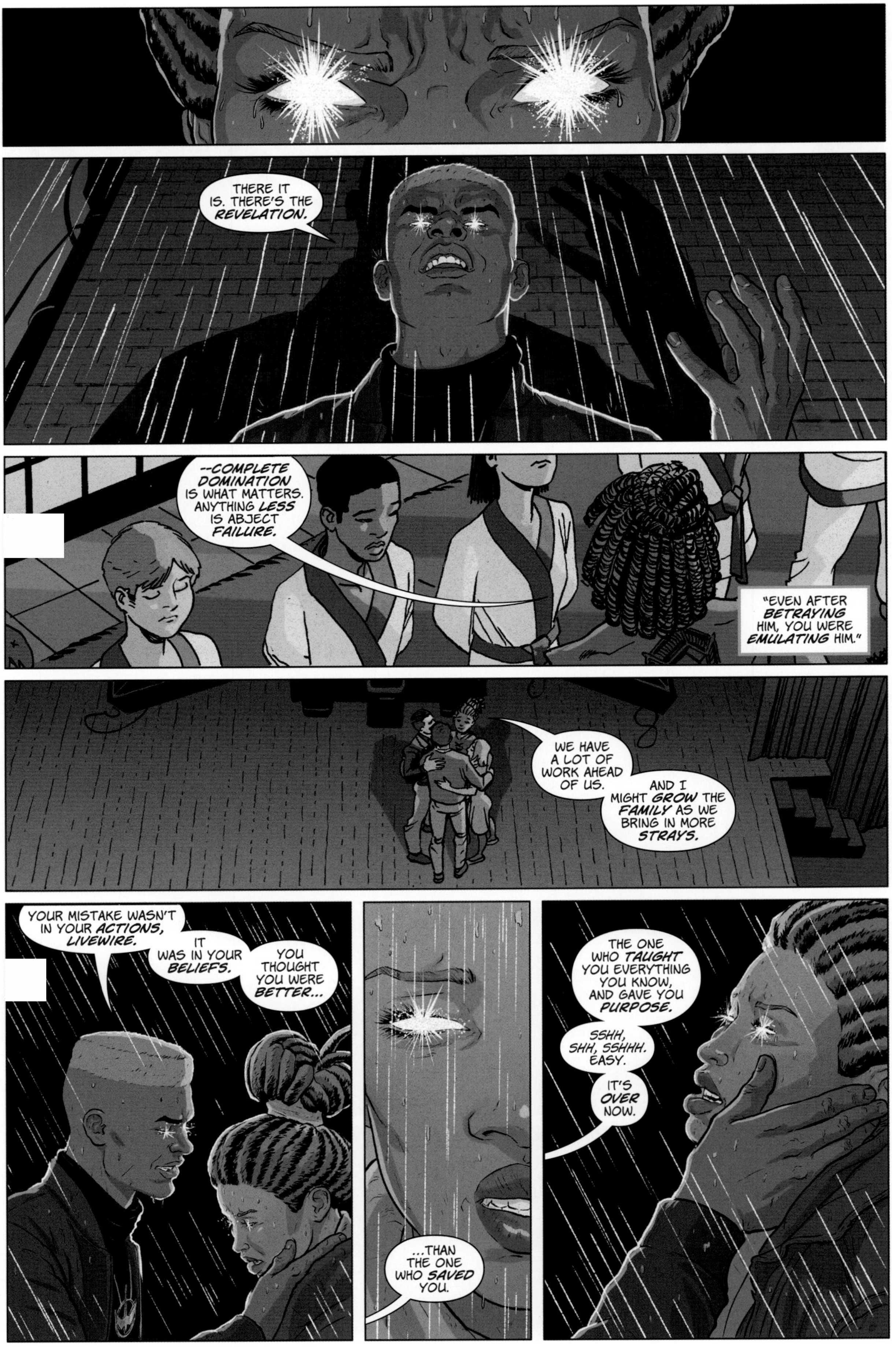
THERE IT IS. THERE'S THE *REVELATION.*
--*COMPLETE DOMINATION* IS WHAT MATTERS. ANYTHING *LESS* IS ABJECT *FAILURE.*
"EVEN AFTER *BETRAYING* HIM, YOU WERE *EMULATING* HIM."
WE HAVE A LOT OF WORK AHEAD OF US.
AND I MIGHT *GROW* THE *FAMILY* AS WE BRING IN MORE *STRAYS.*
YOUR MISTAKE WASN'T IN YOUR *ACTIONS, LIVEWIRE.*
IT WAS IN YOUR *BELIEFS.*
YOU THOUGHT YOU WERE *BETTER...*
...THAN THE ONE WHO *SAVED* YOU.
THE ONE WHO *TAUGHT* YOU EVERYTHING YOU KNOW, AND GAVE YOU *PURPOSE.*
SSHH, SHH, SSHHH. EASY.
IT'S *OVER* NOW.

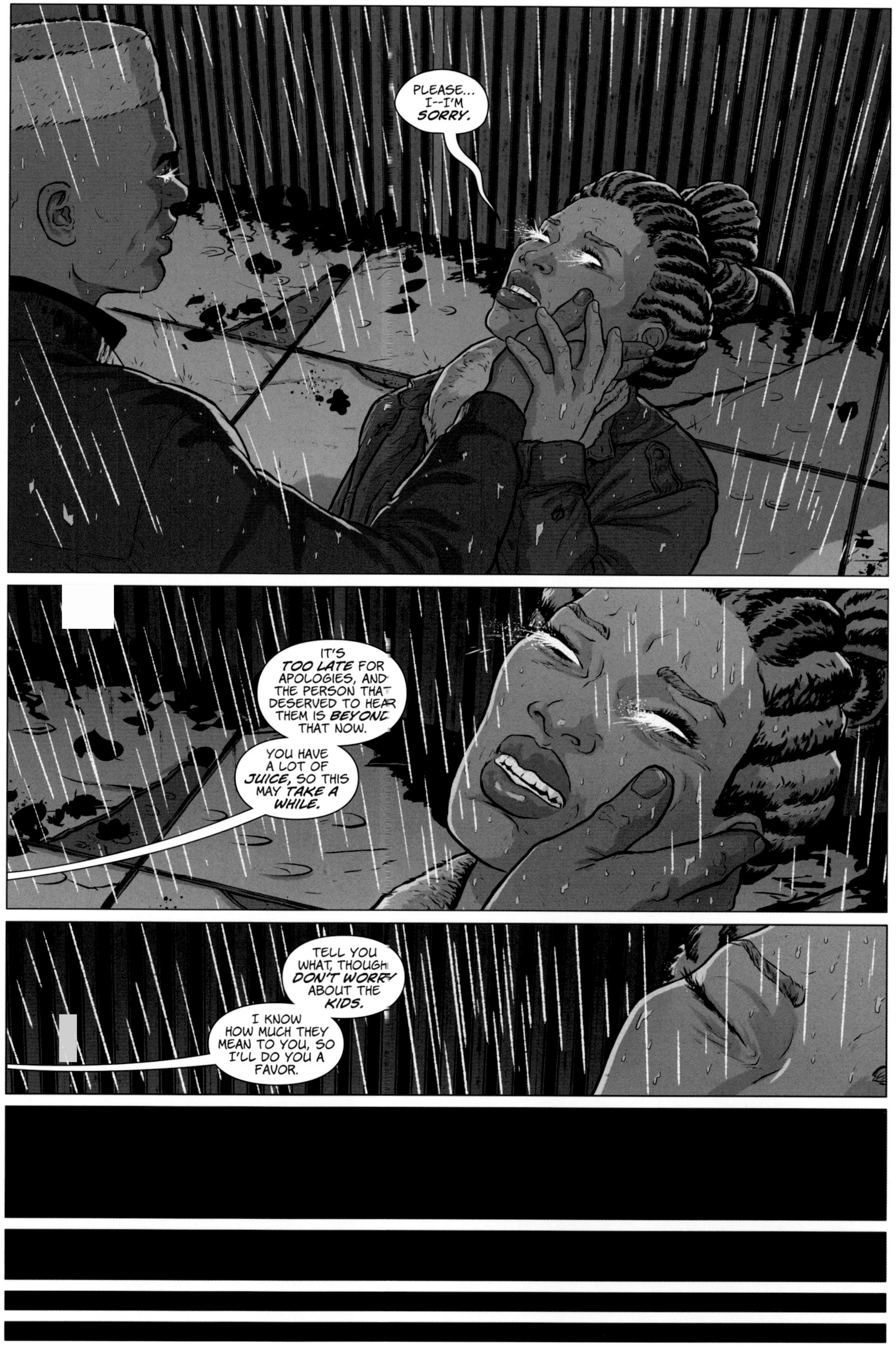
PLEASE... I--I'M SORRY.
IT'S TOO LATE FOR APOLOGIES, AND THE PERSON THAT DESERVED TO HEAR THEM IS BEYOND THAT NOW.
YOU HAVE A LOT OF JUICE, SO THIS MAY TAKE A WHILE.
TELL YOU WHAT, THOUGH. DON'T WORRY ABOUT THE KIDS.
I KNOW HOW MUCH THEY MEAN TO YOU, SO I'LL DO YOU A FAVOR.

[redacted]

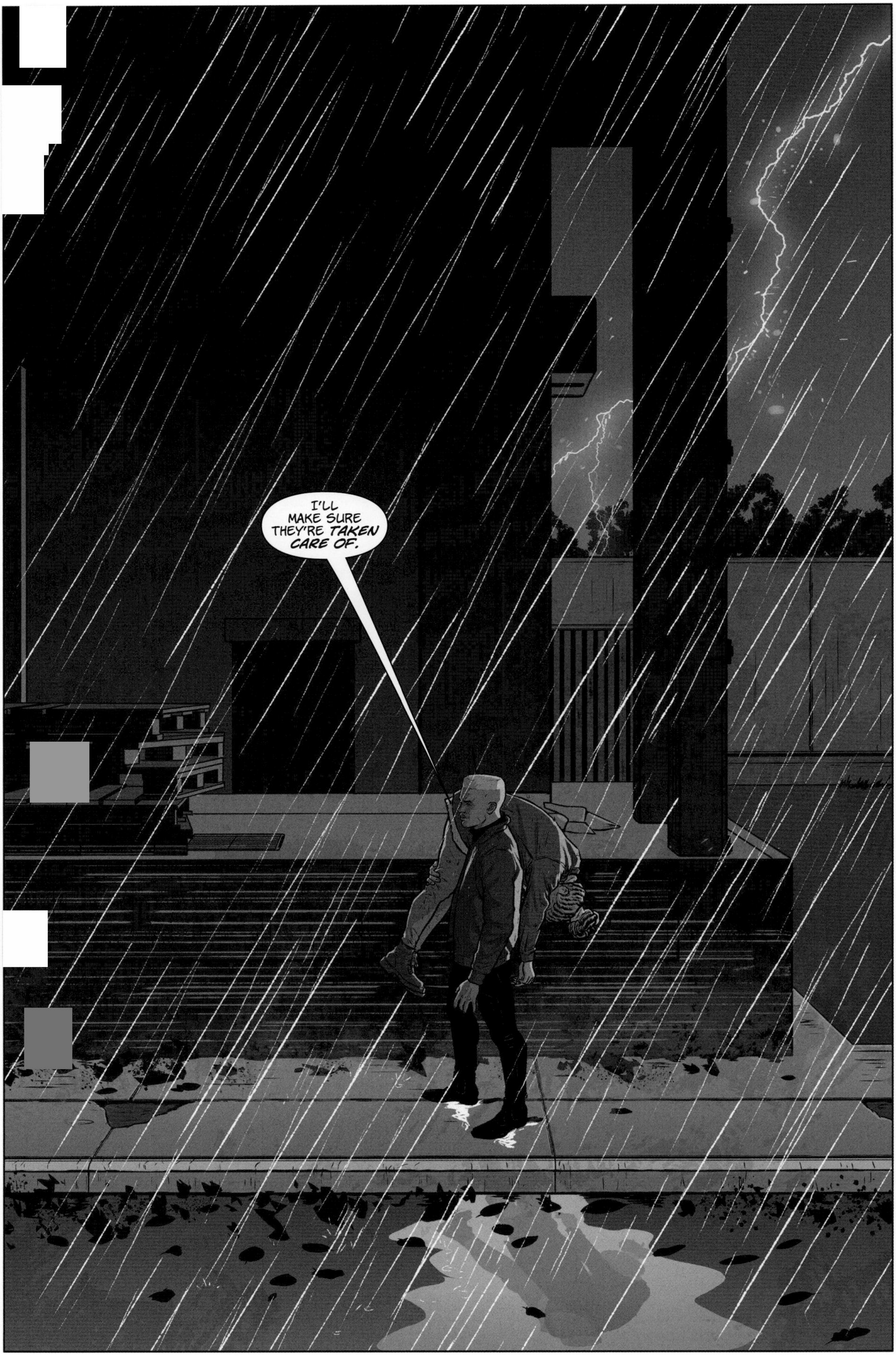
I'LL MAKE SURE THEY'RE *TAKEN CARE OF.*

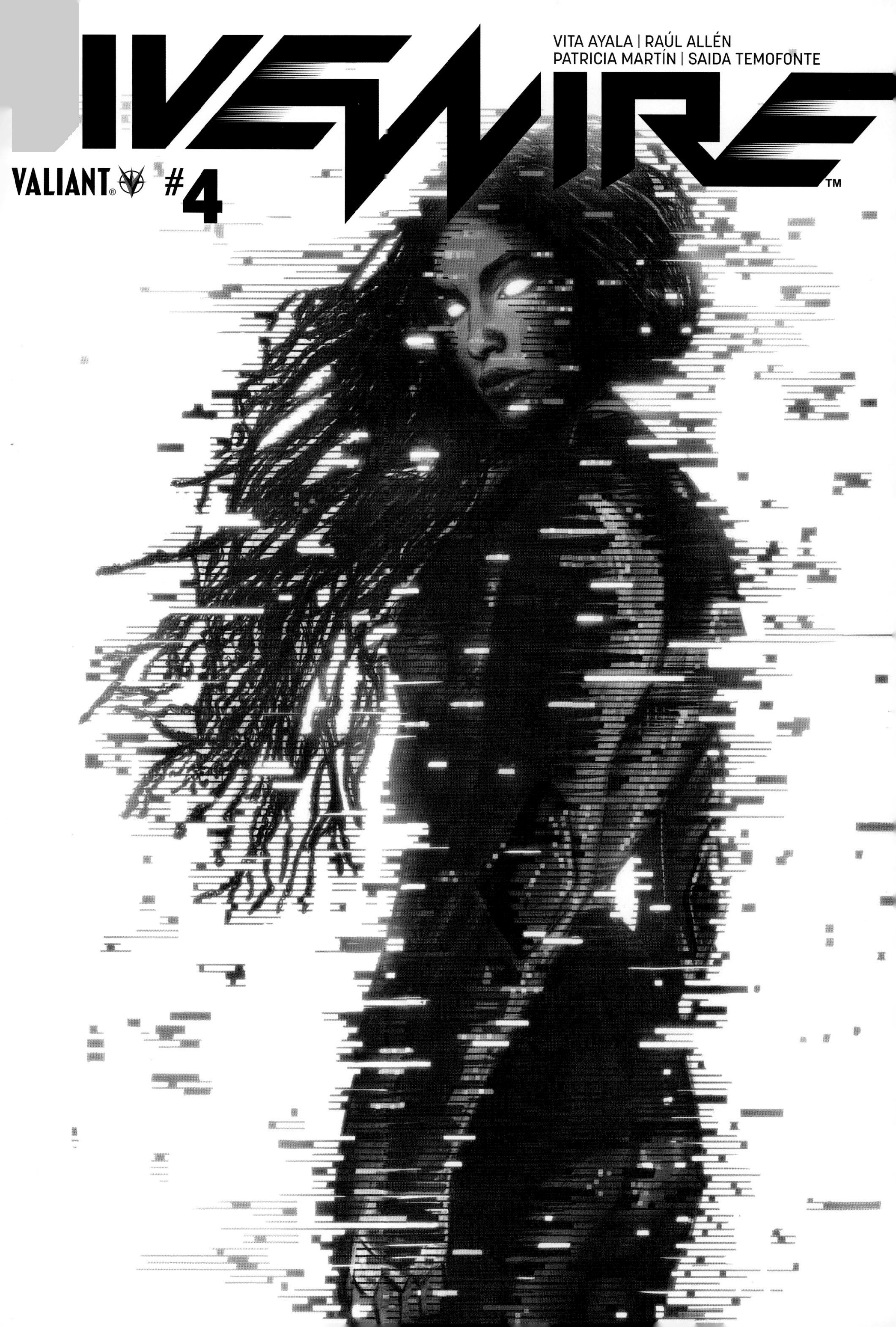
VITA AYALA | RAÚL ALLÉN
PATRICIA MARTÍN | SAIDA TEMOFONTE
IVEWIRE™
VALIANT®
#4

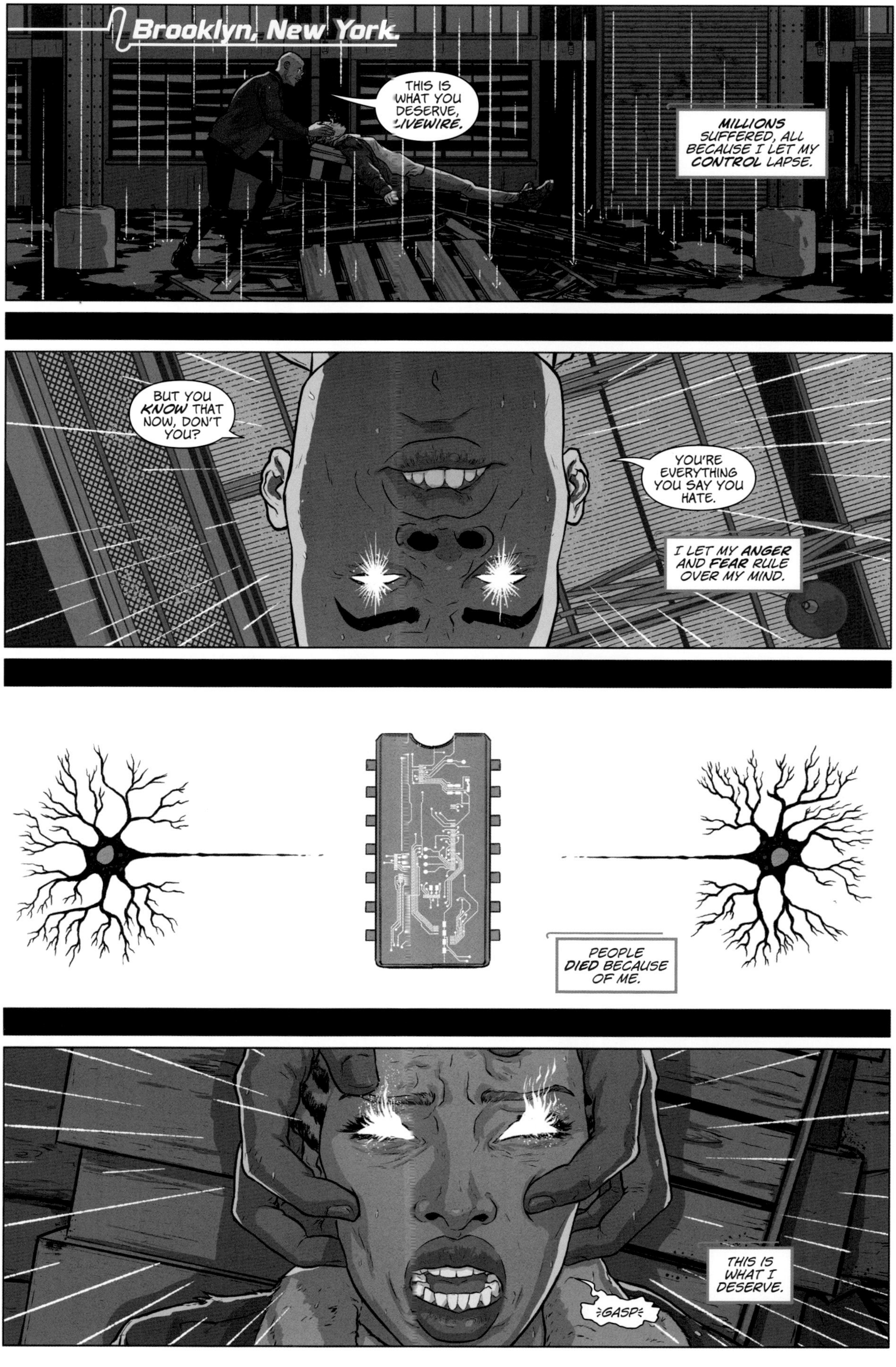
Brooklyn, New York.
THIS IS WHAT YOU DESERVE, LIVEWIRE.
MILLIONS SUFFERED, ALL BECAUSE I LET MY CONTROL LAPSE.
BUT YOU KNOW THAT NOW, DON'T YOU?
YOU'RE EVERYTHING YOU SAY YOU HATE.
I LET MY ANGER AND FEAR RULE OVER MY MIND.
PEOPLE DIED BECAUSE OF ME.
THIS IS WHAT I DESERVE.
GASP

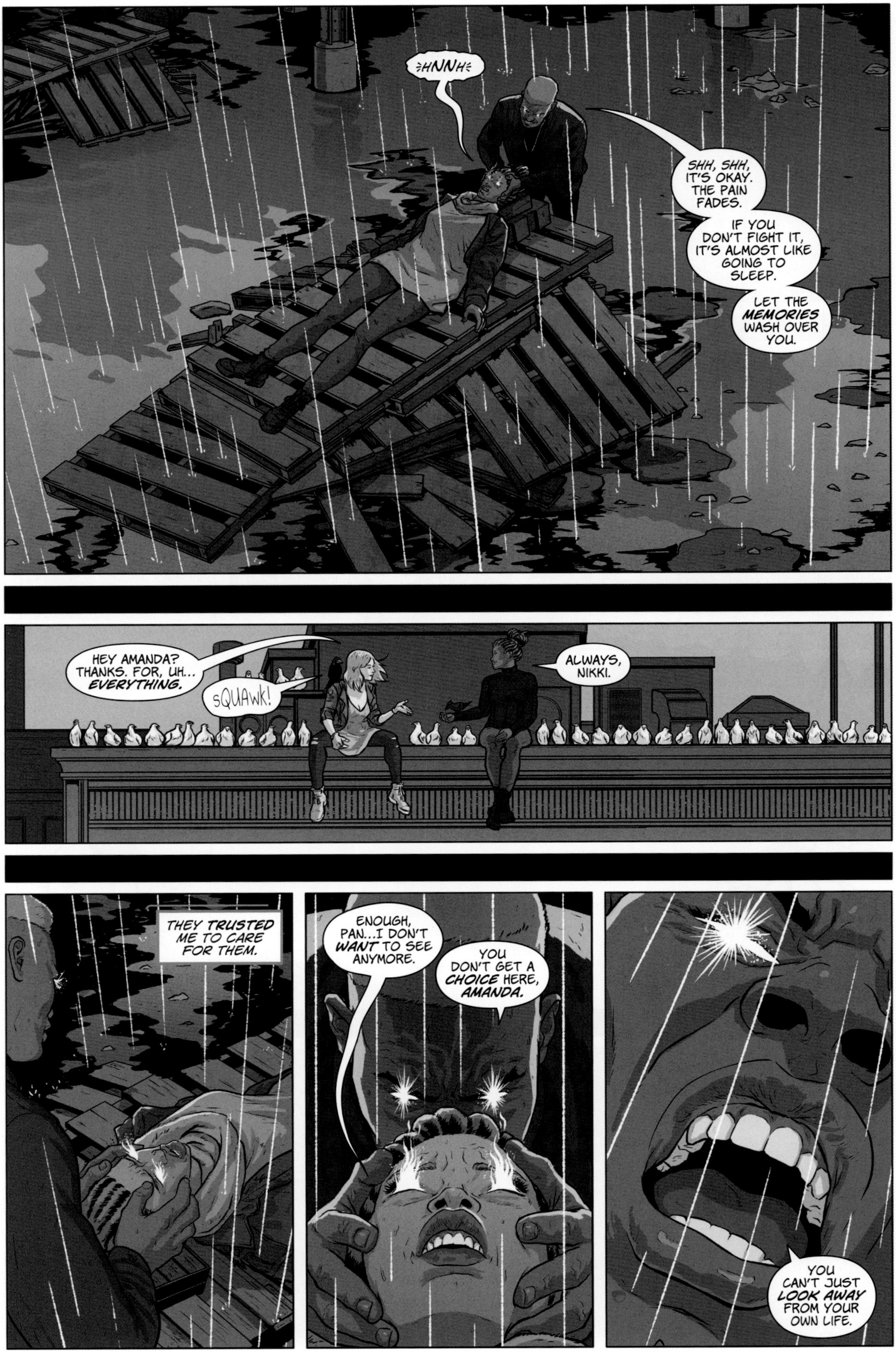
HNNH
SHH, SHH, IT'S OKAY. THE PAIN FADES.
IF YOU DON'T FIGHT IT, IT'S ALMOST LIKE GOING TO SLEEP.
LET THE MEMORIES WASH OVER YOU.
HEY AMANDA? THANKS. FOR, UH... EVERYTHING.
SQUAWK!
ALWAYS, NIKKI.
THEY TRUSTED ME TO CARE FOR THEM.
ENOUGH, PAN...I DON'T WANT TO SEE ANYMORE.
YOU DON'T GET A CHOICE HERE, AMANDA.
YOU CAN'T JUST LOOK AWAY FROM YOUR OWN LIFE.

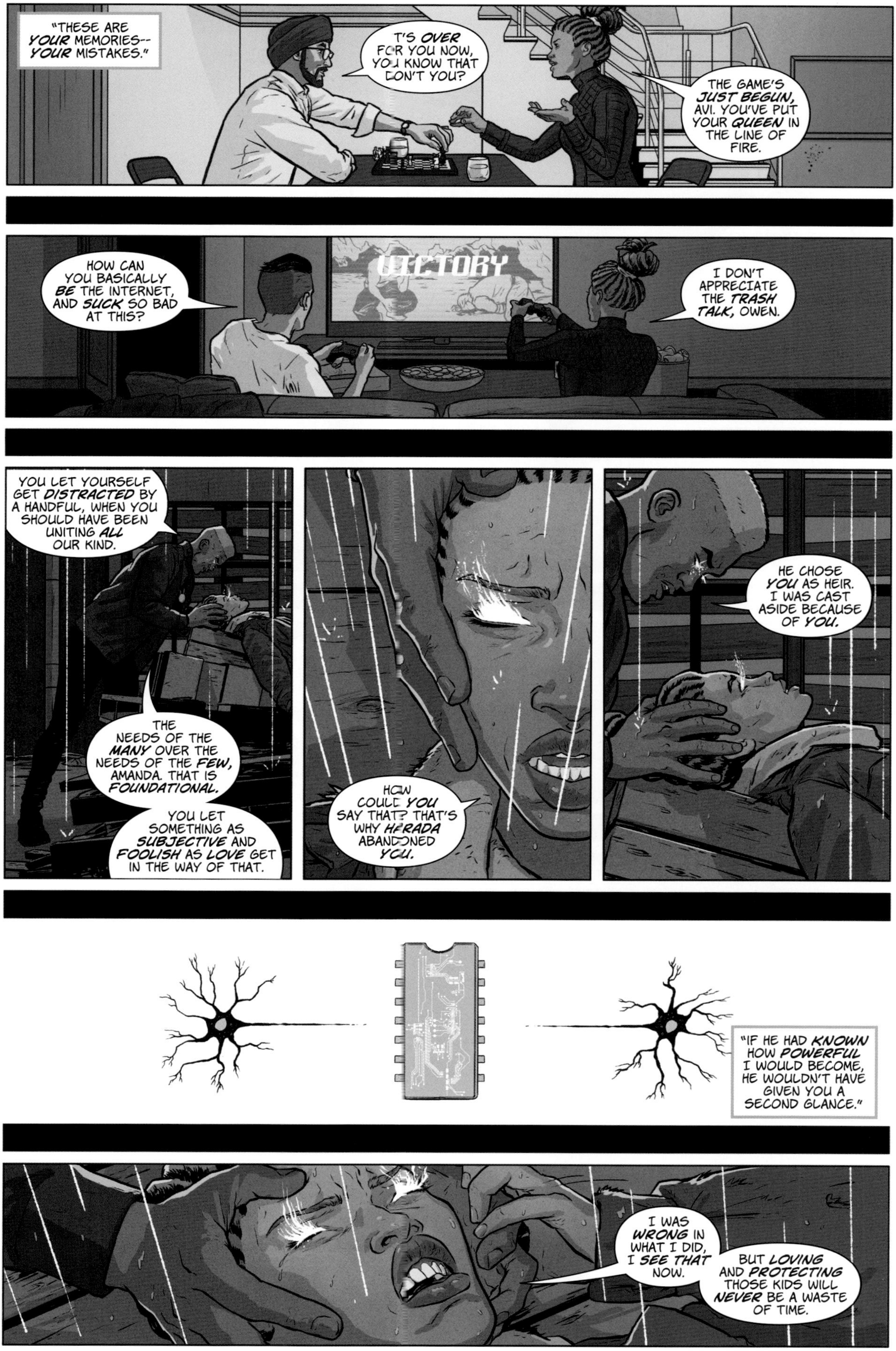
"THESE ARE YOUR MEMORIES-- YOUR MISTAKES."
T'S OVER FOR YOU NOW, YOU KNOW THAT DON'T YOU?
THE GAME'S JUST BEGUN, AVI. YOU'VE PUT YOUR QUEEN IN THE LINE OF FIRE.
VICTORY
HOW CAN YOU BASICALLY BE THE INTERNET, AND SUCK SO BAD AT THIS?
I DON'T APPRECIATE THE TRASH TALK, OWEN.
YOU LET YOURSELF GET DISTRACTED BY A HANDFUL, WHEN YOU SHOULD HAVE BEEN UNITING ALL OUR KIND.
THE NEEDS OF THE MANY OVER THE NEEDS OF THE FEW, AMANDA. THAT IS FOUNDATIONAL.
YOU LET SOMETHING AS SUBJECTIVE AND FOOLISH AS LOVE GET IN THE WAY OF THAT.
HOW COULD YOU SAY THAT? THAT'S WHY HARADA ABANDONED YOU.
HE CHOSE YOU AS HEIR. I WAS CAST ASIDE BECAUSE OF YOU.
"IF HE HAD KNOWN HOW POWERFUL I WOULD BECOME, HE WOULDN'T HAVE GIVEN YOU A SECOND GLANCE."
I WAS WRONG IN WHAT I DID, I SEE THAT NOW.
BUT LOVING AND PROTECTING THOSE KIDS WILL NEVER BE A WASTE OF TIME.

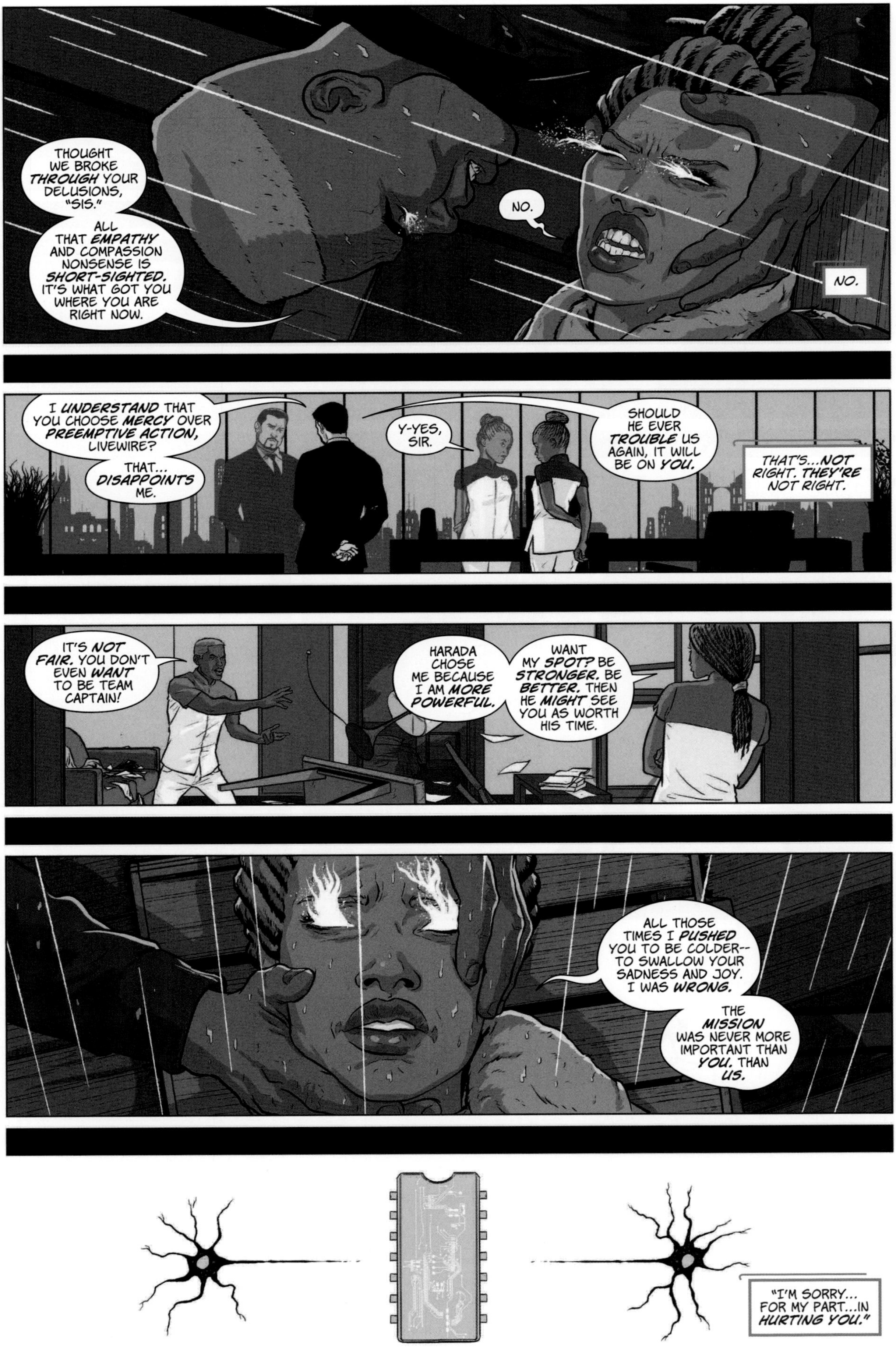
THOUGHT WE BROKE THROUGH YOUR DELUSIONS, "SIS."
ALL THAT EMPATHY AND COMPASSION NONSENSE IS SHORT-SIGHTED. IT'S WHAT GOT YOU WHERE YOU ARE RIGHT NOW.
NO.
NO.
I UNDERSTAND THAT YOU CHOOSE MERCY OVER PREEMPTIVE ACTION, LIVEWIRE?
THAT... DISAPPOINTS ME.
Y-YES, SIR.
SHOULD HE EVER TROUBLE US AGAIN, IT WILL BE ON YOU.
THAT'S...NOT RIGHT. THEY'RE NOT RIGHT.
IT'S NOT FAIR. YOU DON'T EVEN WANT TO BE TEAM CAPTAIN!
HARADA CHOSE ME BECAUSE I AM MORE POWERFUL.
WANT MY SPOT? BE STRONGER. BE BETTER. THEN HE MIGHT SEE YOU AS WORTH HIS TIME.
ALL THOSE TIMES I PUSHED YOU TO BE COLDER--TO SWALLOW YOUR SADNESS AND JOY. I WAS WRONG.
THE MISSION WAS NEVER MORE IMPORTANT THAN YOU. THAN US.
"I'M SORRY... FOR MY PART...IN HURTING YOU."

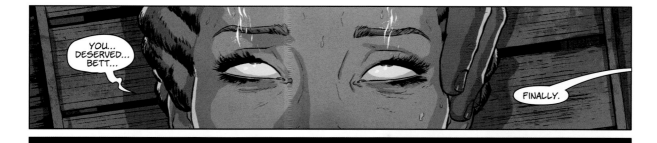

YOU... DESERVED... BETT...

FINALLY.

"I WAS GETTING TIRED OF YOUR MOUTH."

AMANDA MCKEE. THE *MIGHTY LIVEWIRE.*

TCH.

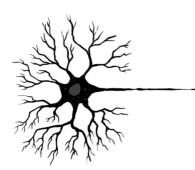

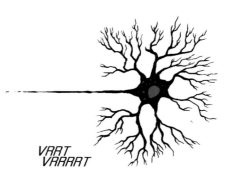

VRRT VRRRT

YEAH. IT'S D--

THE F--?!

THEY'LL HAVE TO CALL YOU BACK.

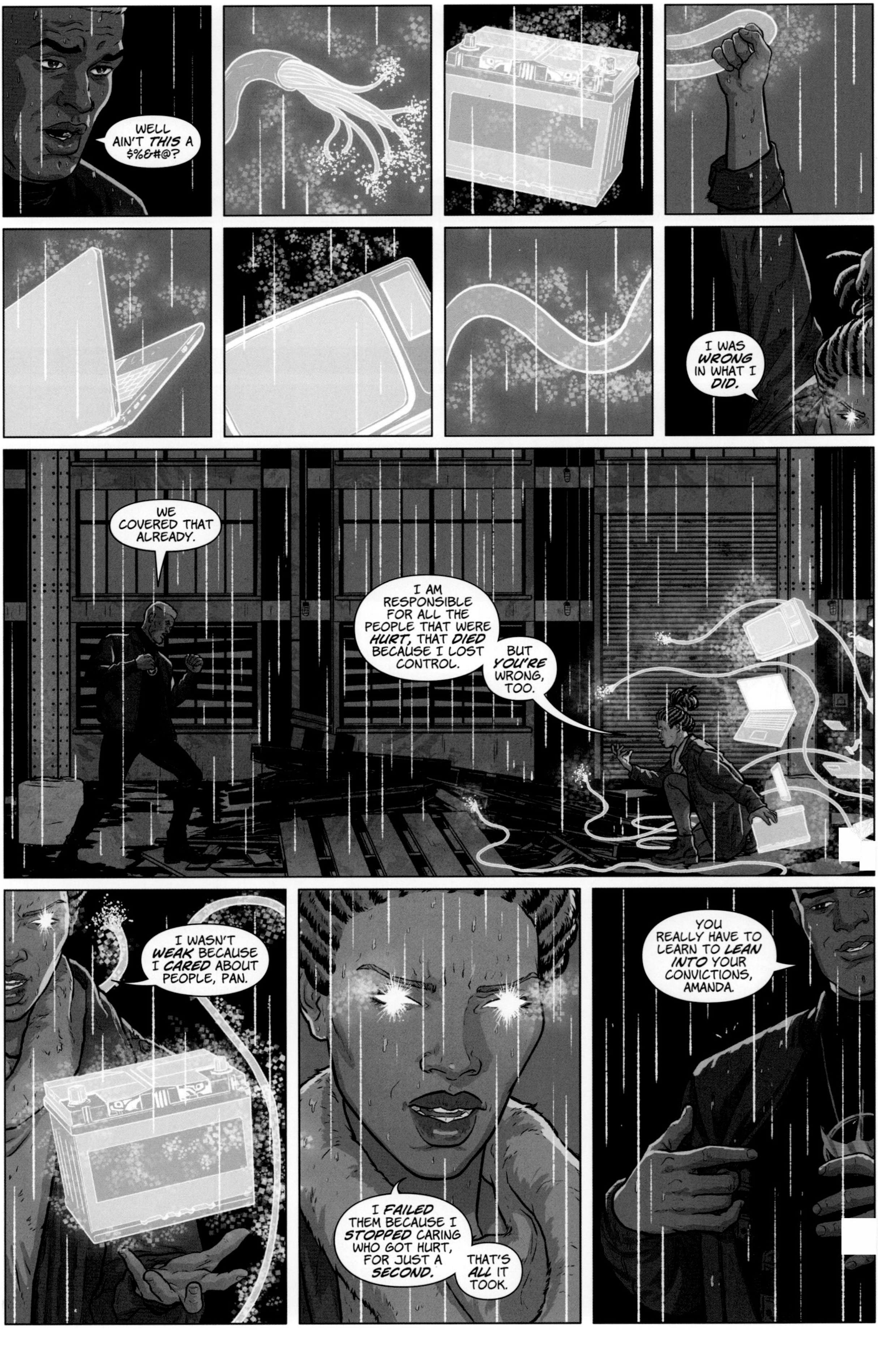
WELL AIN'T *THIS* A $%&#@?
I WAS *WRONG* IN WHAT I *DID.*
WE COVERED THAT ALREADY.
I AM RESPONSIBLE FOR ALL THE PEOPLE THAT WERE *HURT,* THAT *DIED* BECAUSE I LOST CONTROL.
BUT *YOU'RE* WRONG, TOO.
I WASN'T *WEAK* BECAUSE I *CARED* ABOUT PEOPLE, PAN.
I *FAILED* THEM BECAUSE I *STOPPED* CARING WHO GOT HURT, FOR JUST A *SECOND.*
THAT'S *ALL* IT TOOK.
YOU REALLY HAVE TO LEARN TO *LEAN INTO* YOUR CONVICTIONS, AMANDA.

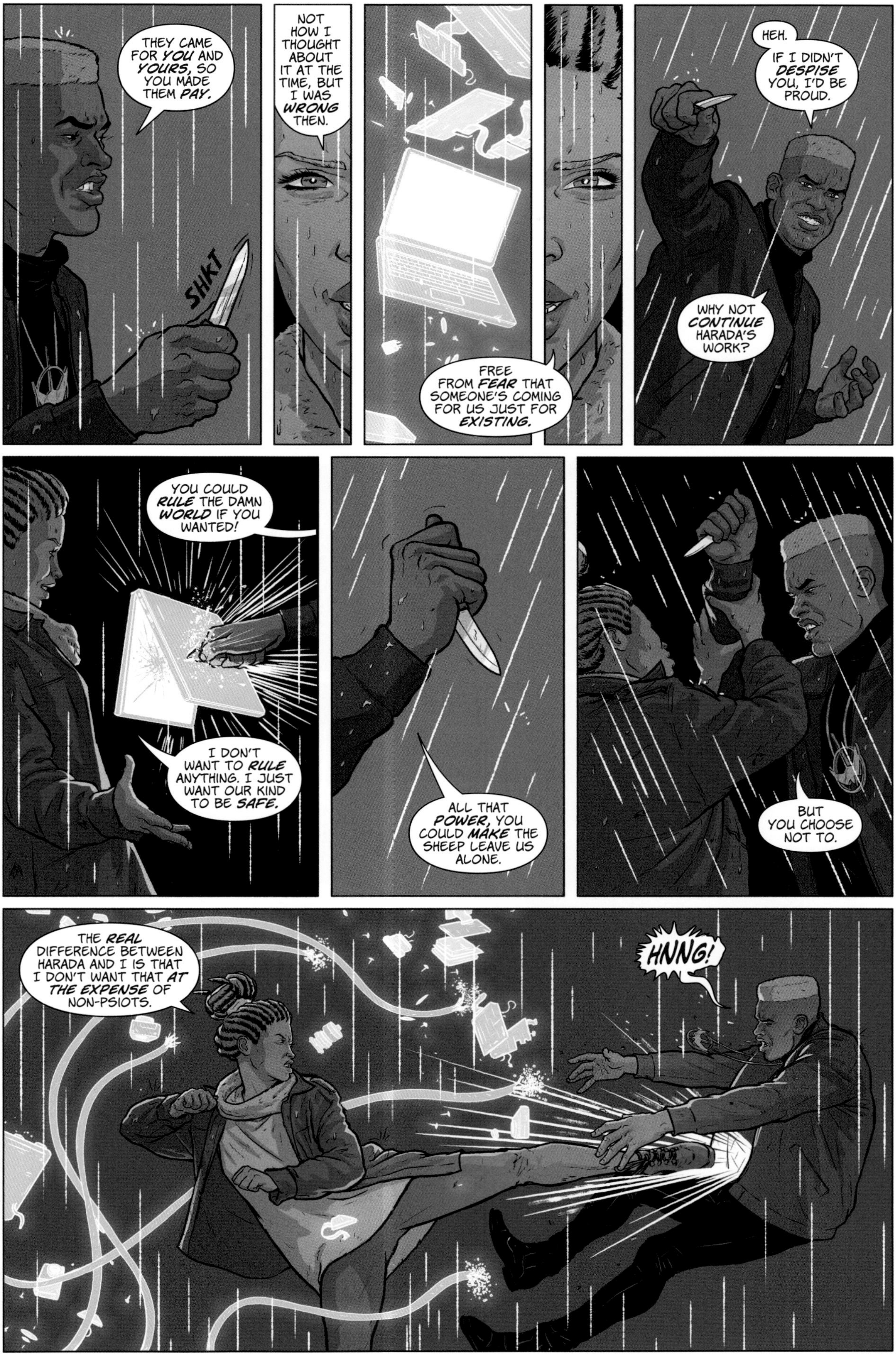
THEY CAME FOR YOU AND YOURS, SO YOU MADE THEM PAY.
SHKT
NOT HOW I THOUGHT ABOUT IT AT THE TIME, BUT I WAS WRONG THEN.
FREE FROM FEAR THAT SOMEONE'S COMING FOR US JUST FOR EXISTING.
HEH.
IF I DIDN'T DESPISE YOU, I'D BE PROUD.
WHY NOT CONTINUE HARADA'S WORK?
YOU COULD RULE THE DAMN WORLD IF YOU WANTED!
I DON'T WANT TO RULE ANYTHING. I JUST WANT OUR KIND TO BE SAFE.
ALL THAT POWER, YOU COULD MAKE THE SHEEP LEAVE US ALONE.
BUT YOU CHOOSE NOT TO.
THE REAL DIFFERENCE BETWEEN HARADA AND I IS THAT I DON'T WANT THAT AT THE EXPENSE OF NON-PSIOTS.
HNNG!

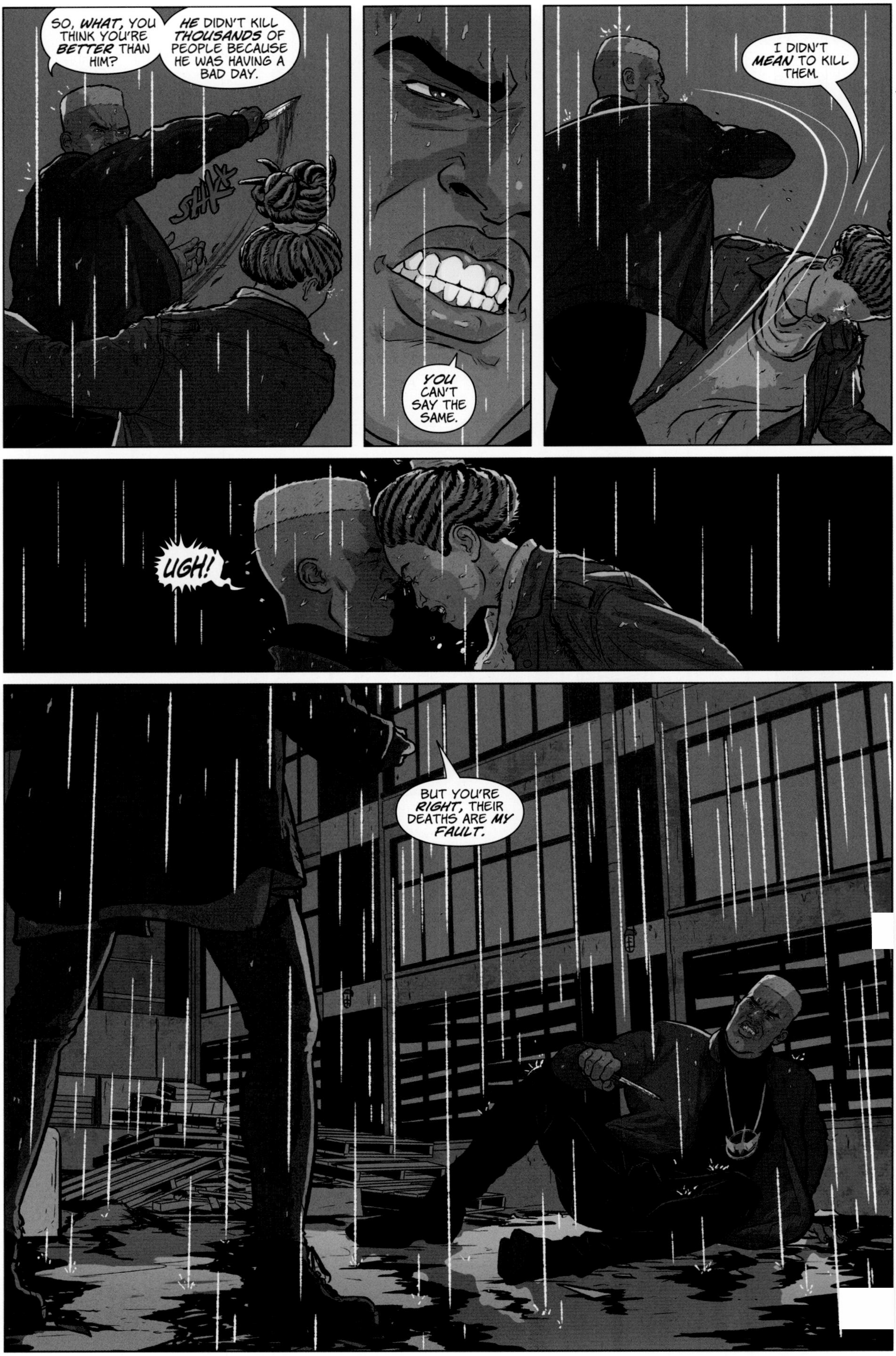
SO, WHAT, YOU THINK YOU'RE BETTER THAN HIM?
HE DIDN'T KILL THOUSANDS OF PEOPLE BECAUSE HE WAS HAVING A BAD DAY.
YOU CAN'T SAY THE SAME.
I DIDN'T MEAN TO KILL THEM.
UGH!
BUT YOU'RE RIGHT, THEIR DEATHS ARE MY FAULT.

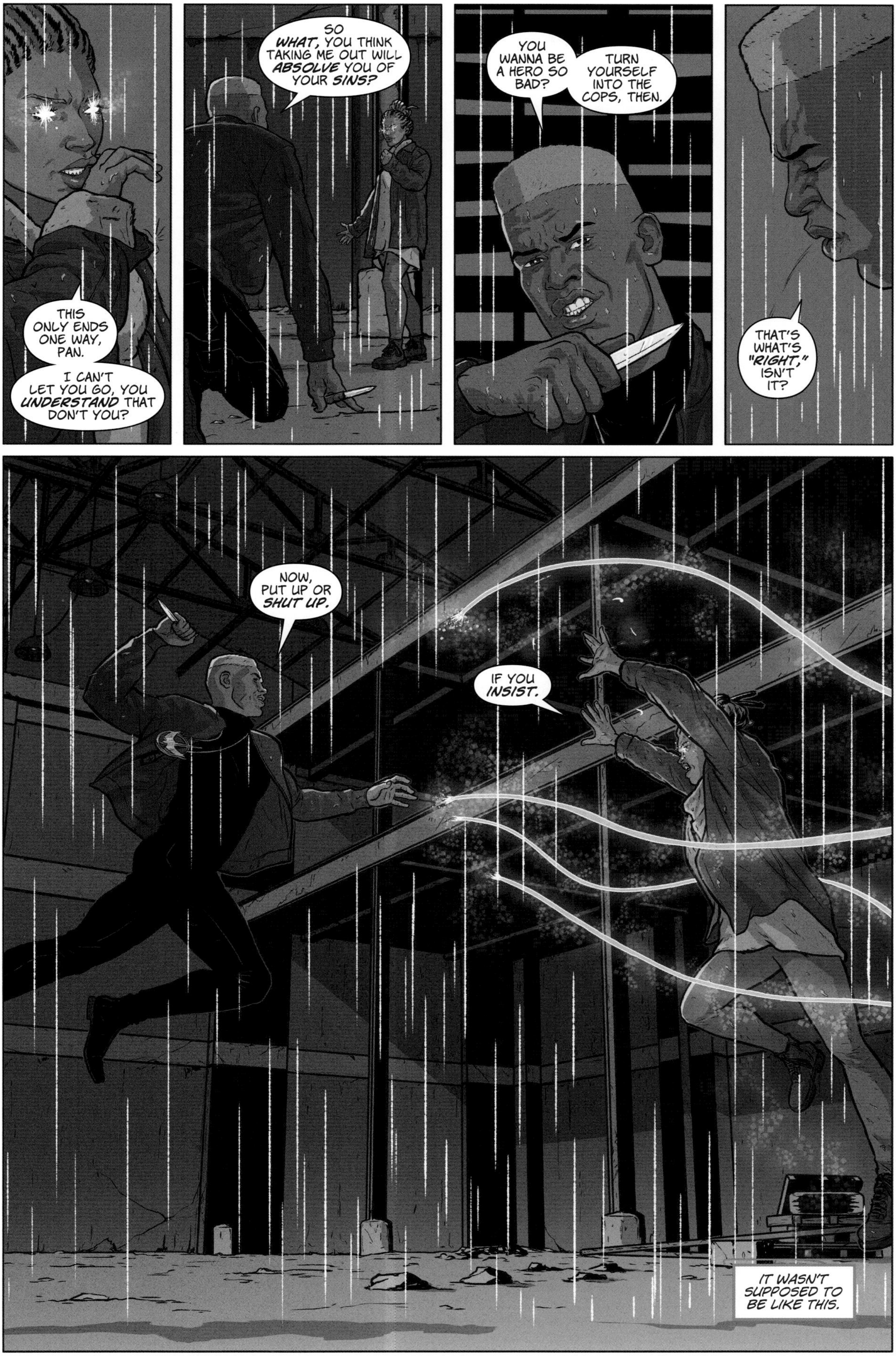
THIS ONLY ENDS ONE WAY, PAN.
I CAN'T LET YOU GO, YOU UNDERSTAND THAT DON'T YOU?
SO WHAT, YOU THINK TAKING ME OUT WILL ABSOLVE YOU OF YOUR SINS?
YOU WANNA BE A HERO SO BAD?
TURN YOURSELF INTO THE COPS, THEN.
THAT'S WHAT'S "RIGHT," ISN'T IT?
NOW, PUT UP OR SHUT UP.
IF YOU INSIST.
IT WASN'T SUPPOSED TO BE LIKE THIS.

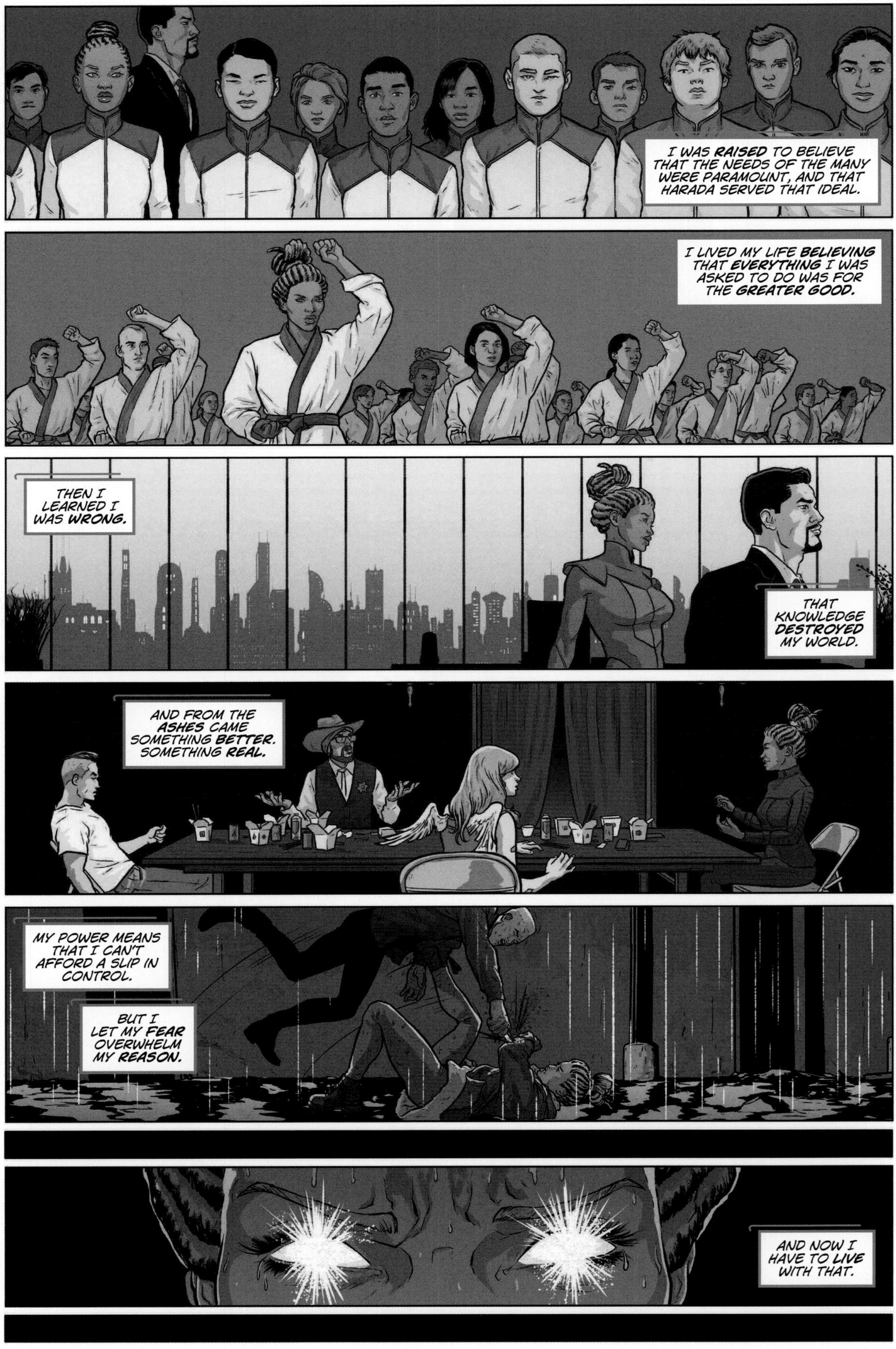
I WAS **RAISED** TO BELIEVE THAT THE NEEDS OF THE MANY WERE PARAMOUNT, AND THAT HARADA SERVED THAT IDEAL.
I LIVED MY LIFE **BELIEVING** THAT **EVERYTHING** I WAS ASKED TO DO WAS FOR THE **GREATER GOOD.**
THEN I LEARNED I WAS **WRONG.**
THAT KNOWLEDGE **DESTROYED** MY WORLD.
AND FROM THE **ASHES** CAME SOMETHING **BETTER.** SOMETHING **REAL.**
MY POWER MEANS THAT I CAN'T AFFORD A SLIP IN CONTROL.
BUT I LET MY **FEAR** OVERWHELM MY **REASON.**
AND NOW I HAVE TO **LIVE** WITH THAT.

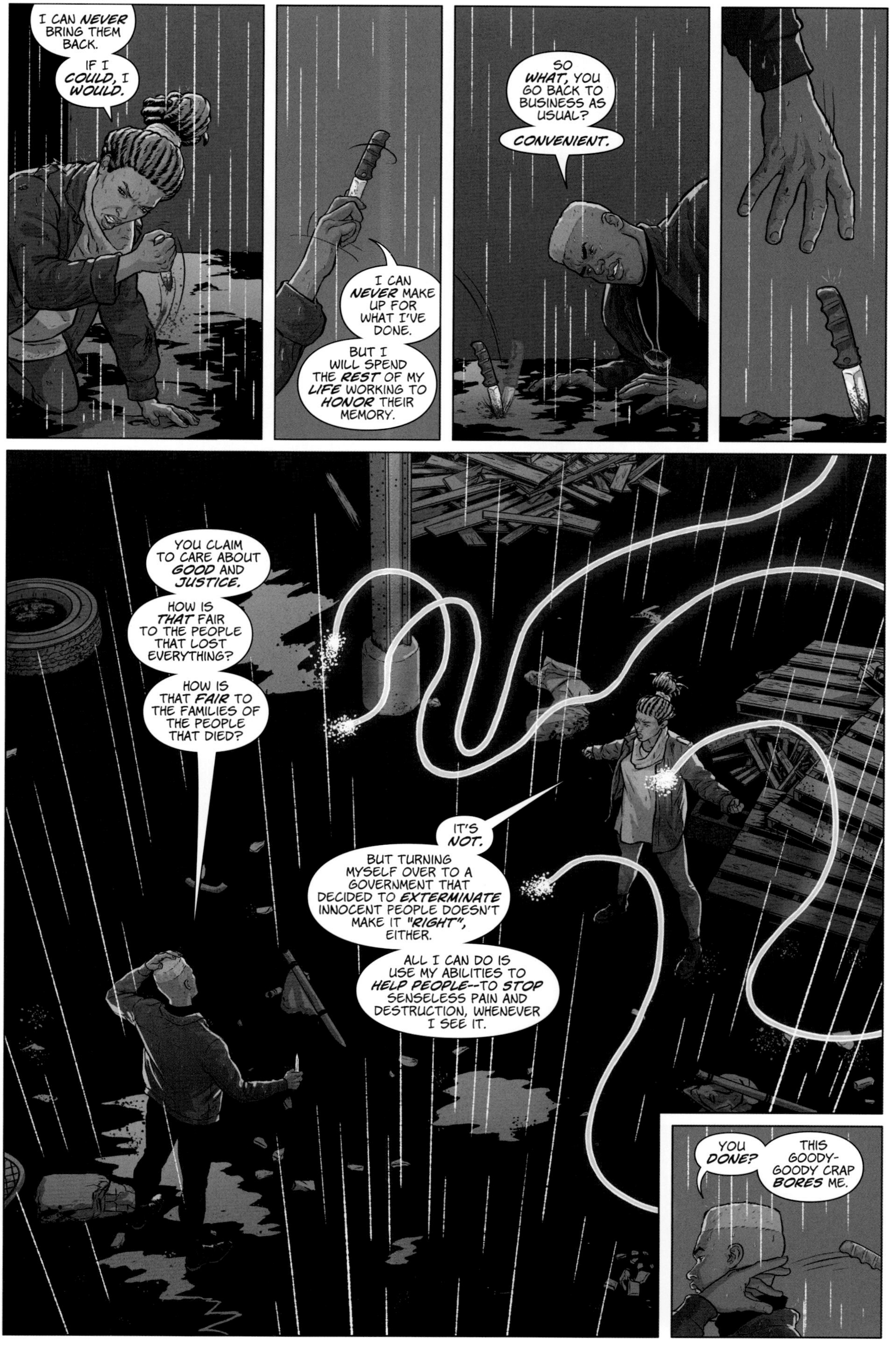
I CAN NEVER BRING THEM BACK.
IF I COULD, I WOULD.
I CAN NEVER MAKE UP FOR WHAT I'VE DONE.
BUT I WILL SPEND THE REST OF MY LIFE WORKING TO HONOR THEIR MEMORY.
SO WHAT, YOU GO BACK TO BUSINESS AS USUAL?
CONVENIENT.
YOU CLAIM TO CARE ABOUT GOOD AND JUSTICE.
HOW IS THAT FAIR TO THE PEOPLE THAT LOST EVERYTHING?
HOW IS THAT FAIR TO THE FAMILIES OF THE PEOPLE THAT DIED?
IT'S NOT.
BUT TURNING MYSELF OVER TO A GOVERNMENT THAT DECIDED TO EXTERMINATE INNOCENT PEOPLE DOESN'T MAKE IT "RIGHT", EITHER.
ALL I CAN DO IS USE MY ABILITIES TO HELP PEOPLE--TO STOP SENSELESS PAIN AND DESTRUCTION, WHENEVER I SEE IT.
YOU DONE?
THIS GOODY-GOODY CRAP BORES ME.

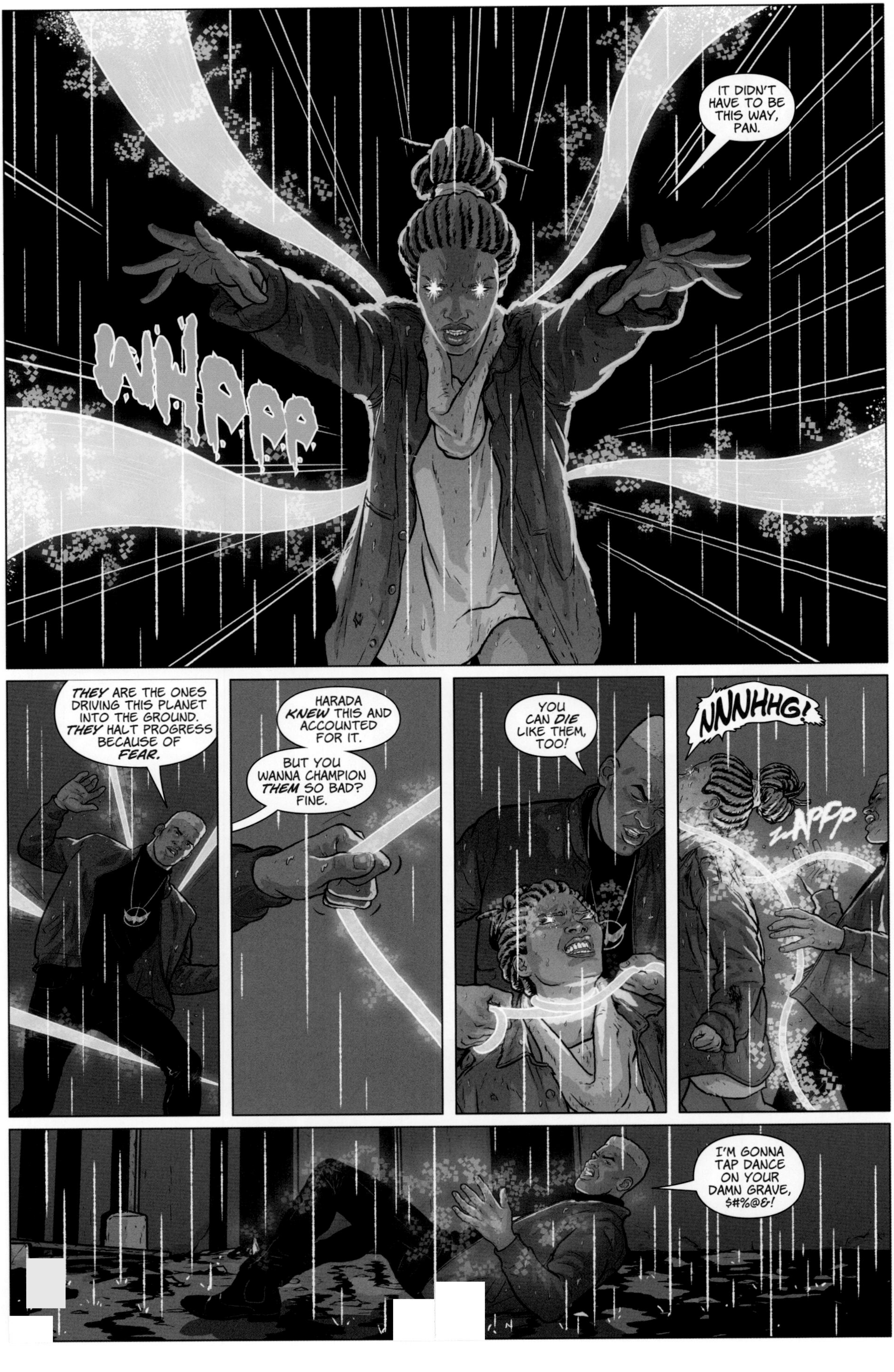
IT DIDN'T HAVE TO BE THIS WAY, PAN.
WHPPP
THEY ARE THE ONES DRIVING THIS PLANET INTO THE GROUND. THEY HALT PROGRESS BECAUSE OF FEAR.
HARADA KNEW THIS AND ACCOUNTED FOR IT.
BUT YOU WANNA CHAMPION THEM SO BAD? FINE.
YOU CAN DIE LIKE THEM, TOO!
NNNHHG!
ZAPPP
I'M GONNA TAP DANCE ON YOUR DAMN GRAVE, $#%@&!

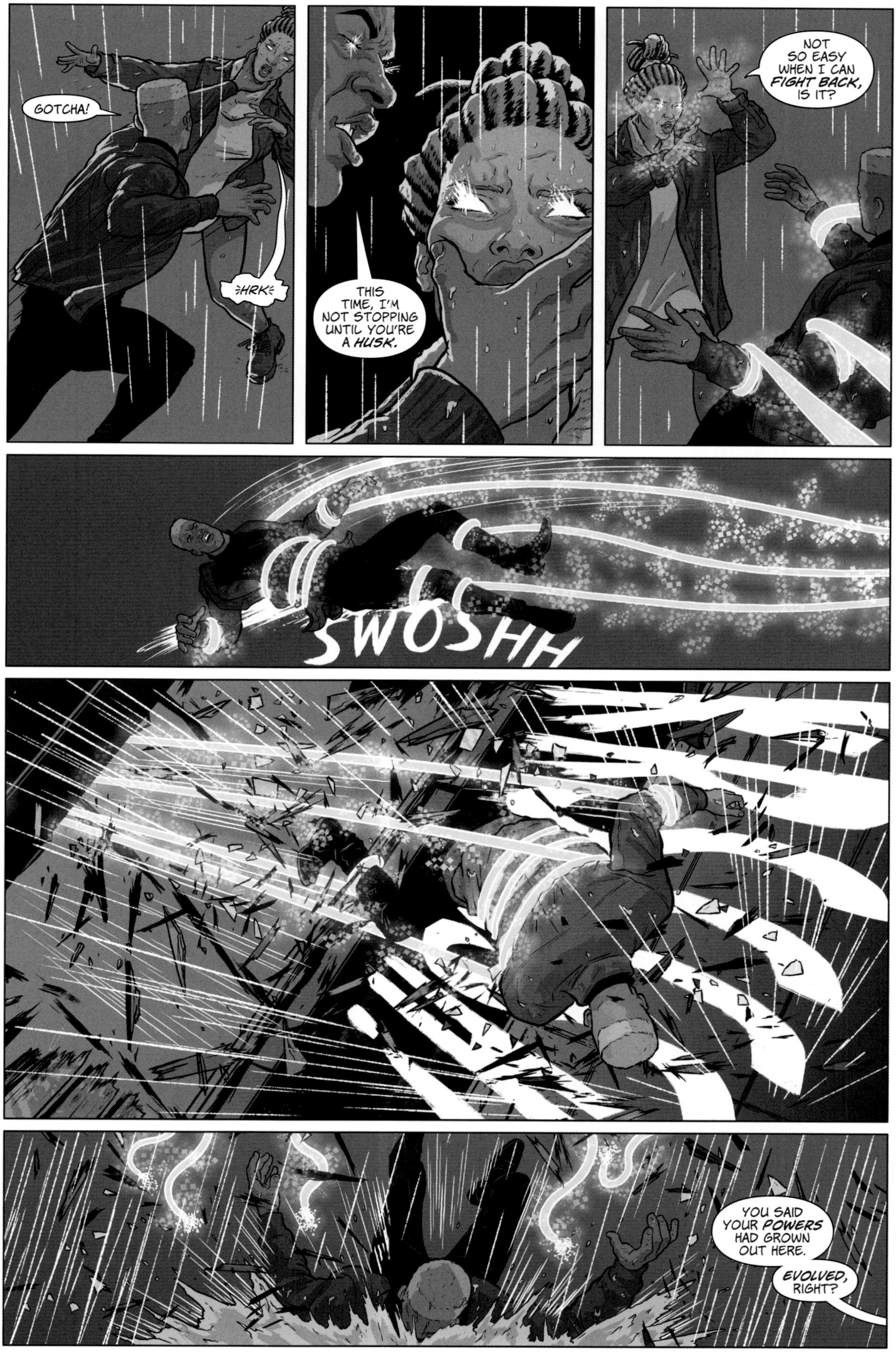
GOTCHA!
HRK
THIS TIME, I'M NOT STOPPING UNTIL YOU'RE A HUSK.
NOT SO EASY WHEN I CAN FIGHT BACK, IS IT?
SWOSHH
YOU SAID YOUR POWERS HAD GROWN OUT HERE.
EVOLVED, RIGHT?

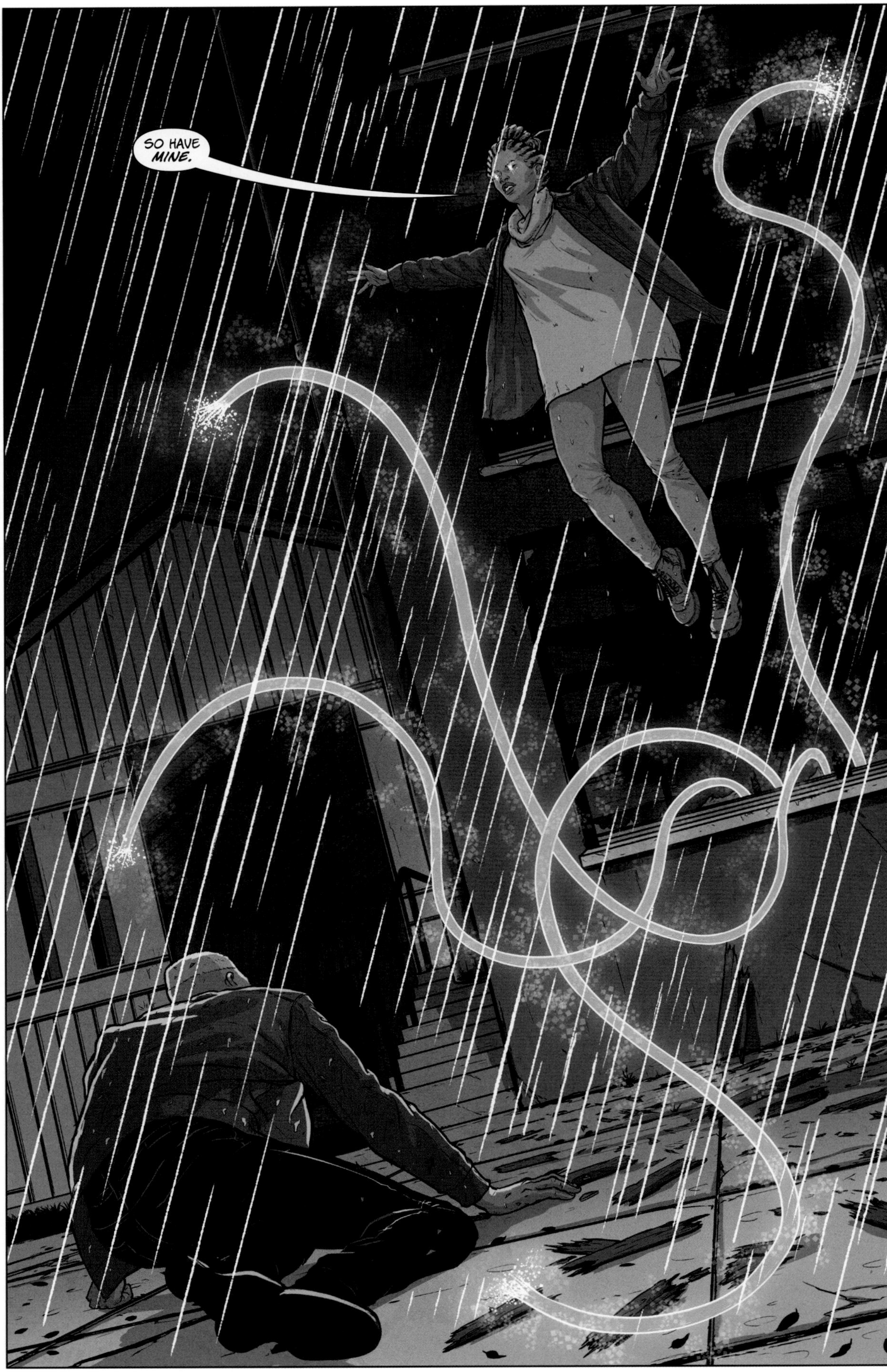
SO HAVE *MINE.*

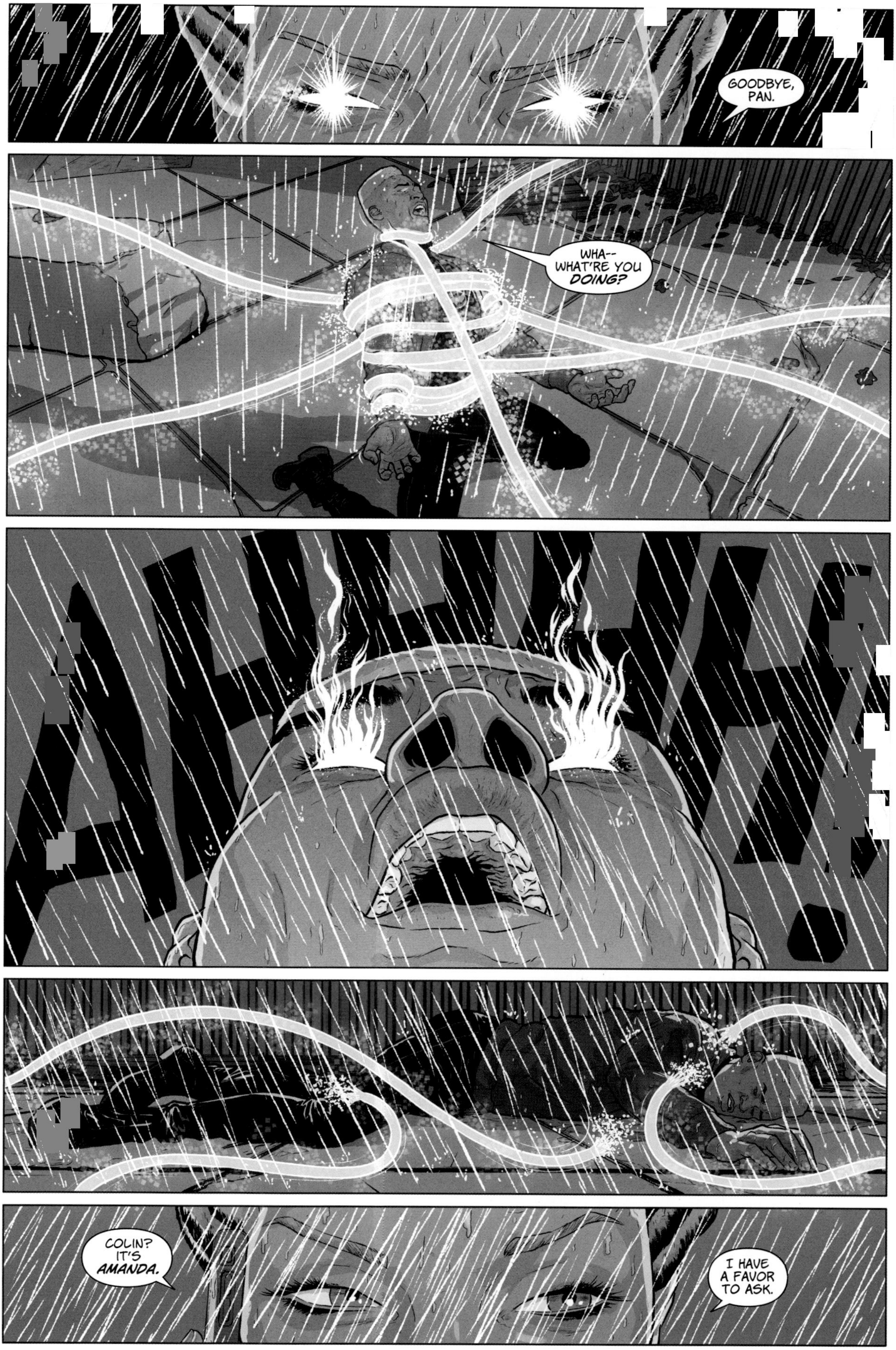
GOODBYE, PAN.
WHA-- WHAT'RE YOU *DOING?*
COLIN? IT'S *AMANDA.*
I HAVE A FAVOR TO ASK.

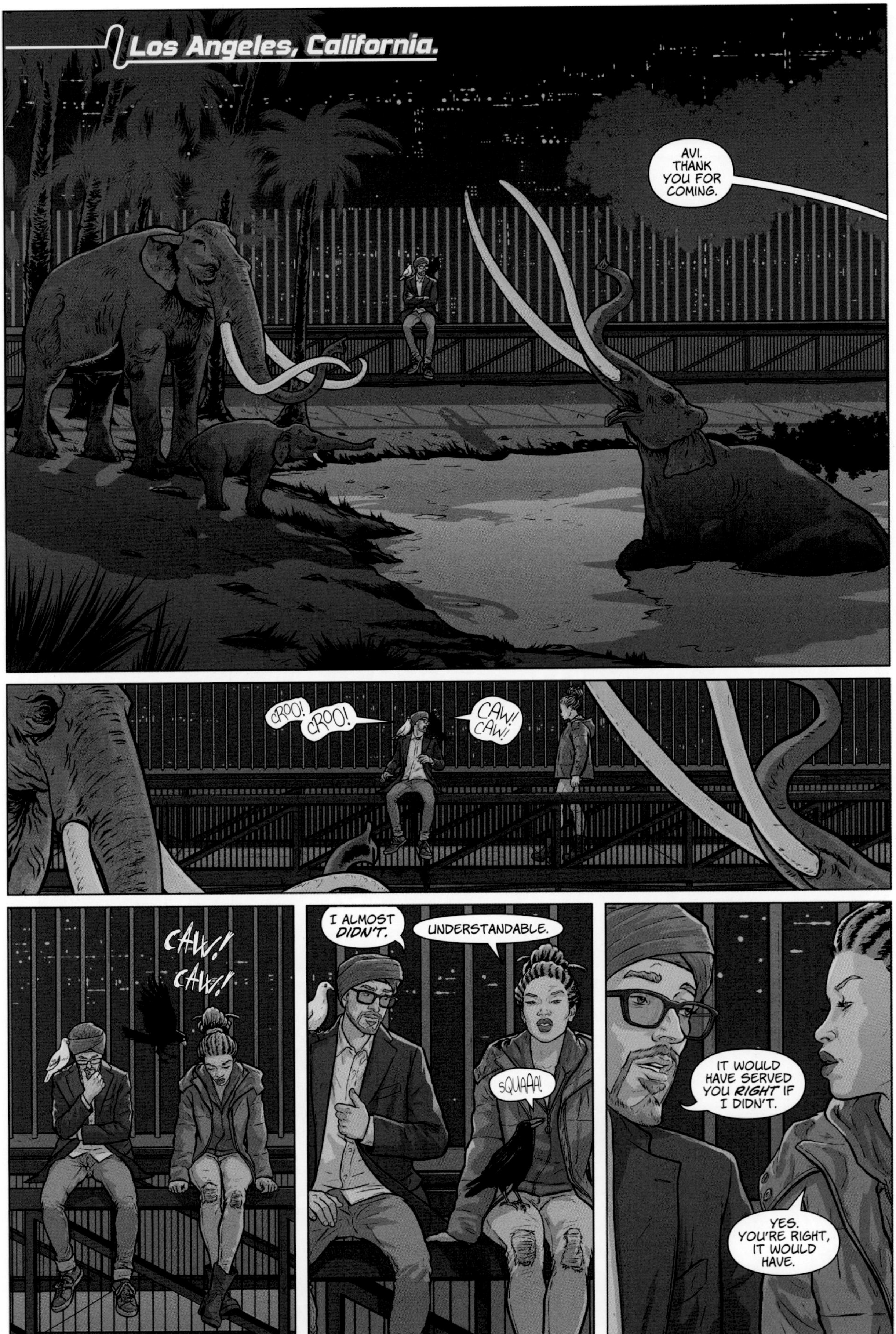
Los Angeles, California.
AVI. THANK YOU FOR COMING.
CROO! CROO!
CAW! CAW!
CAW! CAW!
I ALMOST DIDN'T.
UNDERSTANDABLE.
SQUAAA!
IT WOULD HAVE SERVED YOU RIGHT IF I DIDN'T.
YES. YOU'RE RIGHT, IT WOULD HAVE.

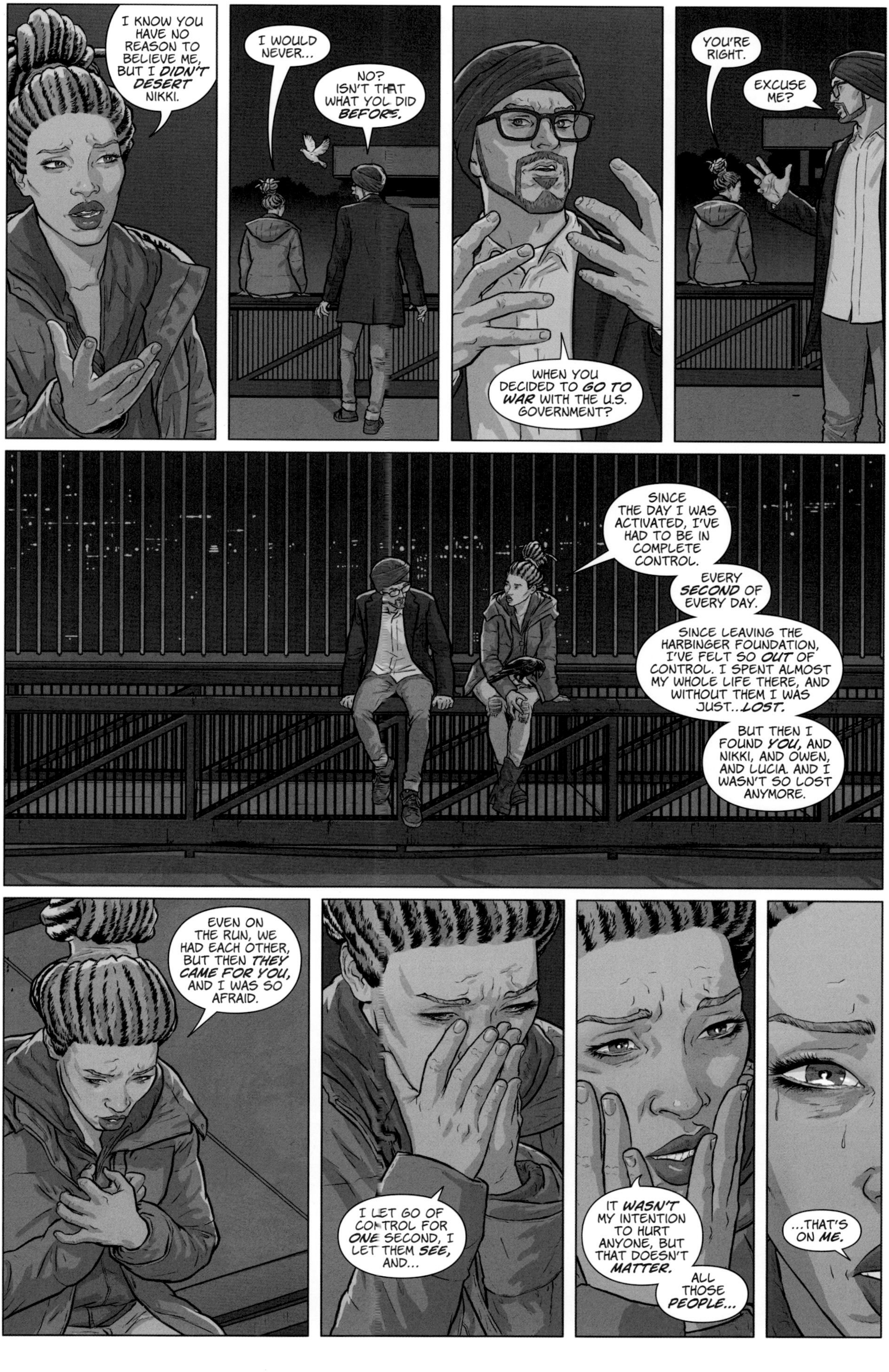

I KNOW YOU HAVE NO REASON TO BELIEVE ME, BUT I *DIDN'T DESERT* NIKKI.
I WOULD NEVER...
NO? ISN'T THAT WHAT YOU DID *BEFORE*.
WHEN YOU DECIDED TO *GO TO WAR* WITH THE U.S. GOVERNMENT?
YOU'RE RIGHT.
EXCUSE ME?
SINCE THE DAY I WAS ACTIVATED, I'VE HAD TO BE IN COMPLETE CONTROL.
EVERY *SECOND* OF EVERY DAY.
SINCE LEAVING THE HARBINGER FOUNDATION, I'VE FELT SO *OUT* OF CONTROL. I SPENT ALMOST MY WHOLE LIFE THERE, AND WITHOUT THEM I WAS JUST...*LOST.*
BUT THEN I FOUND *YOU,* AND NIKKI, AND OWEN, AND LUCIA. AND I WASN'T SO LOST ANYMORE.
EVEN ON THE RUN, WE HAD EACH OTHER, BUT THEN *THEY CAME FOR YOU,* AND I WAS SO AFRAID.
I LET GO OF CONTROL FOR *ONE* SECOND, I LET THEM *SEE,* AND...
IT *WASN'T* MY INTENTION TO HURT ANYONE, BUT THAT DOESN'T *MATTER.*
ALL THOSE *PEOPLE...*
...THAT'S ON *ME.*

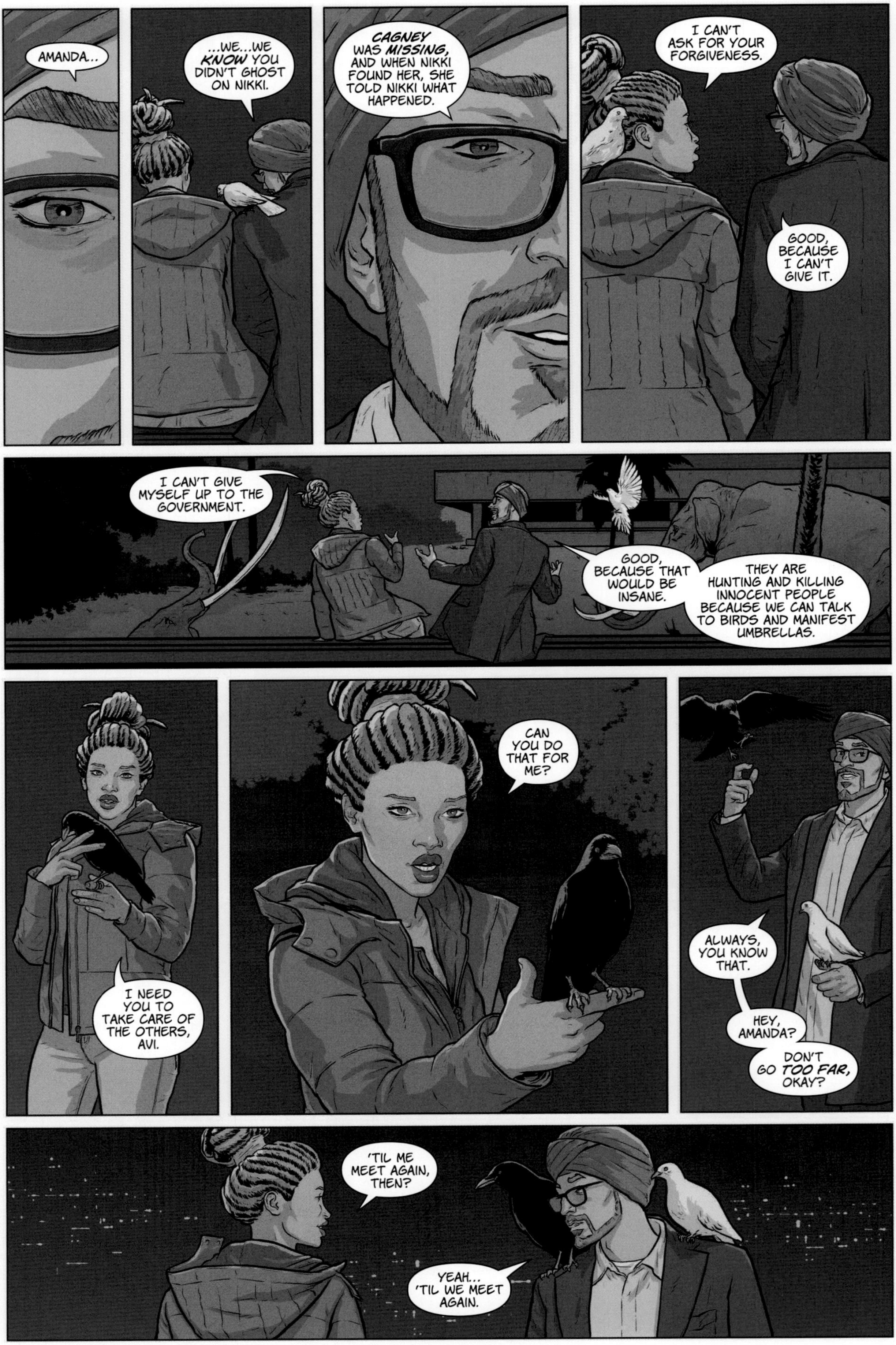
AMANDA...
...WE...WE KNOW YOU DIDN'T GHOST ON NIKKI.
CAGNEY WAS MISSING, AND WHEN NIKKI FOUND HER, SHE TOLD NIKKI WHAT HAPPENED.
I CAN'T ASK FOR YOUR FORGIVENESS.
GOOD, BECAUSE I CAN'T GIVE IT.
I CAN'T GIVE MYSELF UP TO THE GOVERNMENT.
GOOD, BECAUSE THAT WOULD BE INSANE.
THEY ARE HUNTING AND KILLING INNOCENT PEOPLE BECAUSE WE CAN TALK TO BIRDS AND MANIFEST UMBRELLAS.
I NEED YOU TO TAKE CARE OF THE OTHERS, AVI.
CAN YOU DO THAT FOR ME?
ALWAYS, YOU KNOW THAT.
HEY, AMANDA?
DON'T GO TOO FAR, OKAY?
'TIL ME MEET AGAIN, THEN?
YEAH... 'TIL WE MEET AGAIN.

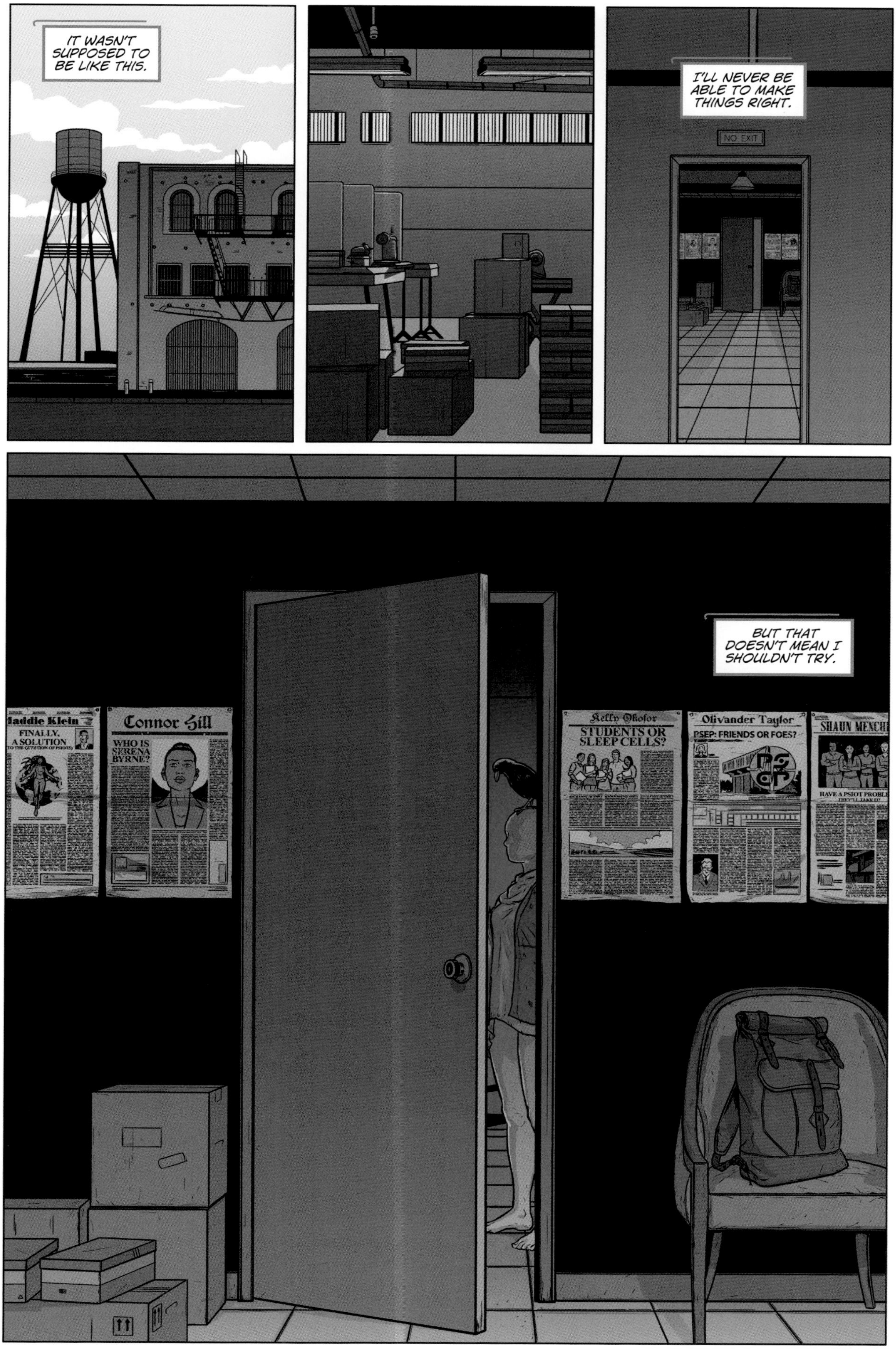
IT WASN'T SUPPOSED TO BE LIKE THIS.
I'LL NEVER BE ABLE TO MAKE THINGS RIGHT.
NO EXIT
BUT THAT DOESN'T MEAN I SHOULDN'T TRY.
FINALLY, A SOLUTION
Connor Hill
WHO IS SERENA BYRNE?
Kelly Okofor
STUDENTS OR SLEEP CELLS?
Olivander Taylor
PSEP: FRIENDS OR FOES?

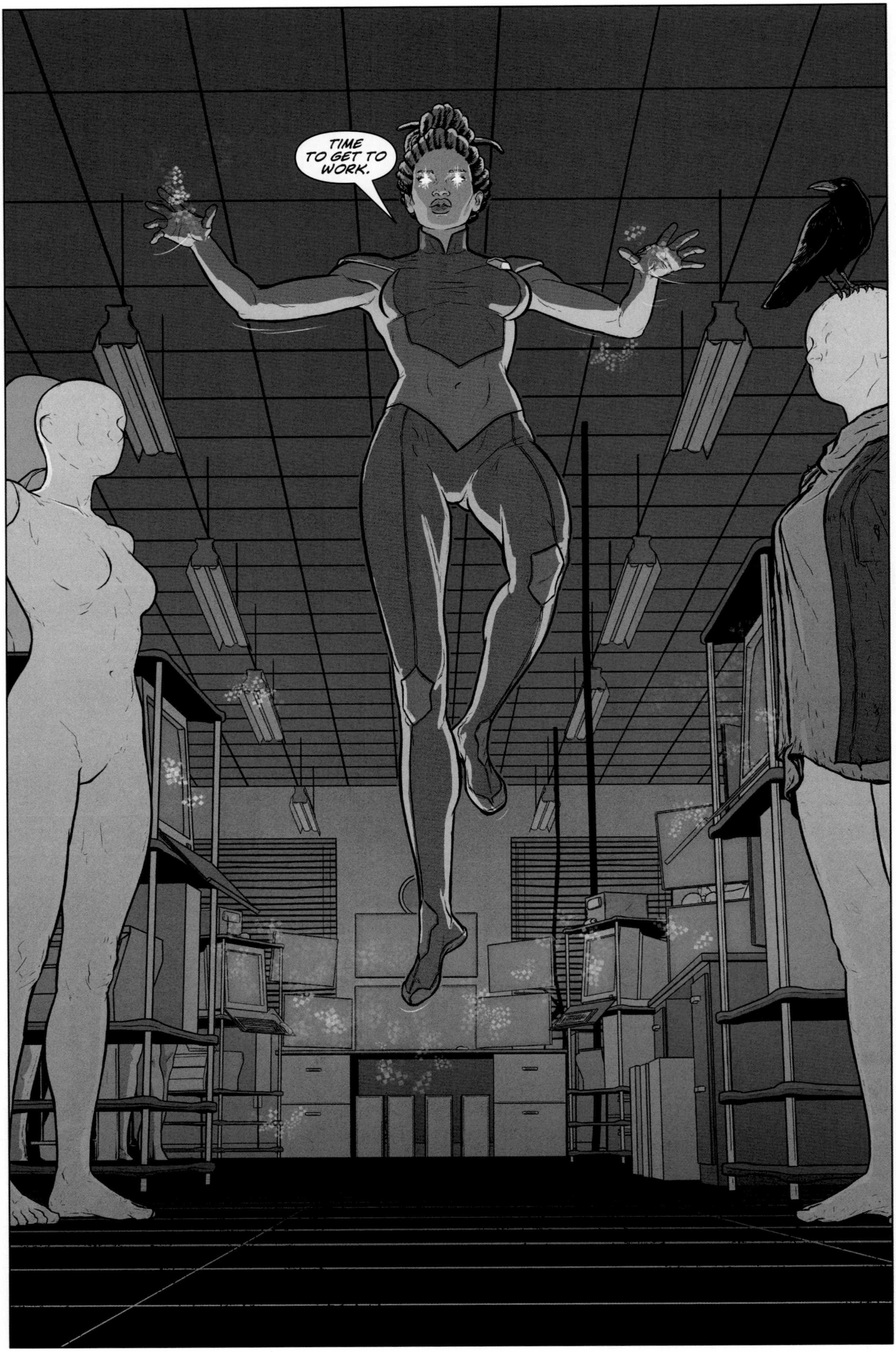
TIME TO GET TO WORK.

GUARDIA

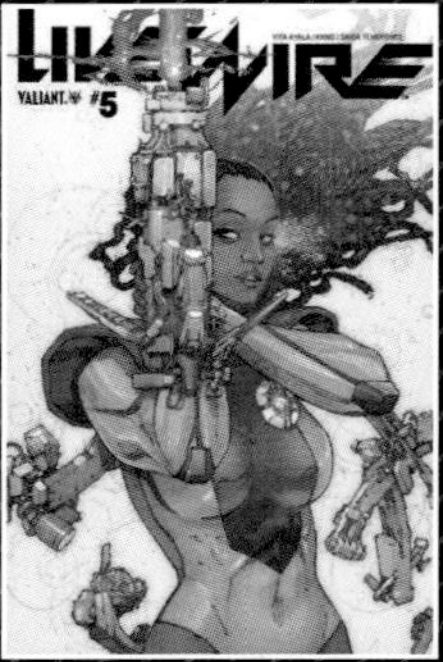
LIVEWIRE
VALIANT
#5

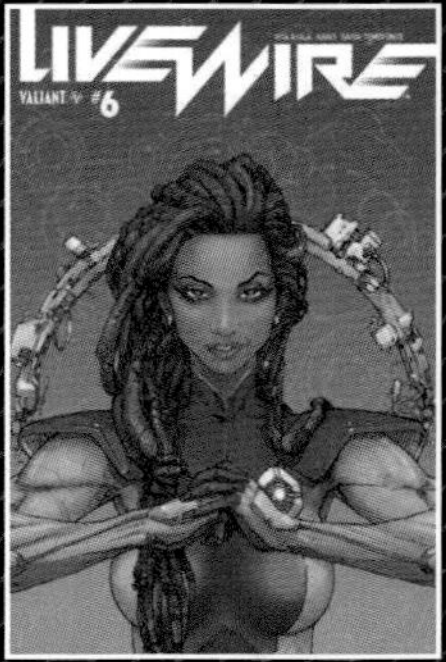
LIVEWIRE
VALIANT
#6

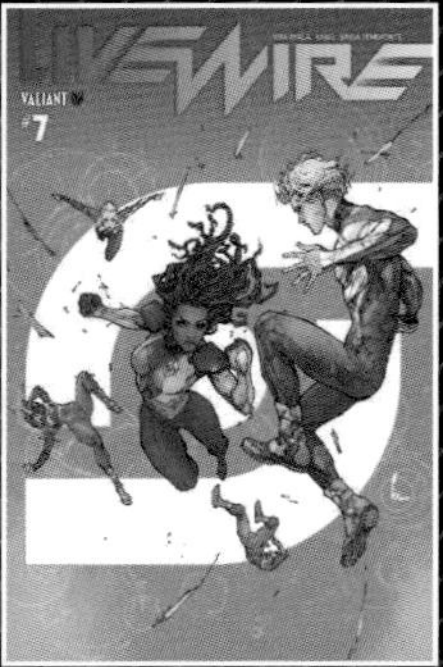
LIVEWIRE
VALIANT
#7

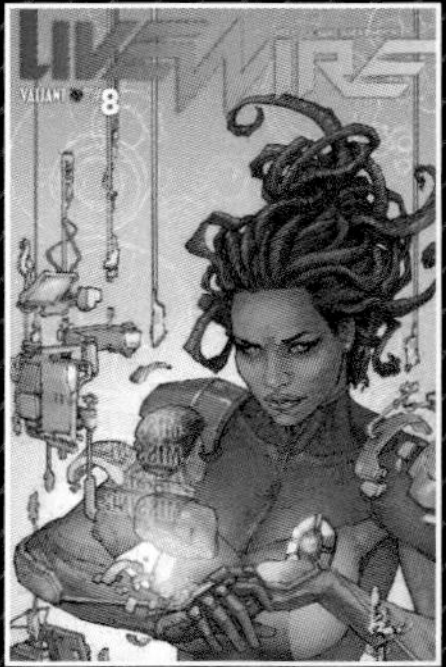
LIVEWIRE
VALIANT
8

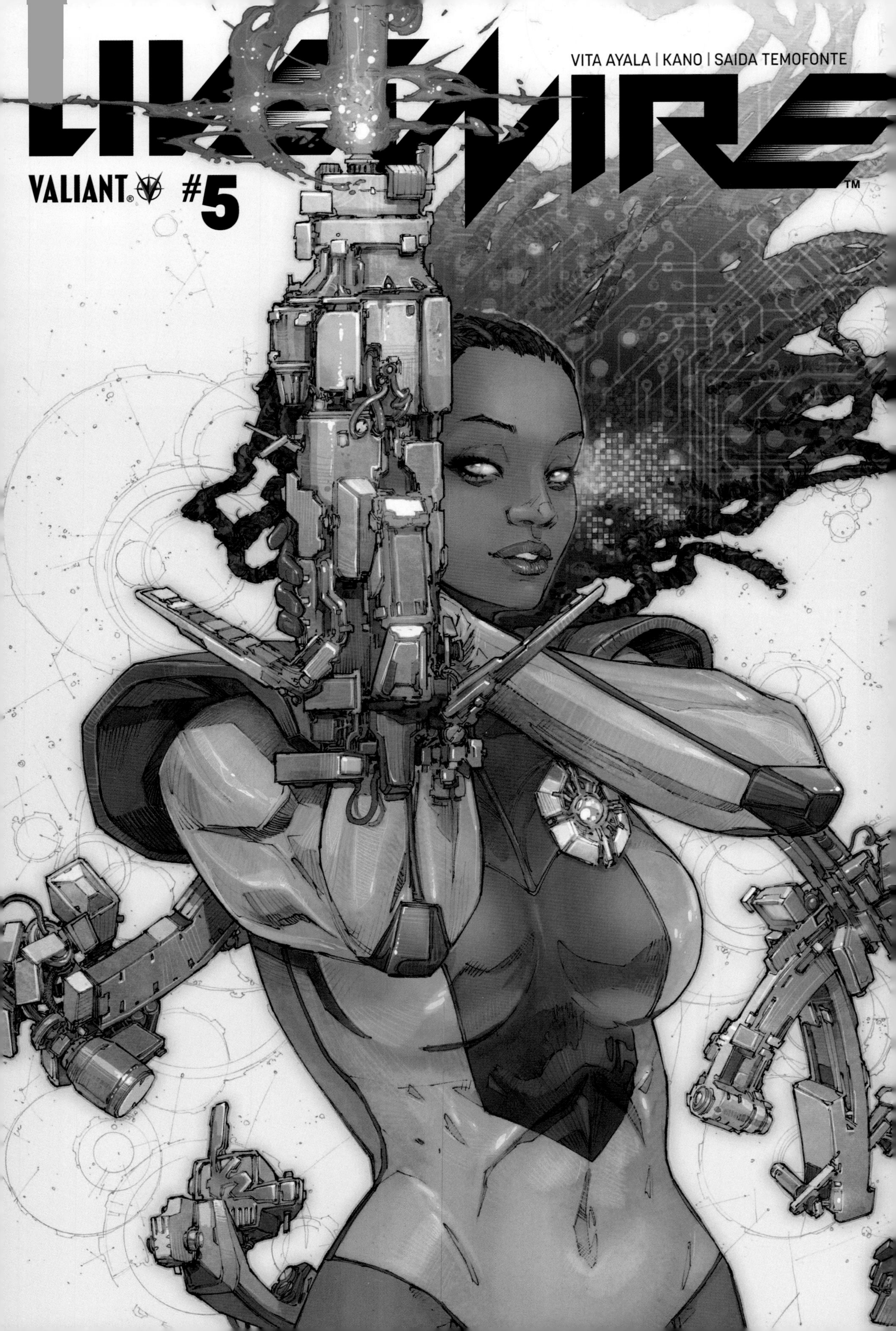
VITA AYALA | KANO | SAIDA TEMOFONTE
LIVEWIRE™
VALIANT®
#5

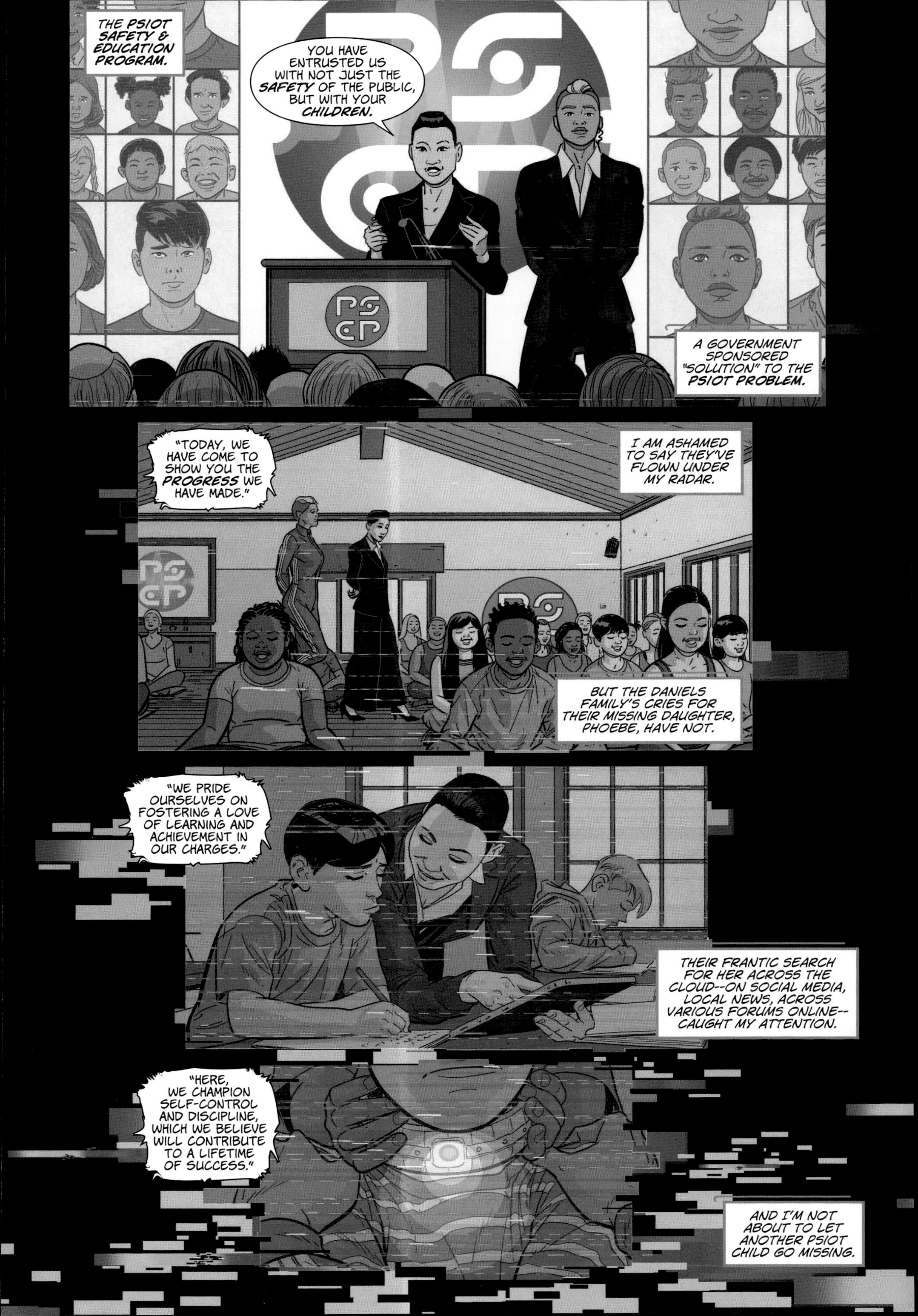
THE PSIOT SAFETY & EDUCATION PROGRAM.
YOU HAVE ENTRUSTED US WITH NOT JUST THE SAFETY OF THE PUBLIC, BUT WITH YOUR CHILDREN.
A GOVERNMENT SPONSORED "SOLUTION" TO THE PSIOT PROBLEM.
"TODAY, WE HAVE COME TO SHOW YOU THE PROGRESS WE HAVE MADE."
I AM ASHAMED TO SAY THEY'VE FLOWN UNDER MY RADAR.
BUT THE DANIELS FAMILY'S CRIES FOR THEIR MISSING DAUGHTER, PHOEBE, HAVE NOT.
"WE PRIDE OURSELVES ON FOSTERING A LOVE OF LEARNING AND ACHIEVEMENT IN OUR CHARGES."
THEIR FRANTIC SEARCH FOR HER ACROSS THE CLOUD--ON SOCIAL MEDIA, LOCAL NEWS, ACROSS VARIOUS FORUMS ONLINE--CAUGHT MY ATTENTION.
"HERE, WE CHAMPION SELF-CONTROL AND DISCIPLINE, WHICH WE BELIEVE WILL CONTRIBUTE TO A LIFETIME OF SUCCESS."
AND I'M NOT ABOUT TO LET ANOTHER PSIOT CHILD GO MISSING.

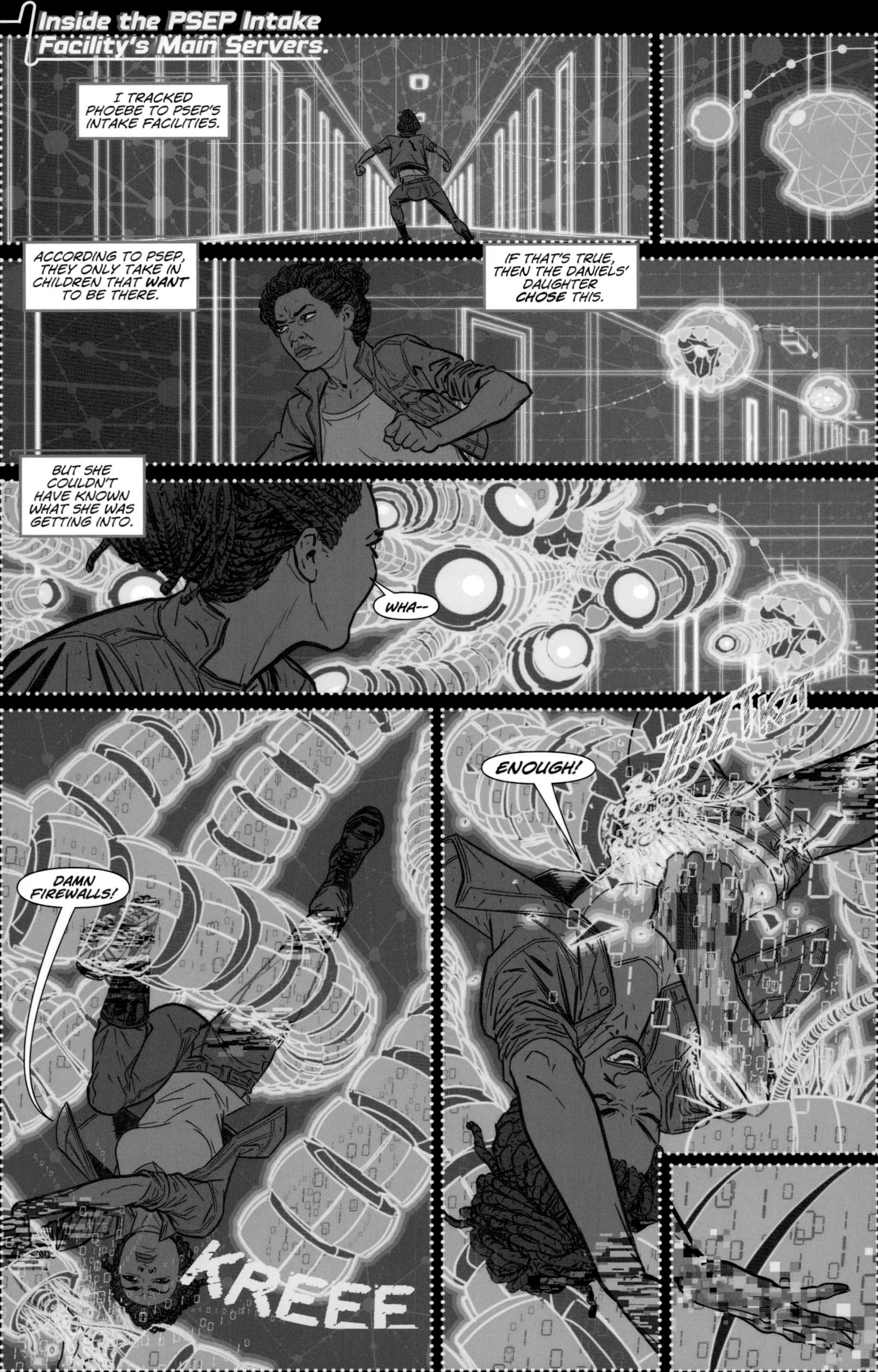
Inside the PSEP Intake Facility's Main Servers.
I TRACKED PHOEBE TO PSEP'S INTAKE FACILITIES.
ACCORDING TO PSEP, THEY ONLY TAKE IN CHILDREN THAT WANT TO BE THERE.
IF THAT'S TRUE, THEN THE DANIELS' DAUGHTER CHOSE THIS.
BUT SHE COULDN'T HAVE KNOWN WHAT SHE WAS GETTING INTO.
WHA--
DAMN FIREWALLS!
KREEE
ENOUGH!
ZZZTKZT

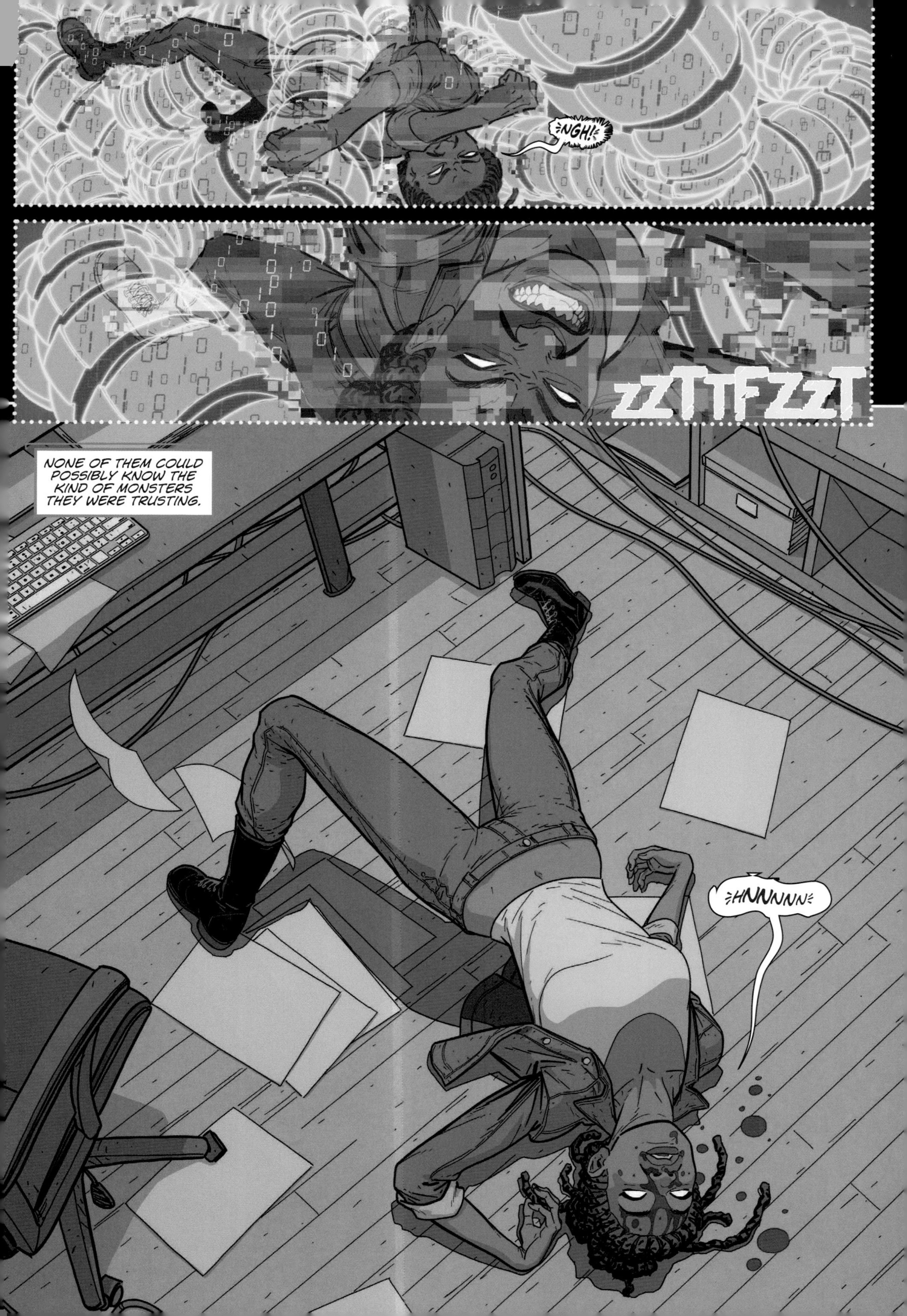
NGH!
zZTTFZzT
NONE OF THEM COULD POSSIBLY KNOW THE KIND OF MONSTERS THEY WERE TRUSTING.
HNNNNN

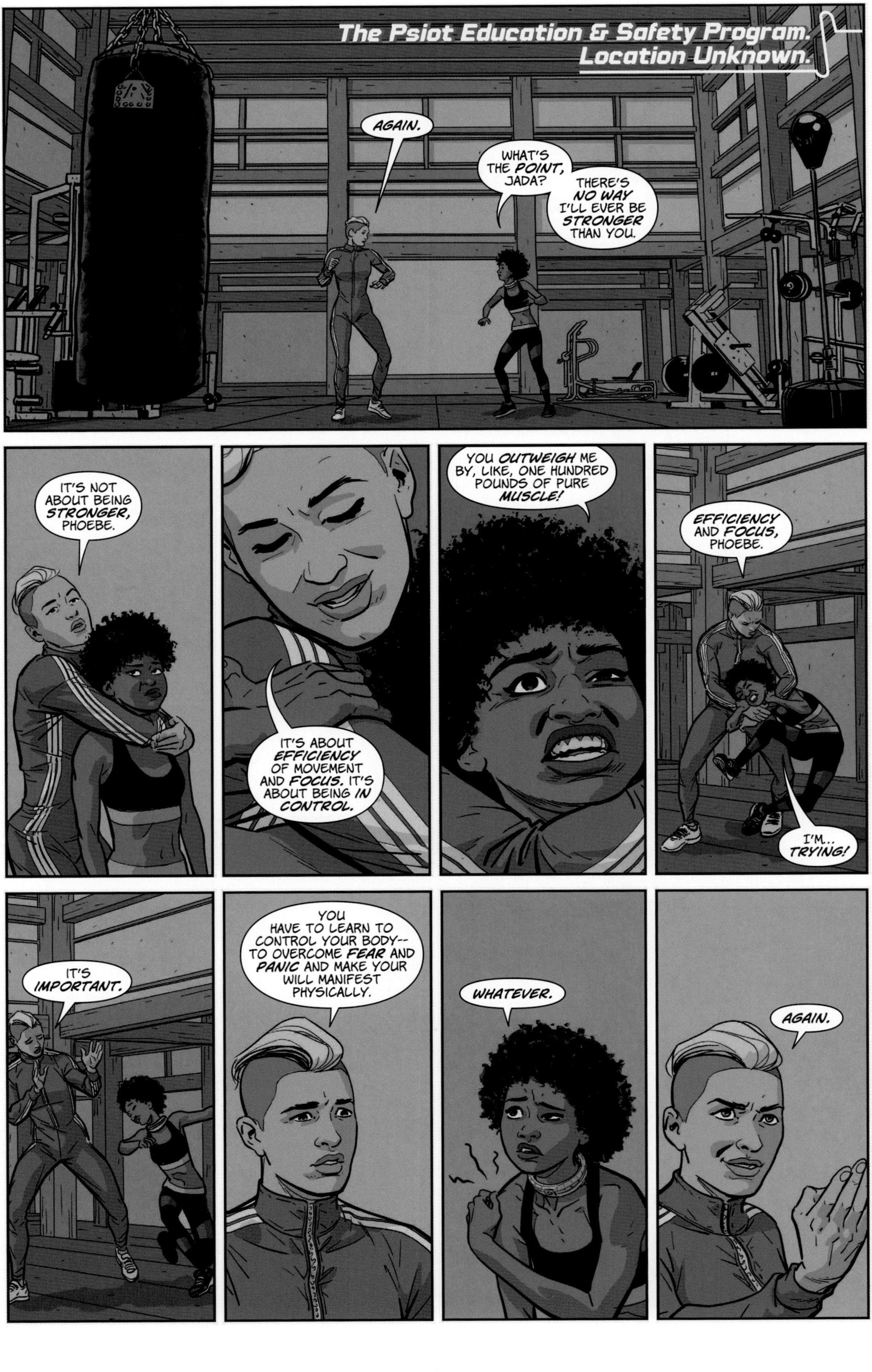
The Psiot Education & Safety Program. Location Unknown.
AGAIN.
WHAT'S THE POINT, JADA?
THERE'S NO WAY I'LL EVER BE STRONGER THAN YOU.
IT'S NOT ABOUT BEING STRONGER, PHOEBE.
IT'S ABOUT EFFICIENCY OF MOVEMENT AND FOCUS. IT'S ABOUT BEING IN CONTROL.
YOU OUTWEIGH ME BY, LIKE, ONE HUNDRED POUNDS OF PURE MUSCLE!
EFFICIENCY AND FOCUS, PHOEBE.
I'M... TRYING!
IT'S IMPORTANT.
YOU HAVE TO LEARN TO CONTROL YOUR BODY-- TO OVERCOME FEAR AND PANIC AND MAKE YOUR WILL MANIFEST PHYSICALLY.
WHATEVER.
AGAIN.

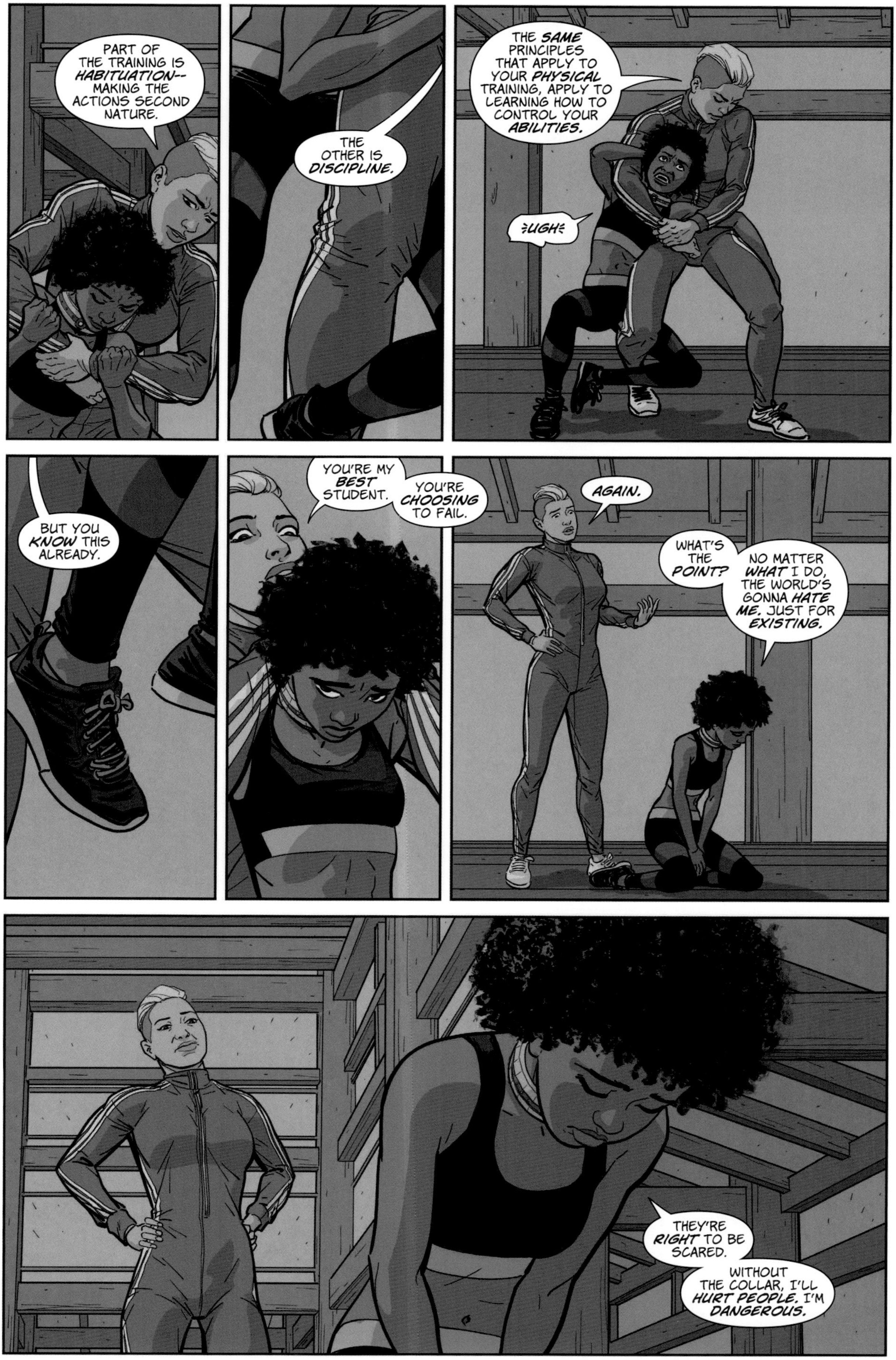
PART OF THE TRAINING IS HABITUATION-- MAKING THE ACTIONS SECOND NATURE.
THE OTHER IS DISCIPLINE.
THE SAME PRINCIPLES THAT APPLY TO YOUR PHYSICAL TRAINING, APPLY TO LEARNING HOW TO CONTROL YOUR ABILITIES.
UGH
BUT YOU KNOW THIS ALREADY.
YOU'RE MY BEST STUDENT.
YOU'RE CHOOSING TO FAIL.
AGAIN.
WHAT'S THE POINT?
NO MATTER WHAT I DO, THE WORLD'S GONNA HATE ME. JUST FOR EXISTING.
THEY'RE RIGHT TO BE SCARED.
WITHOUT THE COLLAR, I'LL HURT PEOPLE. I'M DANGEROUS.

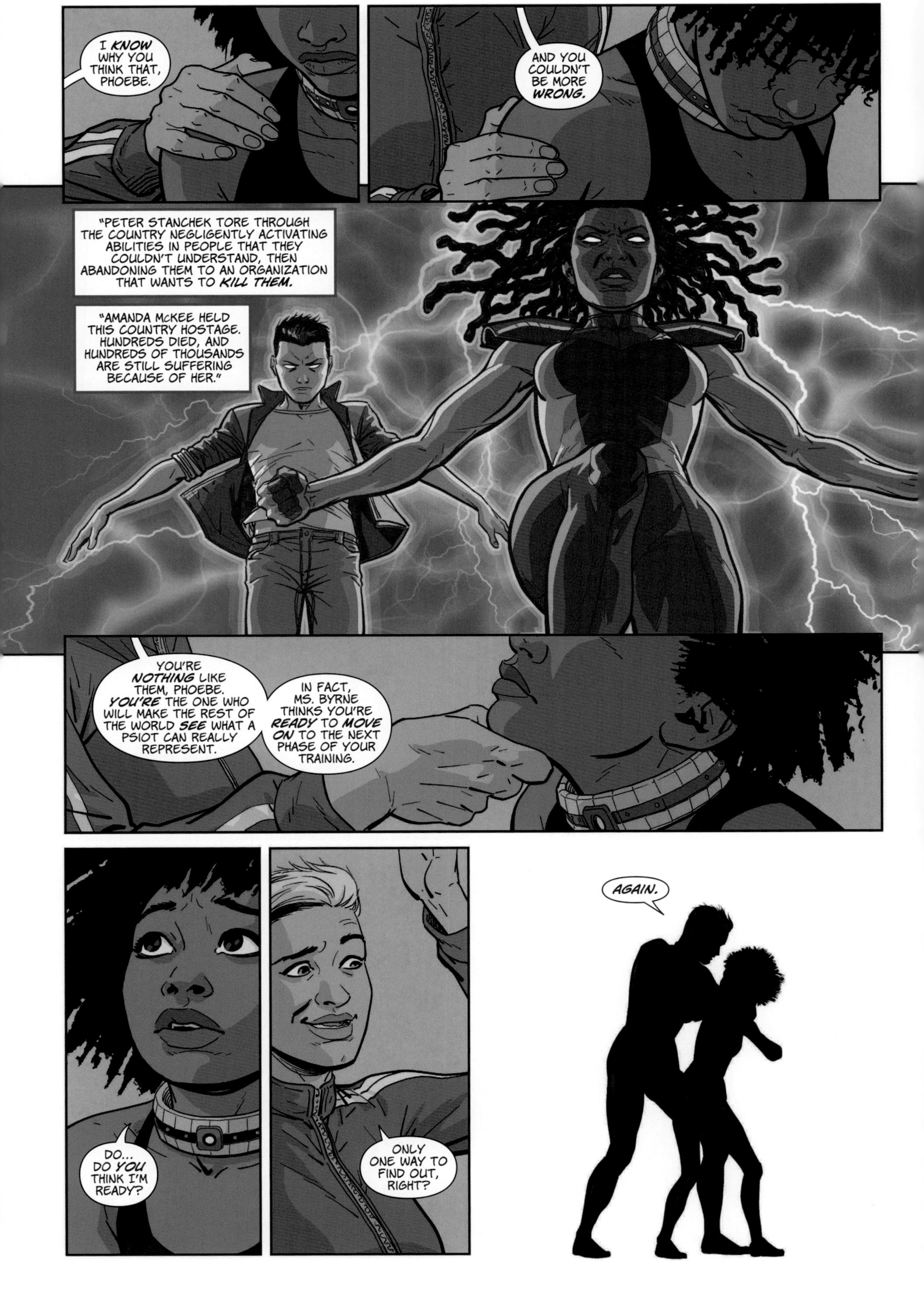

I KNOW WHY YOU THINK THAT, PHOEBE.
AND YOU COULDN'T BE MORE WRONG.
"PETER STANCHEK TORE THROUGH THE COUNTRY NEGLIGENTLY ACTIVATING ABILITIES IN PEOPLE THAT THEY COULDN'T UNDERSTAND, THEN ABANDONING THEM TO AN ORGANIZATION THAT WANTS TO KILL THEM.
"AMANDA McKEE HELD THIS COUNTRY HOSTAGE. HUNDREDS DIED, AND HUNDREDS OF THOUSANDS ARE STILL SUFFERING BECAUSE OF HER."
YOU'RE NOTHING LIKE THEM, PHOEBE. YOU'RE THE ONE WHO WILL MAKE THE REST OF THE WORLD SEE WHAT A PSIOT CAN REALLY REPRESENT.
IN FACT, MS. BYRNE THINKS YOU'RE READY TO MOVE ON TO THE NEXT PHASE OF YOUR TRAINING.
DO... DO YOU THINK I'M READY?
ONLY ONE WAY TO FIND OUT, RIGHT?
AGAIN.

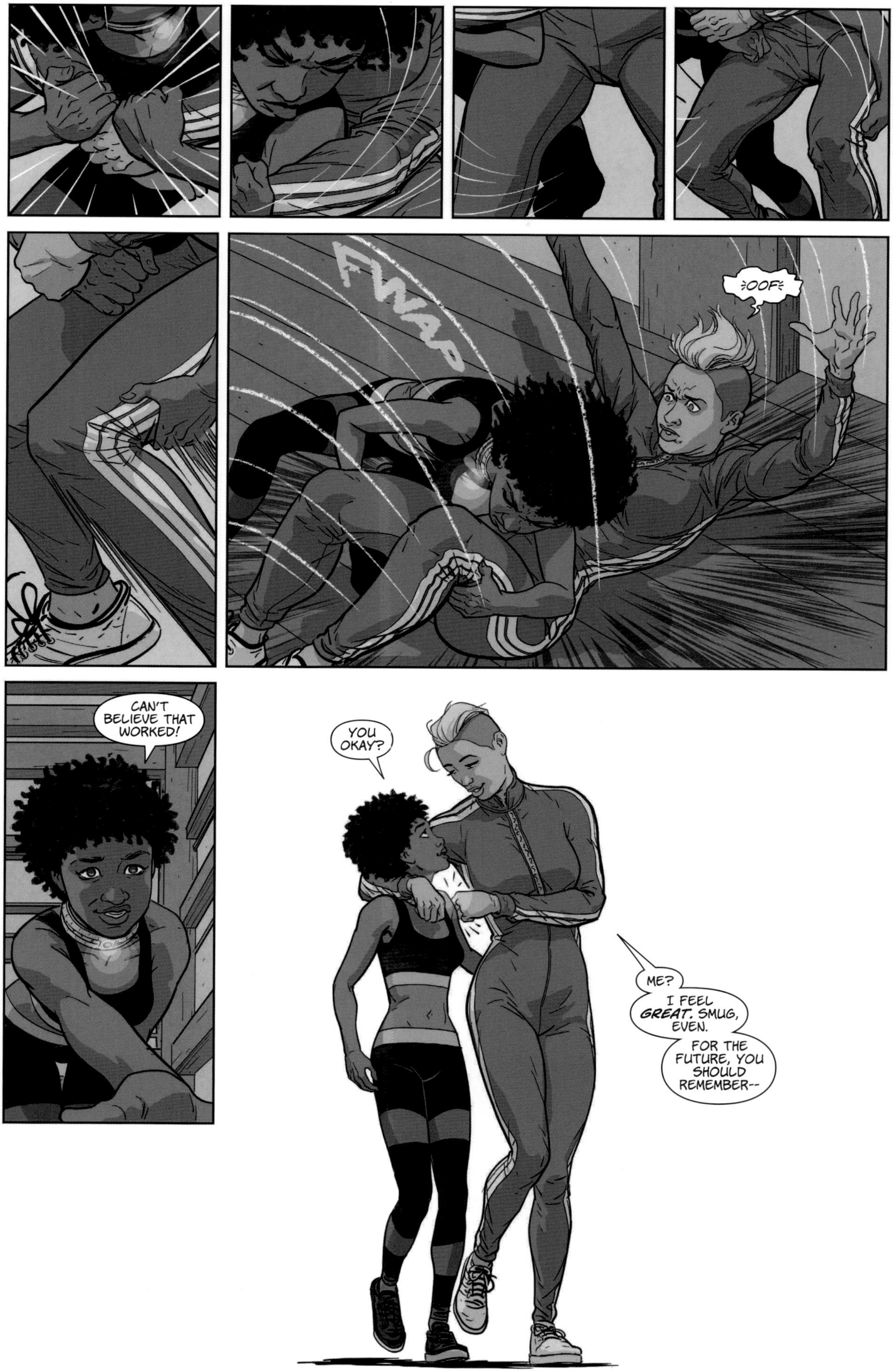
FWAP
OOF
CAN'T BELIEVE THAT WORKED!
YOU OKAY?
ME? I FEEL GREAT. SMUG, EVEN.
FOR THE FUTURE, YOU SHOULD REMEMBER--

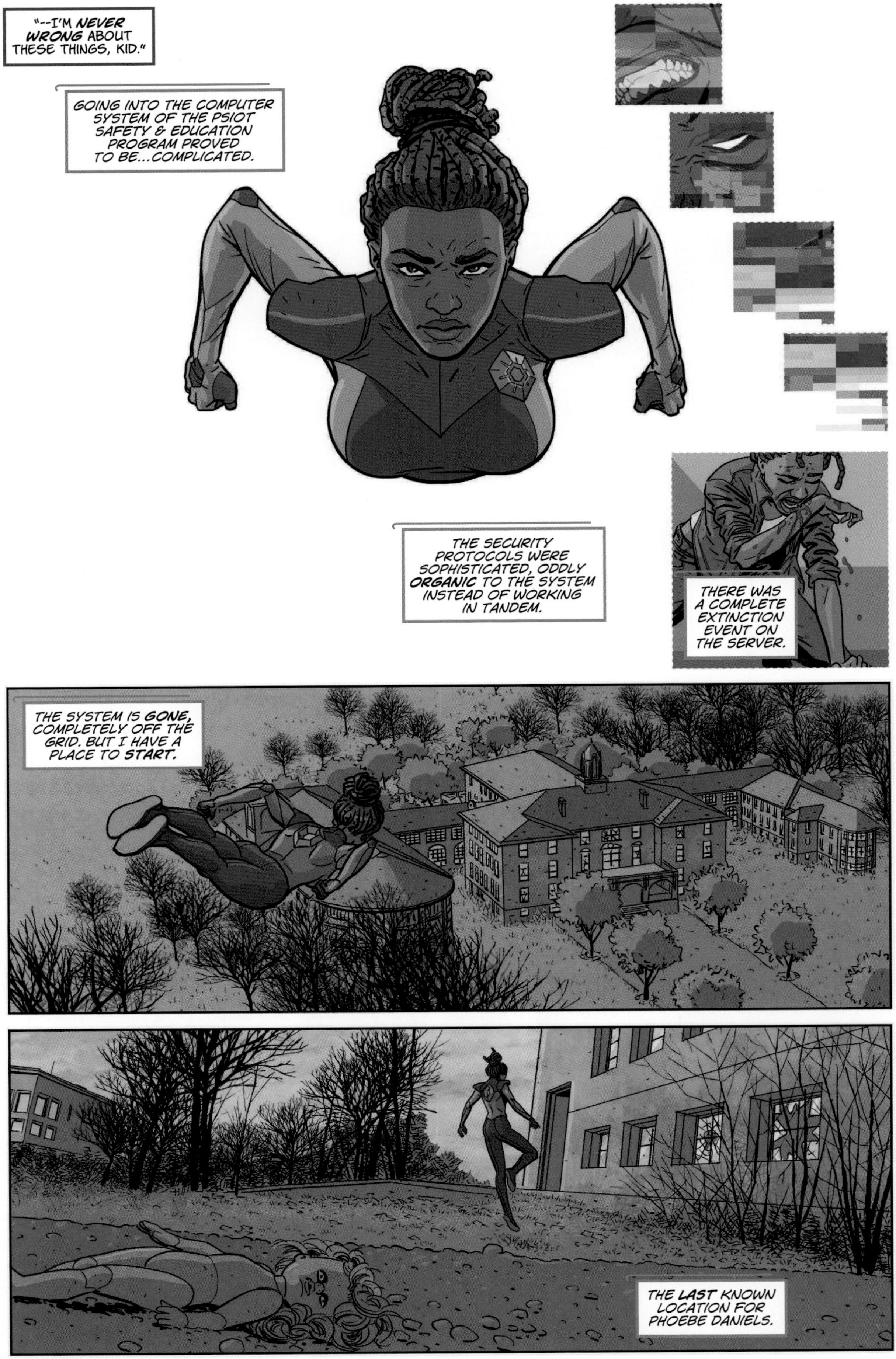
"--I'M NEVER WRONG ABOUT THESE THINGS, KID."
GOING INTO THE COMPUTER SYSTEM OF THE PSIOT SAFETY & EDUCATION PROGRAM PROVED TO BE...COMPLICATED.
THE SECURITY PROTOCOLS WERE SOPHISTICATED, ODDLY ORGANIC TO THE SYSTEM INSTEAD OF WORKING IN TANDEM.
THERE WAS A COMPLETE EXTINCTION EVENT ON THE SERVER.
THE SYSTEM IS GONE, COMPLETELY OFF THE GRID. BUT I HAVE A PLACE TO START.
THE LAST KNOWN LOCATION FOR PHOEBE DANIELS.

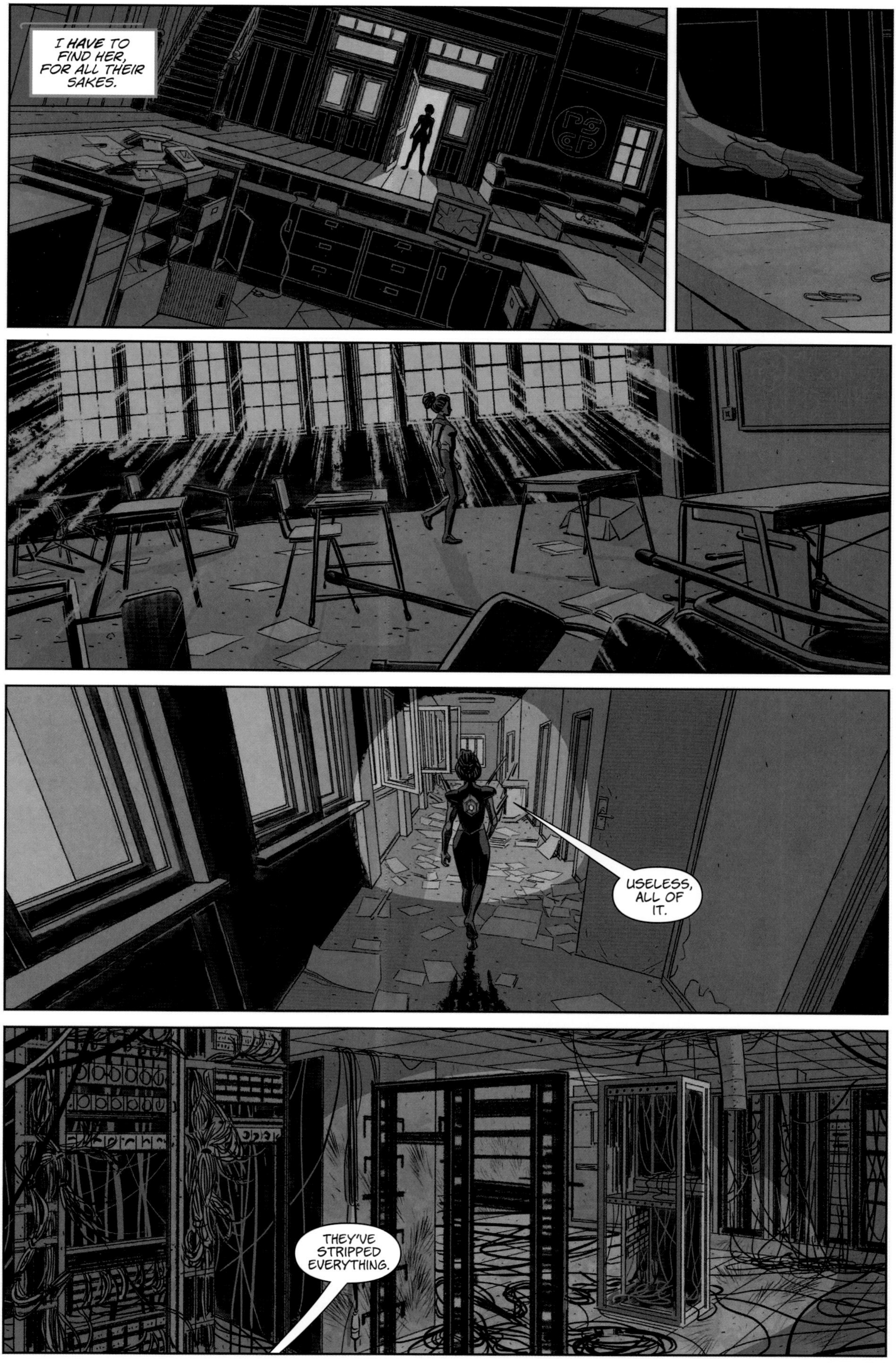
I HAVE TO FIND HER, FOR ALL THEIR SAKES.
USELESS, ALL OF IT.
THEY'VE STRIPPED EVERYTHING.

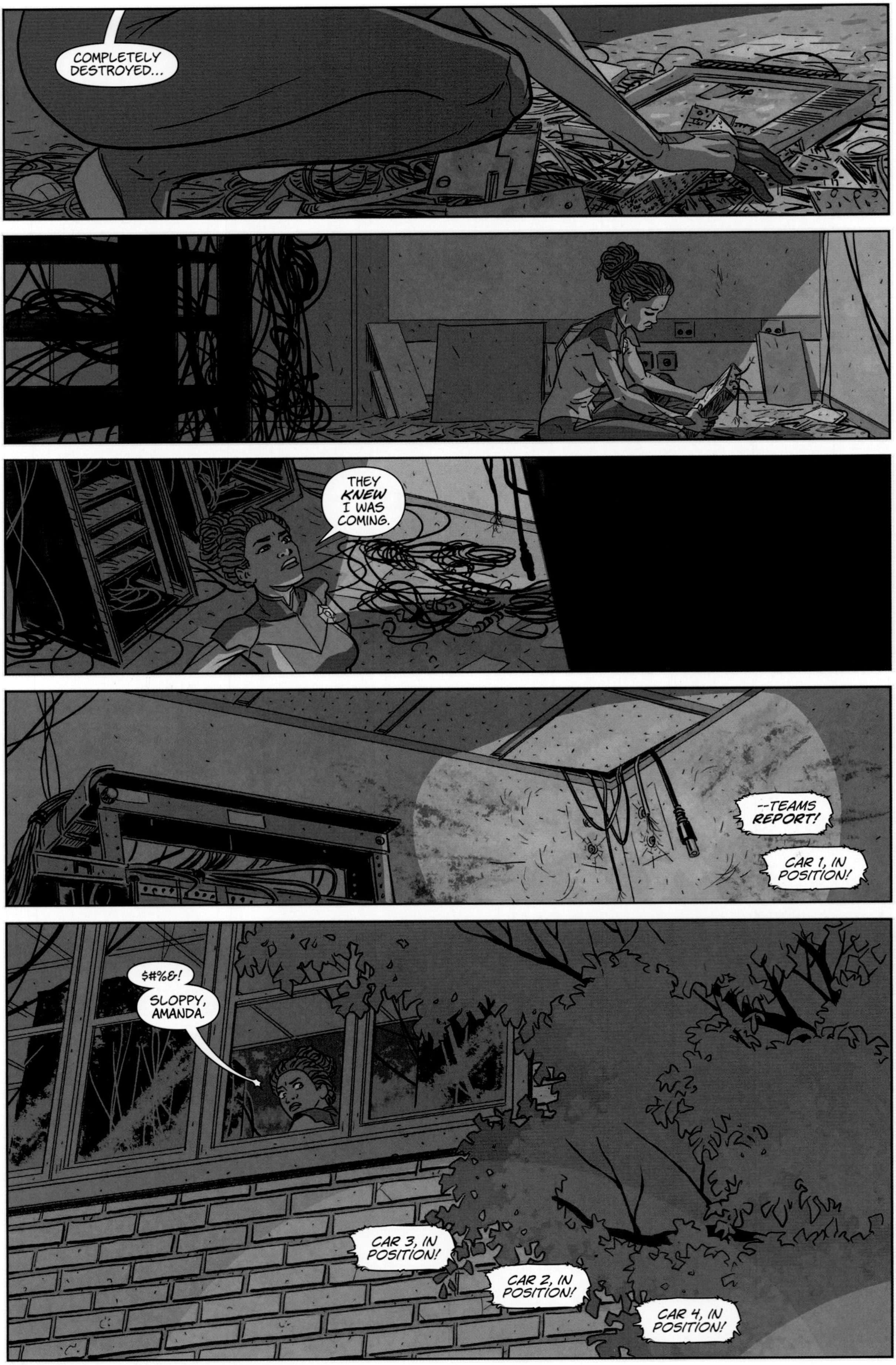
COMPLETELY DESTROYED...
THEY KNEW I WAS COMING.
--TEAMS REPORT!
CAR 1, IN POSITION!
$#%&!
SLOPPY, AMANDA.
CAR 3, IN POSITION!
CAR 2, IN POSITION!
CAR 4, IN POSITION!

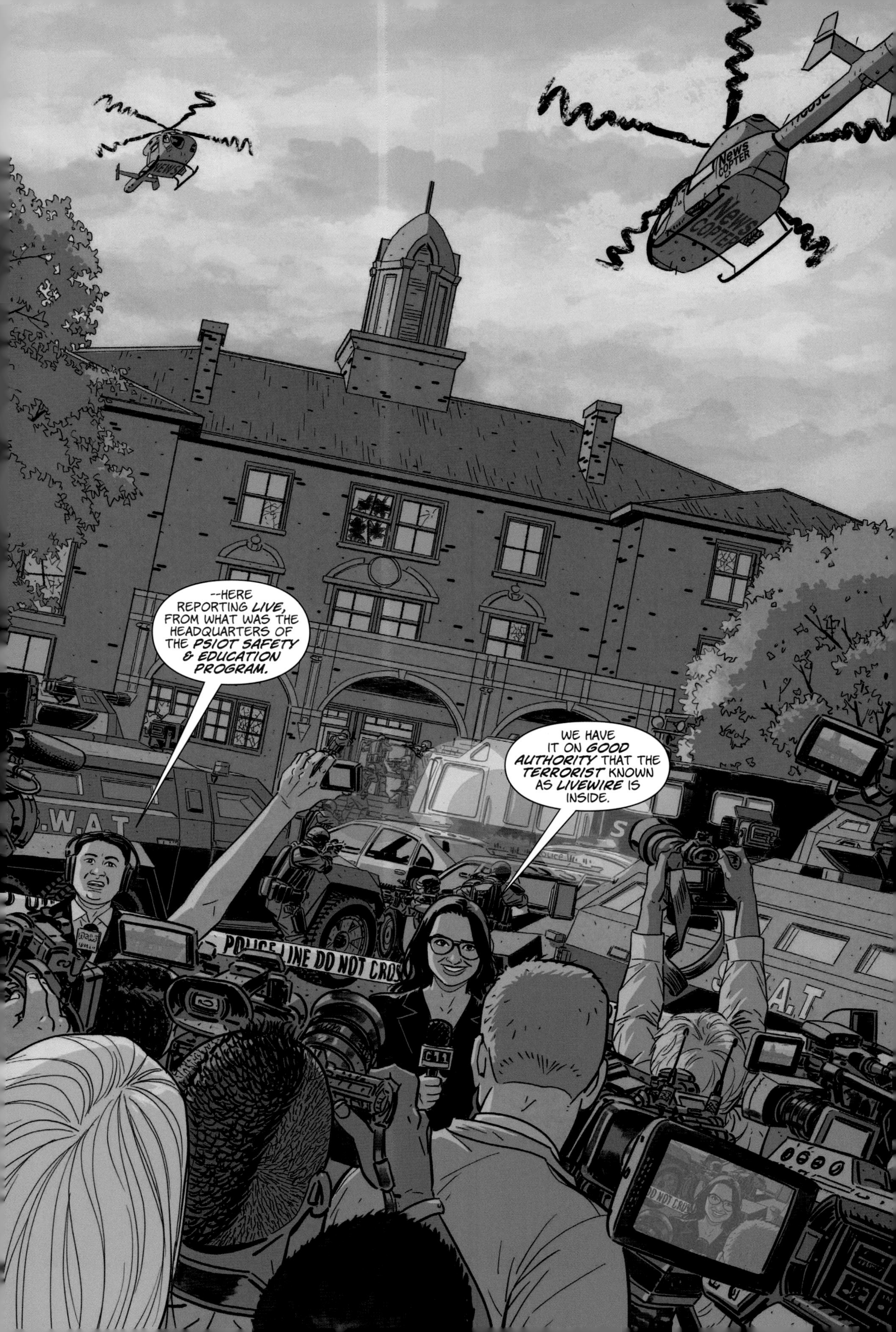

News COPTER
--HERE REPORTING LIVE, FROM WHAT WAS THE HEADQUARTERS OF THE PSIOT SAFETY & EDUCATION PROGRAM.
WE HAVE IT ON GOOD AUTHORITY THAT THE TERRORIST KNOWN AS LIVEWIRE IS INSIDE.
S.W.A.T
POLICE LINE DO NOT CROS
S.W.A.T

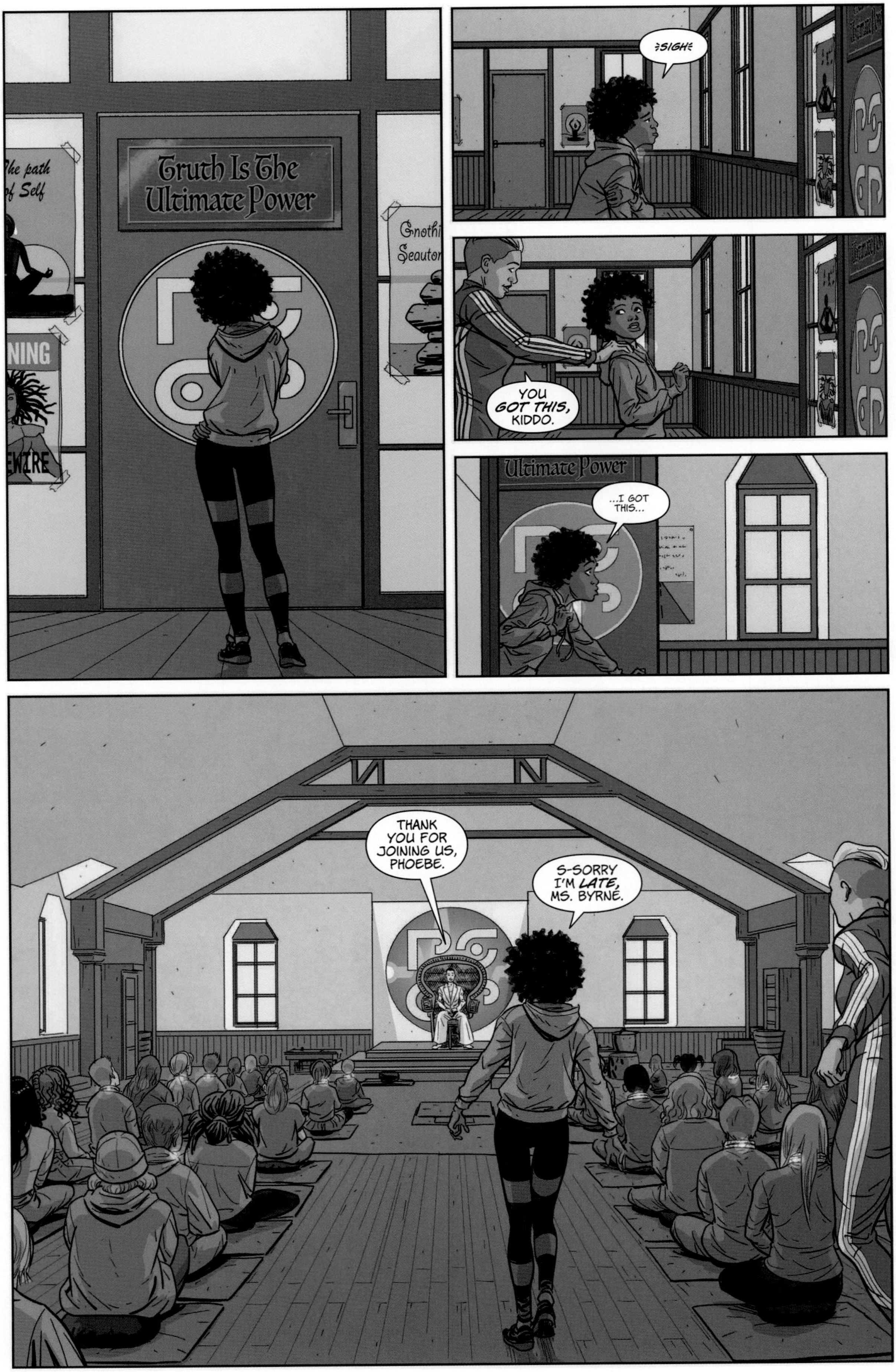
Truth Is The Ultimate Power
The path of Self
Gnothi Seauton
SIGH
YOU GOT THIS, KIDDO.
Ultimate Power
...I GOT THIS...
THANK YOU FOR JOINING US, PHOEBE.
S-SORRY I'M LATE, MS. BYRNE.

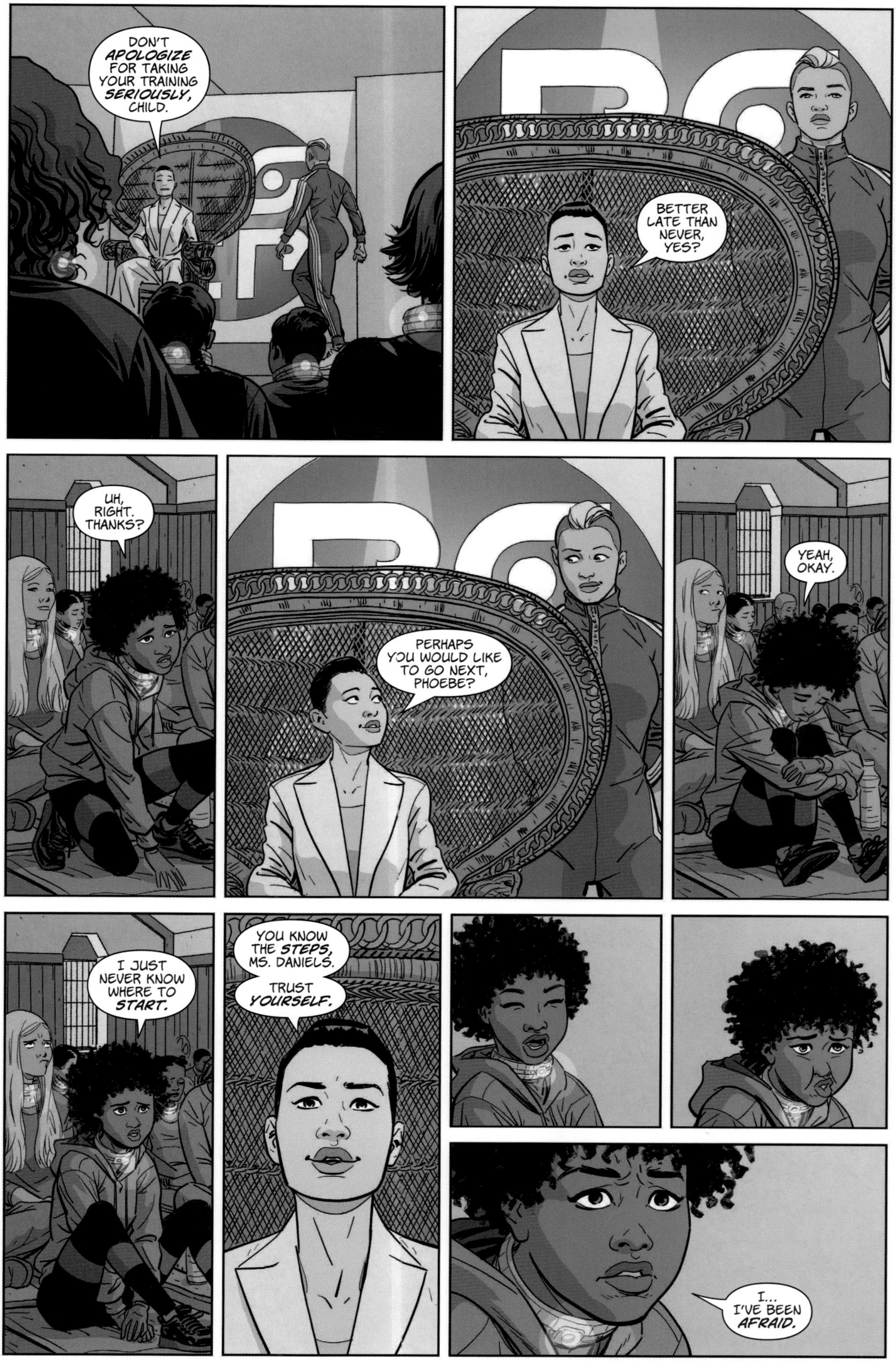
DON'T APOLOGIZE FOR TAKING YOUR TRAINING SERIOUSLY, CHILD.
BETTER LATE THAN NEVER, YES?
UH, RIGHT. THANKS?
PERHAPS YOU WOULD LIKE TO GO NEXT, PHOEBE?
YEAH, OKAY.
I JUST NEVER KNOW WHERE TO START.
YOU KNOW THE STEPS, MS. DANIELS.
TRUST YOURSELF.
I... I'VE BEEN AFRAID.

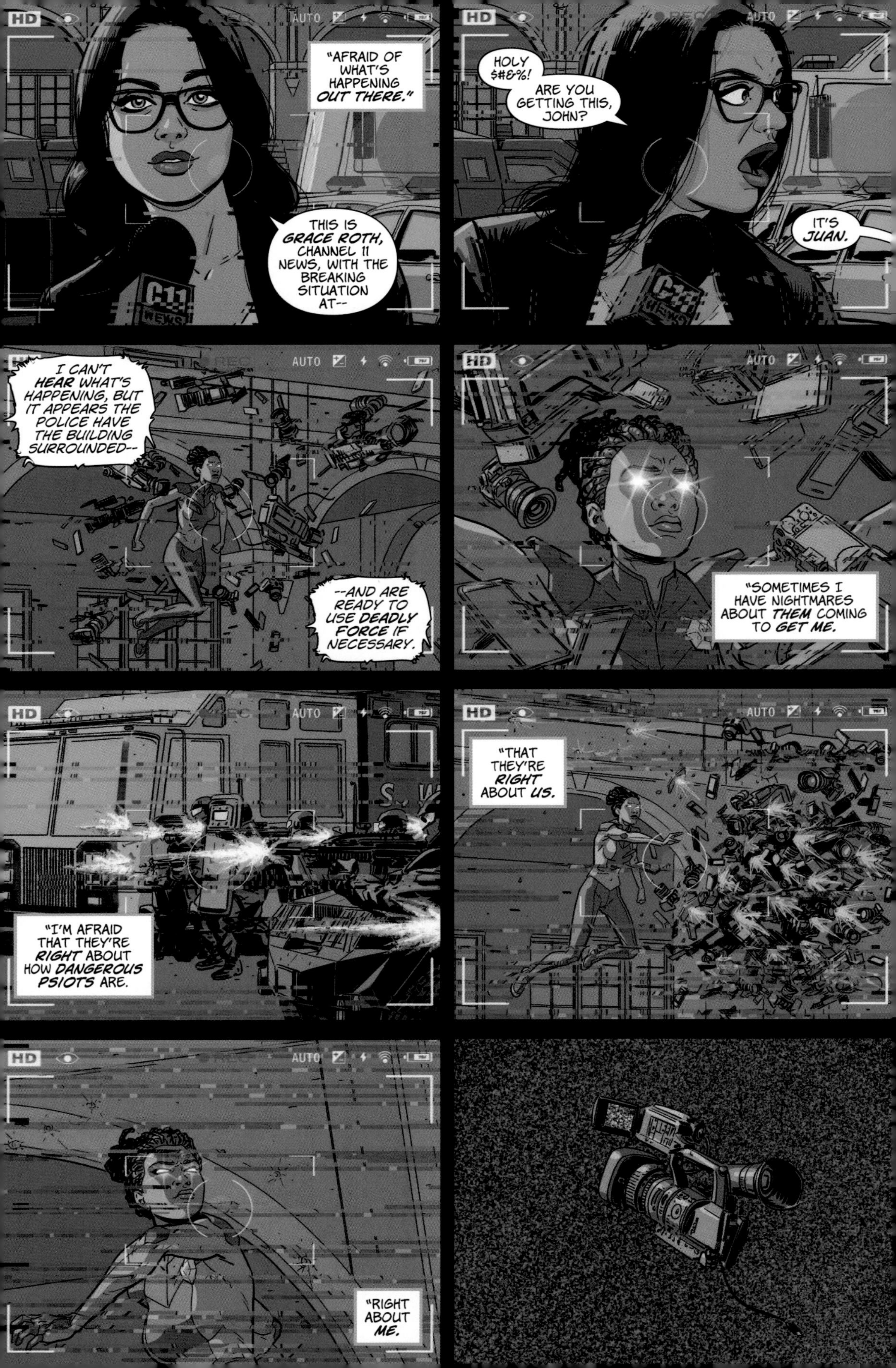
"AFRAID OF WHAT'S HAPPENING *OUT THERE.*"
C11 NEWS
THIS IS *GRACE ROTH,* CHANNEL 11 NEWS, WITH THE BREAKING SITUATION AT--
HOLY $#&%!
ARE YOU GETTING THIS, JOHN?
IT'S *JUAN.*
I CAN'T *HEAR* WHAT'S HAPPENING, BUT IT APPEARS THE POLICE HAVE THE BUILDING SURROUNDED--
--AND ARE READY TO USE *DEADLY FORCE* IF NECESSARY.
"SOMETIMES I HAVE NIGHTMARES ABOUT *THEM* COMING TO *GET ME.*
"I'M AFRAID THAT THEY'RE *RIGHT* ABOUT HOW *DANGEROUS PSIOTS* ARE.
"THAT THEY'RE *RIGHT* ABOUT *US.*
"RIGHT ABOUT *ME.*

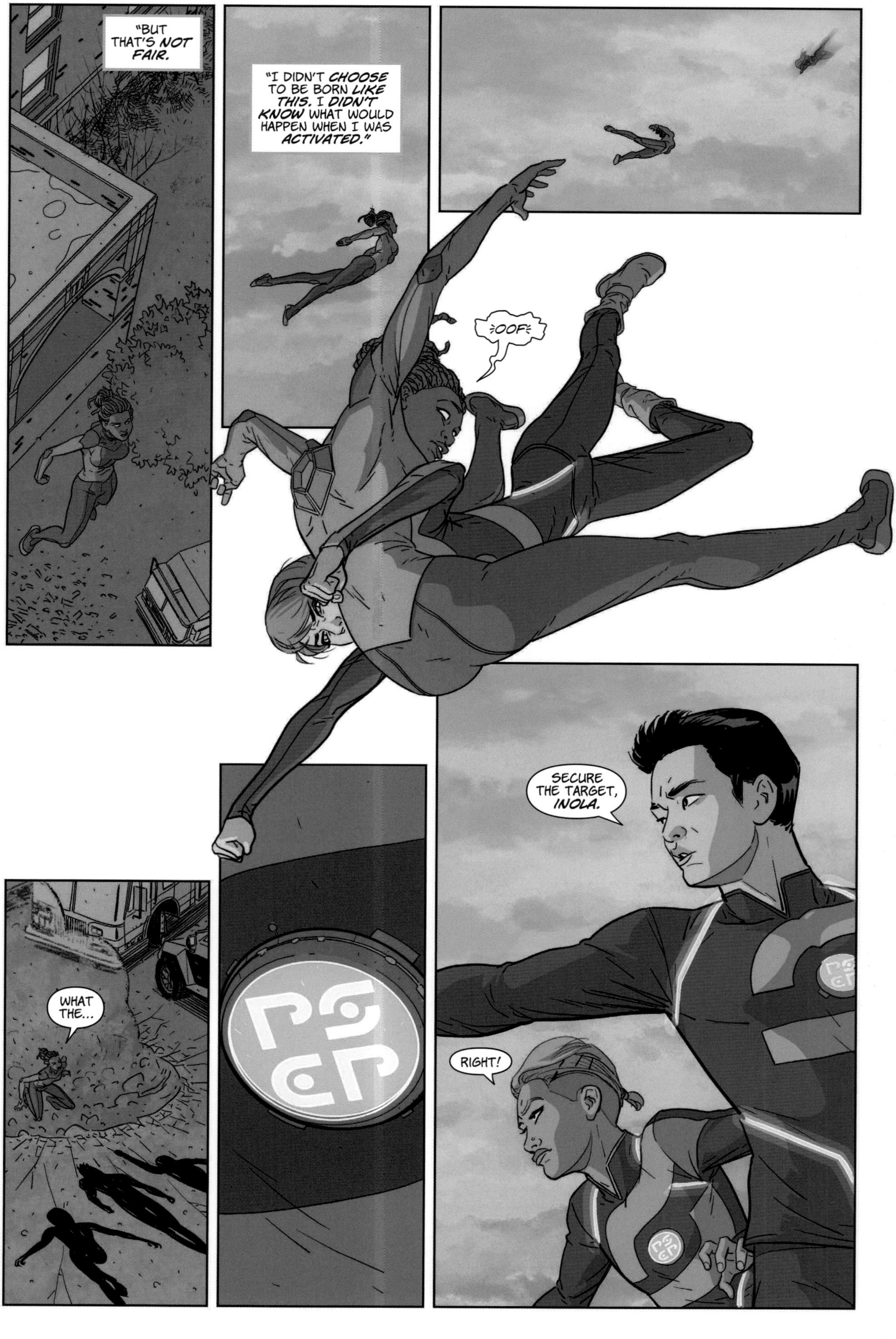
"BUT THAT'S NOT FAIR.
"I DIDN'T CHOOSE TO BE BORN LIKE THIS. I DIDN'T KNOW WHAT WOULD HAPPEN WHEN I WAS ACTIVATED."
OOF
SECURE THE TARGET, INOLA.
RIGHT!
WHAT THE...

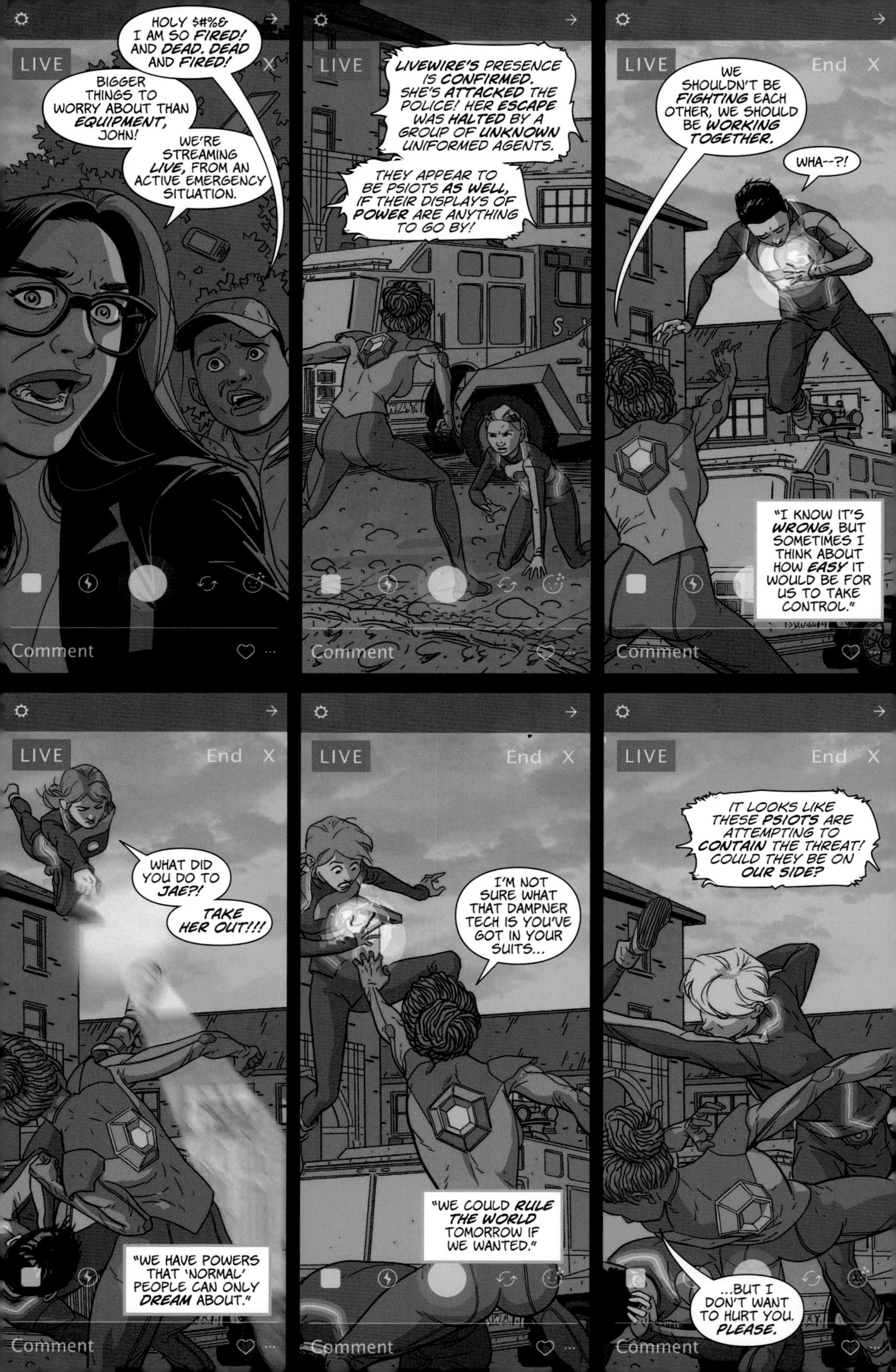
LIVE
X
HOLY $#%& I AM SO FIRED! AND DEAD. DEAD AND FIRED!
BIGGER THINGS TO WORRY ABOUT THAN EQUIPMENT, JOHN!
WE'RE STREAMING LIVE, FROM AN ACTIVE EMERGENCY SITUATION.
Comment
LIVE
LIVEWIRE'S PRESENCE IS CONFIRMED. SHE'S ATTACKED THE POLICE! HER ESCAPE WAS HALTED BY A GROUP OF UNKNOWN UNIFORMED AGENTS.
THEY APPEAR TO BE PSIOTS AS WELL, IF THEIR DISPLAYS OF POWER ARE ANYTHING TO GO BY!
Comment
LIVE
End X
WE SHOULDN'T BE FIGHTING EACH OTHER, WE SHOULD BE WORKING TOGETHER.
WHA--?!
"I KNOW IT'S WRONG, BUT SOMETIMES I THINK ABOUT HOW EASY IT WOULD BE FOR US TO TAKE CONTROL."
Comment
LIVE
End X
WHAT DID YOU DO TO JAE?!
TAKE HER OUT!!!
"WE HAVE POWERS THAT 'NORMAL' PEOPLE CAN ONLY DREAM ABOUT."
Comment
LIVE
End X
I'M NOT SURE WHAT THAT DAMPNER TECH IS YOU'VE GOT IN YOUR SUITS...
"WE COULD RULE THE WORLD TOMORROW IF WE WANTED."
Comment
LIVE
End X
IT LOOKS LIKE THESE PSIOTS ARE ATTEMPTING TO CONTAIN THE THREAT! COULD THEY BE ON OUR SIDE?
...BUT I DON'T WANT TO HURT YOU. PLEASE.
Comment

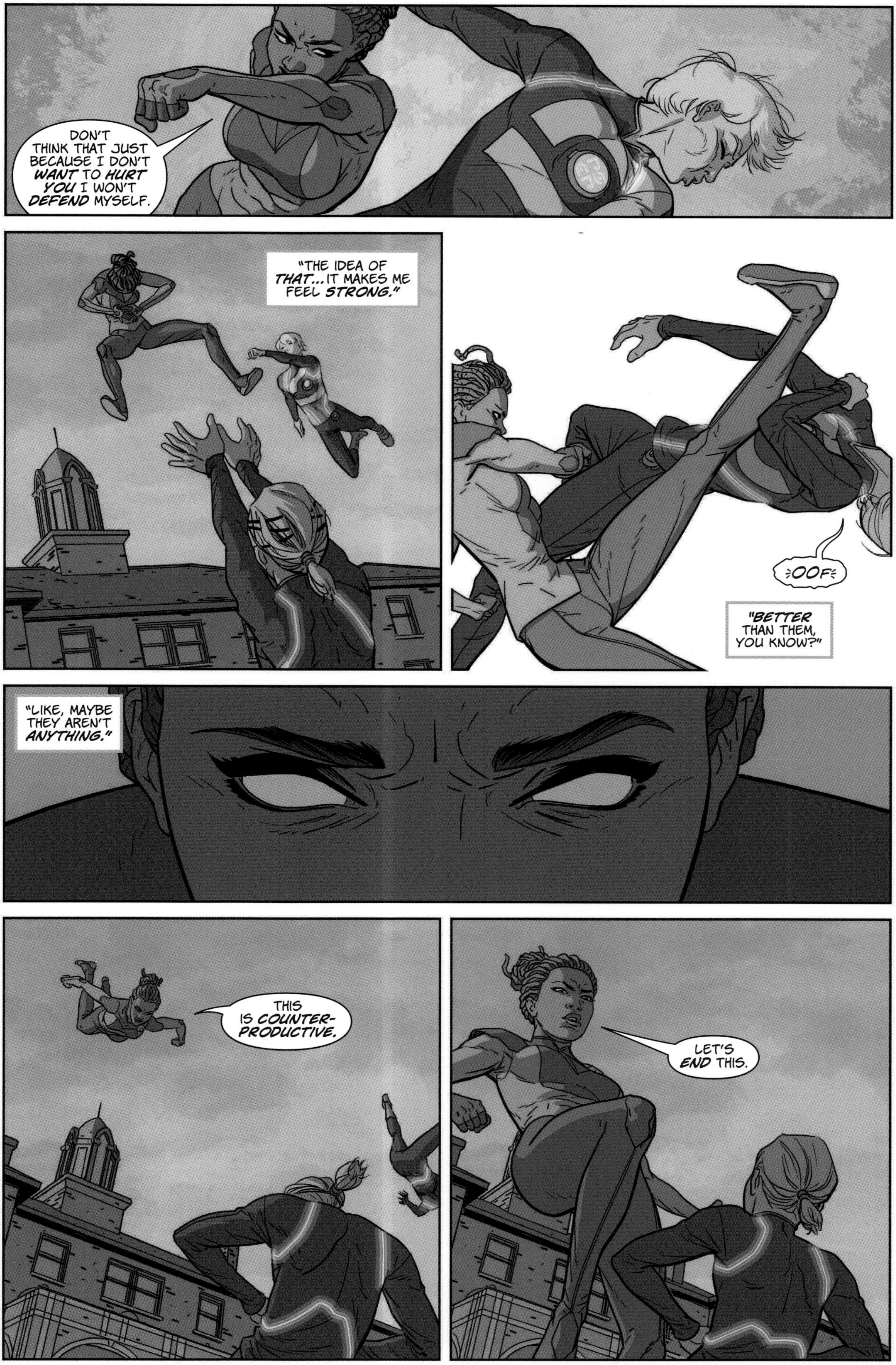
DON'T THINK THAT JUST BECAUSE I DON'T **WANT** TO **HURT YOU** I WON'T **DEFEND** MYSELF.
"THE IDEA OF **THAT...** IT MAKES ME FEEL **STRONG.**"
OOF
"**BETTER** THAN THEM, YOU KNOW?"
"LIKE, MAYBE THEY AREN'T **ANYTHING.**"
THIS IS **COUNTER-PRODUCTIVE.**
LET'S **END** THIS.

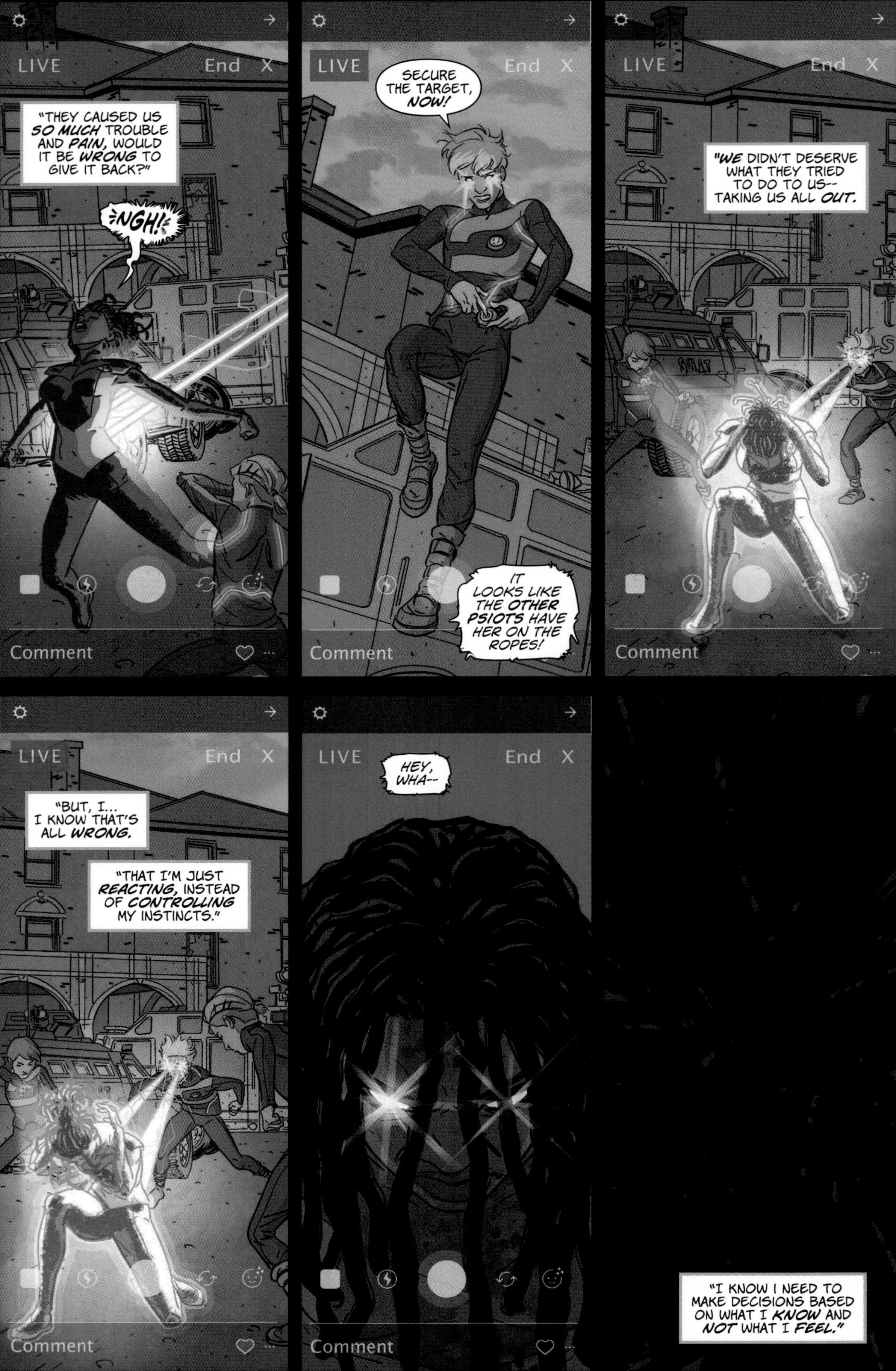

"THEY CAUSED US SO MUCH TROUBLE AND PAIN, WOULD IT BE WRONG TO GIVE IT BACK?"
NGH!
SECURE THE TARGET, NOW!
IT LOOKS LIKE THE OTHER PSIOTS HAVE HER ON THE ROPES!
"WE DIDN'T DESERVE WHAT THEY TRIED TO DO TO US-- TAKING US ALL OUT.
"BUT, I... I KNOW THAT'S ALL WRONG.
"THAT I'M JUST REACTING, INSTEAD OF CONTROLLING MY INSTINCTS."
HEY, WHA--
"I KNOW I NEED TO MAKE DECISIONS BASED ON WHAT I KNOW AND NOT WHAT I FEEL."

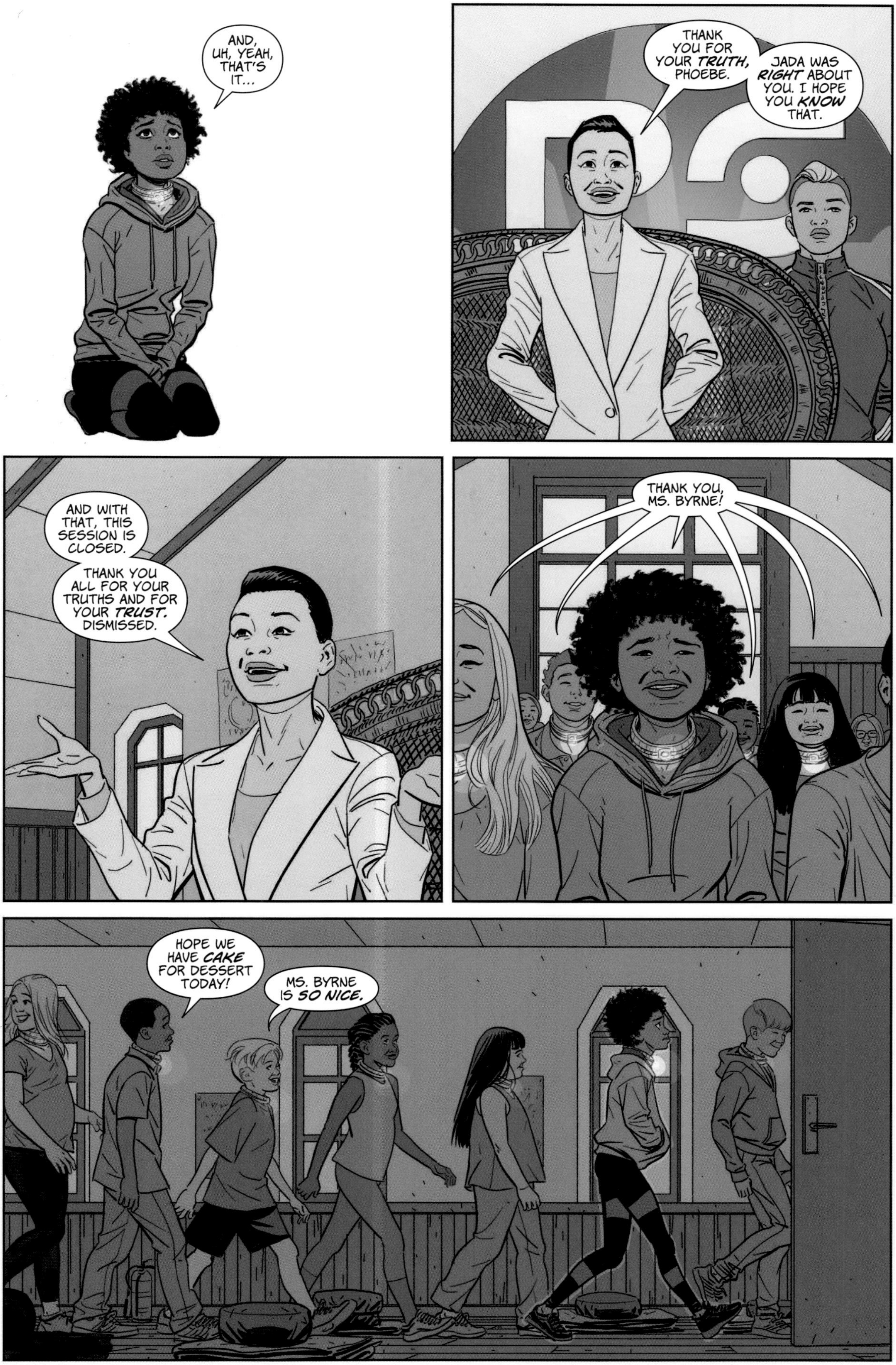
AND, UH, YEAH, THAT'S IT...
THANK YOU FOR YOUR *TRUTH,* PHOEBE.
JADA WAS *RIGHT* ABOUT YOU. I HOPE YOU *KNOW* THAT.
AND WITH THAT, THIS SESSION IS CLOSED.
THANK YOU ALL FOR YOUR TRUTHS AND FOR YOUR *TRUST.* DISMISSED.
THANK YOU, MS. BYRNE!
HOPE WE HAVE *CAKE* FOR DESSERT TODAY!
MS. BYRNE IS *SO NICE.*

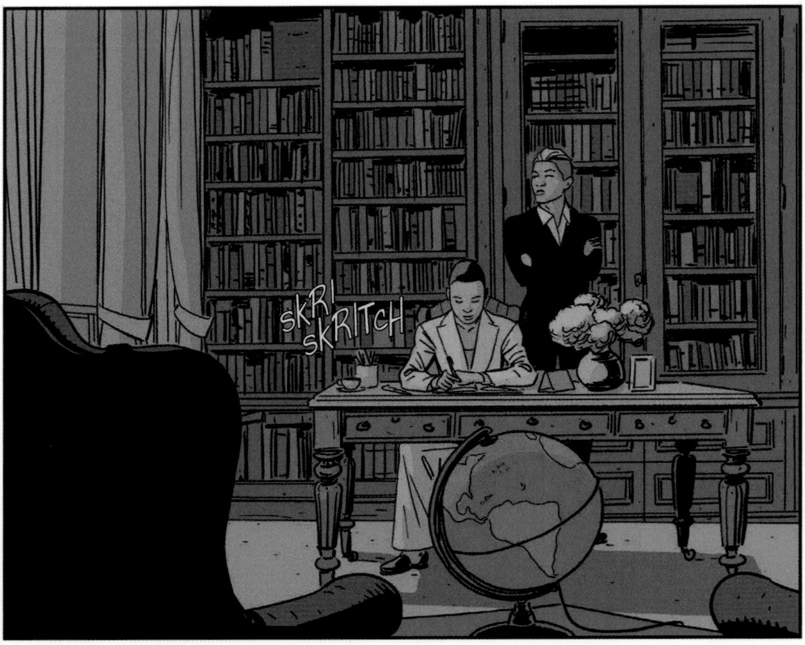
SKRI
SKRITCH
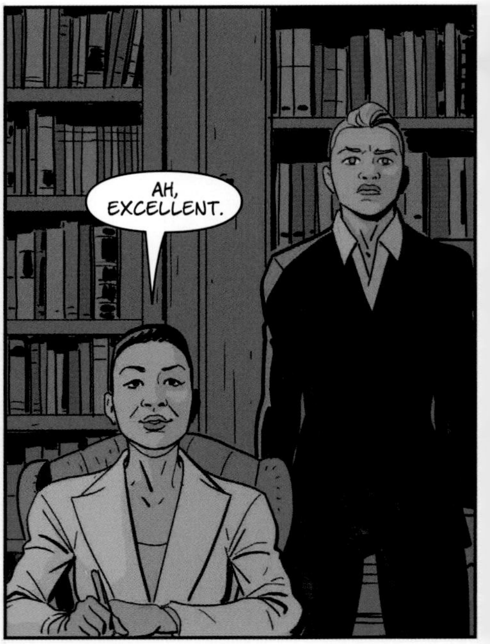
AH, EXCELLENT.
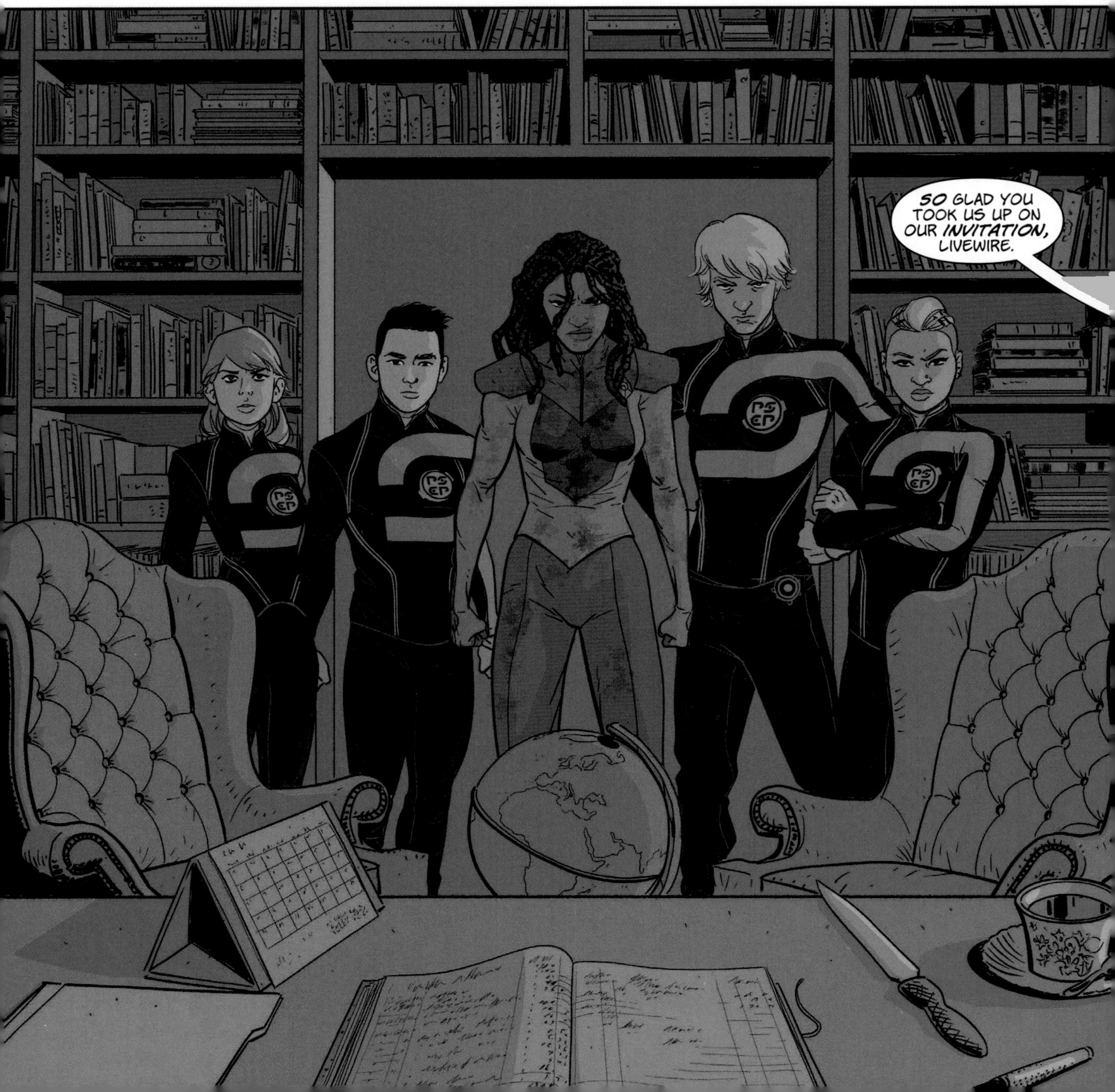
SO GLAD YOU TOOK US UP ON OUR INVITATION, LIVEWIRE.

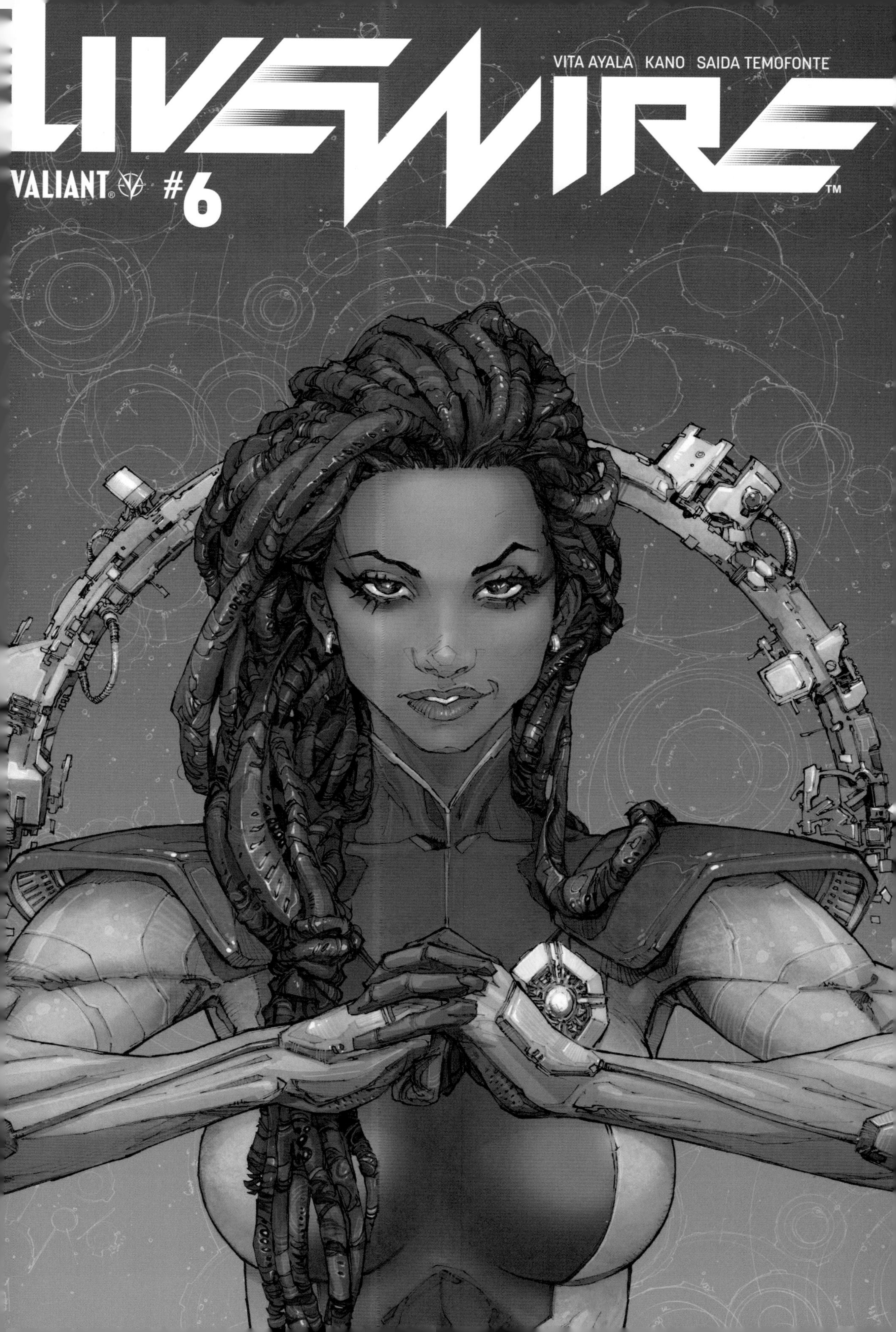
LIVEWIRE™
VITA AYALA | KANO | SAIDA TEMOFONTE
VALIANT®
#6

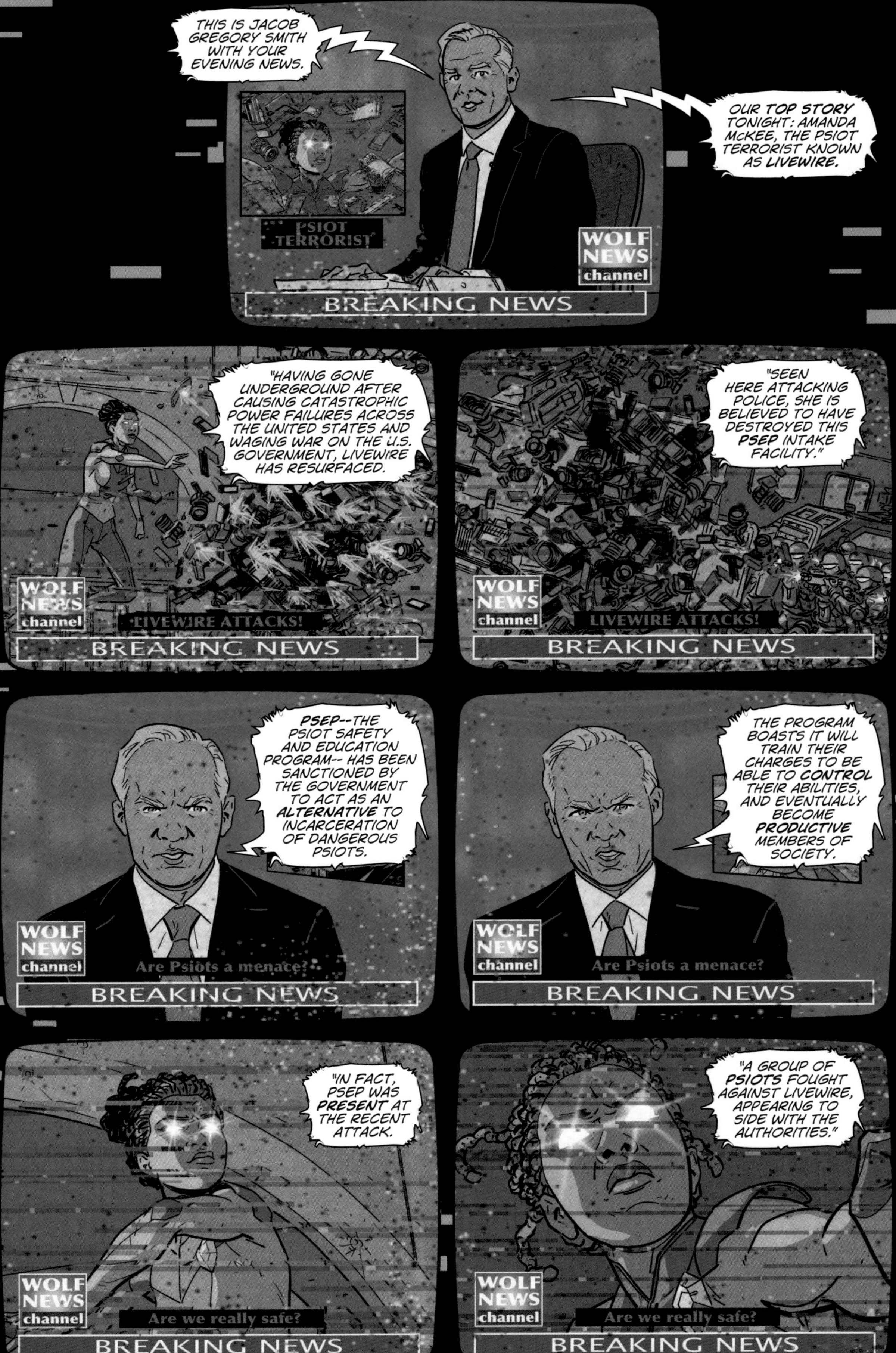
THIS IS JACOB GREGORY SMITH WITH YOUR EVENING NEWS.
PSIOT TERRORIST
OUR TOP STORY TONIGHT: AMANDA McKEE, THE PSIOT TERRORIST KNOWN AS LIVEWIRE.
WOLF NEWS channel
BREAKING NEWS
"HAVING GONE UNDERGROUND AFTER CAUSING CATASTROPHIC POWER FAILURES ACROSS THE UNITED STATES AND WAGING WAR ON THE U.S. GOVERNMENT, LIVEWIRE HAS RESURFACED.
WOLF NEWS channel
LIVEWIRE ATTACKS!
BREAKING NEWS
"SEEN HERE ATTACKING POLICE, SHE IS BELIEVED TO HAVE DESTROYED THIS PSEP INTAKE FACILITY."
WOLF NEWS channel
LIVEWIRE ATTACKS!
BREAKING NEWS
PSEP--THE PSIOT SAFETY AND EDUCATION PROGRAM-- HAS BEEN SANCTIONED BY THE GOVERNMENT TO ACT AS AN ALTERNATIVE TO INCARCERATION OF DANGEROUS PSIOTS.
WOLF NEWS channel
Are Psiots a menace?
BREAKING NEWS
THE PROGRAM BOASTS IT WILL TRAIN THEIR CHARGES TO BE ABLE TO CONTROL THEIR ABILITIES, AND EVENTUALLY BECOME PRODUCTIVE MEMBERS OF SOCIETY.
WOLF NEWS channel
Are Psiots a menace?
BREAKING NEWS
"IN FACT, PSEP WAS PRESENT AT THE RECENT ATTACK.
WOLF NEWS channel
Are we really safe?
BREAKING NEWS
"A GROUP OF PSIOTS FOUGHT AGAINST LIVEWIRE, APPEARING TO SIDE WITH THE AUTHORITIES."
WOLF NEWS channel
Are we really safe?
BREAKING NEWS

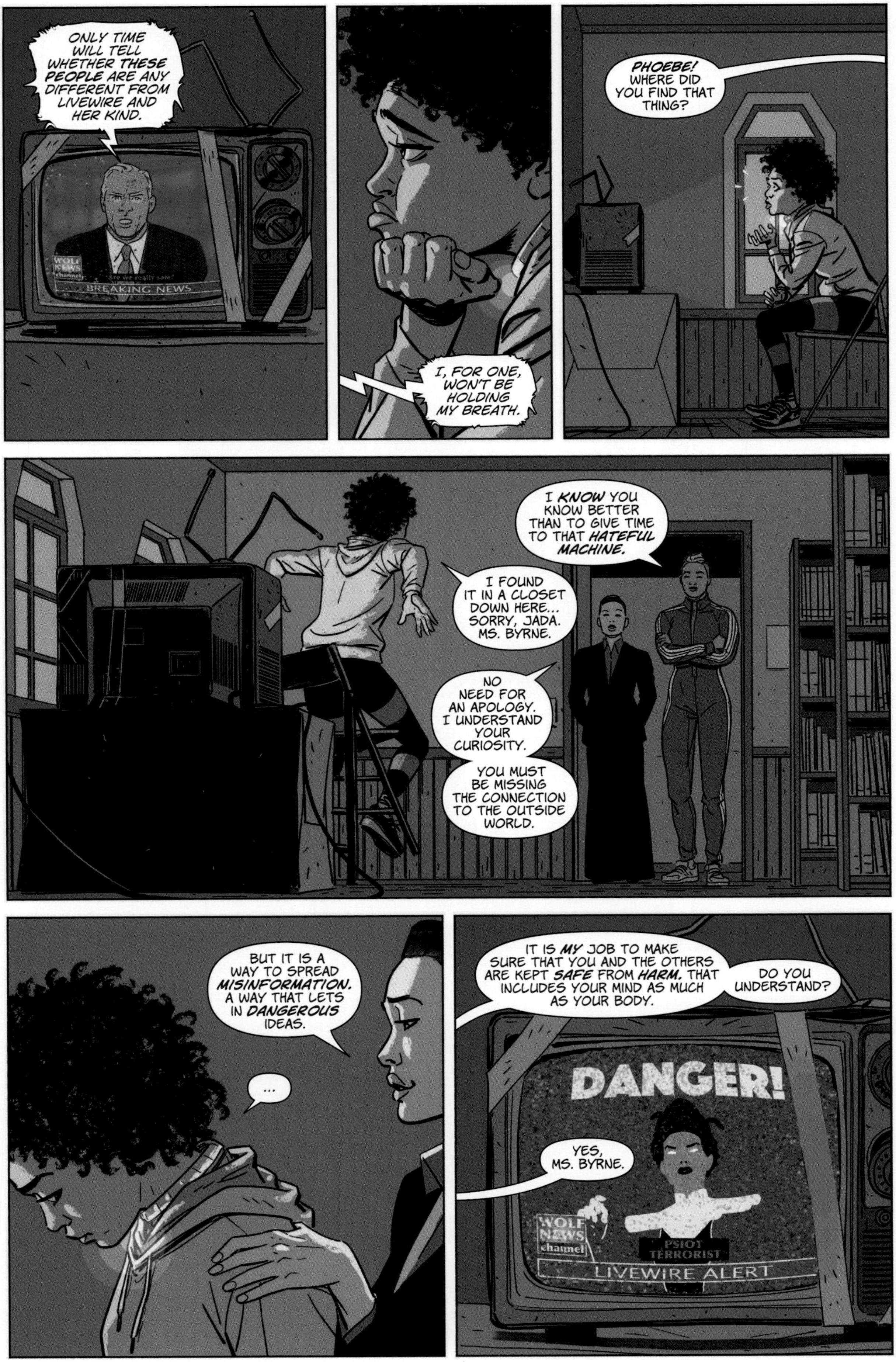
ONLY TIME WILL TELL WHETHER THESE PEOPLE ARE ANY DIFFERENT FROM LIVEWIRE AND HER KIND.
WOLF NEWS channel
BREAKING NEWS
I, FOR ONE, WON'T BE HOLDING MY BREATH.
PHOEBE! WHERE DID YOU FIND THAT THING?
I KNOW YOU KNOW BETTER THAN TO GIVE TIME TO THAT HATEFUL MACHINE.
I FOUND IT IN A CLOSET DOWN HERE... SORRY, JADA. MS. BYRNE.
NO NEED FOR AN APOLOGY. I UNDERSTAND YOUR CURIOSITY.
YOU MUST BE MISSING THE CONNECTION TO THE OUTSIDE WORLD.
BUT IT IS A WAY TO SPREAD MISINFORMATION. A WAY THAT LETS IN DANGEROUS IDEAS.
...
IT IS MY JOB TO MAKE SURE THAT YOU AND THE OTHERS ARE KEPT SAFE FROM HARM. THAT INCLUDES YOUR MIND AS MUCH AS YOUR BODY.
DO YOU UNDERSTAND?
DANGER!
YES, MS. BYRNE.
WOLF NEWS channel
PSIOT TERRORIST
LIVEWIRE ALERT

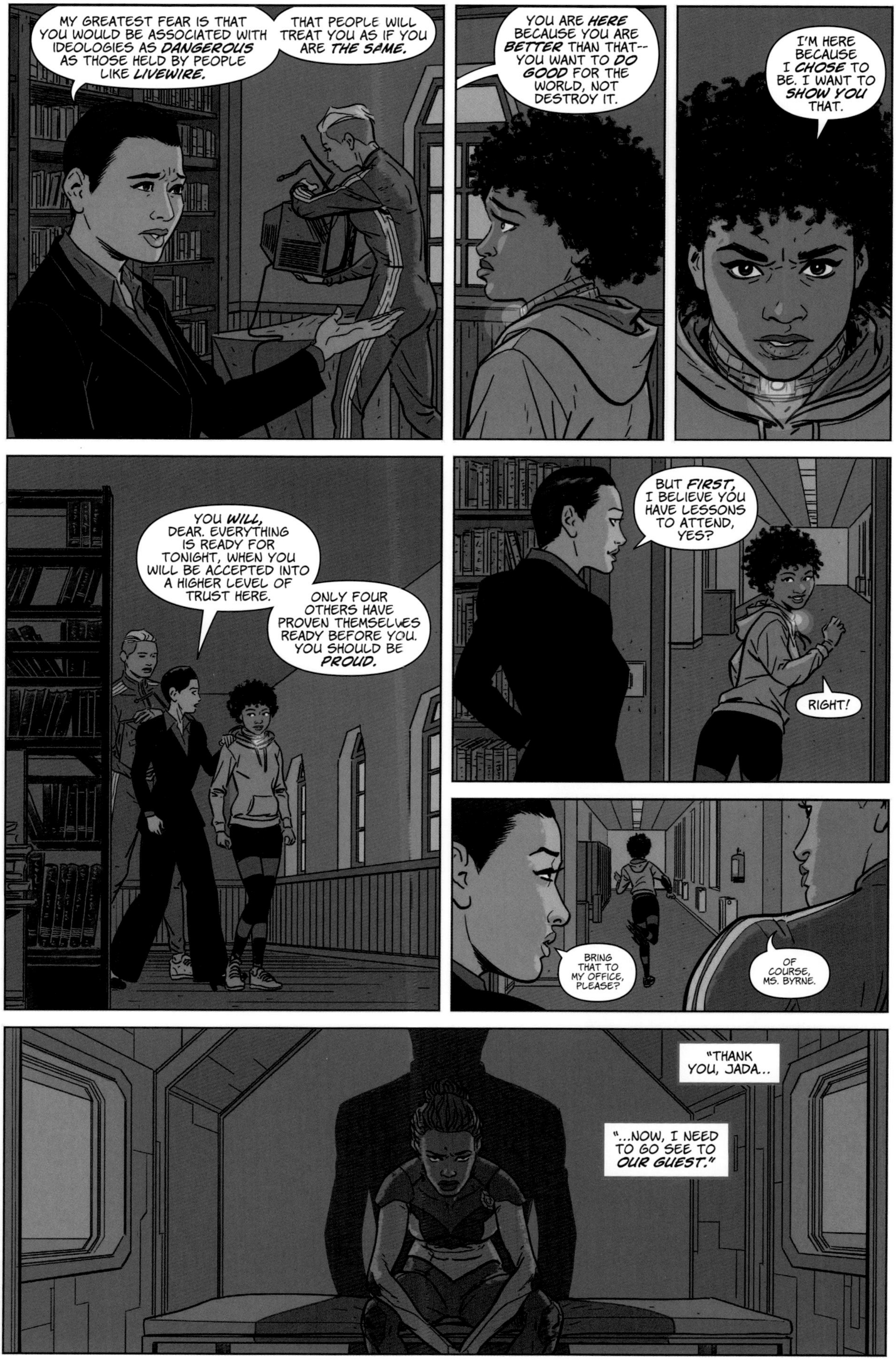
MY GREATEST FEAR IS THAT YOU WOULD BE ASSOCIATED WITH IDEOLOGIES AS DANGEROUS AS THOSE HELD BY PEOPLE LIKE LIVEWIRE.
THAT PEOPLE WILL TREAT YOU AS IF YOU ARE THE SAME.
YOU ARE HERE BECAUSE YOU ARE BETTER THAN THAT--YOU WANT TO DO GOOD FOR THE WORLD, NOT DESTROY IT.
I'M HERE BECAUSE I CHOSE TO BE. I WANT TO SHOW YOU THAT.
YOU WILL, DEAR. EVERYTHING IS READY FOR TONIGHT, WHEN YOU WILL BE ACCEPTED INTO A HIGHER LEVEL OF TRUST HERE.
ONLY FOUR OTHERS HAVE PROVEN THEMSELVES READY BEFORE YOU. YOU SHOULD BE PROUD.
BUT FIRST, I BELIEVE YOU HAVE LESSONS TO ATTEND, YES?
RIGHT!
BRING THAT TO MY OFFICE, PLEASE?
OF COURSE, MS. BYRNE.
"THANK YOU, JADA...
"...NOW, I NEED TO GO SEE TO OUR GUEST."

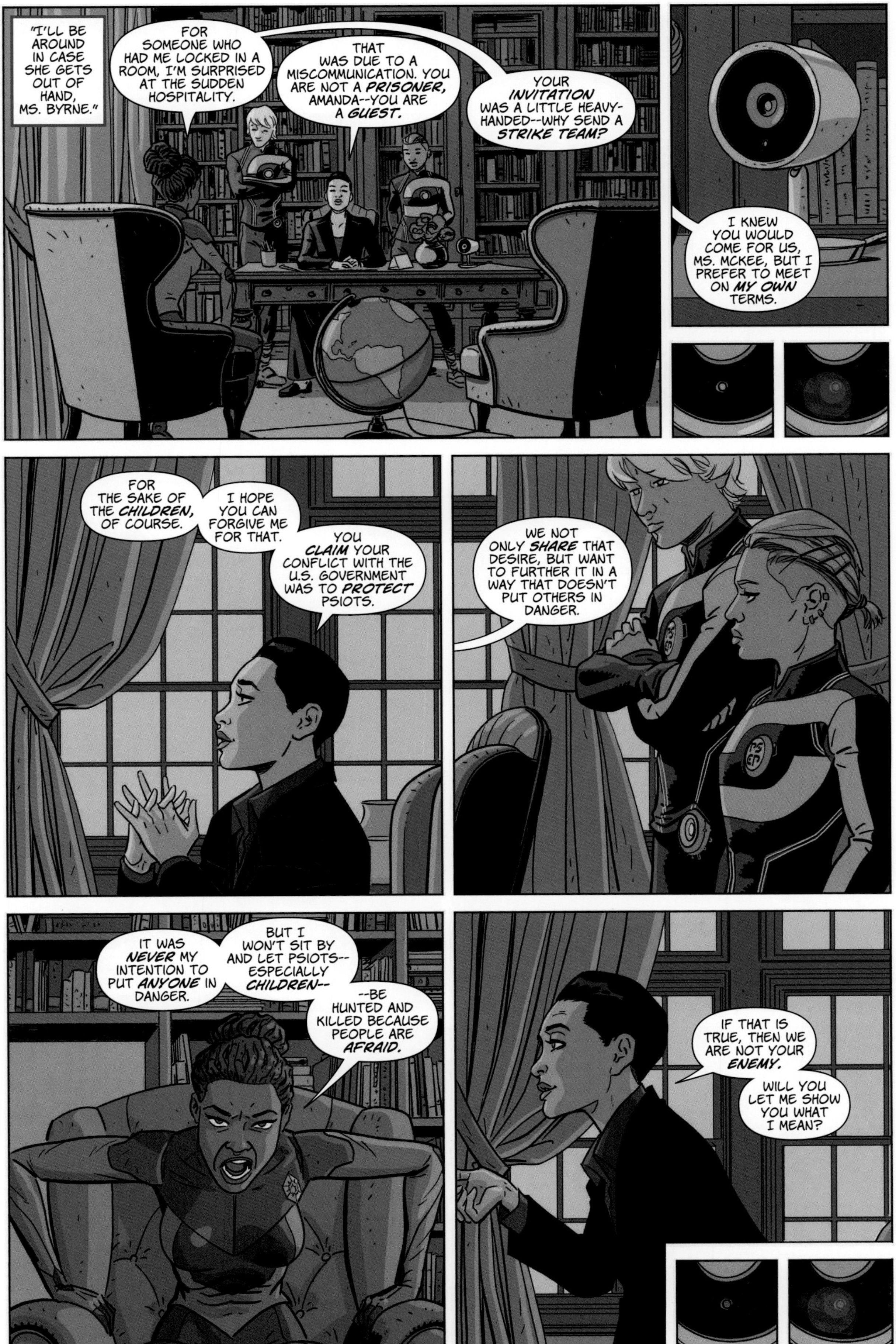
"I'LL BE AROUND IN CASE SHE GETS OUT OF HAND, MS. BYRNE."
FOR SOMEONE WHO HAD ME LOCKED IN A ROOM, I'M SURPRISED AT THE SUDDEN HOSPITALITY.
THAT WAS DUE TO A MISCOMMUNICATION. YOU ARE NOT A PRISONER, AMANDA--YOU ARE A GUEST.
YOUR INVITATION WAS A LITTLE HEAVY-HANDED--WHY SEND A STRIKE TEAM?
I KNEW YOU WOULD COME FOR US, MS. MCKEE, BUT I PREFER TO MEET ON MY OWN TERMS.
FOR THE SAKE OF THE CHILDREN, OF COURSE.
I HOPE YOU CAN FORGIVE ME FOR THAT.
YOU CLAIM YOUR CONFLICT WITH THE U.S. GOVERNMENT WAS TO PROTECT PSIOTS.
WE NOT ONLY SHARE THAT DESIRE, BUT WANT TO FURTHER IT IN A WAY THAT DOESN'T PUT OTHERS IN DANGER.
IT WAS NEVER MY INTENTION TO PUT ANYONE IN DANGER.
BUT I WON'T SIT BY AND LET PSIOTS--ESPECIALLY CHILDREN--
--BE HUNTED AND KILLED BECAUSE PEOPLE ARE AFRAID.
IF THAT IS TRUE, THEN WE ARE NOT YOUR ENEMY.
WILL YOU LET ME SHOW YOU WHAT I MEAN?

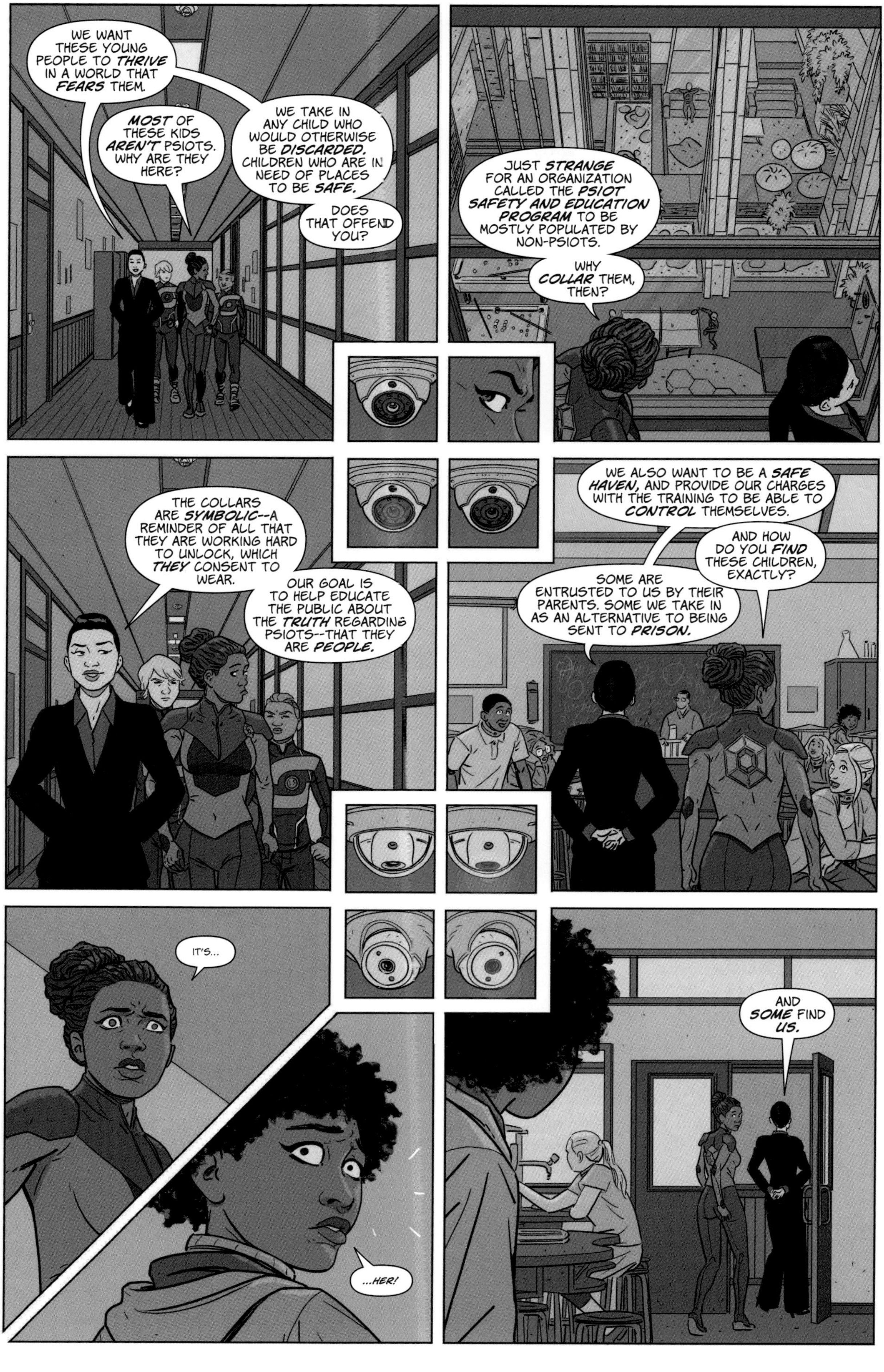
WE WANT THESE YOUNG PEOPLE TO THRIVE IN A WORLD THAT FEARS THEM.
MOST OF THESE KIDS AREN'T PSIOTS. WHY ARE THEY HERE?
WE TAKE IN ANY CHILD WHO WOULD OTHERWISE BE DISCARDED. CHILDREN WHO ARE IN NEED OF PLACES TO BE SAFE.
DOES THAT OFFEND YOU?
JUST STRANGE FOR AN ORGANIZATION CALLED THE PSIOT SAFETY AND EDUCATION PROGRAM TO BE MOSTLY POPULATED BY NON-PSIOTS.
WHY COLLAR THEM, THEN?
THE COLLARS ARE SYMBOLIC--A REMINDER OF ALL THAT THEY ARE WORKING HARD TO UNLOCK, WHICH THEY CONSENT TO WEAR.
OUR GOAL IS TO HELP EDUCATE THE PUBLIC ABOUT THE TRUTH REGARDING PSIOTS--THAT THEY ARE PEOPLE.
WE ALSO WANT TO BE A SAFE HAVEN, AND PROVIDE OUR CHARGES WITH THE TRAINING TO BE ABLE TO CONTROL THEMSELVES.
AND HOW DO YOU FIND THESE CHILDREN, EXACTLY?
SOME ARE ENTRUSTED TO US BY THEIR PARENTS. SOME WE TAKE IN AS AN ALTERNATIVE TO BEING SENT TO PRISON.
IT'S...
...HER!
AND SOME FIND US.

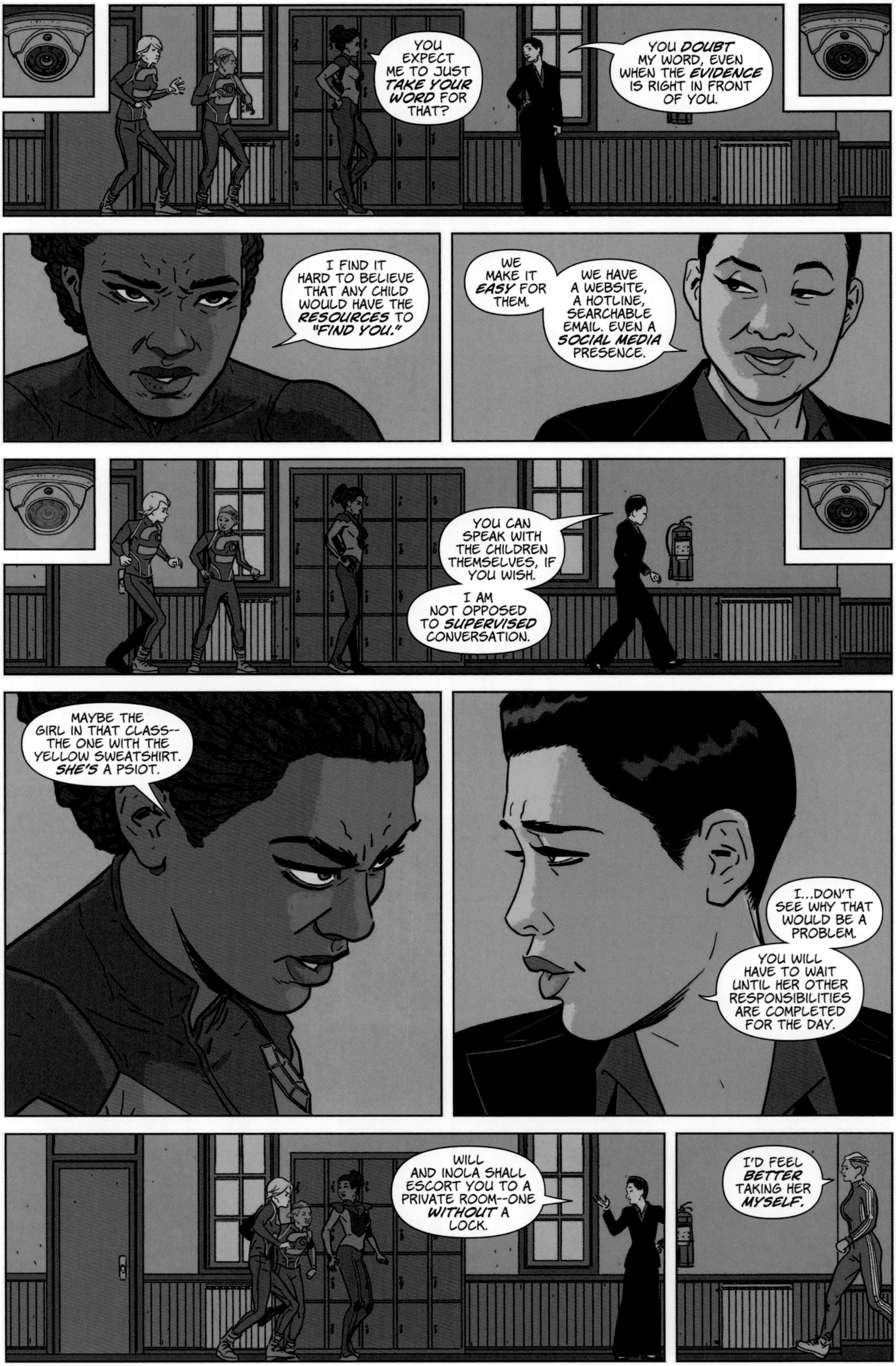
YOU EXPECT ME TO JUST TAKE YOUR WORD FOR THAT?
YOU DOUBT MY WORD, EVEN WHEN THE EVIDENCE IS RIGHT IN FRONT OF YOU.
I FIND IT HARD TO BELIEVE THAT ANY CHILD WOULD HAVE THE RESOURCES TO "FIND YOU."
WE MAKE IT EASY FOR THEM.
WE HAVE A WEBSITE, A HOTLINE, SEARCHABLE EMAIL. EVEN A SOCIAL MEDIA PRESENCE.
YOU CAN SPEAK WITH THE CHILDREN THEMSELVES, IF YOU WISH.
I AM NOT OPPOSED TO SUPERVISED CONVERSATION.
MAYBE THE GIRL IN THAT CLASS-- THE ONE WITH THE YELLOW SWEATSHIRT. SHE'S A PSIOT.
I...DON'T SEE WHY THAT WOULD BE A PROBLEM.
YOU WILL HAVE TO WAIT UNTIL HER OTHER RESPONSIBILITIES ARE COMPLETED FOR THE DAY.
WILL AND INOLA SHALL ESCORT YOU TO A PRIVATE ROOM--ONE WITHOUT A LOCK.
I'D FEEL BETTER TAKING HER MYSELF.

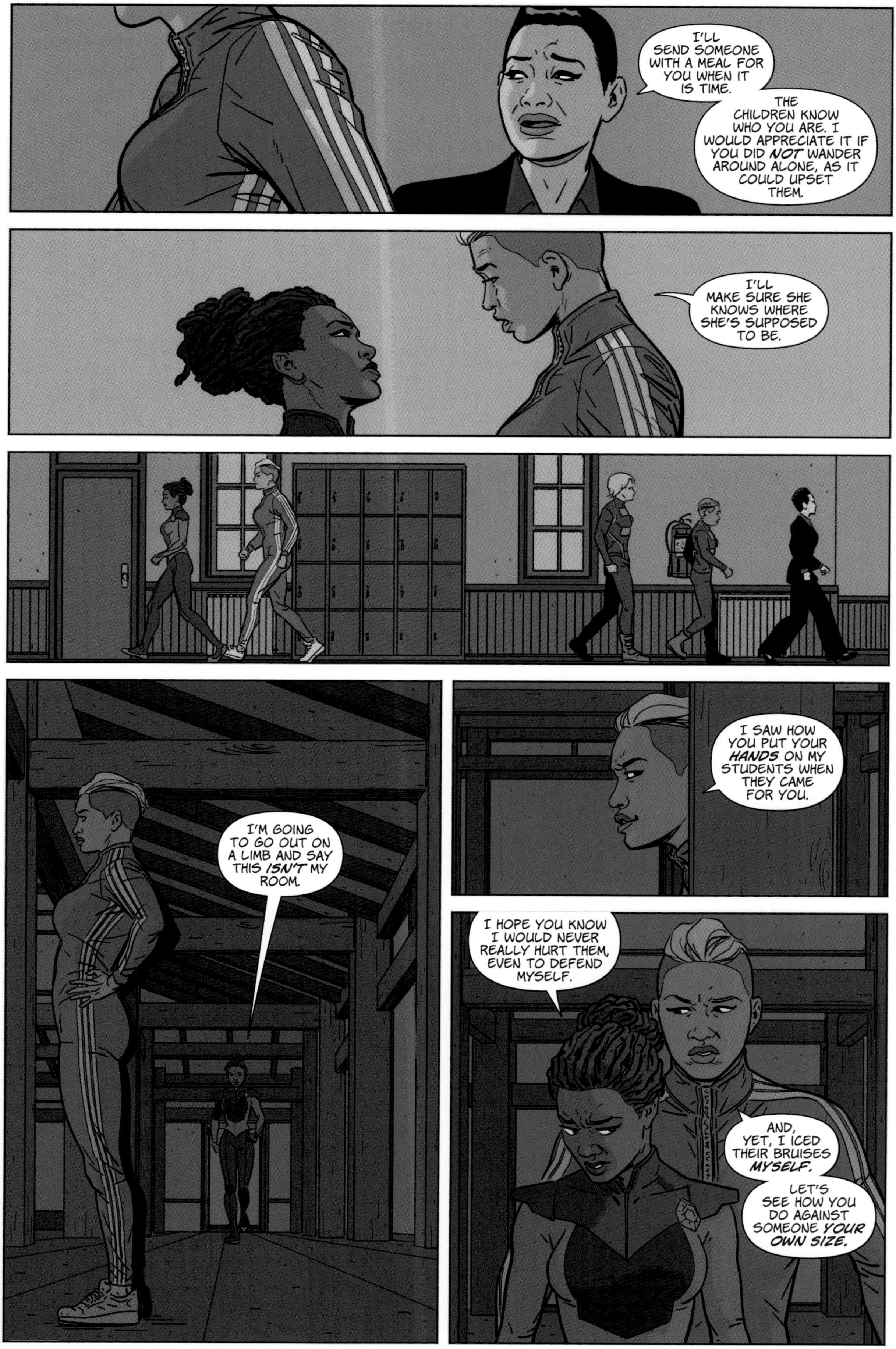
I'LL SEND SOMEONE WITH A MEAL FOR YOU WHEN IT IS TIME.
THE CHILDREN KNOW WHO YOU ARE. I WOULD APPRECIATE IT IF YOU DID *NOT* WANDER AROUND ALONE, AS IT COULD UPSET THEM.
I'LL MAKE SURE SHE KNOWS WHERE SHE'S SUPPOSED TO BE.
I'M GOING TO GO OUT ON A LIMB AND SAY THIS *ISN'T* MY ROOM.
I SAW HOW YOU PUT YOUR ***HANDS*** ON MY STUDENTS WHEN THEY CAME FOR YOU.
I HOPE YOU KNOW I WOULD NEVER REALLY HURT THEM, EVEN TO DEFEND MYSELF.
AND, YET, I ICED THEIR BRUISES ***MYSELF.***
LET'S SEE HOW YOU DO AGAINST SOMEONE ***YOUR OWN SIZE.***

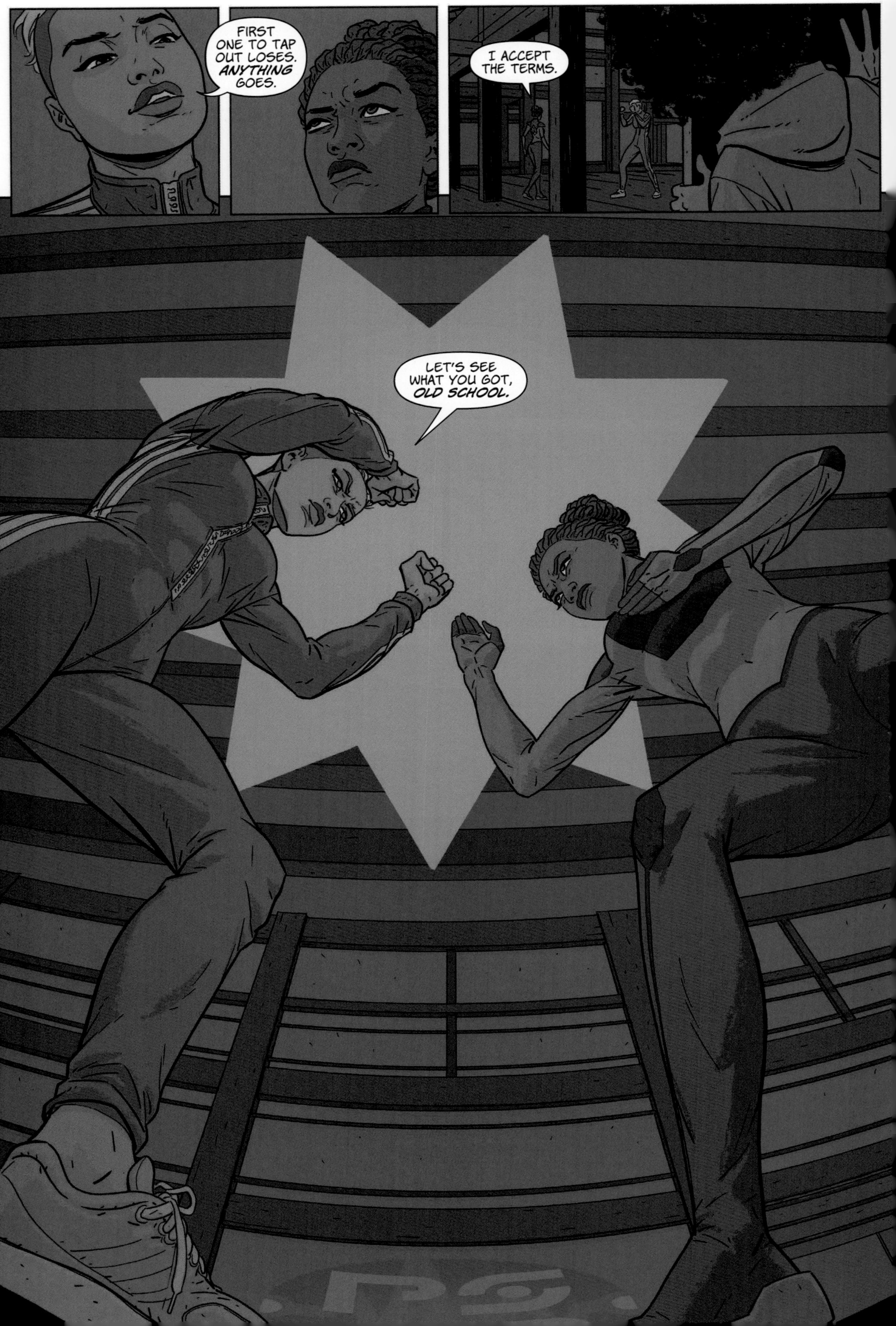
FIRST ONE TO TAP OUT LOSES. ANYTHING GOES.
I ACCEPT THE TERMS.
LET'S SEE WHAT YOU GOT, OLD SCHOOL.

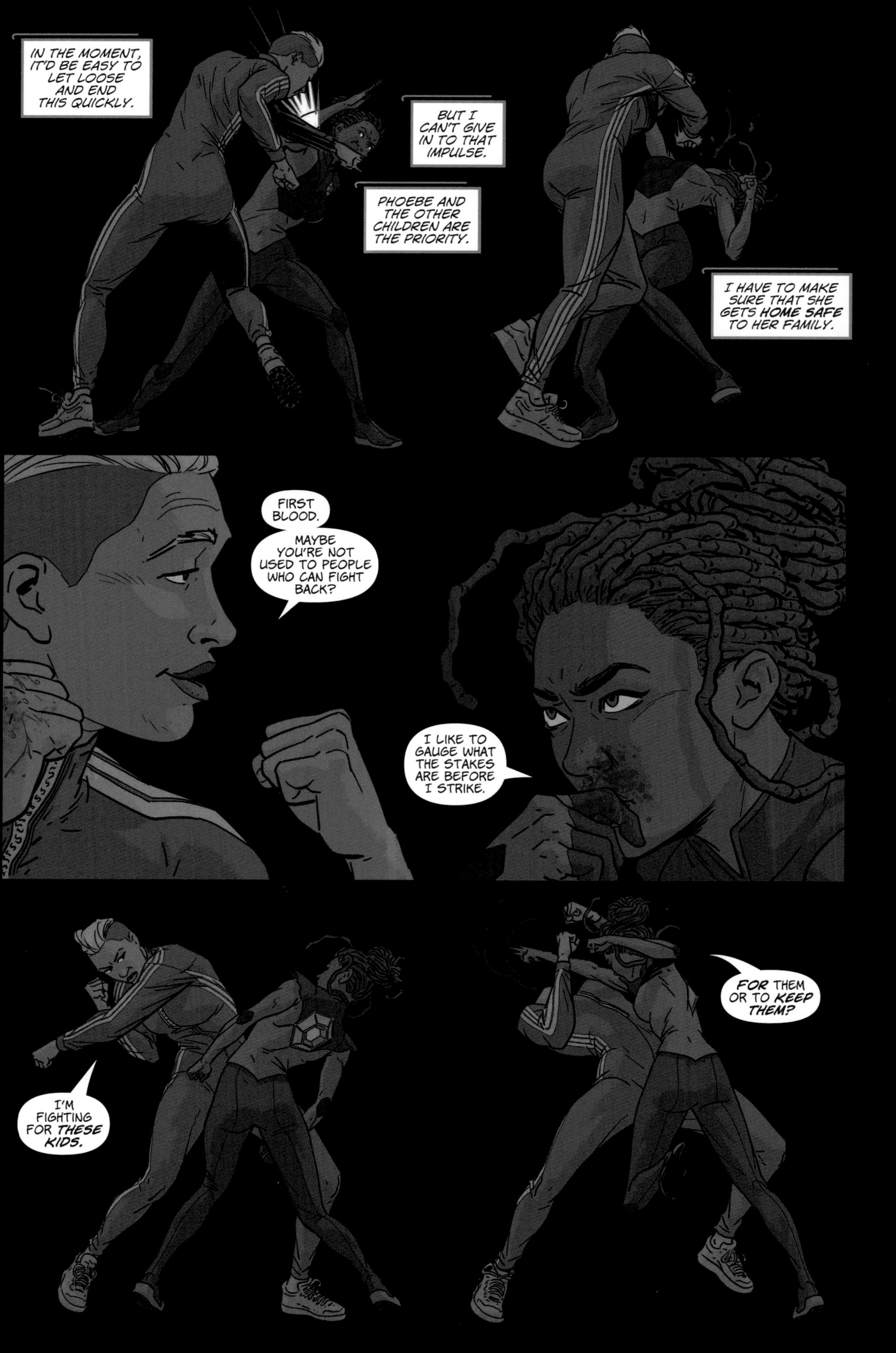
IN THE MOMENT, IT'D BE EASY TO LET LOOSE AND END THIS QUICKLY.
BUT I CAN'T GIVE IN TO THAT IMPULSE.
PHOEBE AND THE OTHER CHILDREN ARE THE PRIORITY.
I HAVE TO MAKE SURE THAT SHE GETS **HOME SAFE** TO HER FAMILY.
FIRST BLOOD.
MAYBE YOU'RE NOT USED TO PEOPLE WHO CAN FIGHT BACK?
I LIKE TO GAUGE WHAT THE STAKES ARE BEFORE I STRIKE.
I'M FIGHTING FOR ***THESE KIDS.***
FOR THEM OR TO ***KEEP THEM?***

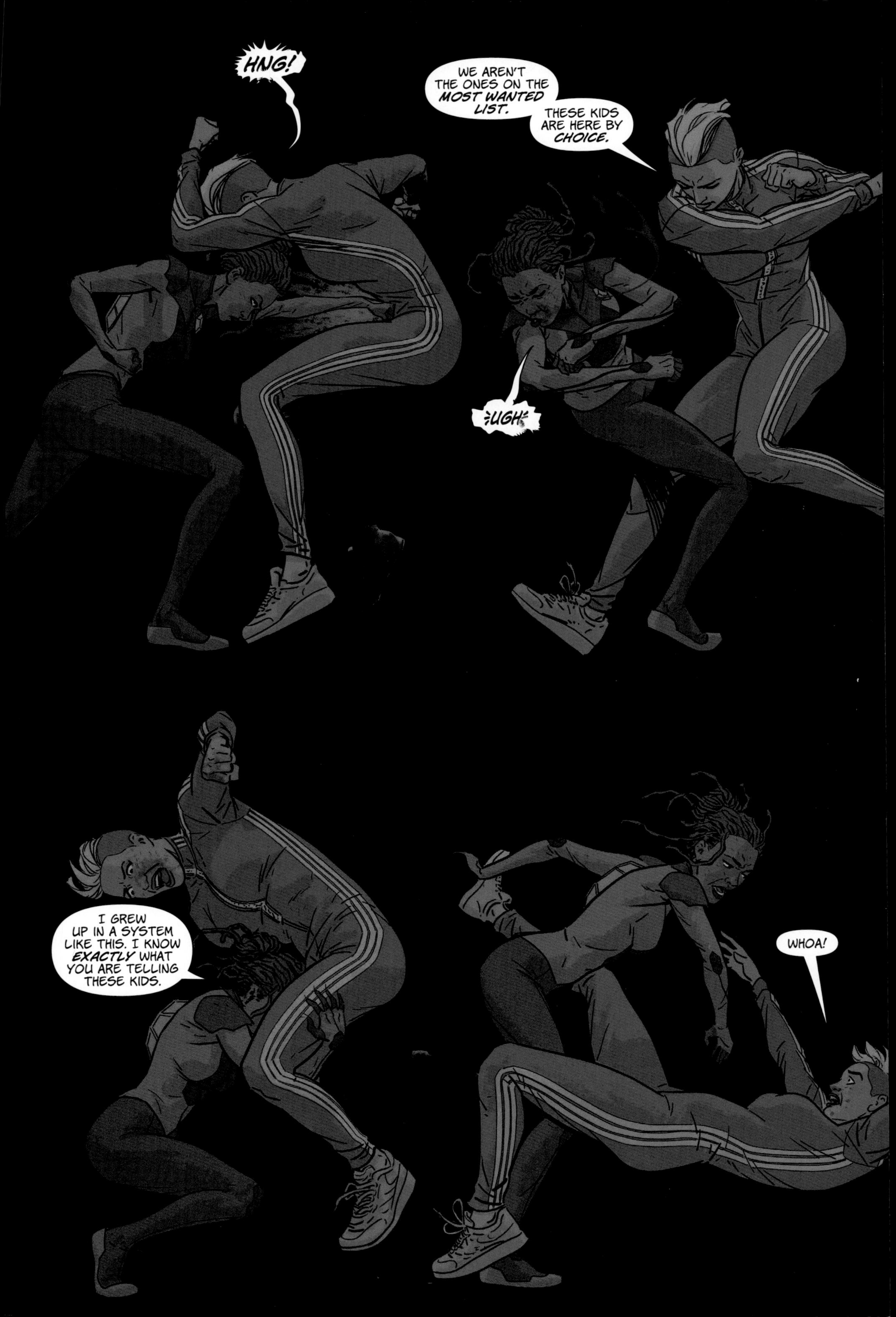

HNG!
WE AREN'T THE ONES ON THE MOST WANTED LIST.
THESE KIDS ARE HERE BY CHOICE.
UGH
I GREW UP IN A SYSTEM LIKE THIS. I KNOW EXACTLY WHAT YOU ARE TELLING THESE KIDS.
WHOA!

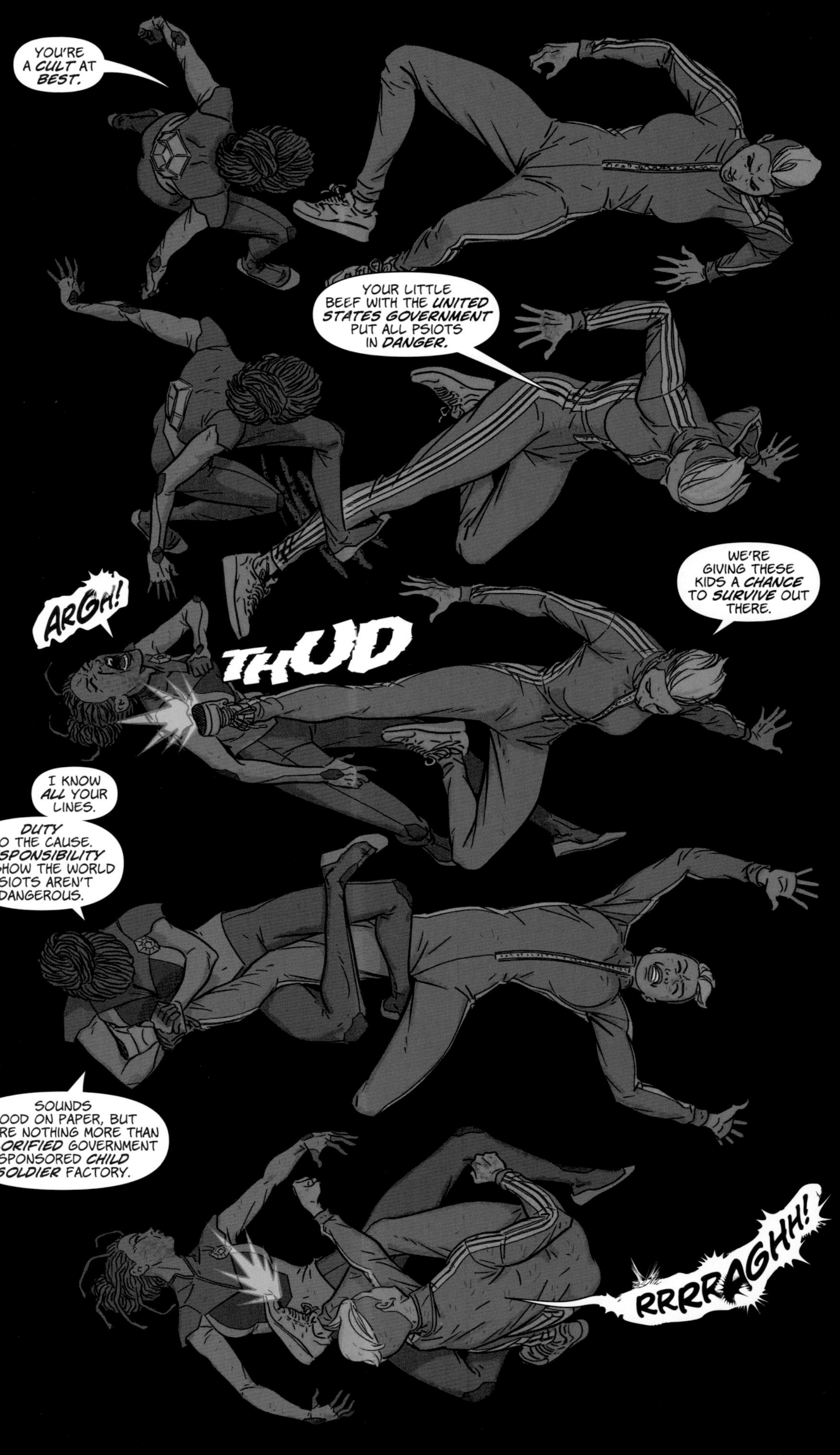
YOU'RE A CULT AT BEST.
YOUR LITTLE BEEF WITH THE UNITED STATES GOVERNMENT PUT ALL PSIOTS IN DANGER.
ARGH!
THUD
WE'RE GIVING THESE KIDS A CHANCE TO SURVIVE OUT THERE.
I KNOW ALL YOUR LINES.
DUTY TO THE CAUSE. RESPONSIBILITY TO SHOW THE WORLD PSIOTS AREN'T DANGEROUS.
SOUNDS GOOD ON PAPER, BUT YOU'RE NOTHING MORE THAN A GLORIFIED GOVERNMENT SPONSORED CHILD SOLDIER FACTORY.
RRRRAGHH!

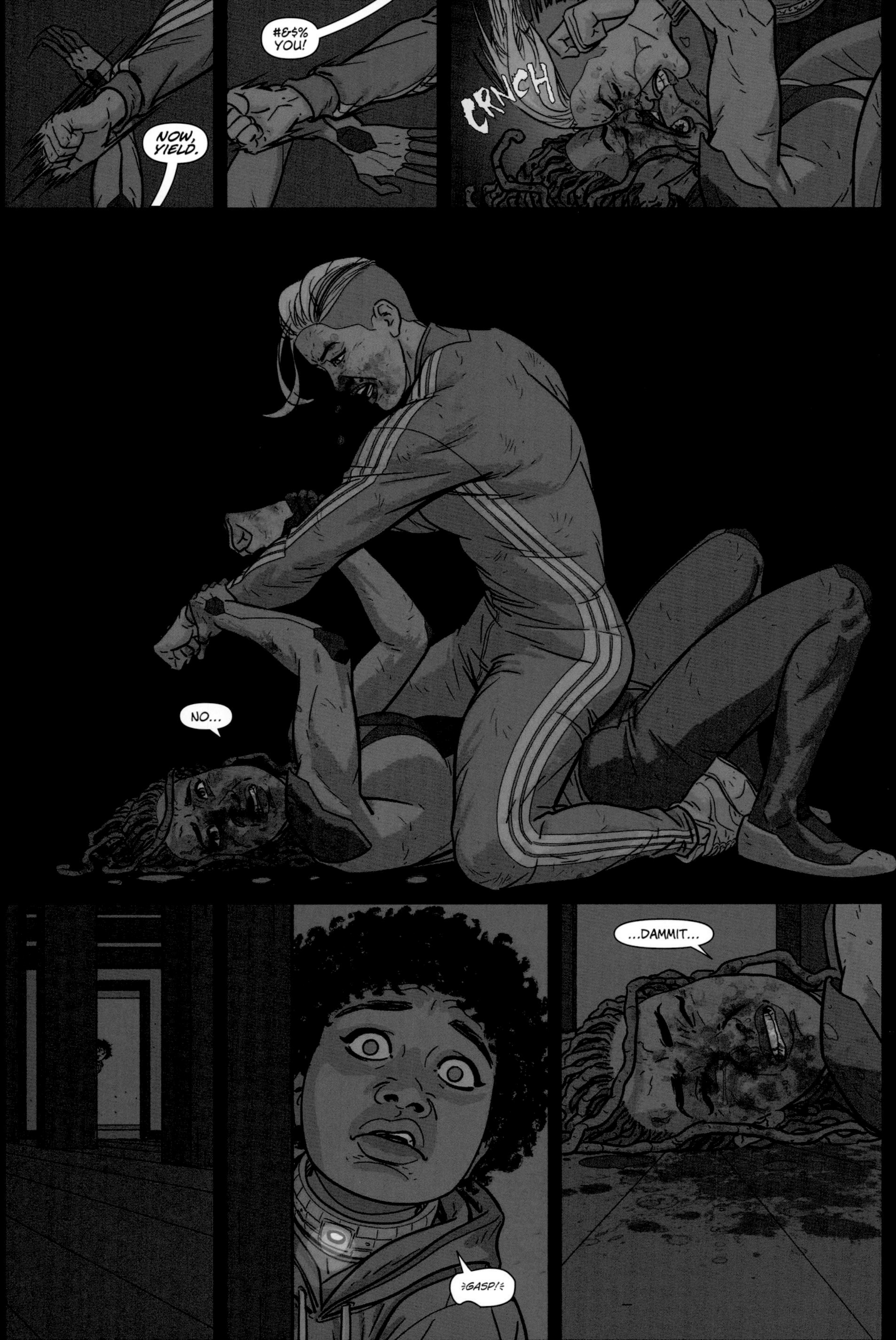
NOW, YIELD.
#&$% YOU!
CRNCH
NO...
...DAMMIT...
GASP!

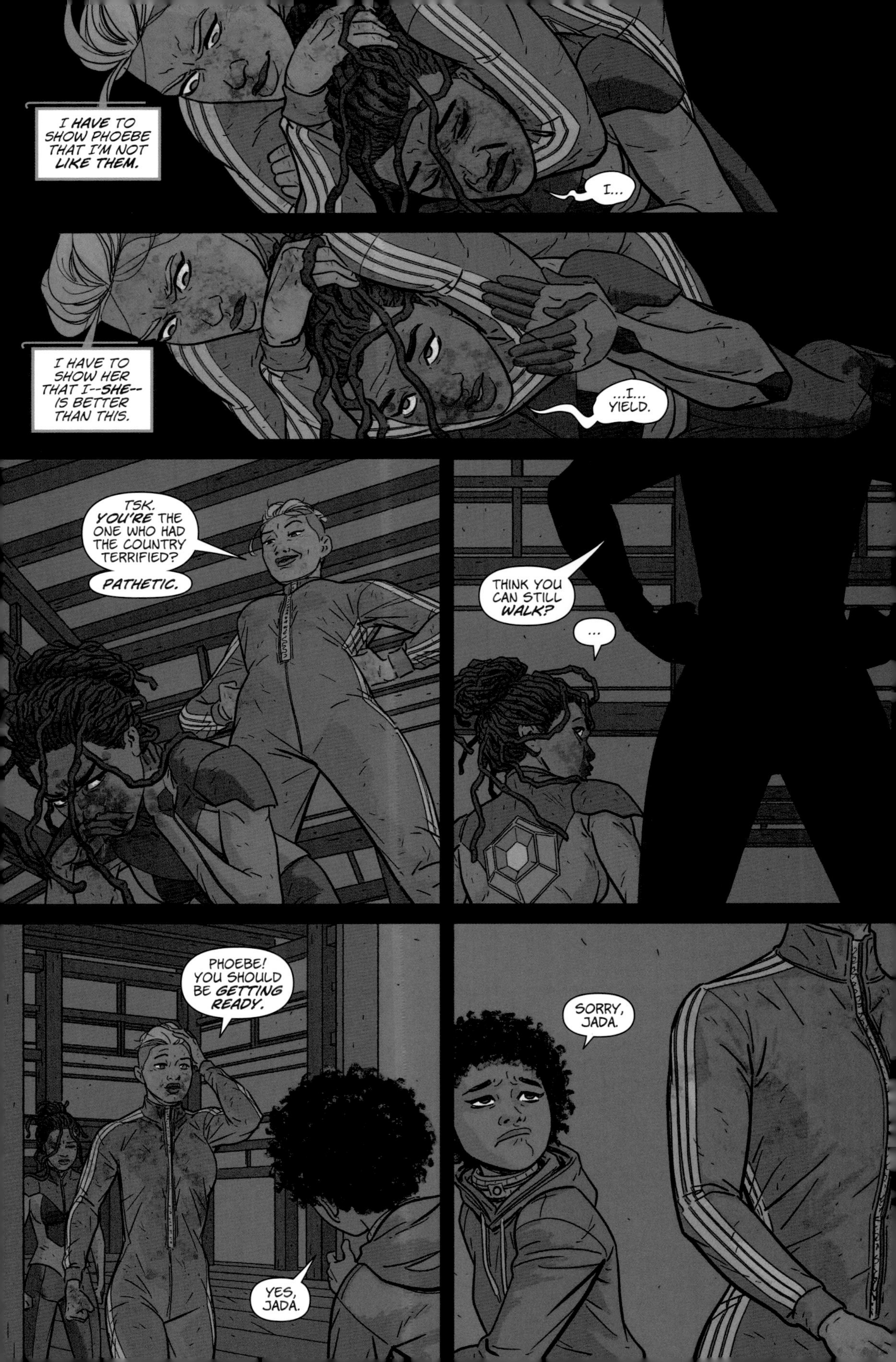
I HAVE TO SHOW PHOEBE THAT I'M NOT LIKE THEM.
I...
I HAVE TO SHOW HER THAT I--SHE--IS BETTER THAN THIS.
...I... YIELD.
TSK. YOU'RE THE ONE WHO HAD THE COUNTRY TERRIFIED?
PATHETIC.
THINK YOU CAN STILL WALK?
...
PHOEBE! YOU SHOULD BE GETTING READY.
YES, JADA.
SORRY, JADA.

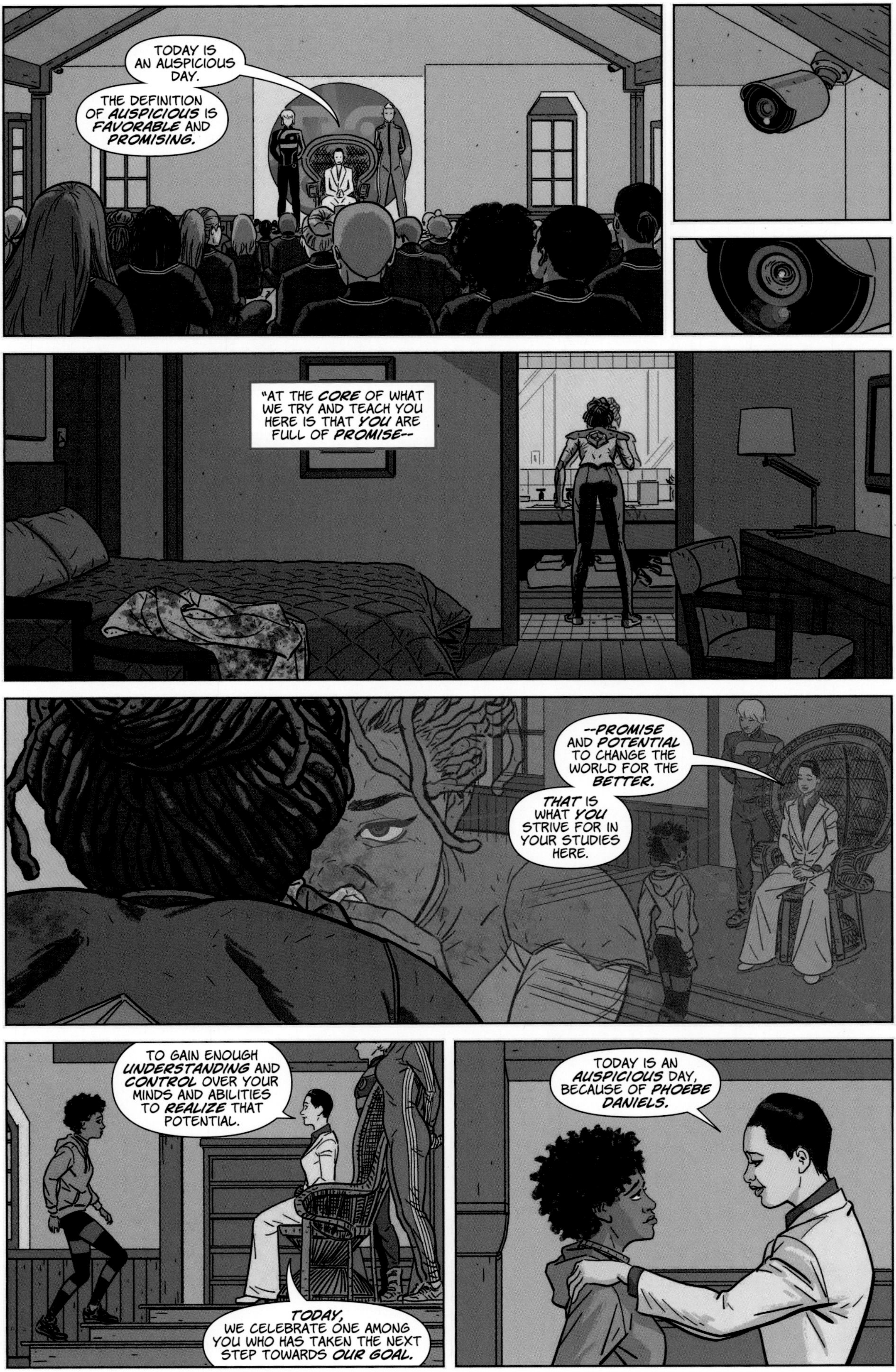
TODAY IS AN AUSPICIOUS DAY.
THE DEFINITION OF AUSPICIOUS IS FAVORABLE AND PROMISING.
"AT THE CORE OF WHAT WE TRY AND TEACH YOU HERE IS THAT YOU ARE FULL OF PROMISE--
--PROMISE AND POTENTIAL TO CHANGE THE WORLD FOR THE BETTER.
THAT IS WHAT YOU STRIVE FOR IN YOUR STUDIES HERE.
TO GAIN ENOUGH UNDERSTANDING AND CONTROL OVER YOUR MINDS AND ABILITIES TO REALIZE THAT POTENTIAL.
TODAY, WE CELEBRATE ONE AMONG YOU WHO HAS TAKEN THE NEXT STEP TOWARDS OUR GOAL.
TODAY IS AN AUSPICIOUS DAY, BECAUSE OF PHOEBE DANIELS.

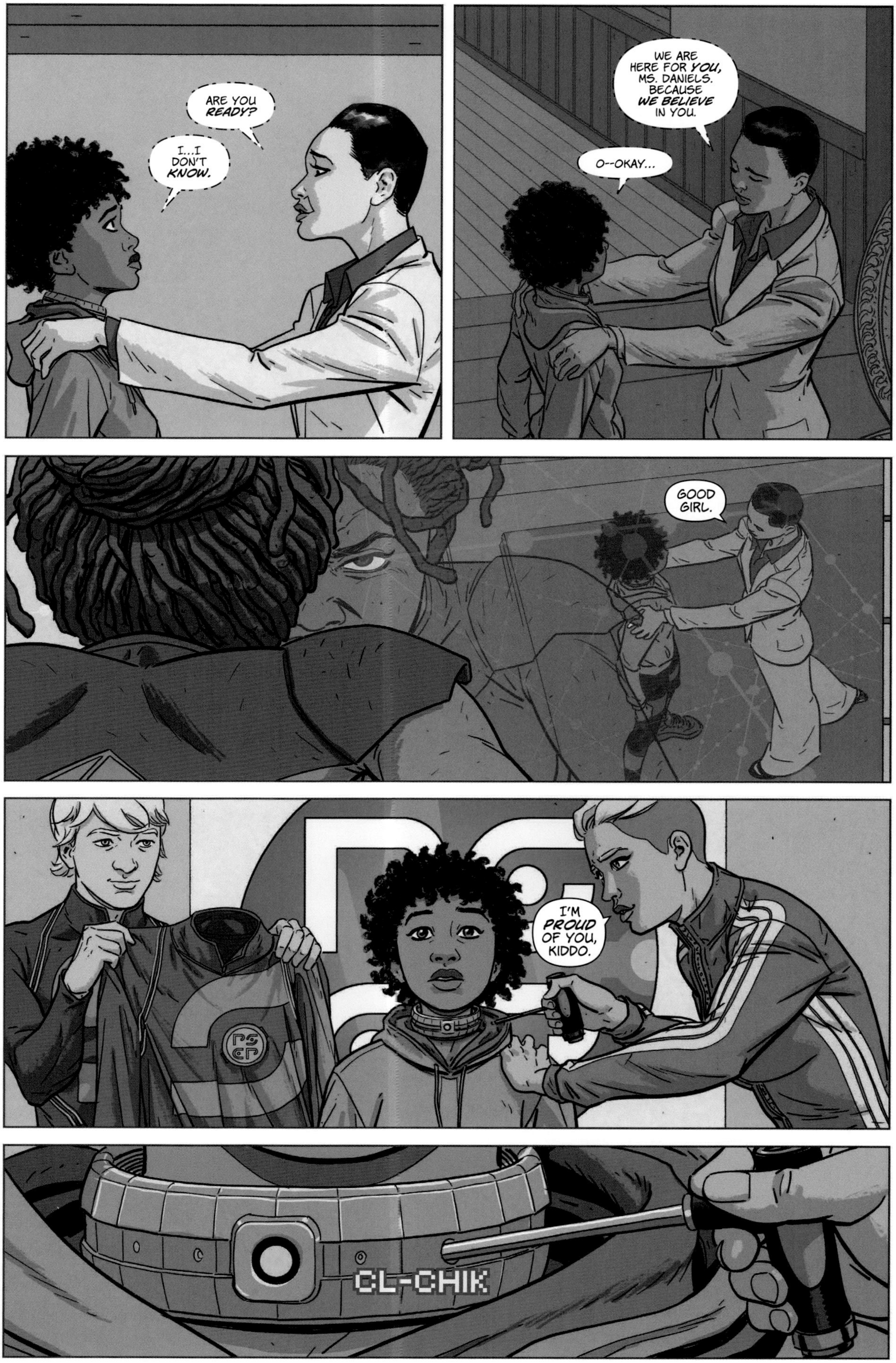
ARE YOU READY?
I...I DON'T KNOW.
WE ARE HERE FOR YOU, MS. DANIELS. BECAUSE WE BELIEVE IN YOU.
O--OKAY...
GOOD GIRL.
I'M PROUD OF YOU, KIDDO.
CL-CHIK

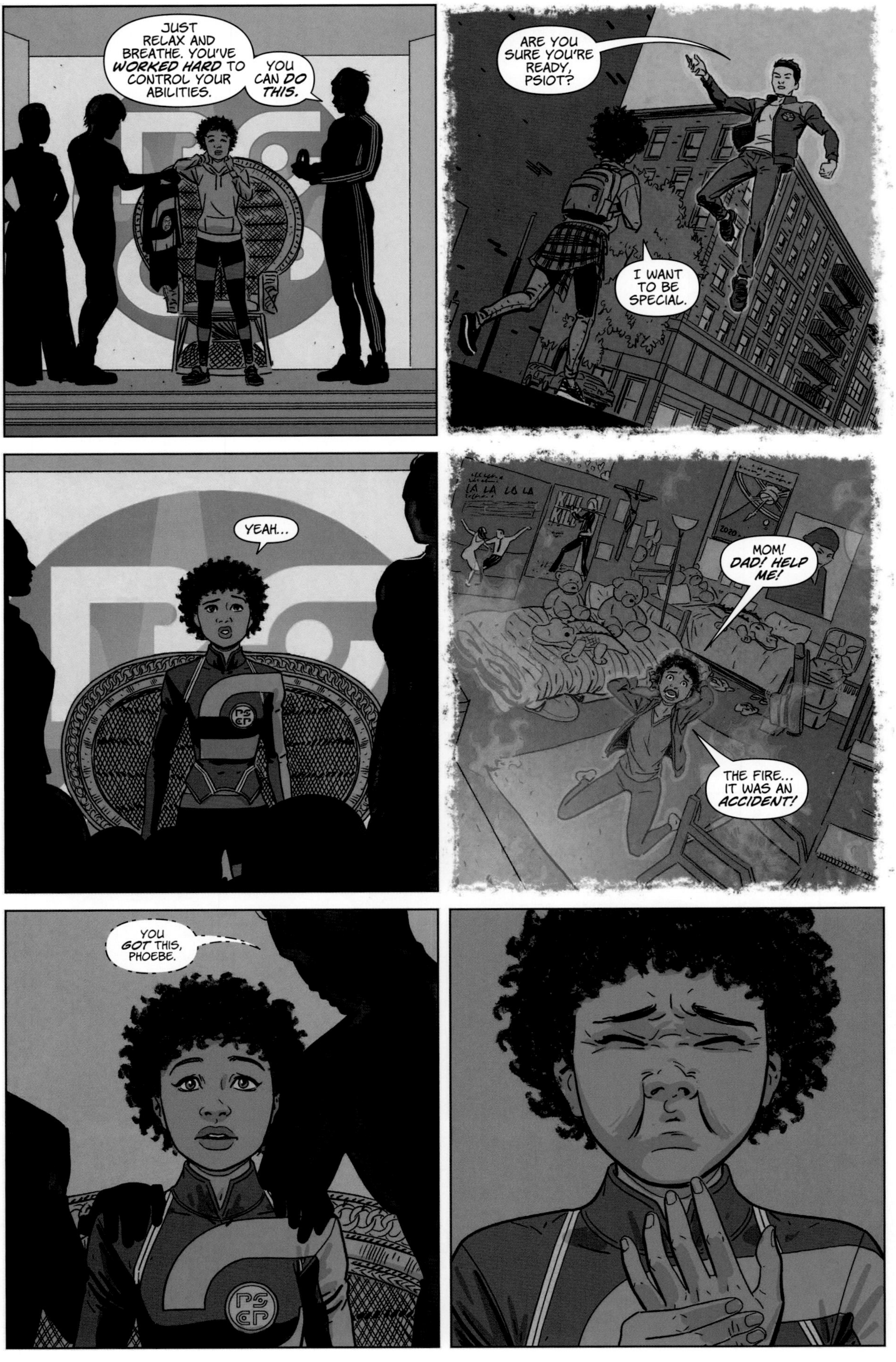
JUST RELAX AND BREATHE. YOU'VE **WORKED HARD** TO CONTROL YOUR ABILITIES.
YOU CAN **DO THIS.**
ARE YOU SURE YOU'RE READY, PSIOT?
I WANT TO BE SPECIAL.
YEAH...
LA LA LO LA
2020
MOM! **DAD! HELP ME!**
THE FIRE... IT WAS AN **ACCIDENT!**
YOU **GOT** THIS, PHOEBE.

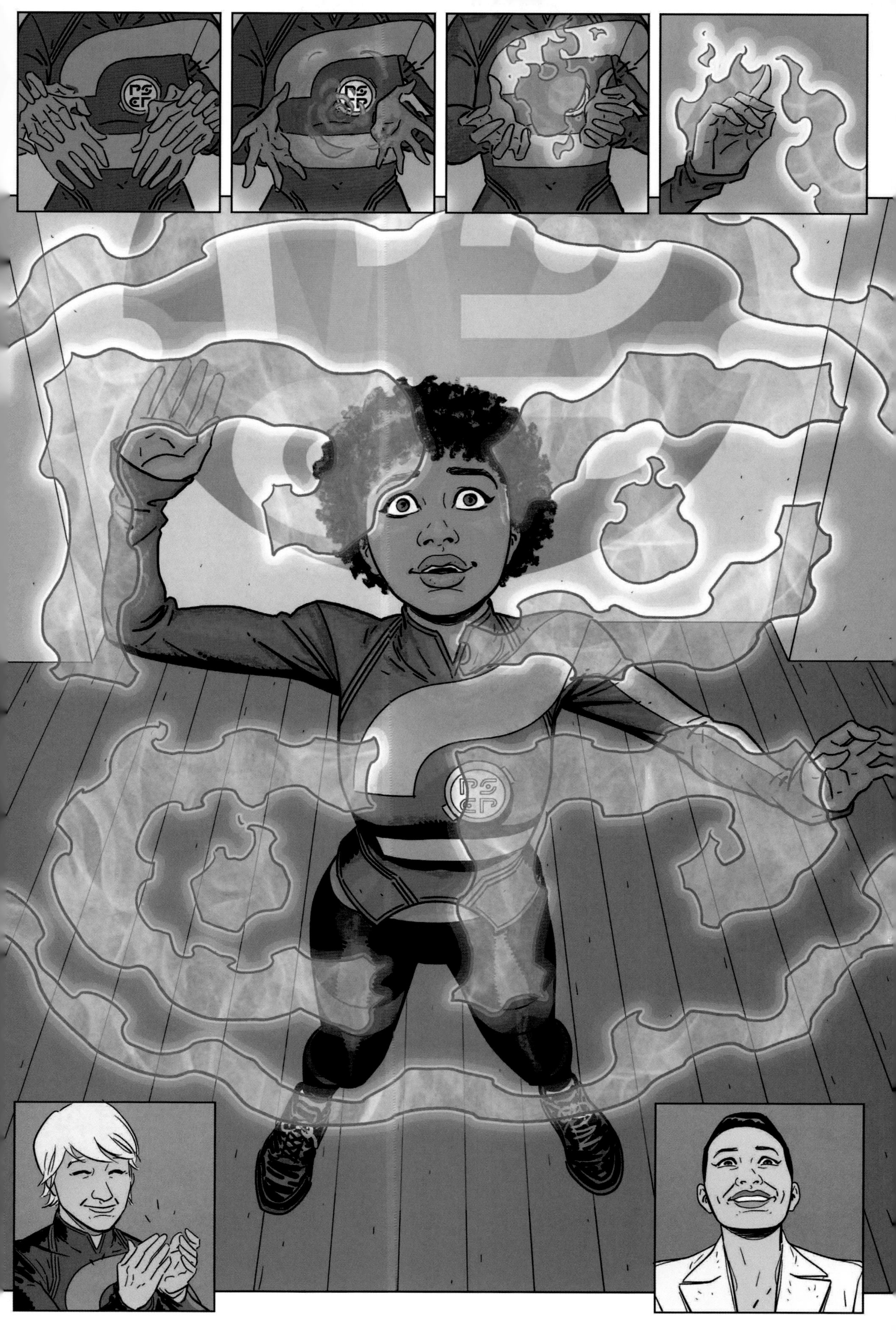

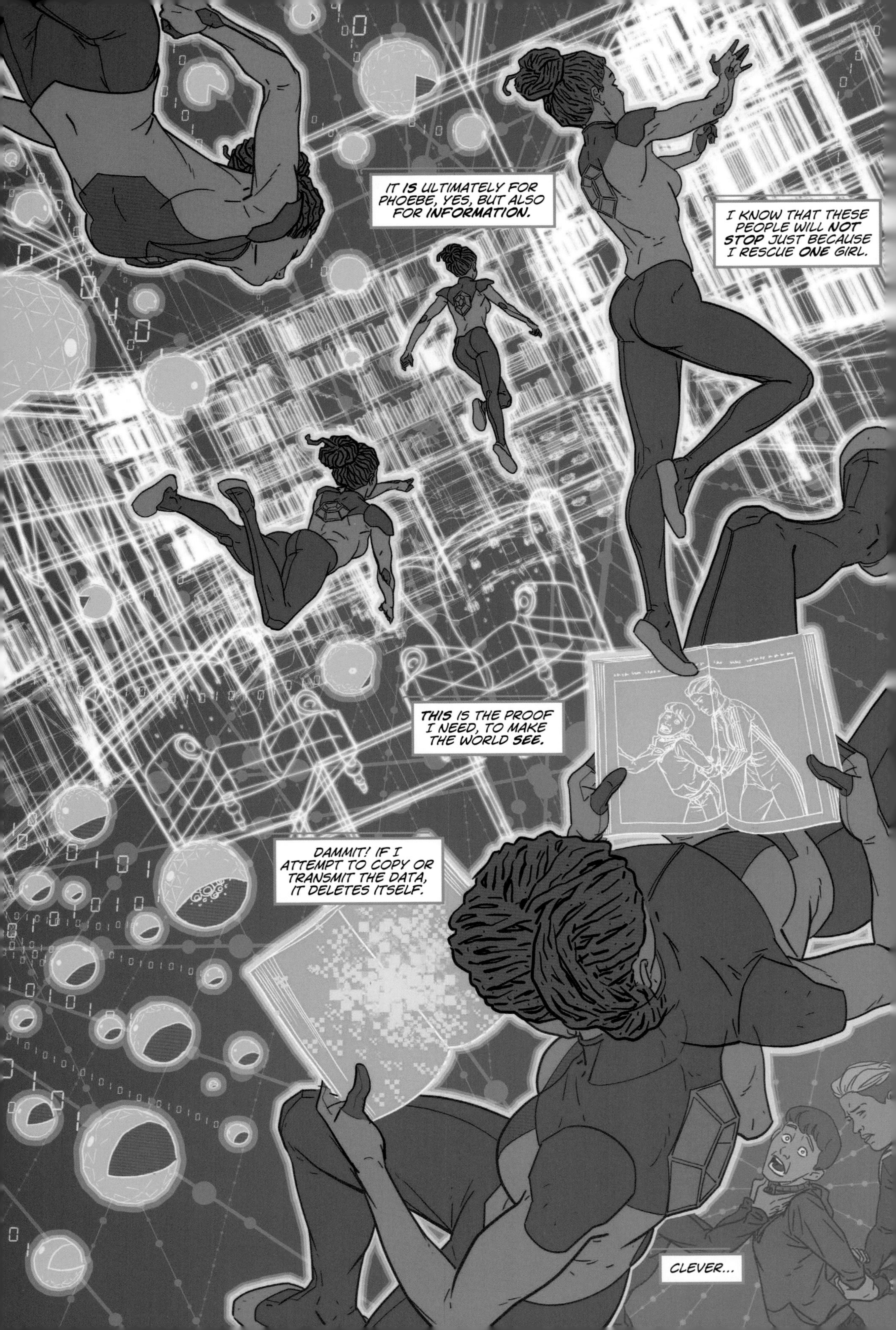
IT IS ULTIMATELY FOR PHOEBE, YES, BUT ALSO FOR INFORMATION.
I KNOW THAT THESE PEOPLE WILL NOT STOP JUST BECAUSE I RESCUE ONE GIRL.
THIS IS THE PROOF I NEED, TO MAKE THE WORLD SEE.
DAMMIT! IF I ATTEMPT TO COPY OR TRANSMIT THE DATA, IT DELETES ITSELF.
CLEVER...

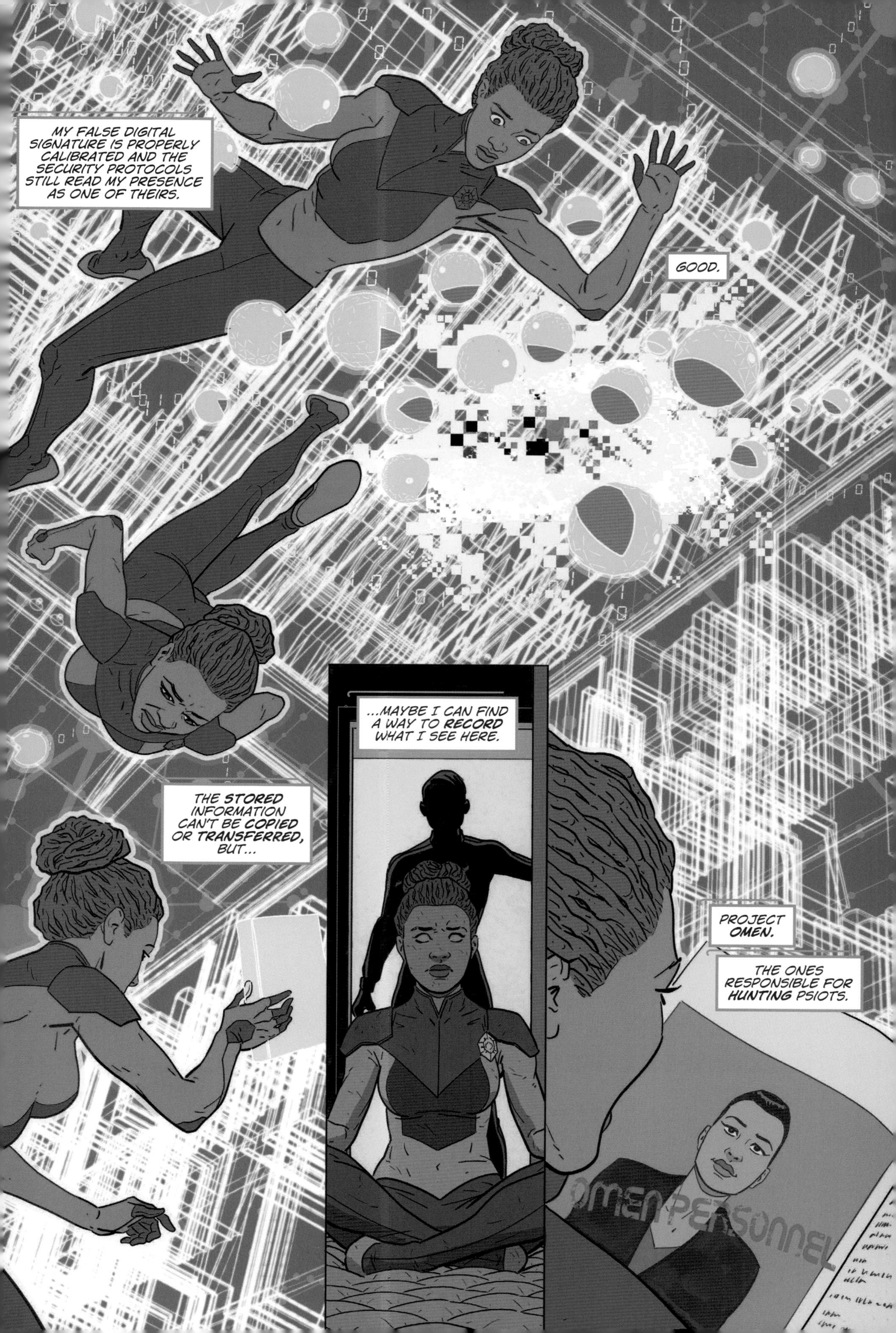
MY FALSE DIGITAL SIGNATURE IS PROPERLY CALIBRATED AND THE SECURITY PROTOCOLS STILL READ MY PRESENCE AS ONE OF THEIRS.
GOOD.
THE STORED INFORMATION CAN'T BE COPIED OR TRANSFERRED, BUT...
...MAYBE I CAN FIND A WAY TO RECORD WHAT I SEE HERE.
PROJECT OMEN.
THE ONES RESPONSIBLE FOR HUNTING PSIOTS.
OMEN PERSONNEL

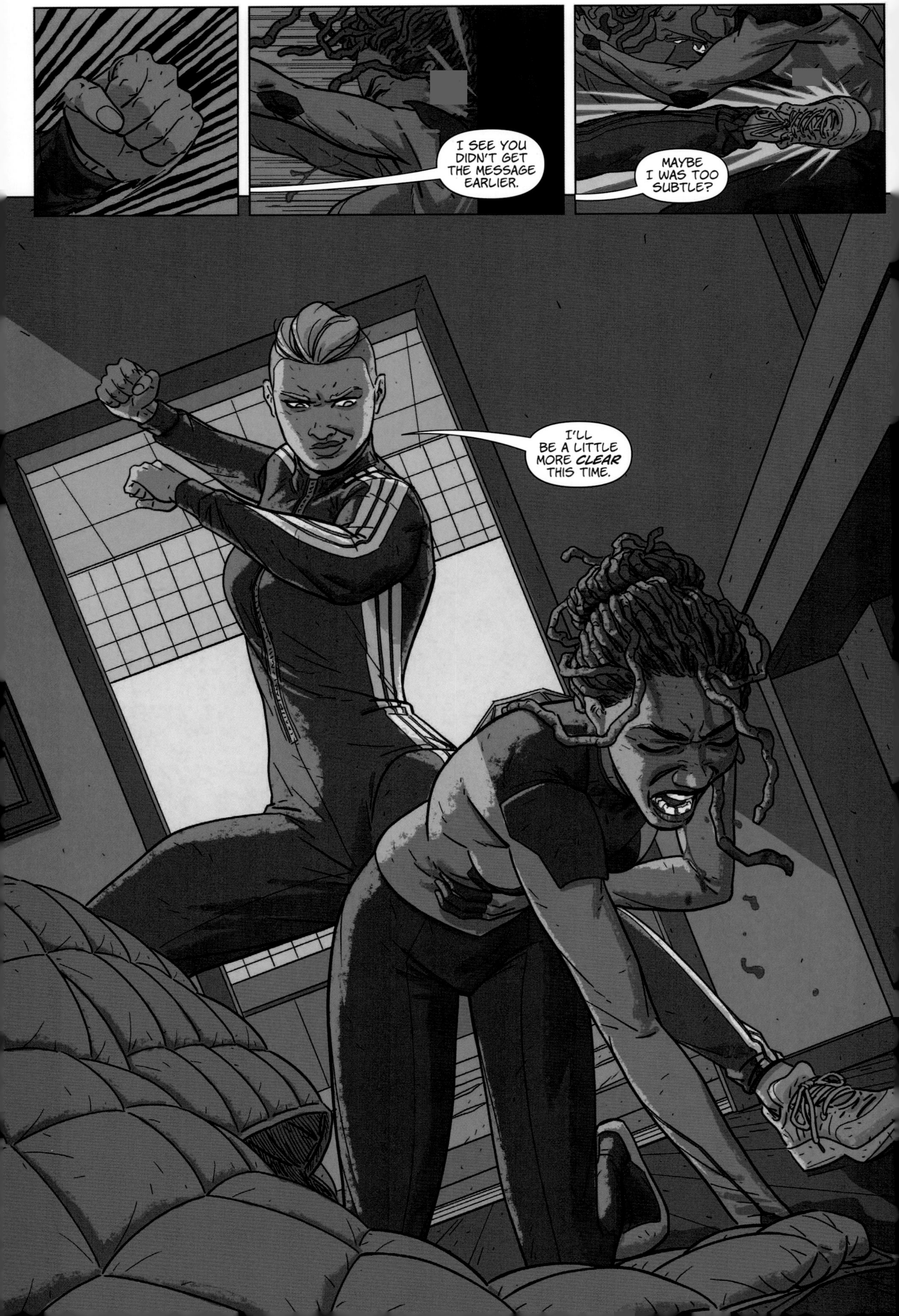
I SEE YOU DIDN'T GET THE MESSAGE EARLIER.
MAYBE I WAS TOO SUBTLE?
I'LL BE A LITTLE MORE *CLEAR* THIS TIME.

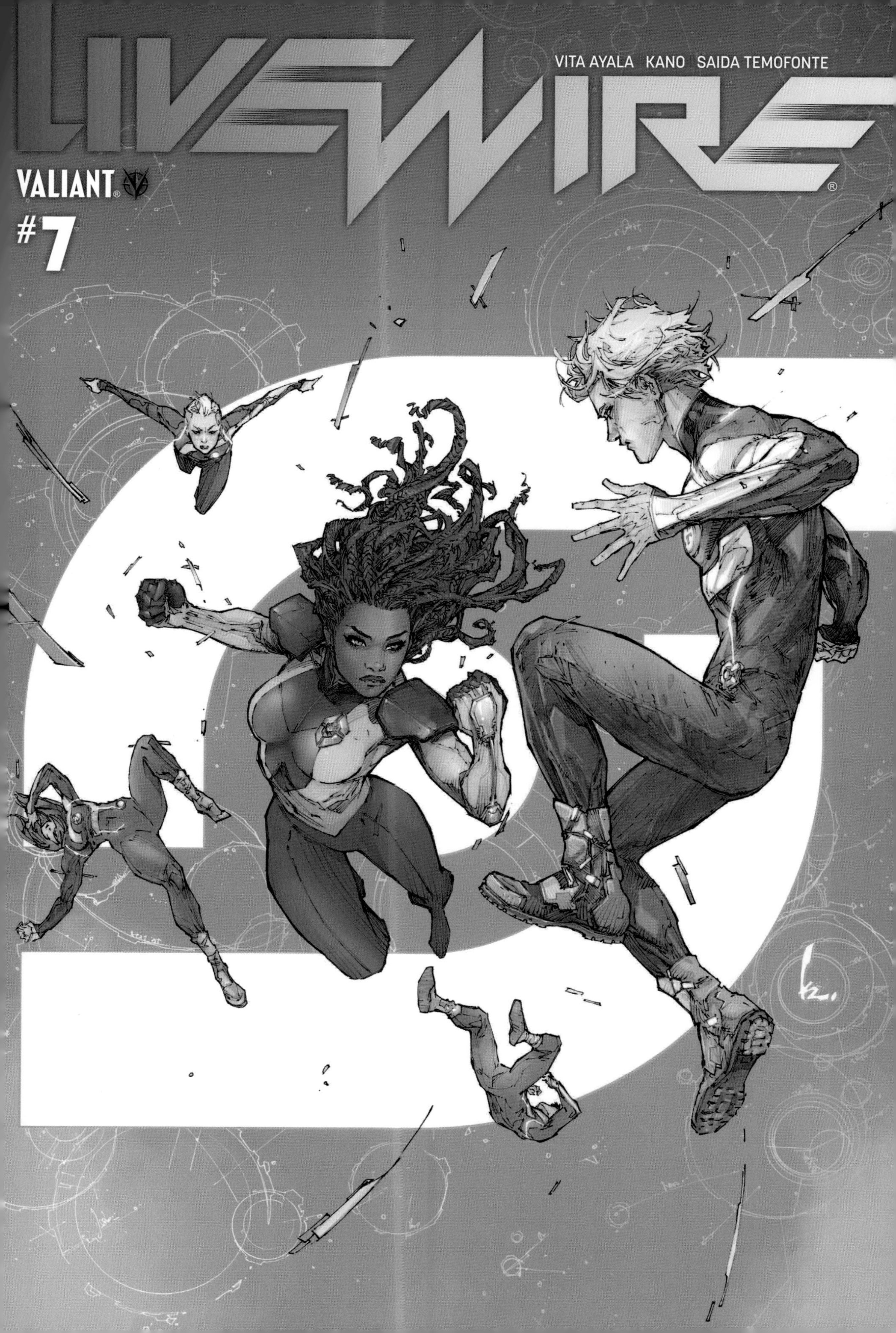
LIVEWIRE
VITA AYALA KANO SAIDA TEMOFONTE
VALIANT
#7

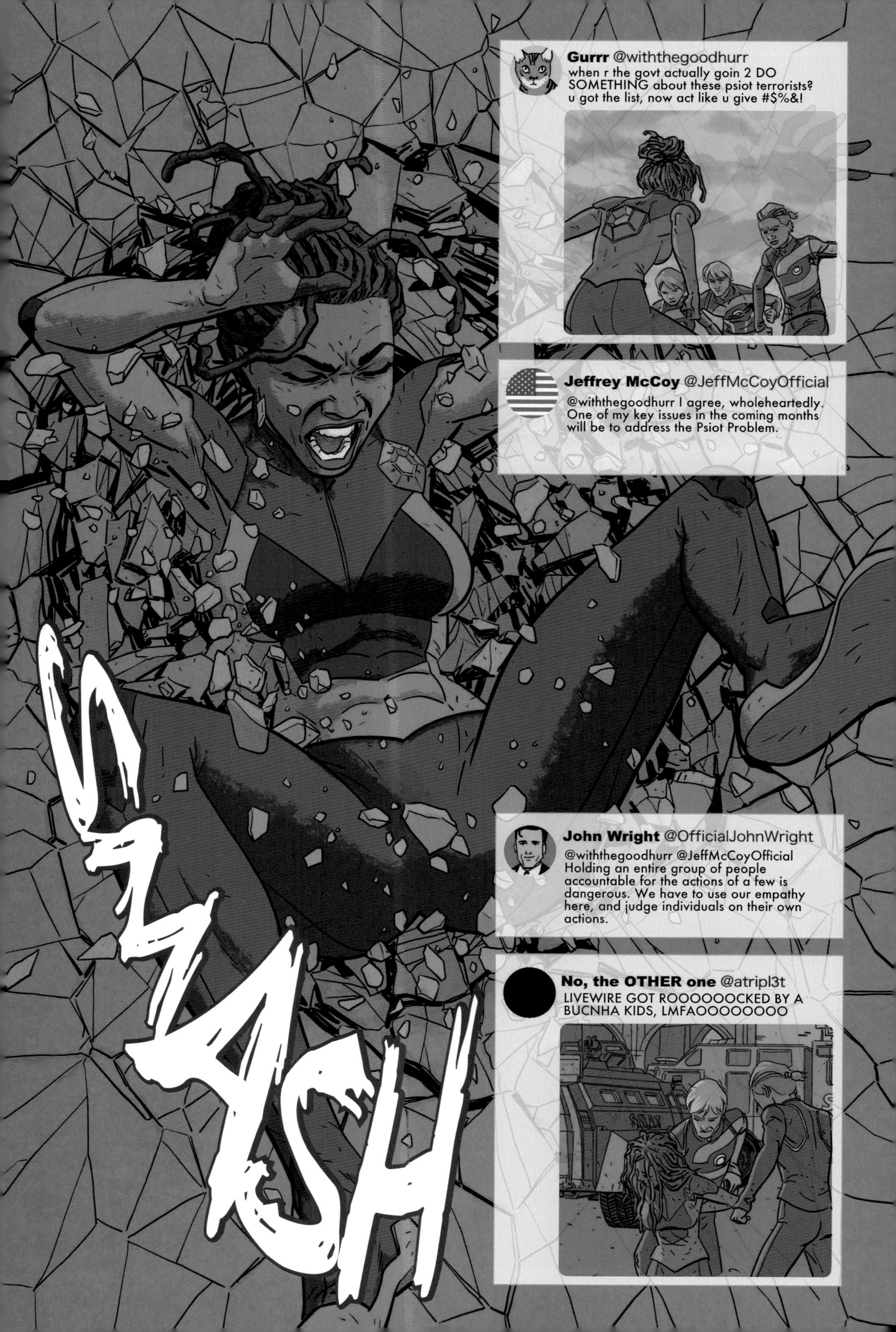
Gurrr @withthegoodhurr
when r the govt actually goin 2 DO SOMETHING about these psiot terrorists? u got the list, now act like u give #$%&!
Jeffrey McCoy @JeffMcCoyOfficial
@withthegoodhurr I agree, wholeheartedly. One of my key issues in the coming months will be to address the Psiot Problem.
SMASH
John Wright @OfficialJohnWright
@withthegoodhurr @JeffMcCoyOfficial Holding an entire group of people accountable for the actions of a few is dangerous. We have to use our empathy here, and judge individuals on their own actions.
No, the OTHER one @atripl3t
LIVEWIRE GOT ROOOOOOCKED BY A BUCNHA KIDS, LMFAOOOOOOOO

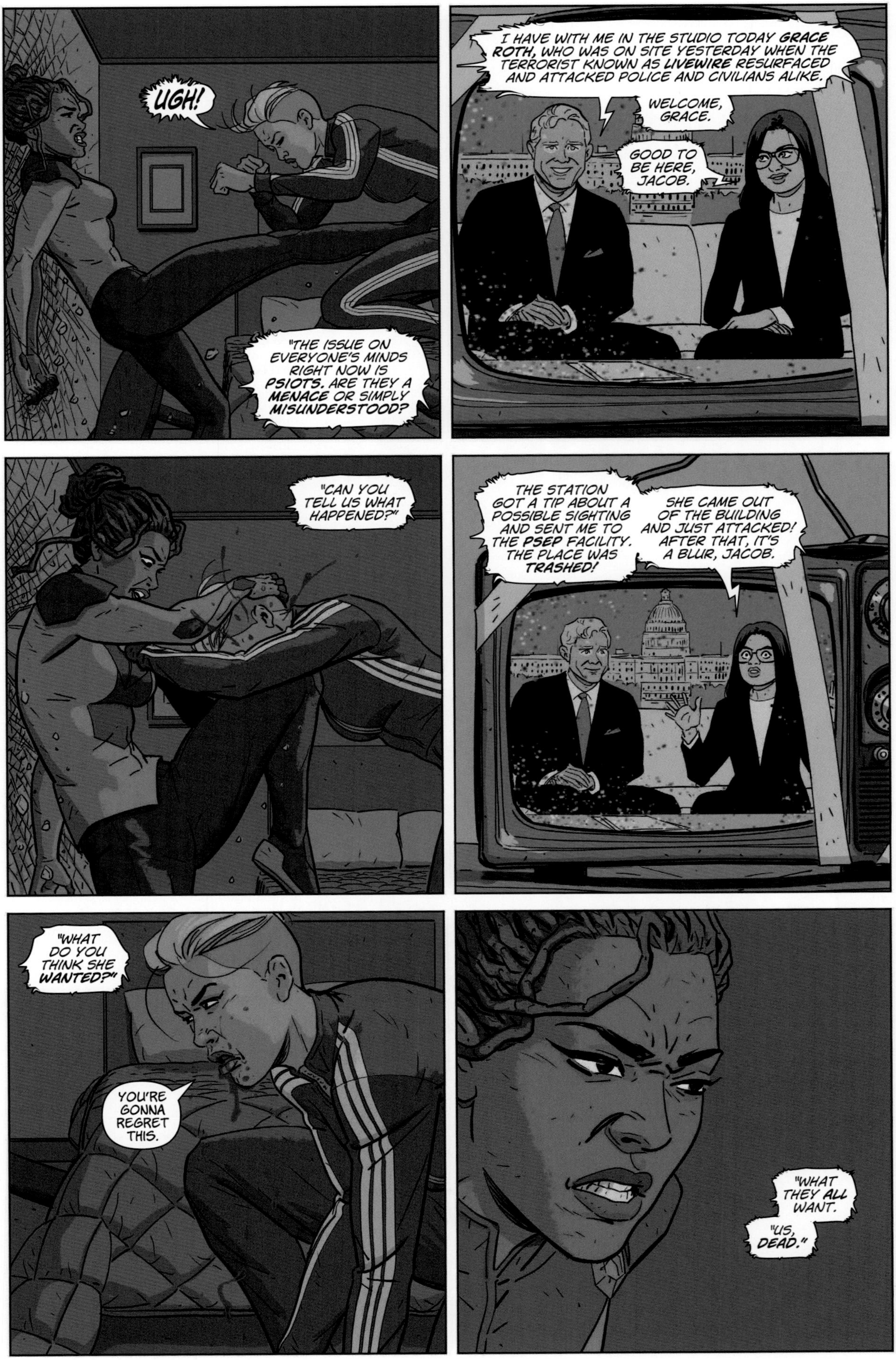
UGH!
"THE ISSUE ON EVERYONE'S MINDS RIGHT NOW IS PSIOTS. ARE THEY A MENACE OR SIMPLY MISUNDERSTOOD?
I HAVE WITH ME IN THE STUDIO TODAY GRACE ROTH, WHO WAS ON SITE YESTERDAY WHEN THE TERRORIST KNOWN AS LIVEWIRE RESURFACED AND ATTACKED POLICE AND CIVILIANS ALIKE.
WELCOME, GRACE.
GOOD TO BE HERE, JACOB.
"CAN YOU TELL US WHAT HAPPENED?"
THE STATION GOT A TIP ABOUT A POSSIBLE SIGHTING AND SENT ME TO THE PSEP FACILITY. THE PLACE WAS TRASHED!
SHE CAME OUT OF THE BUILDING AND JUST ATTACKED! AFTER THAT, IT'S A BLUR, JACOB.
"WHAT DO YOU THINK SHE WANTED?"
YOU'RE GONNA REGRET THIS.
"WHAT THEY ALL WANT.
"US, DEAD."

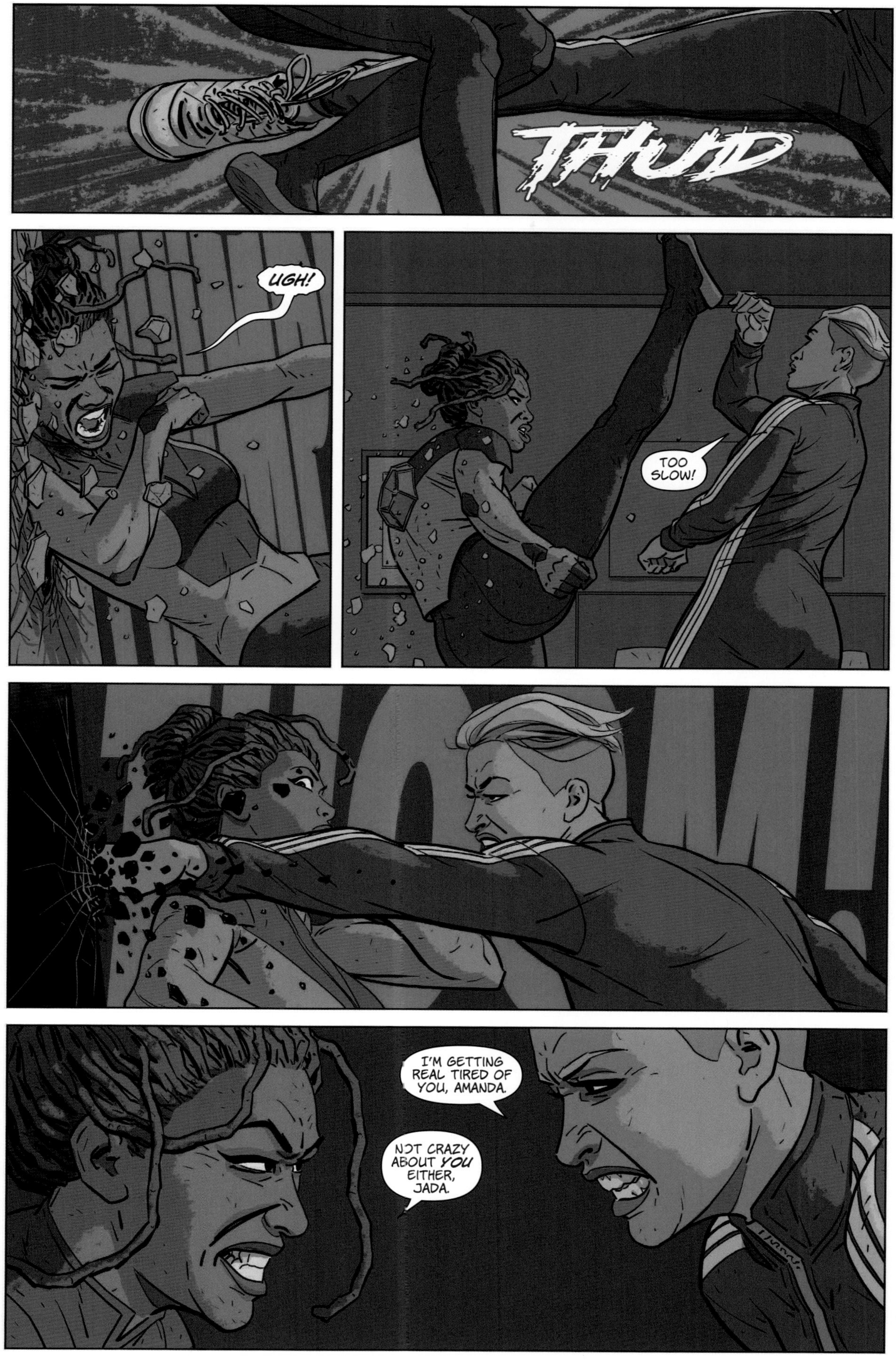
THUD
UGH!
TOO SLOW!
I'M GETTING REAL TIRED OF YOU, AMANDA.
NOT CRAZY ABOUT *YOU* EITHER, JADA.

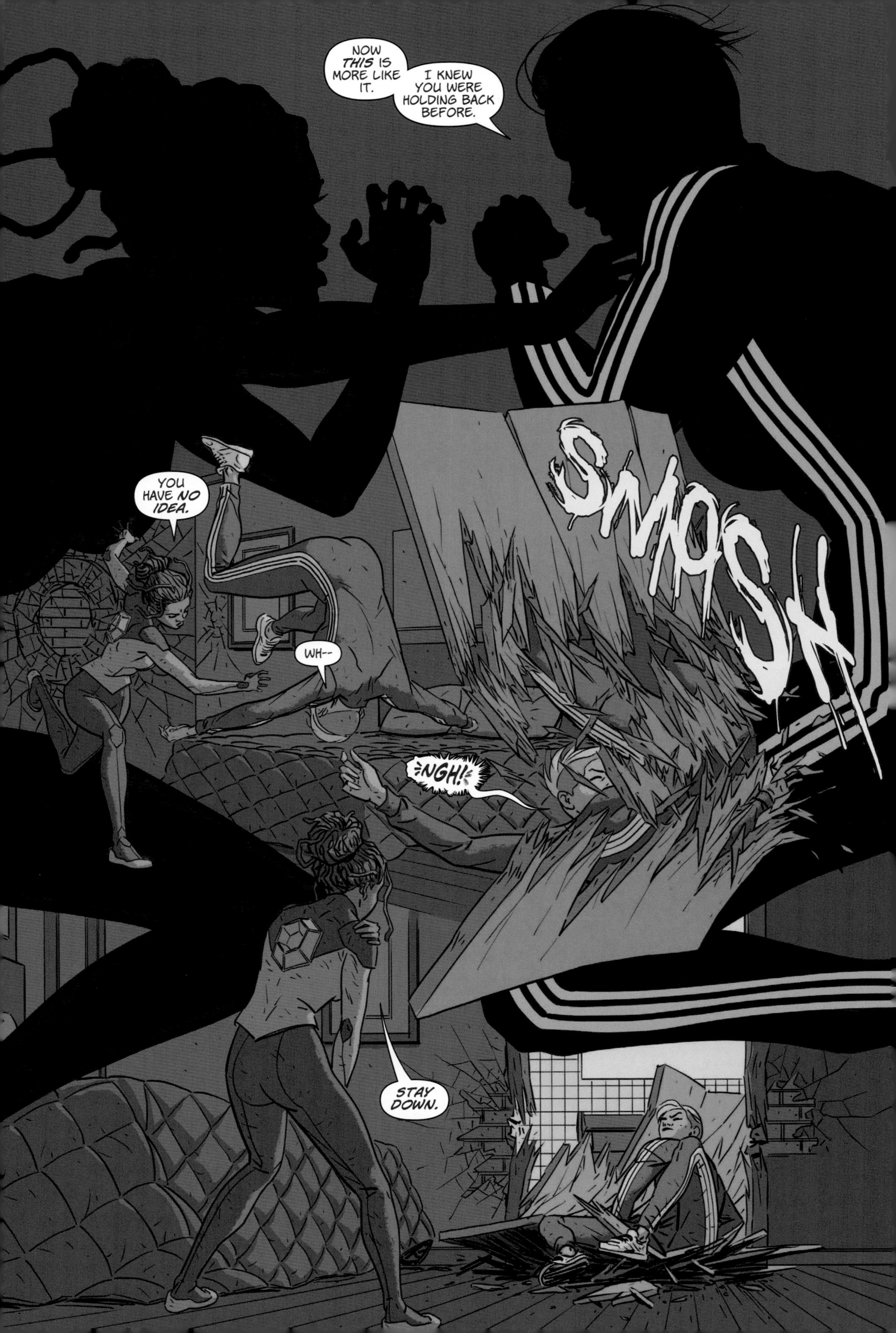
NOW *THIS* IS MORE LIKE IT.
I KNEW YOU WERE HOLDING BACK BEFORE.
YOU HAVE *NO IDEA.*
SMASH
WH--
NGH!
STAY DOWN.

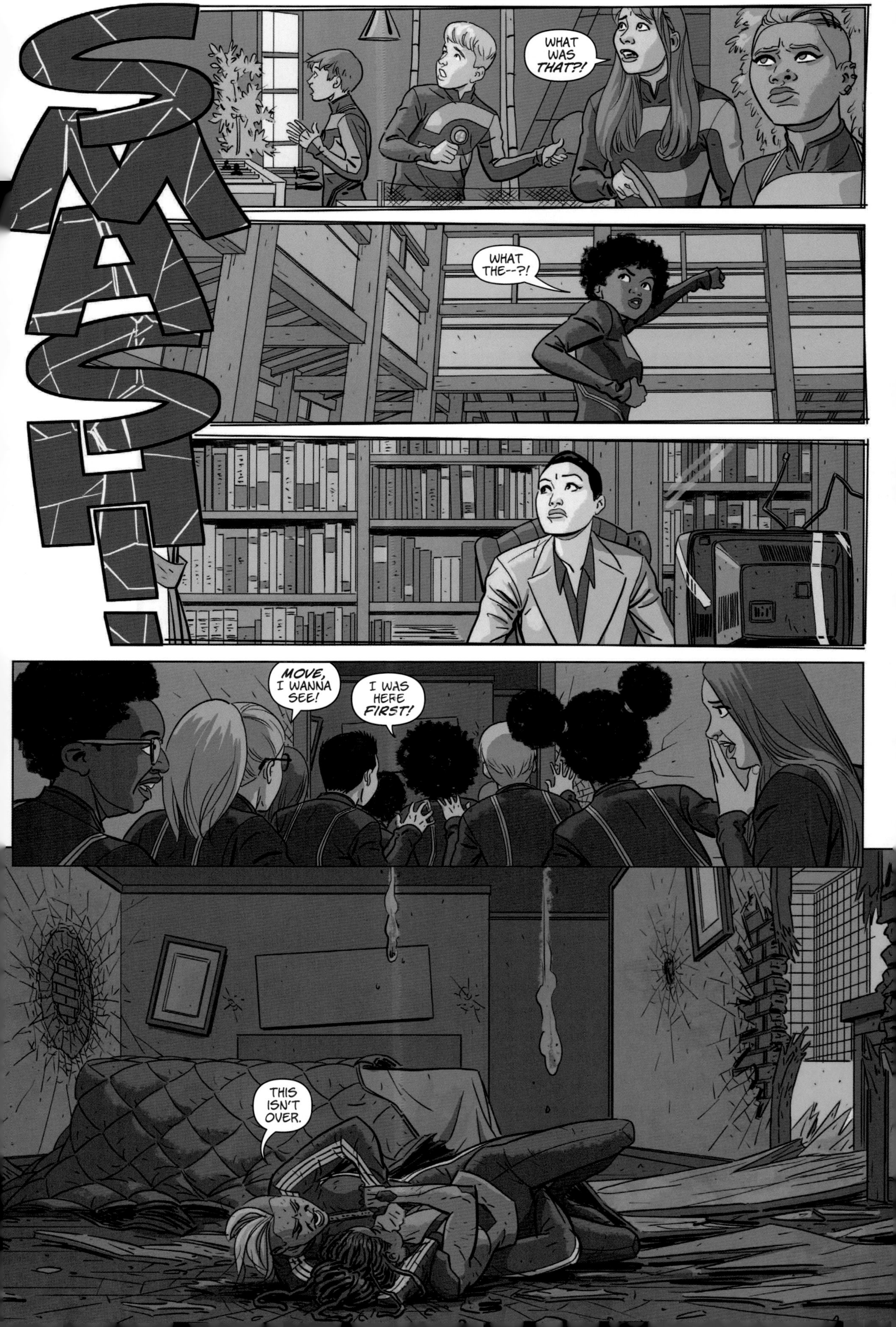
SMASH!
WHAT WAS *THAT?!*
WHAT THE--?!
MOVE, I WANNA SEE!
I WAS HERE *FIRST!*
THIS ISN'T OVER.

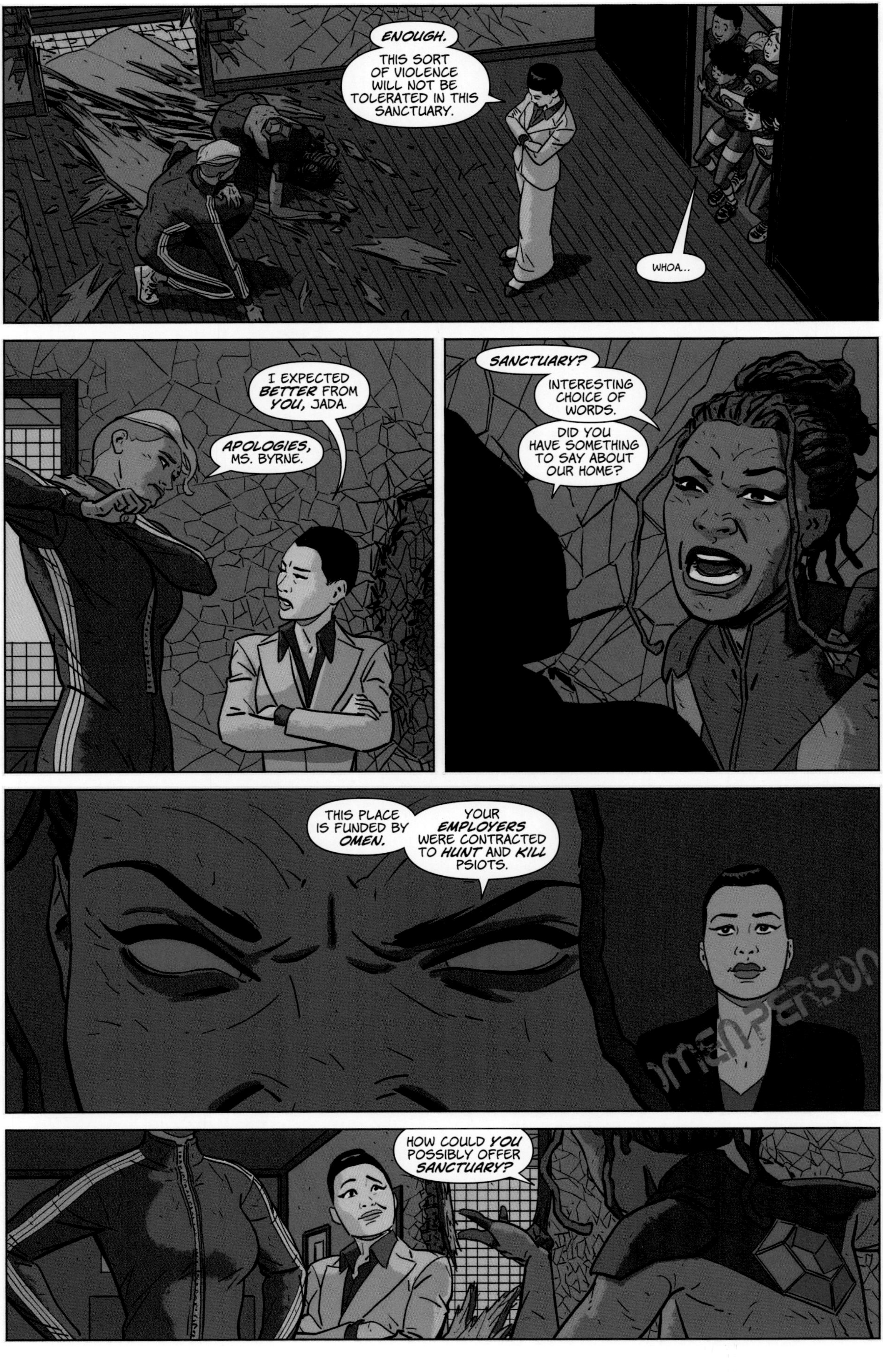
ENOUGH.
THIS SORT OF VIOLENCE WILL NOT BE TOLERATED IN THIS SANCTUARY.
WHOA...
I EXPECTED BETTER FROM YOU, JADA.
APOLOGIES, MS. BYRNE.
SANCTUARY?
INTERESTING CHOICE OF WORDS.
DID YOU HAVE SOMETHING TO SAY ABOUT OUR HOME?
THIS PLACE IS FUNDED BY OMEN.
YOUR EMPLOYERS WERE CONTRACTED TO HUNT AND KILL PSIOTS.
HOW COULD YOU POSSIBLY OFFER SANCTUARY?

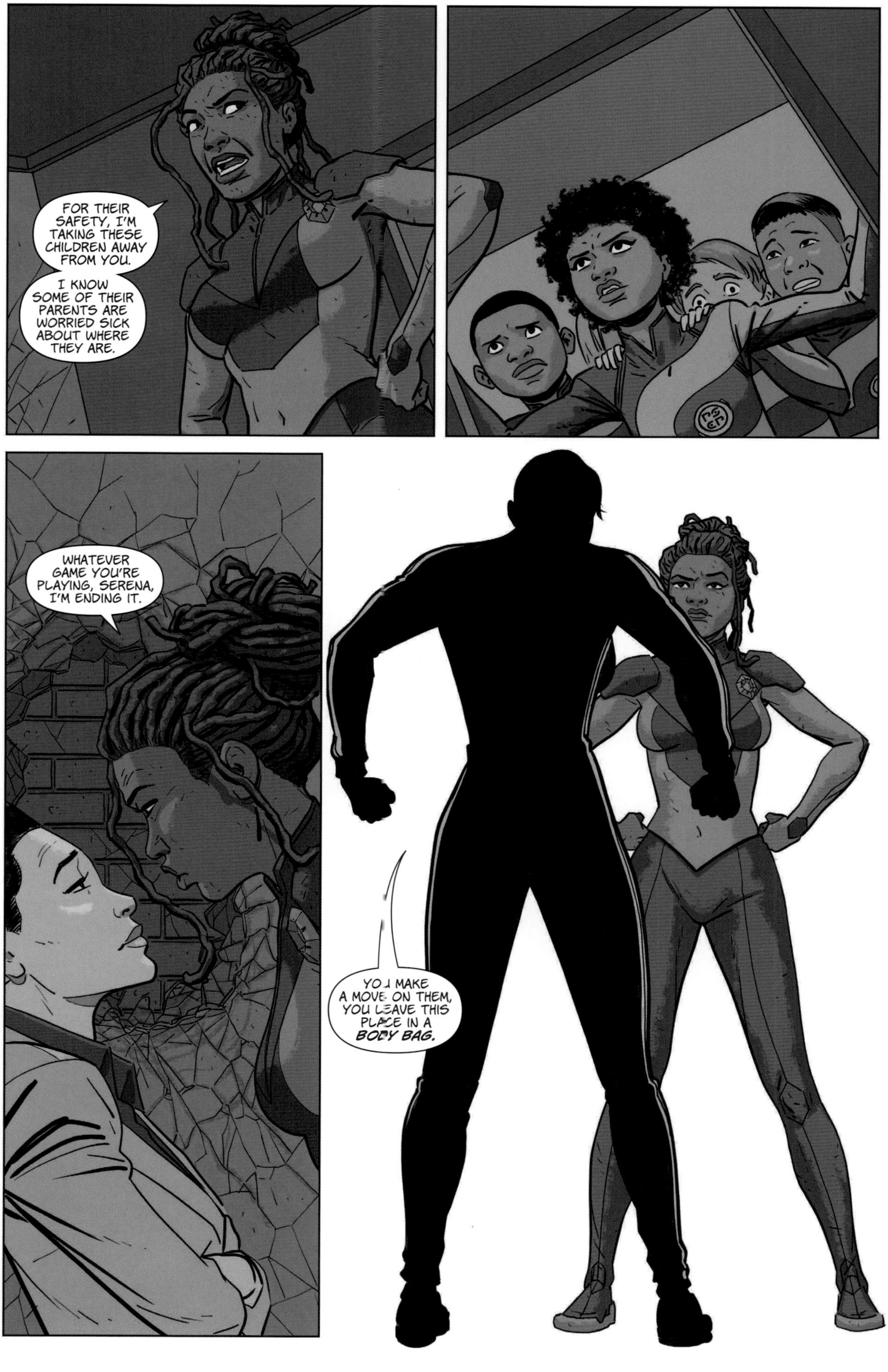
FOR THEIR SAFETY, I'M TAKING THESE CHILDREN AWAY FROM YOU.
I KNOW SOME OF THEIR PARENTS ARE WORRIED SICK ABOUT WHERE THEY ARE.
WHATEVER GAME YOU'RE PLAYING, SERENA, I'M ENDING IT.
YOU MAKE A MOVE ON THEM, YOU LEAVE THIS PLACE IN A *BODY BAG.*

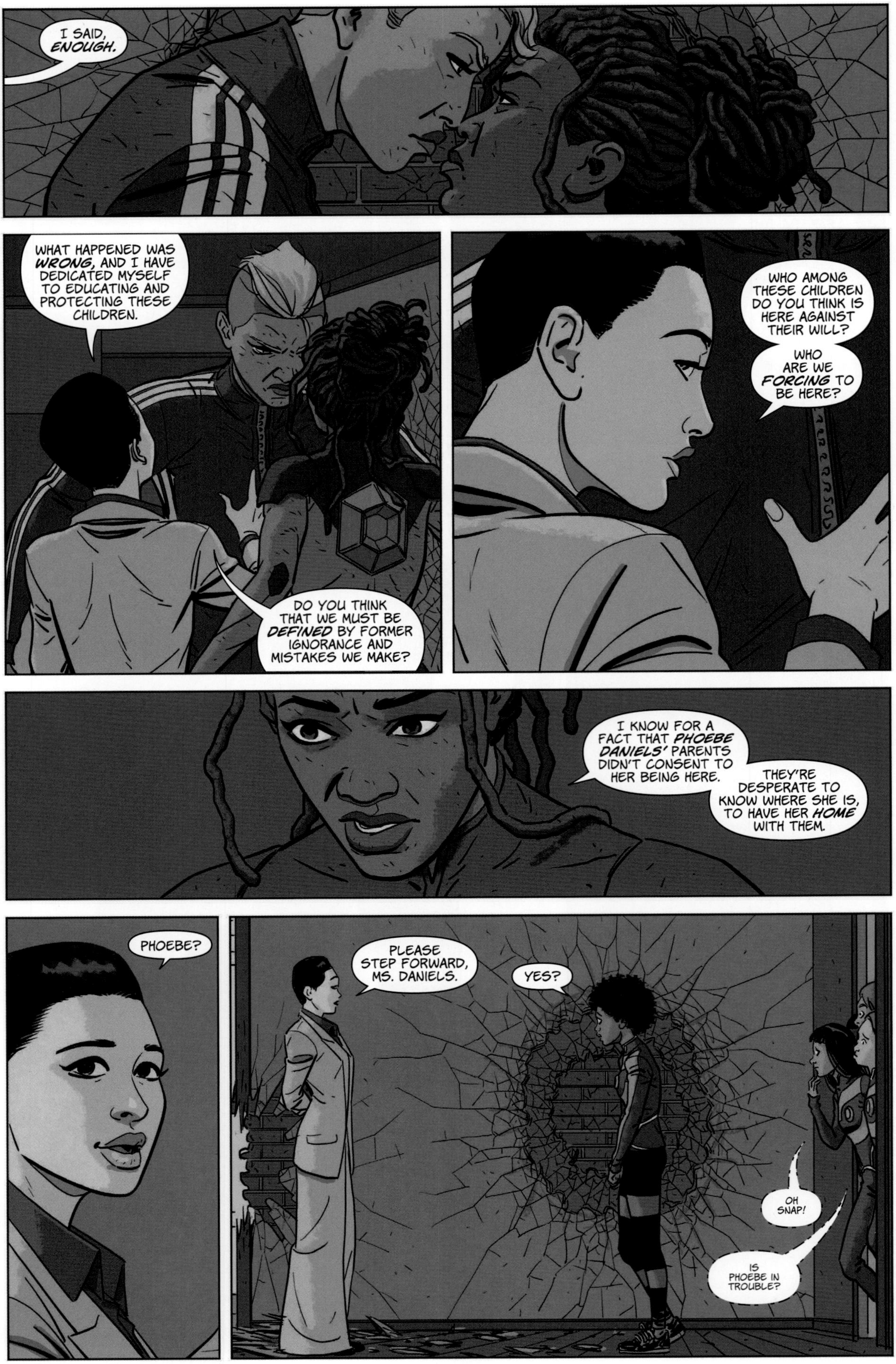
I SAID, ENOUGH.
WHAT HAPPENED WAS WRONG, AND I HAVE DEDICATED MYSELF TO EDUCATING AND PROTECTING THESE CHILDREN.
DO YOU THINK THAT WE MUST BE DEFINED BY FORMER IGNORANCE AND MISTAKES WE MAKE?
WHO AMONG THESE CHILDREN DO YOU THINK IS HERE AGAINST THEIR WILL?
WHO ARE WE FORCING TO BE HERE?
I KNOW FOR A FACT THAT PHOEBE DANIELS' PARENTS DIDN'T CONSENT TO HER BEING HERE.
THEY'RE DESPERATE TO KNOW WHERE SHE IS, TO HAVE HER HOME WITH THEM.
PHOEBE?
PLEASE STEP FORWARD, MS. DANIELS.
YES?
OH SNAP!
IS PHOEBE IN TROUBLE?

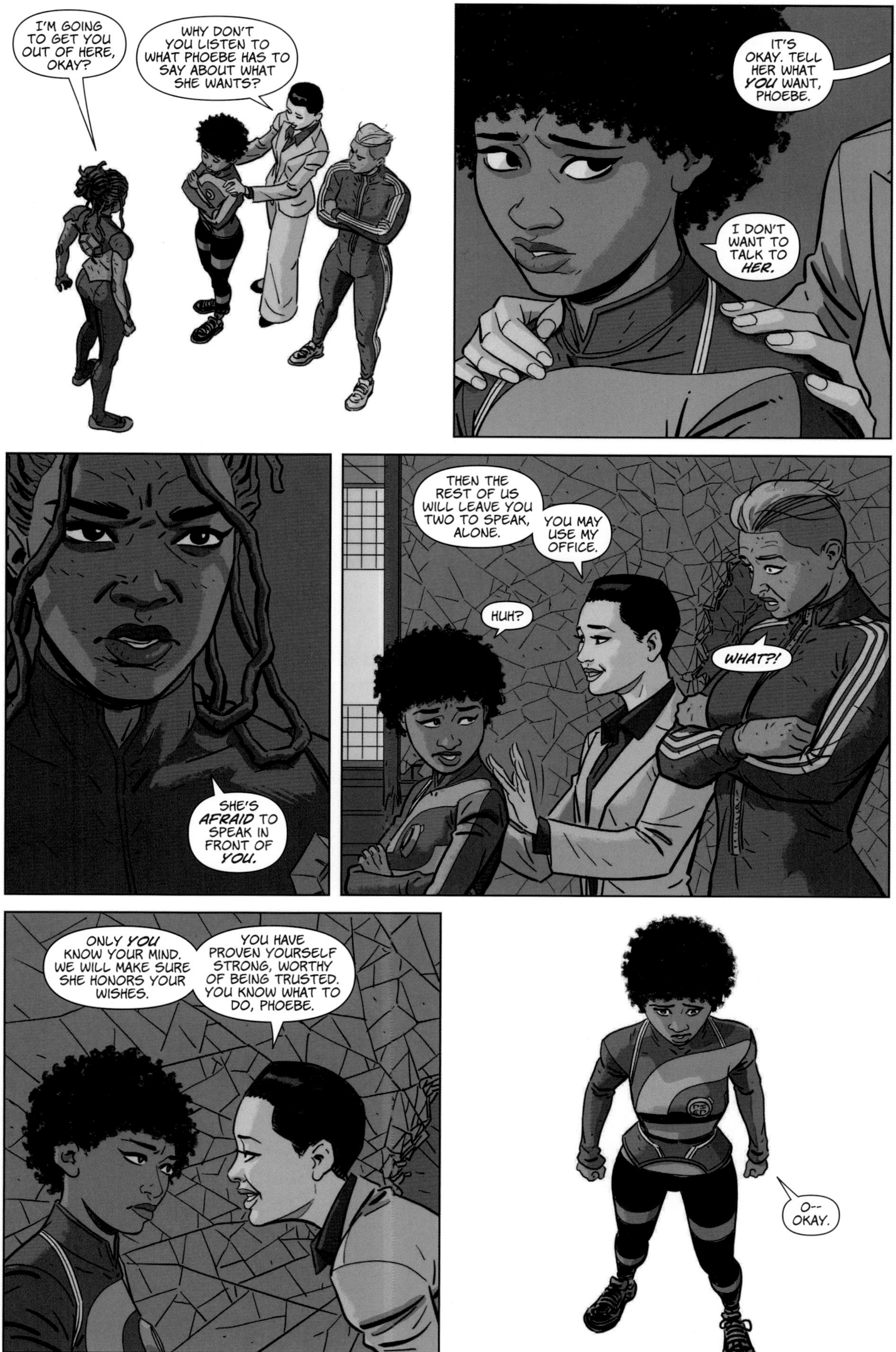
I'M GOING TO GET YOU OUT OF HERE, OKAY?
WHY DON'T YOU LISTEN TO WHAT PHOEBE HAS TO SAY ABOUT WHAT SHE WANTS?
IT'S OKAY. TELL HER WHAT YOU WANT, PHOEBE.
I DON'T WANT TO TALK TO HER.
SHE'S AFRAID TO SPEAK IN FRONT OF YOU.
THEN THE REST OF US WILL LEAVE YOU TWO TO SPEAK, ALONE.
YOU MAY USE MY OFFICE.
HUH?
WHAT?!
ONLY YOU KNOW YOUR MIND. WE WILL MAKE SURE SHE HONORS YOUR WISHES.
YOU HAVE PROVEN YOURSELF STRONG, WORTHY OF BEING TRUSTED. YOU KNOW WHAT TO DO, PHOEBE.
O-- OKAY.

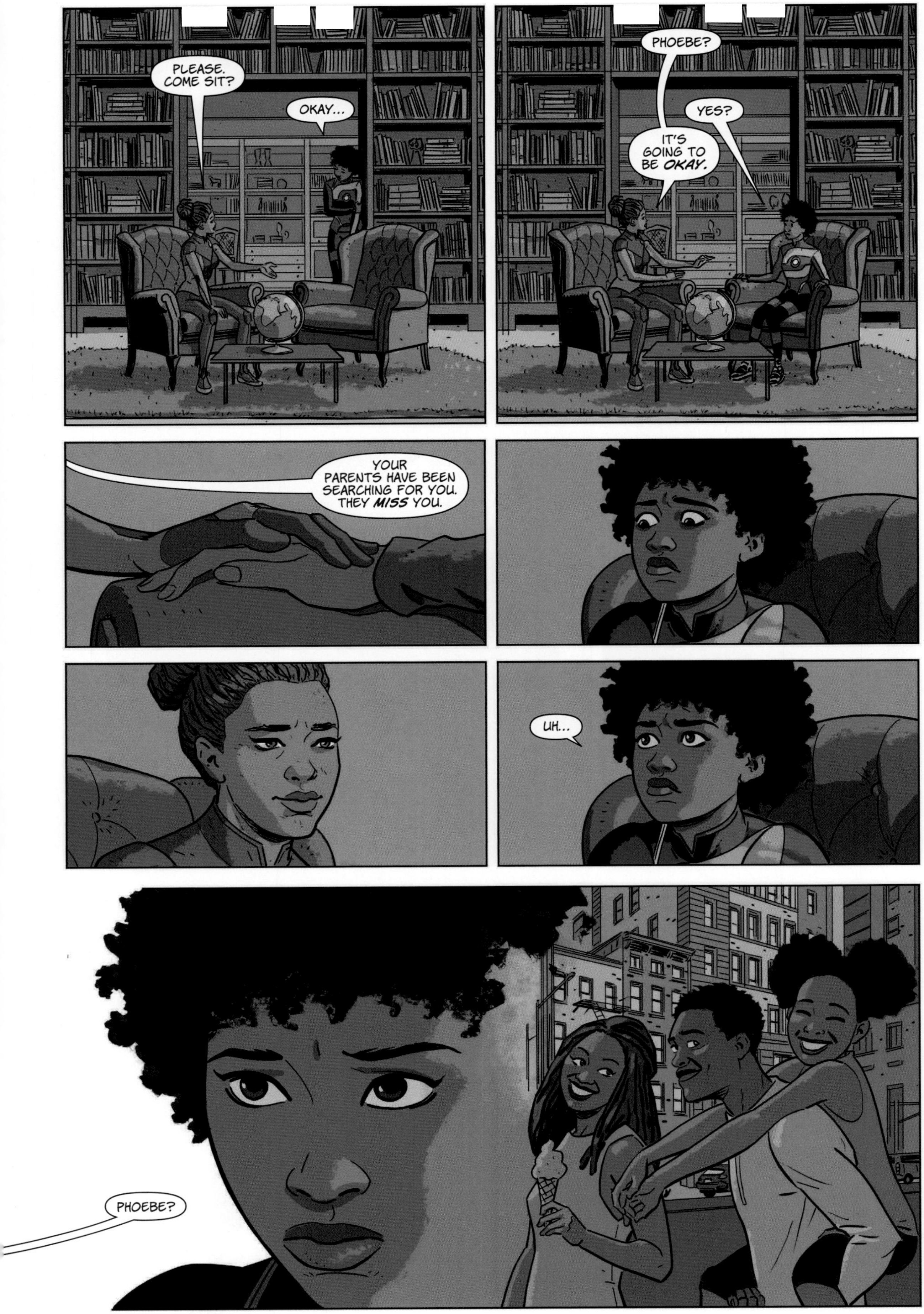
PLEASE. COME SIT?
OKAY...
PHOEBE?
YES?
IT'S GOING TO BE *OKAY.*
YOUR PARENTS HAVE BEEN SEARCHING FOR YOU. THEY *MISS* YOU.
UH...
PHOEBE?

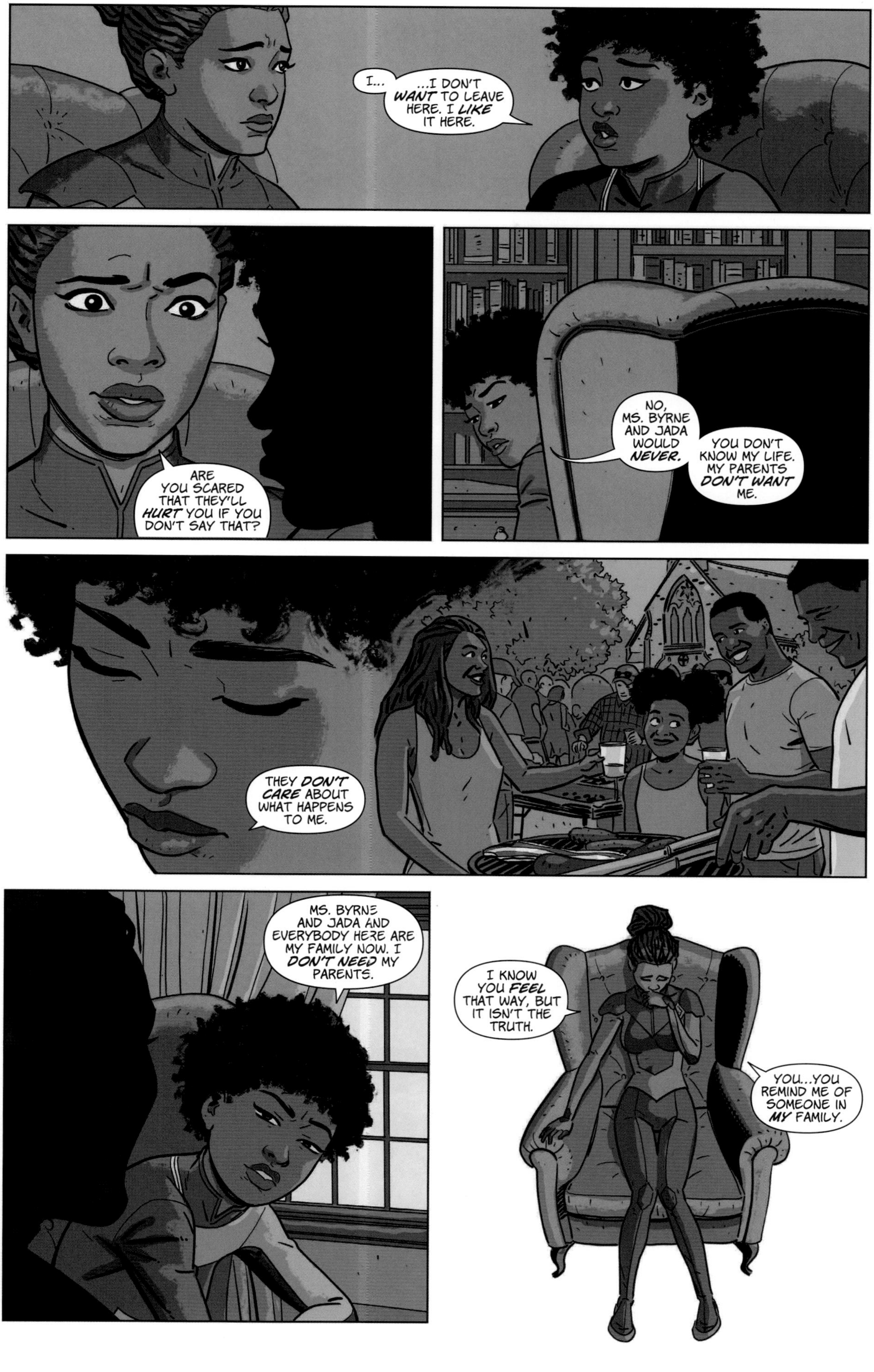
I...
...I DON'T WANT TO LEAVE HERE. I LIKE IT HERE.
ARE YOU SCARED THAT THEY'LL HURT YOU IF YOU DON'T SAY THAT?
NO, MS. BYRNE AND JADA WOULD NEVER.
YOU DON'T KNOW MY LIFE. MY PARENTS DON'T WANT ME.
THEY DON'T CARE ABOUT WHAT HAPPENS TO ME.
MS. BYRNE AND JADA AND EVERYBODY HERE ARE MY FAMILY NOW. I DON'T NEED MY PARENTS.
I KNOW YOU FEEL THAT WAY, BUT IT ISN'T THE TRUTH.
YOU...YOU REMIND ME OF SOMEONE IN MY FAMILY.

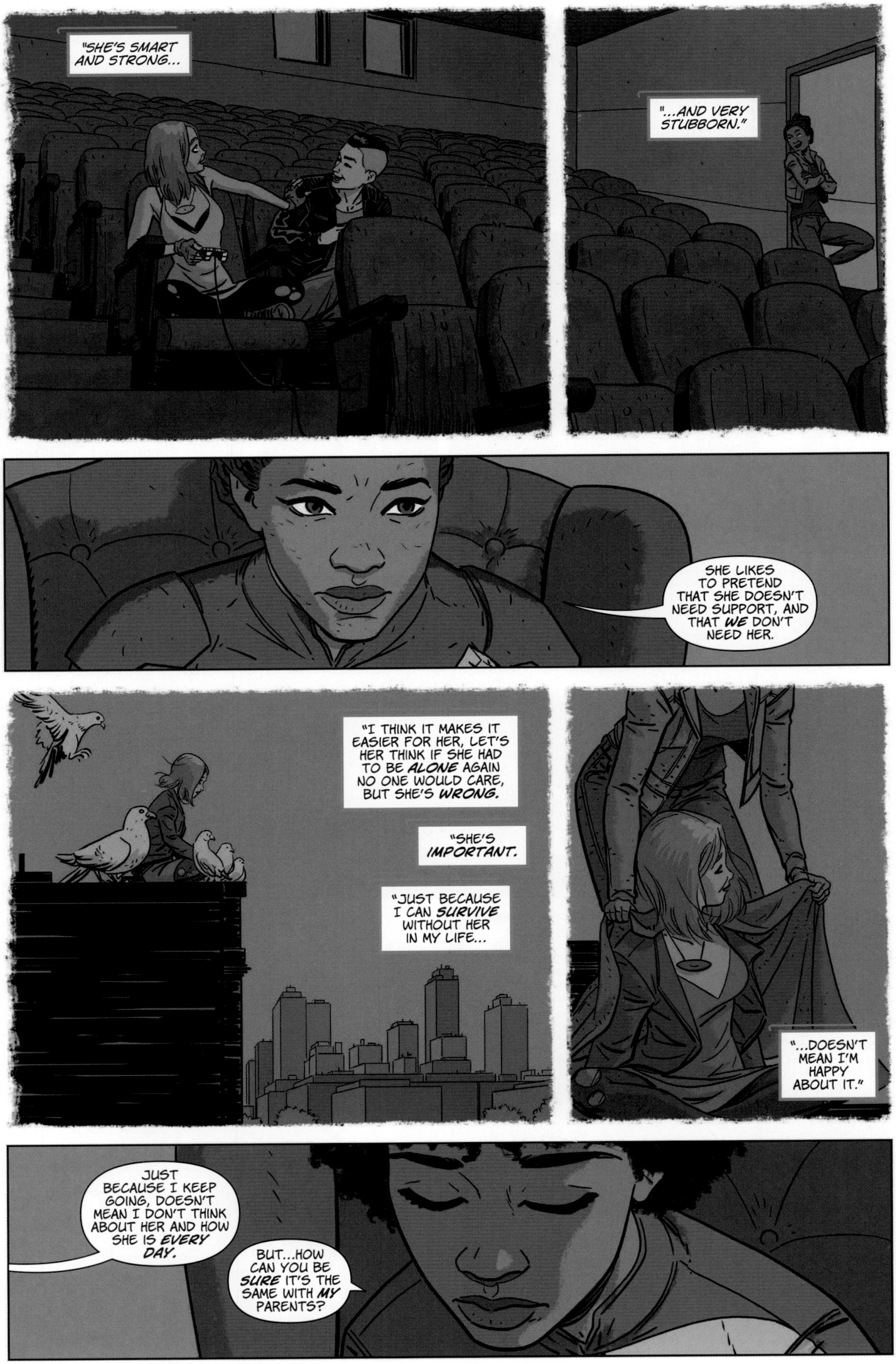
"SHE'S SMART AND STRONG...
"...AND VERY STUBBORN."
SHE LIKES TO PRETEND THAT SHE DOESN'T NEED SUPPORT, AND THAT WE DON'T NEED HER.
"I THINK IT MAKES IT EASIER FOR HER, LET'S HER THINK IF SHE HAD TO BE ALONE AGAIN NO ONE WOULD CARE, BUT SHE'S WRONG.
"SHE'S IMPORTANT.
"JUST BECAUSE I CAN SURVIVE WITHOUT HER IN MY LIFE...
"...DOESN'T MEAN I'M HAPPY ABOUT IT."
JUST BECAUSE I KEEP GOING, DOESN'T MEAN I DON'T THINK ABOUT HER AND HOW SHE IS EVERY DAY.
BUT...HOW CAN YOU BE SURE IT'S THE SAME WITH MY PARENTS?

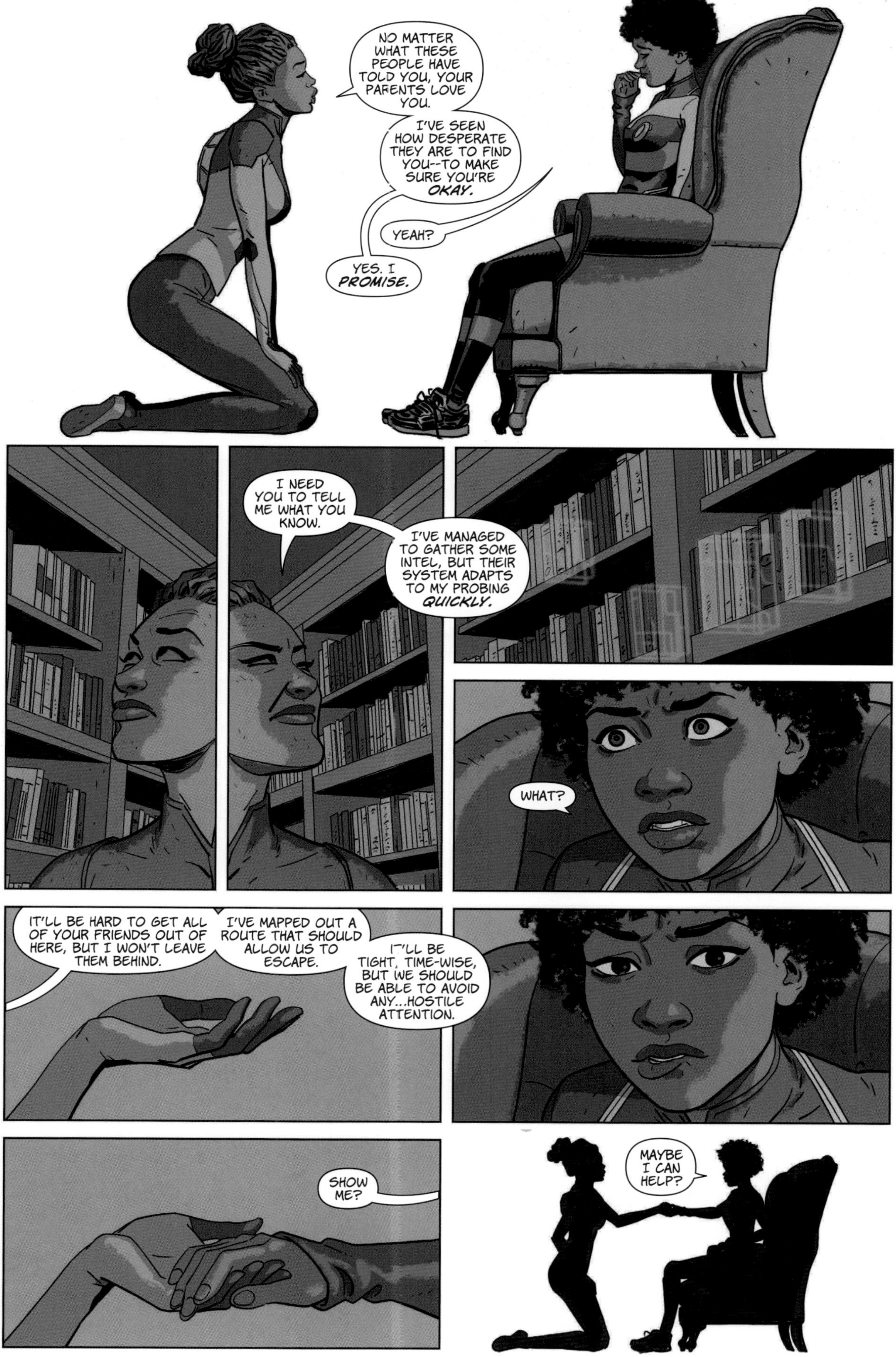
NO MATTER WHAT THESE PEOPLE HAVE TOLD YOU, YOUR PARENTS LOVE YOU.
I'VE SEEN HOW DESPERATE THEY ARE TO FIND YOU--TO MAKE SURE YOU'RE OKAY.
YEAH?
YES. I PROMISE.
I NEED YOU TO TELL ME WHAT YOU KNOW.
I'VE MANAGED TO GATHER SOME INTEL, BUT THEIR SYSTEM ADAPTS TO MY PROBING QUICKLY.
WHAT?
IT'LL BE HARD TO GET ALL OF YOUR FRIENDS OUT OF HERE, BUT I WON'T LEAVE THEM BEHIND.
I'VE MAPPED OUT A ROUTE THAT SHOULD ALLOW US TO ESCAPE.
IT'LL BE TIGHT, TIME-WISE, BUT WE SHOULD BE ABLE TO AVOID ANY...HOSTILE ATTENTION.
SHOW ME?
MAYBE I CAN HELP?

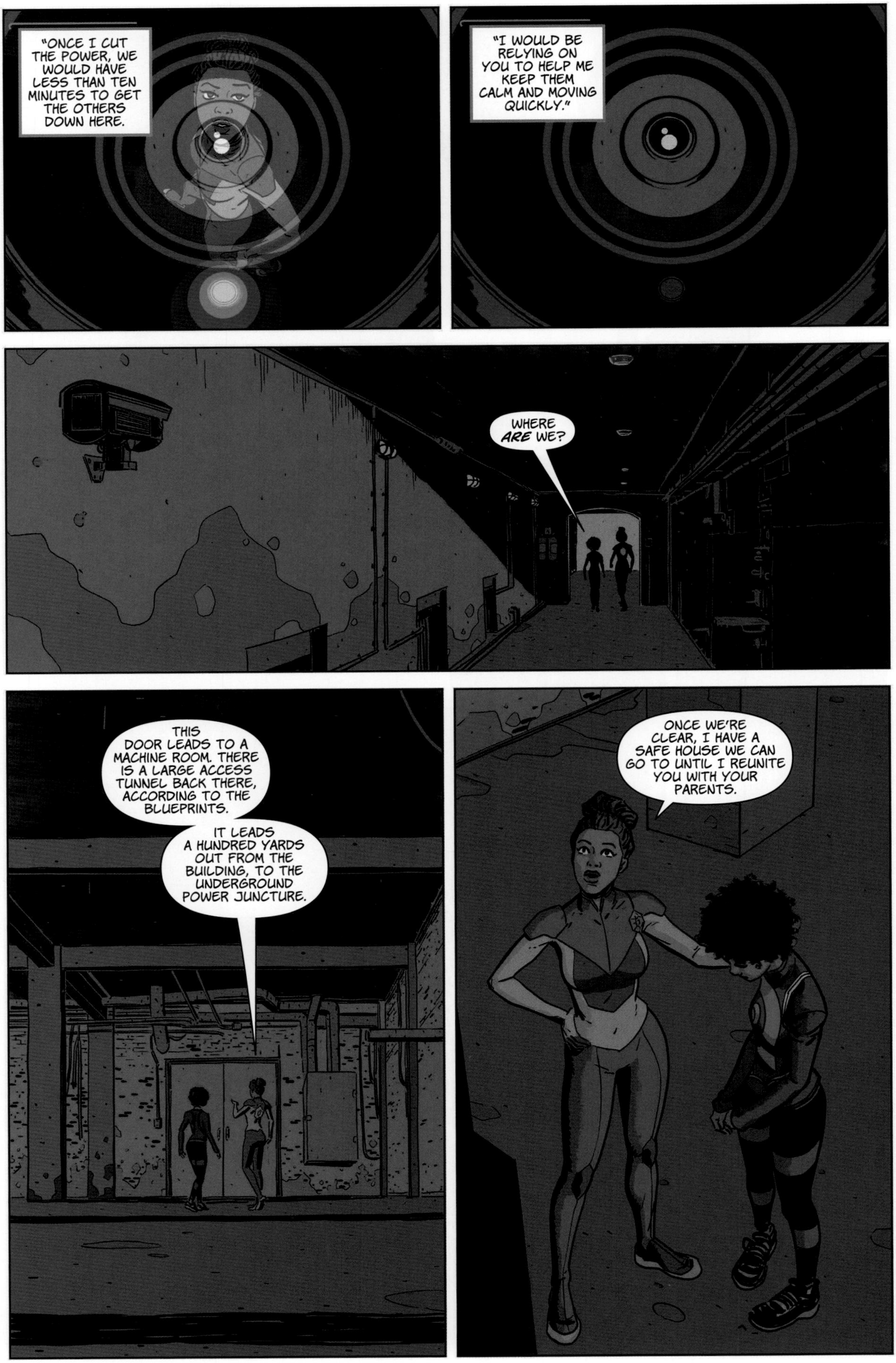
"ONCE I CUT THE POWER, WE WOULD HAVE LESS THAN TEN MINUTES TO GET THE OTHERS DOWN HERE.
"I WOULD BE RELYING ON YOU TO HELP ME KEEP THEM CALM AND MOVING QUICKLY."
WHERE *ARE* WE?
THIS DOOR LEADS TO A MACHINE ROOM. THERE IS A LARGE ACCESS TUNNEL BACK THERE, ACCORDING TO THE BLUEPRINTS.
IT LEADS A HUNDRED YARDS OUT FROM THE BUILDING, TO THE UNDERGROUND POWER JUNCTURE.
ONCE WE'RE CLEAR, I HAVE A SAFE HOUSE WE CAN GO TO UNTIL I REUNITE YOU WITH YOUR PARENTS.

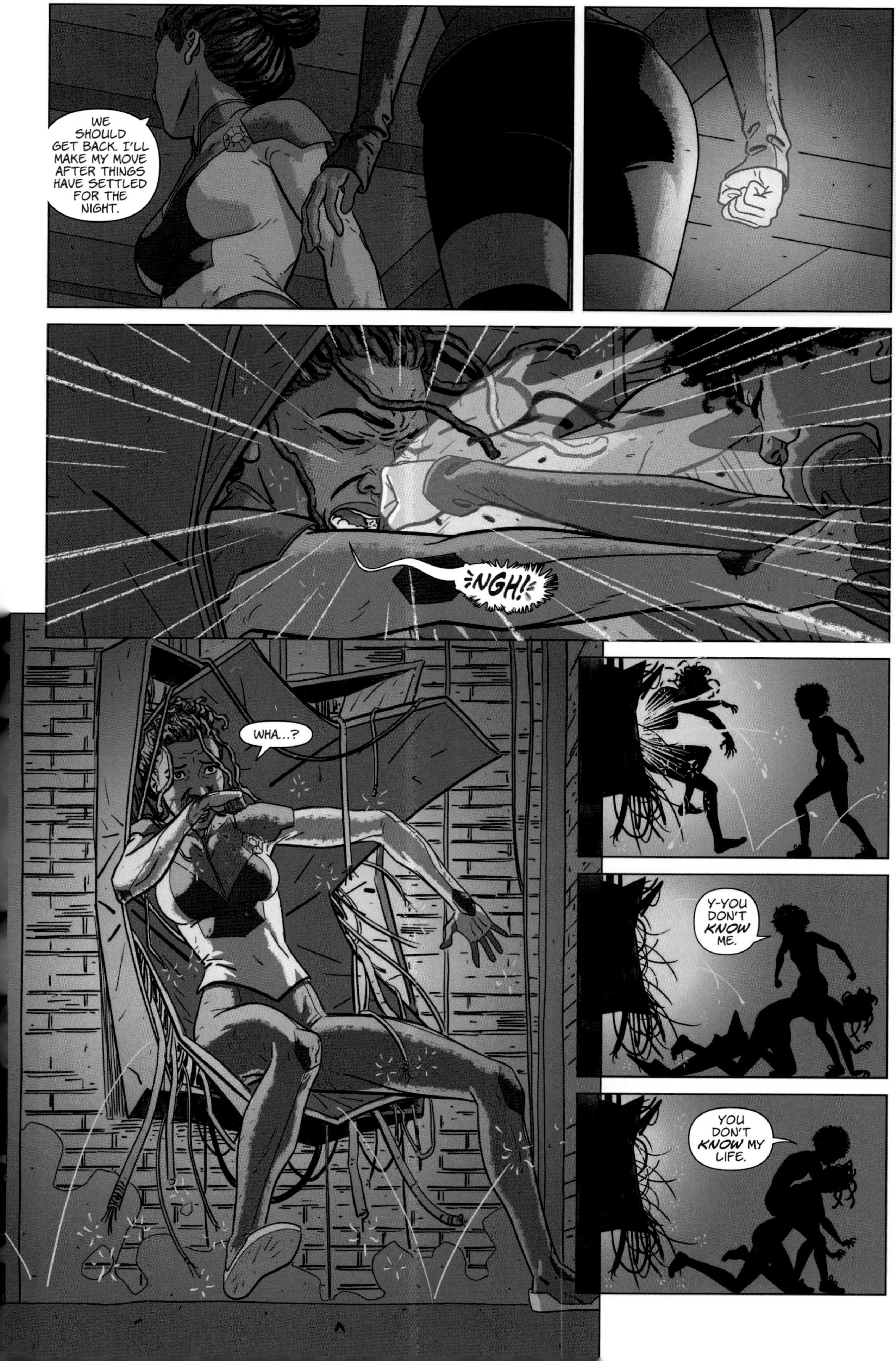
WE SHOULD GET BACK. I'LL MAKE MY MOVE AFTER THINGS HAVE SETTLED FOR THE NIGHT.
NGH!
WHA..?
Y-YOU DON'T KNOW ME.
YOU DON'T KNOW MY LIFE.

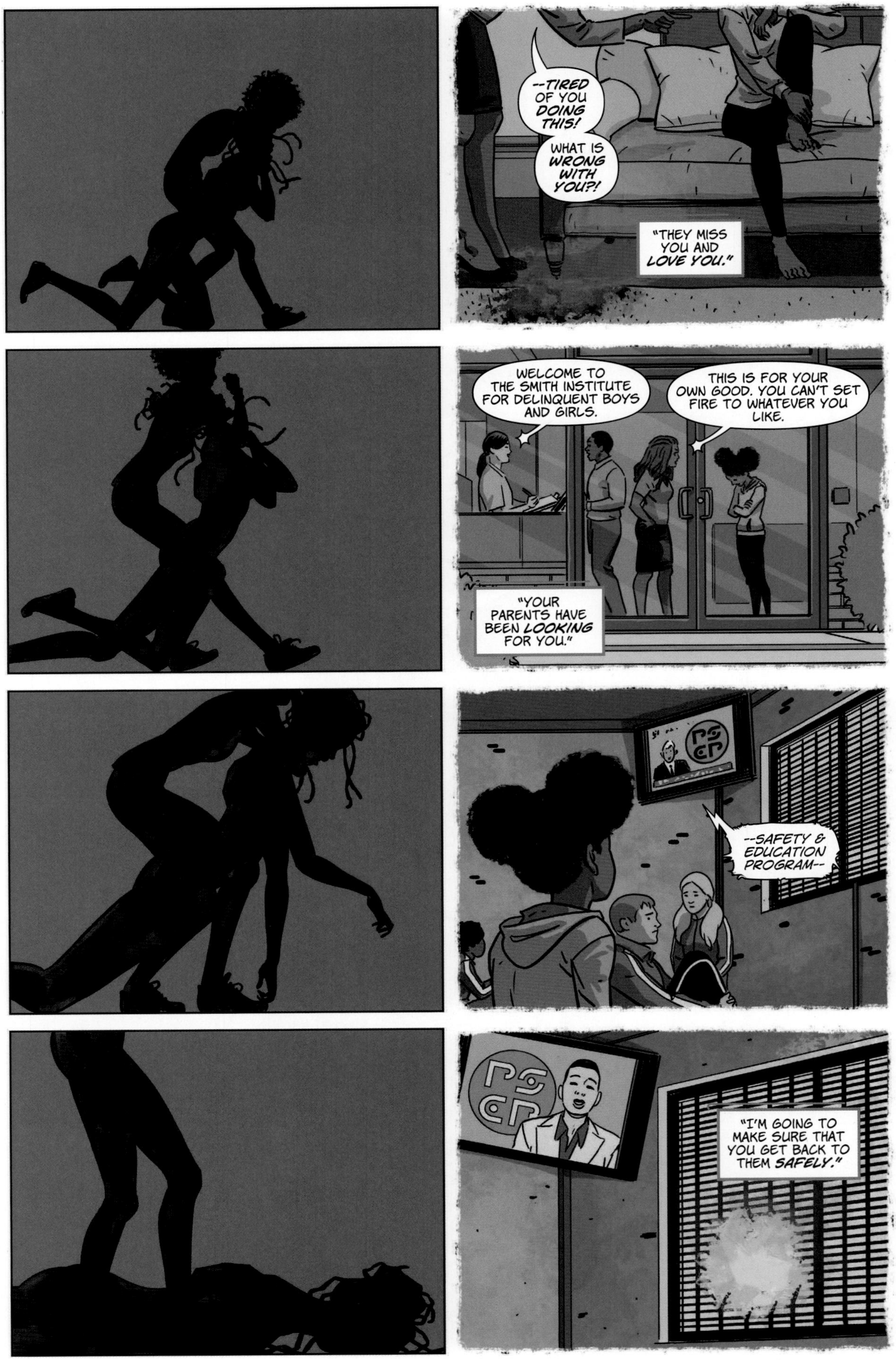
--TIRED OF YOU DOING THIS!
WHAT IS WRONG WITH YOU?!
"THEY MISS YOU AND LOVE YOU."
WELCOME TO THE SMITH INSTITUTE FOR DELINQUENT BOYS AND GIRLS.
THIS IS FOR YOUR OWN GOOD. YOU CAN'T SET FIRE TO WHATEVER YOU LIKE.
"YOUR PARENTS HAVE BEEN LOOKING FOR YOU."
--SAFETY & EDUCATION PROGRAM--
"I'M GOING TO MAKE SURE THAT YOU GET BACK TO THEM SAFELY."

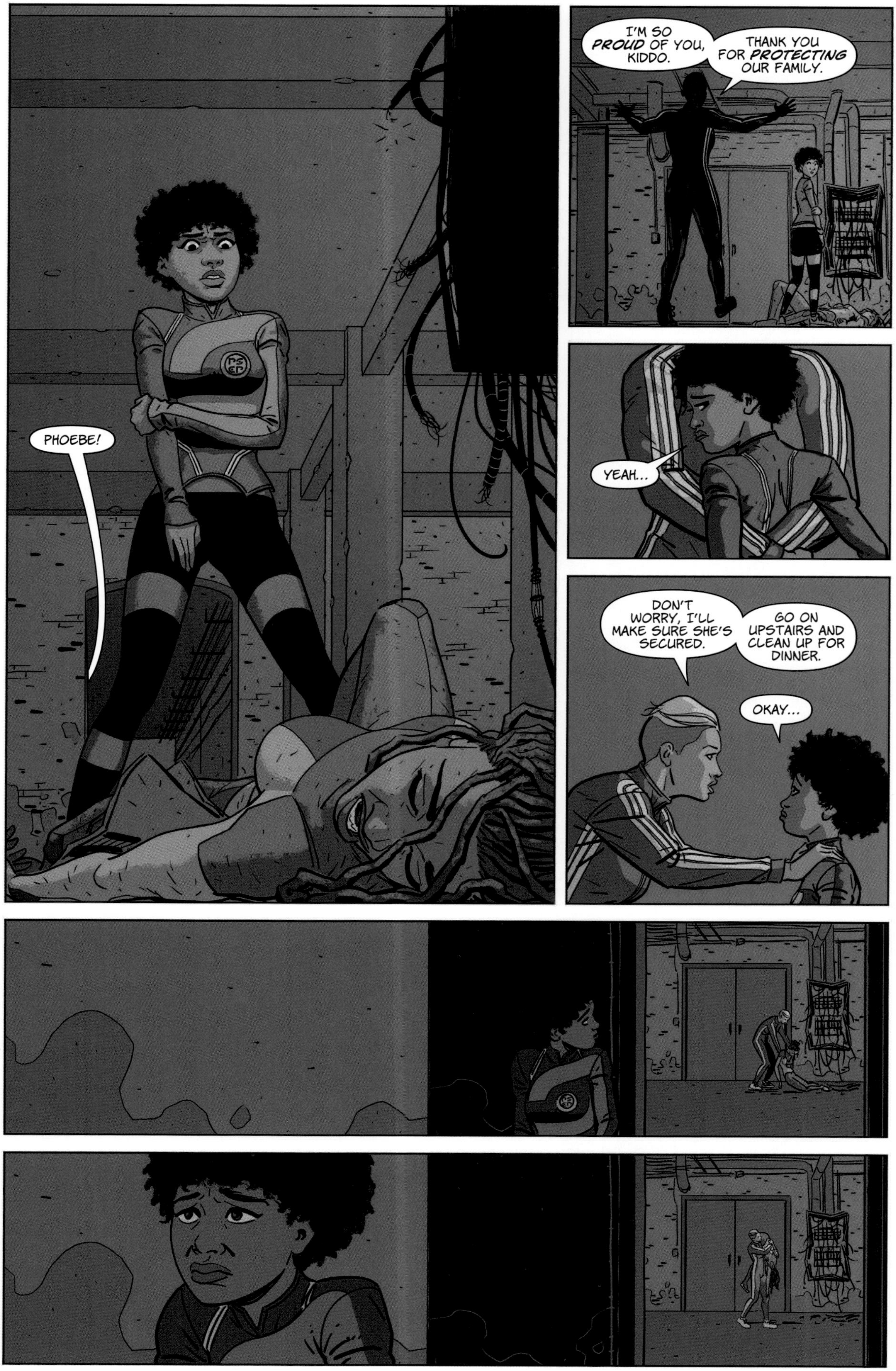
PHOEBE!
I'M SO PROUD OF YOU, KIDDO.
THANK YOU FOR PROTECTING OUR FAMILY.
YEAH...
DON'T WORRY, I'LL MAKE SURE SHE'S SECURED.
GO ON UPSTAIRS AND CLEAN UP FOR DINNER.
OKAY...

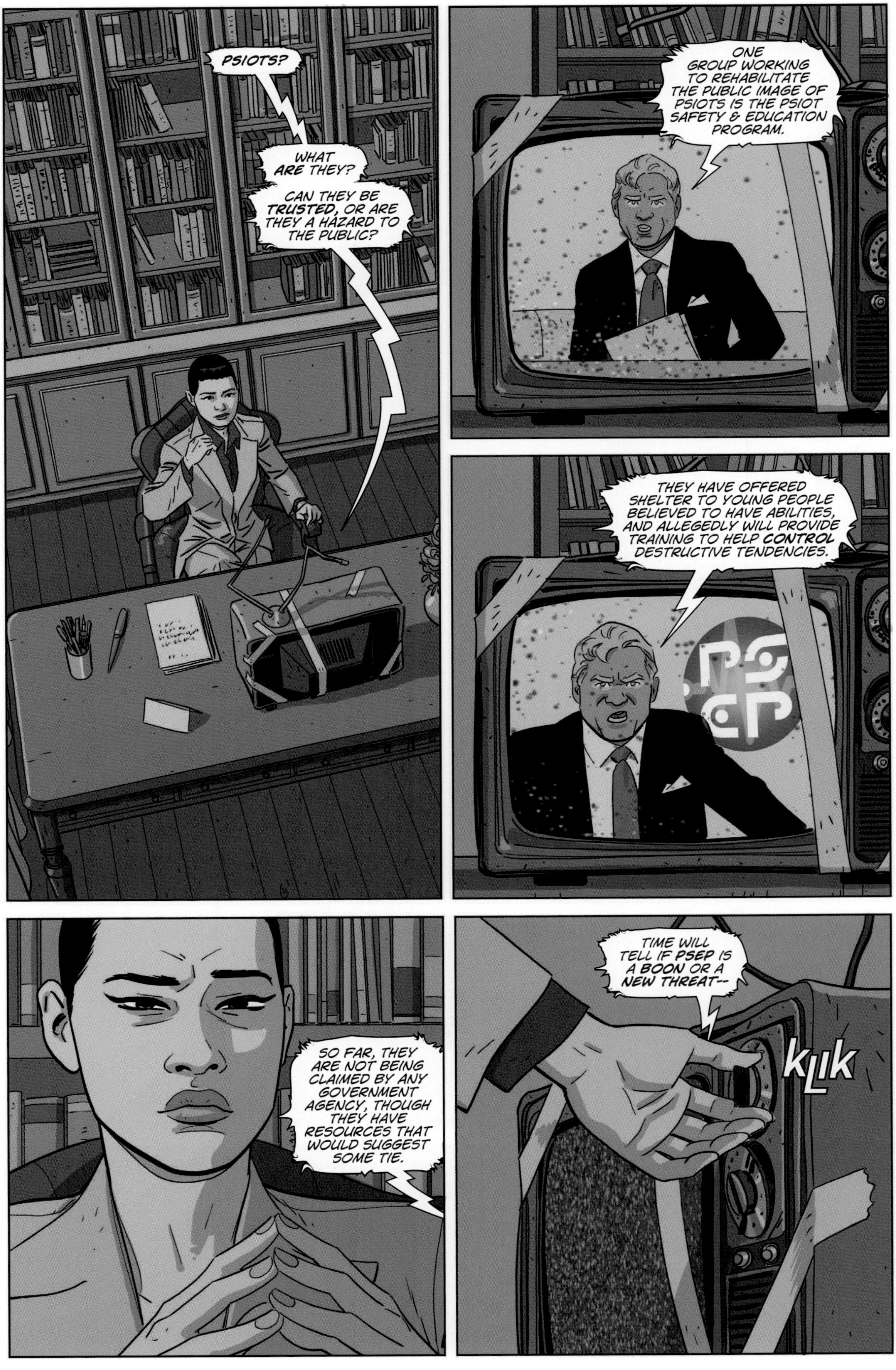
PSIOTS?
WHAT ARE THEY?
CAN THEY BE TRUSTED, OR ARE THEY A HAZARD TO THE PUBLIC?
ONE GROUP WORKING TO REHABILITATE THE PUBLIC IMAGE OF PSIOTS IS THE PSIOT SAFETY & EDUCATION PROGRAM.
THEY HAVE OFFERED SHELTER TO YOUNG PEOPLE BELIEVED TO HAVE ABILITIES, AND ALLEGEDLY WILL PROVIDE TRAINING TO HELP CONTROL DESTRUCTIVE TENDENCIES.
SO FAR, THEY ARE NOT BEING CLAIMED BY ANY GOVERNMENT AGENCY, THOUGH THEY HAVE RESOURCES THAT WOULD SUGGEST SOME TIE.
TIME WILL TELL IF PSEP IS A BOON OR A NEW THREAT--
KLIK

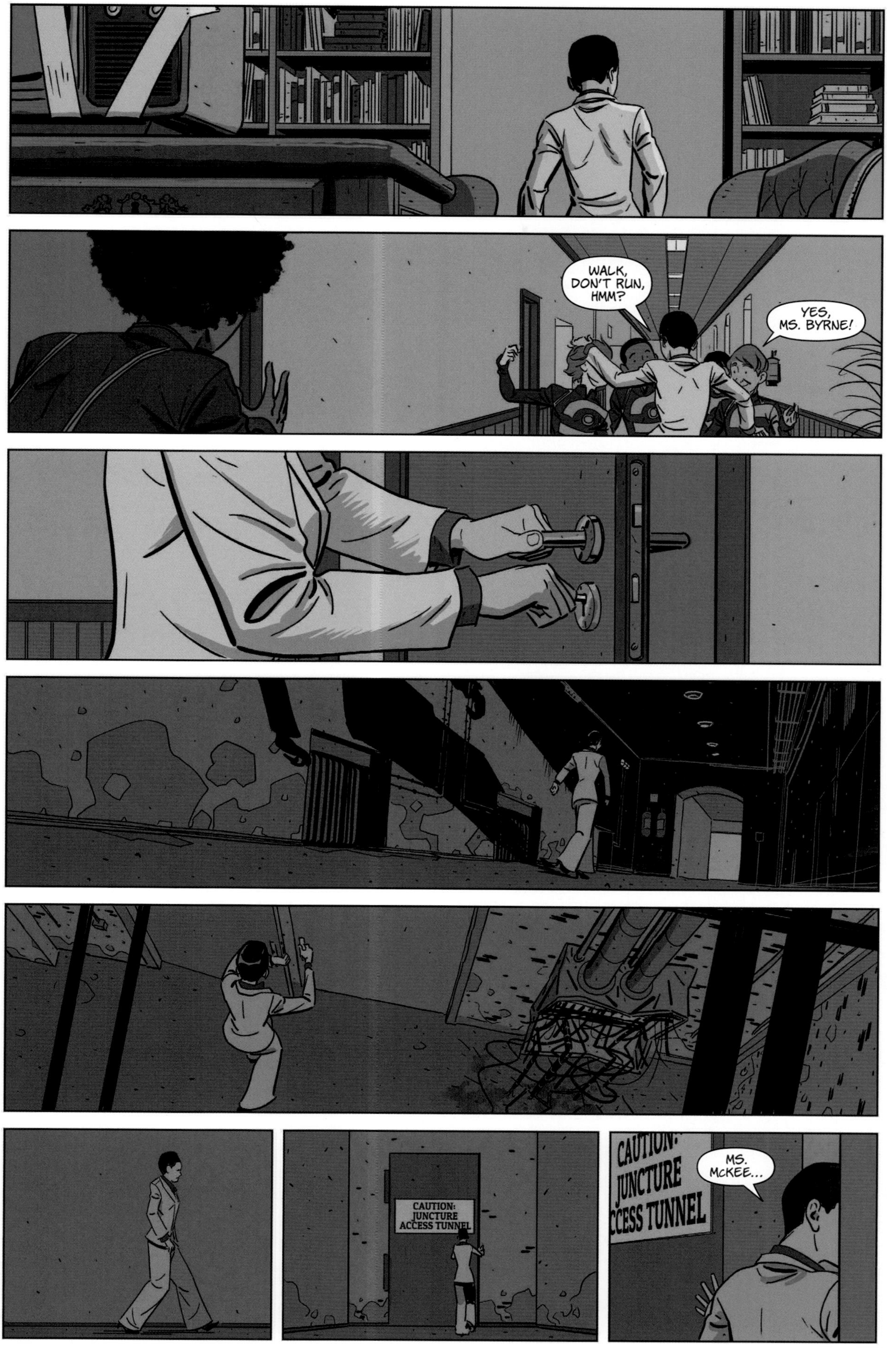
WALK, DON'T RUN, HMM?
YES, MS. BYRNE!
CAUTION: JUNCTURE ACCESS TUNNEL
CAUTION: JUNCTURE CCESS TUNNEL
MS. McKEE...

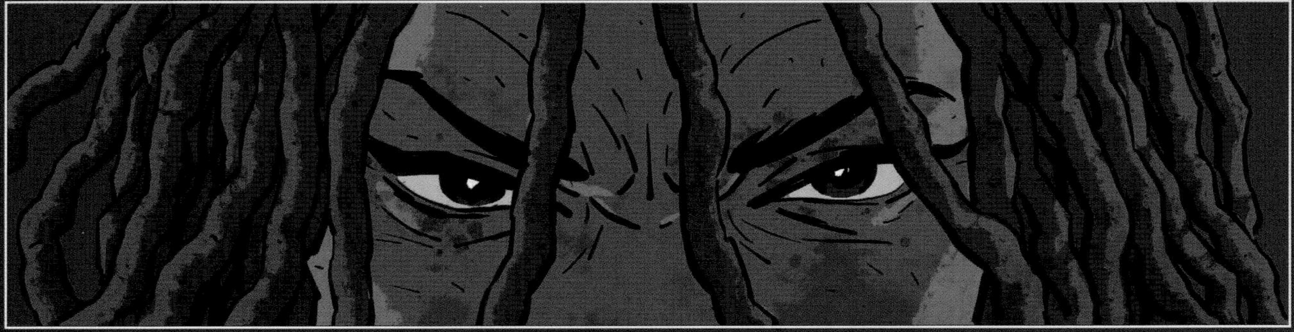

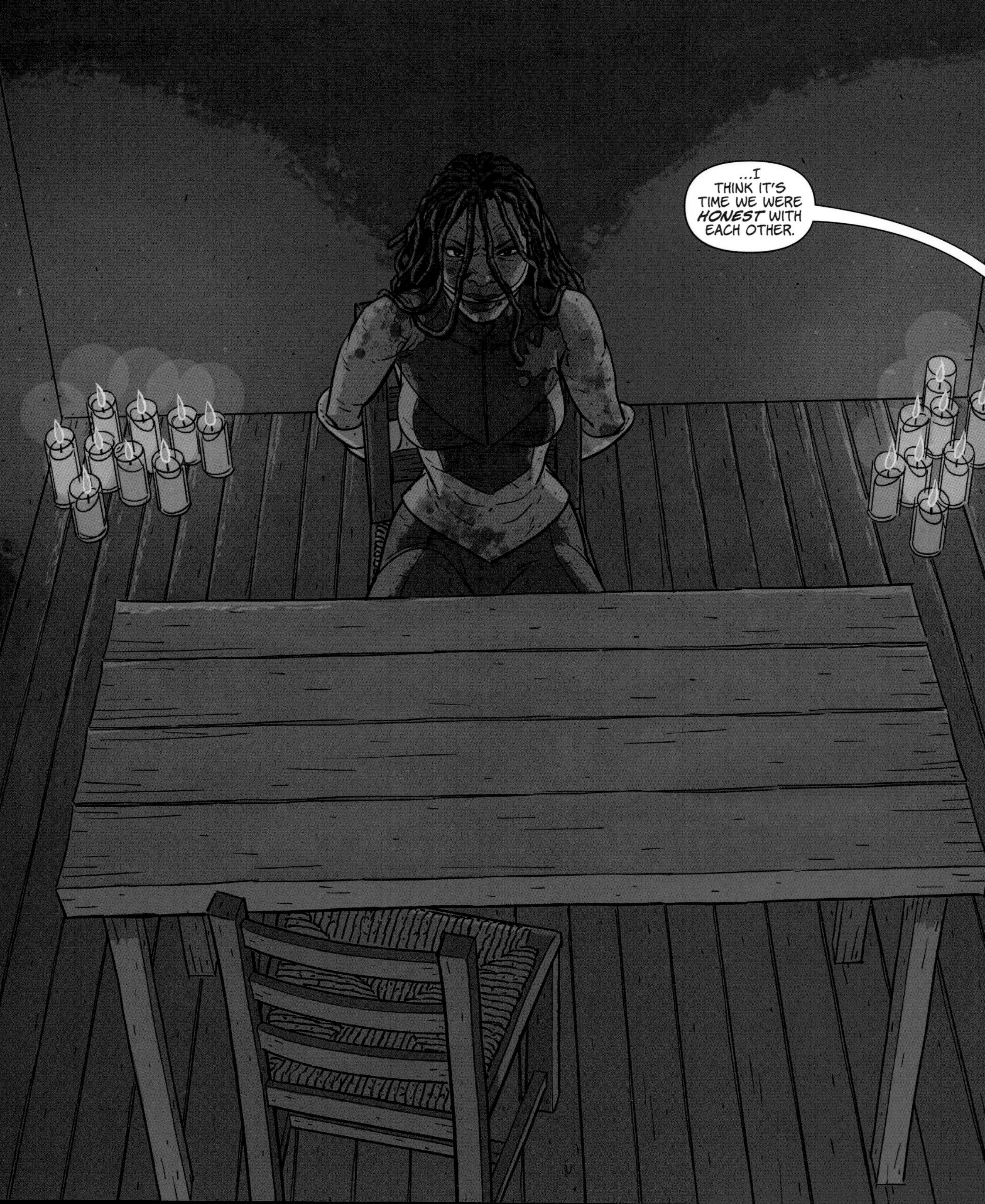
...I THINK IT'S TIME WE WERE HONEST WITH EACH OTHER.

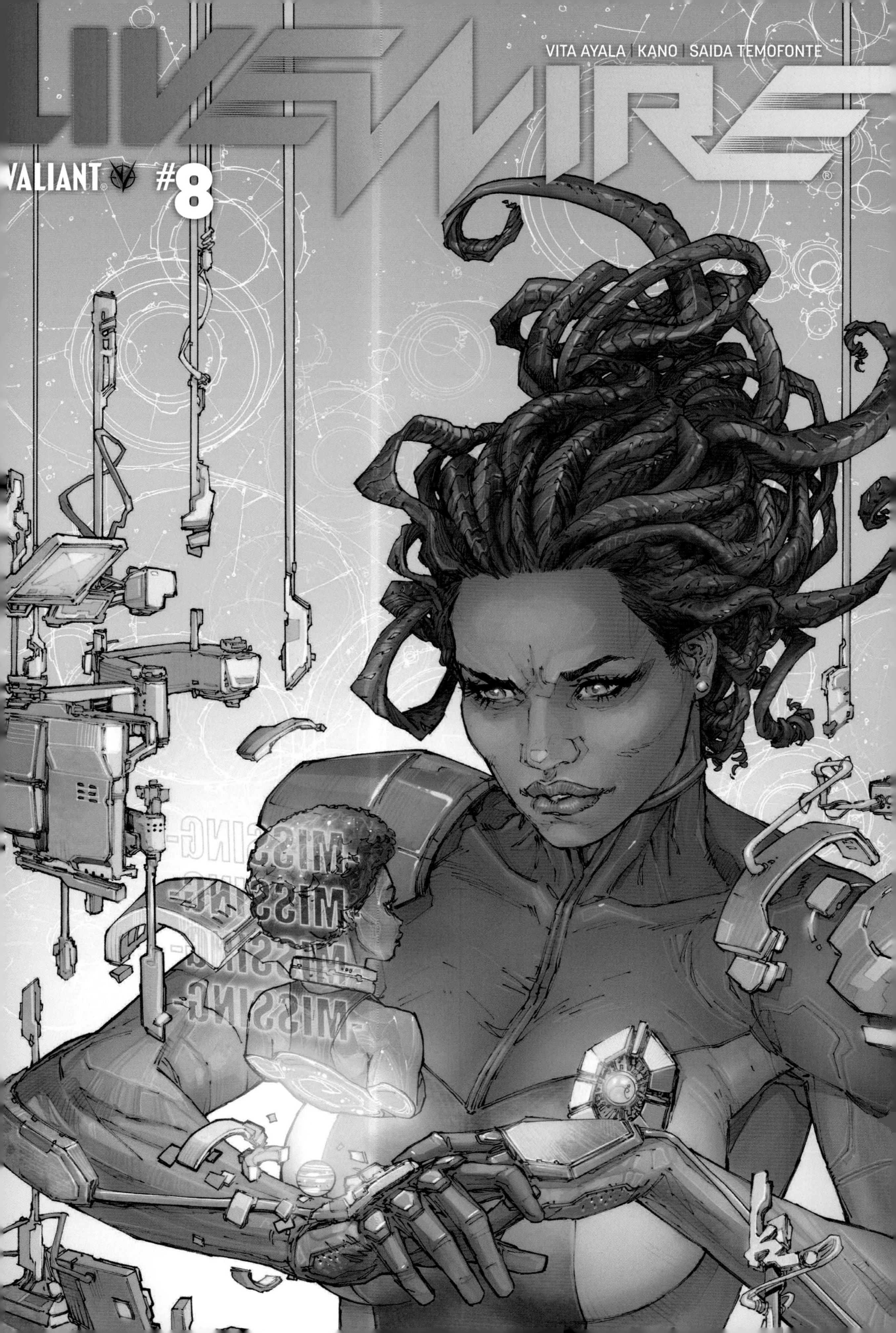
LIVEWIRE
VITA AYALA | KANO | SAIDA TEMOFONTE
VALIANT
#8

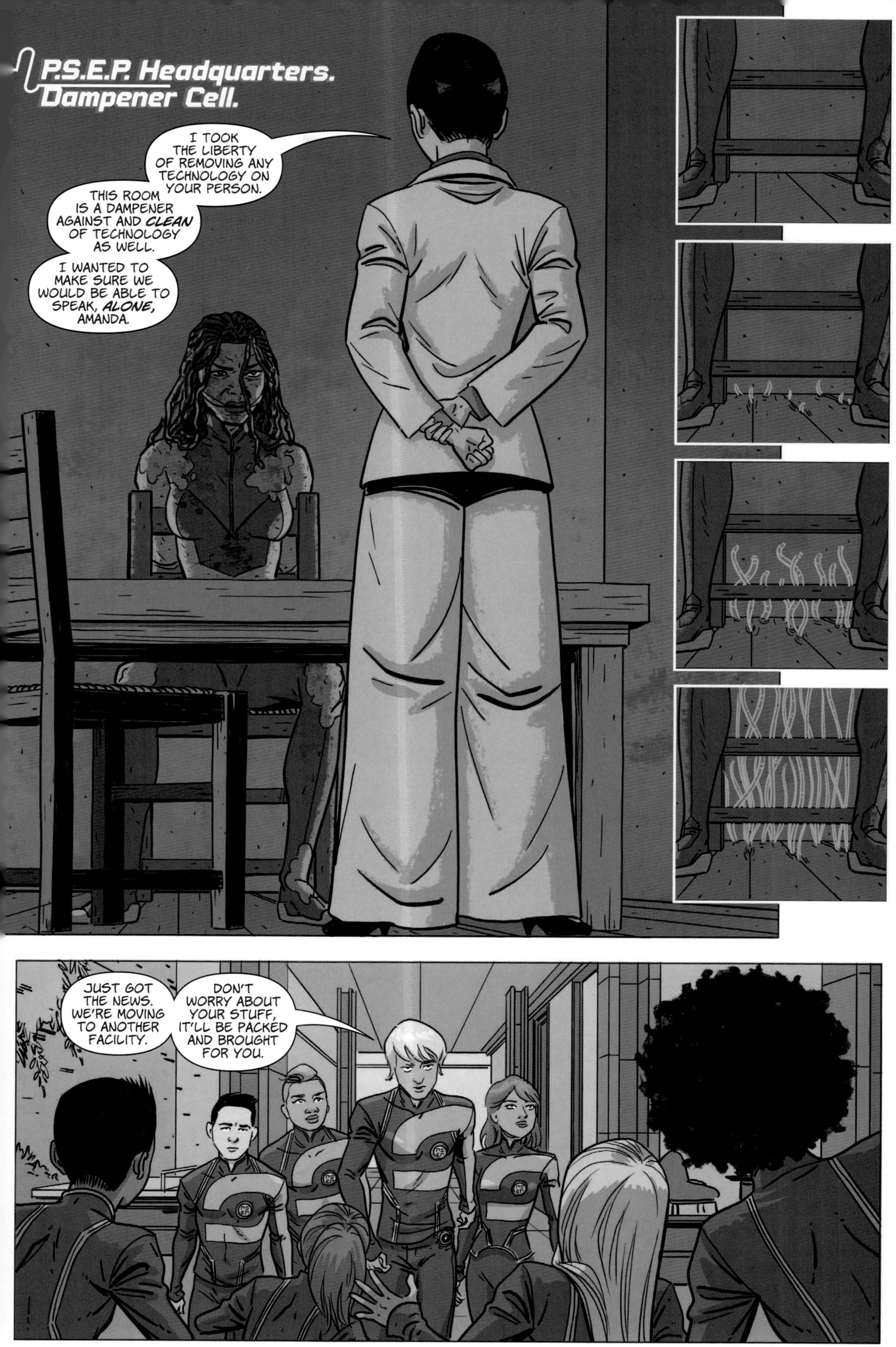
P.S.E.P. Headquarters. Dampener Cell.
I TOOK THE LIBERTY OF REMOVING ANY TECHNOLOGY ON YOUR PERSON.
THIS ROOM IS A DAMPENER AGAINST AND CLEAN OF TECHNOLOGY AS WELL.
I WANTED TO MAKE SURE WE WOULD BE ABLE TO SPEAK, ALONE, AMANDA.
JUST GOT THE NEWS. WE'RE MOVING TO ANOTHER FACILITY.
DON'T WORRY ABOUT YOUR STUFF, IT'LL BE PACKED AND BROUGHT FOR YOU.

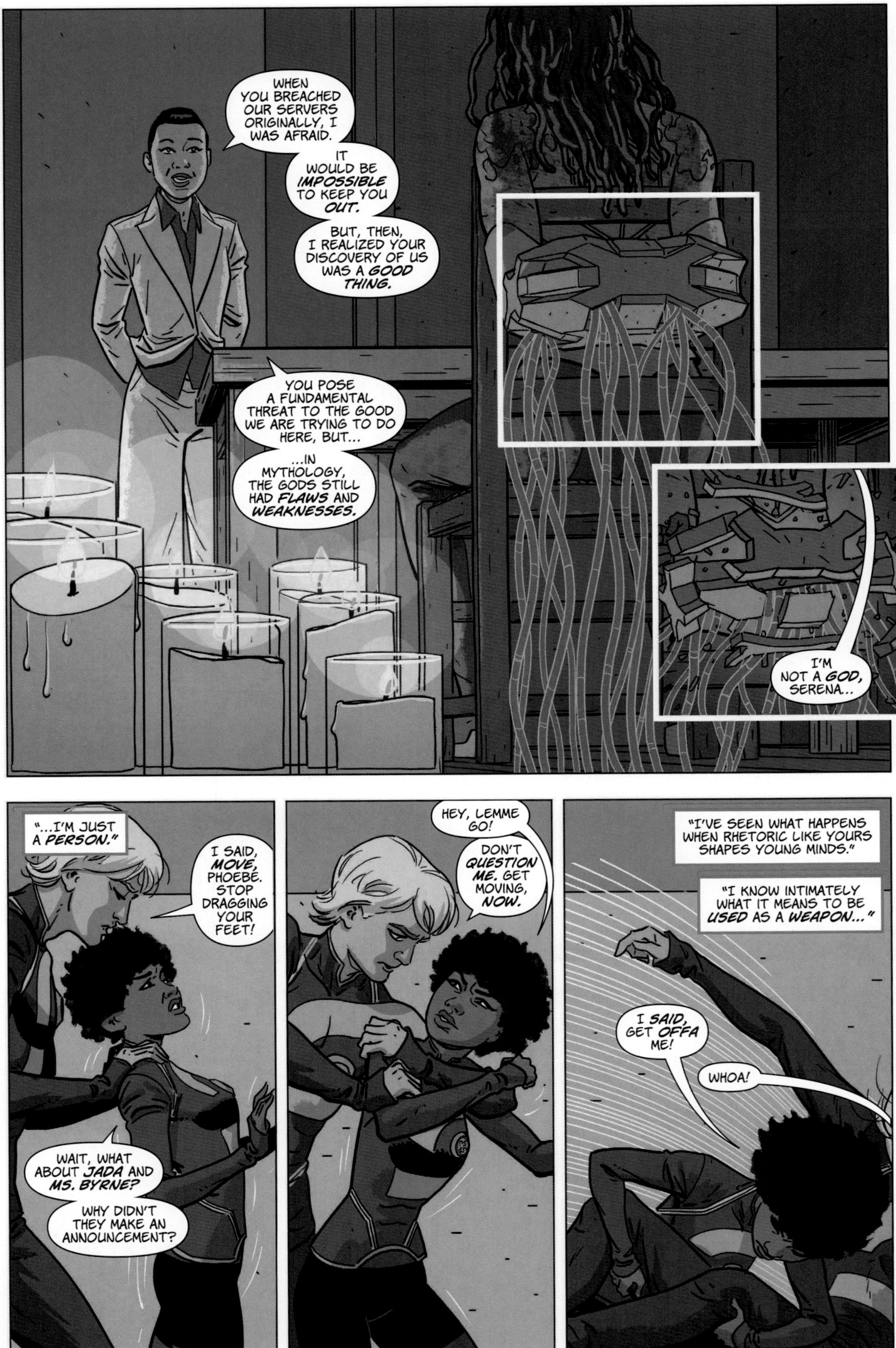
WHEN YOU BREACHED OUR SERVERS ORIGINALLY, I WAS AFRAID.
IT WOULD BE IMPOSSIBLE TO KEEP YOU OUT.
BUT, THEN, I REALIZED YOUR DISCOVERY OF US WAS A GOOD THING.
YOU POSE A FUNDAMENTAL THREAT TO THE GOOD WE ARE TRYING TO DO HERE, BUT...
...IN MYTHOLOGY, THE GODS STILL HAD FLAWS AND WEAKNESSES.
I'M NOT A GOD, SERENA...
"...I'M JUST A PERSON."
I SAID, MOVE, PHOEBE. STOP DRAGGING YOUR FEET!
WAIT, WHAT ABOUT JADA AND MS. BYRNE?
WHY DIDN'T THEY MAKE AN ANNOUNCEMENT?
HEY, LEMME GO!
DON'T QUESTION ME. GET MOVING, NOW.
"I'VE SEEN WHAT HAPPENS WHEN RHETORIC LIKE YOURS SHAPES YOUNG MINDS."
"I KNOW INTIMATELY WHAT IT MEANS TO BE USED AS A WEAPON..."
I SAID, GET OFFA ME!
WHOA!

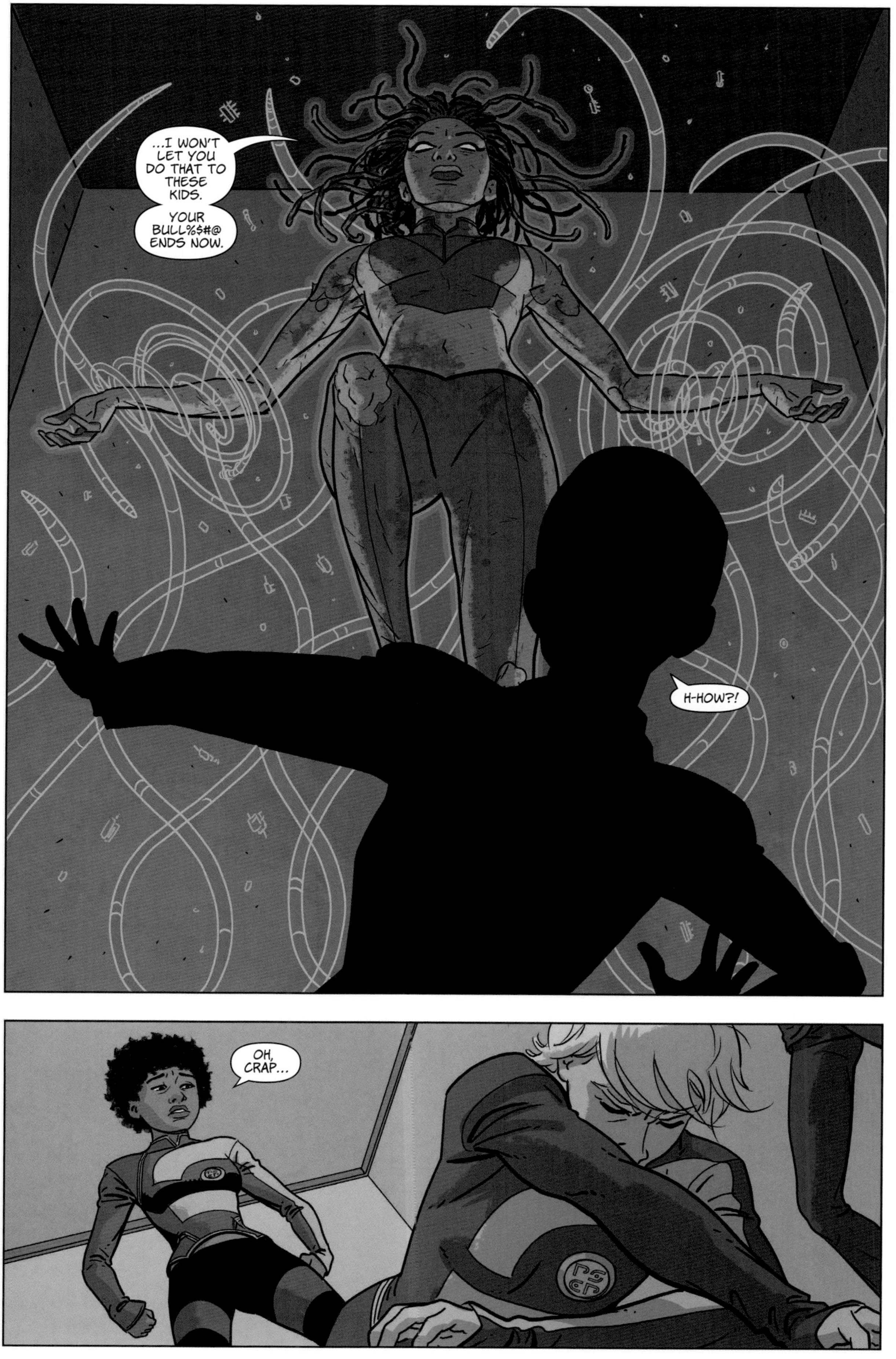
...I WON'T LET YOU DO THAT TO THESE KIDS.
YOUR BULL%$#@ ENDS NOW.
H-HOW?!
OH, CRAP...

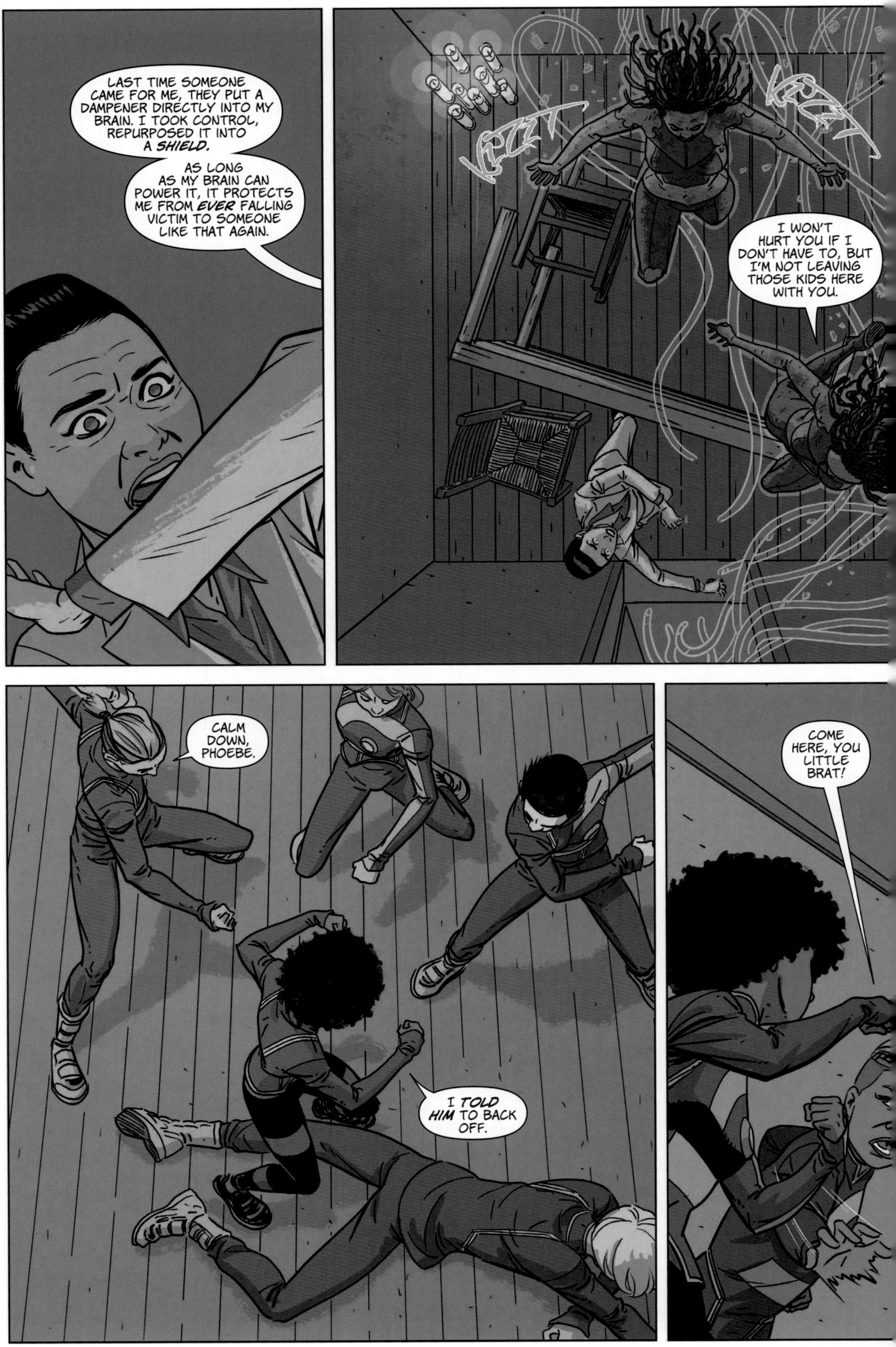
LAST TIME SOMEONE CAME FOR ME, THEY PUT A DAMPENER DIRECTLY INTO MY BRAIN. I TOOK CONTROL, REPURPOSED IT INTO A *SHIELD.*
AS LONG AS MY BRAIN CAN POWER IT, IT PROTECTS ME FROM *EVER* FALLING VICTIM TO SOMEONE LIKE THAT AGAIN.
VZZZT
KZZZT
I WON'T HURT YOU IF I DON'T HAVE TO, BUT I'M NOT LEAVING THOSE KIDS HERE WITH YOU.
CALM DOWN, PHOEBE.
I *TOLD HIM* TO BACK OFF.
COME HERE, YOU LITTLE BRAT!

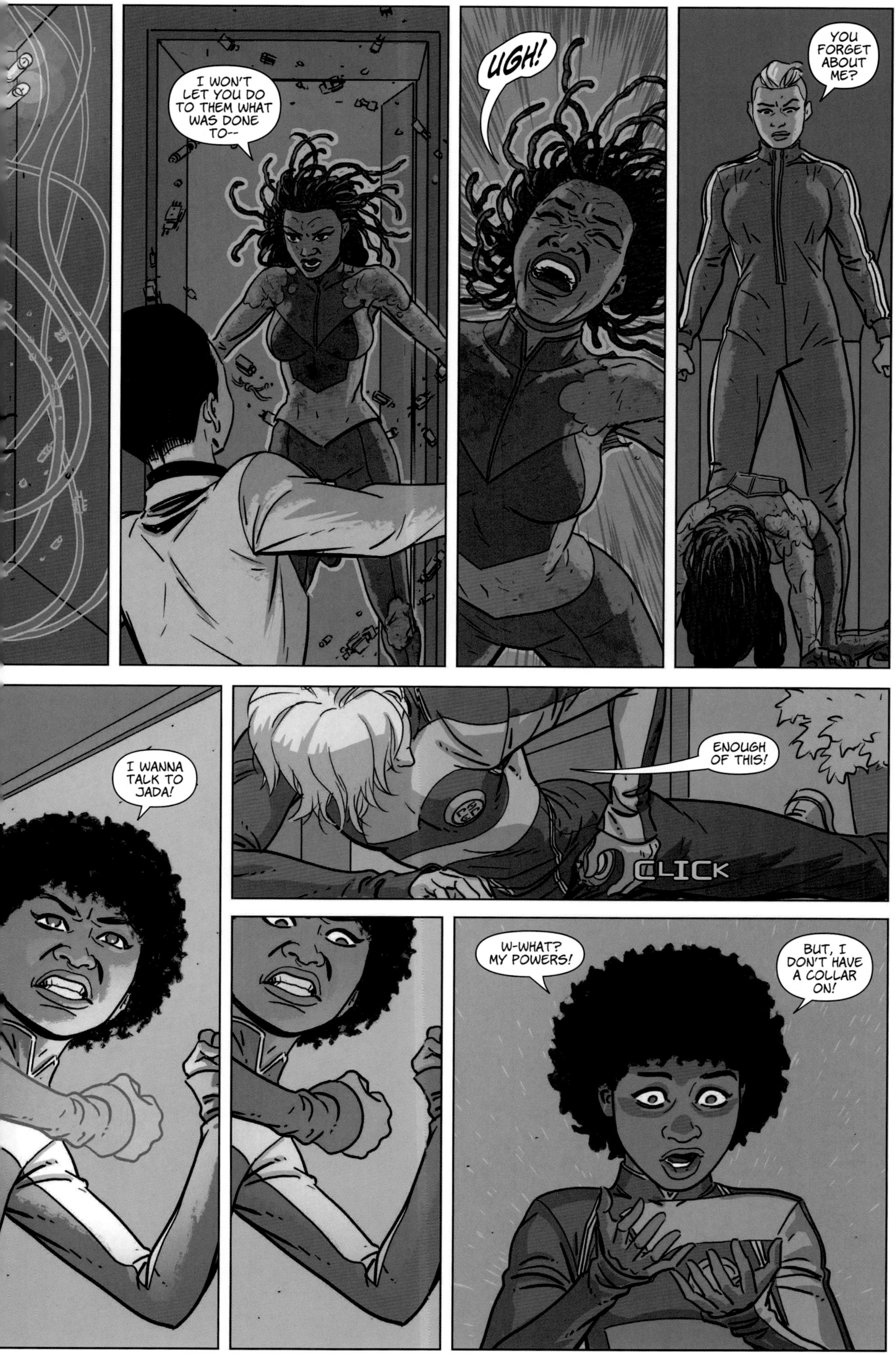
I WON'T LET YOU DO TO THEM WHAT WAS DONE TO--
UGH!
YOU FORGET ABOUT ME?
I WANNA TALK TO JADA!
ENOUGH OF THIS!
CLICK
W-WHAT? MY POWERS!
BUT, I DON'T HAVE A COLLAR ON!

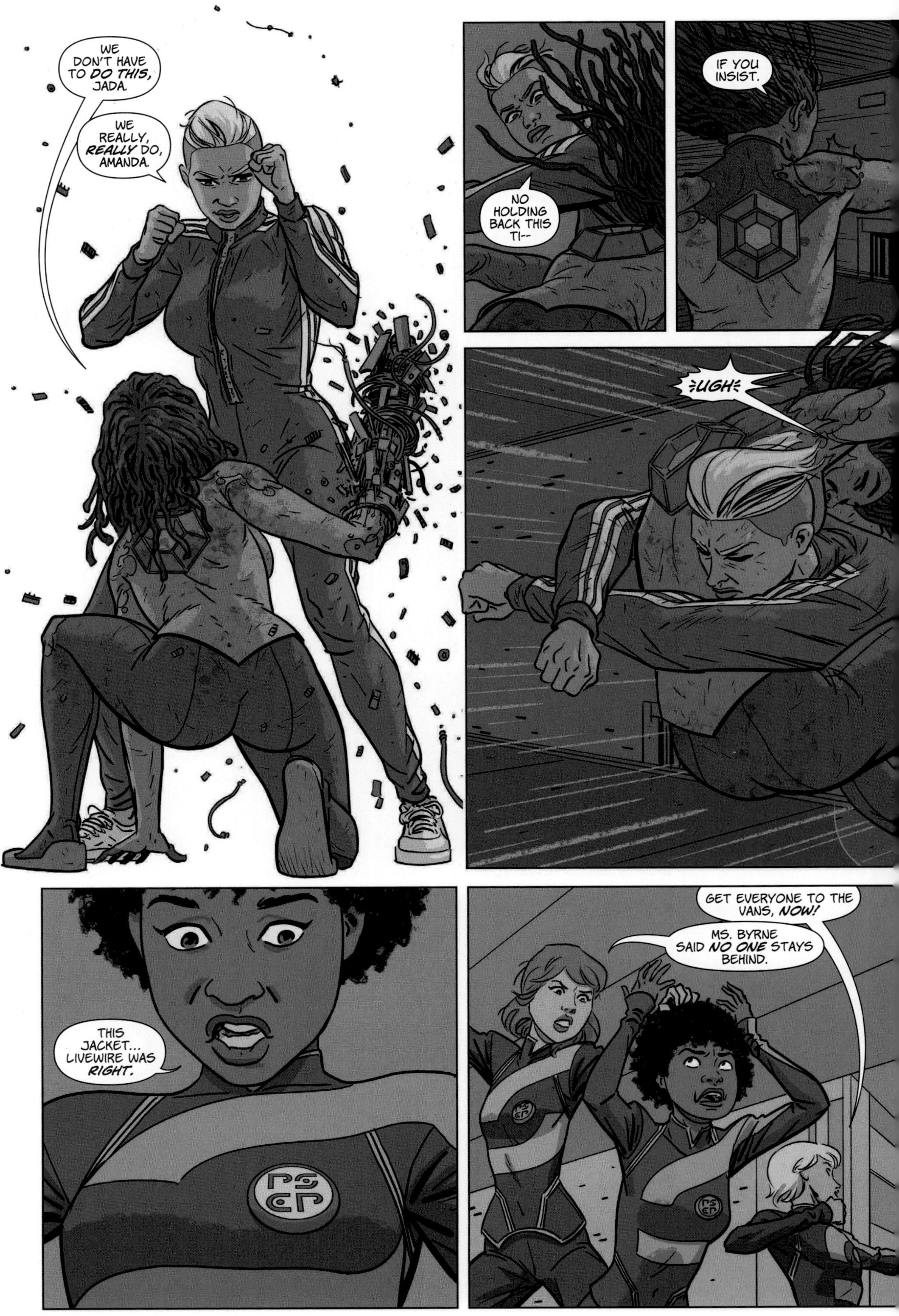
WE DON'T HAVE TO DO THIS, JADA.
WE REALLY, REALLY DO, AMANDA.
NO HOLDING BACK THIS TI--
IF YOU INSIST.
UGH
THIS JACKET... LIVEWIRE WAS RIGHT.
GET EVERYONE TO THE VANS, NOW!
MS. BYRNE SAID NO ONE STAYS BEHIND.

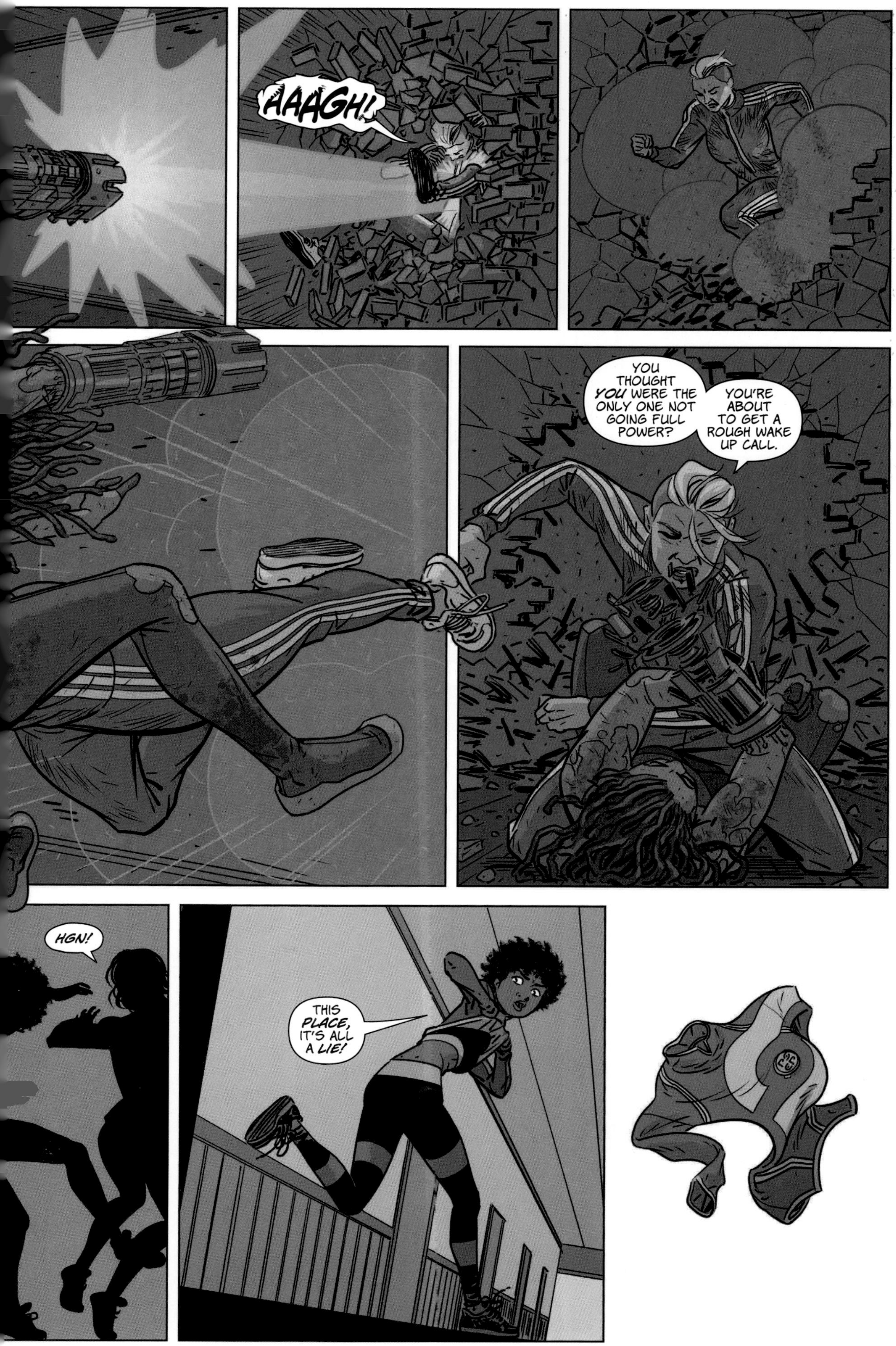
AAAGH!
YOU THOUGHT YOU WERE THE ONLY ONE NOT GOING FULL POWER?
YOU'RE ABOUT TO GET A ROUGH WAKE UP CALL.
HGN!
THIS PLACE, IT'S ALL A LIE!

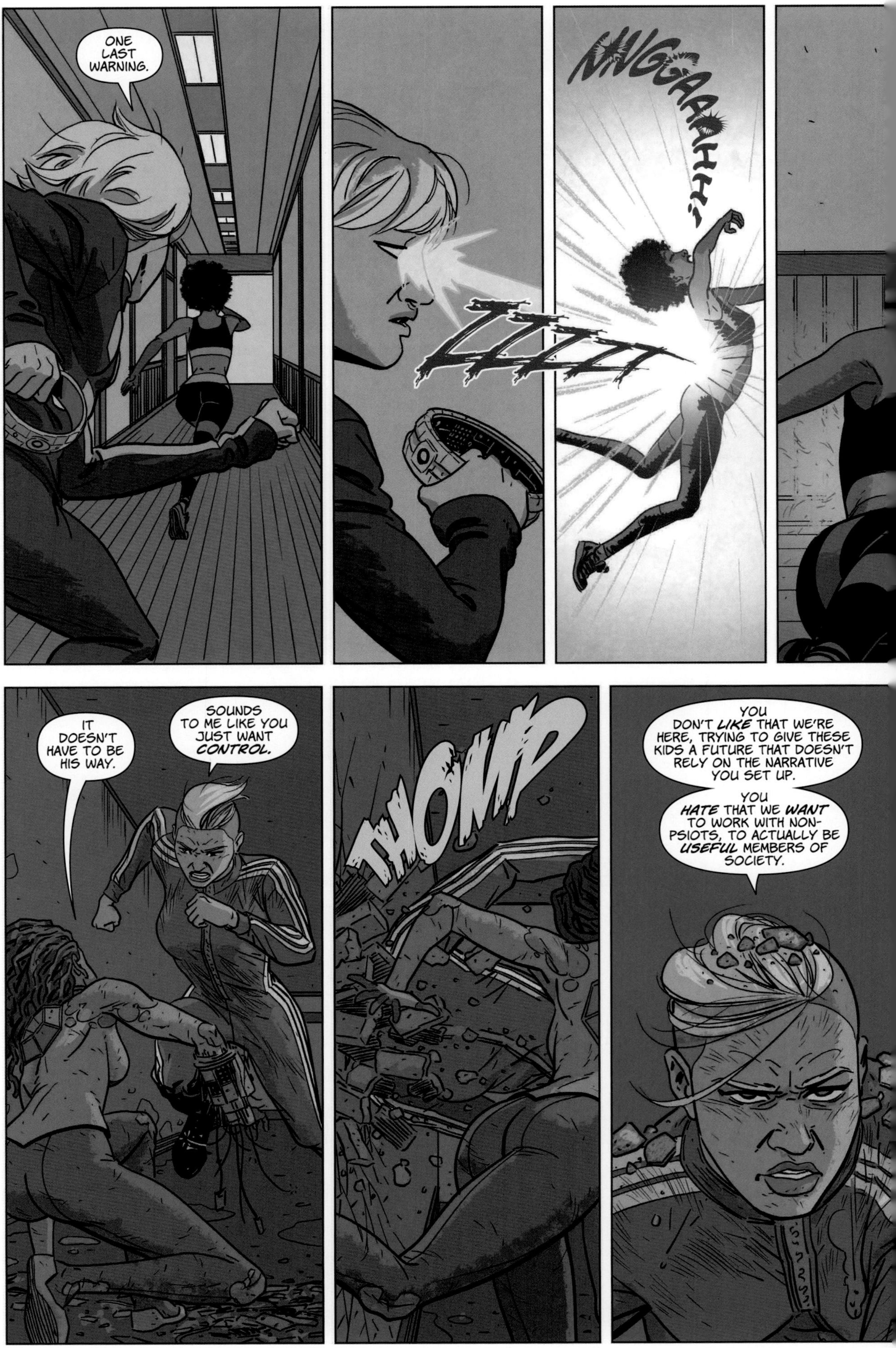
ONE LAST WARNING.
ZZZZT
NNGGAAAHHH!!
IT DOESN'T HAVE TO BE HIS WAY.
SOUNDS TO ME LIKE YOU JUST WANT CONTROL.
THOMP
YOU DON'T LIKE THAT WE'RE HERE, TRYING TO GIVE THESE KIDS A FUTURE THAT DOESN'T RELY ON THE NARRATIVE YOU SET UP.
YOU HATE THAT WE WANT TO WORK WITH NON-PSIOTS, TO ACTUALLY BE USEFUL MEMBERS OF SOCIETY.

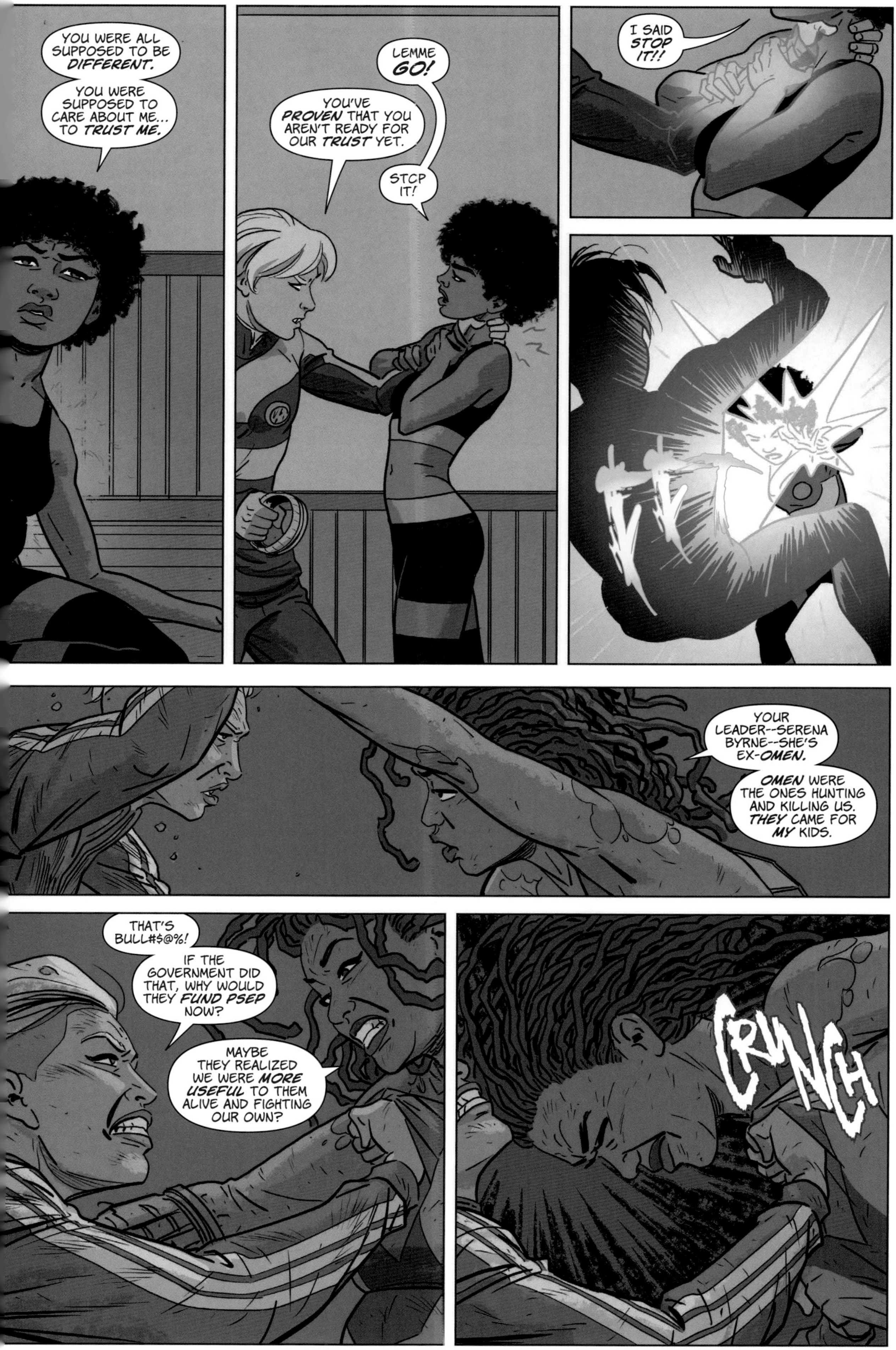

YOU WERE ALL SUPPOSED TO BE *DIFFERENT.*
YOU WERE SUPPOSED TO CARE ABOUT ME... TO *TRUST ME.*
LEMME *GO!*
YOU'VE *PROVEN* THAT YOU AREN'T READY FOR OUR *TRUST* YET.
STCP IT!
I SAID *STOP IT!!*
YOUR LEADER--SERENA BYRNE--SHE'S EX-*OMEN.*
OMEN WERE THE ONES HUNTING AND KILLING US. *THEY* CAME FOR *MY* KIDS.
THAT'S BULL#$@%!
IF THE GOVERNMENT DID THAT, WHY WOULD THEY *FUND PSEP* NOW?
MAYBE THEY REALIZED WE WERE *MORE USEFUL* TO THEM ALIVE AND FIGHTING OUR OWN?
CRUNCH

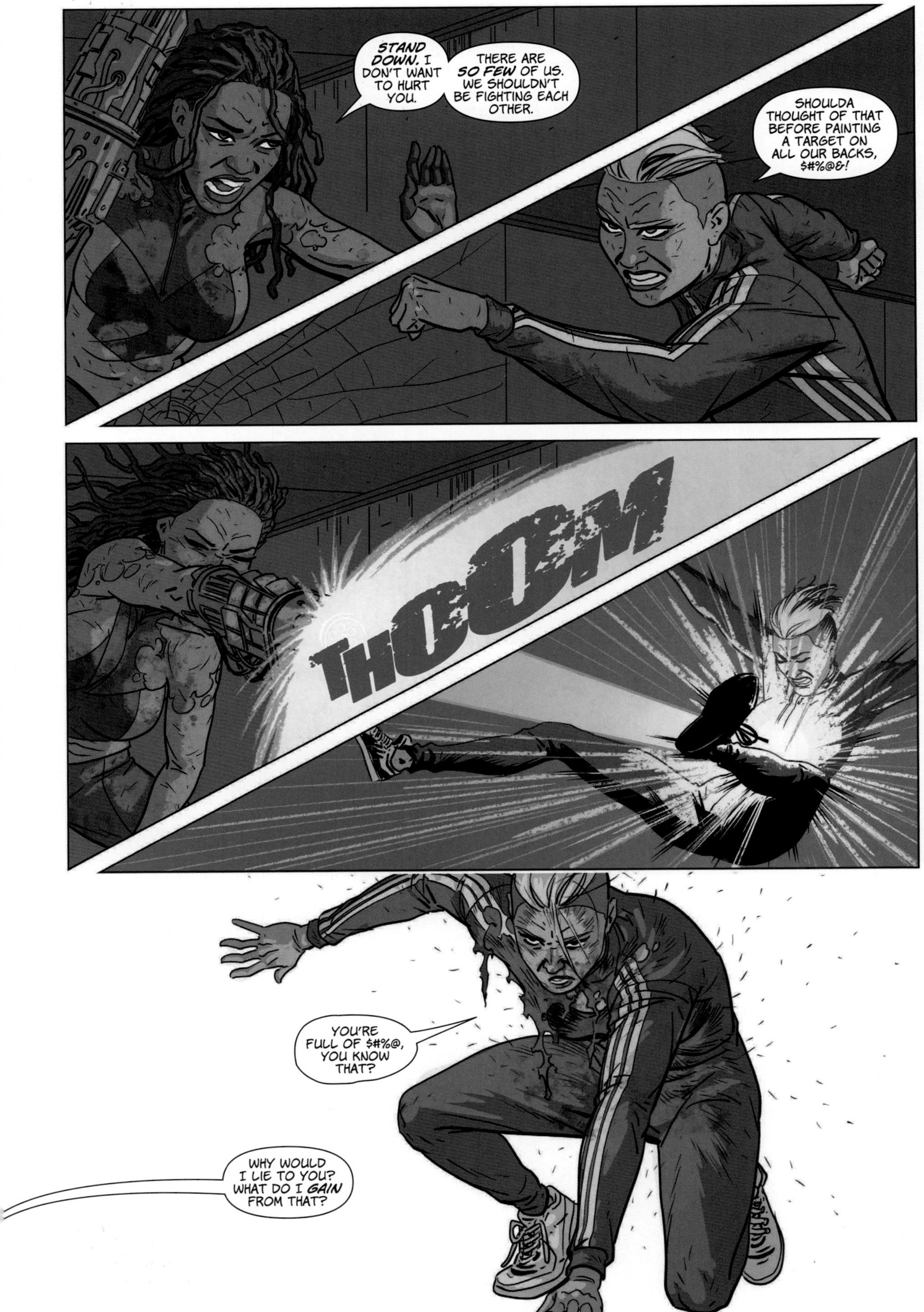
STAND DOWN. I DON'T WANT TO HURT YOU.
THERE ARE SO FEW OF US. WE SHOULDN'T BE FIGHTING EACH OTHER.
SHOULDA THOUGHT OF THAT BEFORE PAINTING A TARGET ON ALL OUR BACKS, $#%@&!
THOOM
YOU'RE FULL OF $#%@, YOU KNOW THAT?
WHY WOULD I LIE TO YOU? WHAT DO I GAIN FROM THAT?

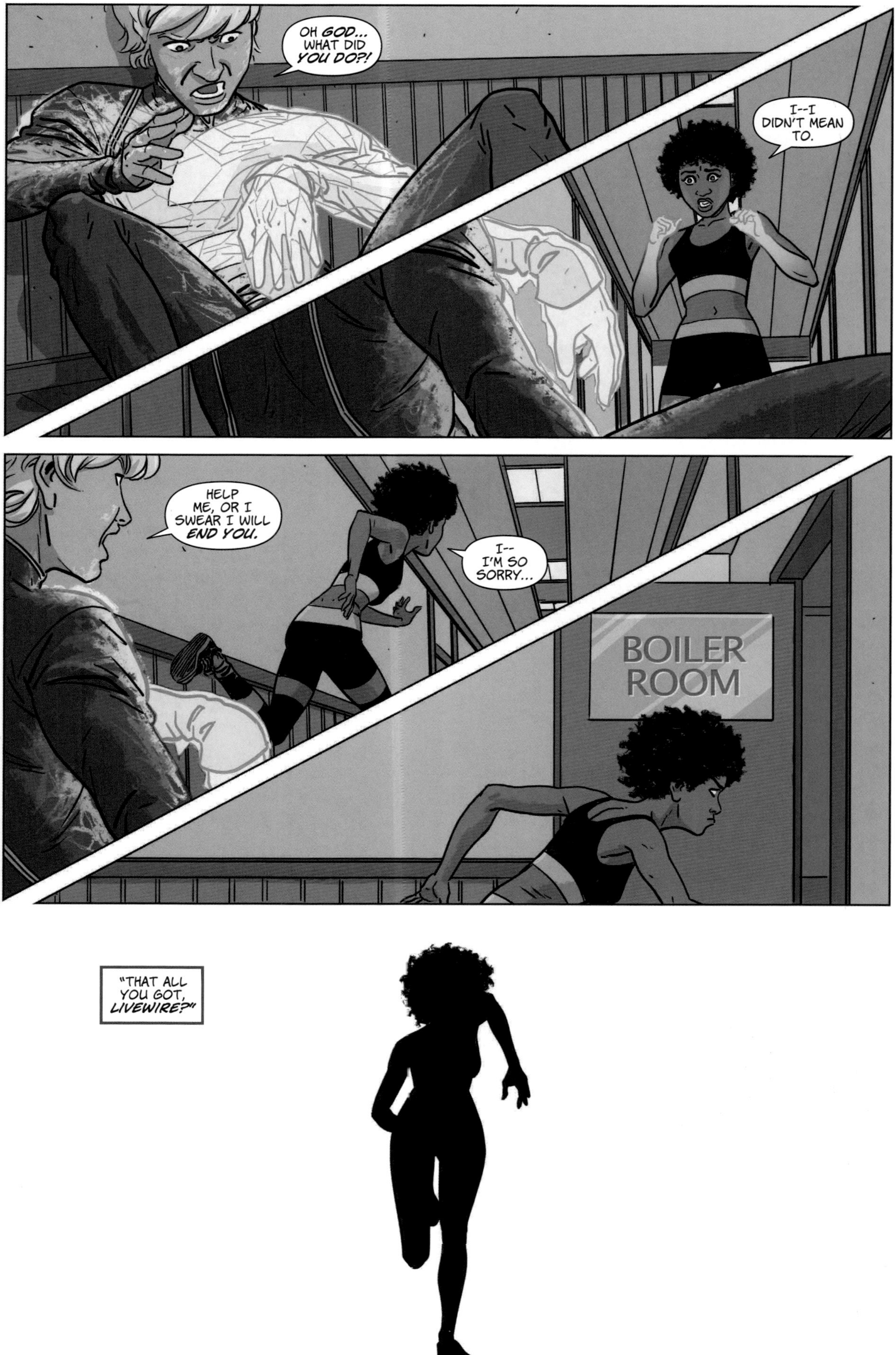
OH GOD... WHAT DID YOU DO?!
I--I DIDN'T MEAN TO.
HELP ME, OR I SWEAR I WILL END YOU.
I-- I'M SO SORRY...
BOILER ROOM
"THAT ALL YOU GOT, LIVEWIRE?"

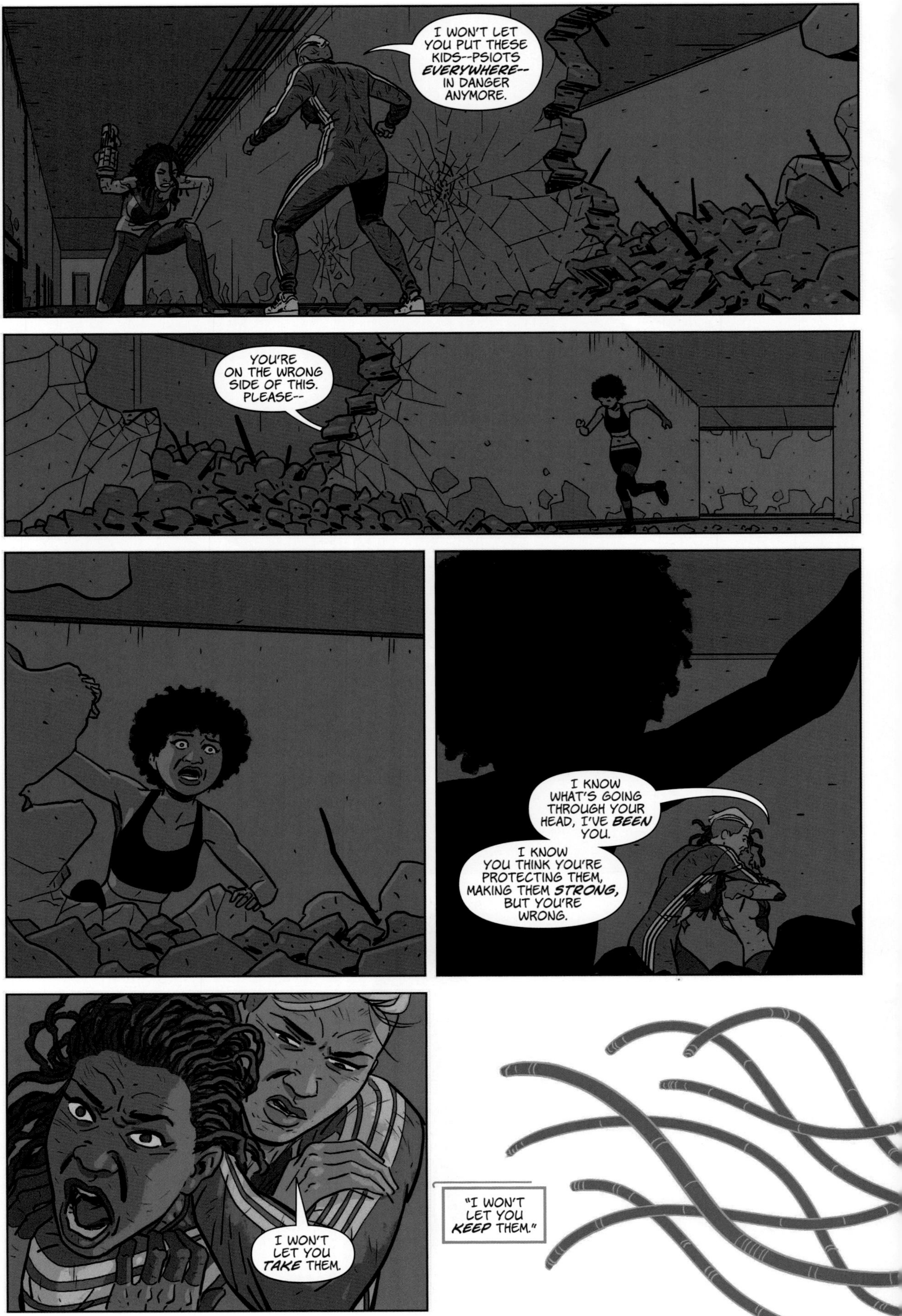
I WON'T LET YOU PUT THESE KIDS--PSIOTS EVERYWHERE-- IN DANGER ANYMORE.
YOU'RE ON THE WRONG SIDE OF THIS. PLEASE--
I KNOW WHAT'S GOING THROUGH YOUR HEAD, I'VE BEEN YOU.
I KNOW YOU THINK YOU'RE PROTECTING THEM, MAKING THEM STRONG, BUT YOU'RE WRONG.
I WON'T LET YOU TAKE THEM.
"I WON'T LET YOU KEEP THEM."

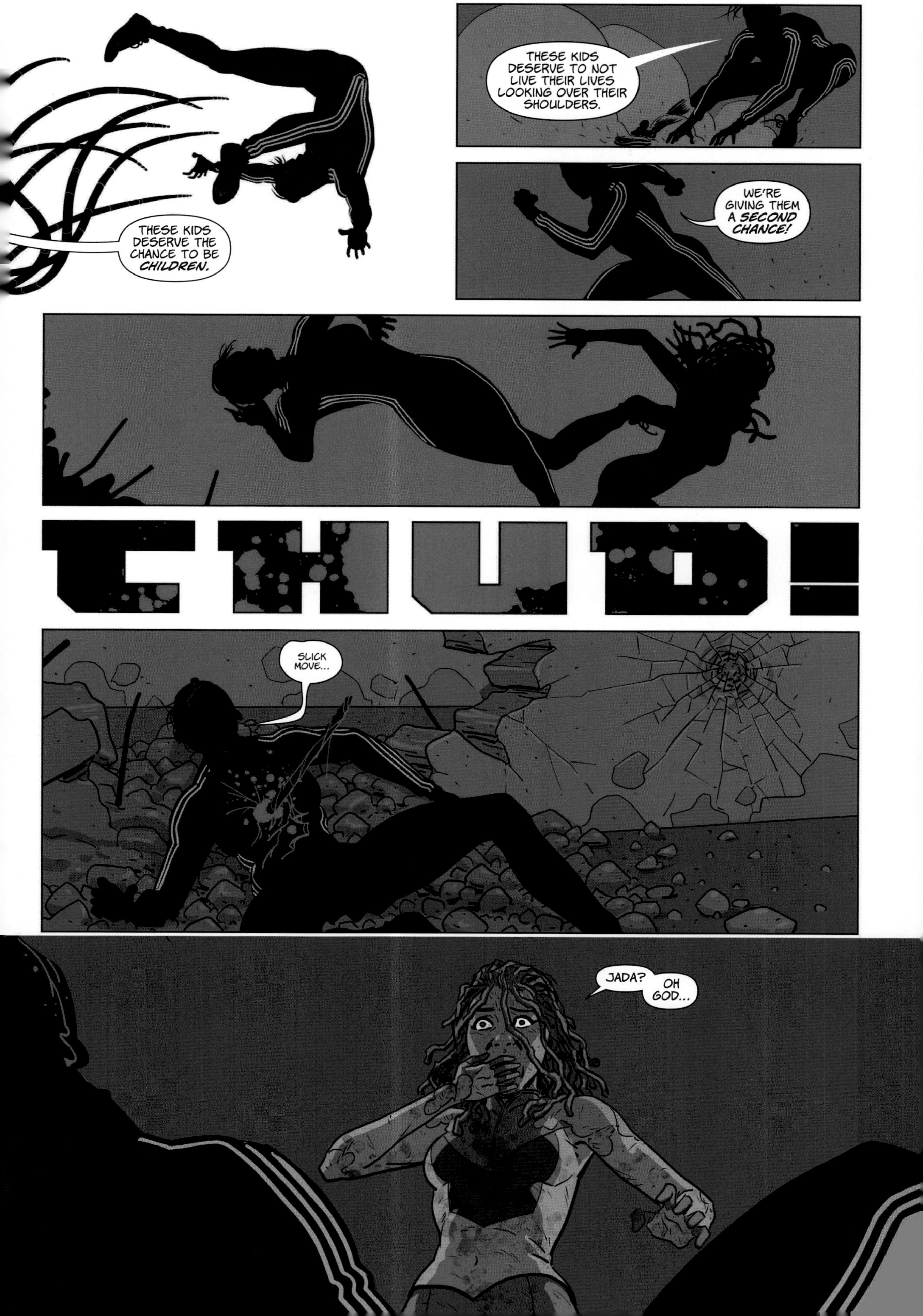

THESE KIDS DESERVE THE CHANCE TO BE *CHILDREN.*
THESE KIDS DESERVE TO NOT LIVE THEIR LIVES LOOKING OVER THEIR SHOULDERS.
WE'RE GIVING THEM A *SECOND CHANCE!*
THUD!
SLICK MOVE...
JADA?
OH GOD...

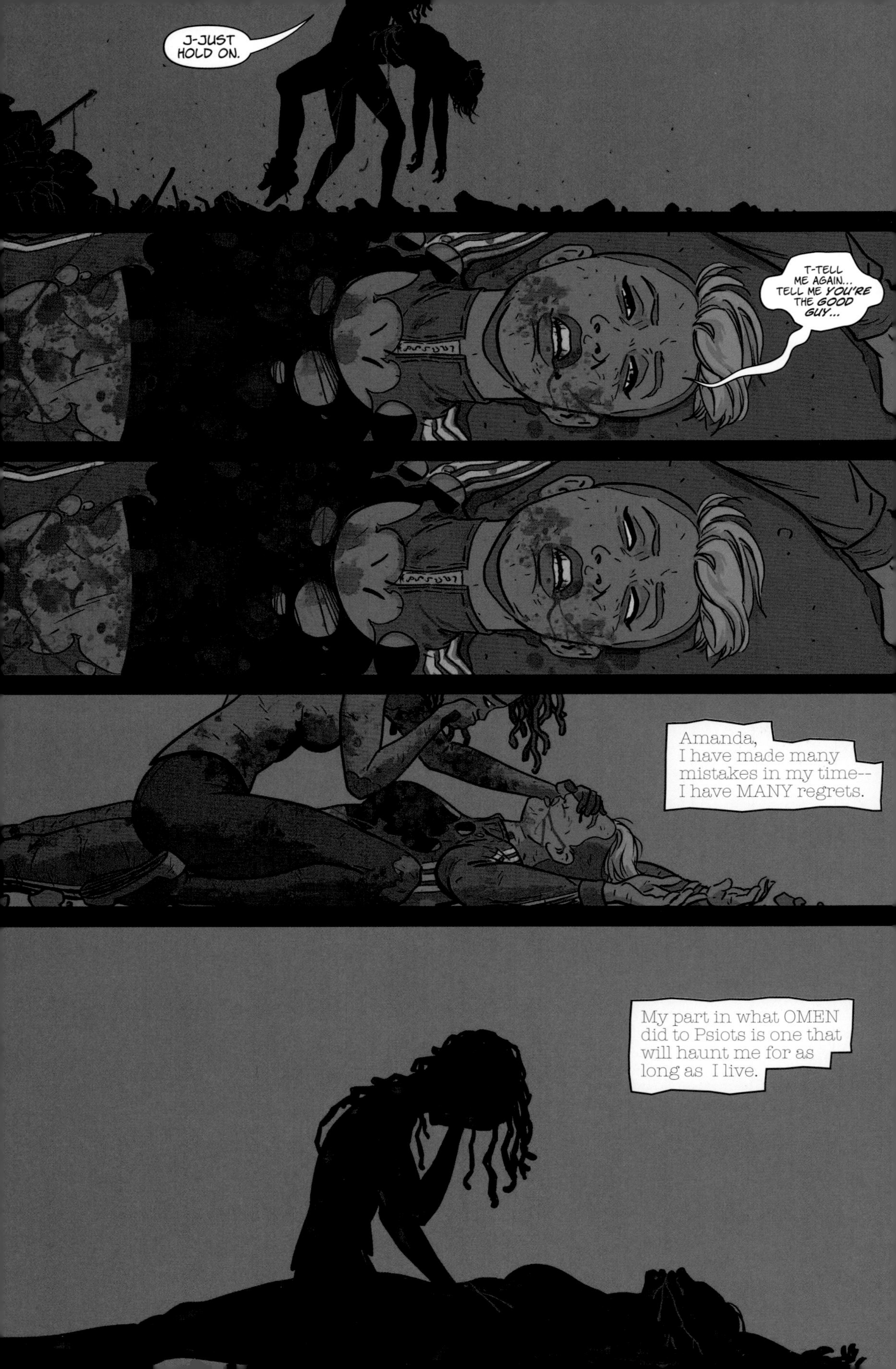
J-JUST HOLD ON.
T-TELL ME AGAIN... TELL ME YOU'RE THE GOOD GUY...
Amanda, I have made many mistakes in my time-- I have MANY regrets.
My part in what OMEN did to Psiots is one that will haunt me for as long as I live.

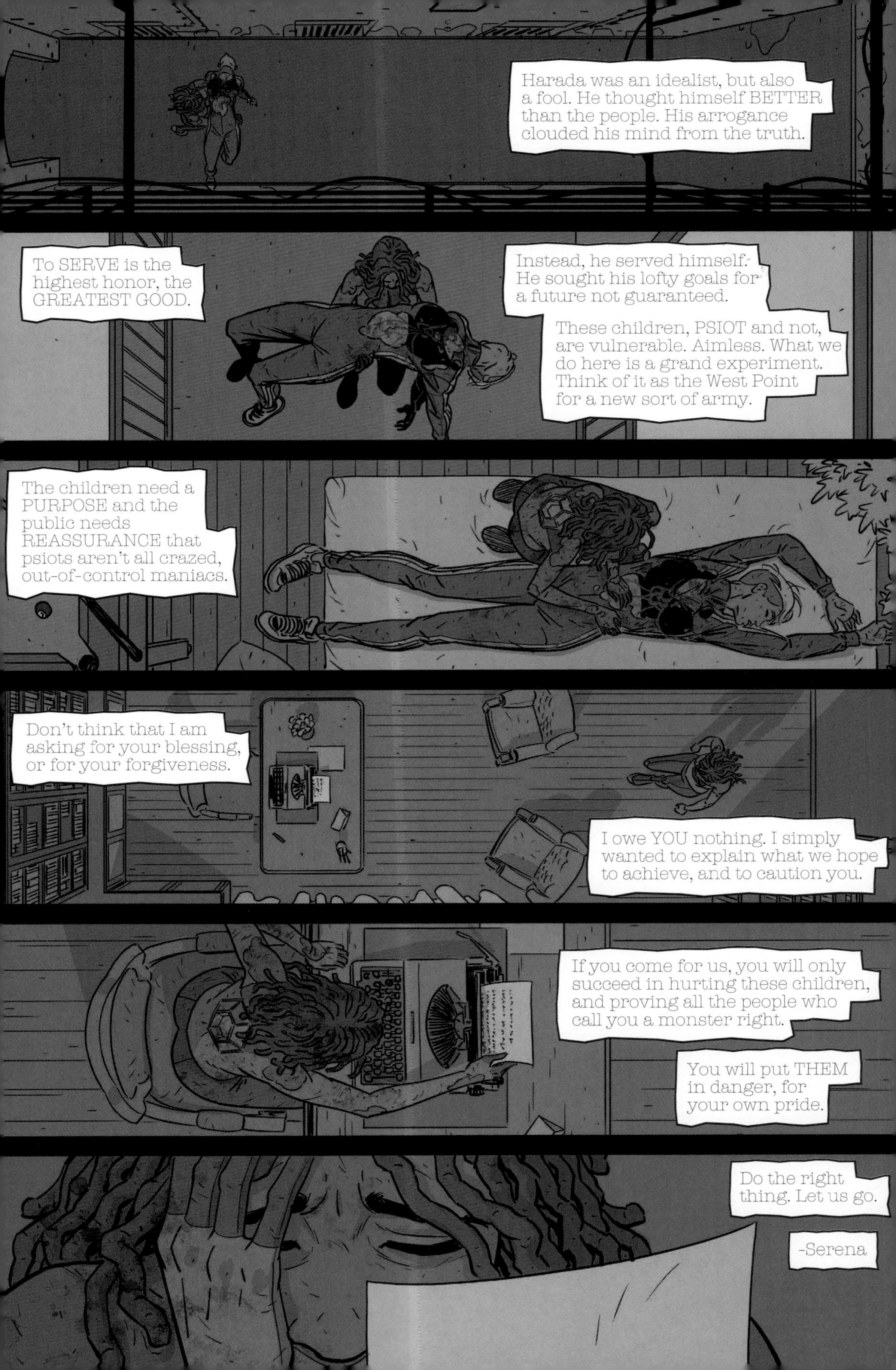
Harada was an idealist, but also a fool. He thought himself BETTER than the people. His arrogance clouded his mind from the truth.
To SERVE is the highest honor, the GREATEST GOOD.
Instead, he served himself. He sought his lofty goals for a future not guaranteed.
These children, PSIOT and not, are vulnerable. Aimless. What we do here is a grand experiment. Think of it as the West Point for a new sort of army.
The children need a PURPOSE and the public needs REASSURANCE that psiots aren't all crazed, out-of-control maniacs.
Don't think that I am asking for your blessing, or for your forgiveness.
I owe YOU nothing. I simply wanted to explain what we hope to achieve, and to caution you.
If you come for us, you will only succeed in hurting these children, and proving all the people who call you a monster right.
You will put THEM in danger, for your own pride.
Do the right thing. Let us go.
-Serena

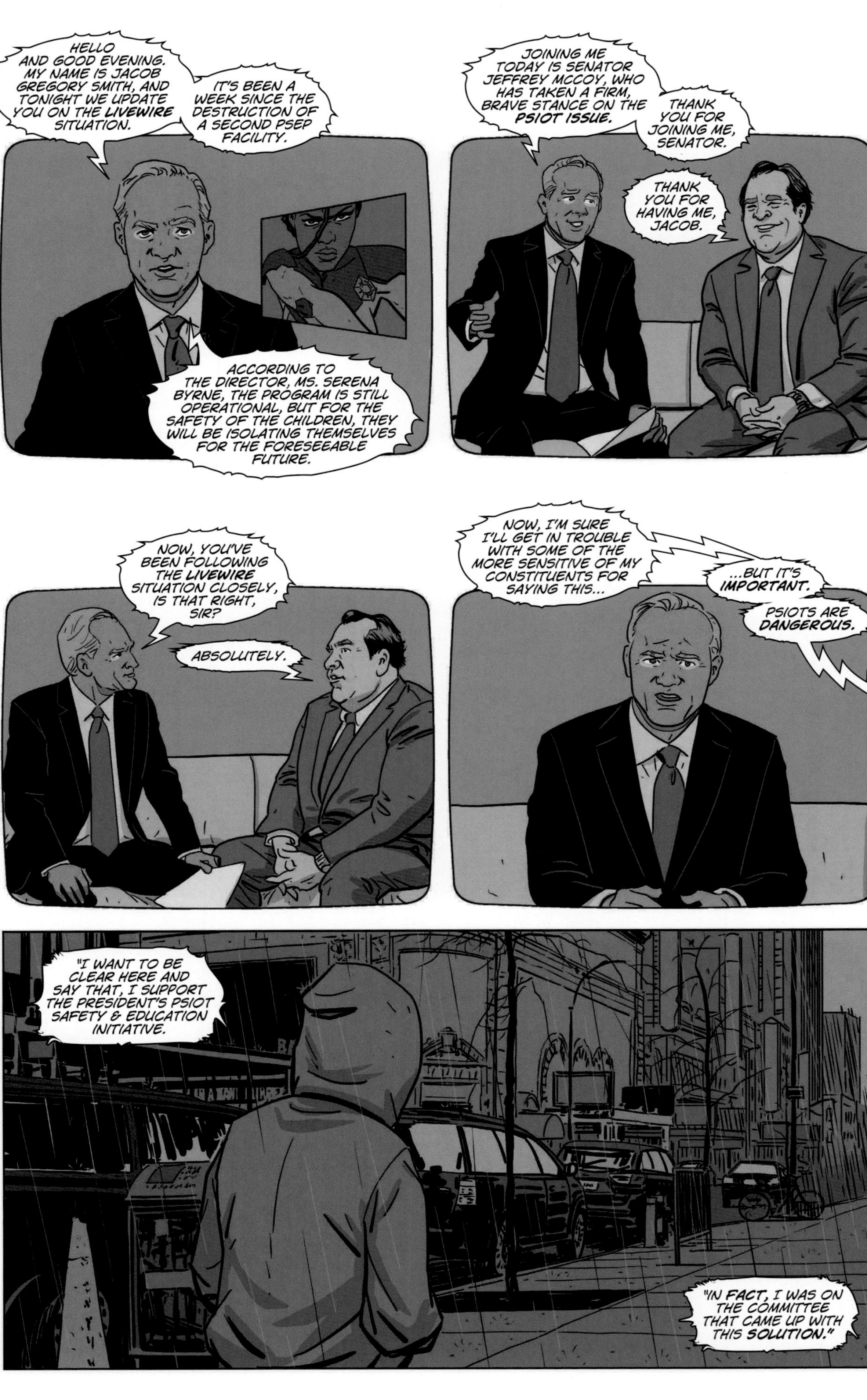
HELLO AND GOOD EVENING. MY NAME IS JACOB GREGORY SMITH, AND TONIGHT WE UPDATE YOU ON THE LIVEWIRE SITUATION.
IT'S BEEN A WEEK SINCE THE DESTRUCTION OF A SECOND PSEP FACILITY.
ACCORDING TO THE DIRECTOR, MS. SERENA BYRNE, THE PROGRAM IS STILL OPERATIONAL, BUT FOR THE SAFETY OF THE CHILDREN, THEY WILL BE ISOLATING THEMSELVES FOR THE FORESEEABLE FUTURE.
JOINING ME TODAY IS SENATOR JEFFREY MCCOY, WHO HAS TAKEN A FIRM, BRAVE STANCE ON THE PSIOT ISSUE.
THANK YOU FOR JOINING ME, SENATOR.
THANK YOU FOR HAVING ME, JACOB.
NOW, YOU'VE BEEN FOLLOWING THE LIVEWIRE SITUATION CLOSELY, IS THAT RIGHT, SIR?
ABSOLUTELY.
NOW, I'M SURE I'LL GET IN TROUBLE WITH SOME OF THE MORE SENSITIVE OF MY CONSTITUENTS FOR SAYING THIS...
...BUT IT'S IMPORTANT.
PSIOTS ARE DANGEROUS.
"I WANT TO BE CLEAR HERE AND SAY THAT, I SUPPORT THE PRESIDENT'S PSIOT SAFETY & EDUCATION INITIATIVE.
"IN FACT, I WAS ON THE COMMITTEE THAT CAME UP WITH THIS SOLUTION."

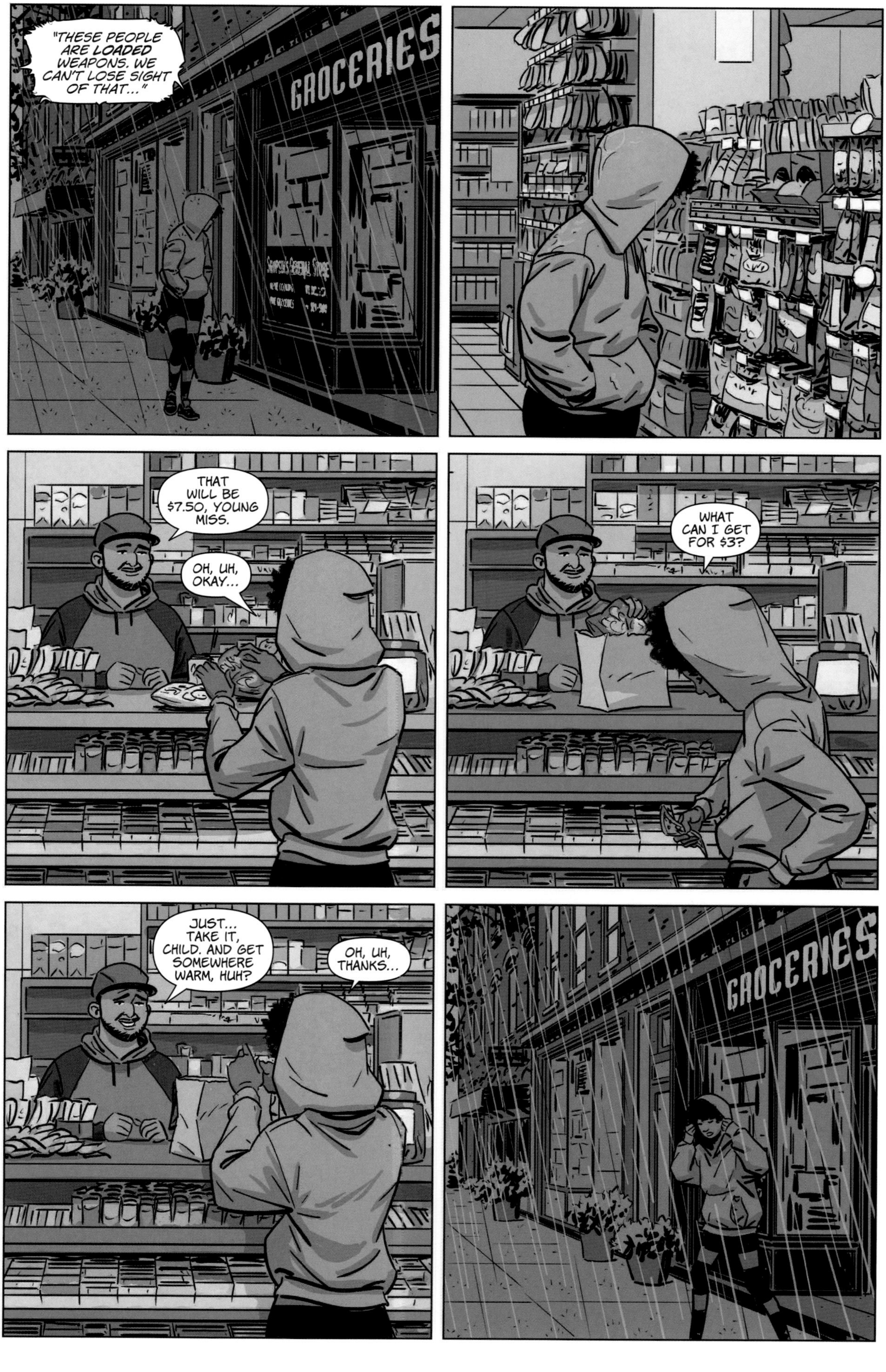
"THESE PEOPLE ARE LOADED WEAPONS. WE CAN'T LOSE SIGHT OF THAT..."
GROCERIES
THAT WILL BE $7.50, YOUNG MISS.
OH, UH, OKAY...
WHAT CAN I GET FOR $3?
JUST... TAKE IT, CHILD. AND GET SOMEWHERE WARM, HUH?
OH, UH, THANKS...
GROCERIES

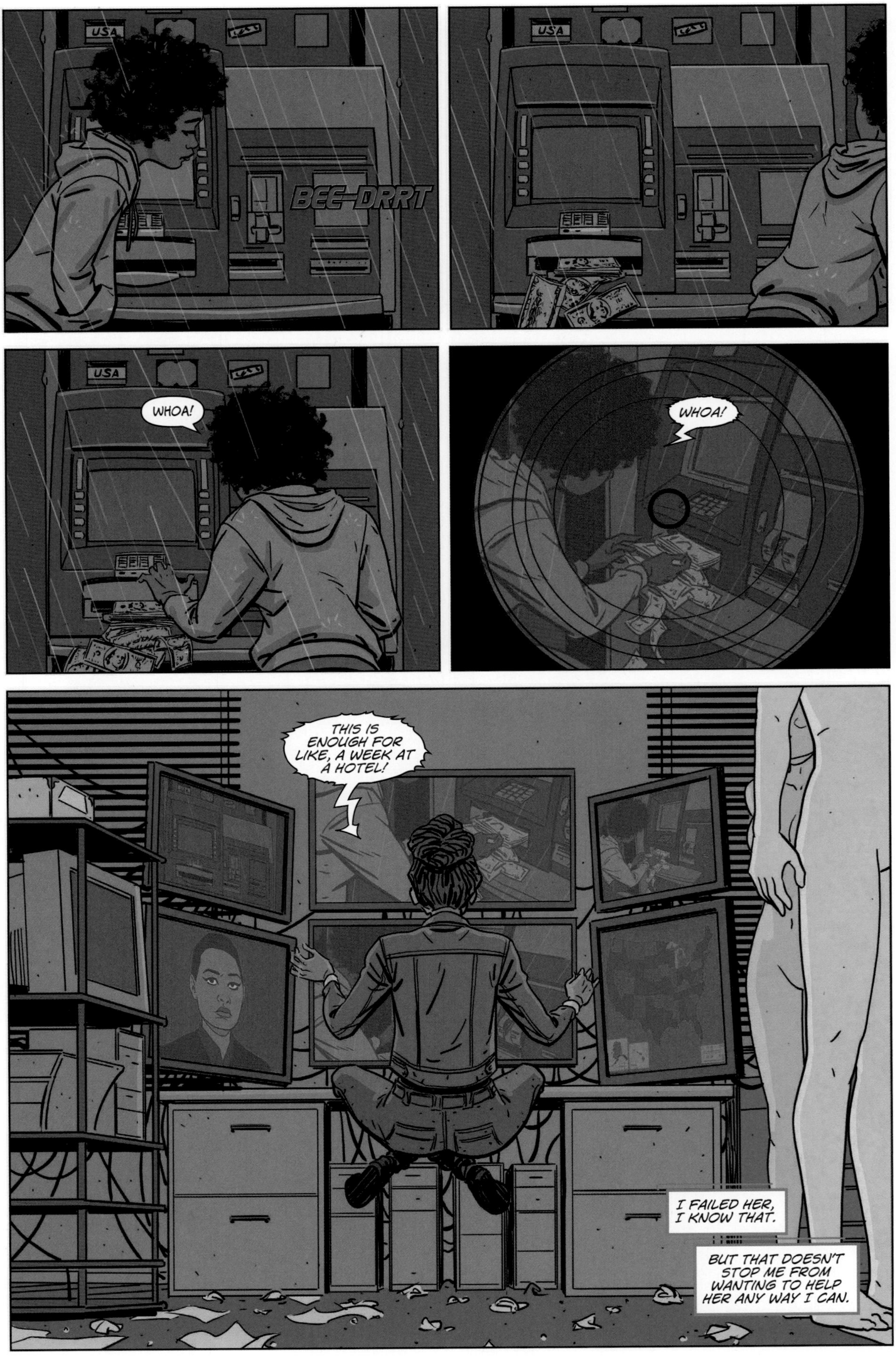
USA
BEE-DRRT
USA
USA
WHOA!
WHOA!
THIS IS ENOUGH FOR LIKE, A WEEK AT A HOTEL!
I FAILED HER, I KNOW THAT.
BUT THAT DOESN'T STOP ME FROM WANTING TO HELP HER ANY WAY I CAN.

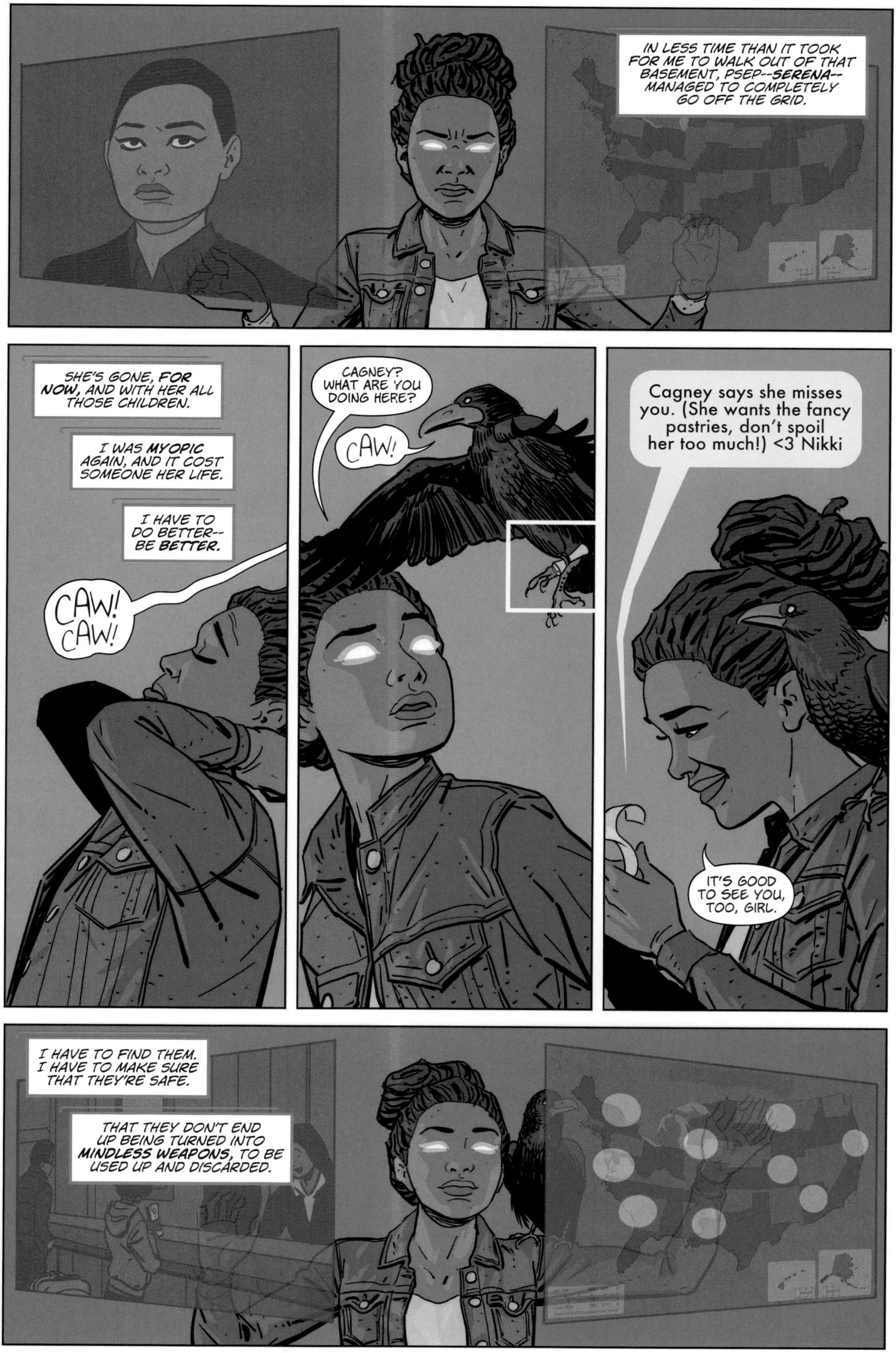
IN LESS TIME THAN IT TOOK FOR ME TO WALK OUT OF THAT BASEMENT, PSEP--SERENA--MANAGED TO COMPLETELY GO OFF THE GRID.
SHE'S GONE, FOR NOW, AND WITH HER ALL THOSE CHILDREN.
I WAS MYOPIC AGAIN, AND IT COST SOMEONE HER LIFE.
I HAVE TO DO BETTER--BE BETTER.
CAW! CAW!
CAGNEY? WHAT ARE YOU DOING HERE?
CAW!
Cagney says she misses you. (She wants the fancy pastries, don't spoil her too much!) <3 Nikki
IT'S GOOD TO SEE YOU, TOO, GIRL.
I HAVE TO FIND THEM. I HAVE TO MAKE SURE THAT THEY'RE SAFE.
THAT THEY DON'T END UP BEING TURNED INTO MINDLESS WEAPONS, TO BE USED UP AND DISCARDED.

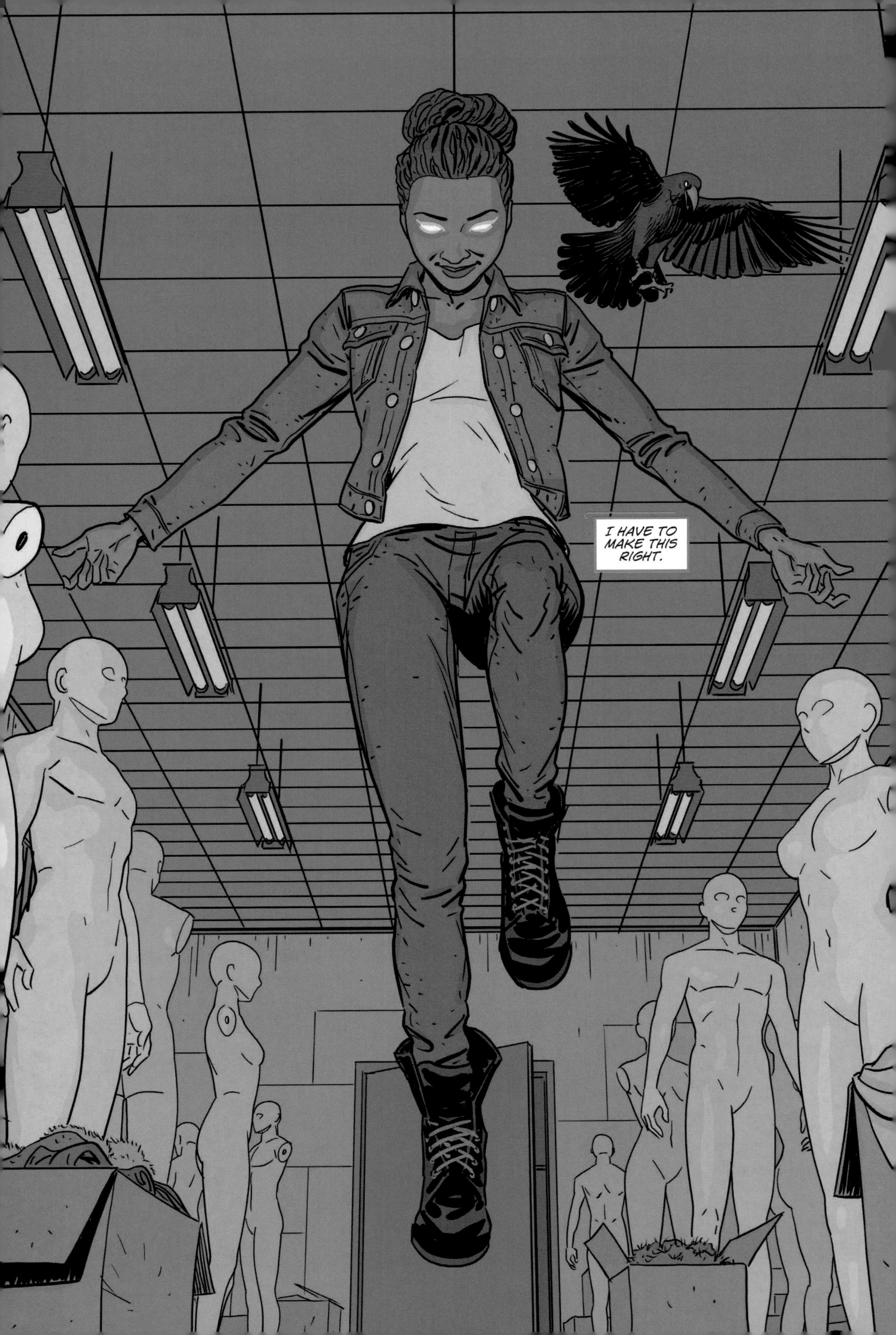
I HAVE TO MAKE THIS RIGHT.

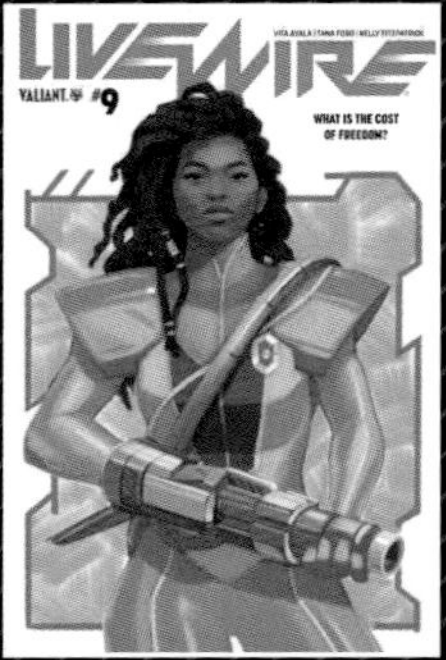
LIVEWIRE
VALIANT
#9
WHAT IS THE COST OF FREEDOM?

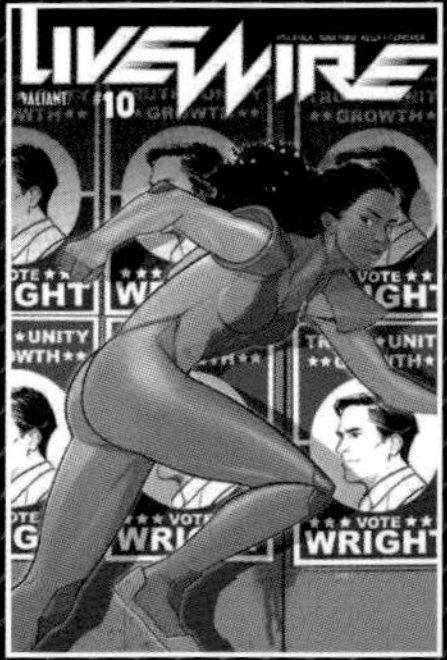
LIVEWIRE
VALIANT
#10
VOTE
WRIGHT

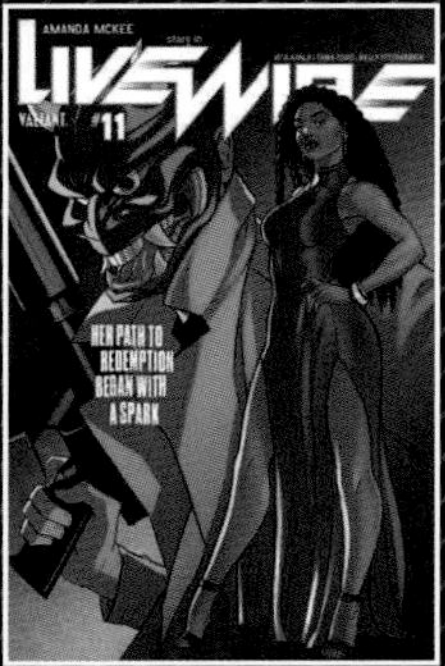
AMANDA MCKEE
LIVEWIRE
VALIANT
#11
HER PATH TO REDEMPTION BEGAN WITH A SPARK

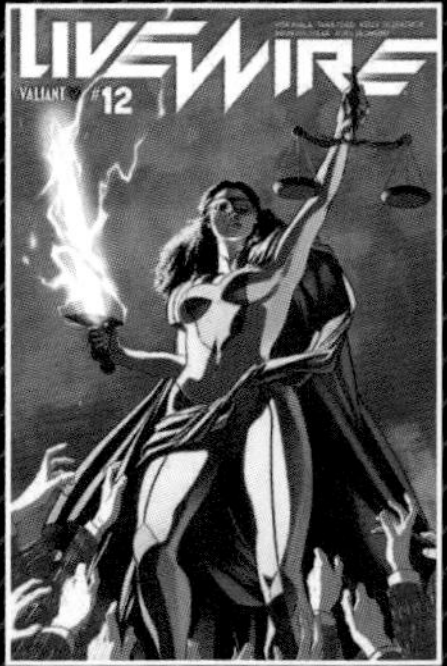
LIVEWIRE
VALIANT
#12

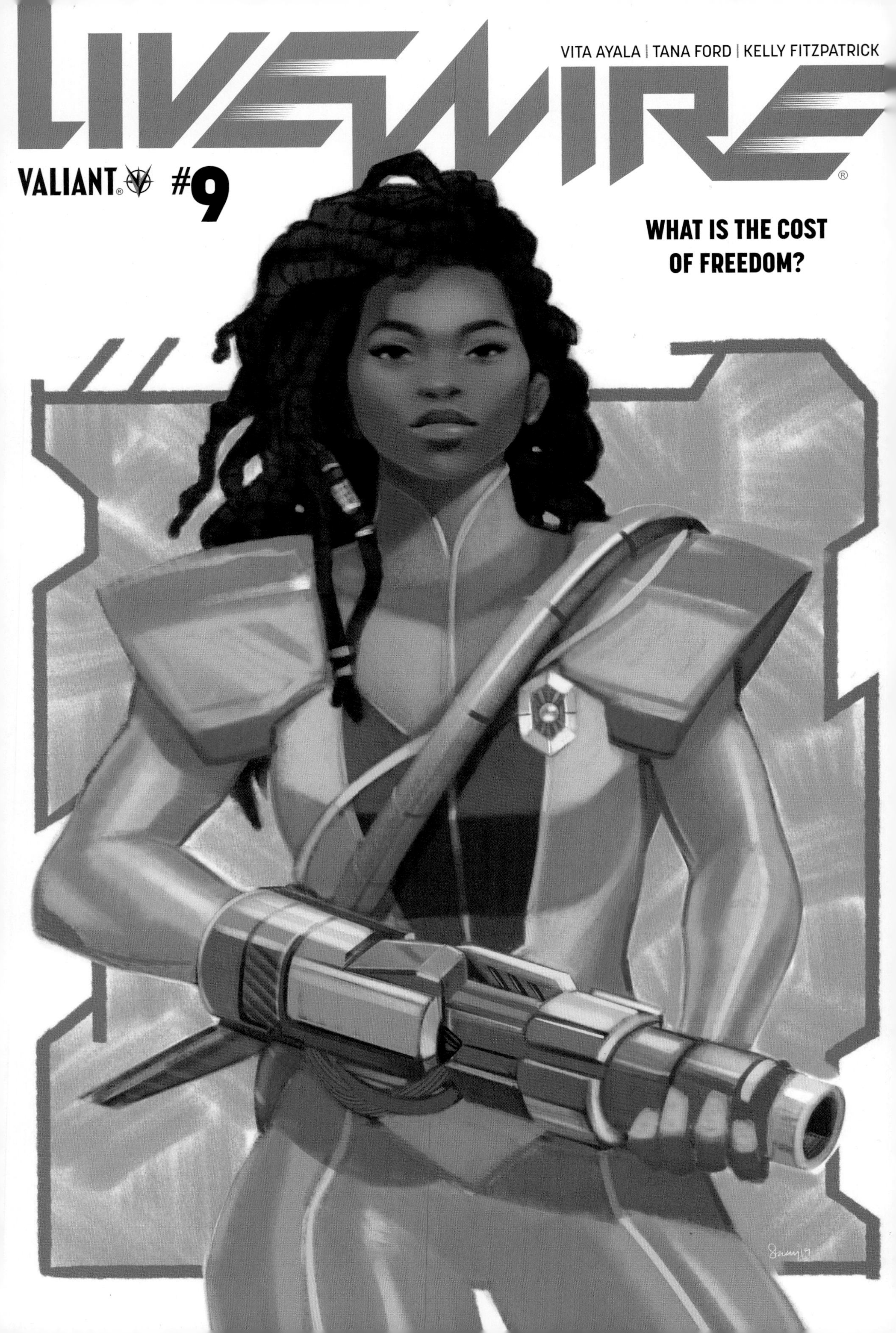

LIVEWIRE
VITA AYALA | TANA FORD | KELLY FITZPATRICK
VALIANT
#9
WHAT IS THE COST
OF FREEDOM?

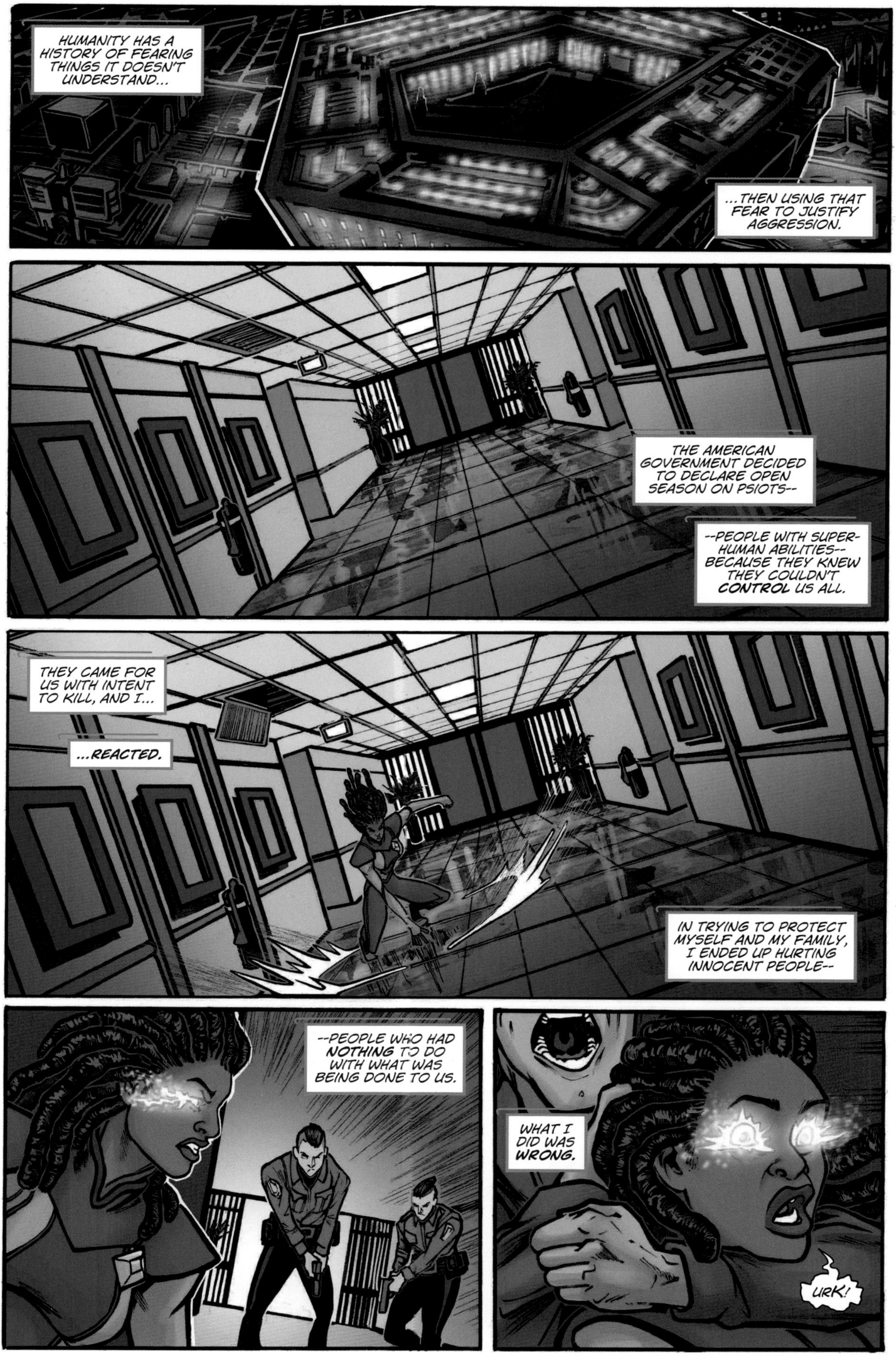
HUMANITY HAS A HISTORY OF FEARING THINGS IT DOESN'T UNDERSTAND...
...THEN USING THAT FEAR TO JUSTIFY AGGRESSION.
THE AMERICAN GOVERNMENT DECIDED TO DECLARE OPEN SEASON ON PSIOTS--
--PEOPLE WITH SUPER-HUMAN ABILITIES--BECAUSE THEY KNEW THEY COULDN'T **CONTROL** US ALL.
THEY CAME FOR US WITH INTENT TO KILL, AND I...
...**REACTED.**
IN TRYING TO PROTECT MYSELF AND MY FAMILY, I ENDED UP HURTING INNOCENT PEOPLE--
--PEOPLE WHO HAD **NOTHING** TO DO WITH WHAT WAS BEING DONE TO US.
WHAT I DID WAS **WRONG.**
URK!

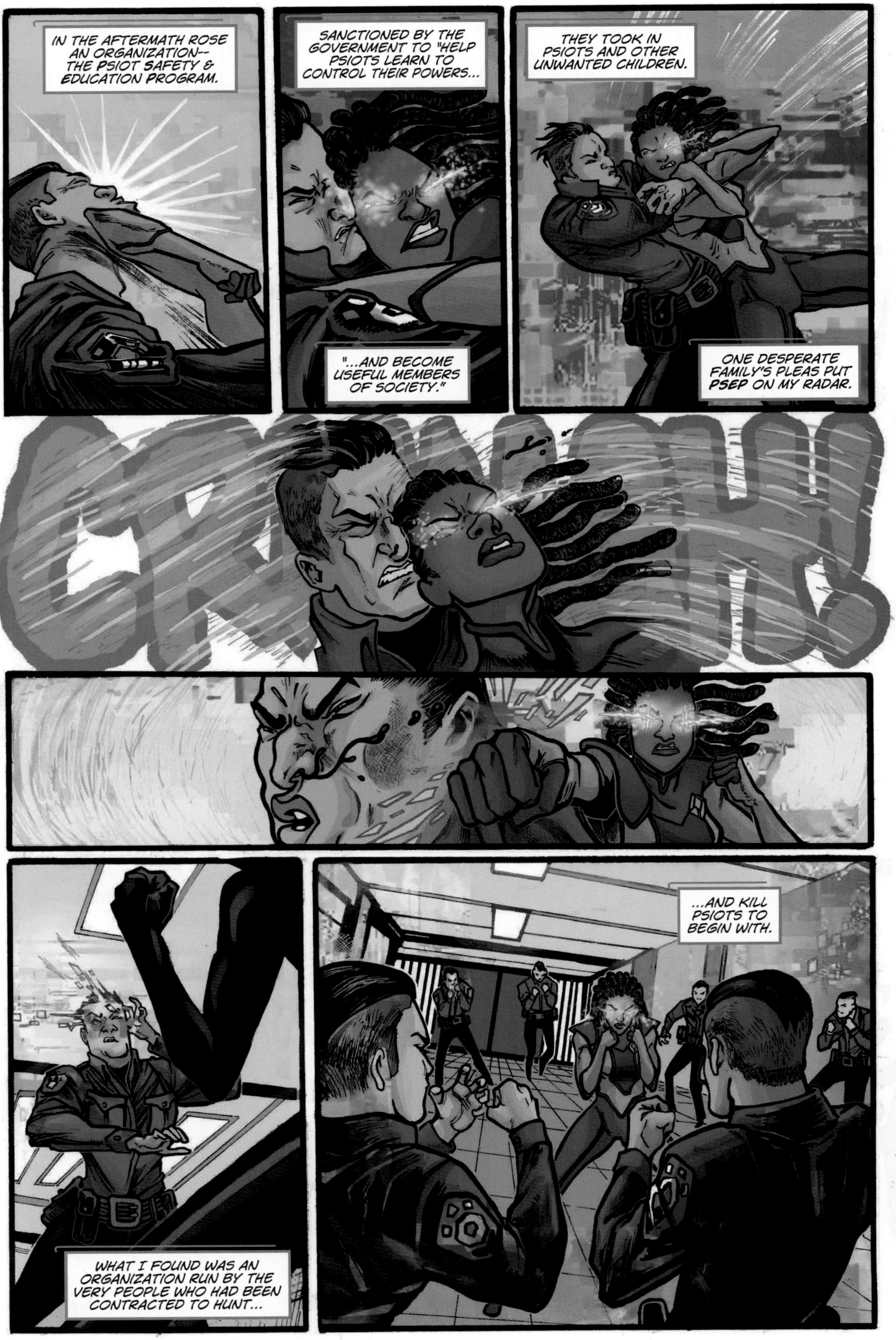
IN THE AFTERMATH ROSE AN ORGANIZATION-- THE PSIOT SAFETY & EDUCATION PROGRAM.
SANCTIONED BY THE GOVERNMENT TO "HELP PSIOTS LEARN TO CONTROL THEIR POWERS...
"...AND BECOME USEFUL MEMBERS OF SOCIETY."
THEY TOOK IN PSIOTS AND OTHER UNWANTED CHILDREN.
ONE DESPERATE FAMILY'S PLEAS PUT PSEP ON MY RADAR.
WHAT I FOUND WAS AN ORGANIZATION RUN BY THE VERY PEOPLE WHO HAD BEEN CONTRACTED TO HUNT...
...AND KILL PSIOTS TO BEGIN WITH.

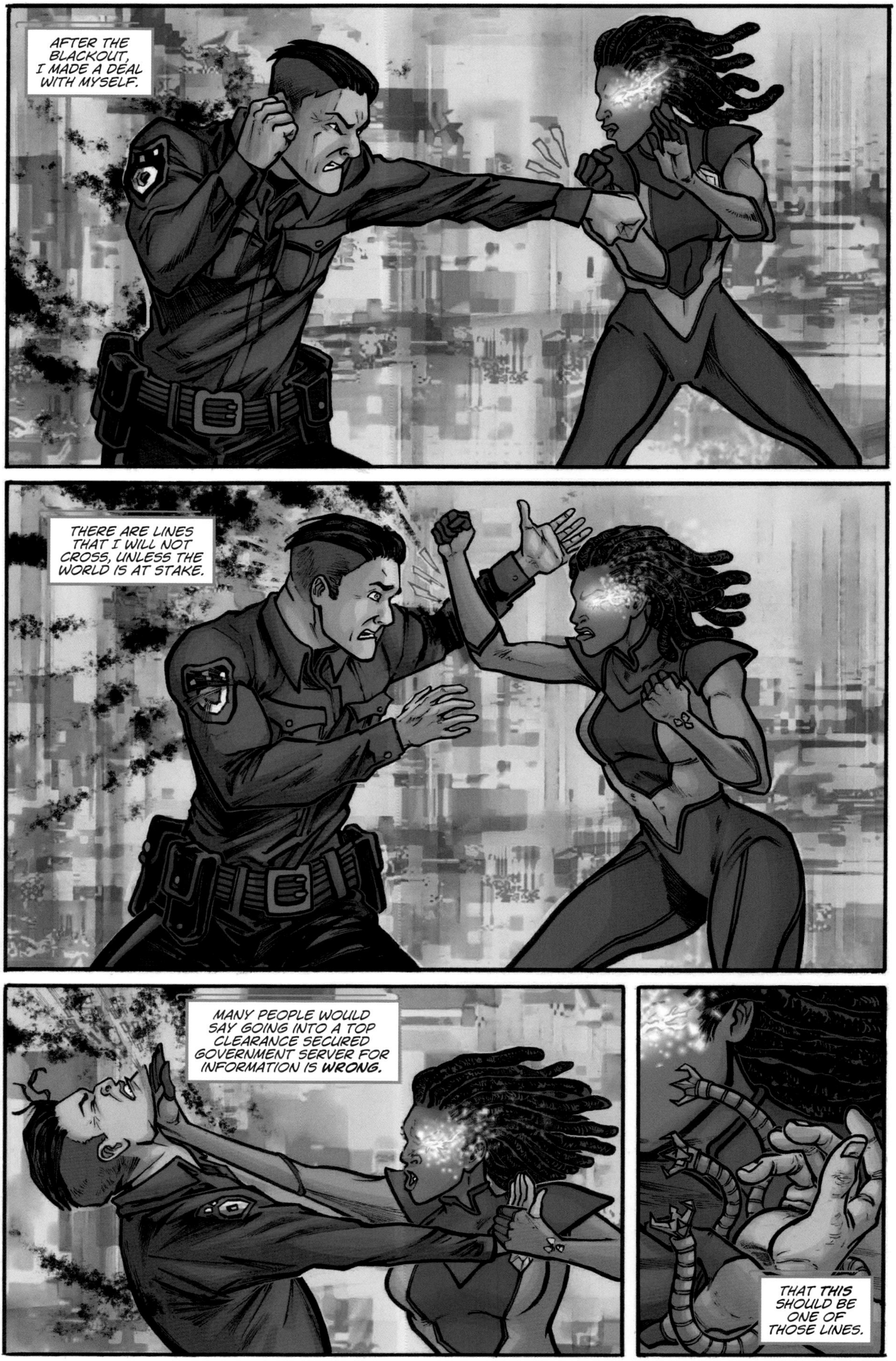
AFTER THE BLACKOUT, I MADE A DEAL WITH MYSELF.
THERE ARE LINES THAT I WILL NOT CROSS, UNLESS THE WORLD IS AT STAKE.
MANY PEOPLE WOULD SAY GOING INTO A TOP CLEARANCE SECURED GOVERNMENT SERVER FOR INFORMATION IS **WRONG**.
THAT **THIS** SHOULD BE ONE OF THOSE LINES.

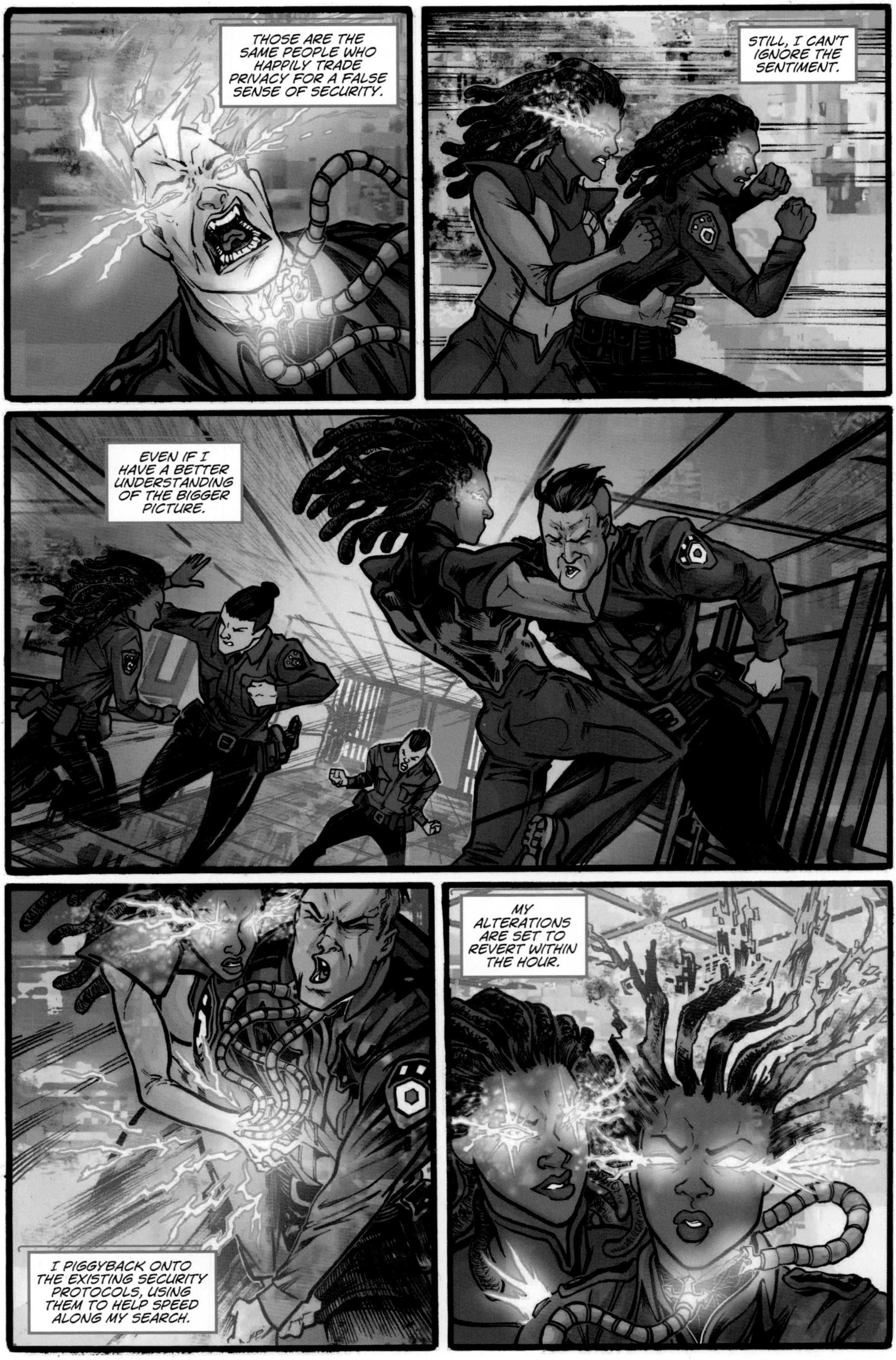
THOSE ARE THE SAME PEOPLE WHO HAPPILY TRADE PRIVACY FOR A FALSE SENSE OF SECURITY.
STILL, I CAN'T IGNORE THE SENTIMENT.
EVEN IF I HAVE A BETTER UNDERSTANDING OF THE BIGGER PICTURE.
I PIGGYBACK ONTO THE EXISTING SECURITY PROTOCOLS, USING THEM TO HELP SPEED ALONG MY SEARCH.
MY ALTERATIONS ARE SET TO REVERT WITHIN THE HOUR.

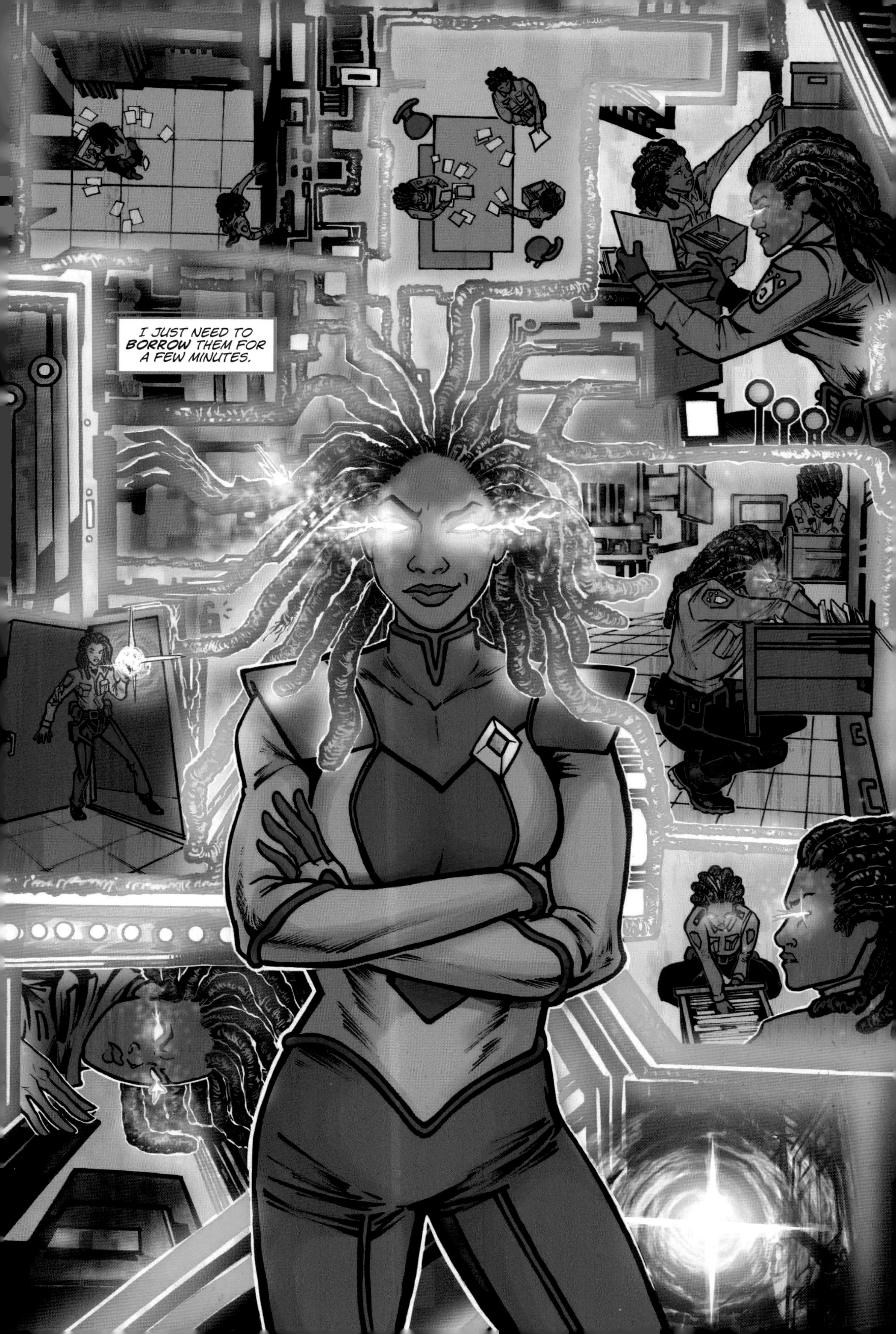
I JUST NEED TO BORROW THEM FOR A FEW MINUTES.

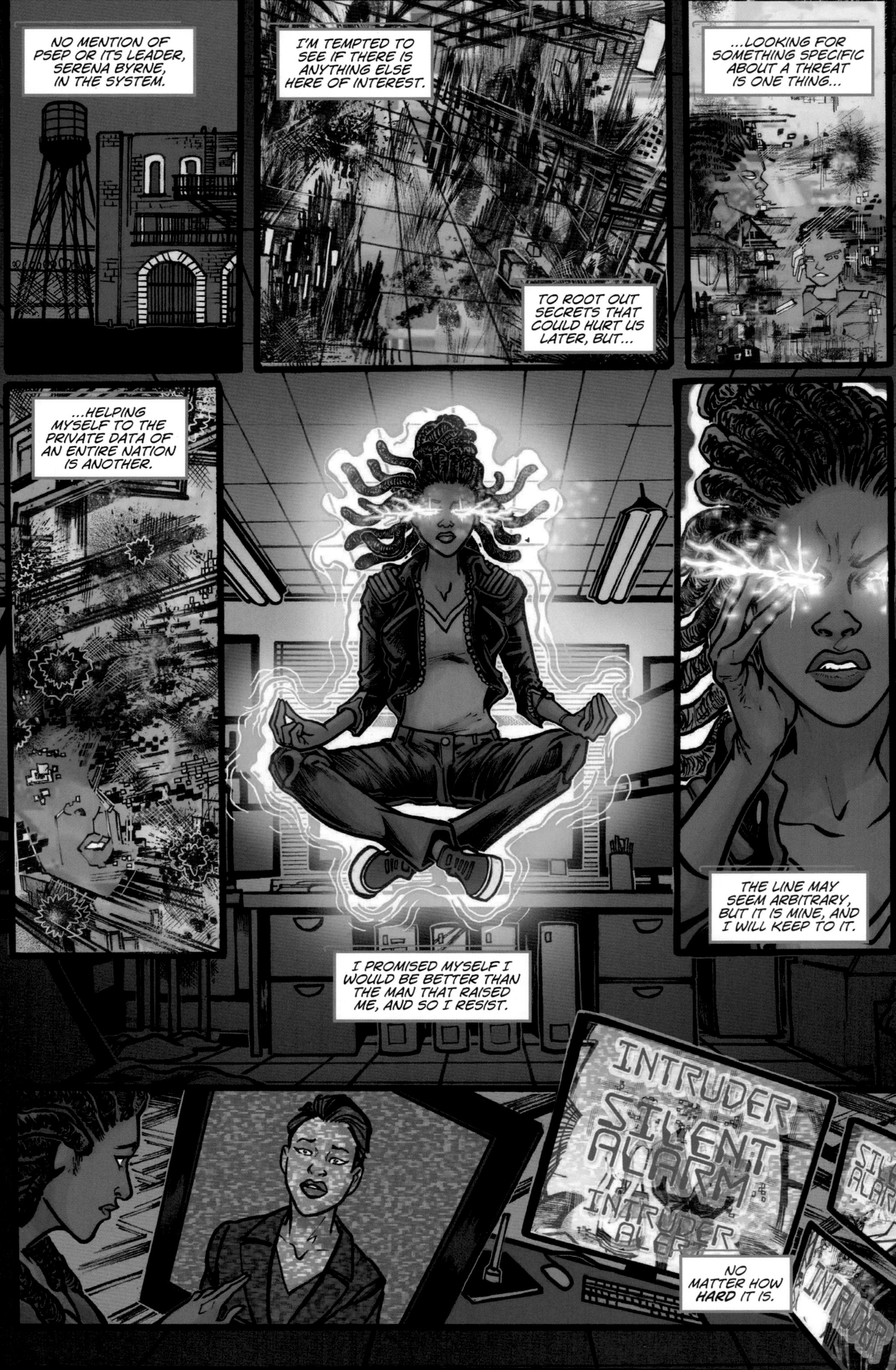
NO MENTION OF PSEP OR ITS LEADER, SERENA BYRNE, IN THE SYSTEM.
I'M TEMPTED TO SEE IF THERE IS ANYTHING ELSE HERE OF INTEREST.
TO ROOT OUT SECRETS THAT COULD HURT US LATER, BUT...
...LOOKING FOR SOMETHING SPECIFIC ABOUT A THREAT IS ONE THING...
...HELPING MYSELF TO THE PRIVATE DATA OF AN ENTIRE NATION IS ANOTHER.
I PROMISED MYSELF I WOULD BE BETTER THAN THE MAN THAT RAISED ME, AND SO I RESIST.
THE LINE MAY SEEM ARBITRARY, BUT IT IS MINE, AND I WILL KEEP TO IT.
INTRUDER
SILENT ALARM
INTRUDER ALERT
NO MATTER HOW HARD IT IS.

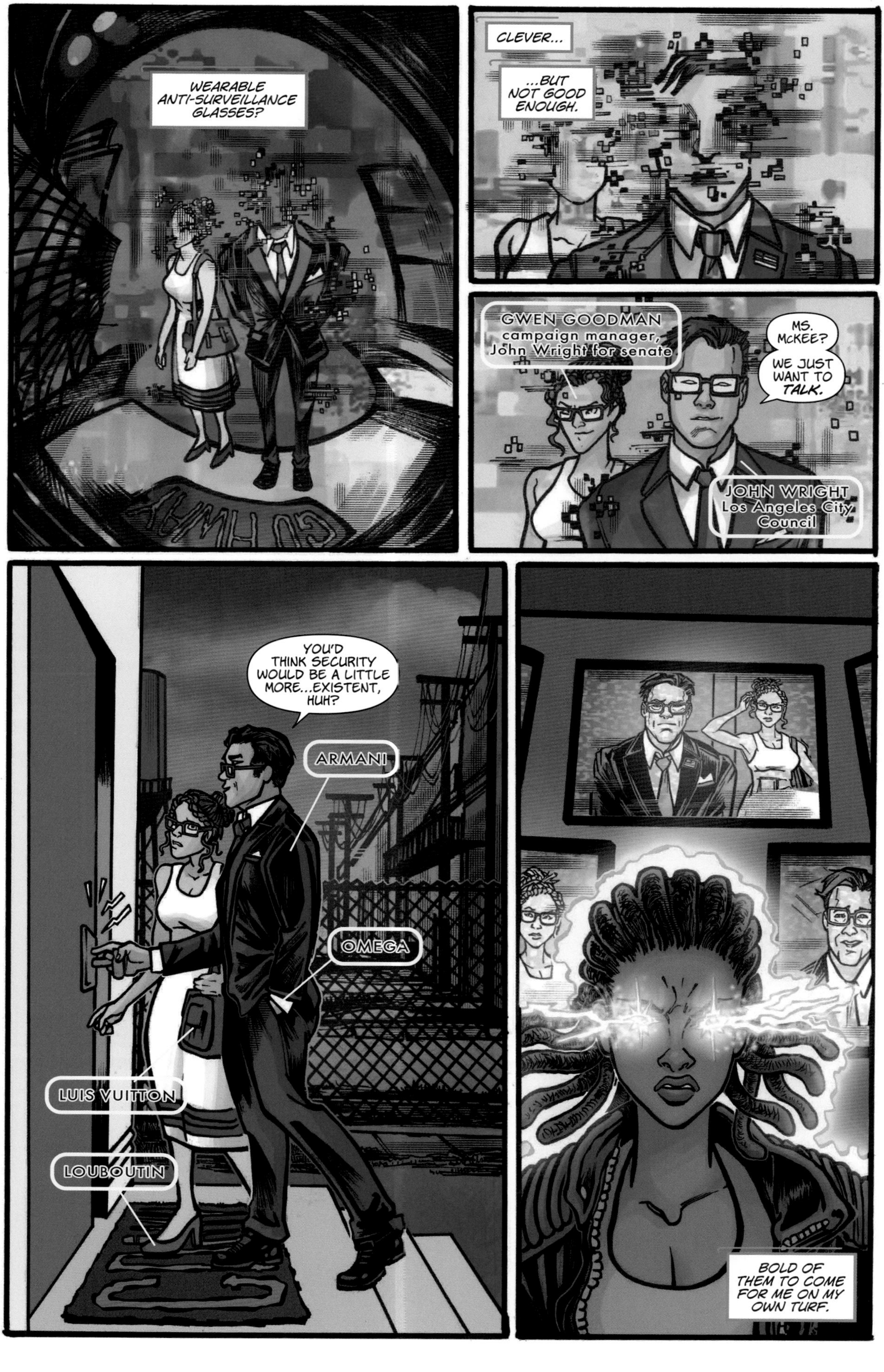
WEARABLE ANTI-SURVEILLANCE GLASSES?
CLEVER...
...BUT NOT GOOD ENOUGH.
GWEN GOODMAN
campaign manager, John Wright for senate
MS. McKEE?
WE JUST WANT TO *TALK.*
JOHN WRIGHT
Los Angeles City Council
YOU'D THINK SECURITY WOULD BE A LITTLE MORE...EXISTENT, HUH?
ARMANI
OMEGA
LUIS VUITTON
LOUBOUTIN
BOLD OF THEM TO COME FOR ME ON MY OWN TURF.

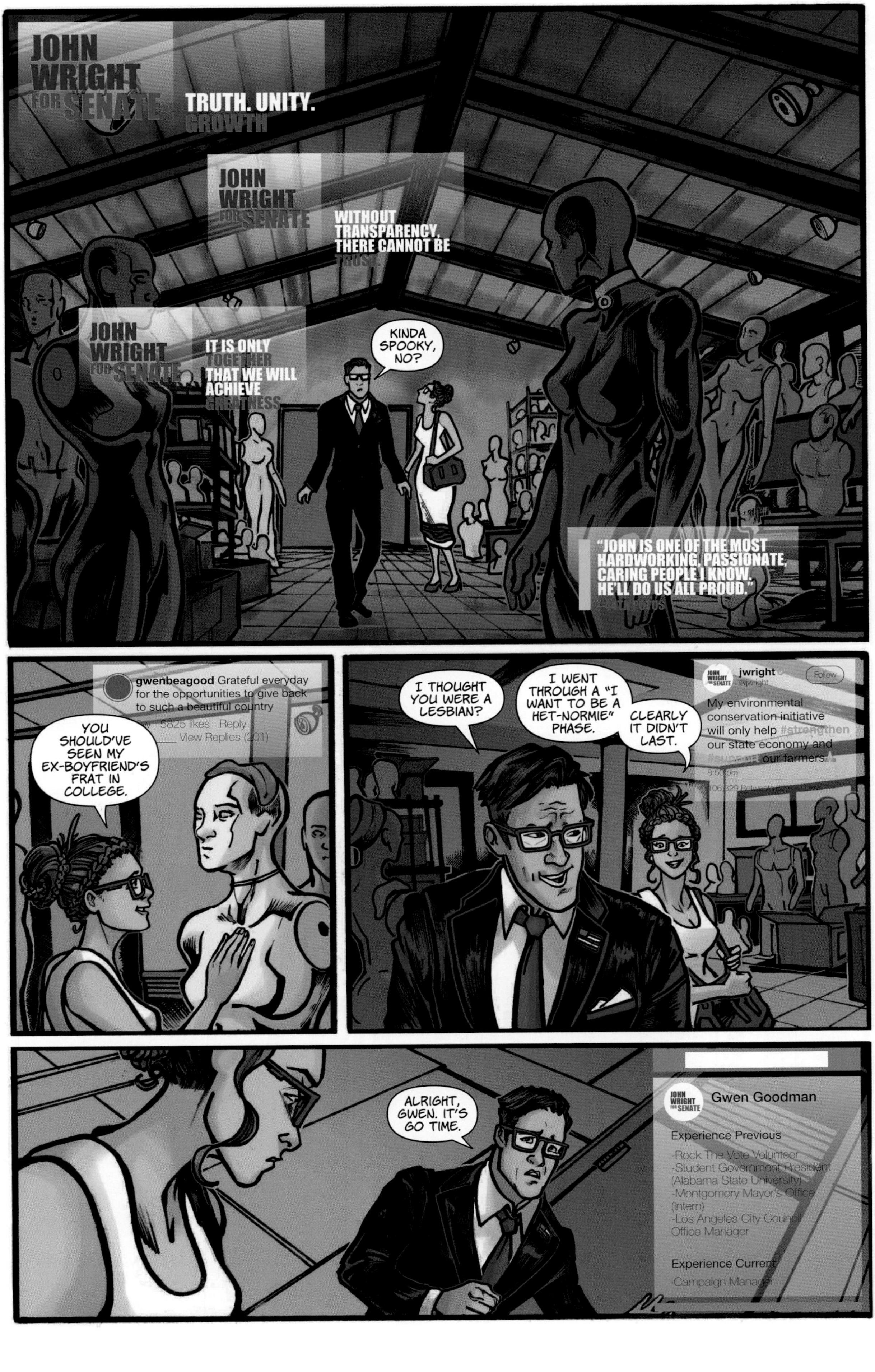
JOHN WRIGHT FOR SENATE
TRUTH. UNITY. GROWTH
JOHN WRIGHT FOR SENATE
WITHOUT TRANSPARENCY, THERE CANNOT BE TRUST.
JOHN WRIGHT FOR SENATE
IT IS ONLY TOGETHER THAT WE WILL ACHIEVE GREATNESS
KINDA SPOOKY, NO?
"JOHN IS ONE OF THE MOST HARDWORKING, PASSIONATE, CARING PEOPLE I KNOW. HE'LL DO US ALL PROUD."
gwenbeagood Grateful everyday for the opportunities to give back to such a beautiful country
5825 likes Reply
View Replies (201)
YOU SHOULD'VE SEEN MY EX-BOYFRIEND'S FRAT IN COLLEGE.
I THOUGHT YOU WERE A LESBIAN?
I WENT THROUGH A "I WANT TO BE A HET-NORMIE" PHASE.
CLEARLY IT DIDN'T LAST.
JOHN WRIGHT FOR SENATE
jwright
@jwright
Follow
My environmental conservation initiative will only help #strengthen our state economy and #support our farmers
8:50 pm
ALRIGHT, GWEN. IT'S GO TIME.
JOHN WRIGHT FOR SENATE
Gwen Goodman
Experience Previous
-Rock The Vote Volunteer
-Student Government President (Alabama State University)
-Montgomery Mayor's Office (Intern)
-Los Angeles City Council Office Manager
Experience Current
-Campaign Manager

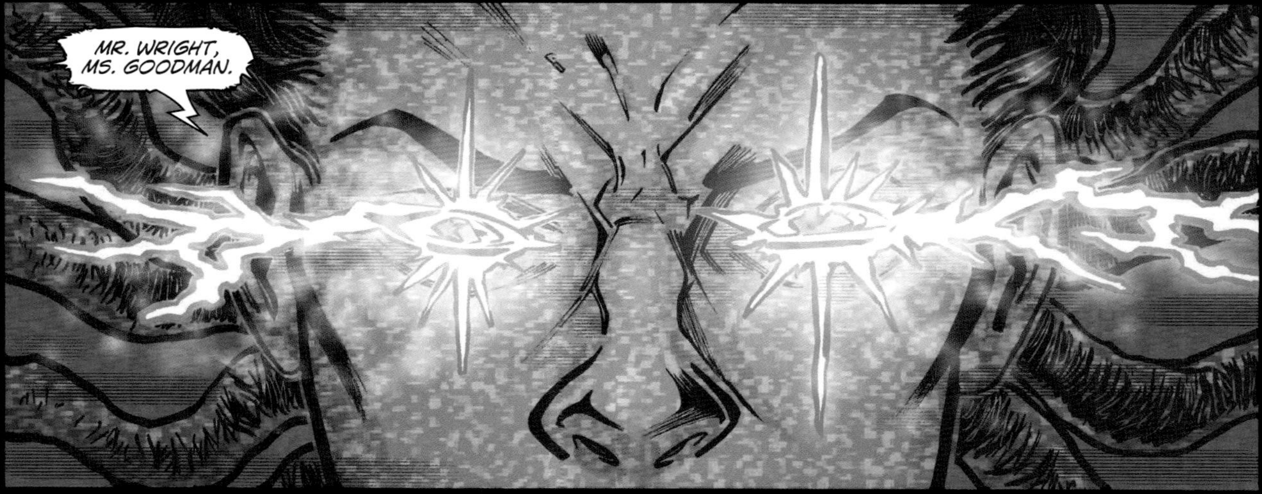
MR. WRIGHT, MS. GOODMAN.
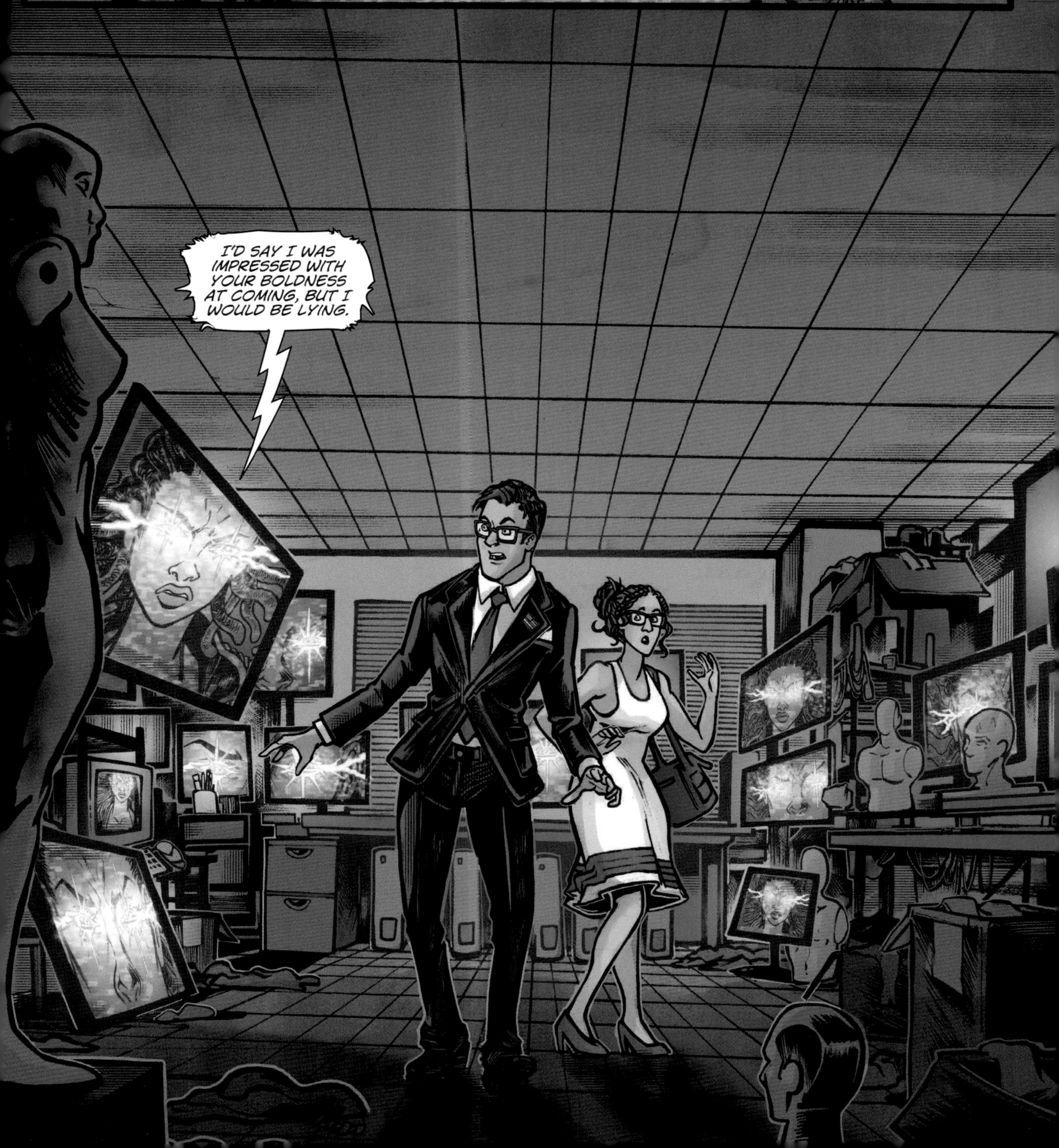
I'D SAY I WAS IMPRESSED WITH YOUR BOLDNESS AT COMING, BUT I WOULD BE LYING.

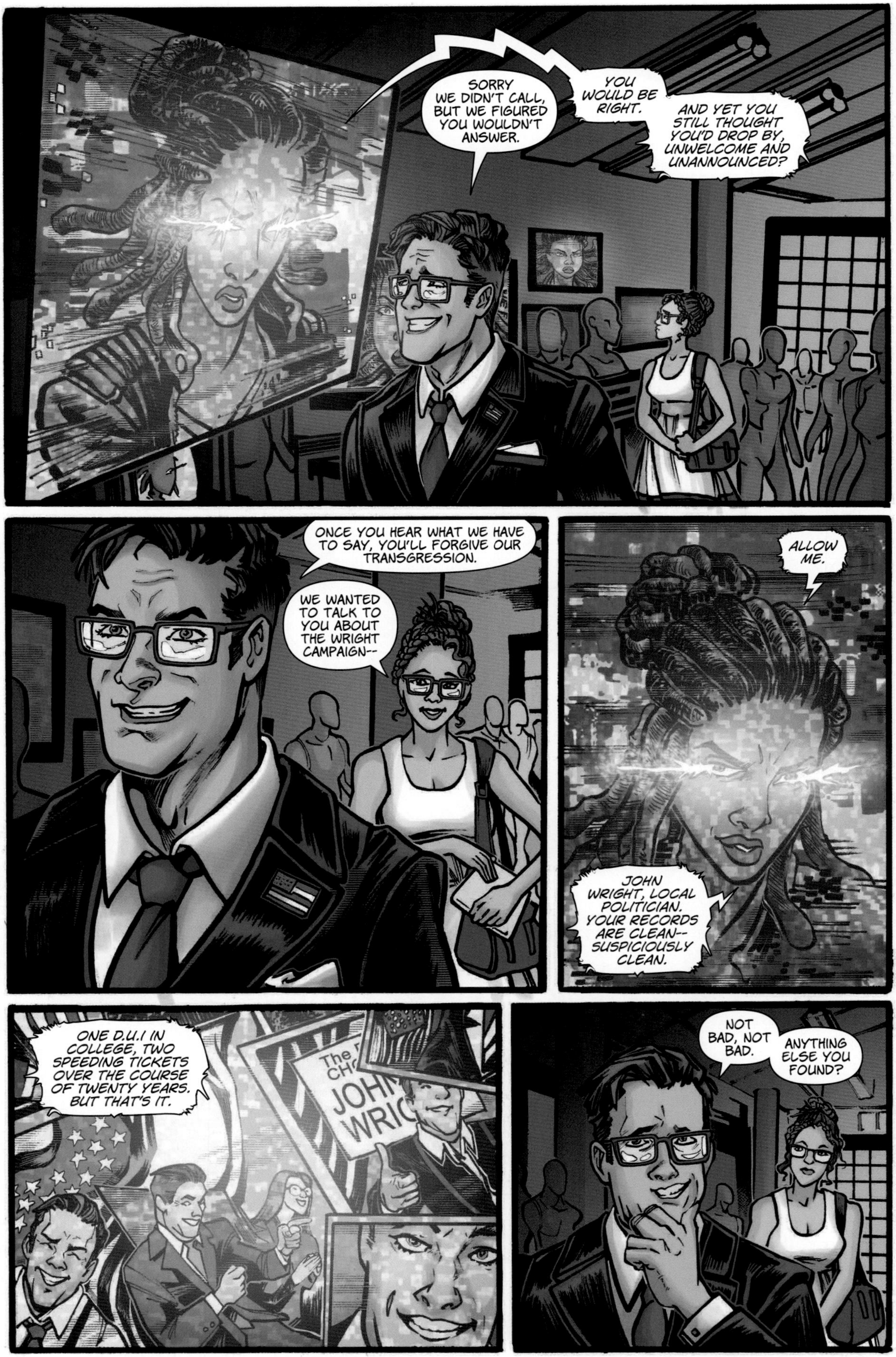
SORRY WE DIDN'T CALL, BUT WE FIGURED YOU WOULDN'T ANSWER.
YOU WOULD BE RIGHT.
AND YET YOU STILL THOUGHT YOU'D DROP BY, UNWELCOME AND UNANNOUNCED?
ONCE YOU HEAR WHAT WE HAVE TO SAY, YOU'LL FORGIVE OUR TRANSGRESSION.
WE WANTED TO TALK TO YOU ABOUT THE WRIGHT CAMPAIGN--
ALLOW ME.
JOHN WRIGHT, LOCAL POLITICIAN. YOUR RECORDS ARE CLEAN-- SUSPICIOUSLY CLEAN.
ONE D.U.I IN COLLEGE, TWO SPEEDING TICKETS OVER THE COURSE OF TWENTY YEARS. BUT THAT'S IT.
NOT BAD, NOT BAD.
ANYTHING ELSE YOU FOUND?

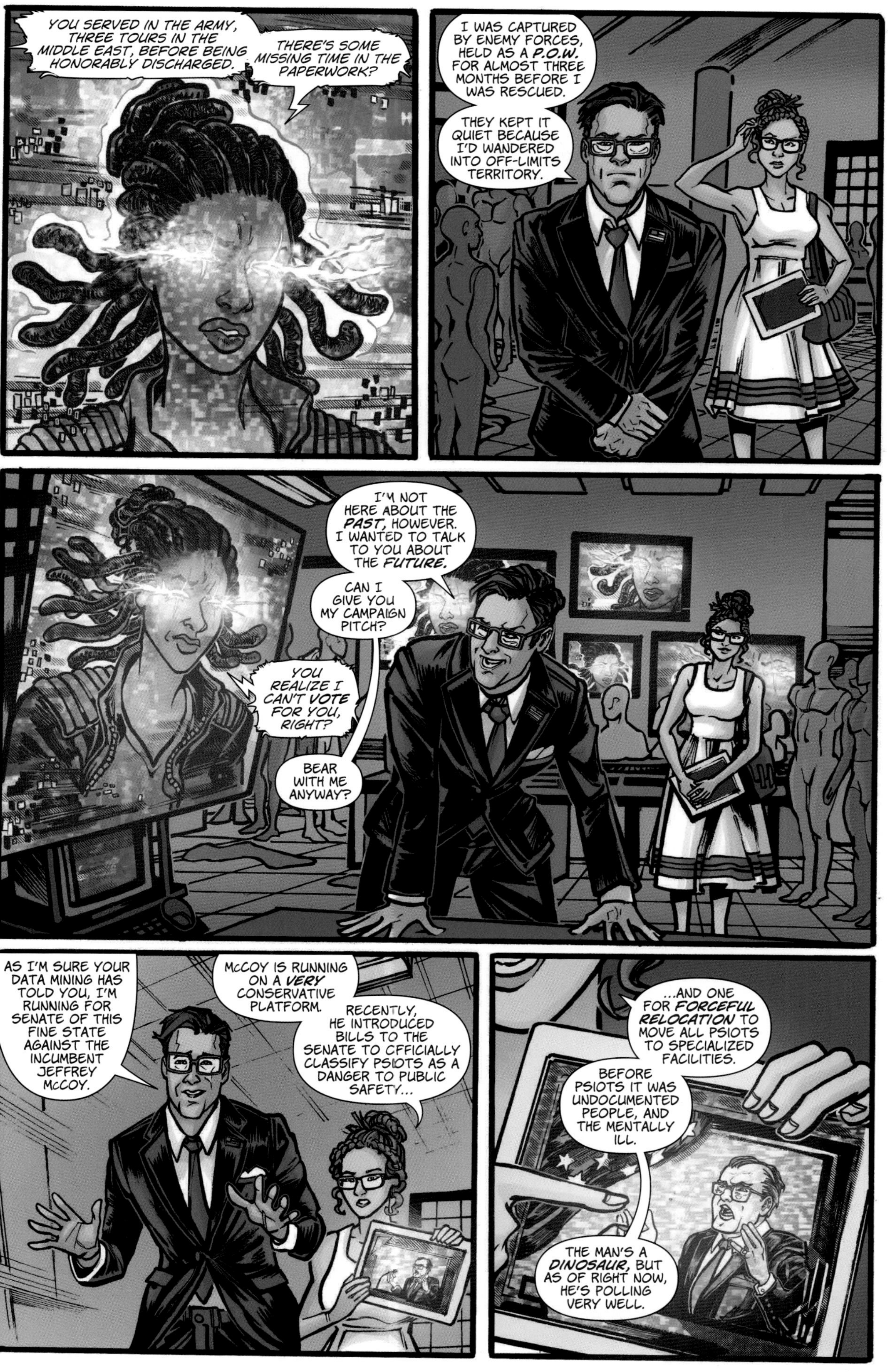
YOU SERVED IN THE ARMY, THREE TOURS IN THE MIDDLE EAST, BEFORE BEING HONORABLY DISCHARGED.
THERE'S SOME MISSING TIME IN THE PAPERWORK?
I WAS CAPTURED BY ENEMY FORCES, HELD AS A *P.O.W.* FOR ALMOST THREE MONTHS BEFORE I WAS RESCUED.
THEY KEPT IT QUIET BECAUSE I'D WANDERED INTO OFF-LIMITS TERRITORY.
I'M NOT HERE ABOUT THE *PAST,* HOWEVER. I WANTED TO TALK TO YOU ABOUT THE *FUTURE.*
CAN I GIVE YOU MY CAMPAIGN PITCH?
YOU REALIZE I CAN'T *VOTE* FOR YOU, RIGHT?
BEAR WITH ME ANYWAY?
AS I'M SURE YOUR DATA MINING HAS TOLD YOU, I'M RUNNING FOR SENATE OF THIS FINE STATE AGAINST THE INCUMBENT JEFFREY McCOY.
McCOY IS RUNNING ON A *VERY* CONSERVATIVE PLATFORM.
RECENTLY, HE INTRODUCED BILLS TO THE SENATE TO CFFICIALLY CLASSIFY PSIOTS AS A DANGER TO PUBLIC SAFETY...
...AND ONE FOR *FORCEFUL RELOCATION* TO MOVE ALL PSIOTS TO SPECIALIZED FACILITIES.
BEFORE PSIOTS IT WAS UNDOCUMENTED PEOPLE, AND THE MENTALLY ILL.
THE MAN'S A *DINOSAUR,* BUT AS OF RIGHT NOW, HE'S POLLING VERY WELL.

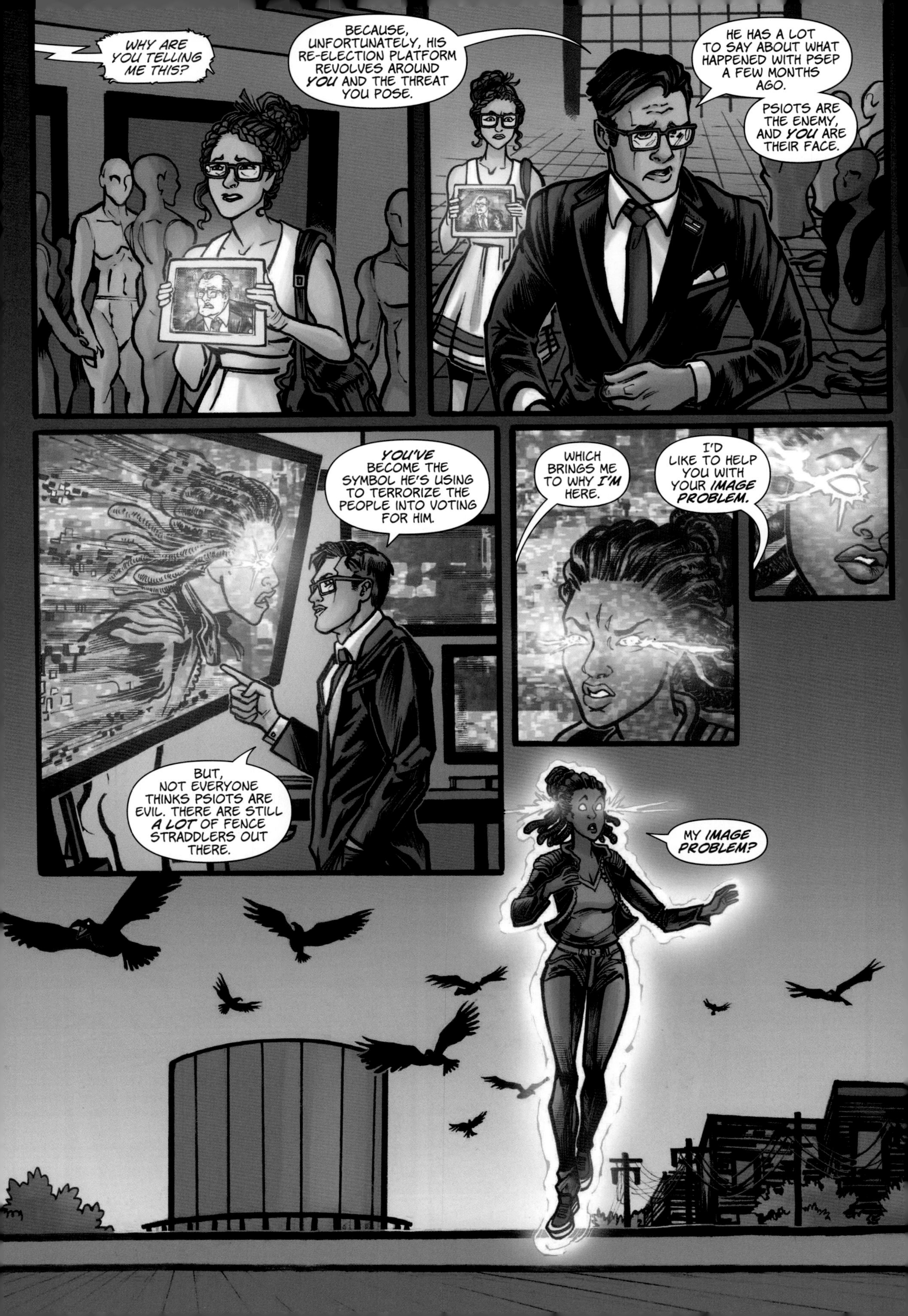
WHY ARE YOU TELLING ME THIS?
BECAUSE, UNFORTUNATELY, HIS RE-ELECTION PLATFORM REVOLVES AROUND YOU AND THE THREAT YOU POSE.
HE HAS A LOT TO SAY ABOUT WHAT HAPPENED WITH PSEP A FEW MONTHS AGO.
PSIOTS ARE THE ENEMY, AND YOU ARE THEIR FACE.
YOU'VE BECOME THE SYMBOL HE'S USING TO TERRORIZE THE PEOPLE INTO VOTING FOR HIM.
BUT, NOT EVERYONE THINKS PSIOTS ARE EVIL. THERE ARE STILL A LOT OF FENCE STRADDLERS OUT THERE.
WHICH BRINGS ME TO WHY I'M HERE.
I'D LIKE TO HELP YOU WITH YOUR IMAGE PROBLEM.
MY IMAGE PROBLEM?

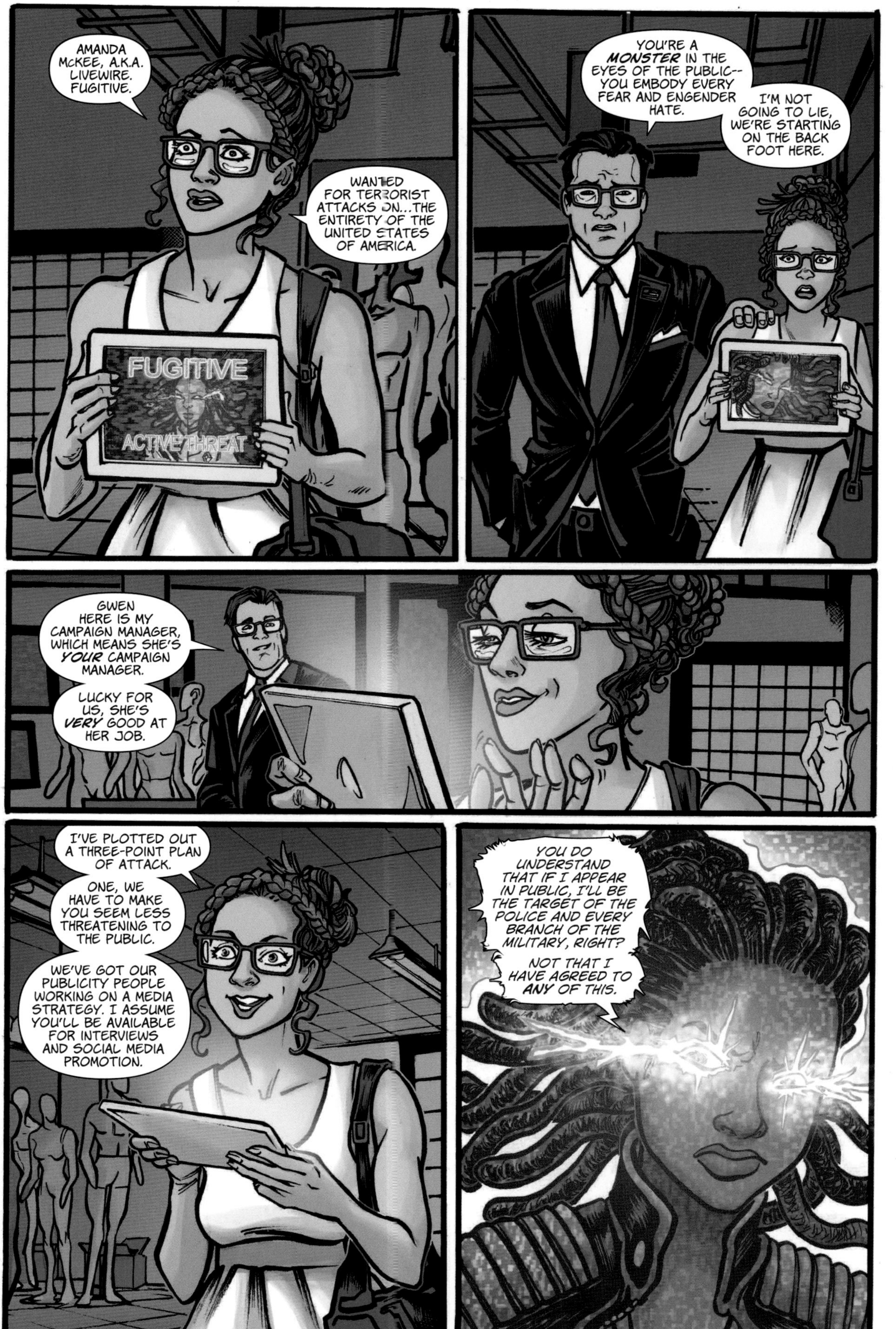
AMANDA McKEE, A.K.A. LIVEWIRE. FUGITIVE.
WANTED FOR TERRORIST ATTACKS ON...THE ENTIRETY OF THE UNITED STATES OF AMERICA.
FUGITIVE
ACTIVE THREAT
YOU'RE A MONSTER IN THE EYES OF THE PUBLIC--YOU EMBODY EVERY FEAR AND ENGENDER HATE.
I'M NOT GOING TO LIE, WE'RE STARTING ON THE BACK FOOT HERE.
GWEN HERE IS MY CAMPAIGN MANAGER, WHICH MEANS SHE'S YOUR CAMPAIGN MANAGER.
LUCKY FOR US, SHE'S VERY GOOD AT HER JOB.
I'VE PLOTTED OUT A THREE-POINT PLAN OF ATTACK.
ONE, WE HAVE TO MAKE YOU SEEM LESS THREATENING TO THE PUBLIC.
WE'VE GOT OUR PUBLICITY PEOPLE WORKING ON A MEDIA STRATEGY. I ASSUME YOU'LL BE AVAILABLE FOR INTERVIEWS AND SOCIAL MEDIA PROMOTION.
YOU DO UNDERSTAND THAT IF I APPEAR IN PUBLIC, I'LL BE THE TARGET OF THE POLICE AND EVERY BRANCH OF THE MILITARY, RIGHT?
NOT THAT I HAVE AGREED TO ANY OF THIS.

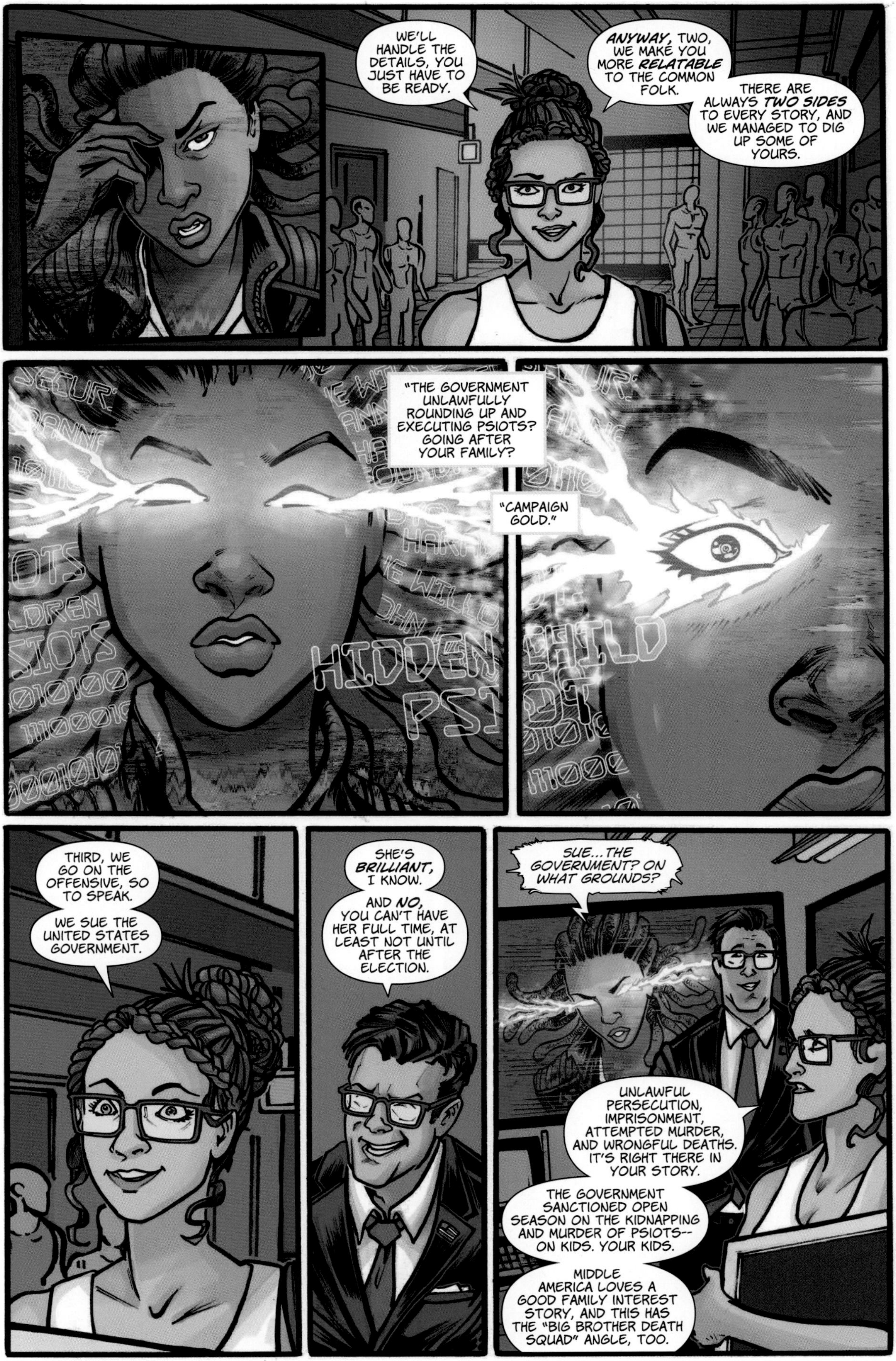
WE'LL HANDLE THE DETAILS, YOU JUST HAVE TO BE READY.
ANYWAY, TWO, WE MAKE YOU MORE RELATABLE TO THE COMMON FOLK.
THERE ARE ALWAYS TWO SIDES TO EVERY STORY, AND WE MANAGED TO DIG UP SOME OF YOURS.
"THE GOVERNMENT UNLAWFULLY ROUNDING UP AND EXECUTING PSIOTS? GOING AFTER YOUR FAMILY?
"CAMPAIGN GOLD."
HIDDEN
PSIOTS
CHILD
THIRD, WE GO ON THE OFFENSIVE, SO TO SPEAK.
WE SUE THE UNITED STATES GOVERNMENT.
SHE'S BRILLIANT, I KNOW.
AND NO, YOU CAN'T HAVE HER FULL TIME, AT LEAST NOT UNTIL AFTER THE ELECTION.
SUE...THE GOVERNMENT? ON WHAT GROUNDS?
UNLAWFUL PERSECUTION, IMPRISONMENT, ATTEMPTED MURDER, AND WRONGFUL DEATHS. IT'S RIGHT THERE IN YOUR STORY.
THE GOVERNMENT SANCTIONED OPEN SEASON ON THE KIDNAPPING AND MURDER OF PSIOTS-- ON KIDS. YOUR KIDS.
MIDDLE AMERICA LOVES A GOOD FAMILY INTEREST STORY, AND THIS HAS THE "BIG BROTHER DEATH SQUAD" ANGLE, TOO.

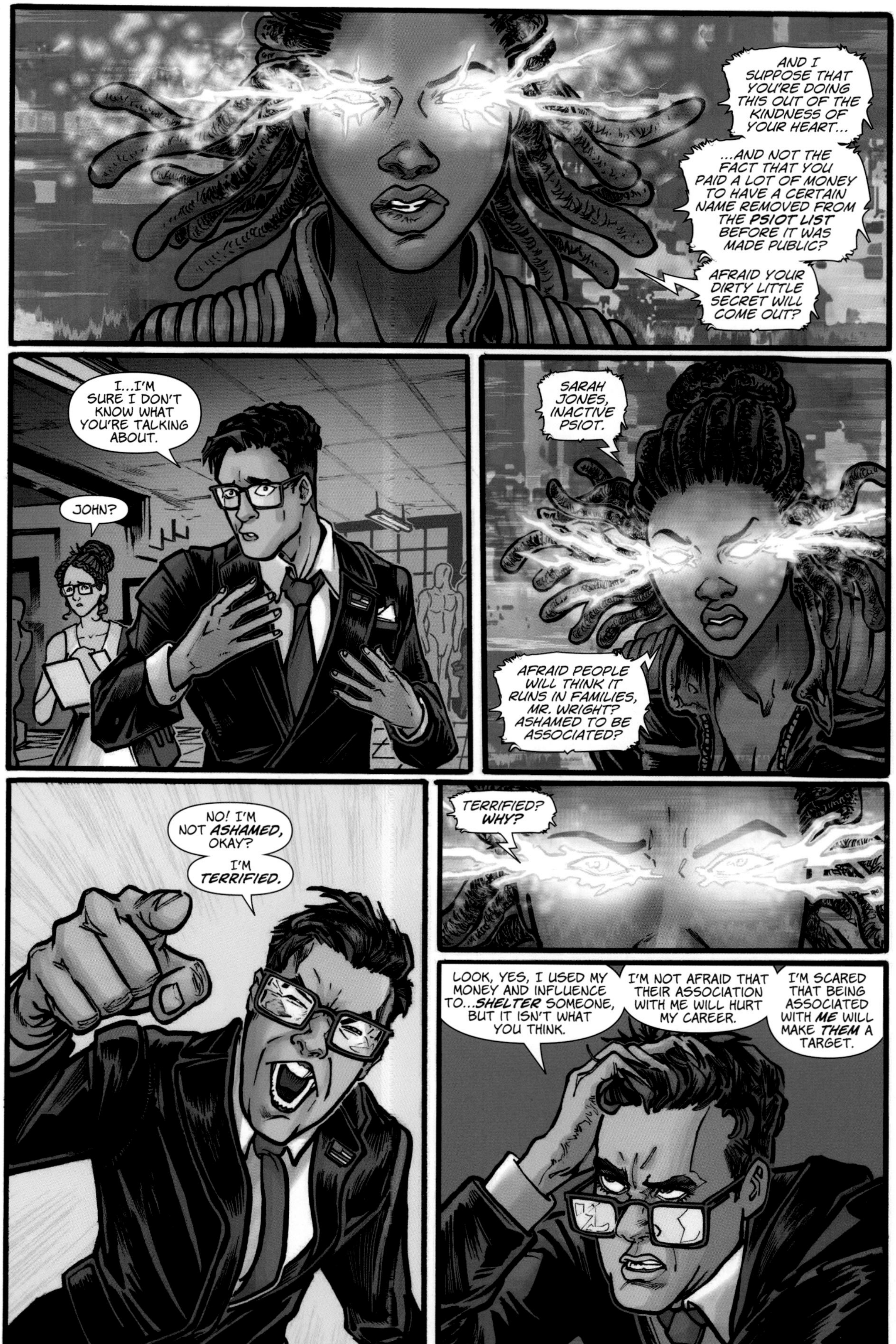
AND I SUPPOSE THAT YOU'RE DOING THIS OUT OF THE KINDNESS OF YOUR HEART...
...AND NOT THE FACT THAT YOU PAID A LOT OF MONEY TO HAVE A CERTAIN NAME REMOVED FROM THE **PSIOT LIST** BEFORE IT WAS MADE PUBLIC?
AFRAID YOUR DIRTY LITTLE SECRET WILL COME OUT?
I...I'M SURE I DON'T KNOW WHAT YOU'RE TALKING ABOUT.
JOHN?
SARAH JONES, INACTIVE PSIOT.
AFRAID PEOPLE WILL THINK IT RUNS IN FAMILIES, MR. WRIGHT? ASHAMED TO BE ASSOCIATED?
NO! I'M NOT ***ASHAMED,*** OKAY?
I'M ***TERRIFIED.***
TERRIFIED? ***WHY?***
LOOK, YES, I USED MY MONEY AND INFLUENCE TO...***SHELTER*** SOMEONE, BUT IT ISN'T WHAT YOU THINK.
I'M NOT AFRAID THAT THEIR ASSOCIATION WITH ME WILL HURT MY CAREER.
I'M SCARED THAT BEING ASSOCIATED WITH ***ME*** WILL MAKE ***THEM*** A TARGET.

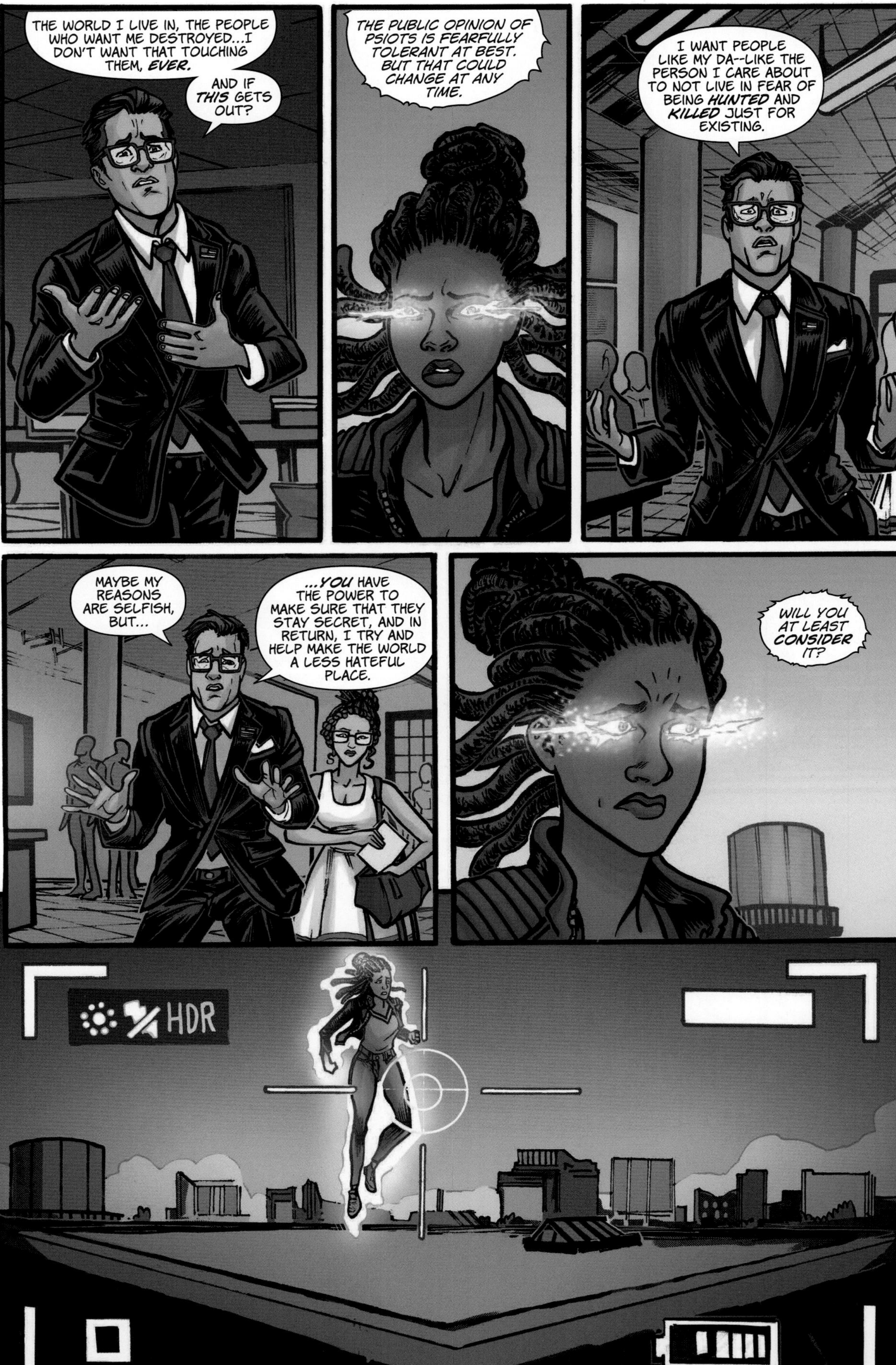
THE WORLD I LIVE IN, THE PEOPLE WHO WANT ME DESTROYED...I DON'T WANT THAT TOUCHING THEM, **EVER.**
AND IF **THIS** GETS OUT?
*THE PUBLIC OPINION OF PSIOTS IS **FEARFULLY** TOLERANT AT BEST. BUT THAT COULD CHANGE AT ANY TIME.*
I WANT PEOPLE LIKE MY DA--LIKE THE PERSON I CARE ABOUT TO NOT LIVE IN FEAR OF BEING **HUNTED** AND **KILLED** JUST FOR EXISTING.
MAYBE MY REASONS ARE SELFISH, BUT...
...YOU HAVE THE POWER TO MAKE SURE THAT THEY STAY SECRET, AND IN RETURN, I TRY AND HELP MAKE THE WORLD A LESS HATEFUL PLACE.
*WILL YOU AT LEAST **CONSIDER** IT?*
HDR

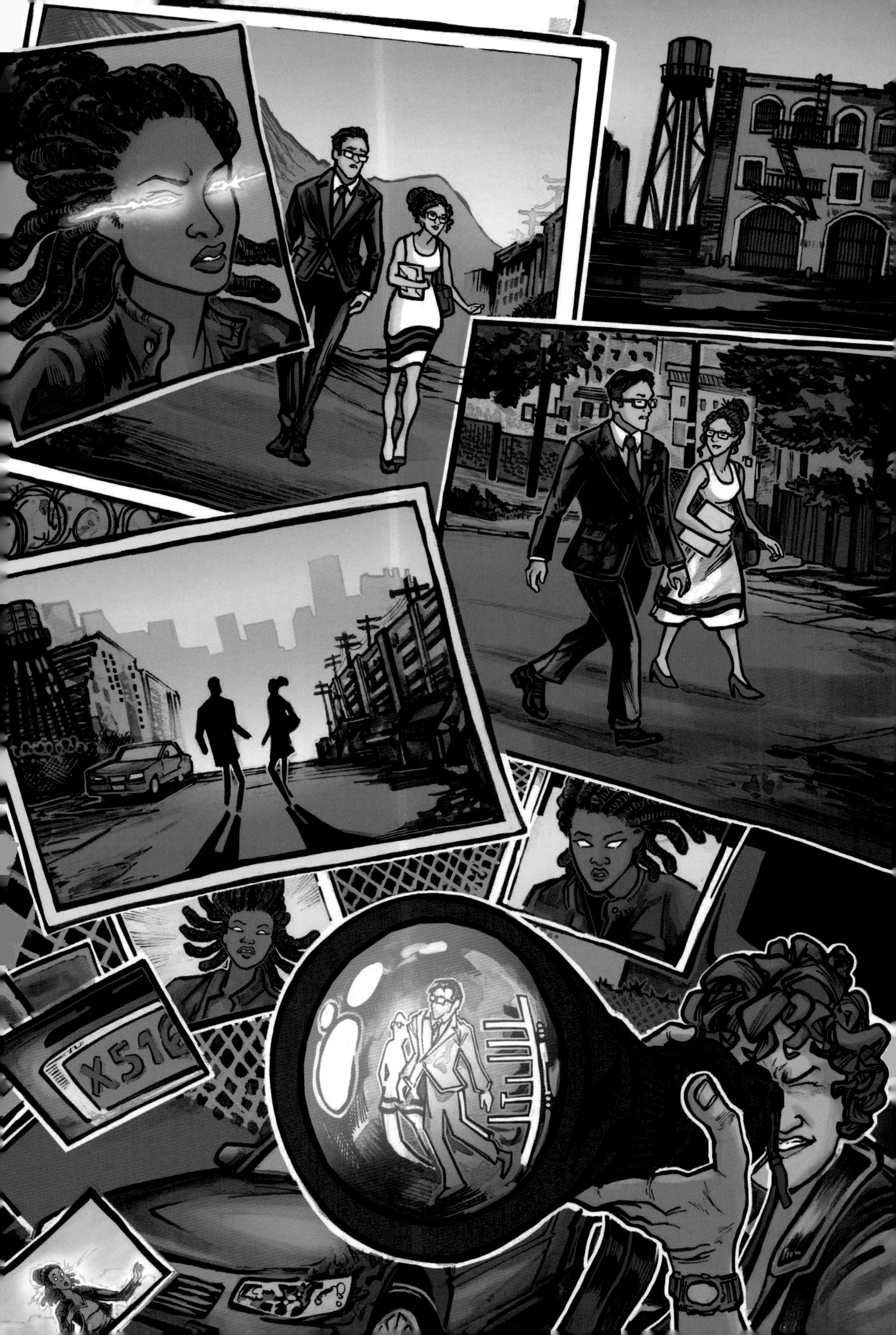

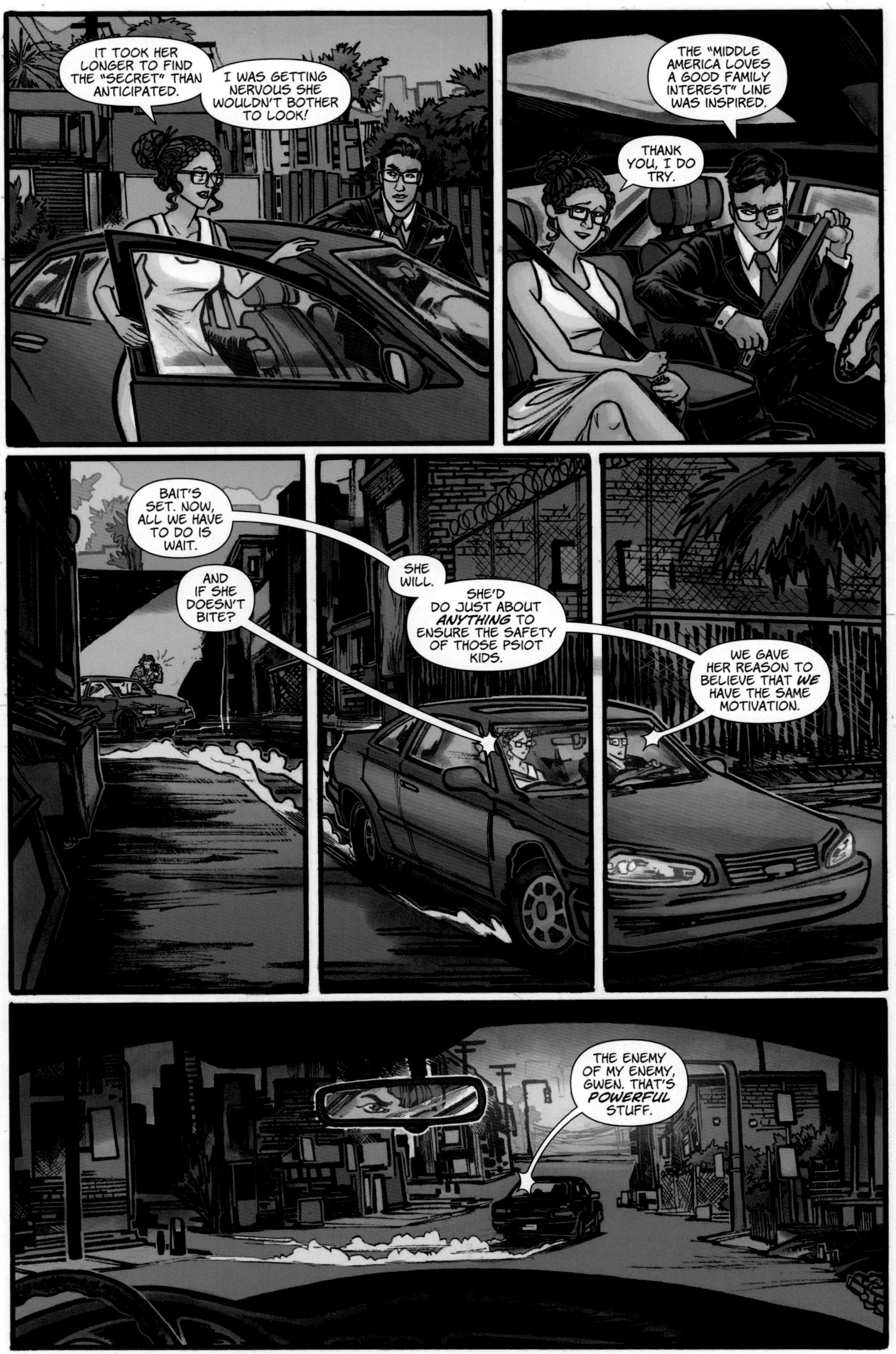
IT TOOK HER LONGER TO FIND THE "SECRET" THAN ANTICIPATED.
I WAS GETTING NERVOUS SHE WOULDN'T BOTHER TO LOOK!
THE "MIDDLE AMERICA LOVES A GOOD FAMILY INTEREST" LINE WAS INSPIRED.
THANK YOU, I DO TRY.
BAIT'S SET. NOW, ALL WE HAVE TO DO IS WAIT.
AND IF SHE DOESN'T BITE?
SHE WILL.
SHE'D DO JUST ABOUT *ANYTHING* TO ENSURE THE SAFETY OF THOSE PSIOT KIDS.
WE GAVE HER REASON TO BELIEVE THAT *WE* HAVE THE SAME MOTIVATION.
THE ENEMY OF MY ENEMY, GWEN. THAT'S *POWERFUL* STUFF.

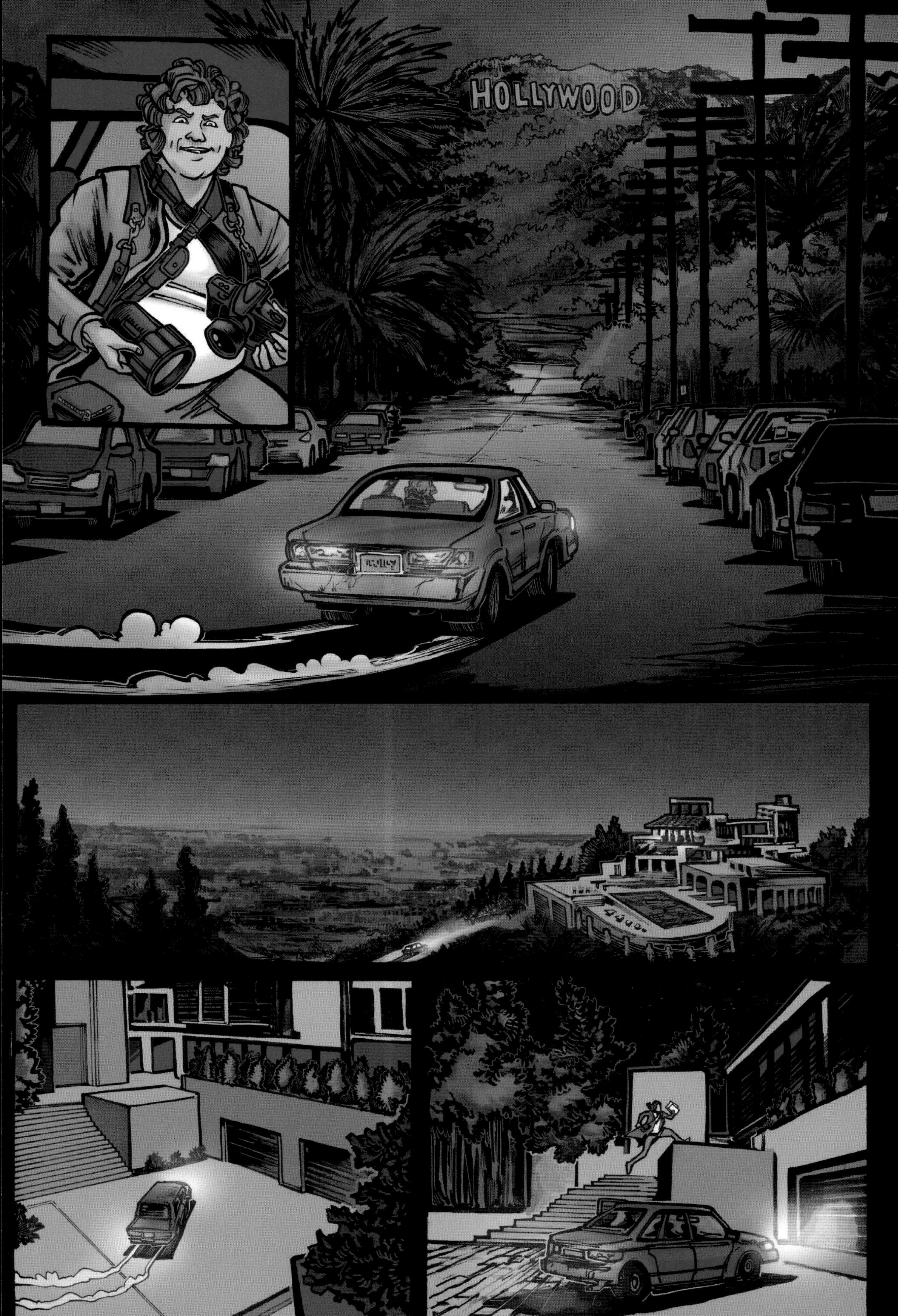
HOLLYWOOD

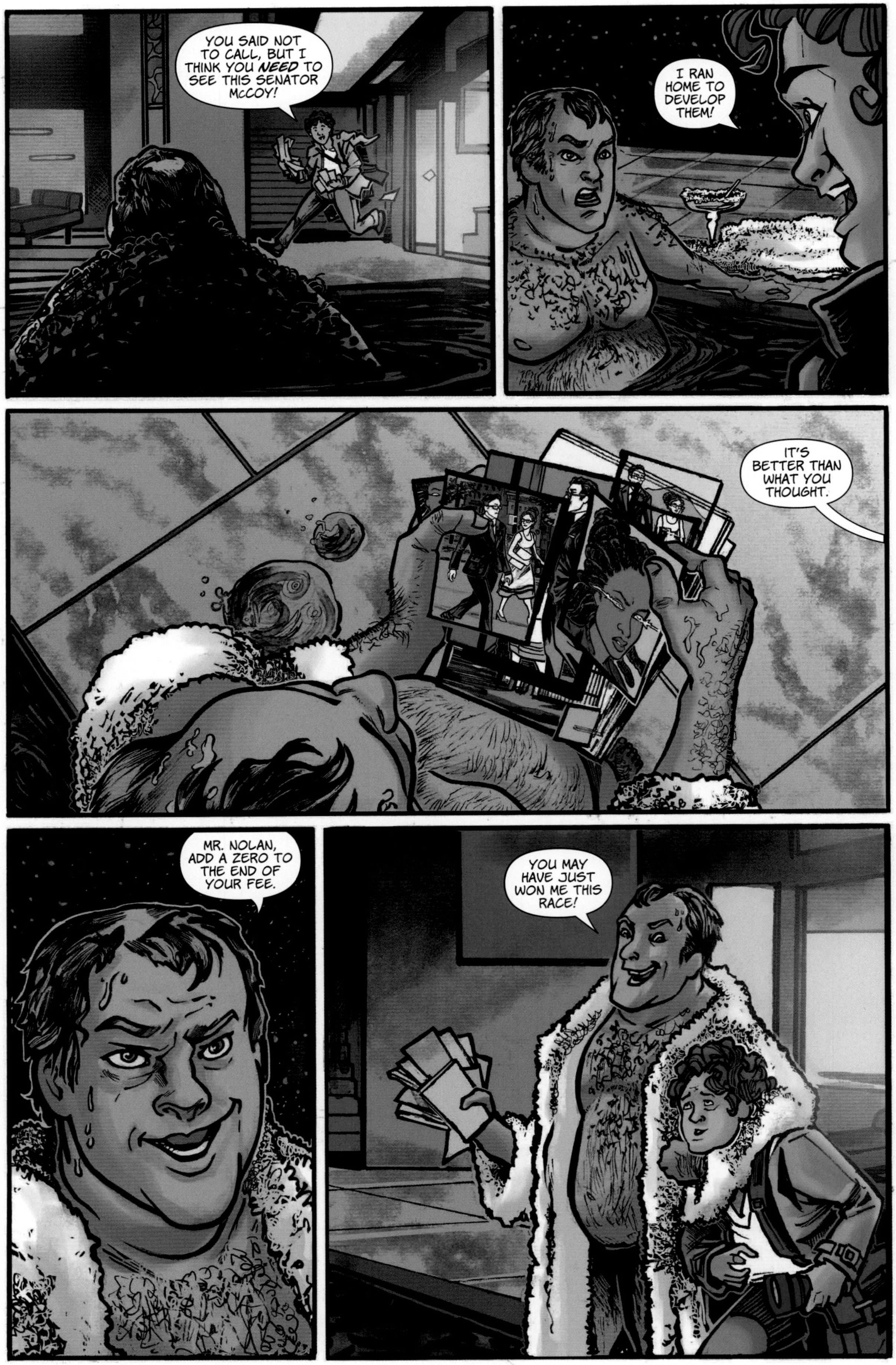
YOU SAID NOT TO CALL, BUT I THINK YOU NEED TO SEE THIS SENATOR McCOY!
I RAN HOME TO DEVELOP THEM!
IT'S BETTER THAN WHAT YOU THOUGHT.
MR. NOLAN, ADD A ZERO TO THE END OF YOUR FEE.
YOU MAY HAVE JUST WON ME THIS RACE!

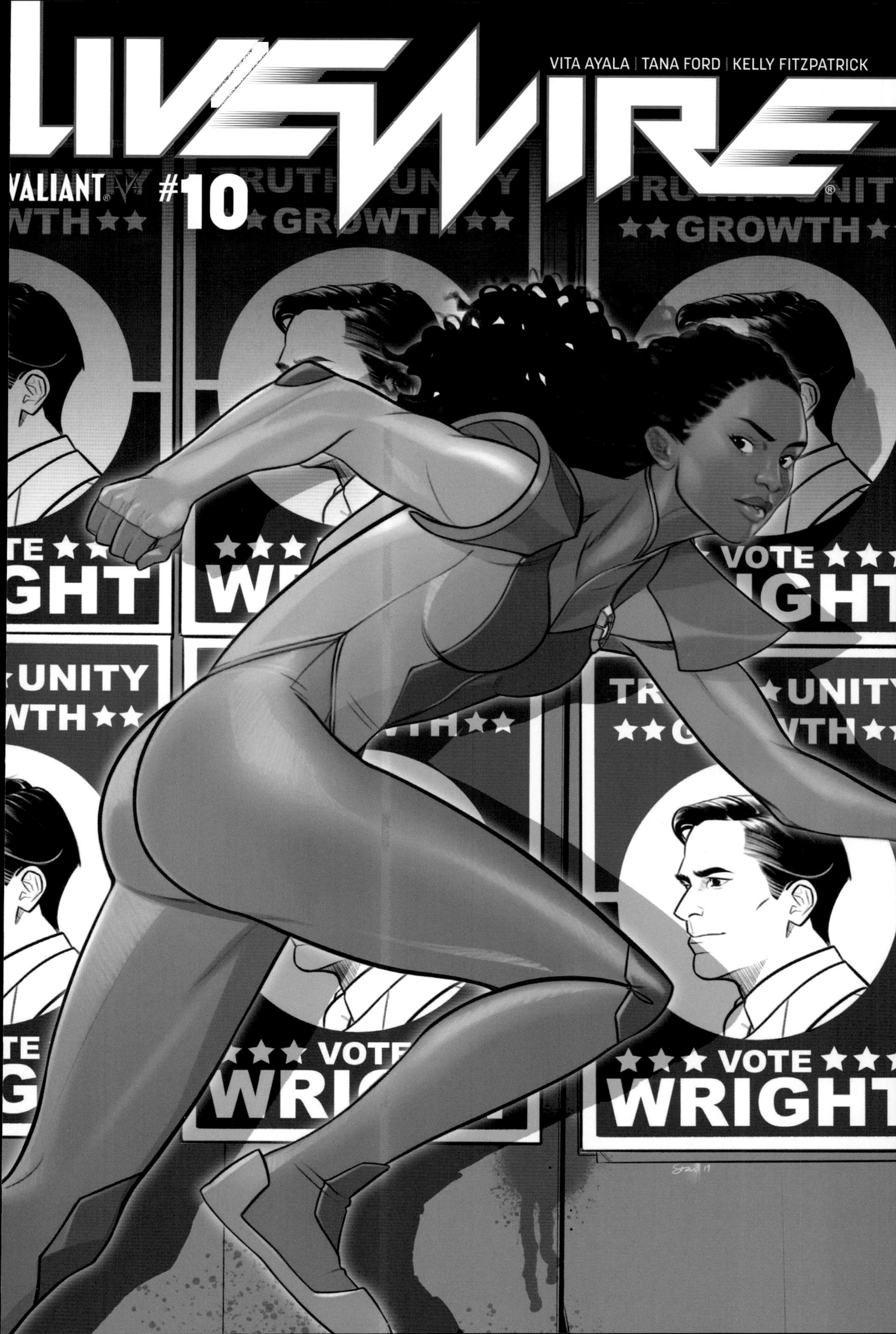
LIVEWIRE
VITA AYALA | TANA FORD | KELLY FITZPATRICK
VALIANT
#10
GROWTH
VOTE
WRIGHT
UNITY
VOTE
WRIGHT

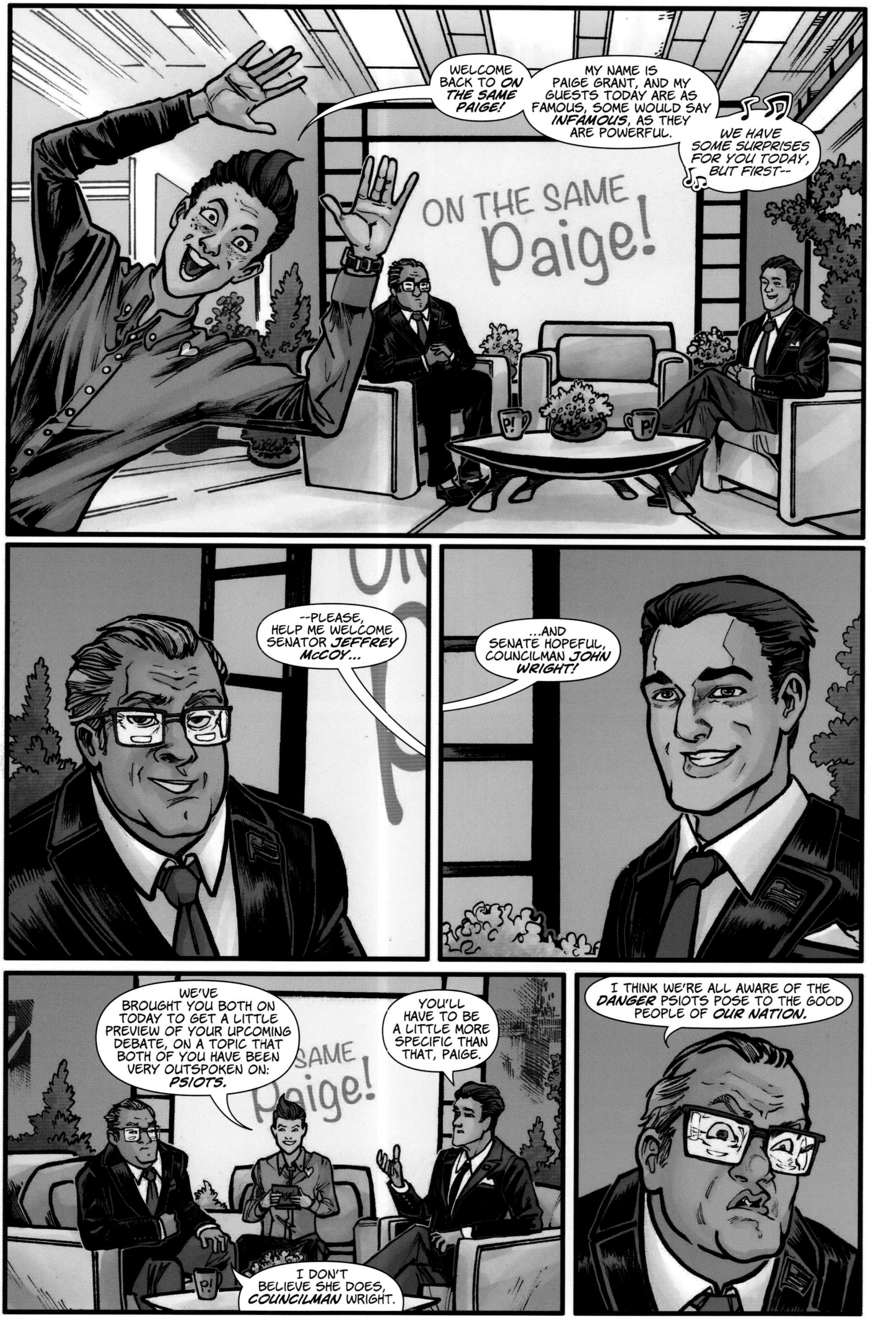
WELCOME BACK TO ON THE SAME PAIGE!
MY NAME IS PAIGE GRANT, AND MY GUESTS TODAY ARE AS FAMOUS, SOME WOULD SAY INFAMOUS, AS THEY ARE POWERFUL.
WE HAVE SOME SURPRISES FOR YOU TODAY, BUT FIRST--
ON THE SAME Paige!
--PLEASE, HELP ME WELCOME SENATOR JEFFREY McCOY...
...AND SENATE HOPEFUL, COUNCILMAN JOHN WRIGHT!
WE'VE BROUGHT YOU BOTH ON TODAY TO GET A LITTLE PREVIEW OF YOUR UPCOMING DEBATE, ON A TOPIC THAT BOTH OF YOU HAVE BEEN VERY OUTSPOKEN ON: PSIOTS.
YOU'LL HAVE TO BE A LITTLE MORE SPECIFIC THAN THAT, PAIGE.
I DON'T BELIEVE SHE DOES, COUNCILMAN WRIGHT.
I THINK WE'RE ALL AWARE OF THE DANGER PSIOTS POSE TO THE GOOD PEOPLE OF OUR NATION.

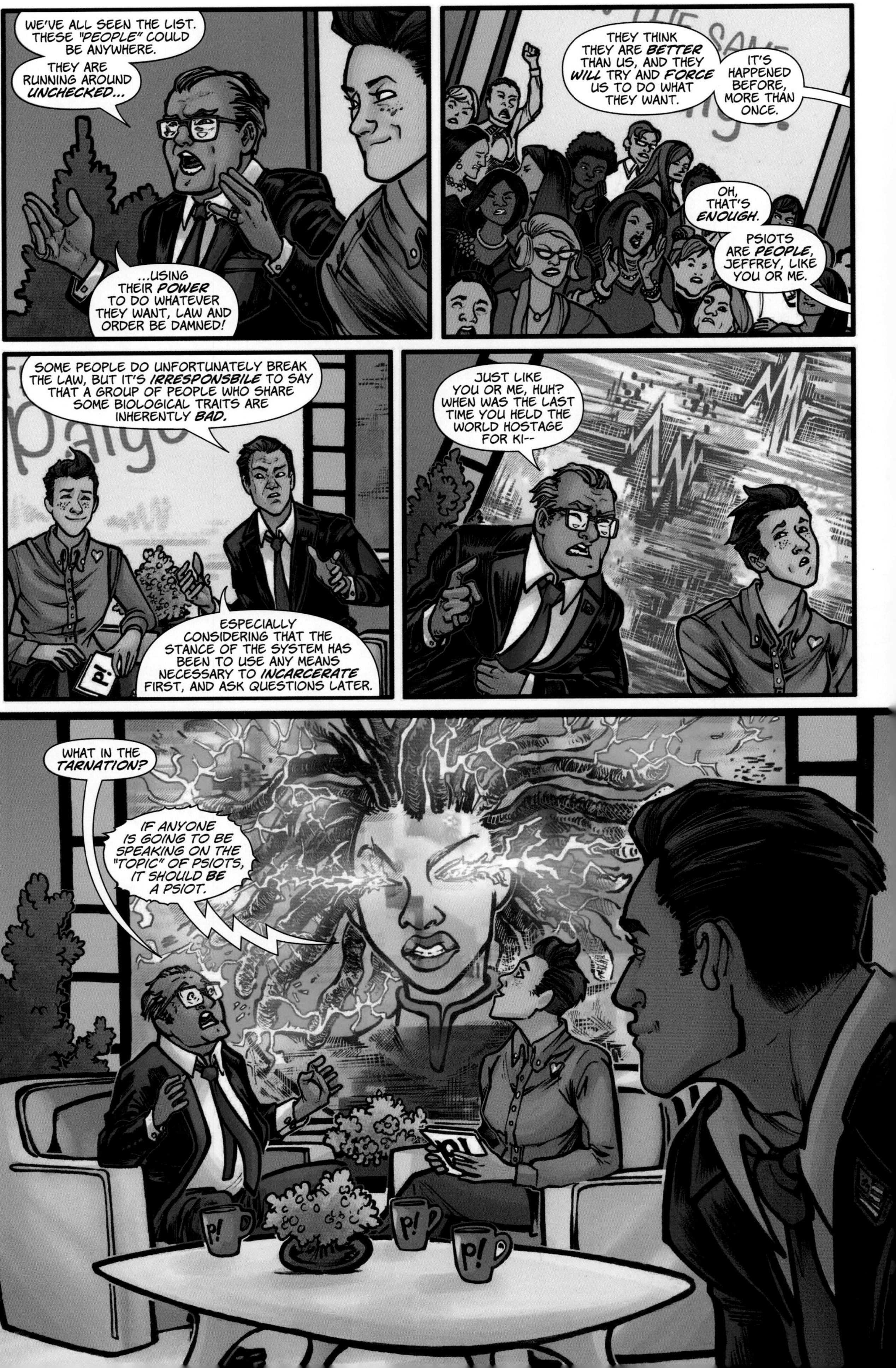
WE'VE ALL SEEN THE LIST. THESE "PEOPLE" COULD BE ANYWHERE.
THEY ARE RUNNING AROUND *UNCHECKED...*
...USING THEIR *POWER* TO DO WHATEVER THEY WANT, LAW AND ORDER BE DAMNED!
THEY THINK THEY ARE *BETTER* THAN US, AND THEY *WILL* TRY AND *FORCE* US TO DO WHAT THEY WANT.
IT'S HAPPENED BEFORE, MORE THAN ONCE.
OH, THAT'S *ENOUGH.*
PSIOTS ARE *PEOPLE,* JEFFREY, LIKE YOU OR ME.
SOME PEOPLE DO UNFORTUNATELY BREAK THE LAW, BUT IT'S *IRRESPONSBILE* TO SAY THAT A GROUP OF PEOPLE WHO SHARE SOME BIOLOGICAL TRAITS ARE INHERENTLY *BAD.*
ESPECIALLY CONSIDERING THAT THE STANCE OF THE SYSTEM HAS BEEN TO USE ANY MEANS NECESSARY TO *INCARCERATE* FIRST, AND ASK QUESTIONS LATER.
JUST LIKE YOU OR ME, HUH? WHEN WAS THE LAST TIME YOU HELD THE WORLD HOSTAGE FOR KI--
WHAT IN THE *TARNATION?*
*IF ANYONE IS GOING TO BE SPEAKING ON THE "TOPIC" OF PSIOTS, IT SHOULD **BE** A PSIOT.*

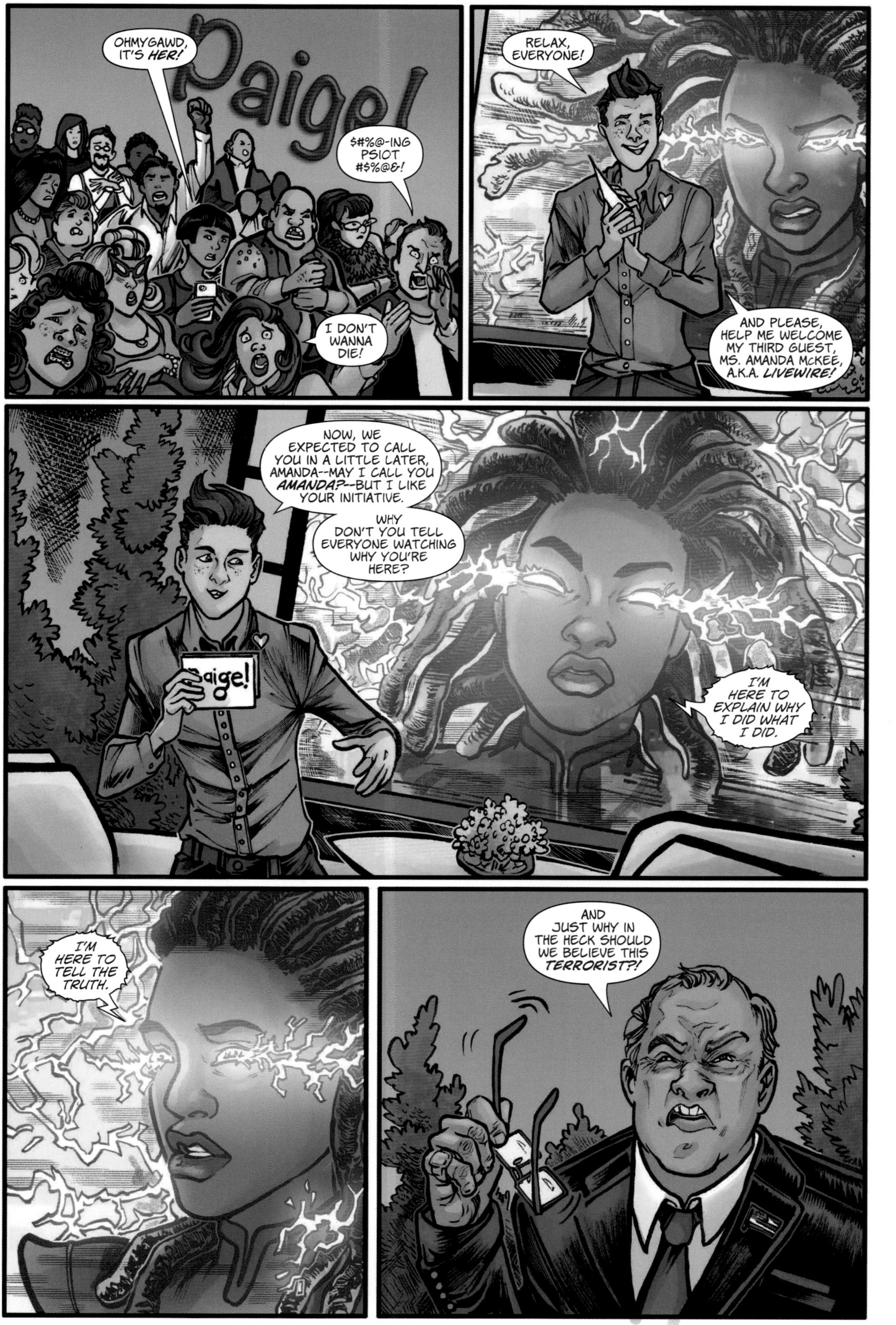
Paige!
OHMYGAWD, IT'S HER!
$#%@-ING PSIOT #$%@&!
I DON'T WANNA DIE!
RELAX, EVERYONE!
AND PLEASE, HELP ME WELCOME MY THIRD GUEST, MS. AMANDA McKEE, A.K.A. LIVEWIRE!
NOW, WE EXPECTED TO CALL YOU IN A LITTLE LATER, AMANDA--MAY I CALL YOU AMANDA?--BUT I LIKE YOUR INITIATIVE.
WHY DON'T YOU TELL EVERYONE WATCHING WHY YOU'RE HERE?
Paige!
I'M HERE TO EXPLAIN WHY I DID WHAT I DID.
I'M HERE TO TELL THE TRUTH.
AND JUST WHY IN THE HECK SHOULD WE BELIEVE THIS TERRORIST?!

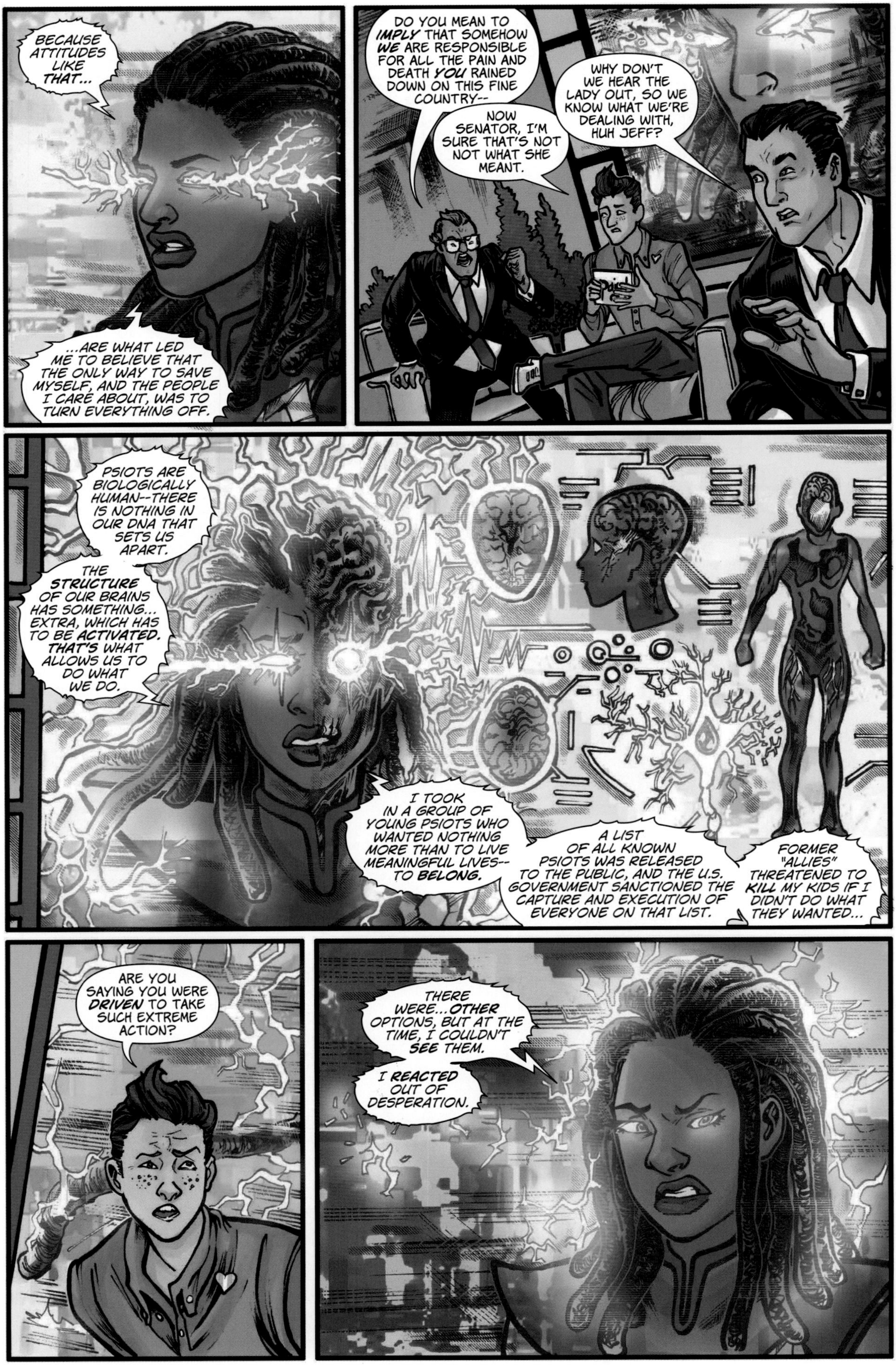

BECAUSE ATTITUDES LIKE THAT...
...ARE WHAT LED ME TO BELIEVE THAT THE ONLY WAY TO SAVE MYSELF, AND THE PEOPLE I CARE ABOUT, WAS TO TURN EVERYTHING OFF.
DO YOU MEAN TO IMPLY THAT SOMEHOW WE ARE RESPONSIBLE FOR ALL THE PAIN AND DEATH YOU RAINED DOWN ON THIS FINE COUNTRY--
NOW SENATOR, I'M SURE THAT'S NOT NOT WHAT SHE MEANT.
WHY DON'T WE HEAR THE LADY OUT, SO WE KNOW WHAT WE'RE DEALING WITH, HUH JEFF?
PSIOTS ARE BIOLOGICALLY HUMAN--THERE IS NOTHING IN OUR DNA THAT SETS US APART.
THE STRUCTURE OF OUR BRAINS HAS SOMETHING... EXTRA, WHICH HAS TO BE ACTIVATED. THAT'S WHAT ALLOWS US TO DO WHAT WE DO.
I TOOK IN A GROUP OF YOUNG PSIOTS WHO WANTED NOTHING MORE THAN TO LIVE MEANINGFUL LIVES-- TO BELONG.
A LIST OF ALL KNOWN PSIOTS WAS RELEASED TO THE PUBLIC, AND THE U.S. GOVERNMENT SANCTIONED THE CAPTURE AND EXECUTION OF EVERYONE ON THAT LIST.
FORMER "ALLIES" THREATENED TO KILL MY KIDS IF I DIDN'T DO WHAT THEY WANTED...
ARE YOU SAYING YOU WERE DRIVEN TO TAKE SUCH EXTREME ACTION?
THERE WERE...OTHER OPTIONS, BUT AT THE TIME, I COULDN'T SEE THEM.
I REACTED OUT OF DESPERATION.

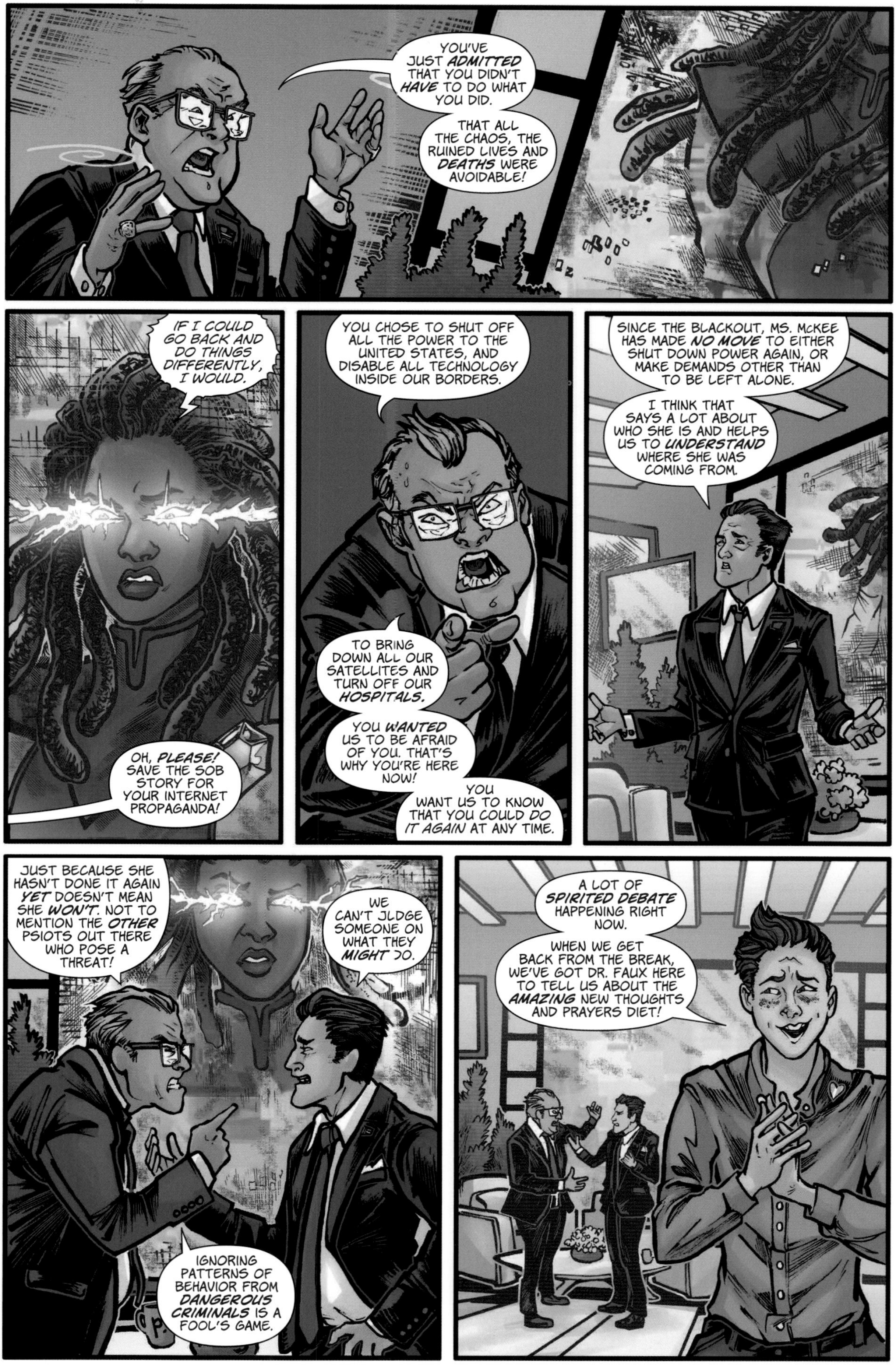
YOU'VE JUST ADMITTED THAT YOU DIDN'T HAVE TO DO WHAT YOU DID.
THAT ALL THE CHAOS, THE RUINED LIVES AND DEATHS WERE AVOIDABLE!
IF I COULD GO BACK AND DO THINGS DIFFERENTLY, I WOULD.
OH, PLEASE! SAVE THE SOB STORY FOR YOUR INTERNET PROPAGANDA!
YOU CHOSE TO SHUT OFF ALL THE POWER TO THE UNITED STATES, AND DISABLE ALL TECHNOLOGY INSIDE OUR BORDERS.
TO BRING DOWN ALL OUR SATELLITES AND TURN OFF OUR HOSPITALS.
YOU WANTED US TO BE AFRAID OF YOU. THAT'S WHY YOU'RE HERE NOW!
YOU WANT US TO KNOW THAT YOU COULD DO IT AGAIN AT ANY TIME.
SINCE THE BLACKOUT, MS. McKEE HAS MADE NO MOVE TO EITHER SHUT DOWN POWER AGAIN, OR MAKE DEMANDS OTHER THAN TO BE LEFT ALONE.
I THINK THAT SAYS A LOT ABOUT WHO SHE IS AND HELPS US TO UNDERSTAND WHERE SHE WAS COMING FROM.
JUST BECAUSE SHE HASN'T DONE IT AGAIN YET DOESN'T MEAN SHE WON'T. NOT TO MENTION THE OTHER PSIOTS OUT THERE WHO POSE A THREAT!
WE CAN'T JUDGE SOMEONE ON WHAT THEY MIGHT DO.
IGNORING PATTERNS OF BEHAVIOR FROM DANGEROUS CRIMINALS IS A FOOL'S GAME.
A LOT OF SPIRITED DEBATE HAPPENING RIGHT NOW.
WHEN WE GET BACK FROM THE BREAK, WE'VE GOT DR. FAUX HERE TO TELL US ABOUT THE AMAZING NEW THOUGHTS AND PRAYERS DIET!

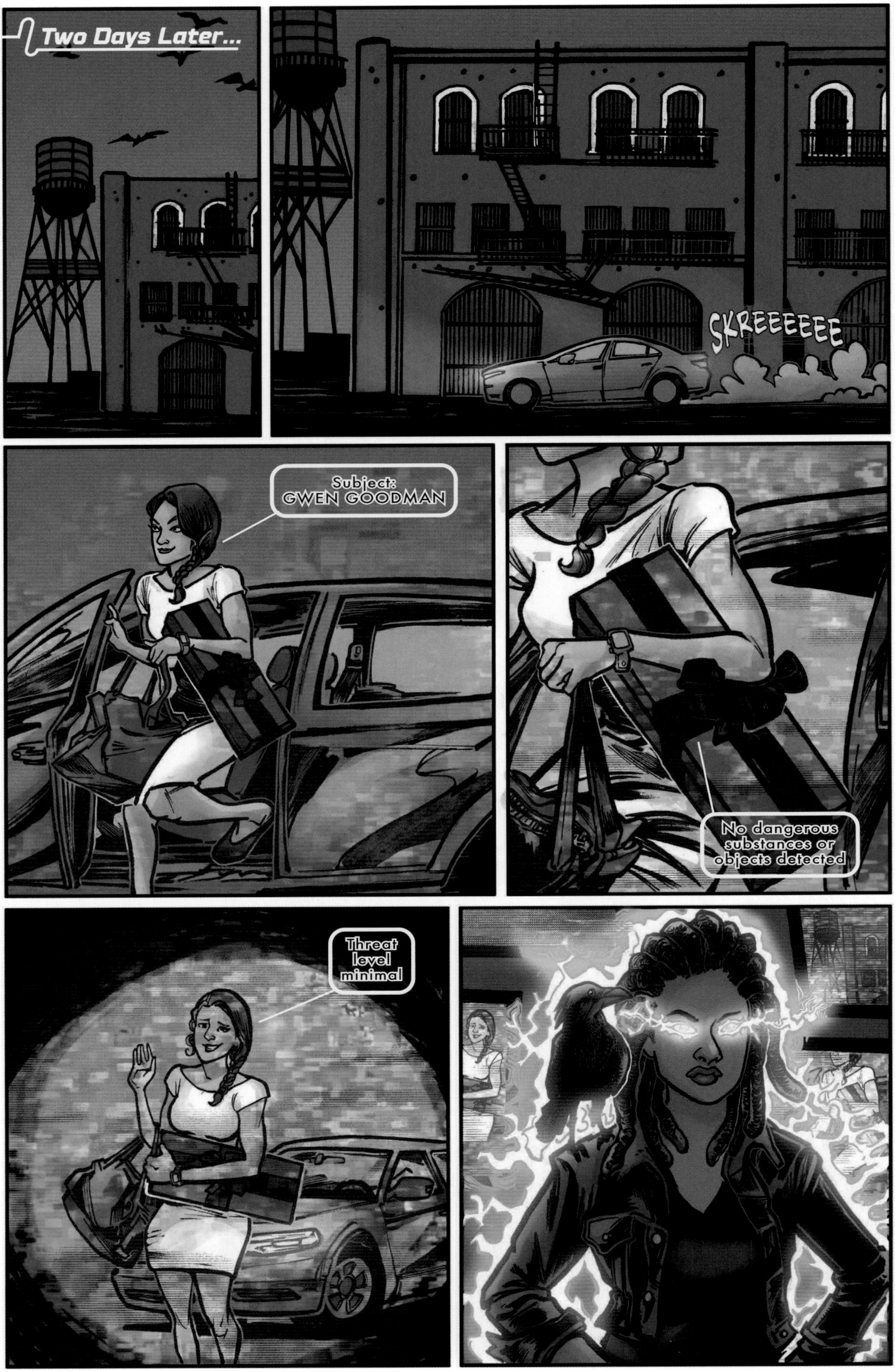
Two Days Later...
SKREEEEEE
Subject: GWEN GOODMAN
No dangerous substances or objects detected
Threat level minimal

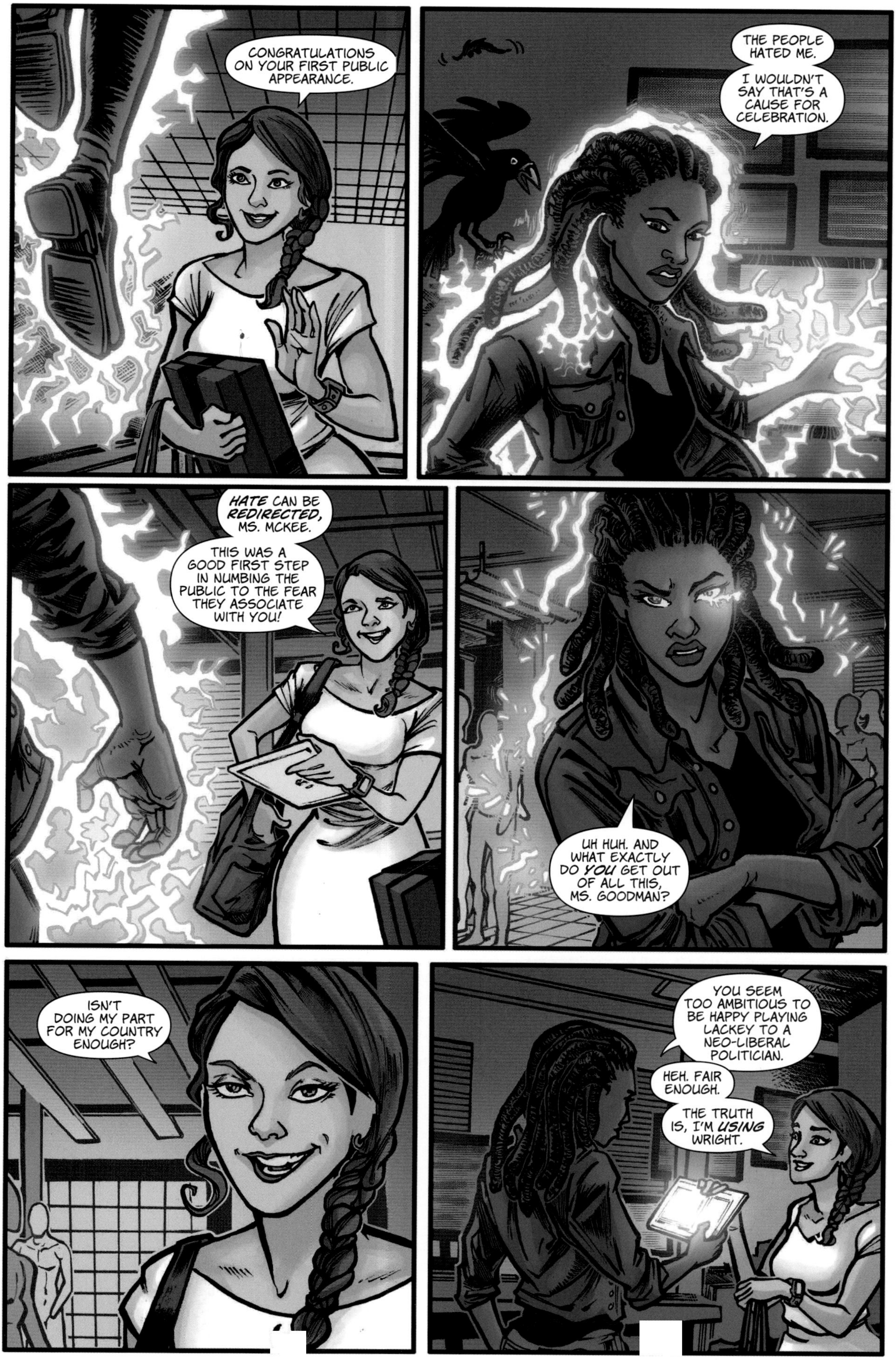

CONGRATULATIONS ON YOUR FIRST PUBLIC APPEARANCE.
THE PEOPLE HATED ME.
I WOULDN'T SAY THAT'S A CAUSE FOR CELEBRATION.
HATE CAN BE *REDIRECTED,* MS. MCKEE.
THIS WAS A GOOD FIRST STEP IN NUMBING THE PUBLIC TO THE FEAR THEY ASSOCIATE WITH YOU!
UH HUH. AND WHAT EXACTLY DO *YOU* GET OUT OF ALL THIS, MS. GOODMAN?
ISN'T DOING MY PART FOR MY COUNTRY ENOUGH?
YOU SEEM TOO AMBITIOUS TO BE HAPPY PLAYING LACKEY TO A NEO-LIBERAL POLITICIAN.
HEH. FAIR ENOUGH.
THE TRUTH IS, I'M *USING* WRIGHT.

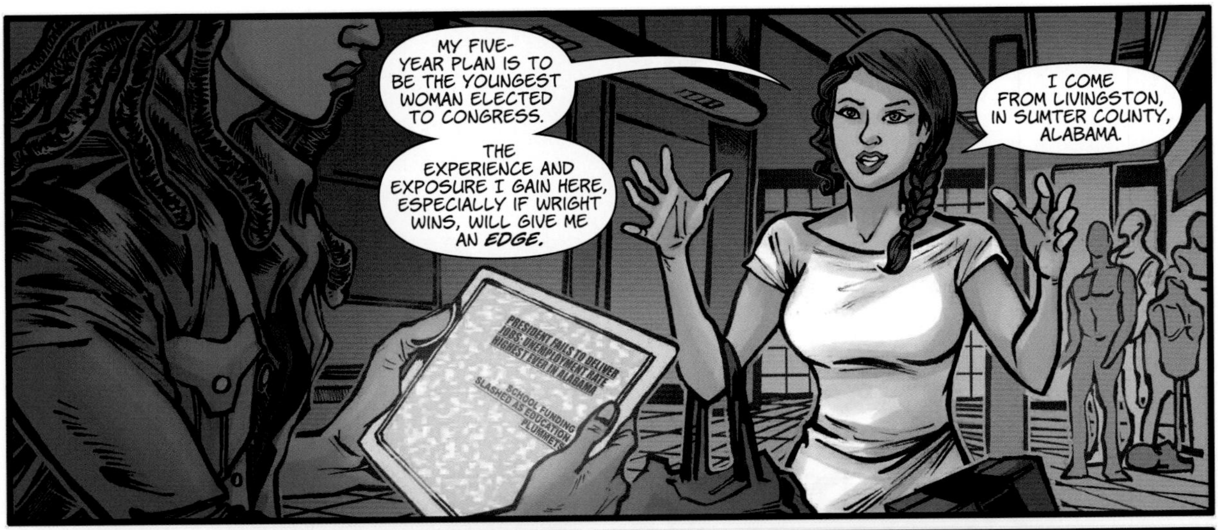
MY FIVE-YEAR PLAN IS TO BE THE YOUNGEST WOMAN ELECTED TO CONGRESS.
THE EXPERIENCE AND EXPOSURE I GAIN HERE, ESPECIALLY IF WRIGHT WINS, WILL GIVE ME AN *EDGE.*
I COME FROM LIVINGSTON, IN SUMTER COUNTY, ALABAMA.
PRESIDENT FAILS TO DELIVER JOBS; UNEMPLOYMENT RATE HIGHEST EVER IN ALABAMA
SCHOOL FUNDING SLASHED AS EDUCATION PLUMMETS

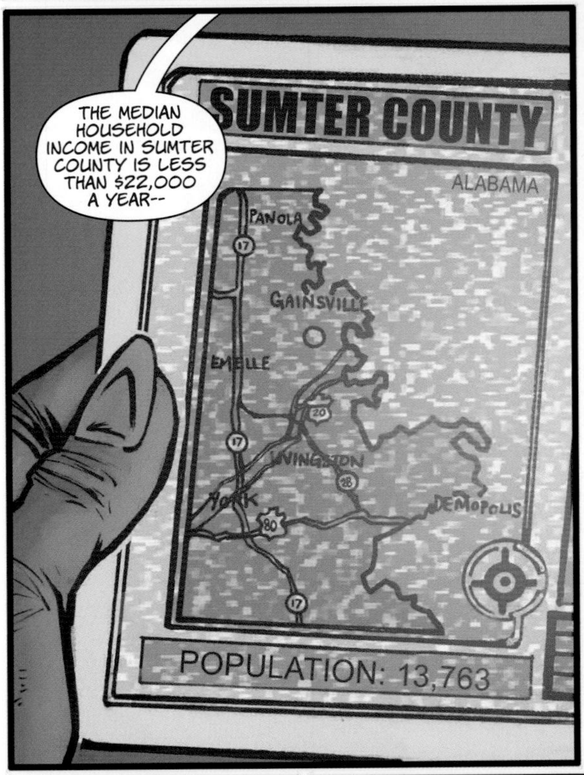
THE MEDIAN HOUSEHOLD INCOME IN SUMTER COUNTY IS LESS THAN $22,000 A YEAR--
SUMTER COUNTY
ALABAMA
PANOLA
GAINSVILLE
EMELLE
LIVINGSTON
YORK
DEMOPOLIS
17
20
28
80
POPULATION: 13,763

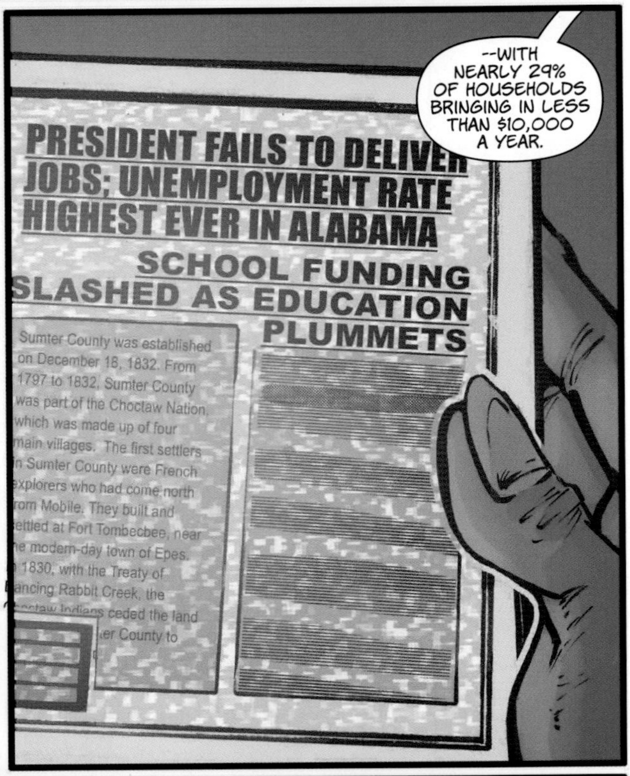
--WITH NEARLY 29% OF HOUSEHOLDS BRINGING IN LESS THAN $10,000 A YEAR.
JOBS; UNEMPLOYMENT RATE
HIGHEST EVER IN ALABAMA
SCHOOL FUNDING
SLASHED AS EDUCATION
PLUMMETS
Sumter County was established
on December 18, 1832. From
1797 to 1832, Sumter County
was part of the Choctaw Nation,
which was made up of four
main villages. The first settlers
in Sumter County were French
explorers who had come north
from Mobile. They built and
settled at Fort Tombecbee, near
the modern-day town of Epes.
1830, with the Treaty of
Rabbit Creek, the
ceded the land

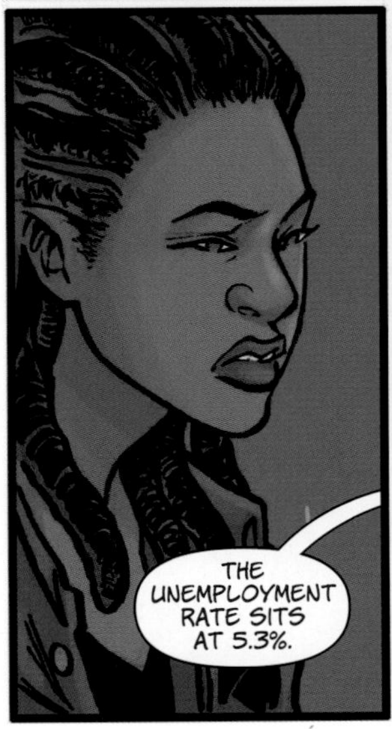
THE UNEMPLOYMENT RATE SITS AT 5.3%.

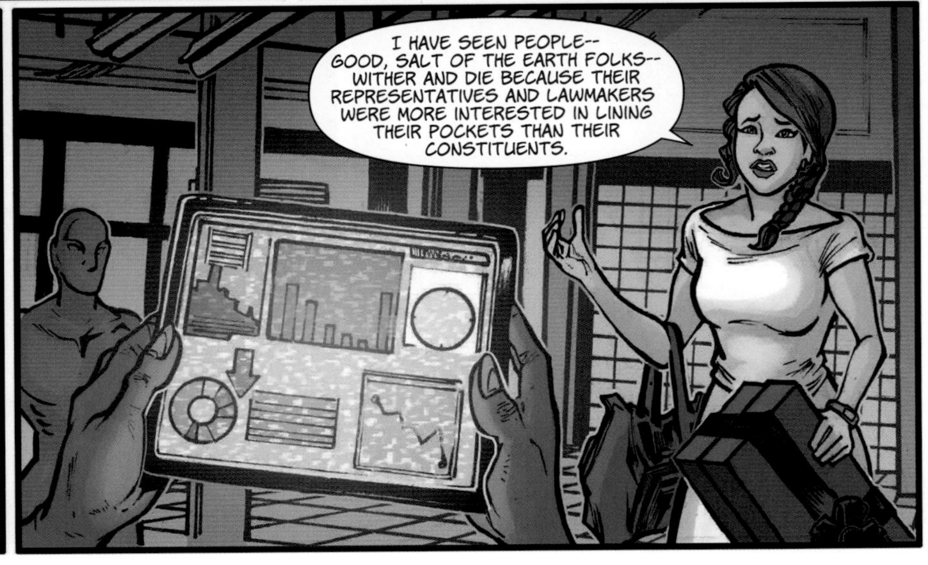
I HAVE SEEN PEOPLE-- GOOD, SALT OF THE EARTH FOLKS-- WITHER AND DIE BECAUSE THEIR REPRESENTATIVES AND LAWMAKERS WERE MORE INTERESTED IN LINING THEIR POCKETS THAN THEIR CONSTITUENTS.

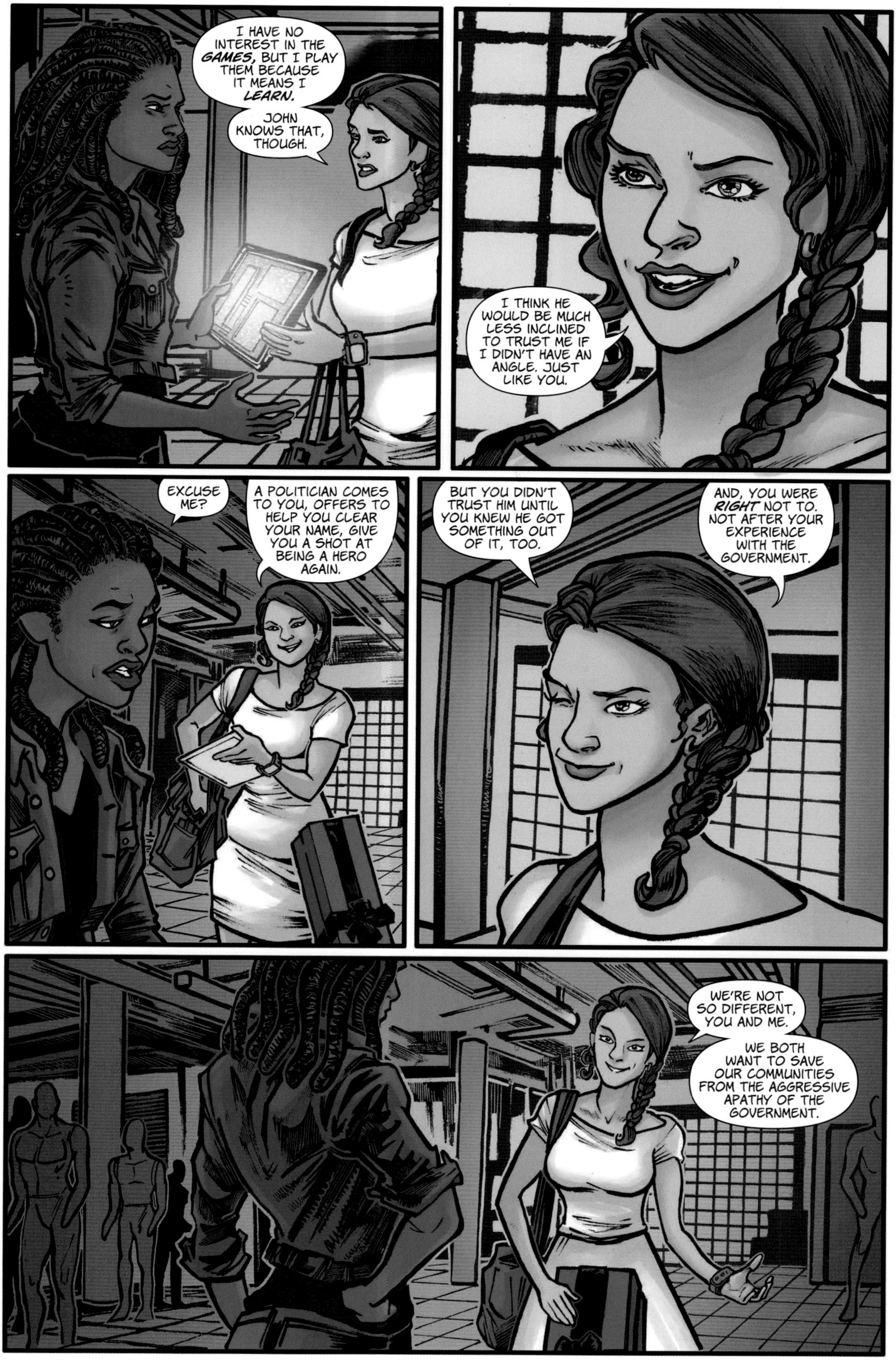
I HAVE NO INTEREST IN THE GAMES, BUT I PLAY THEM BECAUSE IT MEANS I LEARN.
JOHN KNOWS THAT, THOUGH.
I THINK HE WOULD BE MUCH LESS INCLINED TO TRUST ME IF I DIDN'T HAVE AN ANGLE. JUST LIKE YOU.
EXCUSE ME?
A POLITICIAN COMES TO YOU, OFFERS TO HELP YOU CLEAR YOUR NAME, GIVE YOU A SHOT AT BEING A HERO AGAIN.
BUT YOU DIDN'T TRUST HIM UNTIL YOU KNEW HE GOT SOMETHING OUT OF IT, TOO.
AND, YOU WERE RIGHT NOT TO. NOT AFTER YOUR EXPERIENCE WITH THE GOVERNMENT.
WE'RE NOT SO DIFFERENT, YOU AND ME.
WE BOTH WANT TO SAVE OUR COMMUNITIES FROM THE AGGRESSIVE APATHY OF THE GOVERNMENT.

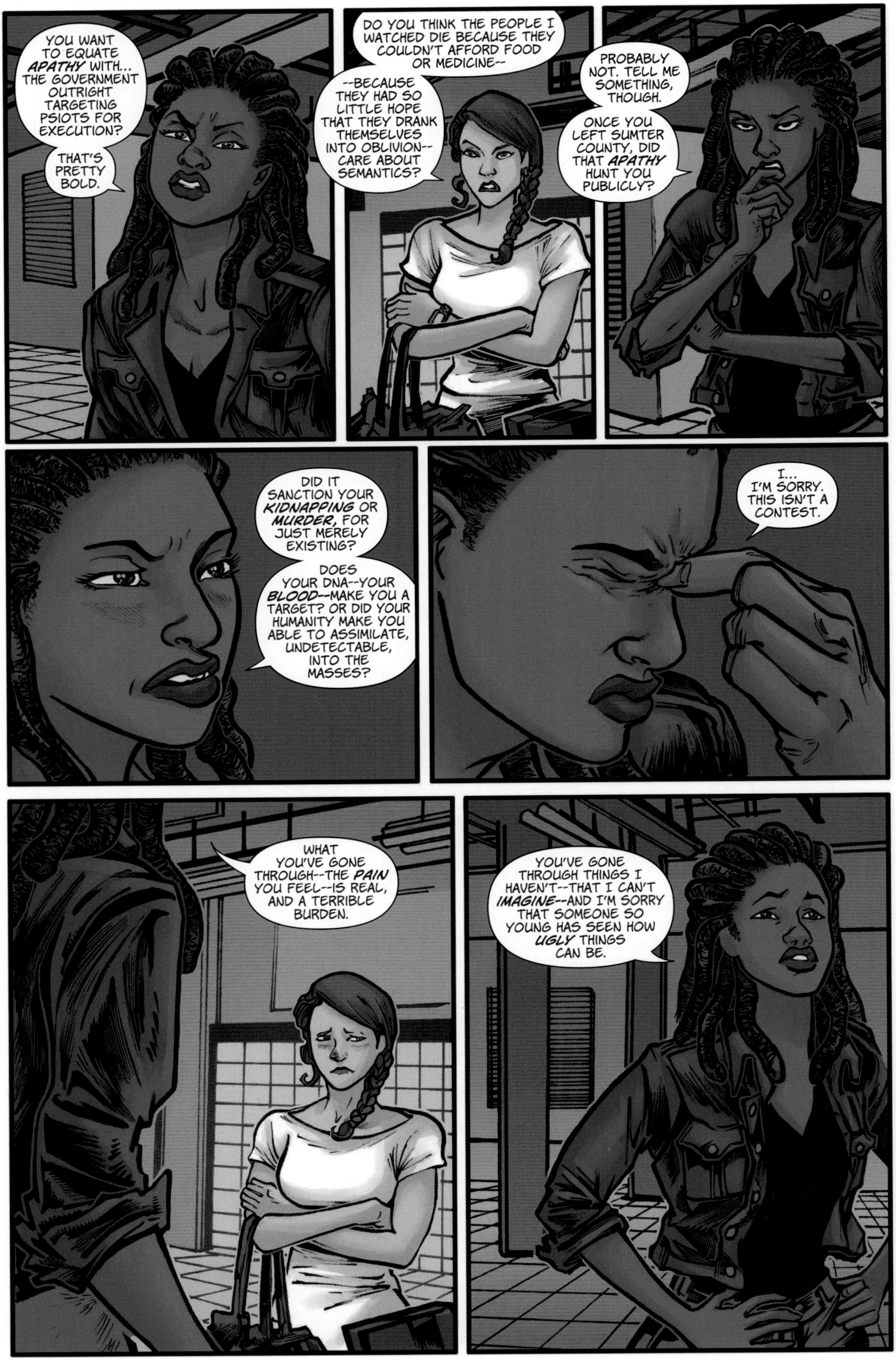
YOU WANT TO EQUATE APATHY WITH... THE GOVERNMENT OUTRIGHT TARGETING PSIOTS FOR EXECUTION?
THAT'S PRETTY BOLD.
DO YOU THINK THE PEOPLE I WATCHED DIE BECAUSE THEY COULDN'T AFFORD FOOD OR MEDICINE--
--BECAUSE THEY HAD SO LITTLE HOPE THAT THEY DRANK THEMSELVES INTO OBLIVION--CARE ABOUT SEMANTICS?
PROBABLY NOT. TELL ME SOMETHING, THOUGH.
ONCE YOU LEFT SUMTER COUNTY, DID THAT APATHY HUNT YOU PUBLICLY?
DID IT SANCTION YOUR KIDNAPPING OR MURDER, FOR JUST MERELY EXISTING?
DOES YOUR DNA--YOUR BLOOD--MAKE YOU A TARGET? OR DID YOUR HUMANITY MAKE YOU ABLE TO ASSIMILATE, UNDETECTABLE, INTO THE MASSES?
I... I'M SORRY. THIS ISN'T A CONTEST.
WHAT YOU'VE GONE THROUGH--THE PAIN YOU FEEL--IS REAL, AND A TERRIBLE BURDEN.
YOU'VE GONE THROUGH THINGS I HAVEN'T--THAT I CAN'T IMAGINE--AND I'M SORRY THAT SOMEONE SO YOUNG HAS SEEN HOW UGLY THINGS CAN BE.

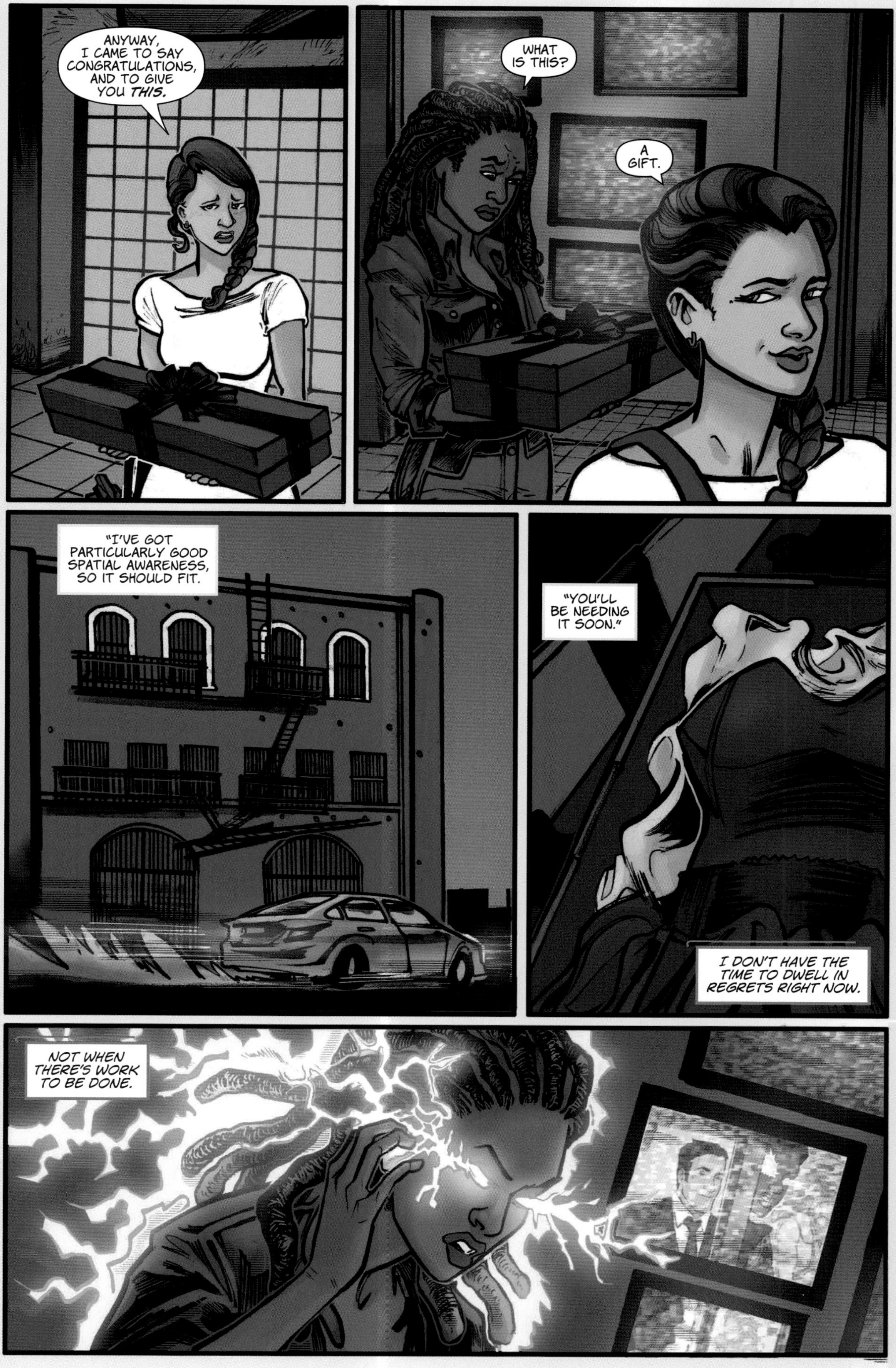
ANYWAY, I CAME TO SAY CONGRATULATIONS, AND TO GIVE YOU *THIS.*
WHAT IS THIS?
A GIFT.
"I'VE GOT PARTICULARLY GOOD SPATIAL AWARENESS, SO IT SHOULD FIT.
"YOU'LL BE NEEDING IT SOON."
I DON'T HAVE THE TIME TO DWELL IN REGRETS RIGHT NOW.
NOT WHEN THERE'S WORK TO BE DONE.

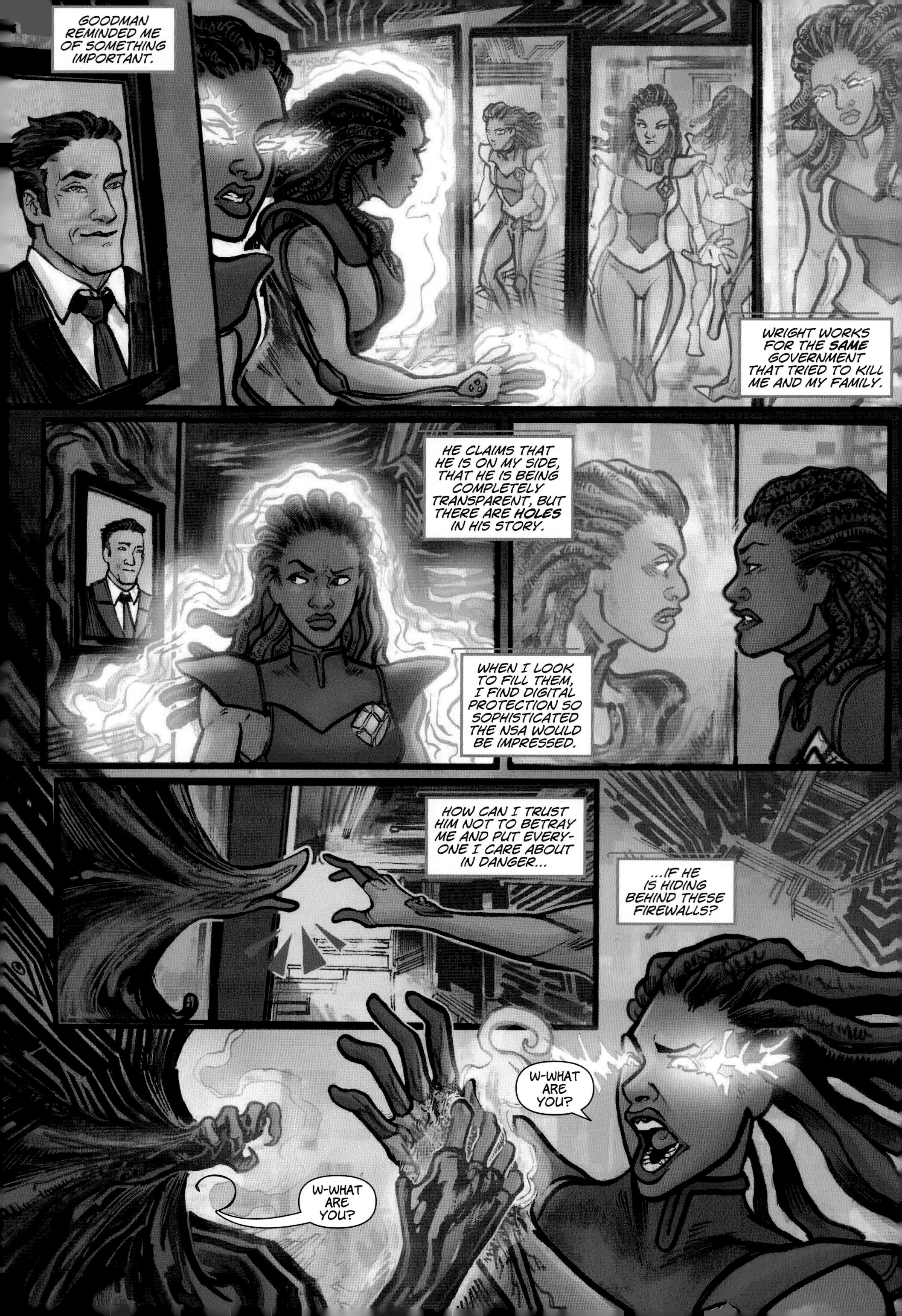
GOODMAN REMINDED ME OF SOMETHING IMPORTANT.
WRIGHT WORKS FOR THE SAME GOVERNMENT THAT TRIED TO KILL ME AND MY FAMILY.
HE CLAIMS THAT HE IS ON MY SIDE, THAT HE IS BEING COMPLETELY TRANSPARENT, BUT THERE ARE HOLES IN HIS STORY.
WHEN I LOOK TO FILL THEM, I FIND DIGITAL PROTECTION SO SOPHISTICATED THE NSA WOULD BE IMPRESSED.
HOW CAN I TRUST HIM NOT TO BETRAY ME AND PUT EVERY-ONE I CARE ABOUT IN DANGER...
...IF HE IS HIDING BEHIND THESE FIREWALLS?
W-WHAT ARE YOU?
W-WHAT ARE YOU?

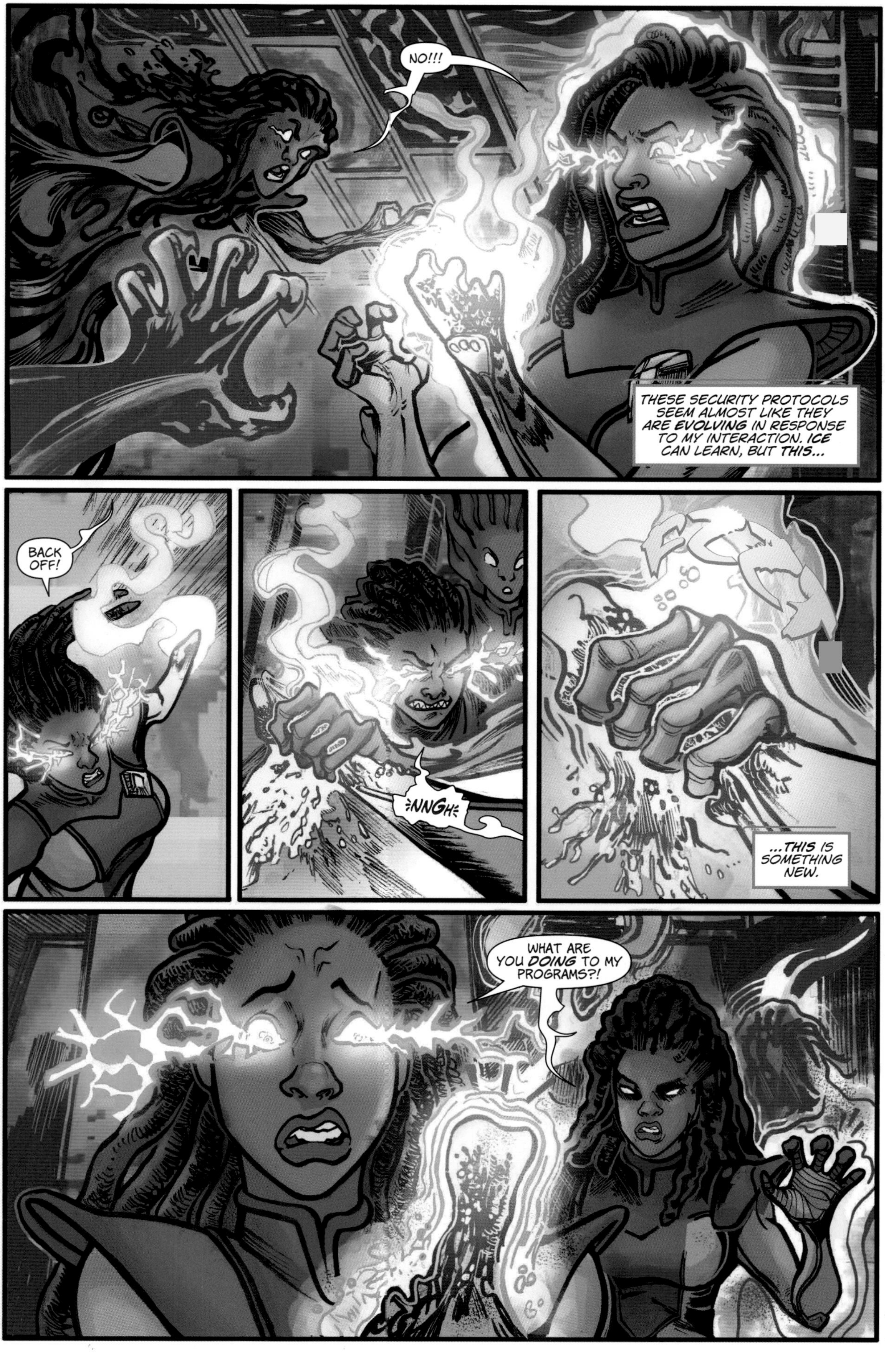
NO!!!
THESE SECURITY PROTOCOLS SEEM ALMOST LIKE THEY ARE EVOLVING IN RESPONSE TO MY INTERACTION. ICE CAN LEARN, BUT THIS...
BACK OFF!
NNGH!
...THIS IS SOMETHING NEW.
WHAT ARE YOU DOING TO MY PROGRAMS?!

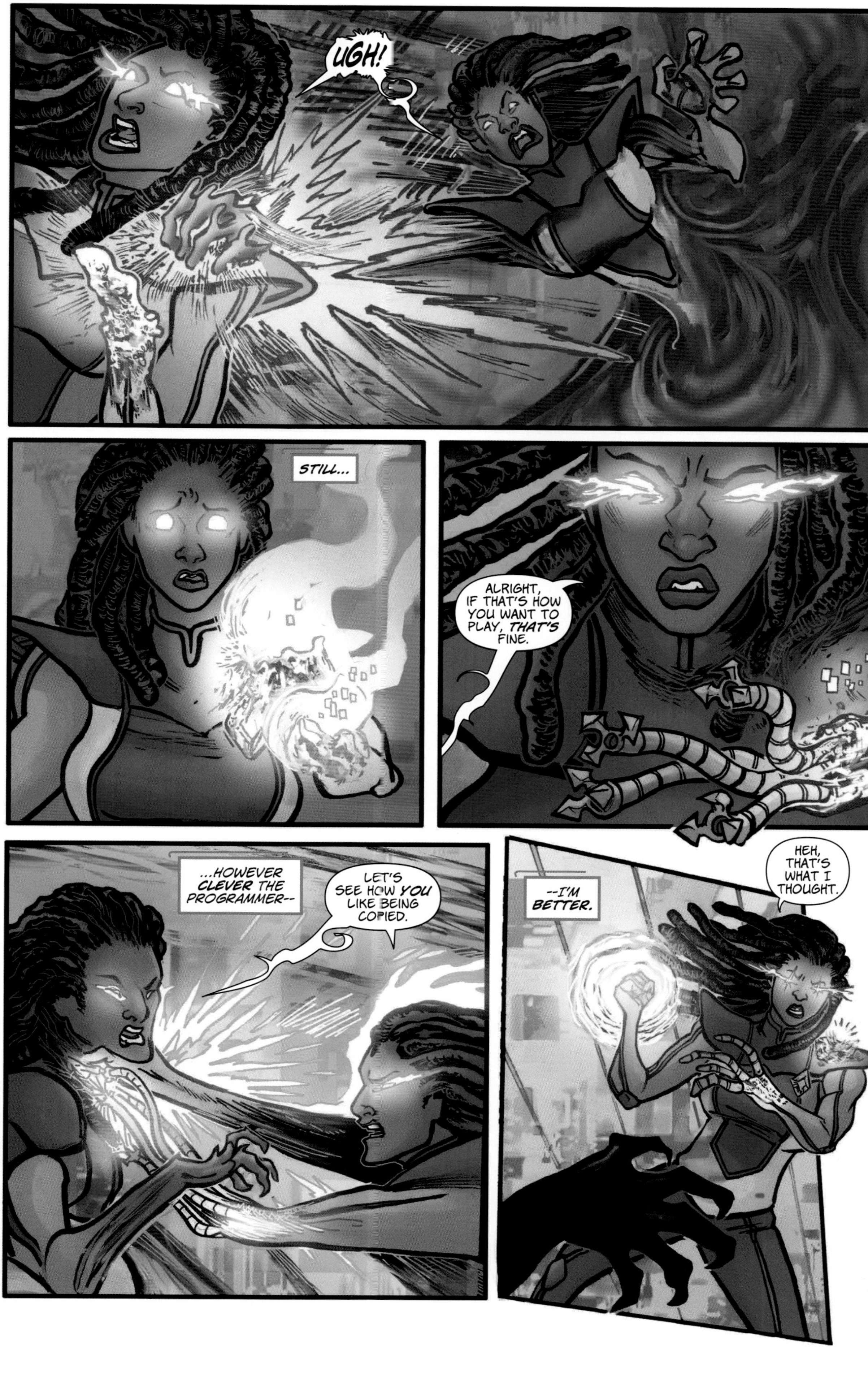
UGH!
STILL...
ALRIGHT, IF THAT'S HOW YOU WANT TO PLAY, THAT'S FINE.
...HOWEVER CLEVER THE PROGRAMMER--
LET'S SEE HOW YOU LIKE BEING COPIED.
--I'M BETTER.
HEH, THAT'S WHAT I THOUGHT.

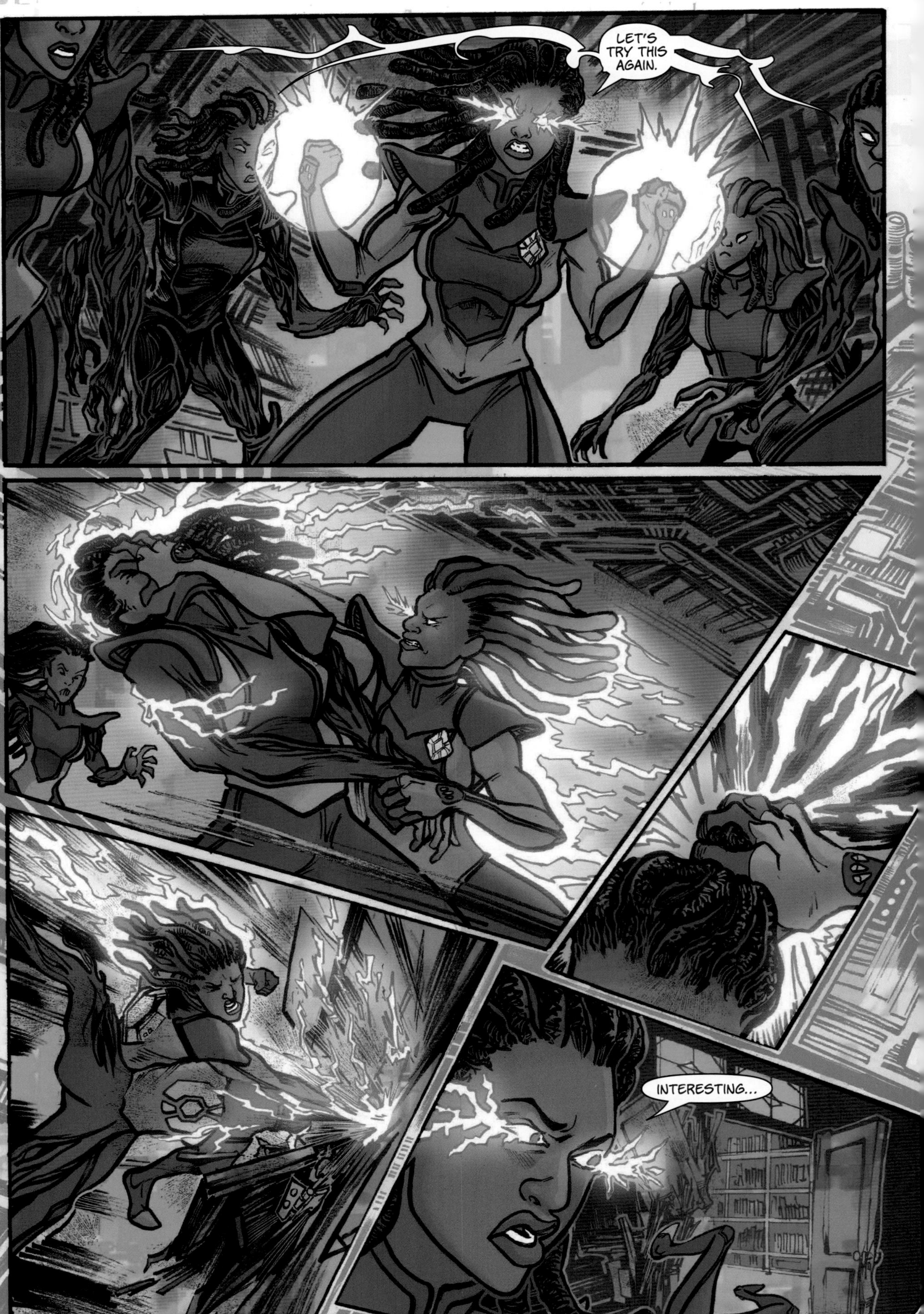
LET'S TRY THIS AGAIN.
INTERESTING...

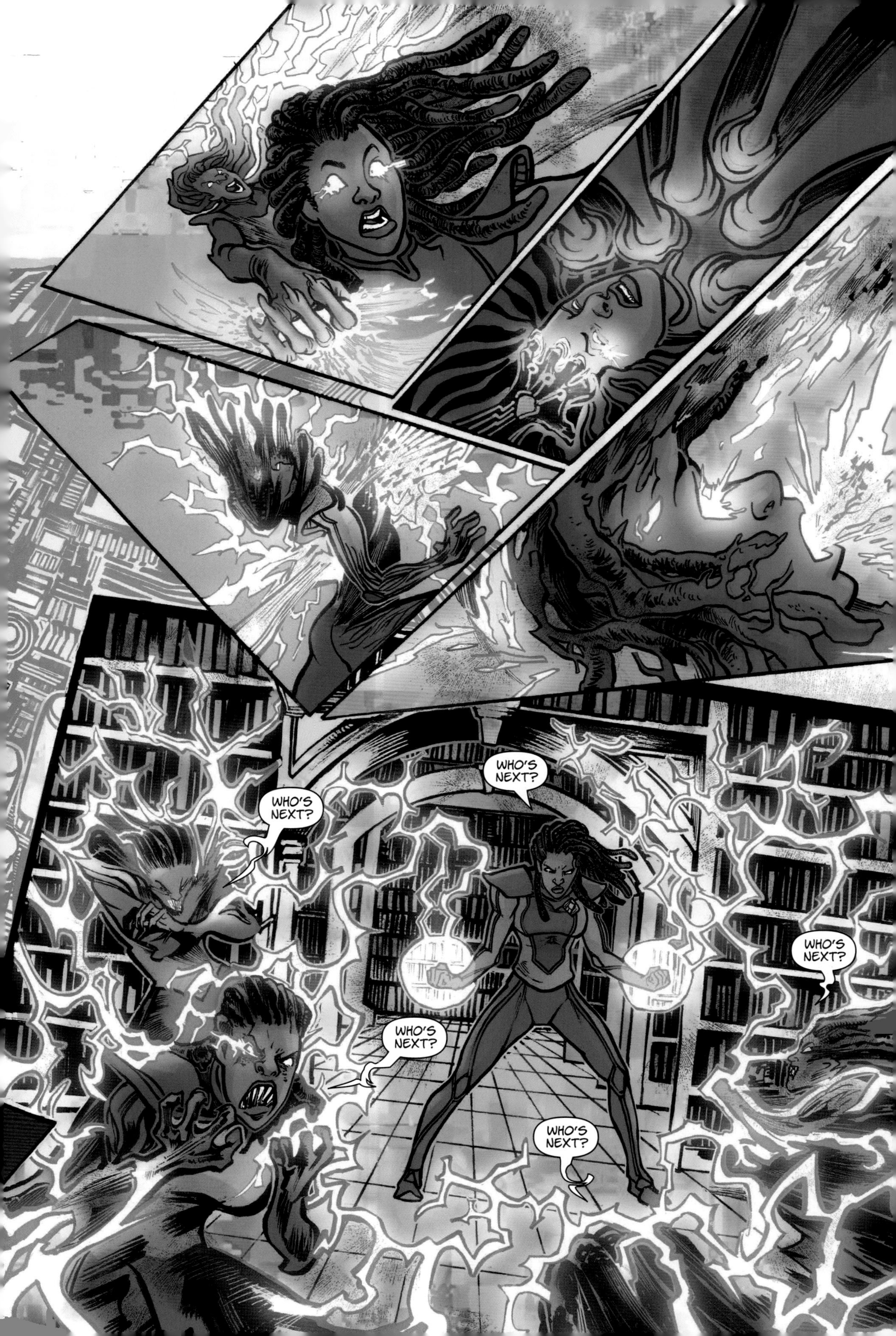
WHO'S NEXT?
WHO'S NEXT?
WHO'S NEXT?
WHO'S NEXT?
WHO'S NEXT?

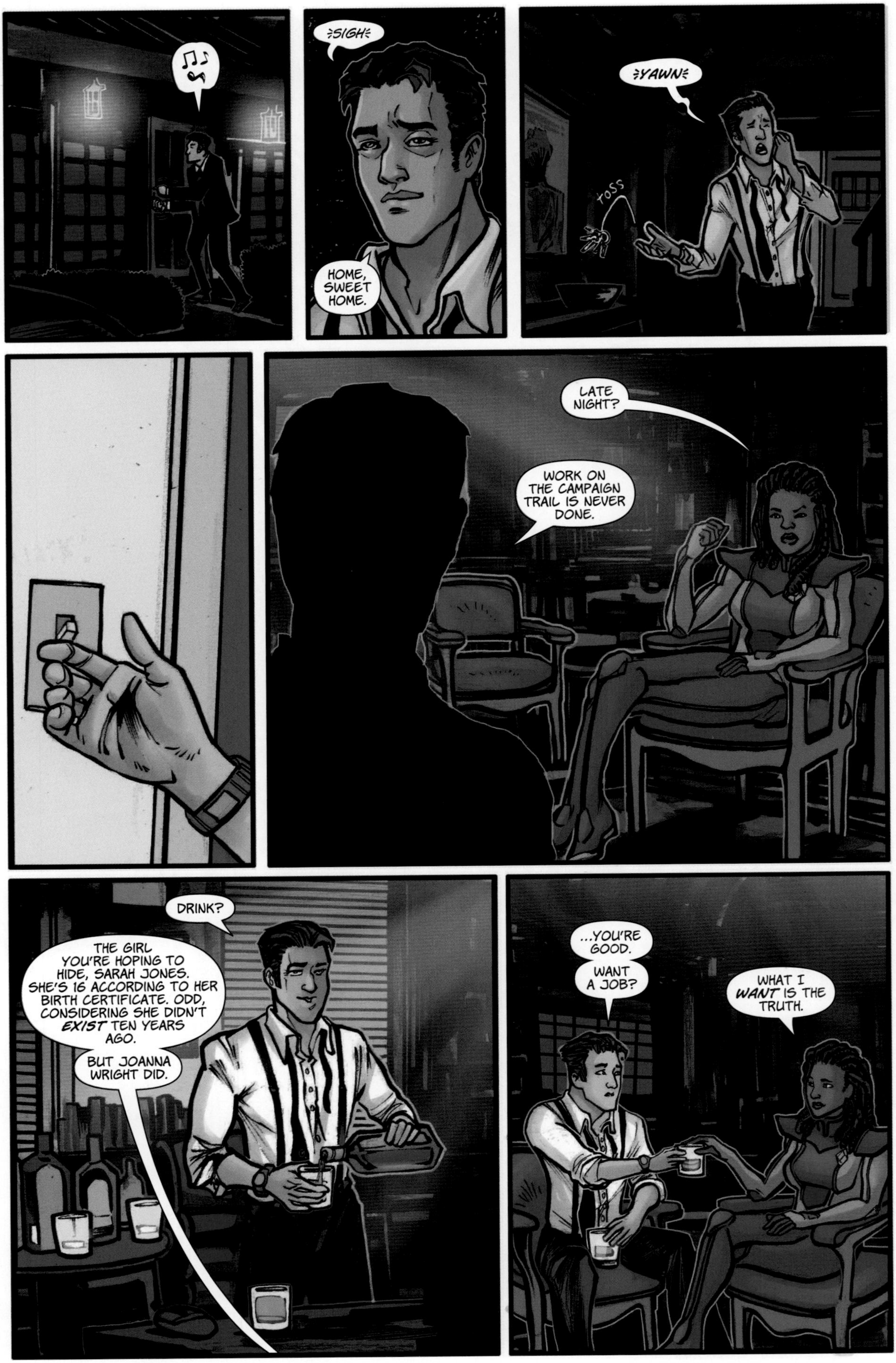

♫♪
SIGH
HOME, SWEET HOME.
YAWN
TOSS
LATE NIGHT?
WORK ON THE CAMPAIGN TRAIL IS NEVER DONE.
DRINK?
THE GIRL YOU'RE HOPING TO HIDE, SARAH JONES. SHE'S 16 ACCORDING TO HER BIRTH CERTIFICATE. ODD, CONSIDERING SHE DIDN'T *EXIST* TEN YEARS AGO.
BUT JOANNA WRIGHT DID.
...YOU'RE GOOD.
WANT A JOB?
WHAT I *WANT* IS THE TRUTH.

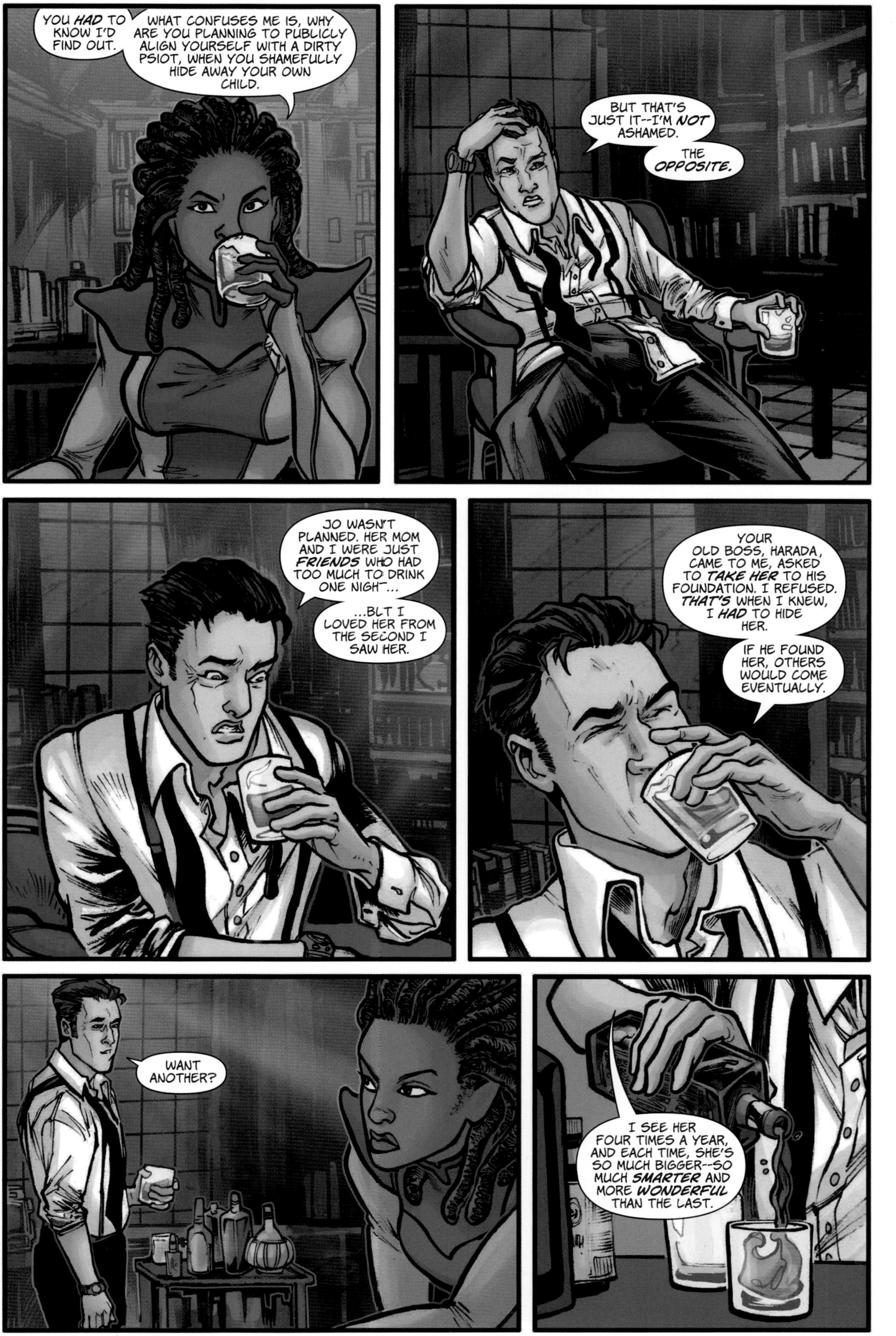
YOU *HAD* TO KNOW I'D FIND OUT.
WHAT CONFUSES ME IS, WHY ARE YOU PLANNING TO PUBLICLY ALIGN YOURSELF WITH A DIRTY PSIOT, WHEN YOU SHAMEFULLY HIDE AWAY YOUR OWN CHILD.
BUT THAT'S JUST IT--I'M *NOT* ASHAMED.
THE *OPPOSITE.*
JO WASN'T PLANNED. HER MOM AND I WERE JUST *FRIENDS* WHO HAD TOO MUCH TO DRINK ONE NIGHT...
...BUT I LOVED HER FROM THE SECOND I SAW HER.
YOUR OLD BOSS, HARADA, CAME TO ME, ASKED TO *TAKE HER* TO HIS FOUNDATION. I REFUSED. *THAT'S* WHEN I KNEW, I *HAD* TO HIDE HER.
IF HE FOUND HER, OTHERS WOULD COME EVENTUALLY.
WANT ANOTHER?
I SEE HER FOUR TIMES A YEAR, AND EACH TIME, SHE'S SO MUCH BIGGER--SO MUCH *SMARTER* AND MORE *WONDERFUL* THAN THE LAST.

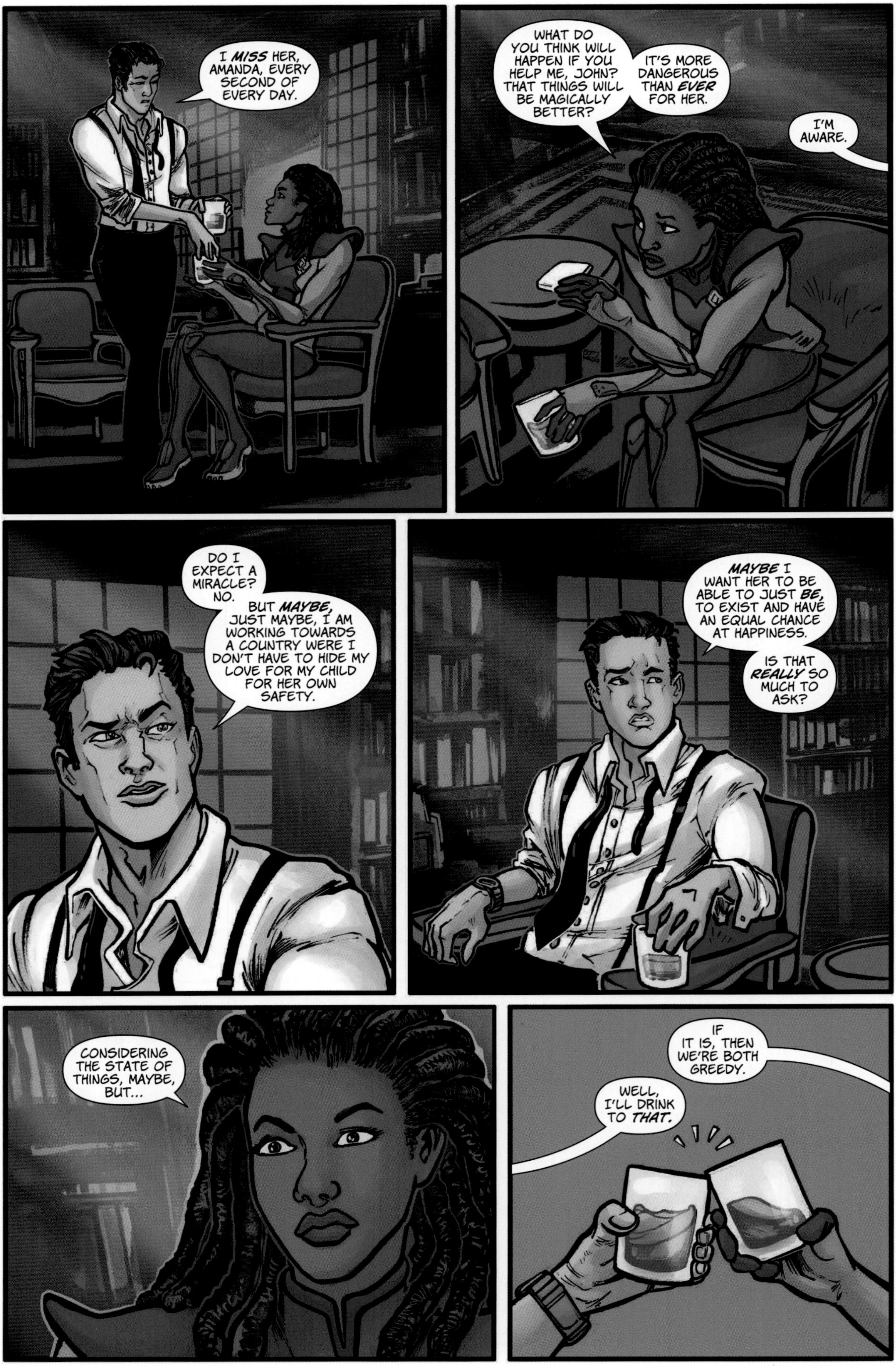
I MISS HER, AMANDA, EVERY SECOND OF EVERY DAY.
WHAT DO YOU THINK WILL HAPPEN IF YOU HELP ME, JOHN? THAT THINGS WILL BE MAGICALLY BETTER?
IT'S MORE DANGEROUS THAN EVER FOR HER.
I'M AWARE.
DO I EXPECT A MIRACLE? NO.
BUT MAYBE, JUST MAYBE, I AM WORKING TOWARDS A COUNTRY WERE I DON'T HAVE TO HIDE MY LOVE FOR MY CHILD FOR HER OWN SAFETY.
MAYBE I WANT HER TO BE ABLE TO JUST BE, TO EXIST AND HAVE AN EQUAL CHANCE AT HAPPINESS.
IS THAT REALLY SO MUCH TO ASK?
CONSIDERING THE STATE OF THINGS, MAYBE, BUT...
IF IT IS, THEN WE'RE BOTH GREEDY.
WELL, I'LL DRINK TO THAT.

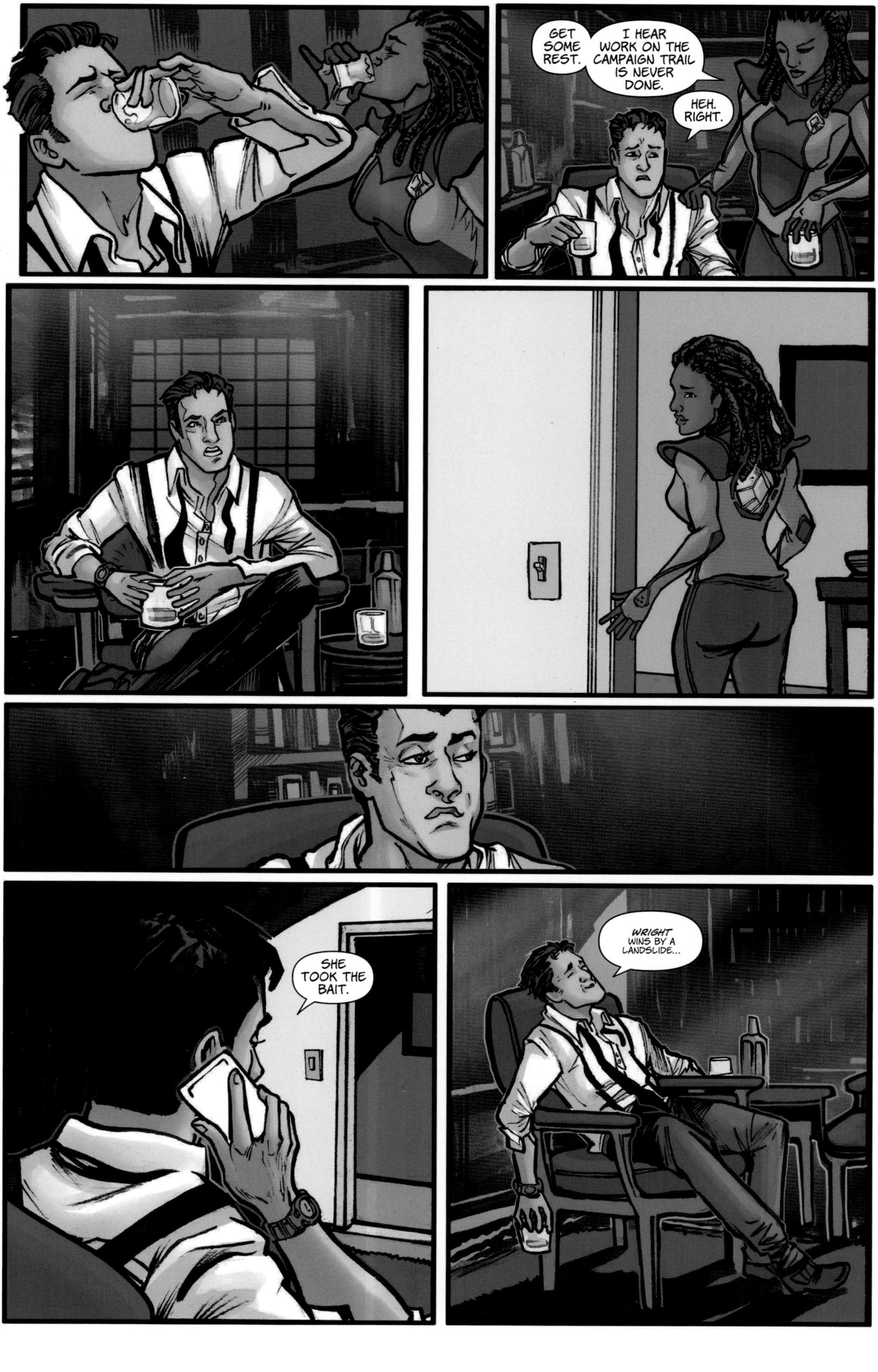
GET SOME REST.
I HEAR WORK ON THE CAMPAIGN TRAIL IS NEVER DONE.
HEH. RIGHT.
SHE TOOK THE BAIT.
WRIGHT WINS BY A LANDSLIDE...

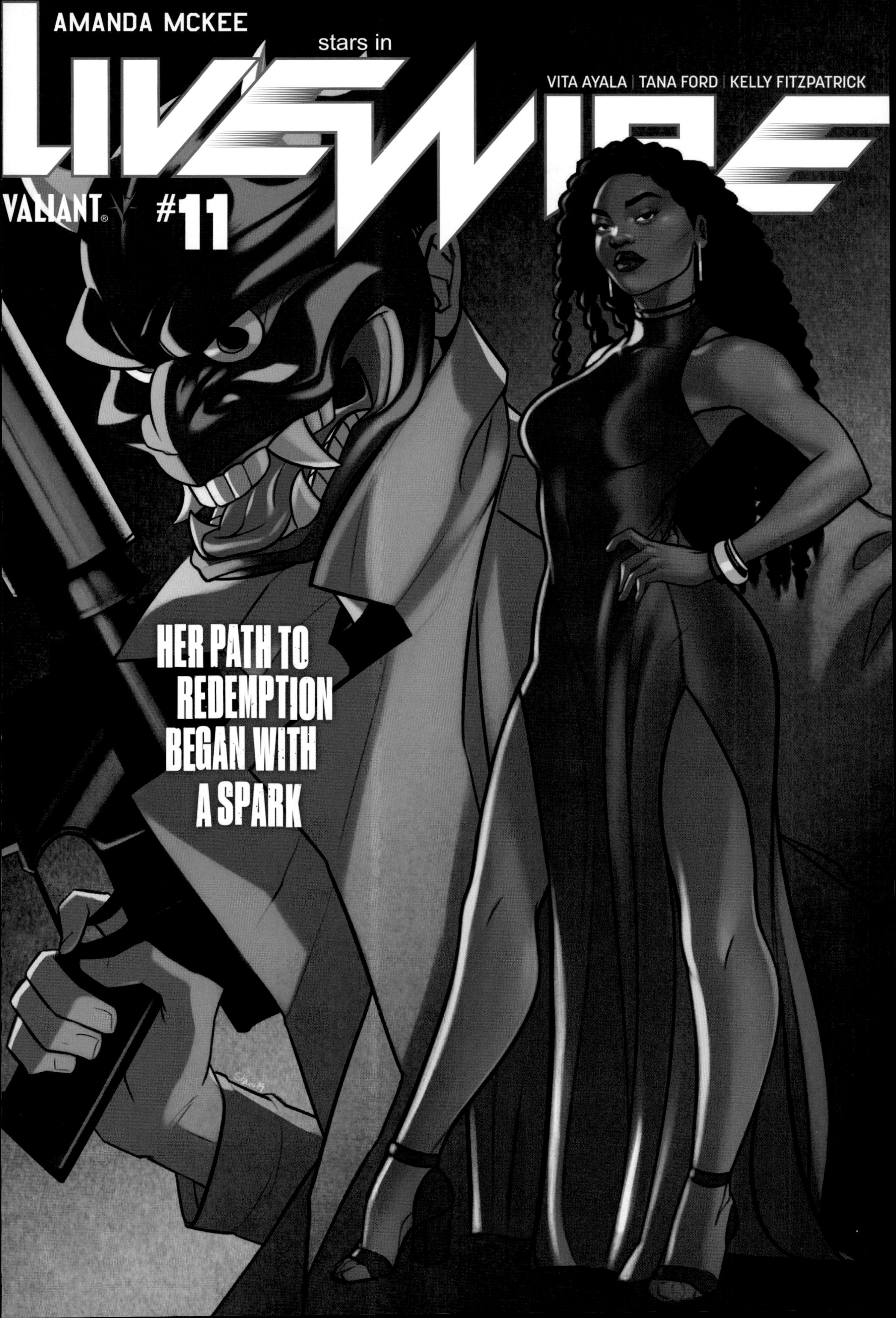
AMANDA MCKEE
stars in
LIVEWIRE
VITA AYALA | TANA FORD | KELLY FITZPATRICK
VALIANT
#11
HER PATH TO REDEMPTION BEGAN WITH A SPARK

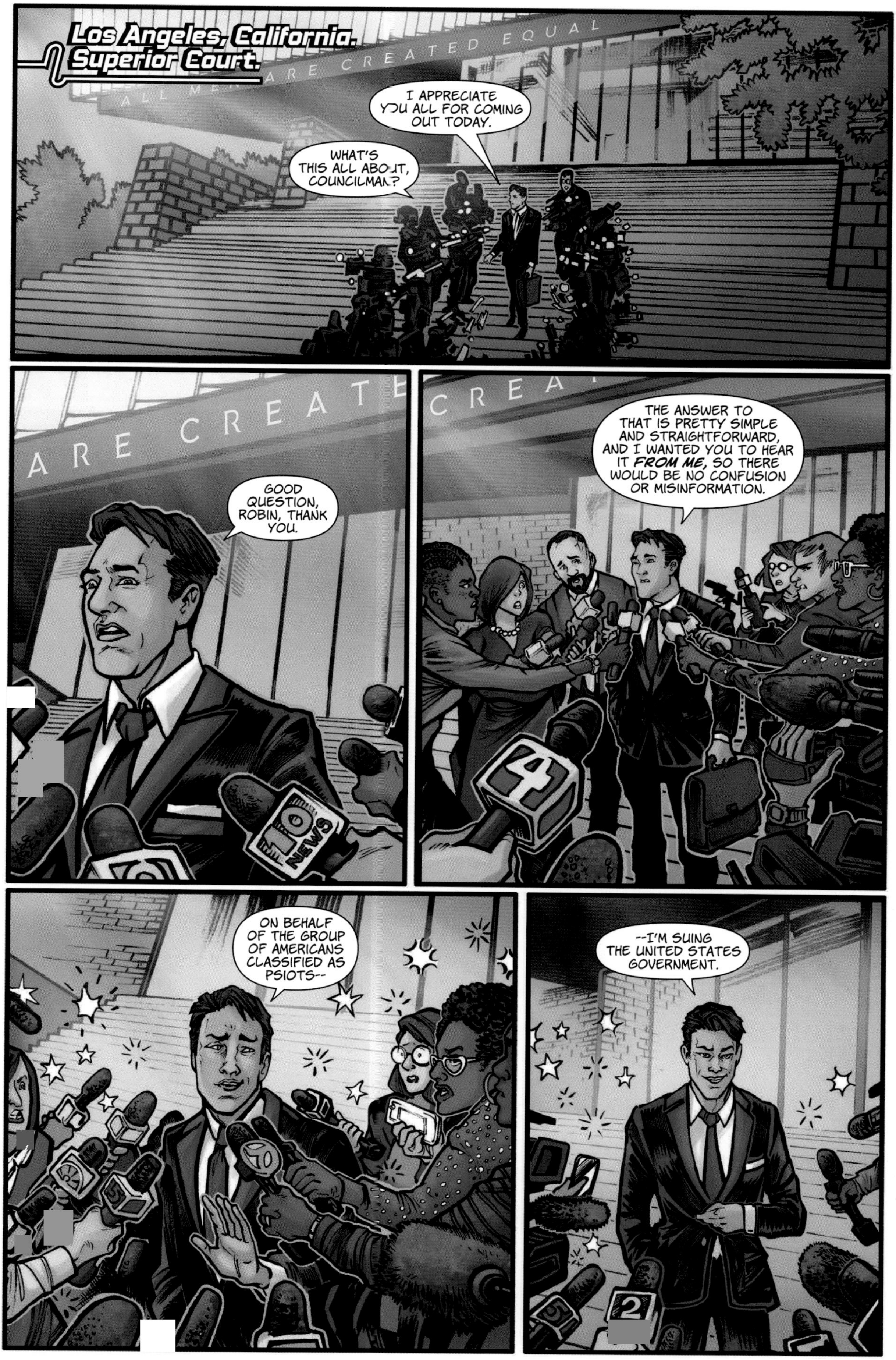
Los Angeles, California. Superior Court.
ARE CREATED EQUAL
I APPRECIATE YOU ALL FOR COMING OUT TODAY.
WHAT'S THIS ALL ABOUT, COUNCILMAN?
GOOD QUESTION, ROBIN, THANK YOU.
THE ANSWER TO THAT IS PRETTY SIMPLE AND STRAIGHTFORWARD, AND I WANTED YOU TO HEAR IT ***FROM ME,*** SO THERE WOULD BE NO CONFUSION OR MISINFORMATION.
ON BEHALF OF THE GROUP OF AMERICANS CLASSIFIED AS PSIOTS--
--I'M SUING THE UNITED STATES GOVERNMENT.

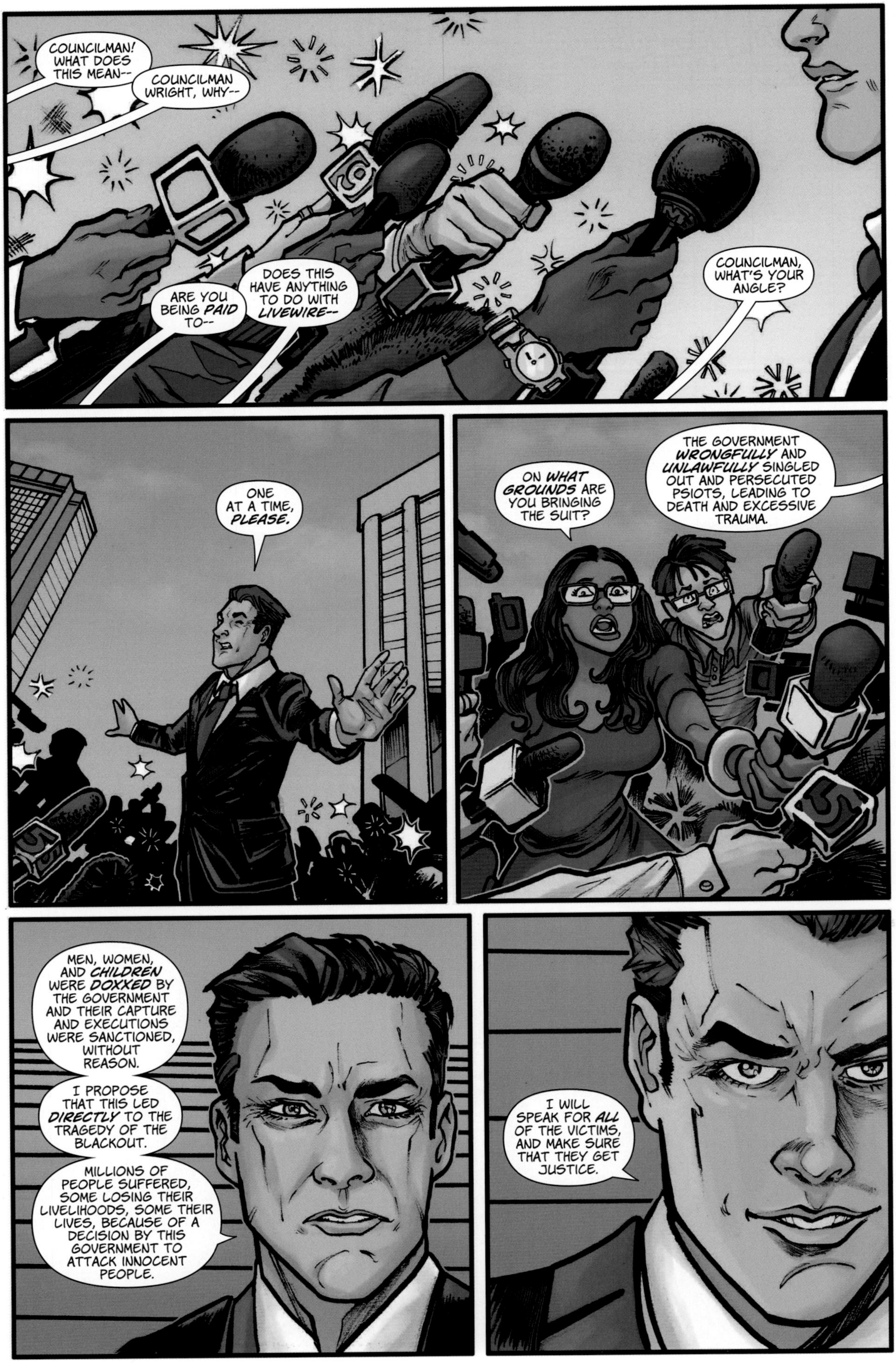
COUNCILMAN! WHAT DOES THIS MEAN--
COUNCILMAN WRIGHT, WHY--
ARE YOU BEING PAID TO--
DOES THIS HAVE ANYTHING TO DO WITH LIVEWIRE--
COUNCILMAN, WHAT'S YOUR ANGLE?
ONE AT A TIME, PLEASE.
ON WHAT GROUNDS ARE YOU BRINGING THE SUIT?
THE GOVERNMENT WRONGFULLY AND UNLAWFULLY SINGLED OUT AND PERSECUTED PSIOTS, LEADING TO DEATH AND EXCESSIVE TRAUMA.
MEN, WOMEN, AND CHILDREN WERE DOXXED BY THE GOVERNMENT AND THEIR CAPTURE AND EXECUTIONS WERE SANCTIONED, WITHOUT REASON.
I PROPOSE THAT THIS LED DIRECTLY TO THE TRAGEDY OF THE BLACKOUT.
MILLIONS OF PEOPLE SUFFERED, SOME LOSING THEIR LIVELIHOODS, SOME THEIR LIVES, BECAUSE OF A DECISION BY THIS GOVERNMENT TO ATTACK INNOCENT PEOPLE.
I WILL SPEAK FOR ALL OF THE VICTIMS, AND MAKE SURE THAT THEY GET JUSTICE.

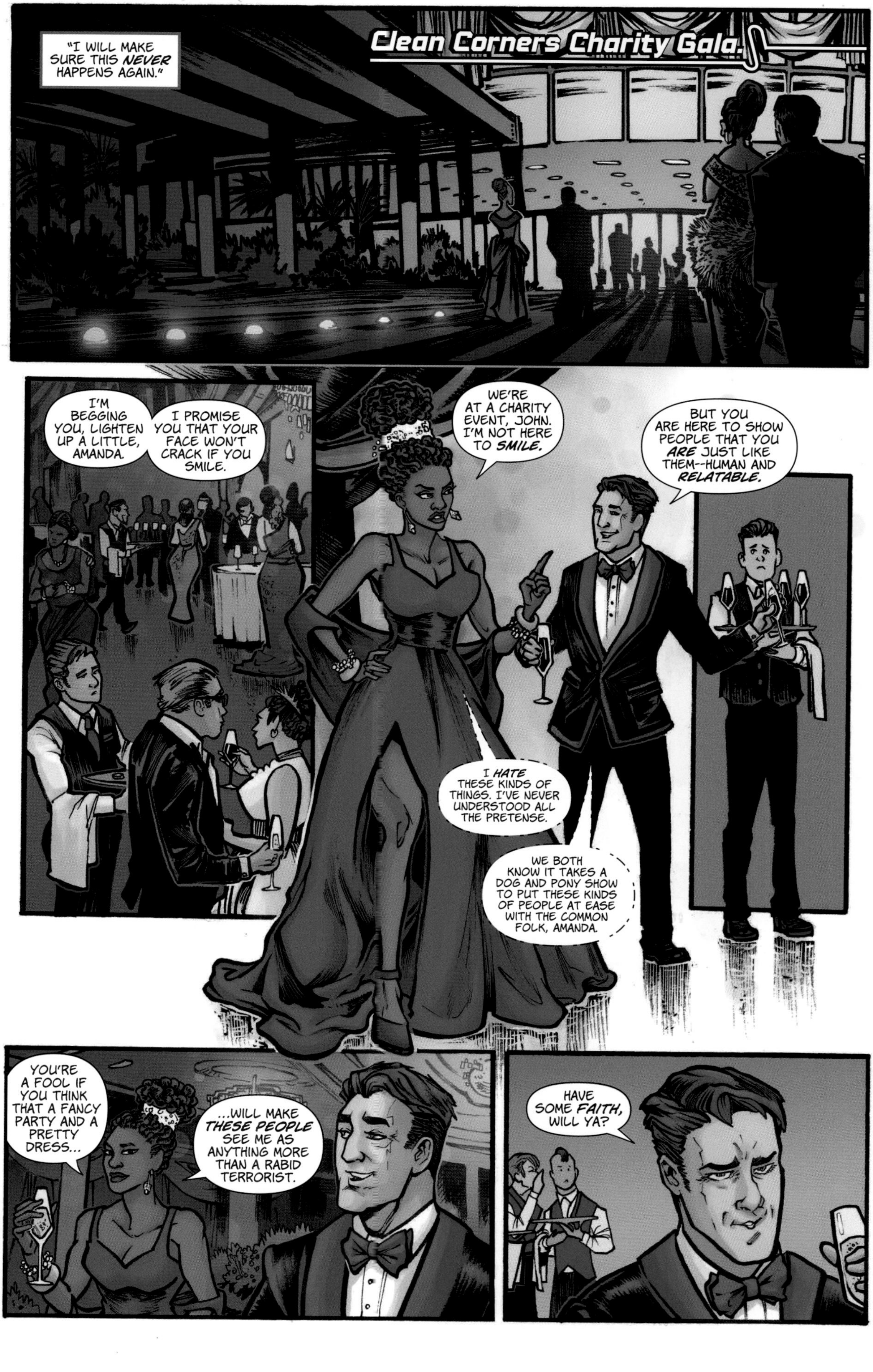

"I WILL MAKE SURE THIS NEVER HAPPENS AGAIN."
Clean Corners Charity Gala.
I'M BEGGING YOU, LIGHTEN UP A LITTLE, AMANDA.
I PROMISE YOU THAT YOUR FACE WON'T CRACK IF YOU SMILE.
WE'RE AT A CHARITY EVENT, JOHN. I'M NOT HERE TO SMILE.
BUT YOU ARE HERE TO SHOW PEOPLE THAT YOU ARE JUST LIKE THEM--HUMAN AND RELATABLE.
I HATE THESE KINDS OF THINGS. I'VE NEVER UNDERSTOOD ALL THE PRETENSE.
WE BOTH KNOW IT TAKES A DOG AND PONY SHOW TO PUT THESE KINDS OF PEOPLE AT EASE WITH THE COMMON FOLK, AMANDA.
YOU'RE A FOOL IF YOU THINK THAT A FANCY PARTY AND A PRETTY DRESS...
...WILL MAKE THESE PEOPLE SEE ME AS ANYTHING MORE THAN A RABID TERRORIST.
HAVE SOME FAITH, WILL YA?

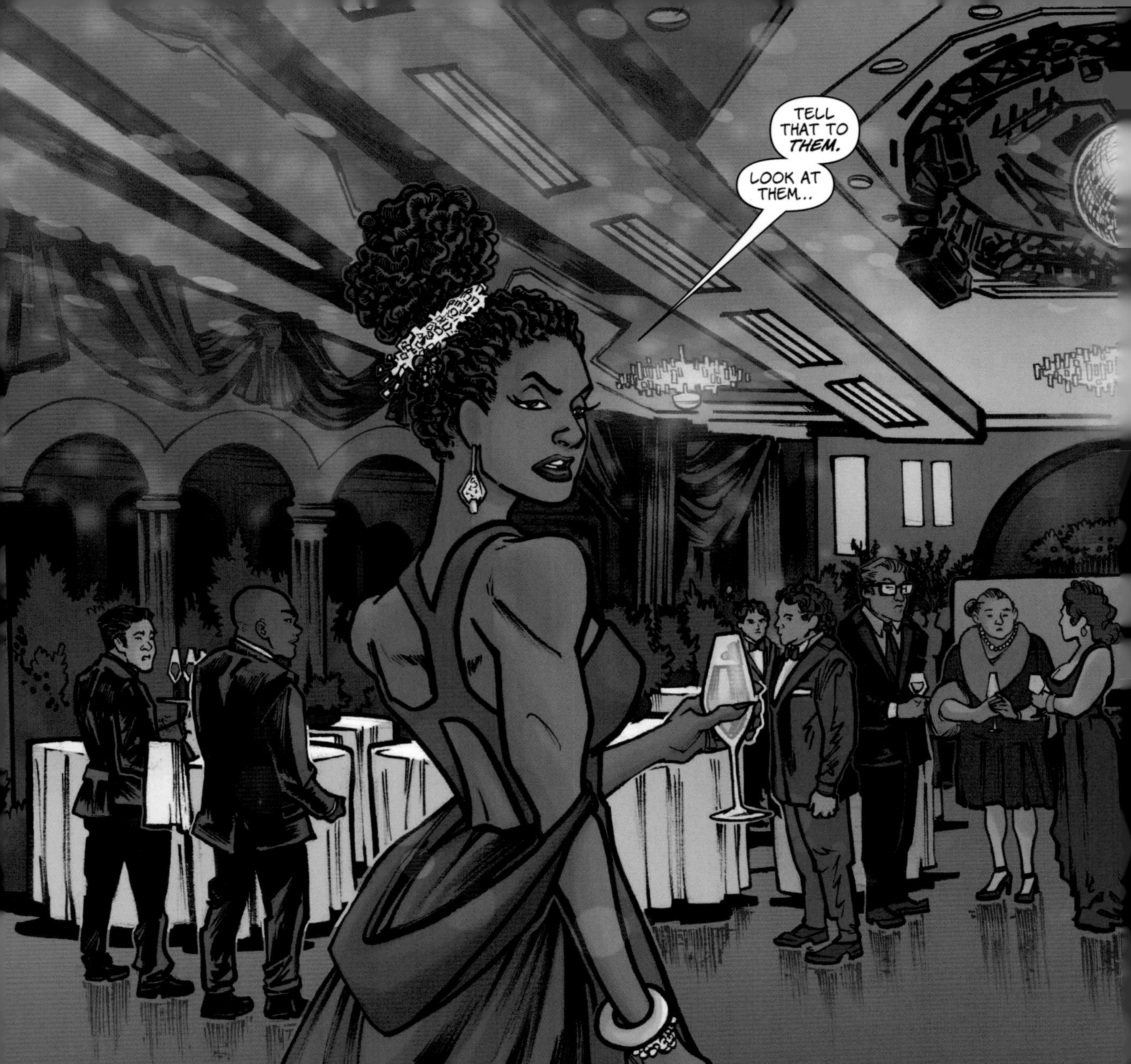
TELL THAT TO *THEM.*
LOOK AT THEM...
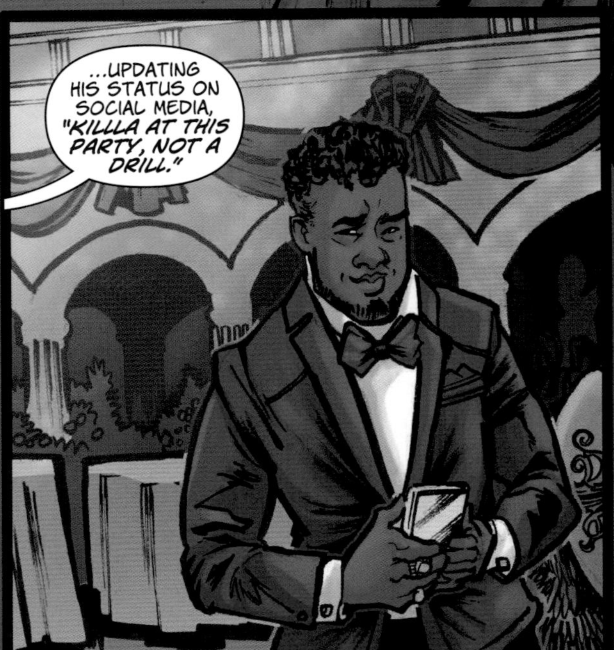
...UPDATING HIS STATUS ON SOCIAL MEDIA, *"KILLLA AT THIS PARTY, NOT A DRILL."*
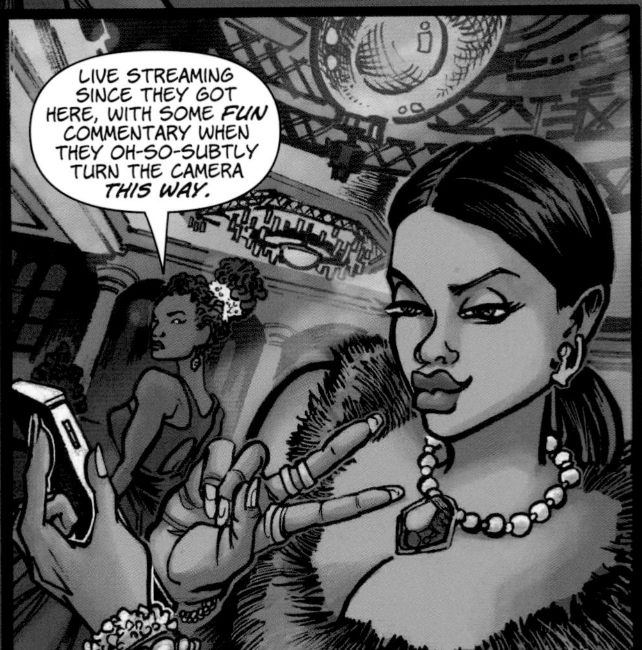
LIVE STREAMING SINCE THEY GOT HERE, WITH SOME *FUN* COMMENTARY WHEN THEY OH-SO-SUBTLY TURN THE CAMERA *THIS WAY.*

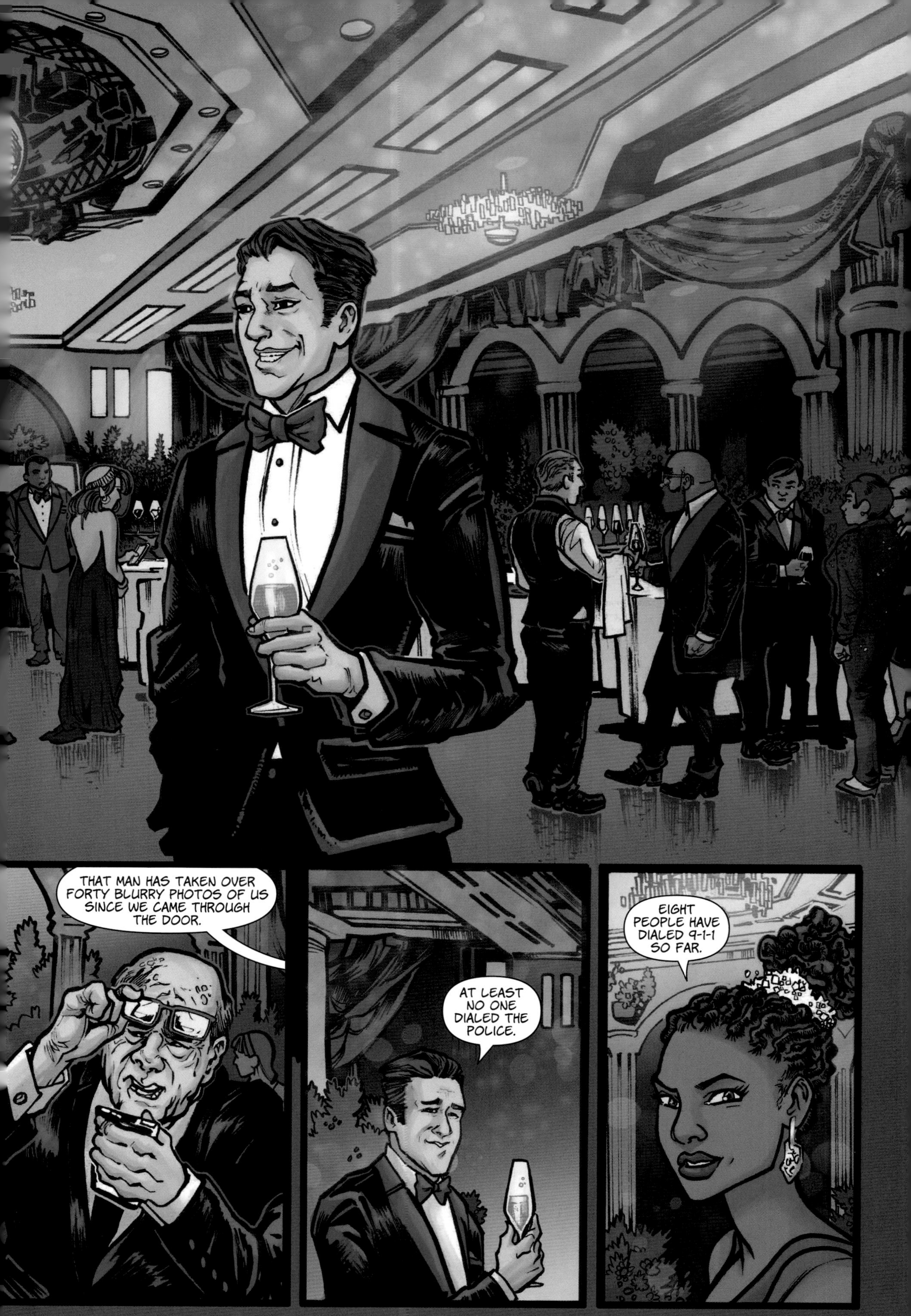
THAT MAN HAS TAKEN OVER FORTY BLURRY PHOTOS OF US SINCE WE CAME THROUGH THE DOOR.
AT LEAST NO ONE DIALED THE POLICE.
EIGHT PEOPLE HAVE DIALED 9-1-1 SO FAR.

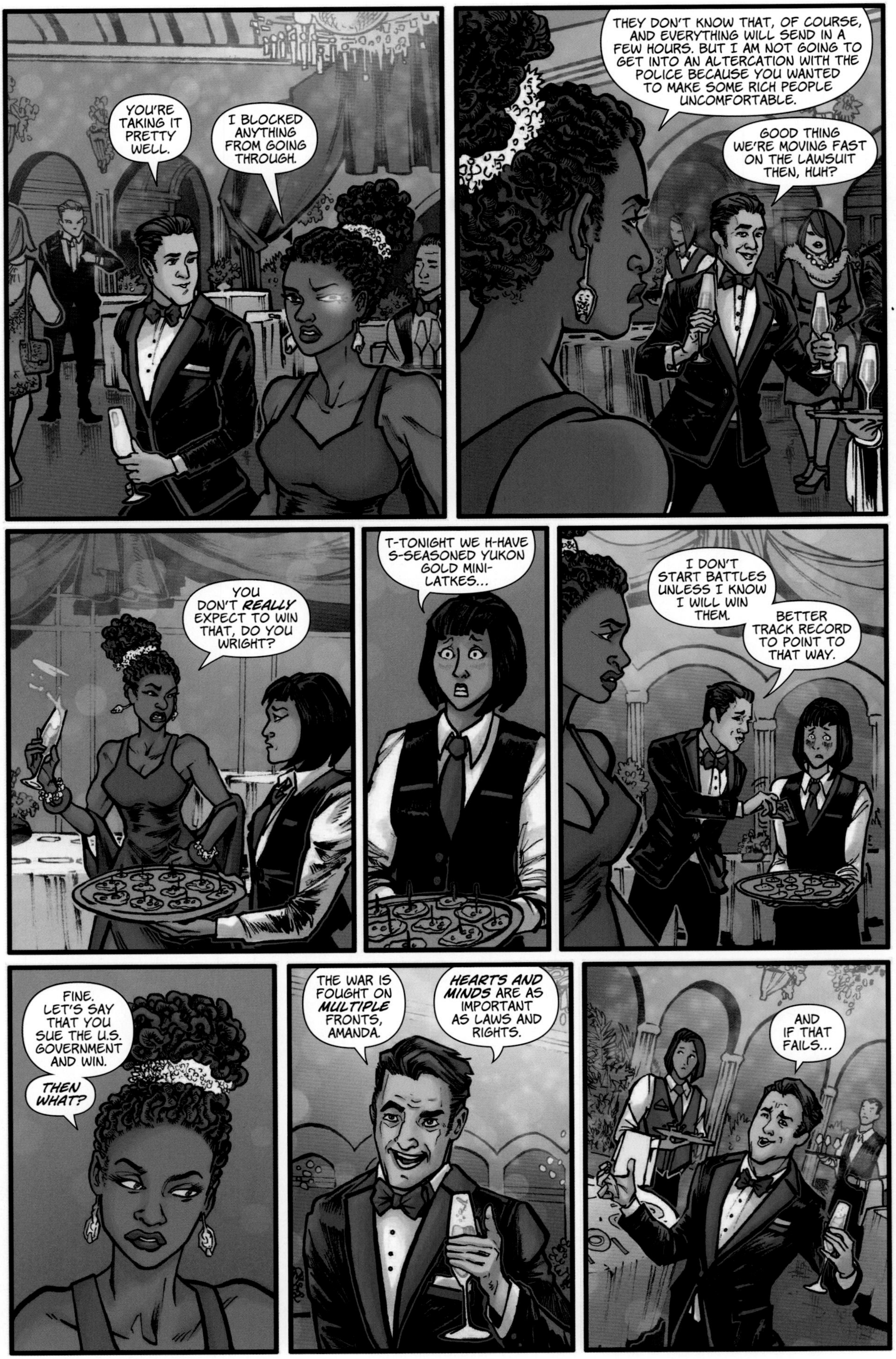
YOU'RE TAKING IT PRETTY WELL.
I BLOCKED ANYTHING FROM GOING THROUGH.
THEY DON'T KNOW THAT, OF COURSE, AND EVERYTHING WILL SEND IN A FEW HOURS. BUT I AM NOT GOING TO GET INTO AN ALTERCATION WITH THE POLICE BECAUSE YOU WANTED TO MAKE SOME RICH PEOPLE UNCOMFORTABLE.
GOOD THING WE'RE MOVING FAST ON THE LAWSUIT THEN, HUH?
YOU DON'T REALLY EXPECT TO WIN THAT, DO YOU WRIGHT?
T-TONIGHT WE H-HAVE S-SEASONED YUKON GOLD MINI-LATKES...
I DON'T START BATTLES UNLESS I KNOW I WILL WIN THEM.
BETTER TRACK RECORD TO POINT TO THAT WAY.
FINE. LET'S SAY THAT YOU SUE THE U.S. GOVERNMENT AND WIN.
THEN WHAT?
THE WAR IS FOUGHT ON MULTIPLE FRONTS, AMANDA.
HEARTS AND MINDS ARE AS IMPORTANT AS LAWS AND RIGHTS.
AND IF THAT FAILS...

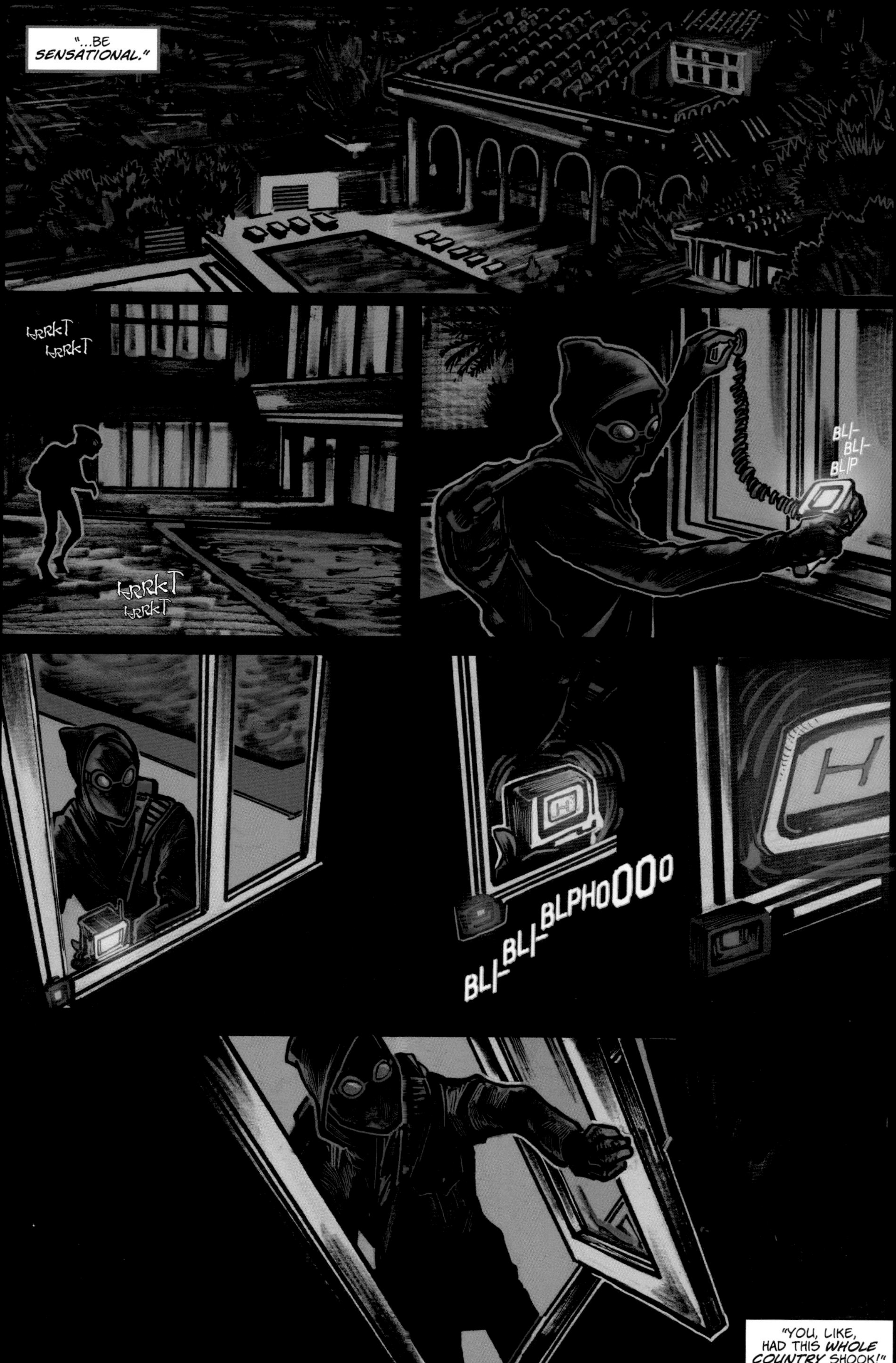
"...BE SENSATIONAL."
LRRKT LRRKT
LRRKT LRRKT
BLI- BLI- BLIP
BLI-BLI-BLPHOOOO
"YOU, LIKE, HAD THIS WHOLE COUNTRY SHOOK!"

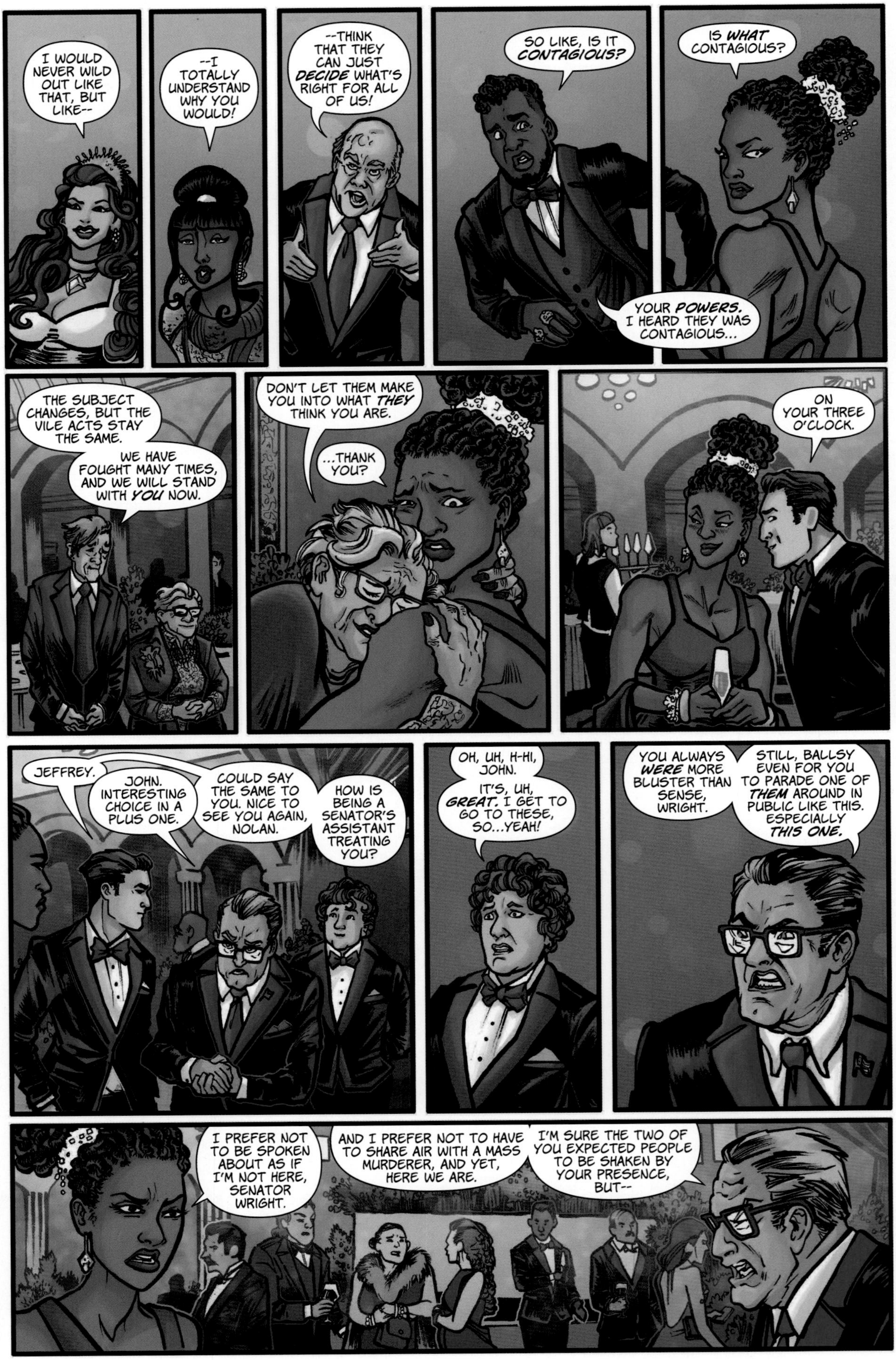
I WOULD NEVER WILD OUT LIKE THAT, BUT LIKE--
--I TOTALLY UNDERSTAND WHY YOU WOULD!
--THINK THAT THEY CAN JUST DECIDE WHAT'S RIGHT FOR ALL OF US!
SO LIKE, IS IT CONTAGIOUS?
IS WHAT CONTAGIOUS?
YOUR POWERS. I HEARD THEY WAS CONTAGIOUS...
THE SUBJECT CHANGES, BUT THE VILE ACTS STAY THE SAME.
WE HAVE FOUGHT MANY TIMES, AND WE WILL STAND WITH YOU NOW.
DON'T LET THEM MAKE YOU INTO WHAT THEY THINK YOU ARE.
...THANK YOU?
ON YOUR THREE O'CLOCK.
JEFFREY.
JOHN. INTERESTING CHOICE IN A PLUS ONE.
COULD SAY THE SAME TO YOU. NICE TO SEE YOU AGAIN, NOLAN.
HOW IS BEING A SENATOR'S ASSISTANT TREATING YOU?
OH, UH, H-HI, JOHN.
IT'S, UH, GREAT. I GET TO GO TO THESE, SO...YEAH!
YOU ALWAYS WERE MORE BLUSTER THAN SENSE, WRIGHT.
STILL, BALLSY EVEN FOR YOU TO PARADE ONE OF THEM AROUND IN PUBLIC LIKE THIS. ESPECIALLY THIS ONE.
I PREFER NOT TO BE SPOKEN ABOUT AS IF I'M NOT HERE, SENATOR WRIGHT.
AND I PREFER NOT TO HAVE TO SHARE AIR WITH A MASS MURDERER, AND YET, HERE WE ARE.
I'M SURE THE TWO OF YOU EXPECTED PEOPLE TO BE SHAKEN BY YOUR PRESENCE, BUT--

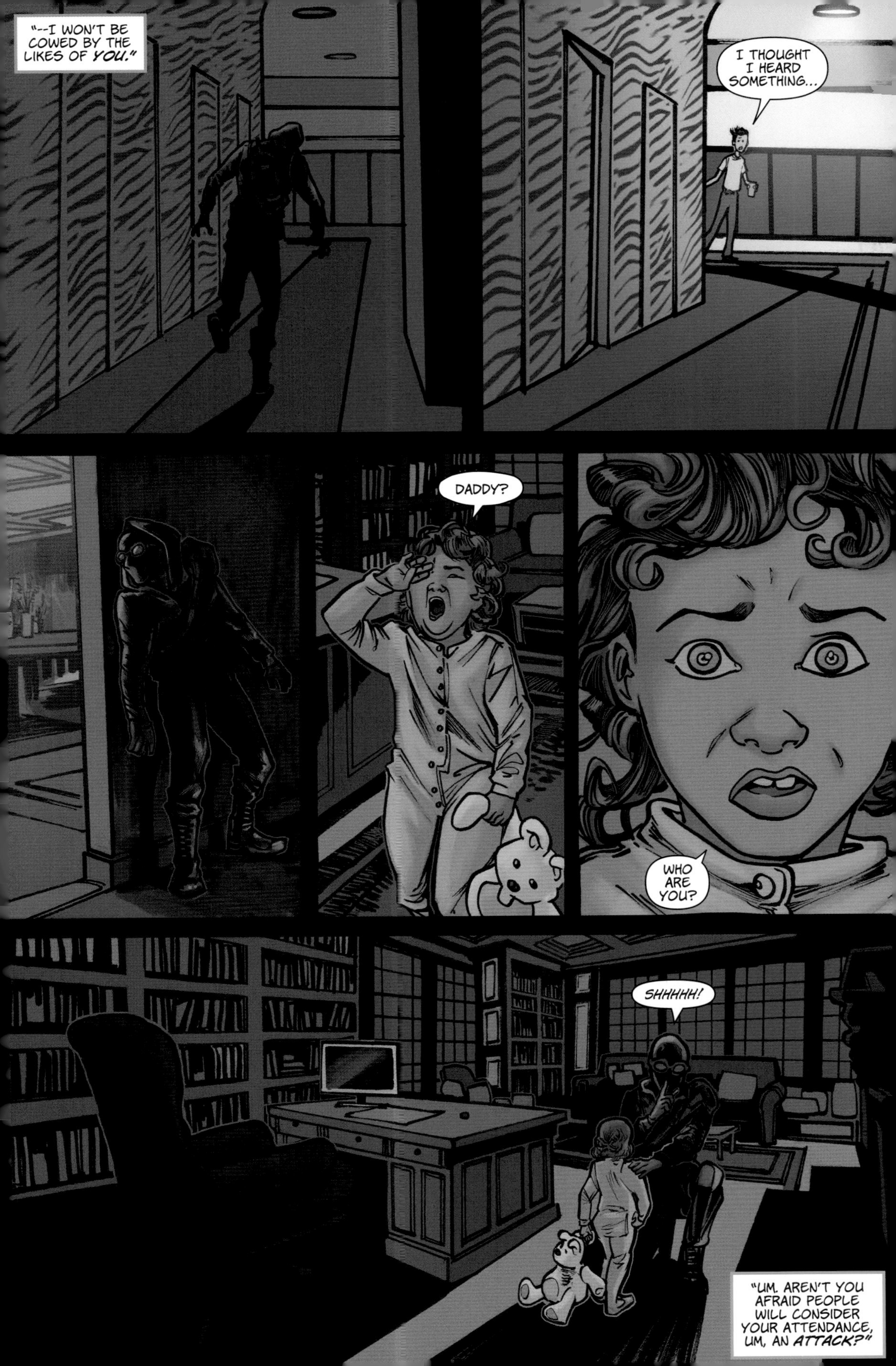
"--I WON'T BE COWED BY THE LIKES OF *YOU.*"
I THOUGHT I HEARD SOMETHING...
DADDY?
WHO ARE YOU?
SHHHHH!
"UM. AREN'T YOU AFRAID PEOPLE WILL CONSIDER YOUR ATTENDANCE, UM, AN *ATTACK?*"

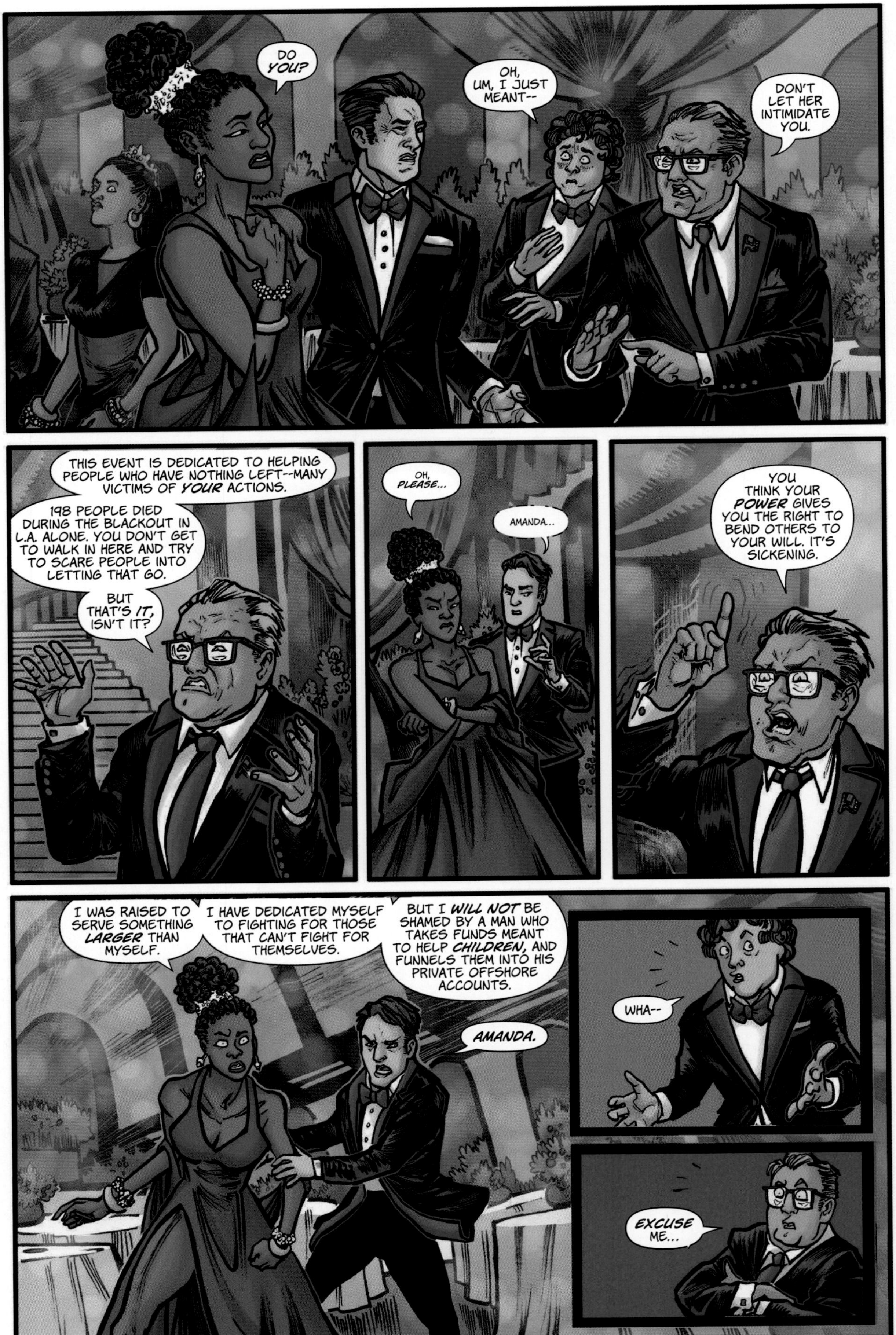
DO *YOU?*
OH, UM, I JUST MEANT--
DON'T LET HER INTIMIDATE YOU.
THIS EVENT IS DEDICATED TO HELPING PEOPLE WHO HAVE NOTHING LEFT--MANY VICTIMS OF ***YOUR*** ACTIONS.
198 PEOPLE DIED DURING THE BLACKOUT IN L.A. ALONE. YOU DON'T GET TO WALK IN HERE AND TRY TO SCARE PEOPLE INTO LETTING THAT GO.
BUT THAT'S *IT,* ISN'T IT?
OH, *PLEASE...*
AMANDA...
YOU THINK YOUR ***POWER*** GIVES YOU THE RIGHT TO BEND OTHERS TO YOUR WILL. IT'S SICKENING.
I WAS RAISED TO SERVE SOMETHING ***LARGER*** THAN MYSELF.
I HAVE DEDICATED MYSELF TO FIGHTING FOR THOSE THAT CAN'T FIGHT FOR THEMSELVES.
BUT I ***WILL NOT*** BE SHAMED BY A MAN WHO TAKES FUNDS MEANT TO HELP ***CHILDREN,*** AND FUNNELS THEM INTO HIS PRIVATE OFFSHORE ACCOUNTS.
AMANDA.
WHA--
EXCUSE ME...

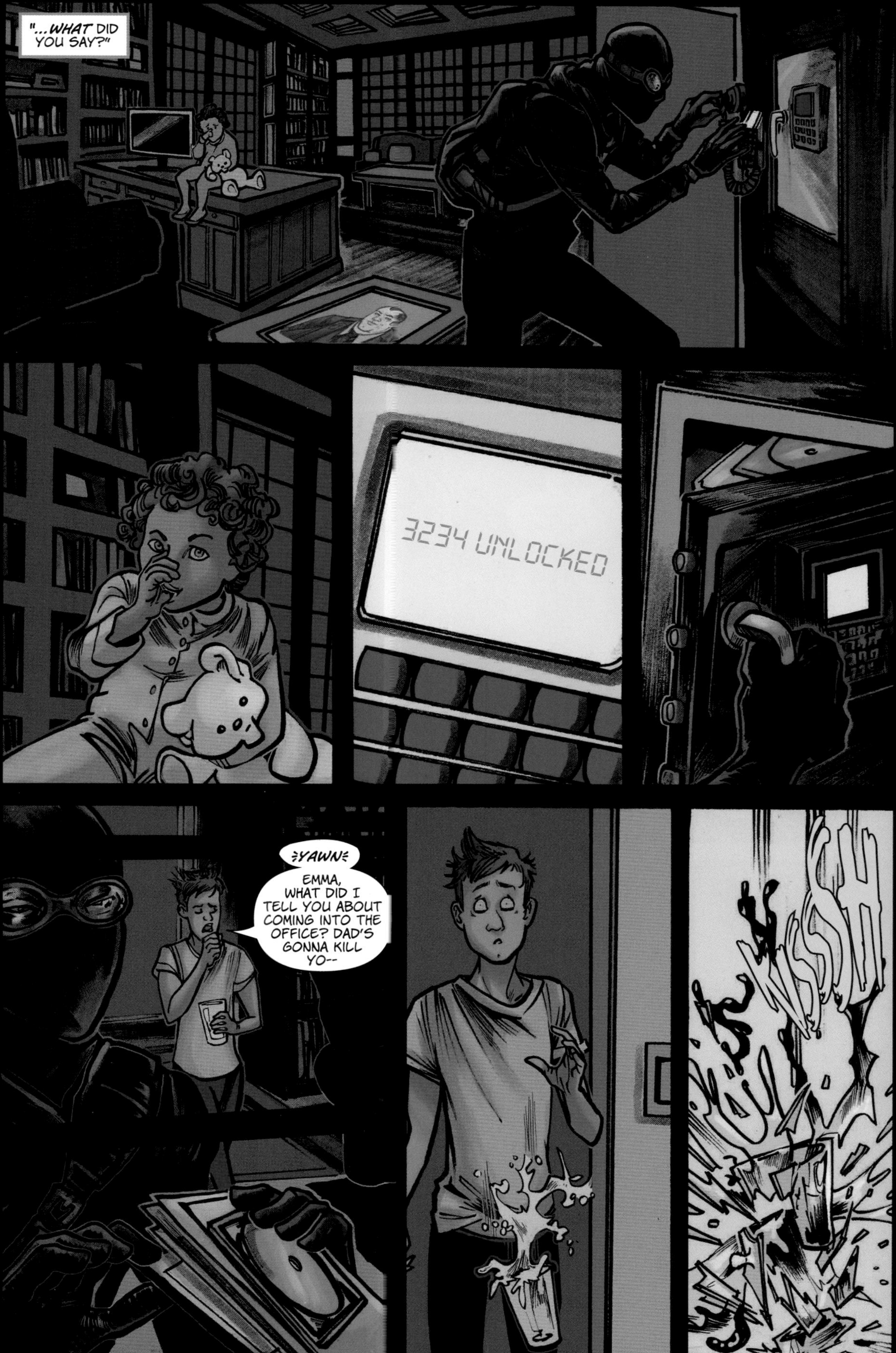
"...WHAT DID YOU SAY?"
3234 UNLOCKED
YAWN
EMMA, WHAT DID I TELL YOU ABOUT COMING INTO THE OFFICE? DAD'S GONNA KILL YO--
KSSH

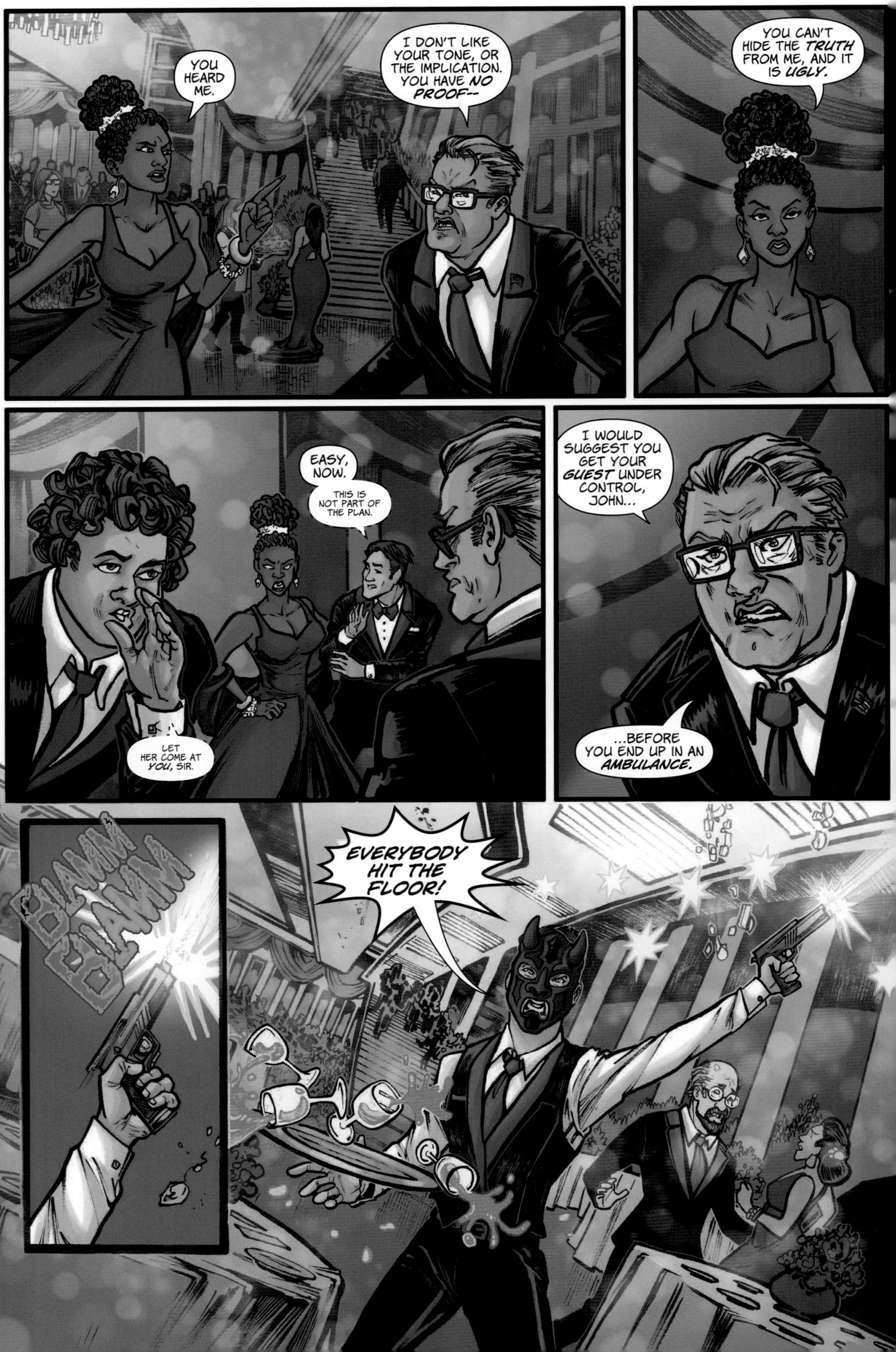
YOU HEARD ME.
I DON'T LIKE YOUR TONE, OR THE IMPLICATION. YOU HAVE *NO PROOF--*
YOU CAN'T HIDE THE *TRUTH* FROM ME, AND IT IS *UGLY.*
EASY, NOW.
THIS IS NOT PART OF THE PLAN.
LET HER COME AT *YOU*, SIR.
I WOULD SUGGEST YOU GET YOUR *GUEST* UNDER CONTROL, JOHN...
...BEFORE YOU END UP IN AN *AMBULANCE.*
BLAMM BLAMM
EVERYBODY HIT THE FLOOR!

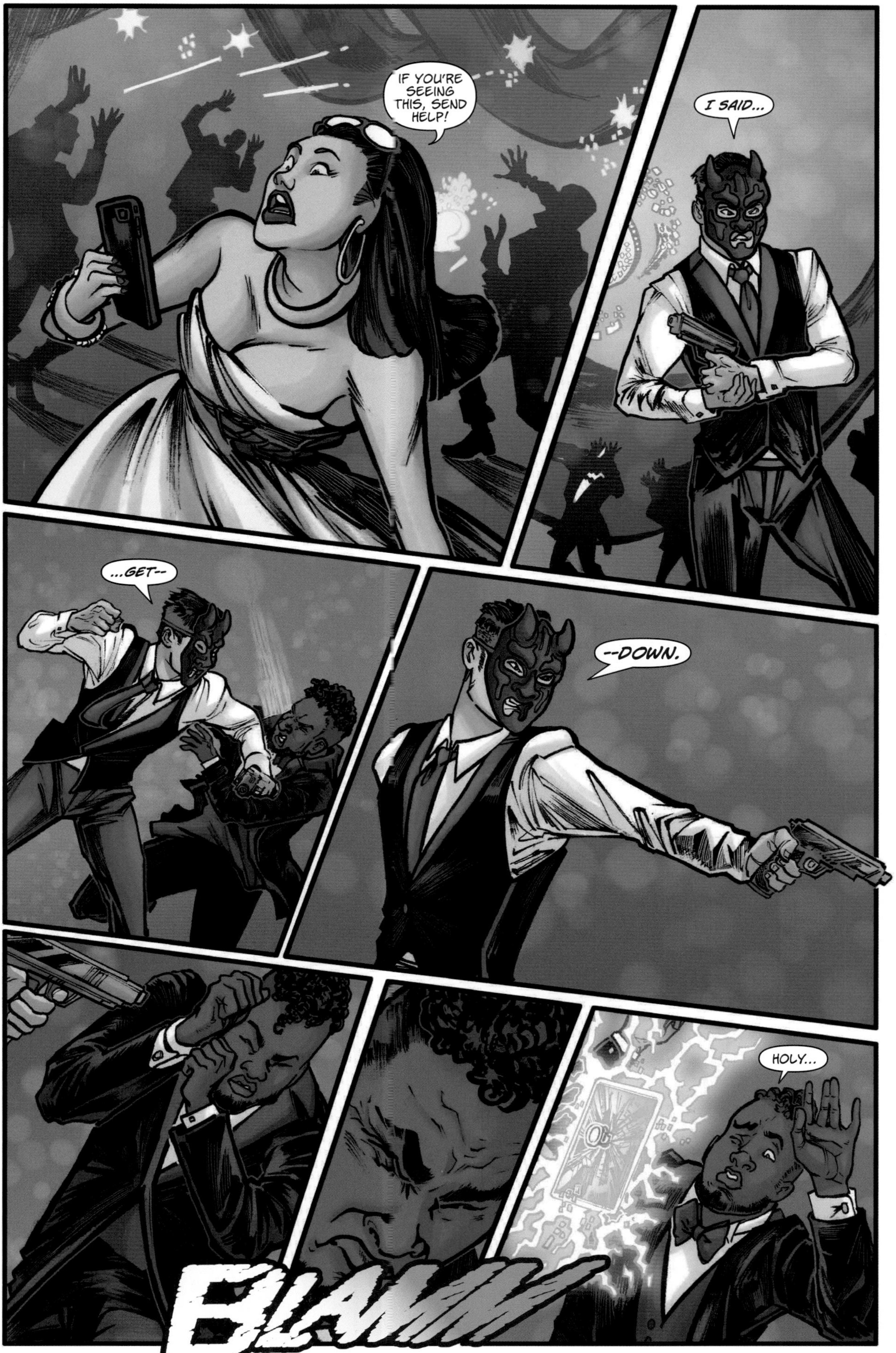
IF YOU'RE SEEING THIS, SEND HELP!
I SAID...
...GET--
--DOWN.
BLAMM
HOLY...

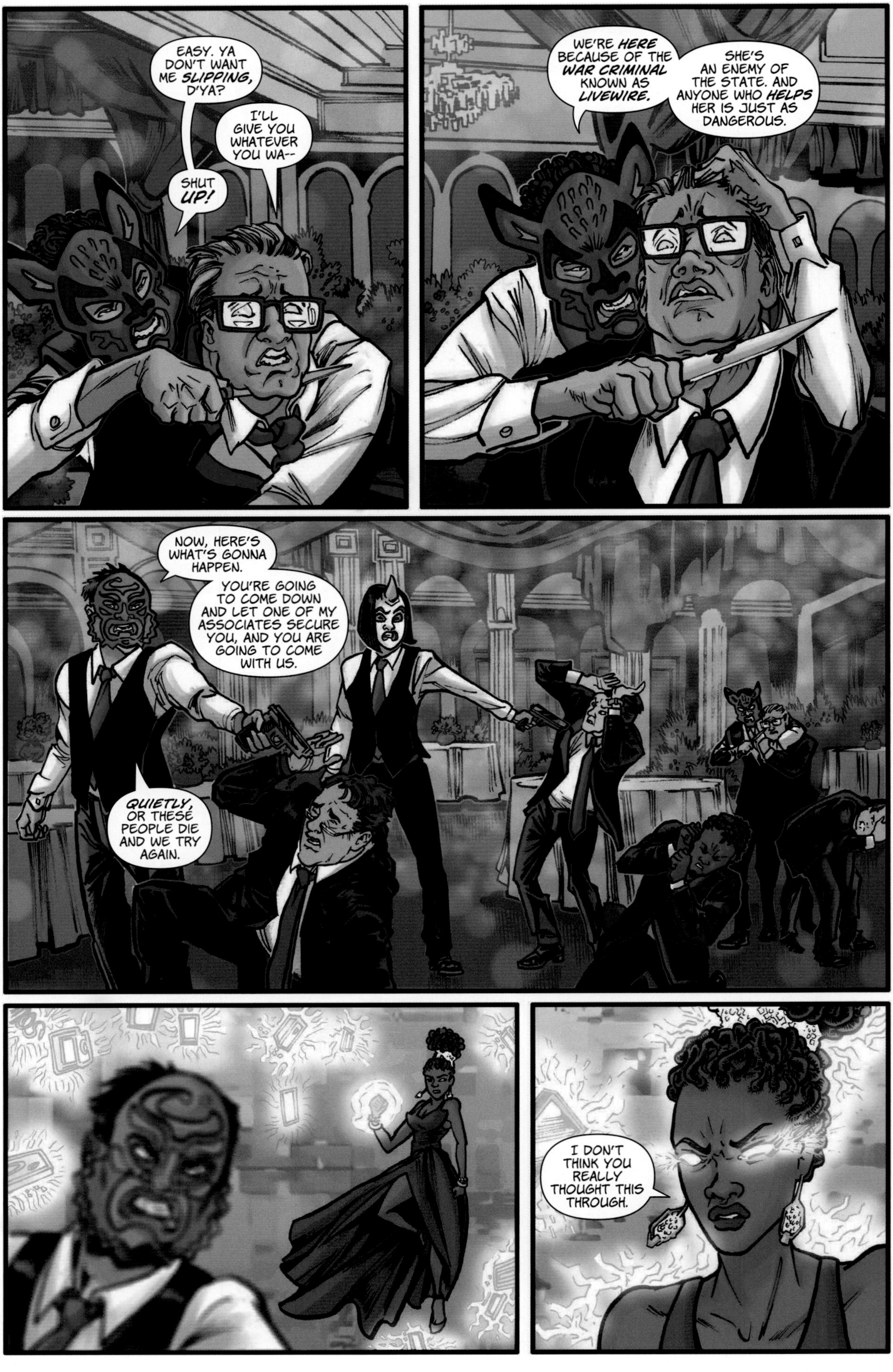
EASY. YA DON'T WANT ME SLIPPING, D'YA?
I'LL GIVE YOU WHATEVER YOU WA--
SHUT UP!
WE'RE HERE BECAUSE OF THE WAR CRIMINAL KNOWN AS LIVEWIRE.
SHE'S AN ENEMY OF THE STATE. AND ANYONE WHO HELPS HER IS JUST AS DANGEROUS.
NOW, HERE'S WHAT'S GONNA HAPPEN.
YOU'RE GOING TO COME DOWN AND LET ONE OF MY ASSOCIATES SECURE YOU, AND YOU ARE GOING TO COME WITH US.
QUIETLY, OR THESE PEOPLE DIE AND WE TRY AGAIN.
I DON'T THINK YOU REALLY THOUGHT THIS THROUGH.

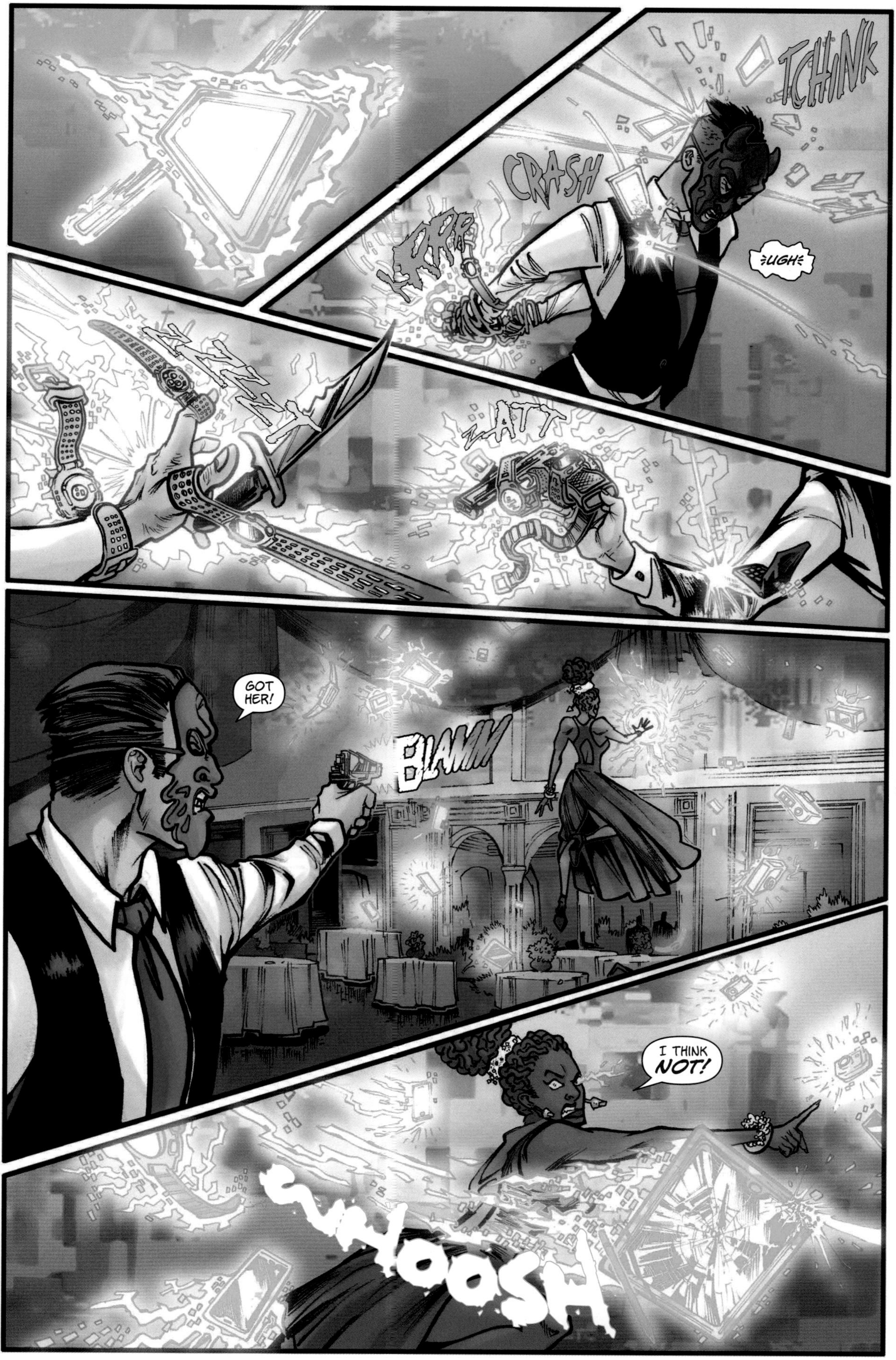
TCHINK
CRASH
UGH
ZATT
GOT HER!
BLAMM
I THINK NOT!

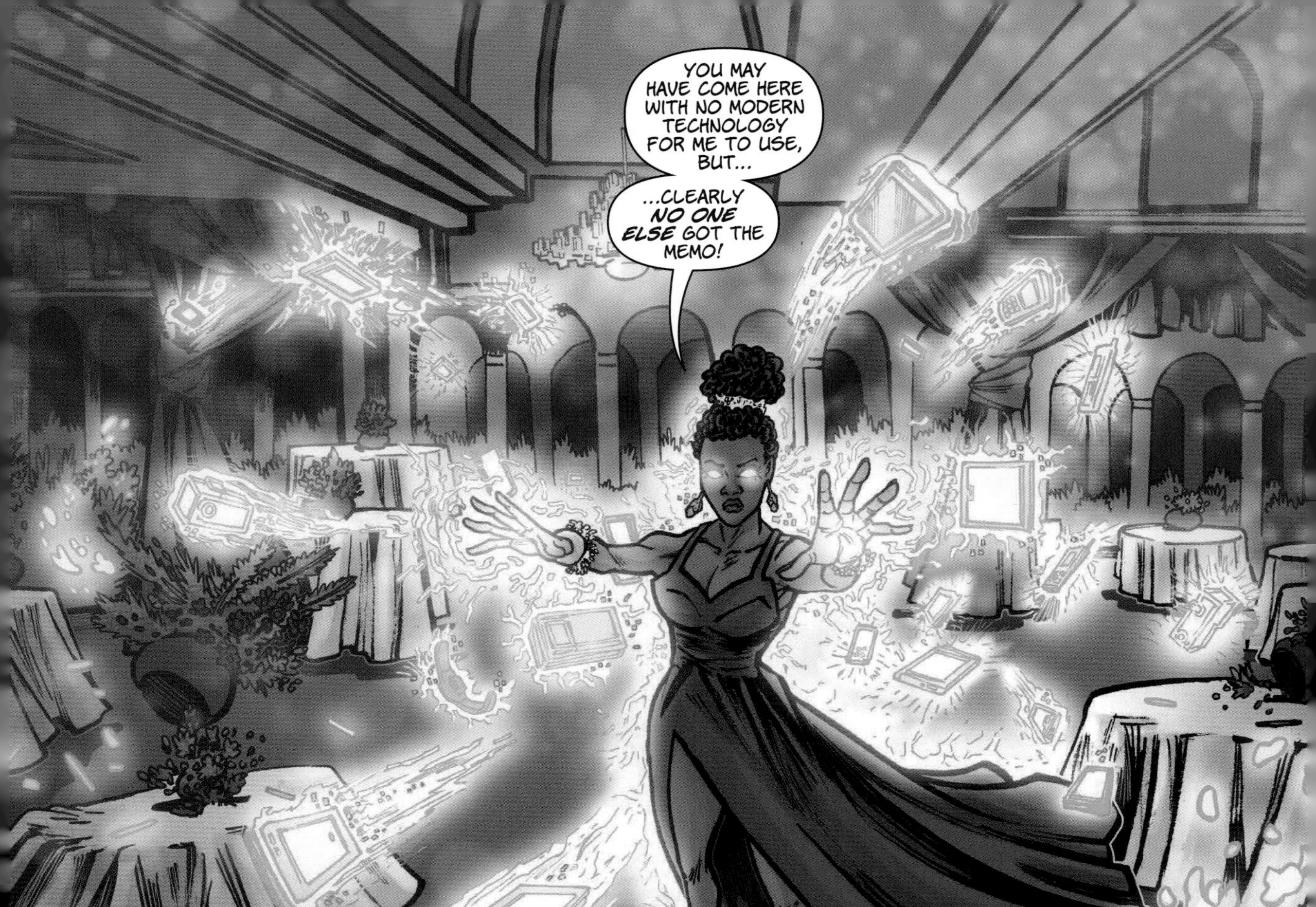
YOU MAY HAVE COME HERE WITH NO MODERN TECHNOLOGY FOR ME TO USE, BUT...
...CLEARLY NO ONE ELSE GOT THE MEMO!
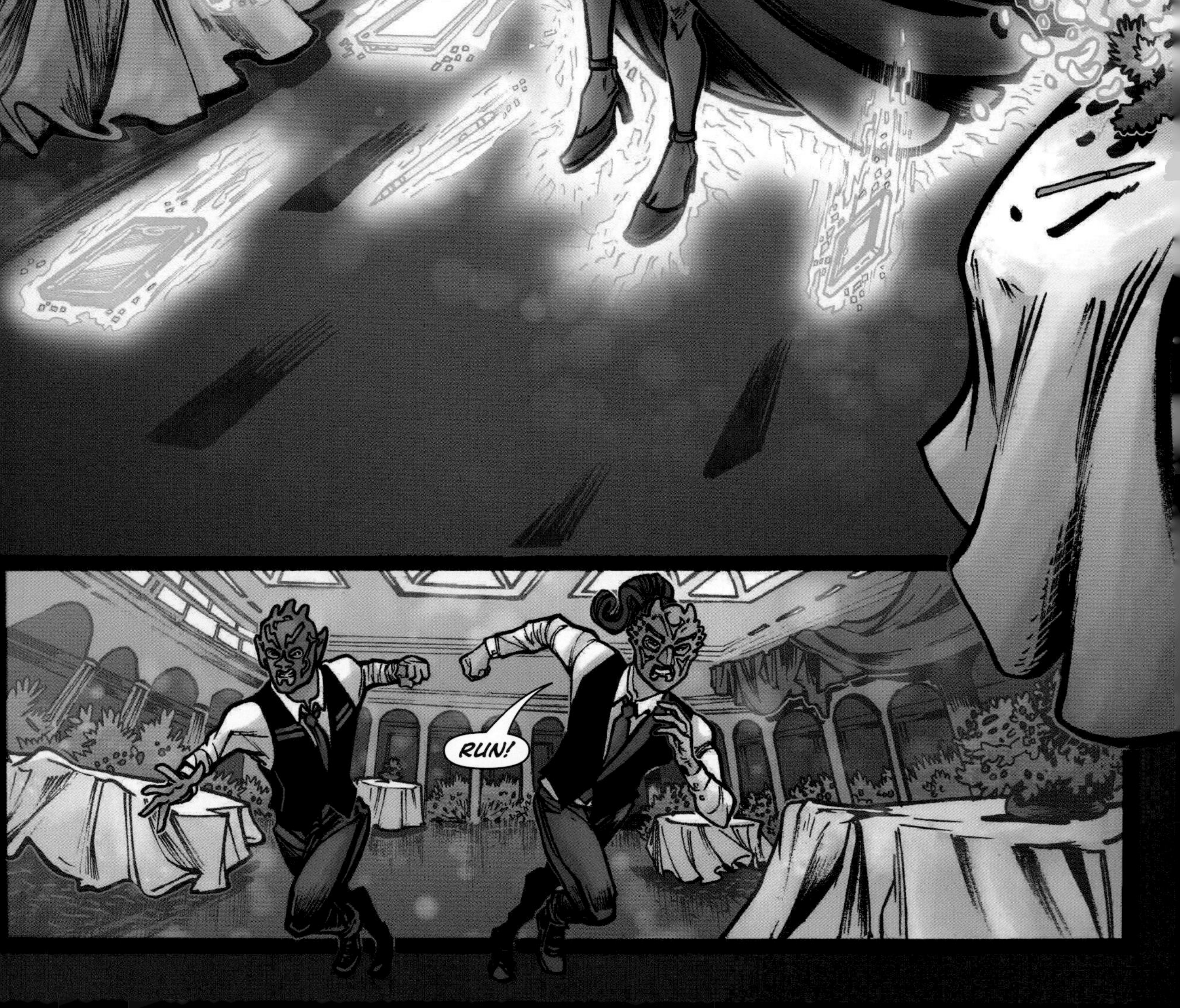
RUN!

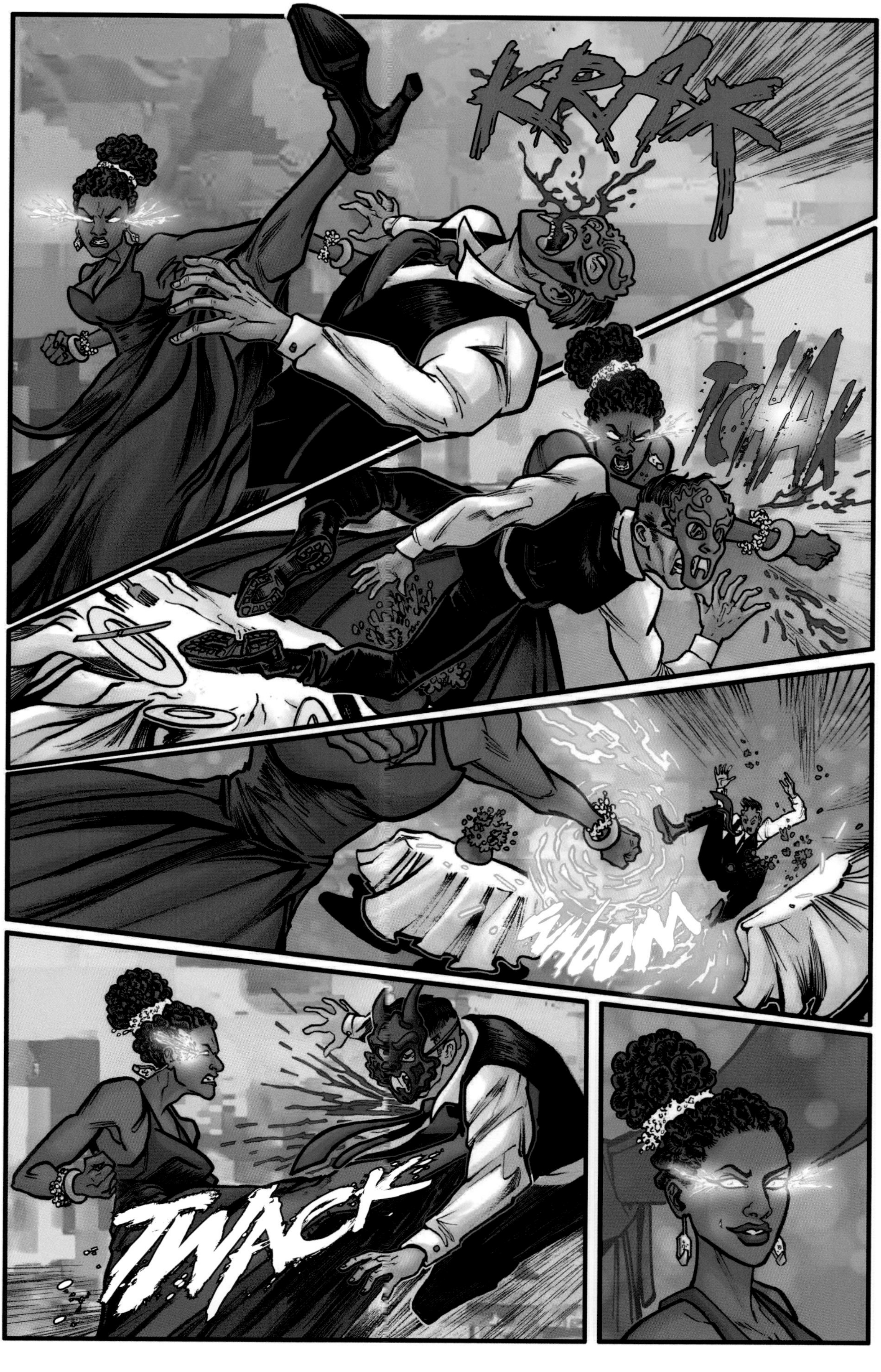
KRAK
TCHAK
SHOOM
TWACK

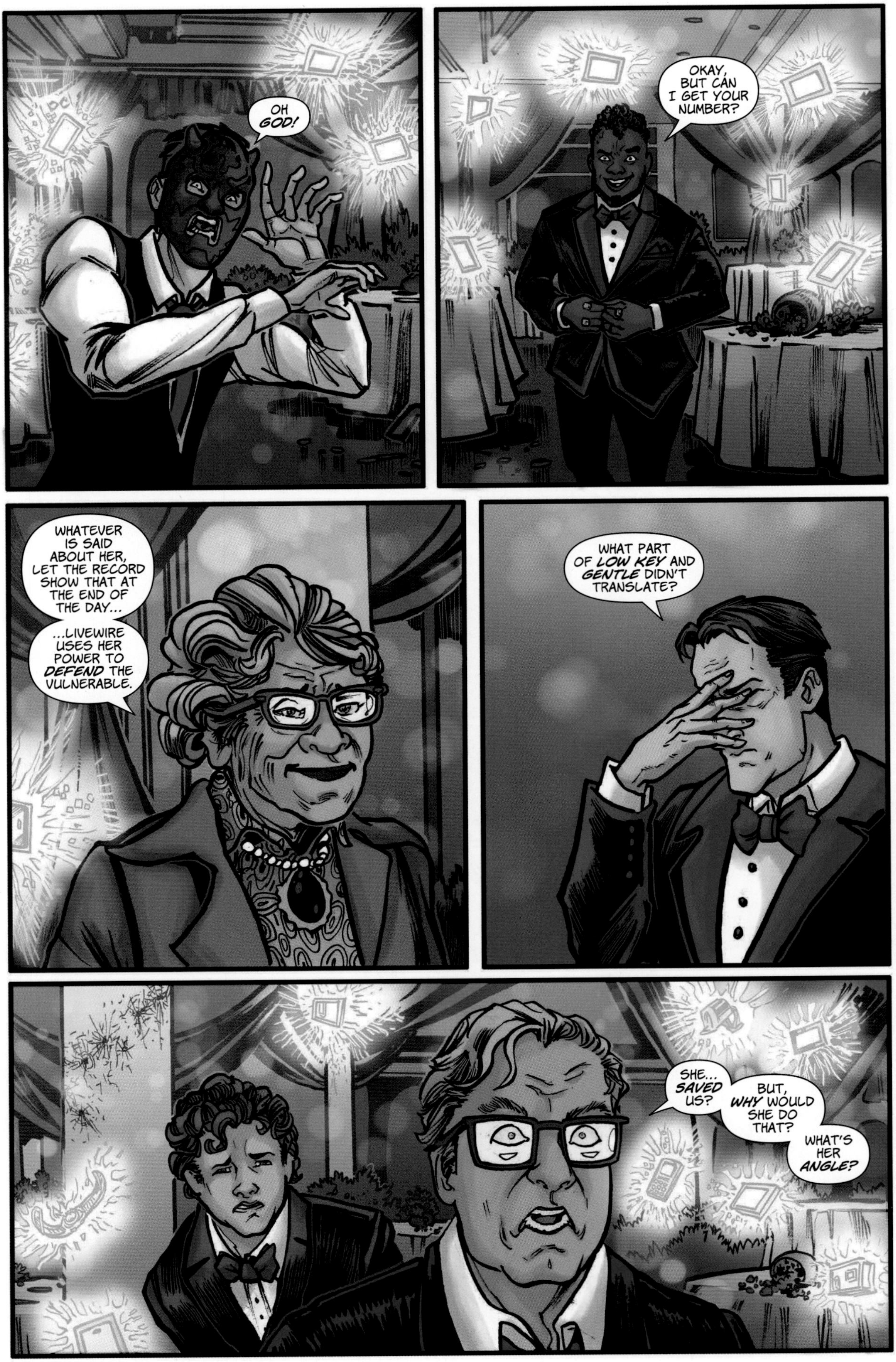
OH *GOD!*
OKAY, BUT CAN I GET YOUR NUMBER?
WHATEVER IS SAID ABOUT HER, LET THE RECORD SHOW THAT AT THE END OF THE DAY...
...LIVEWIRE USES HER POWER TO *DEFEND* THE VULNERABLE.
WHAT PART OF *LOW KEY* AND *GENTLE* DIDN'T TRANSLATE?
SHE... *SAVED* US?
BUT, *WHY* WOULD SHE DO THAT?
WHAT'S HER *ANGLE?*

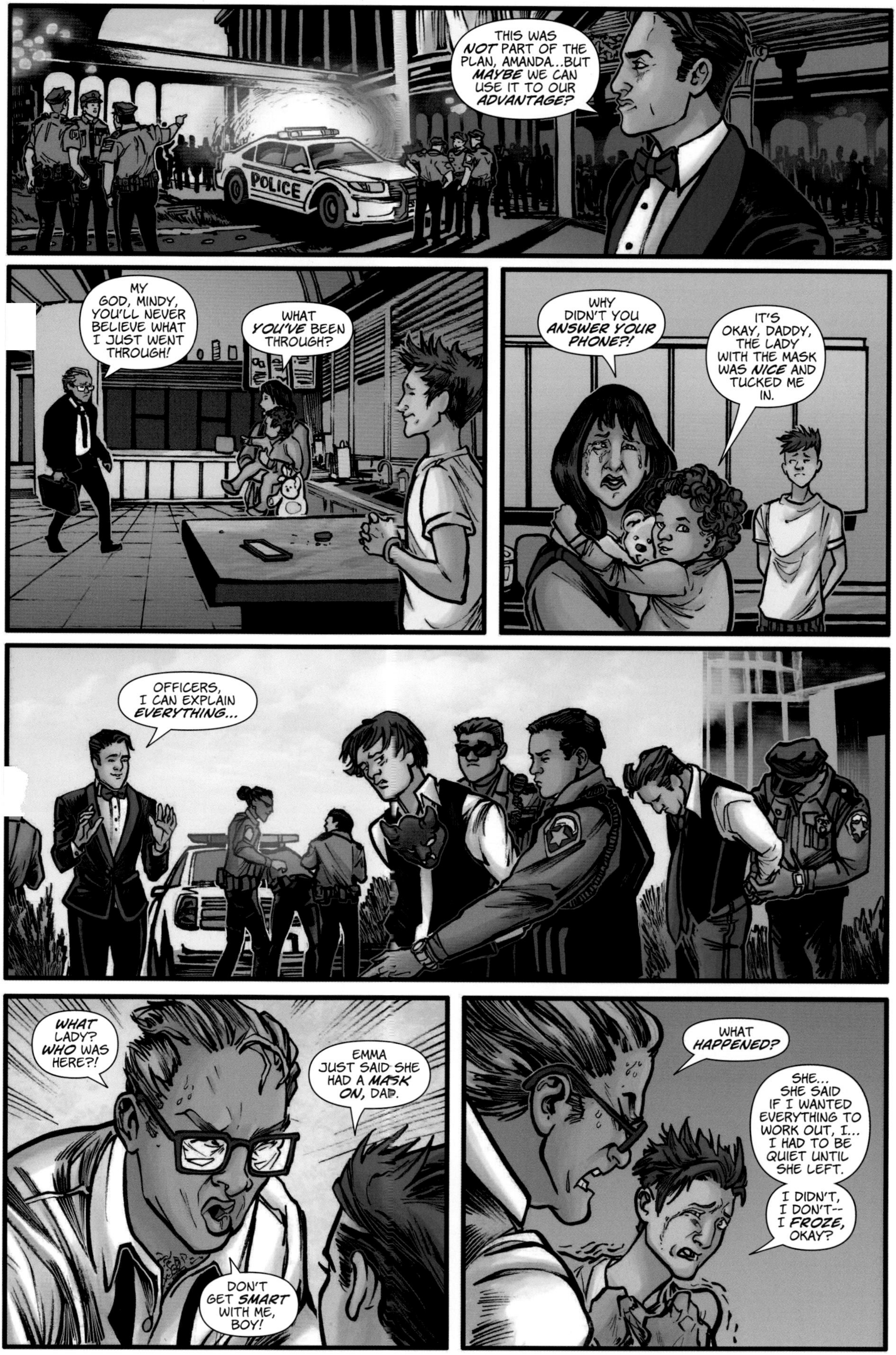
THIS WAS NOT PART OF THE PLAN, AMANDA...BUT MAYBE WE CAN USE IT TO OUR ADVANTAGE?
MY GOD, MINDY, YOU'LL NEVER BELIEVE WHAT I JUST WENT THROUGH!
WHAT YOU'VE BEEN THROUGH?
WHY DIDN'T YOU ANSWER YOUR PHONE?!
IT'S OKAY, DADDY, THE LADY WITH THE MASK WAS NICE AND TUCKED ME IN.
OFFICERS, I CAN EXPLAIN EVERYTHING...
WHAT LADY? WHO WAS HERE?!
EMMA JUST SAID SHE HAD A MASK ON, DAD.
DON'T GET SMART WITH ME, BOY!
WHAT HAPPENED?
SHE... SHE SAID IF I WANTED EVERYTHING TO WORK OUT, I... I HAD TO BE QUIET UNTIL SHE LEFT.
I DIDN'T, I DON'T-- I FROZE, OKAY?

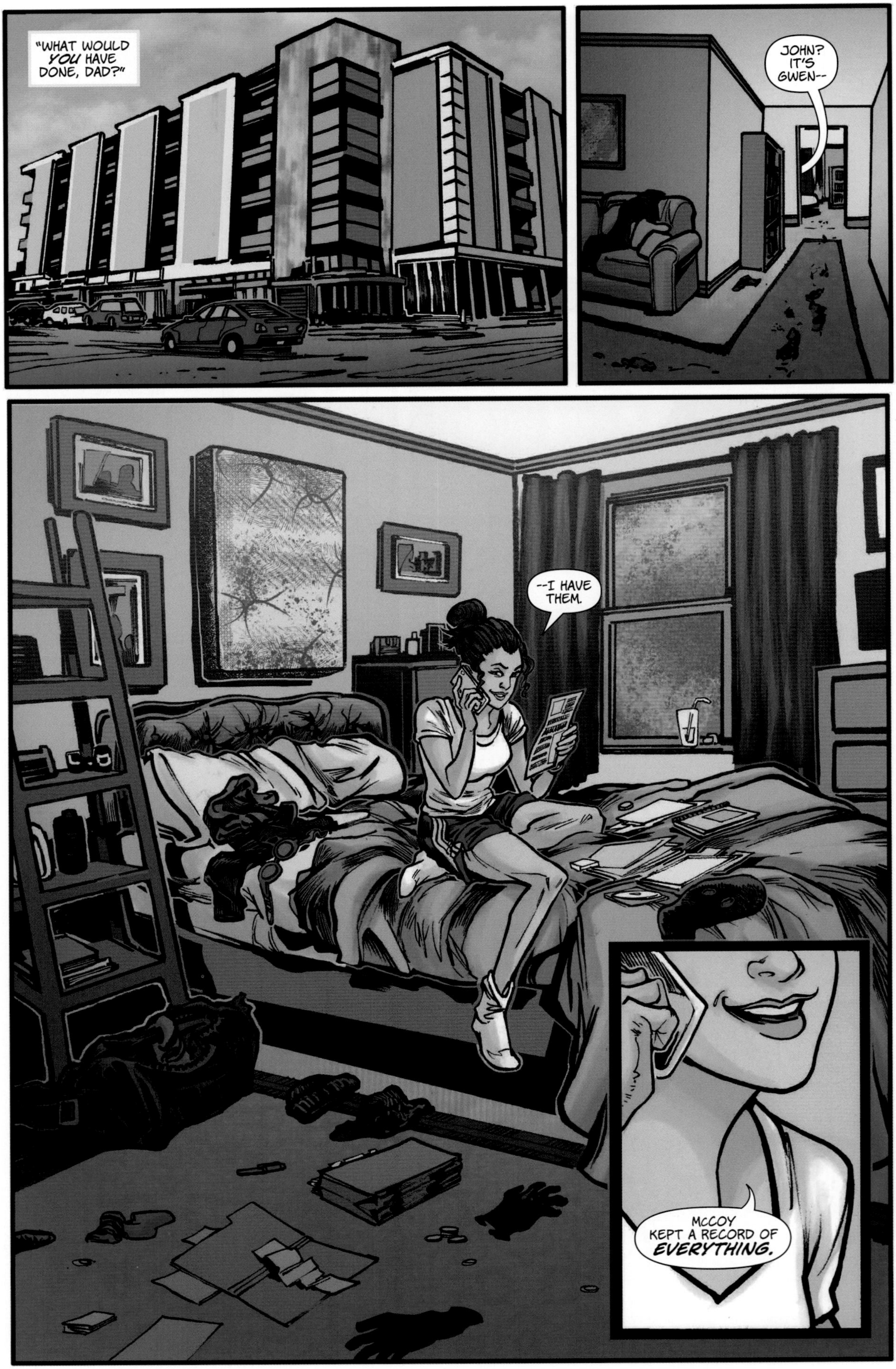
"WHAT WOULD YOU HAVE DONE, DAD?"
JOHN? IT'S GWEN--
--I HAVE THEM.
McCOY KEPT A RECORD OF EVERYTHING.

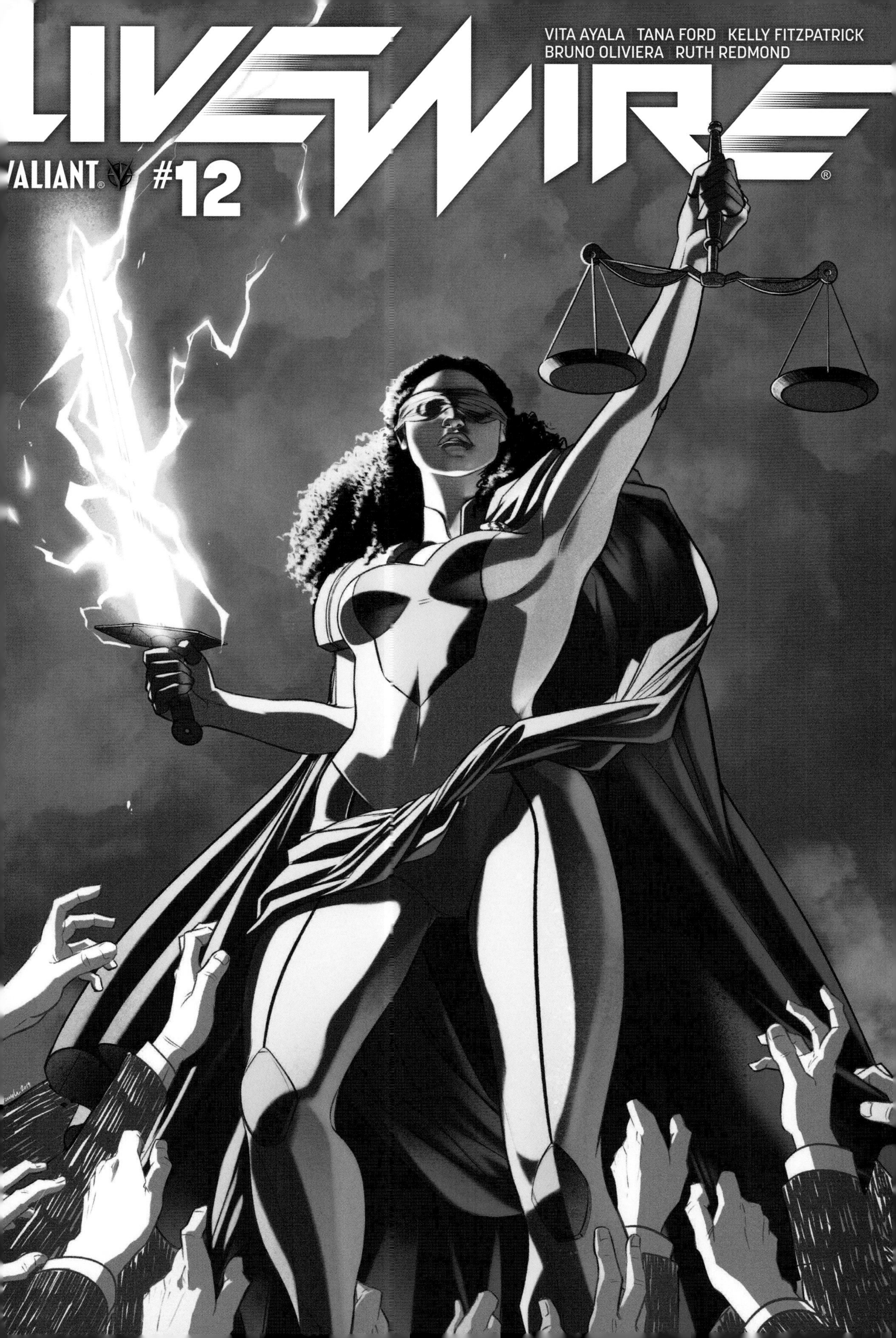
LIVEWIRE®
VITA AYALA | TANA FORD | KELLY FITZPATRICK
BRUNO OLIVIERA | RUTH REDMOND
VALIANT®
#12

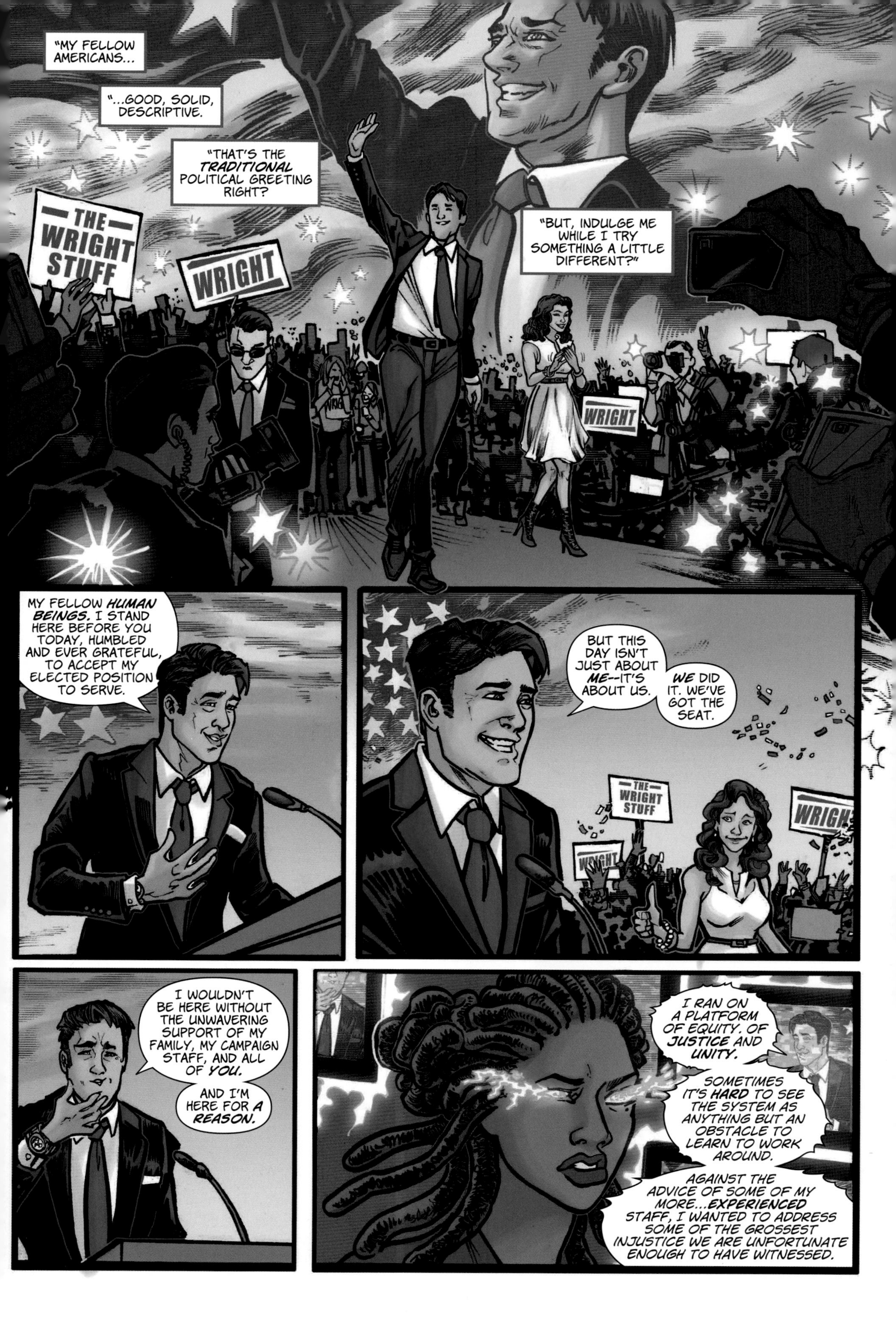
"MY FELLOW AMERICANS...
"...GOOD, SOLID, DESCRIPTIVE.
"THAT'S THE *TRADITIONAL* POLITICAL GREETING RIGHT?
THE WRIGHT STUFF
WRIGHT
"BUT, INDULGE ME WHILE I TRY SOMETHING A LITTLE DIFFERENT?"
WRIGHT
MY FELLOW *HUMAN BEINGS.* I STAND HERE BEFORE YOU TODAY, HUMBLED AND EVER GRATEFUL, TO ACCEPT MY ELECTED POSITION TO SERVE.
BUT THIS DAY ISN'T JUST ABOUT *ME*--IT'S ABOUT US.
WE DID IT. WE'VE GOT THE SEAT.
THE WRIGHT STUFF
WRIGHT
I WOULDN'T BE HERE WITHOUT THE UNWAVERING SUPPORT OF MY FAMILY, MY CAMPAIGN STAFF, AND ALL OF *YOU.*
AND I'M HERE FOR *A REASON.*
I RAN ON A PLATFORM OF EQUITY. OF *JUSTICE* AND *UNITY.*
SOMETIMES IT'S *HARD* TO SEE THE SYSTEM AS ANYTHING BUT AN OBSTACLE TO LEARN TO WORK AROUND.
AGAINST THE ADVICE OF SOME OF MY MORE...*EXPERIENCED* STAFF, I WANTED TO ADDRESS SOME OF THE GROSSEST INJUSTICE WE ARE UNFORTUNATE ENOUGH TO HAVE WITNESSED.

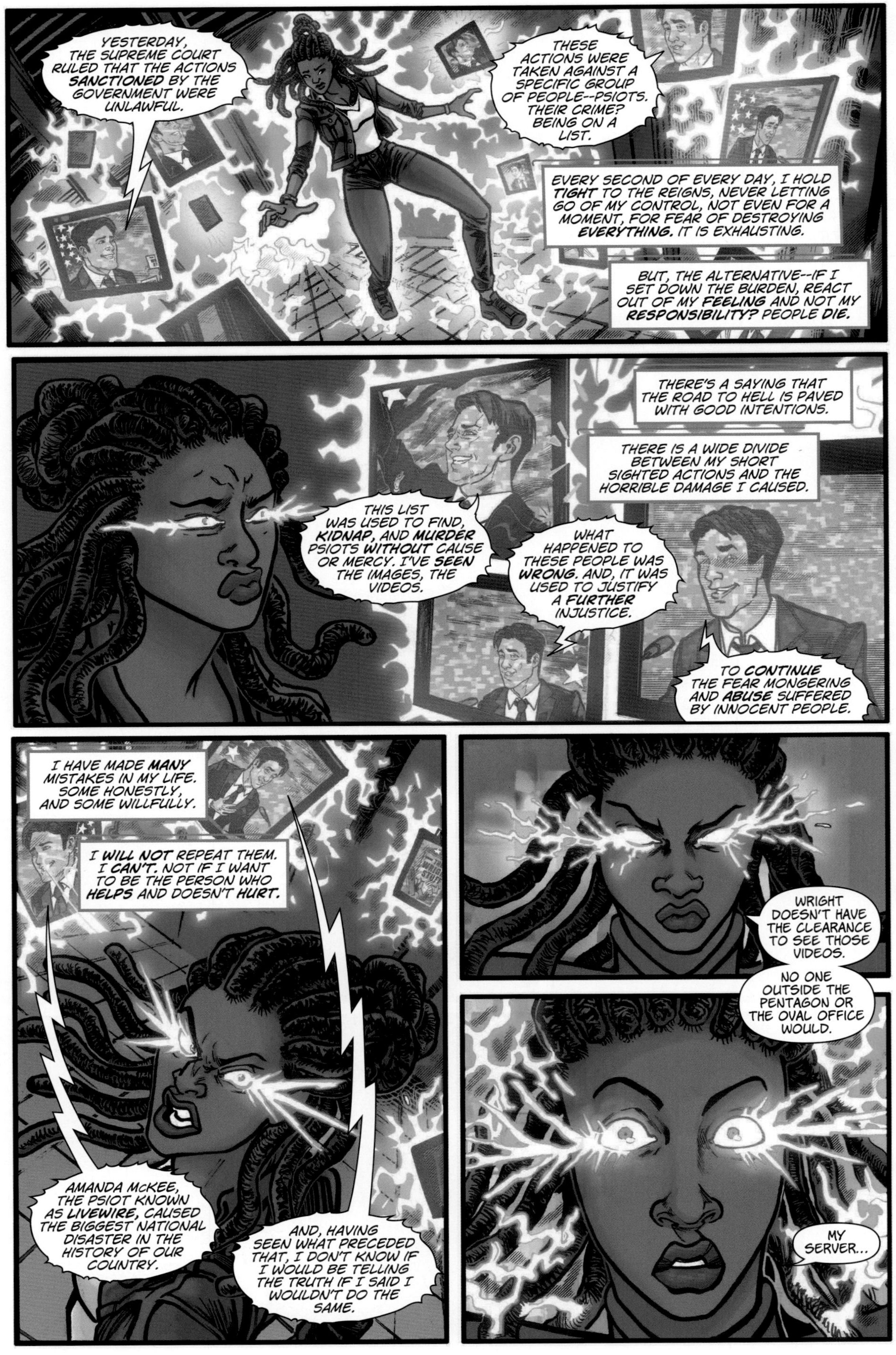
YESTERDAY, THE SUPREME COURT RULED THAT THE ACTIONS SANCTIONED BY THE GOVERNMENT WERE UNLAWFUL.
THESE ACTIONS WERE TAKEN AGAINST A SPECIFIC GROUP OF PEOPLE--PSIOTS. THEIR CRIME? BEING ON A LIST.
EVERY SECOND OF EVERY DAY, I HOLD TIGHT TO THE REIGNS, NEVER LETTING GO OF MY CONTROL, NOT EVEN FOR A MOMENT, FOR FEAR OF DESTROYING EVERYTHING. IT IS EXHAUSTING.
BUT, THE ALTERNATIVE--IF I SET DOWN THE BURDEN, REACT OUT OF MY FEELING AND NOT MY RESPONSIBILITY? PEOPLE DIE.
THERE'S A SAYING THAT THE ROAD TO HELL IS PAVED WITH GOOD INTENTIONS.
THERE IS A WIDE DIVIDE BETWEEN MY SHORT SIGHTED ACTIONS AND THE HORRIBLE DAMAGE I CAUSED.
THIS LIST WAS USED TO FIND, KIDNAP, AND MURDER PSIOTS WITHOUT CAUSE OR MERCY. I'VE SEEN THE IMAGES, THE VIDEOS.
WHAT HAPPENED TO THESE PEOPLE WAS WRONG. AND, IT WAS USED TO JUSTIFY A FURTHER INJUSTICE.
TO CONTINUE THE FEAR MONGERING AND ABUSE SUFFERED BY INNOCENT PEOPLE.
I HAVE MADE MANY MISTAKES IN MY LIFE. SOME HONESTLY, AND SOME WILLFULLY.
I WILL NOT REPEAT THEM. I CAN'T. NOT IF I WANT TO BE THE PERSON WHO HELPS AND DOESN'T HURT.
AMANDA McKEE, THE PSIOT KNOWN AS LIVEWIRE, CAUSED THE BIGGEST NATIONAL DISASTER IN THE HISTORY OF OUR COUNTRY.
AND, HAVING SEEN WHAT PRECEDED THAT, I DON'T KNOW IF I WOULD BE TELLING THE TRUTH IF I SAID I WOULDN'T DO THE SAME.
WRIGHT DOESN'T HAVE THE CLEARANCE TO SEE THOSE VIDEOS.
NO ONE OUTSIDE THE PENTAGON OR THE OVAL OFFICE WOULD.
MY SERVER...

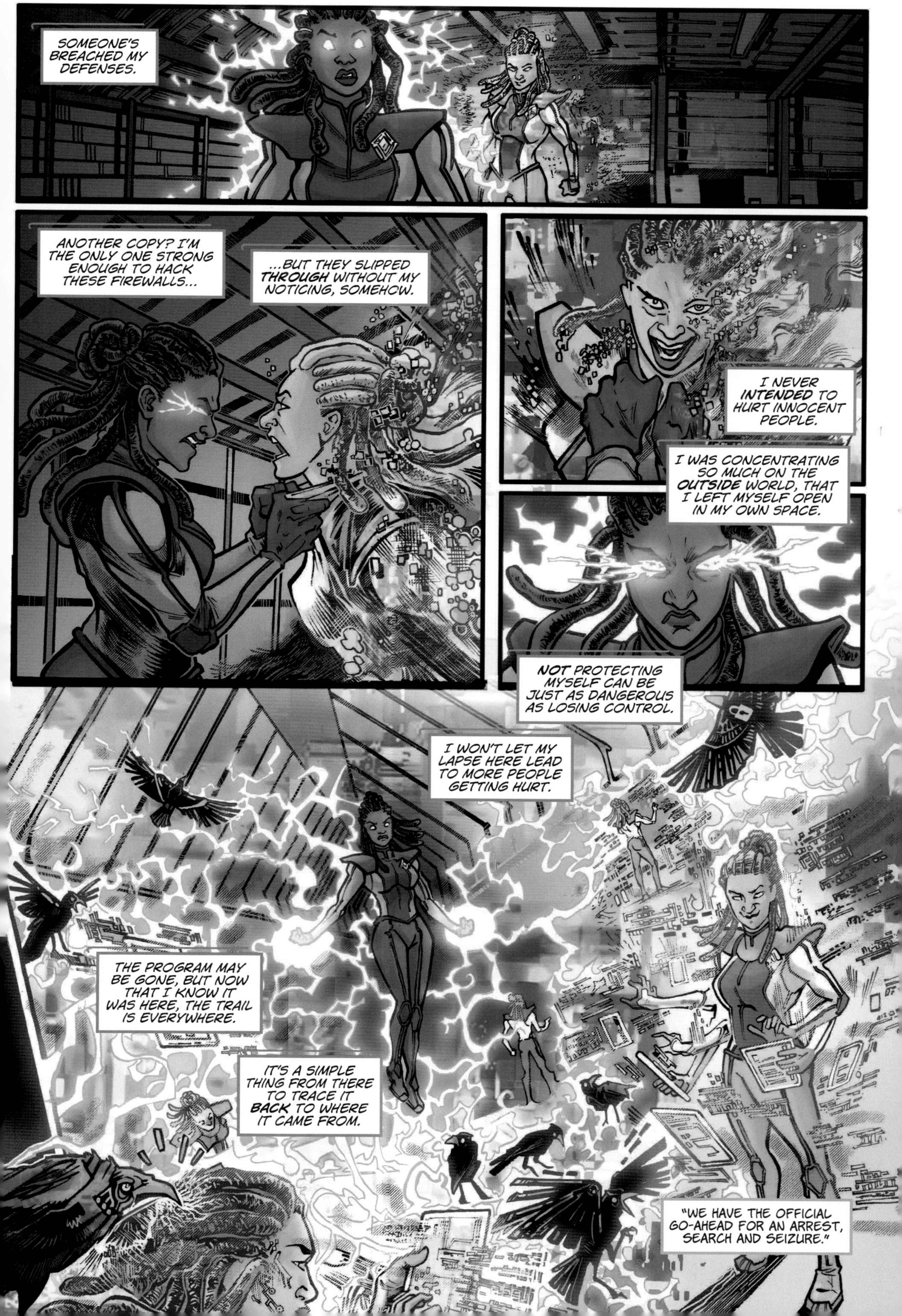
SOMEONE'S BREACHED MY DEFENSES.
ANOTHER COPY? I'M THE ONLY ONE STRONG ENOUGH TO HACK THESE FIREWALLS...
...BUT THEY SLIPPED **THROUGH** WITHOUT MY NOTICING, SOMEHOW.
I NEVER **INTENDED** TO HURT INNOCENT PEOPLE.
I WAS CONCENTRATING SO MUCH ON THE **OUTSIDE** WORLD, THAT I LEFT MYSELF OPEN IN MY OWN SPACE.
NOT PROTECTING MYSELF CAN BE JUST AS DANGEROUS AS LOSING CONTROL.
I WON'T LET MY LAPSE HERE LEAD TO MORE PEOPLE GETTING HURT.
THE PROGRAM MAY BE GONE, BUT NOW THAT I KNOW IT WAS HERE, THE TRAIL IS EVERYWHERE.
IT'S A SIMPLE THING FROM THERE TO TRACE IT **BACK** TO WHERE IT CAME FROM.
"WE HAVE THE OFFICIAL GO-AHEAD FOR AN ARREST, SEARCH AND SEIZURE."

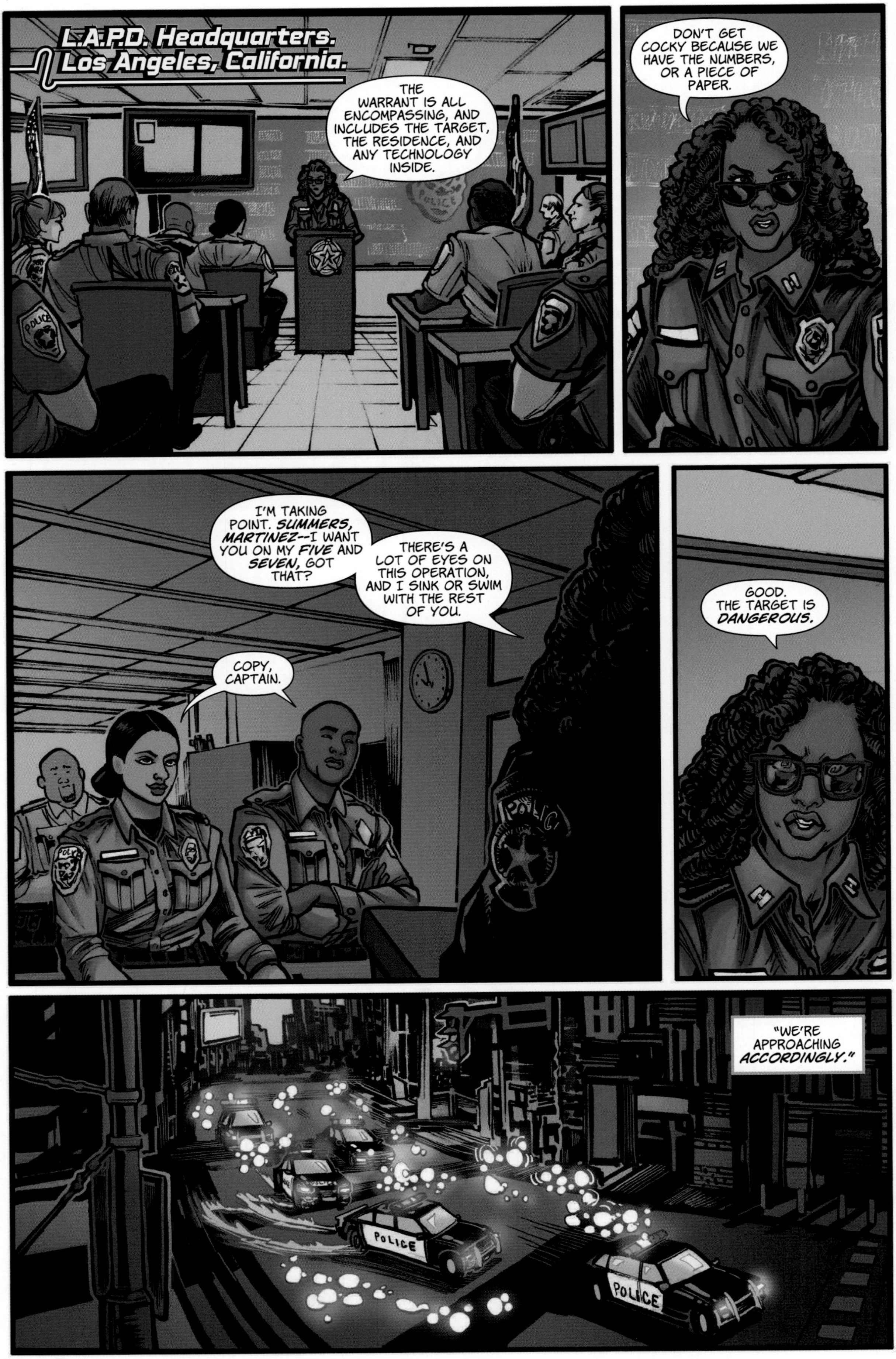
L.A.P.D. Headquarters. Los Angeles, California.
THE WARRANT IS ALL ENCOMPASSING, AND INCLUDES THE TARGET, THE RESIDENCE, AND ANY TECHNOLOGY INSIDE.
DON'T GET COCKY BECAUSE WE HAVE THE NUMBERS, OR A PIECE OF PAPER.
I'M TAKING POINT. SUMMERS, MARTINEZ--I WANT YOU ON MY FIVE AND SEVEN, GOT THAT?
THERE'S A LOT OF EYES ON THIS OPERATION, AND I SINK OR SWIM WITH THE REST OF YOU.
COPY, CAPTAIN.
GOOD. THE TARGET IS DANGEROUS.
"WE'RE APPROACHING ACCORDINGLY."
POLICE
POLICE

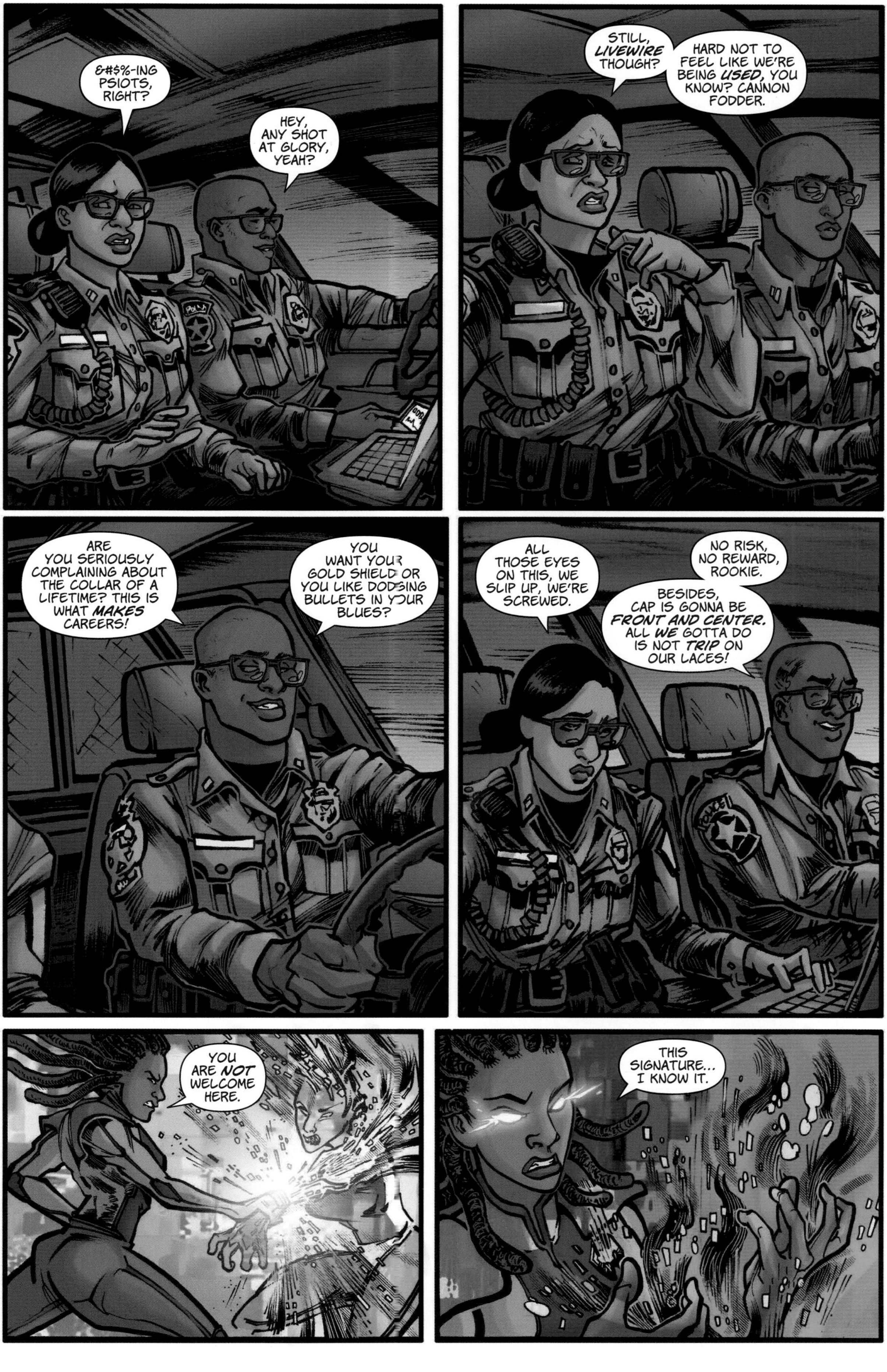
&#$%-ING PSIOTS, RIGHT?
HEY, ANY SHOT AT GLORY, YEAH?
STILL, LIVEWIRE THOUGH?
HARD NOT TO FEEL LIKE WE'RE BEING USED, YOU KNOW? CANNON FODDER.
ARE YOU SERIOUSLY COMPLAINING ABOUT THE COLLAR OF A LIFETIME? THIS IS WHAT MAKES CAREERS!
YOU WANT YOUR GOLD SHIELD OR YOU LIKE DODGING BULLETS IN YOUR BLUES?
ALL THOSE EYES ON THIS, WE SLIP UP, WE'RE SCREWED.
NO RISK, NO REWARD, ROOKIE.
BESIDES, CAP IS GONNA BE FRONT AND CENTER. ALL WE GOTTA DO IS NOT TRIP ON OUR LACES!
YOU ARE NOT WELCOME HERE.
THIS SIGNATURE... I KNOW IT.

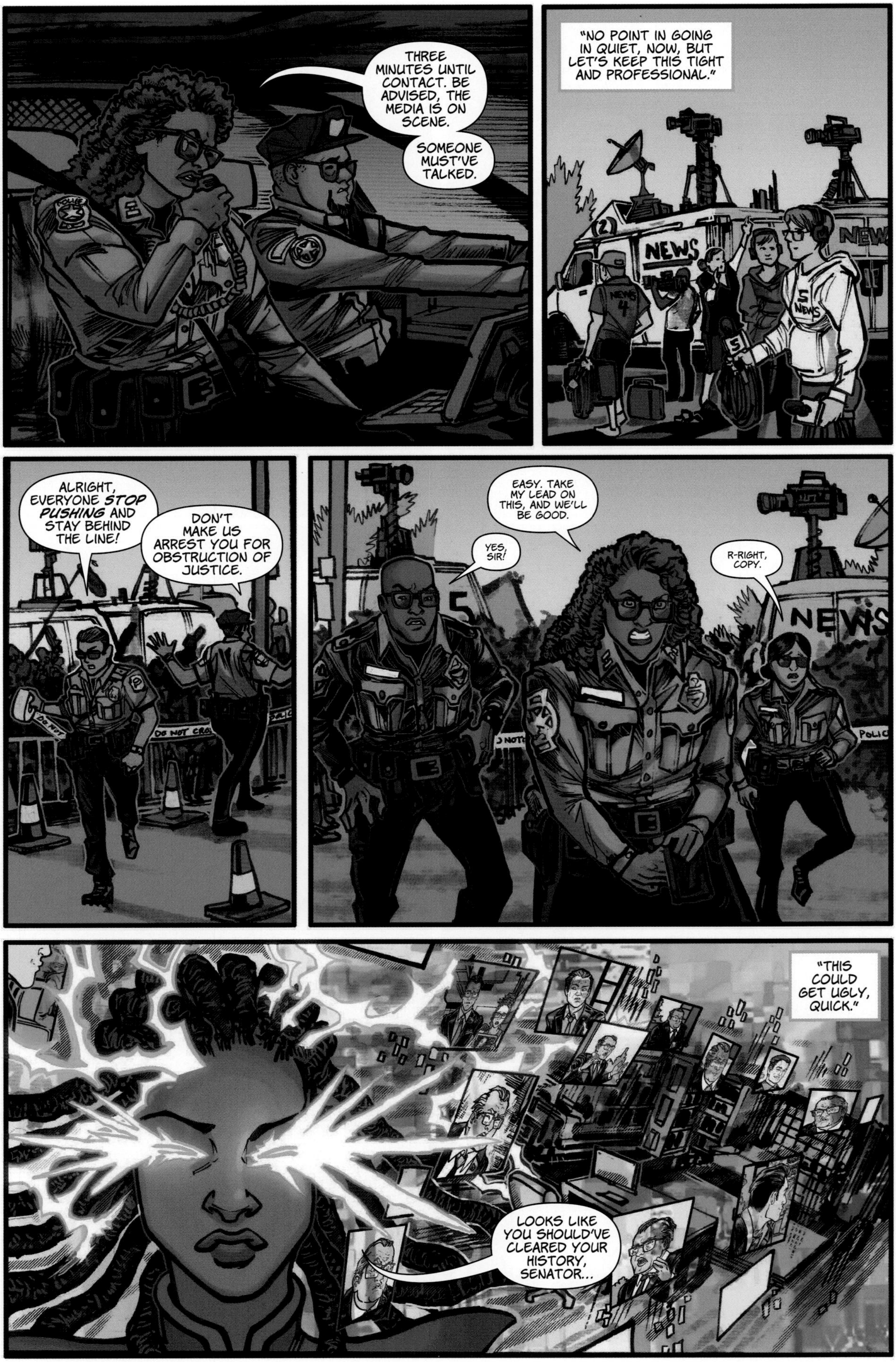
THREE MINUTES UNTIL CONTACT. BE ADVISED, THE MEDIA IS ON SCENE.
SOMEONE MUST'VE TALKED.
"NO POINT IN GOING IN QUIET, NOW, BUT LET'S KEEP THIS TIGHT AND PROFESSIONAL."
NEWS
NEWS 4
5 NEWS
ALRIGHT, EVERYONE *STOP PUSHING* AND STAY BEHIND THE LINE!
DON'T MAKE US ARREST YOU FOR OBSTRUCTION OF JUSTICE.
DO NOT CROSS
YES, SIR!
EASY. TAKE MY LEAD ON THIS, AND WE'LL BE GOOD.
R-RIGHT, COPY.
NEWS
"THIS COULD GET UGLY, QUICK."
LOOKS LIKE YOU SHOULD'VE CLEARED YOUR HISTORY, SENATOR...

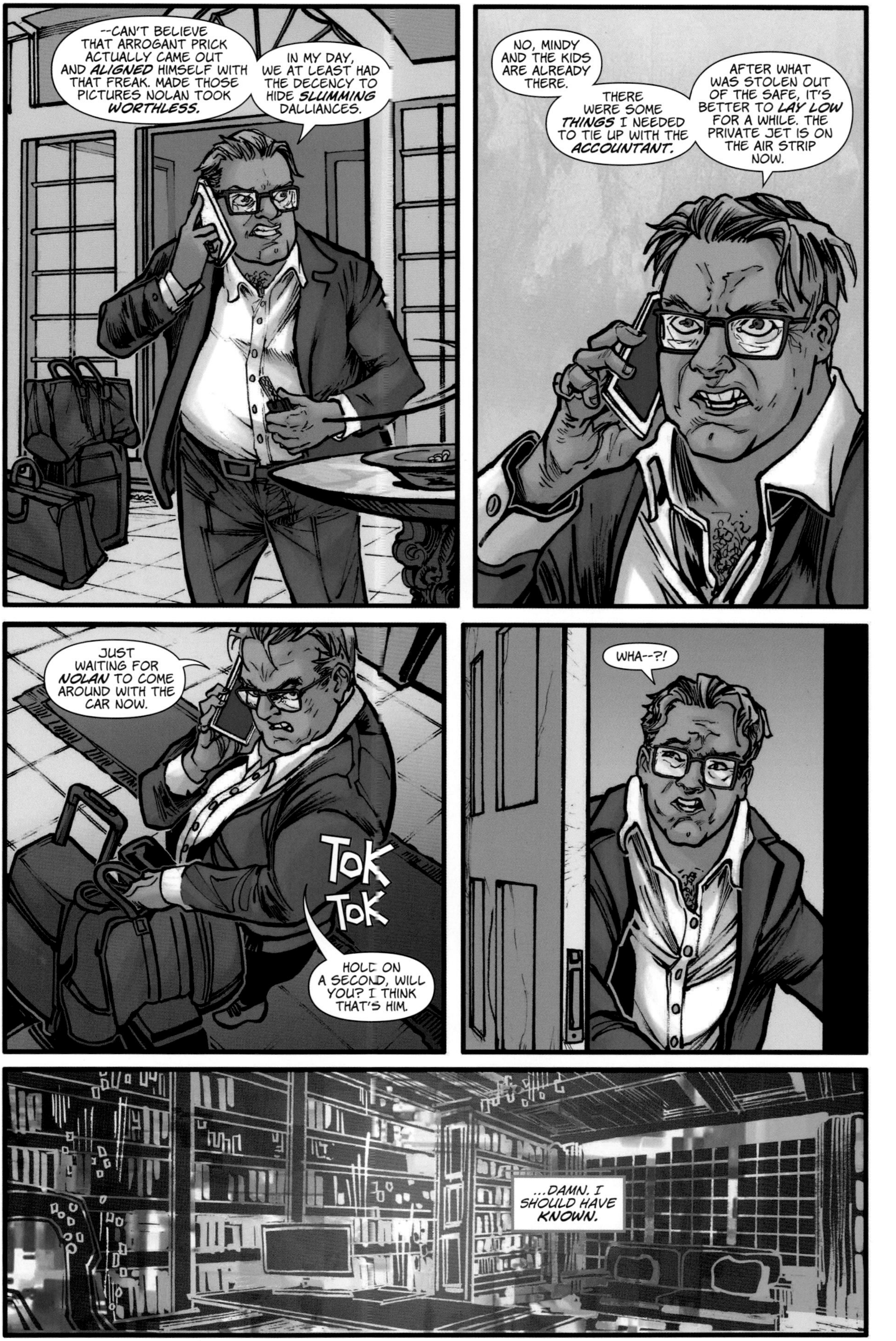
--CAN'T BELIEVE THAT ARROGANT PRICK ACTUALLY CAME OUT AND ALIGNED HIMSELF WITH THAT FREAK. MADE THOSE PICTURES NOLAN TOOK WORTHLESS.
IN MY DAY, WE AT LEAST HAD THE DECENCY TO HIDE SLUMMING DALLIANCES.
NO, MINDY AND THE KIDS ARE ALREADY THERE.
THERE WERE SOME THINGS I NEEDED TO TIE UP WITH THE ACCOUNTANT.
AFTER WHAT WAS STOLEN OUT OF THE SAFE, IT'S BETTER TO LAY LOW FOR A WHILE. THE PRIVATE JET IS ON THE AIR STRIP NOW.
JUST WAITING FOR NOLAN TO COME AROUND WITH THE CAR NOW.
TOK TOK
HOLD ON A SECOND, WILL YOU? I THINK THAT'S HIM.
WHA--?!
...DAMN. I SHOULD HAVE KNOWN.

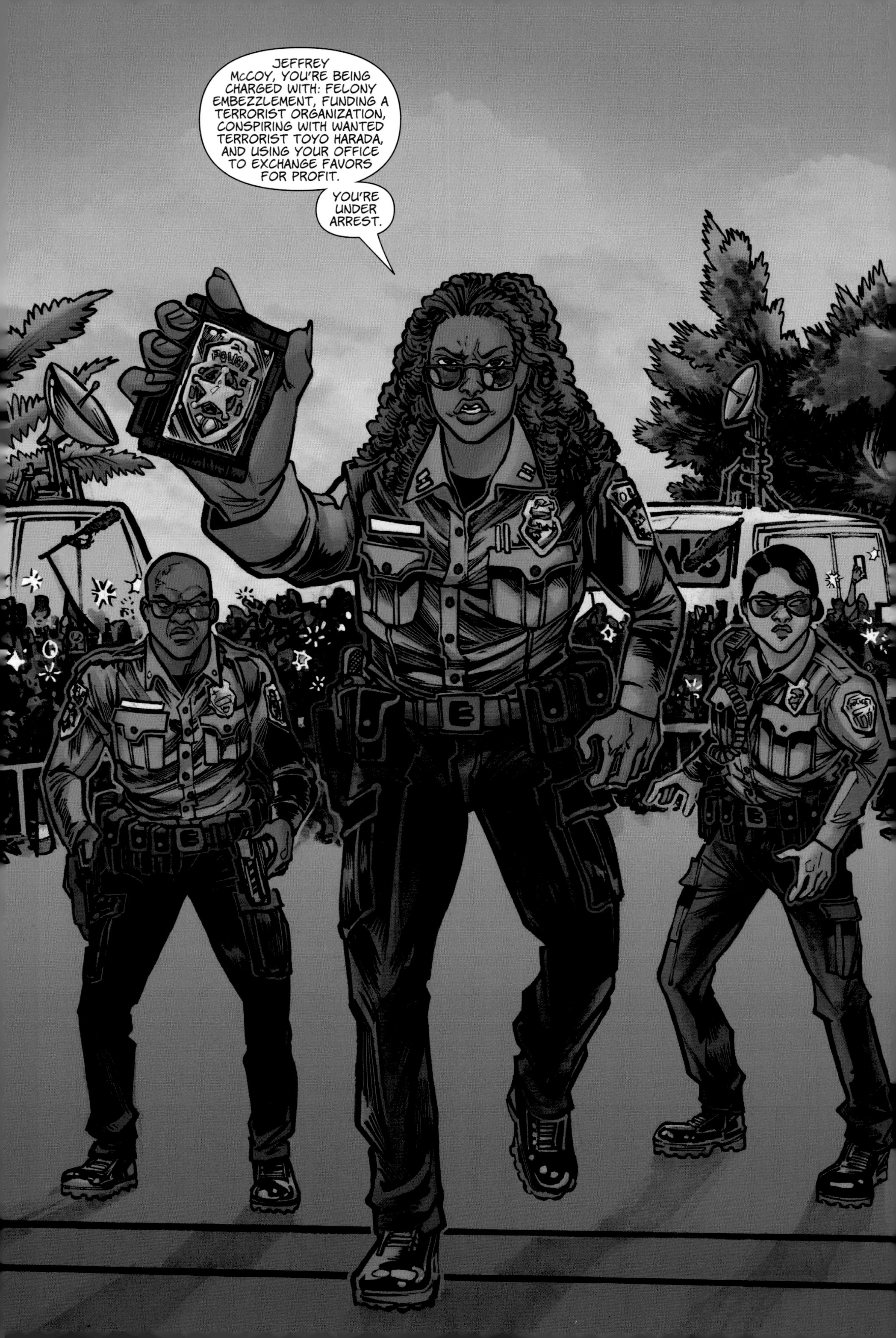
JEFFREY McCOY, YOU'RE BEING CHARGED WITH: FELONY EMBEZZLEMENT, FUNDING A TERRORIST ORGANIZATION, CONSPIRING WITH WANTED TERRORIST TOYO HARADA, AND USING YOUR OFFICE TO EXCHANGE FAVORS FOR PROFIT.
YOU'RE UNDER ARREST.
POLICE

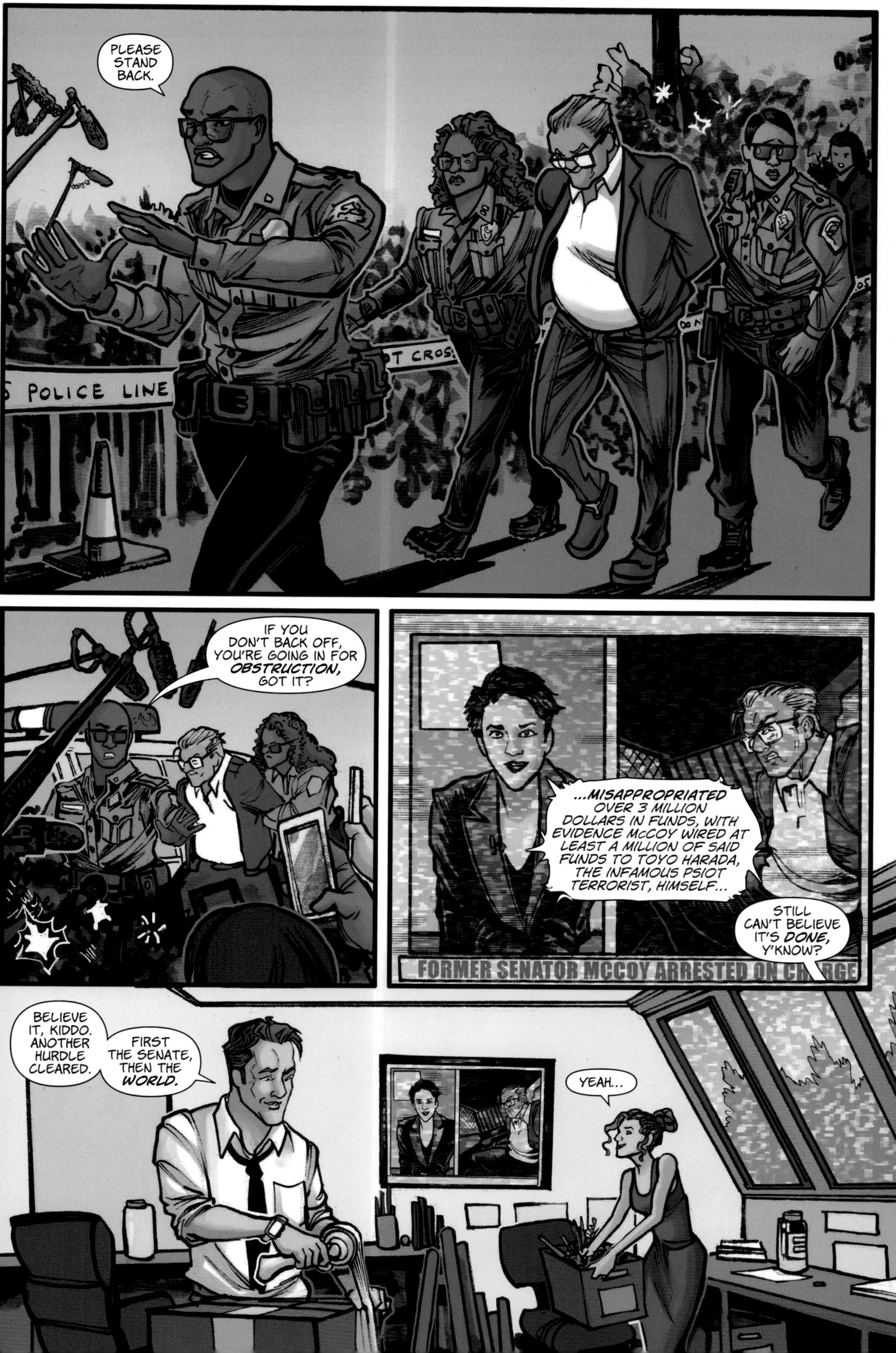
PLEASE STAND BACK.
POLICE LINE
IF YOU DON'T BACK OFF, YOU'RE GOING IN FOR *OBSTRUCTION,* GOT IT?
...MISAPPROPRIATED OVER 3 MILLION DOLLARS IN FUNDS, WITH EVIDENCE McCOY WIRED AT LEAST A MILLION OF SAID FUNDS TO TOYO HARADA, THE INFAMOUS PSIOT TERRORIST, HIMSELF...
FORMER SENATOR MCCOY ARRESTED ON
STILL CAN'T BELIEVE IT'S *DONE,* Y'KNOW?
BELIEVE IT, KIDDO. ANOTHER HURDLE CLEARED.
FIRST THE SENATE, THEN THE *WORLD.*
YEAH...

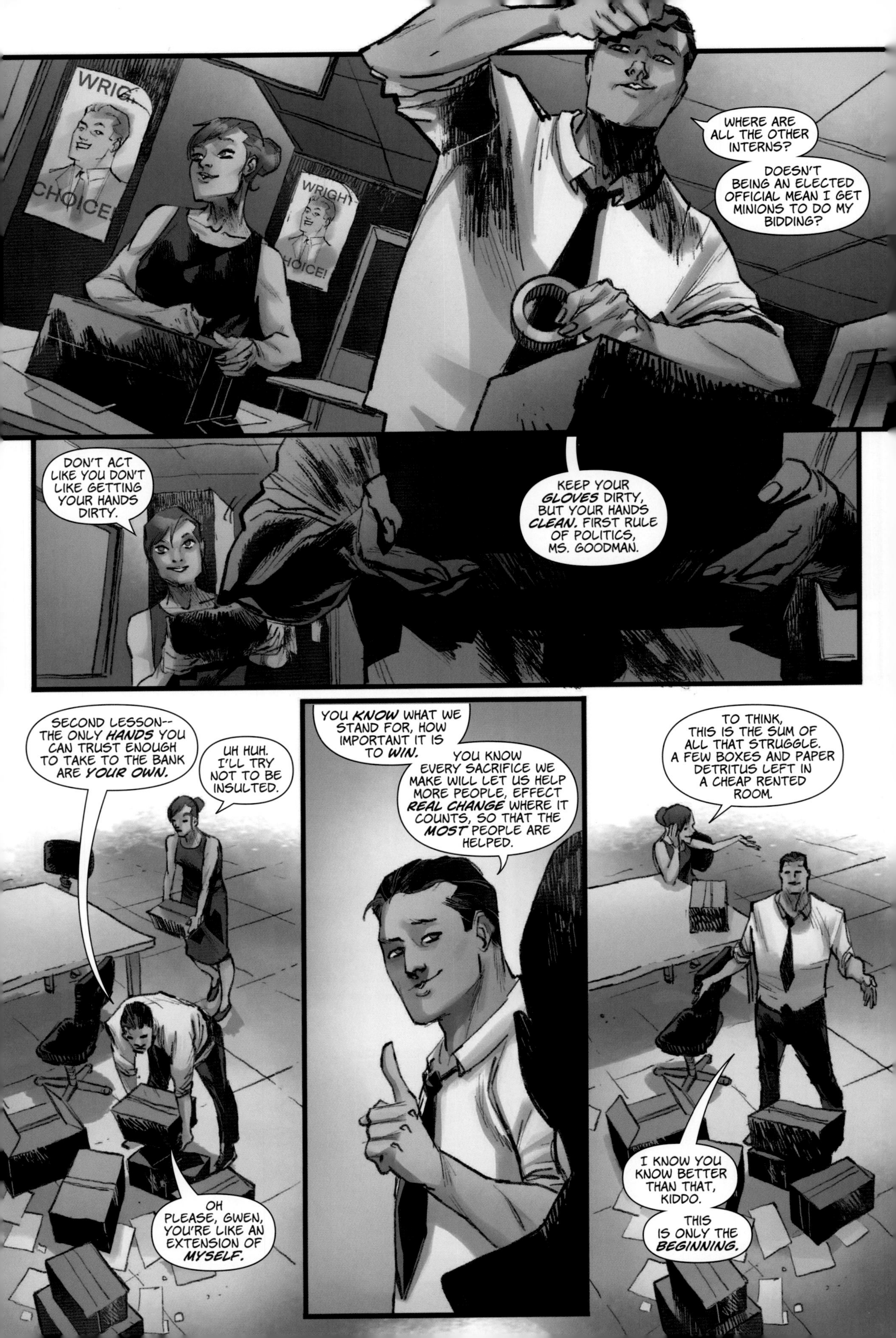
WRIGH
CHOICE!
WRIGHT
CHOICE!
WHERE ARE ALL THE OTHER INTERNS?
DOESN'T BEING AN ELECTED OFFICIAL MEAN I GET MINIONS TO DO MY BIDDING?
DON'T ACT LIKE YOU DON'T LIKE GETTING YOUR HANDS DIRTY.
KEEP YOUR GLOVES DIRTY, BUT YOUR HANDS CLEAN. FIRST RULE OF POLITICS, MS. GOODMAN.
SECOND LESSON-- THE ONLY HANDS YOU CAN TRUST ENOUGH TO TAKE TO THE BANK ARE YOUR OWN.
UH HUH. I'LL TRY NOT TO BE INSULTED.
OH PLEASE, GWEN, YOU'RE LIKE AN EXTENSION OF MYSELF.
YOU KNOW WHAT WE STAND FOR, HOW IMPORTANT IT IS TO WIN.
YOU KNOW EVERY SACRIFICE WE MAKE WILL LET US HELP MORE PEOPLE, EFFECT REAL CHANGE WHERE IT COUNTS, SO THAT THE MOST PEOPLE ARE HELPED.
TO THINK, THIS IS THE SUM OF ALL THAT STRUGGLE. A FEW BOXES AND PAPER DETRITUS LEFT IN A CHEAP RENTED ROOM.
I KNOW YOU KNOW BETTER THAN THAT, KIDDO.
THIS IS ONLY THE BEGINNING.

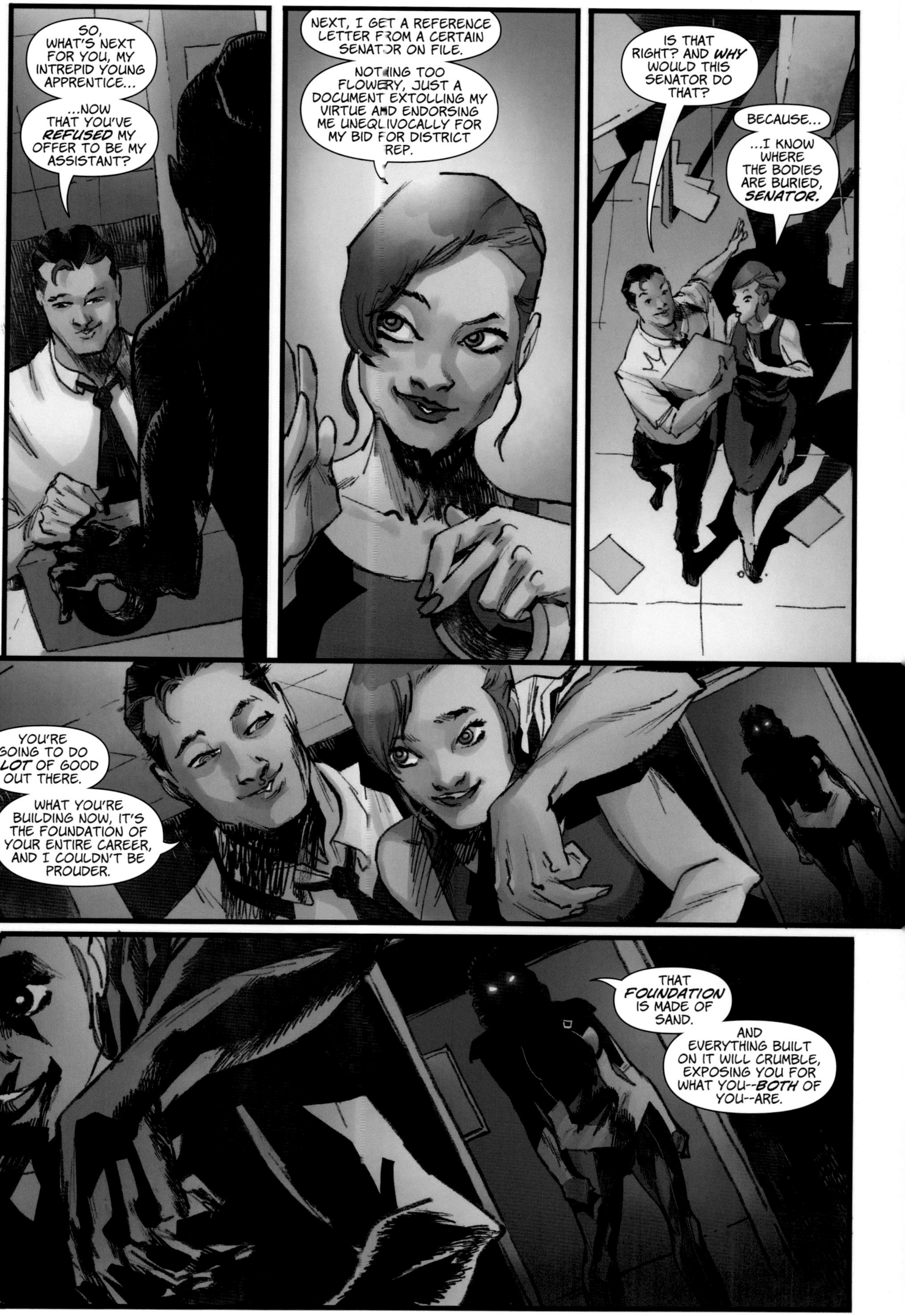
SO, WHAT'S NEXT FOR YOU, MY INTREPID YOUNG APPRENTICE...
...NOW THAT YOU'VE *REFUSED* MY OFFER TO BE MY ASSISTANT?
NEXT, I GET A REFERENCE LETTER FROM A CERTAIN SENATOR ON FILE.
NOTHING TOO FLOWERY, JUST A DOCUMENT EXTOLLING MY VIRTUE AND ENDORSING ME UNEQLIVOCALLY FOR MY BID FOR DISTRICT REP.
IS THAT RIGHT? AND *WHY* WOULD THIS SENATOR DO THAT?
BECAUSE...
...I KNOW WHERE THE BODIES ARE BURIED, ***SENATOR.***
YOU'RE GOING TO DO ***A LOT*** OF GOOD OUT THERE.
WHAT YOU'RE BUILDING NOW, IT'S THE FOUNDATION OF YOUR ENTIRE CAREER, AND I COULDN'T BE PROUDER.
THAT ***FOUNDATION*** IS MADE OF SAND.
AND EVERYTHING BUILT ON IT WILL CRUMBLE, EXPOSING YOU FOR WHAT YOU--***BOTH*** OF YOU--ARE.

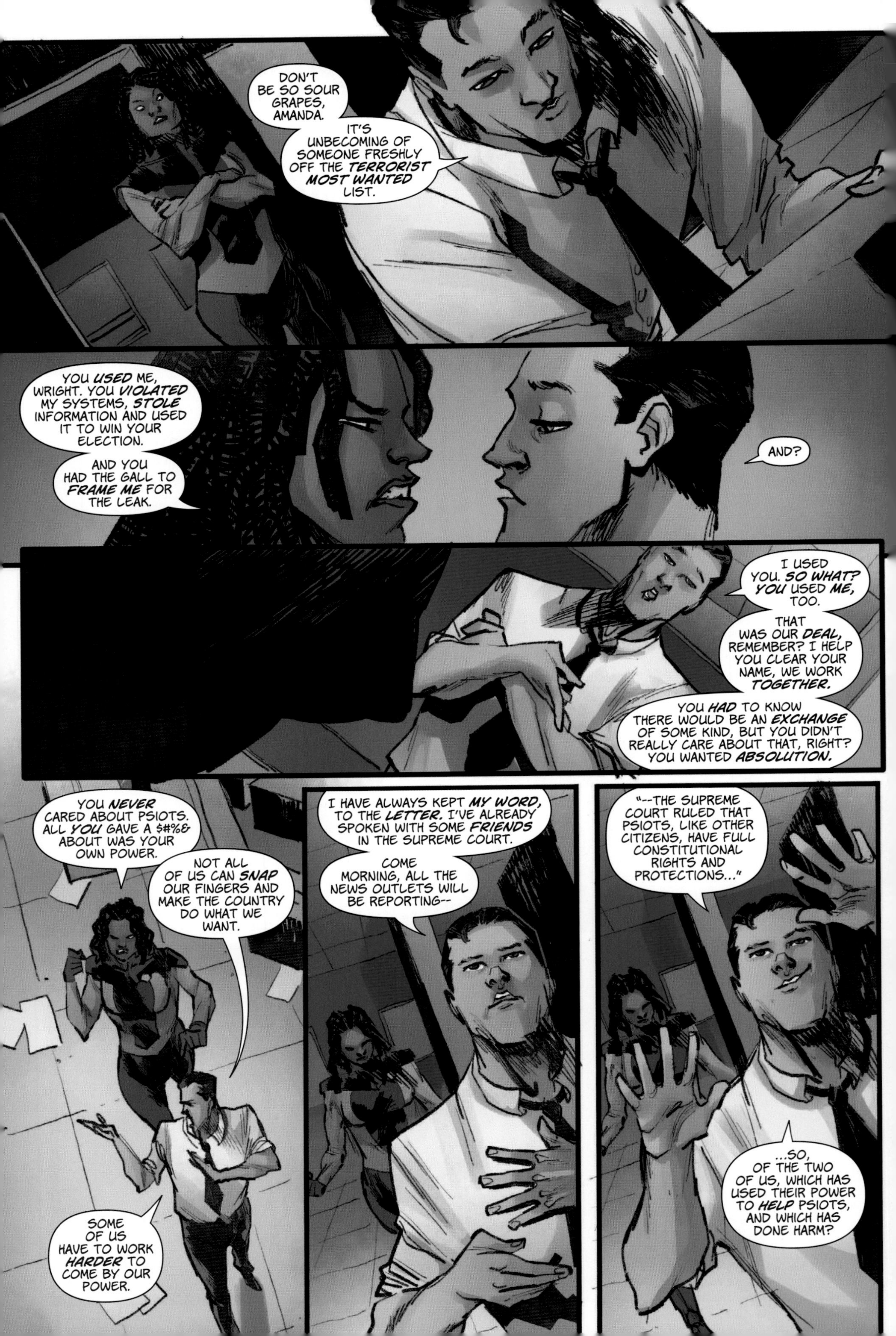
DON'T BE SO SOUR GRAPES, AMANDA.
IT'S UNBECOMING OF SOMEONE FRESHLY OFF THE **TERRORIST MOST WANTED** LIST.
YOU **USED** ME, WRIGHT. YOU **VIOLATED** MY SYSTEMS, **STOLE** INFORMATION AND USED IT TO WIN YOUR ELECTION.
AND YOU HAD THE GALL TO **FRAME ME** FOR THE LEAK.
AND?
I USED YOU. **SO WHAT? YOU** USED **ME,** TOO.
THAT WAS OUR **DEAL,** REMEMBER? I HELP YOU CLEAR YOUR NAME, WE WORK **TOGETHER.**
YOU **HAD** TO KNOW THERE WOULD BE AN **EXCHANGE** OF SOME KIND, BUT YOU DIDN'T REALLY CARE ABOUT THAT, RIGHT? YOU WANTED **ABSOLUTION.**
YOU **NEVER** CARED ABOUT PSIOTS. ALL **YOU** GAVE A $#%& ABOUT WAS YOUR OWN POWER.
NOT ALL OF US CAN **SNAP** OUR FINGERS AND MAKE THE COUNTRY DO WHAT WE WANT.
SOME OF US HAVE TO WORK **HARDER** TO COME BY OUR POWER.
I HAVE ALWAYS KEPT **MY WORD,** TO THE **LETTER.** I'VE ALREADY SPOKEN WITH SOME **FRIENDS** IN THE SUPREME COURT.
COME MORNING, ALL THE NEWS OUTLETS WILL BE REPORTING--
"--THE SUPREME COURT RULED THAT PSIOTS, LIKE OTHER CITIZENS, HAVE FULL CONSTITUTIONAL RIGHTS AND PROTECTIONS..."
...SO, OF THE TWO OF US, WHICH HAS USED THEIR POWER TO **HELP** PSIOTS, AND WHICH HAS DONE HARM?

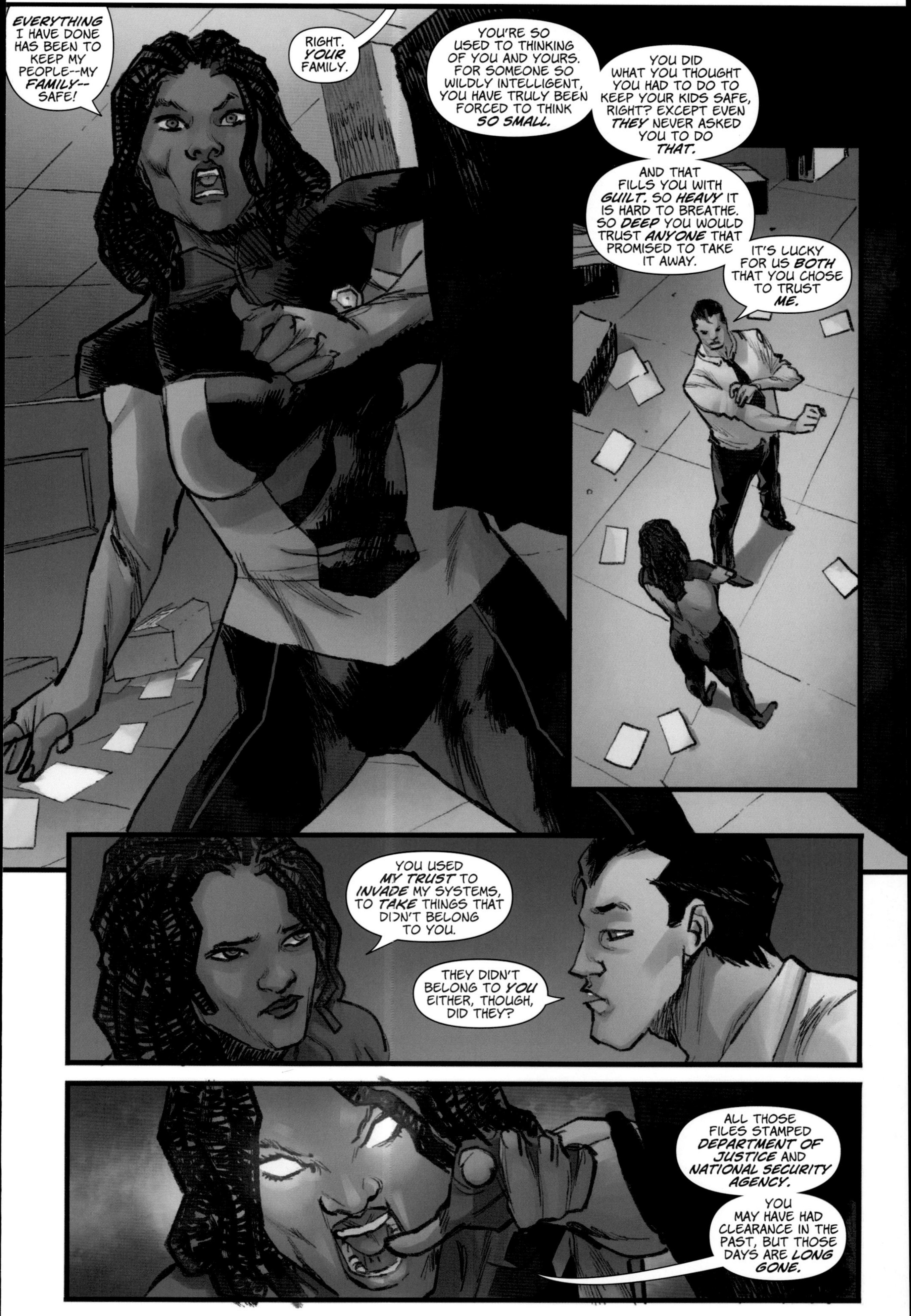
EVERYTHING I HAVE DONE HAS BEEN TO KEEP MY PEOPLE--MY FAMILY--SAFE!
RIGHT. YOUR FAMILY.
YOU'RE SO USED TO THINKING OF YOU AND YOURS. FOR SOMEONE SO WILDLY INTELLIGENT, YOU HAVE TRULY BEEN FORCED TO THINK SO SMALL.
YOU DID WHAT YOU THOUGHT YOU HAD TO DO TO KEEP YOUR KIDS SAFE, RIGHT? EXCEPT EVEN THEY NEVER ASKED YOU TO DO THAT.
AND THAT FILLS YOU WITH GUILT. SO HEAVY IT IS HARD TO BREATHE. SO DEEP YOU WOULD TRUST ANYONE THAT PROMISED TO TAKE IT AWAY.
IT'S LUCKY FOR US BOTH THAT YOU CHOSE TO TRUST ME.
YOU USED MY TRUST TO INVADE MY SYSTEMS, TO TAKE THINGS THAT DIDN'T BELONG TO YOU.
THEY DIDN'T BELONG TO YOU EITHER, THOUGH, DID THEY?
ALL THOSE FILES STAMPED DEPARTMENT OF JUSTICE AND NATIONAL SECURITY AGENCY.
YOU MAY HAVE HAD CLEARANCE IN THE PAST, BUT THOSE DAYS ARE LONG GONE.

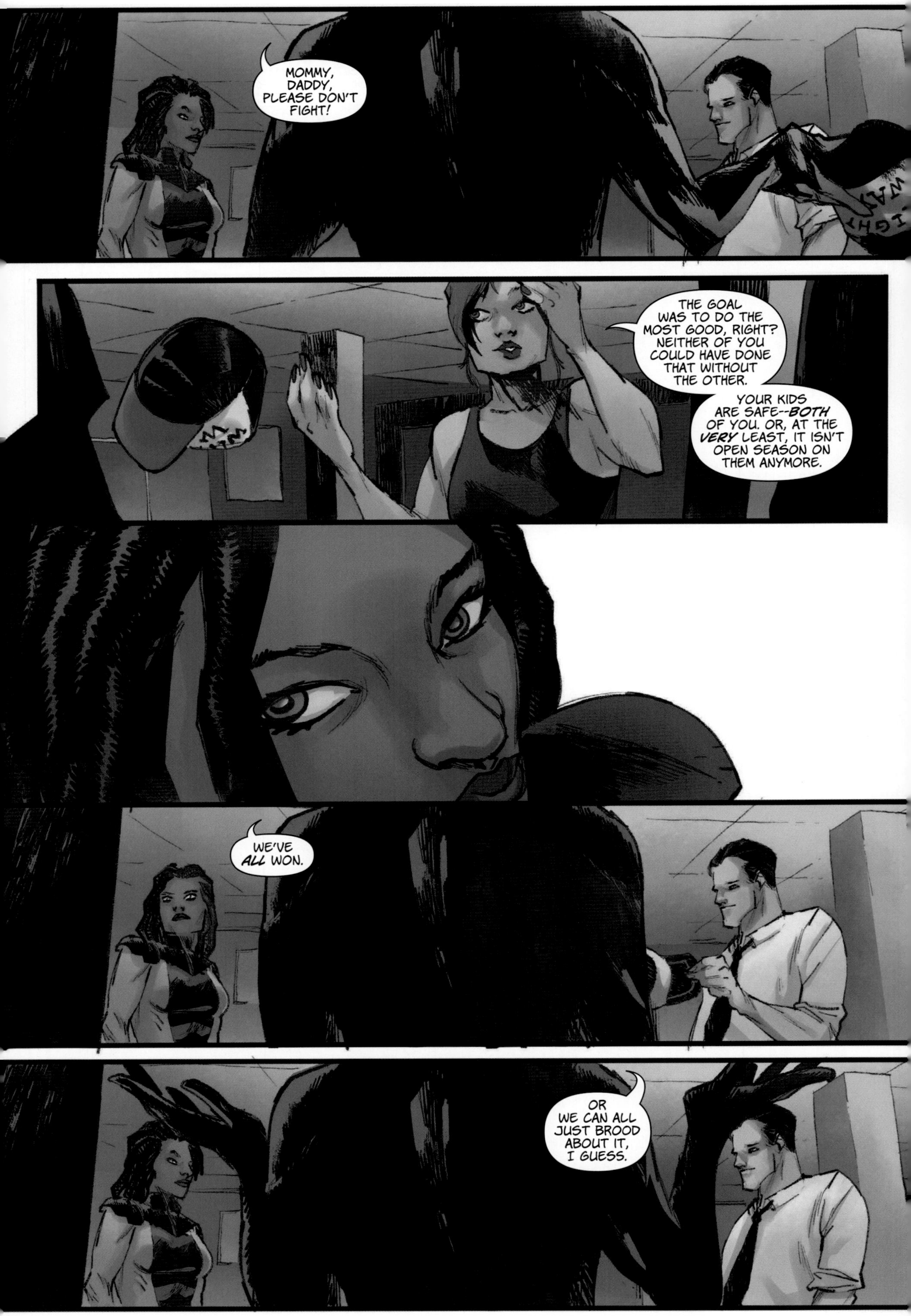
MOMMY, DADDY, PLEASE DON'T FIGHT!
THE GOAL WAS TO DO THE MOST GOOD, RIGHT? NEITHER OF YOU COULD HAVE DONE THAT WITHOUT THE OTHER.
YOUR KIDS ARE SAFE--*BOTH* OF YOU. OR, AT THE *VERY* LEAST, IT ISN'T OPEN SEASON ON THEM ANYMORE.
WE'VE *ALL* WON.
OR WE CAN ALL JUST BROOD ABOUT IT, I GUESS.

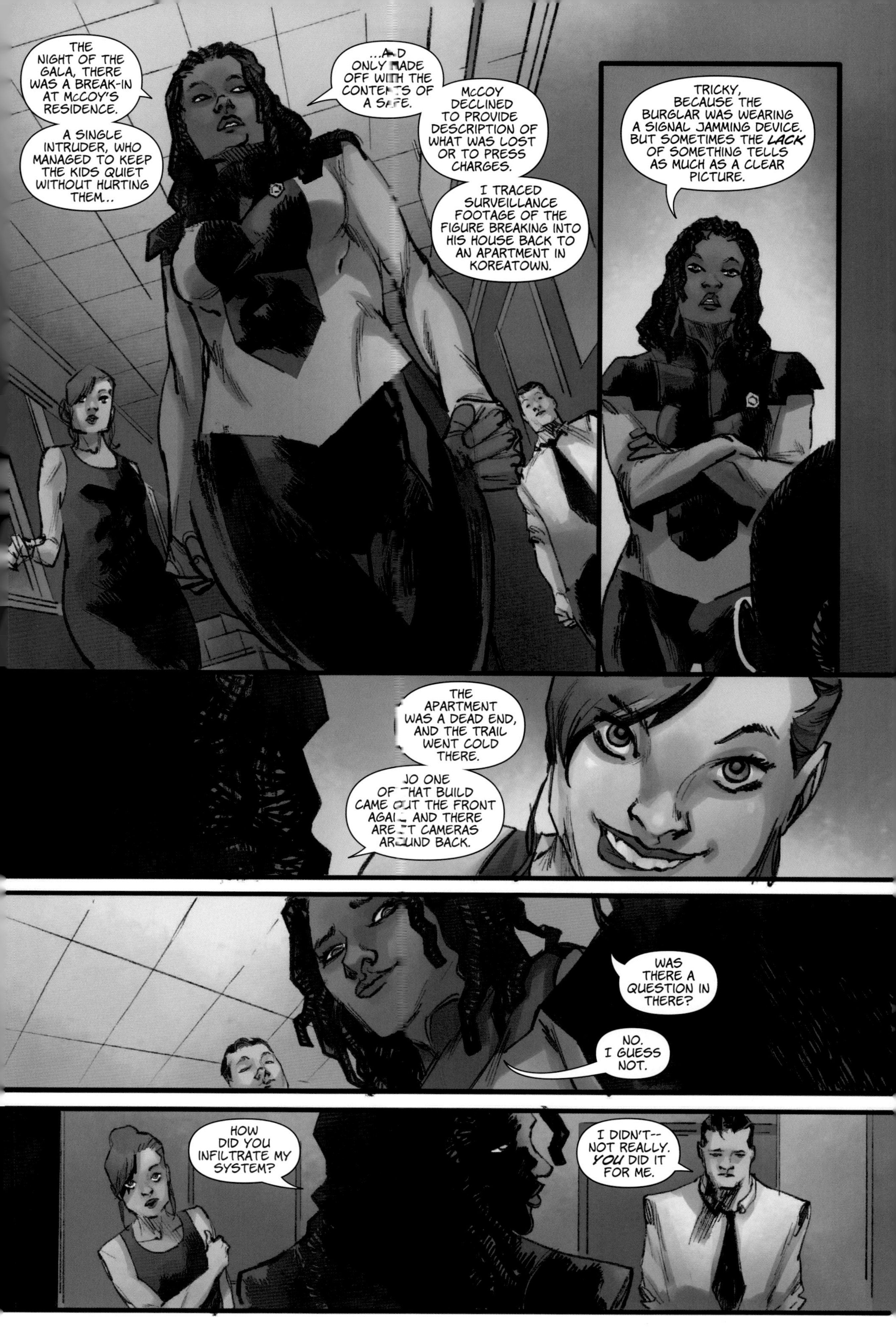

THE NIGHT OF THE GALA, THERE WAS A BREAK-IN AT McCOY'S RESIDENCE.
A SINGLE INTRUDER, WHO MANAGED TO KEEP THE KIDS QUIET WITHOUT HURTING THEM...
...AND ONLY MADE OFF WITH THE CONTENTS OF A SAFE.
McCOY DECLINED TO PROVIDE DESCRIPTION OF WHAT WAS LOST OR TO PRESS CHARGES.
I TRACED SURVEILLANCE FOOTAGE OF THE FIGURE BREAKING INTO HIS HOUSE BACK TO AN APARTMENT IN KOREATOWN.
TRICKY, BECAUSE THE BURGLAR WAS WEARING A SIGNAL JAMMING DEVICE. BUT SOMETIMES THE *LACK* OF SOMETHING TELLS AS MUCH AS A CLEAR PICTURE.
THE APARTMENT WAS A DEAD END, AND THE TRAIL WENT COLD THERE.
NO ONE OF THAT BUILD CAME OUT THE FRONT AGAIN AND THERE AREN'T CAMERAS AROUND BACK.
WAS THERE A QUESTION IN THERE?
NO. I GUESS NOT.
HOW DID YOU INFILTRATE MY SYSTEM?
I DIDN'T-- NOT REALLY. *YOU* DID IT FOR ME.

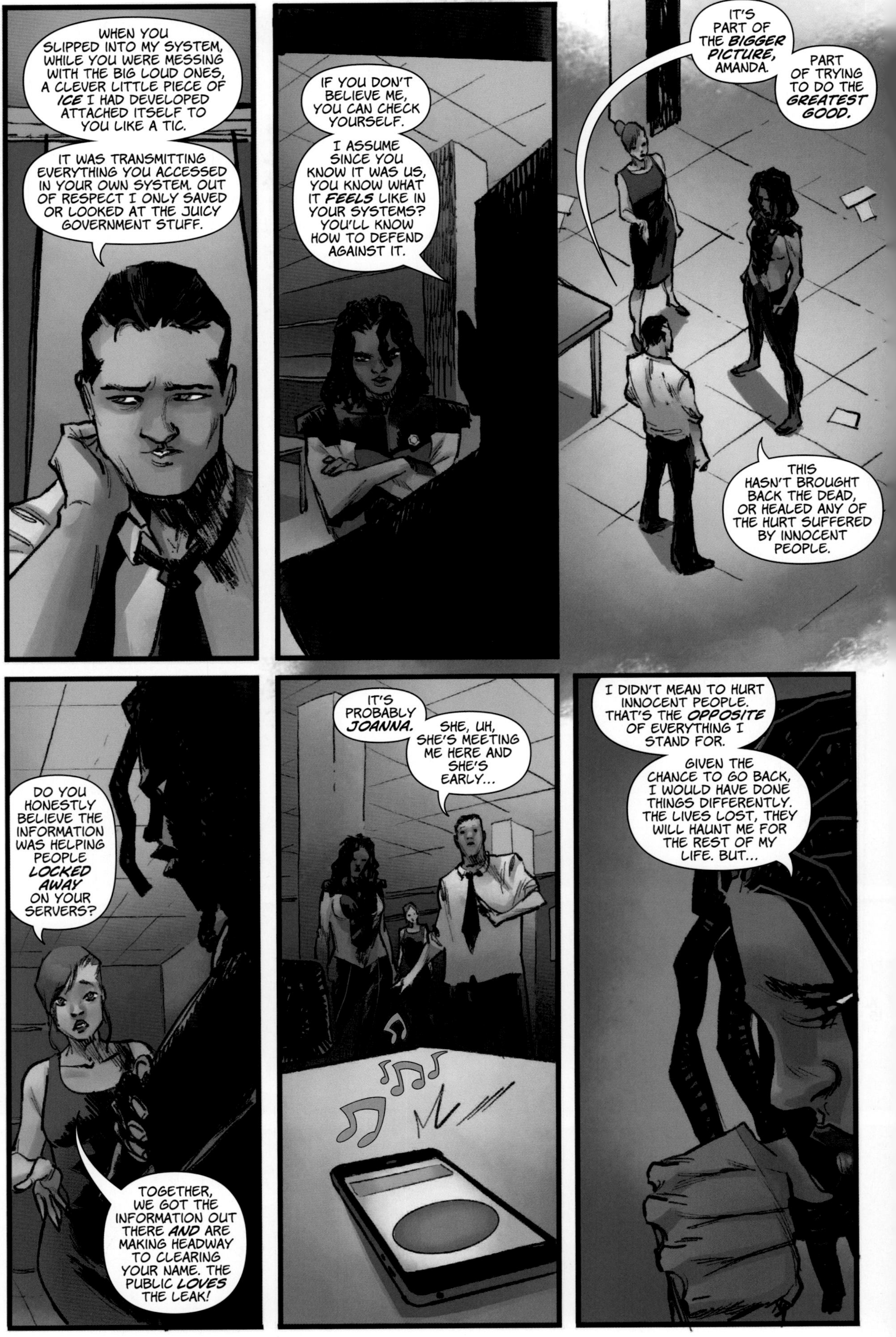
WHEN YOU SLIPPED INTO MY SYSTEM, WHILE YOU WERE MESSING WITH THE BIG LOUD ONES, A CLEVER LITTLE PIECE OF *ICE* I HAD DEVELOPED ATTACHED ITSELF TO YOU LIKE A TIC.
IT WAS TRANSMITTING EVERYTHING YOU ACCESSED IN YOUR OWN SYSTEM. OUT OF RESPECT I ONLY SAVED OR LOOKED AT THE JUICY GOVERNMENT STUFF.
IF YOU DON'T BELIEVE ME, YOU CAN CHECK YOURSELF.
I ASSUME SINCE YOU KNOW IT WAS US, YOU KNOW WHAT IT *FEELS* LIKE IN YOUR SYSTEMS? YOU'LL KNOW HOW TO DEFEND AGAINST IT.
IT'S PART OF THE *BIGGER PICTURE,* AMANDA.
PART OF TRYING TO DO THE *GREATEST GOOD.*
THIS HASN'T BROUGHT BACK THE DEAD, OR HEALED ANY OF THE HURT SUFFERED BY INNOCENT PEOPLE.
DO YOU HONESTLY BELIEVE THE INFORMATION WAS HELPING PEOPLE *LOCKED AWAY* ON YOUR SERVERS?
TOGETHER, WE GOT THE INFORMATION OUT THERE *AND* ARE MAKING HEADWAY TO CLEARING YOUR NAME. THE PUBLIC *LOVES* THE LEAK!
IT'S PROBABLY *JOANNA.*
SHE, UH, SHE'S MEETING ME HERE AND SHE'S EARLY...
I DIDN'T MEAN TO HURT INNOCENT PEOPLE. THAT'S THE *OPPOSITE* OF EVERYTHING I STAND FOR.
GIVEN THE CHANCE TO GO BACK, I WOULD HAVE DONE THINGS DIFFERENTLY. THE LIVES LOST, THEY WILL HAUNT ME FOR THE REST OF MY LIFE. BUT...

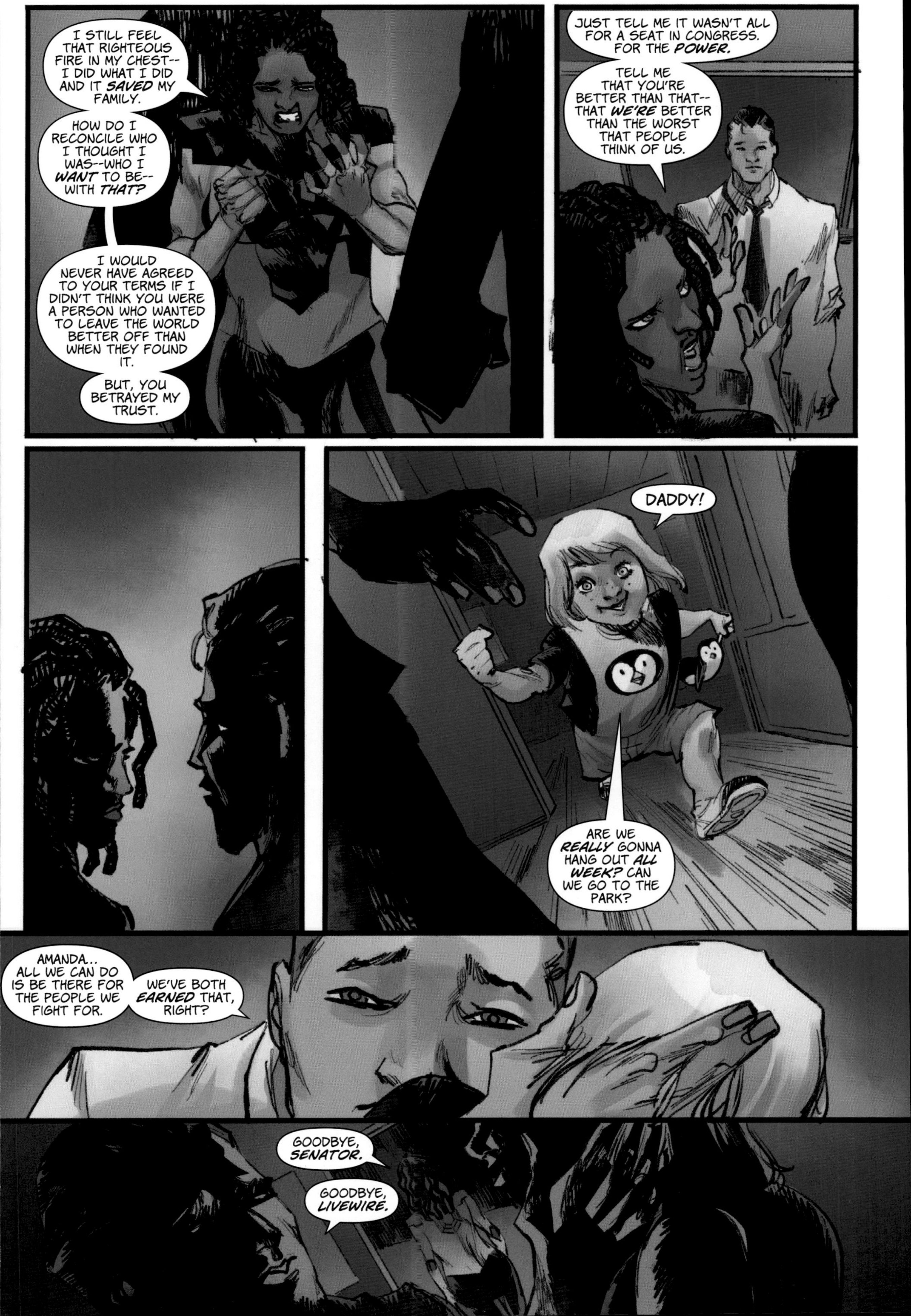
I STILL FEEL THAT RIGHTEOUS FIRE IN MY CHEST-- I DID WHAT I DID AND IT **SAVED** MY FAMILY.
HOW DO I RECONCILE WHO I THOUGHT I WAS--WHO I **WANT** TO BE-- WITH **THAT?**
I WOULD NEVER HAVE AGREED TO YOUR TERMS IF I DIDN'T THINK YOU WERE A PERSON WHO WANTED TO LEAVE THE WORLD BETTER OFF THAN WHEN THEY FOUND IT.
BUT, YOU BETRAYED MY TRUST.
JUST TELL ME IT WASN'T ALL FOR A SEAT IN CONGRESS. FOR THE **POWER.**
TELL ME THAT YOU'RE BETTER THAN THAT-- THAT **WE'RE** BETTER THAN THE WORST THAT PEOPLE THINK OF US.
DADDY!
ARE WE **REALLY** GONNA HANG OUT **ALL WEEK?** CAN WE GO TO THE PARK?
AMANDA.. ALL WE CAN DO IS BE THERE FOR THE PEOPLE WE FIGHT FOR.
WE'VE BOTH **EARNED** THAT, RIGHT?
GOODBYE, **SENATOR.**
GOODBYE, **LIVEWIRE.**

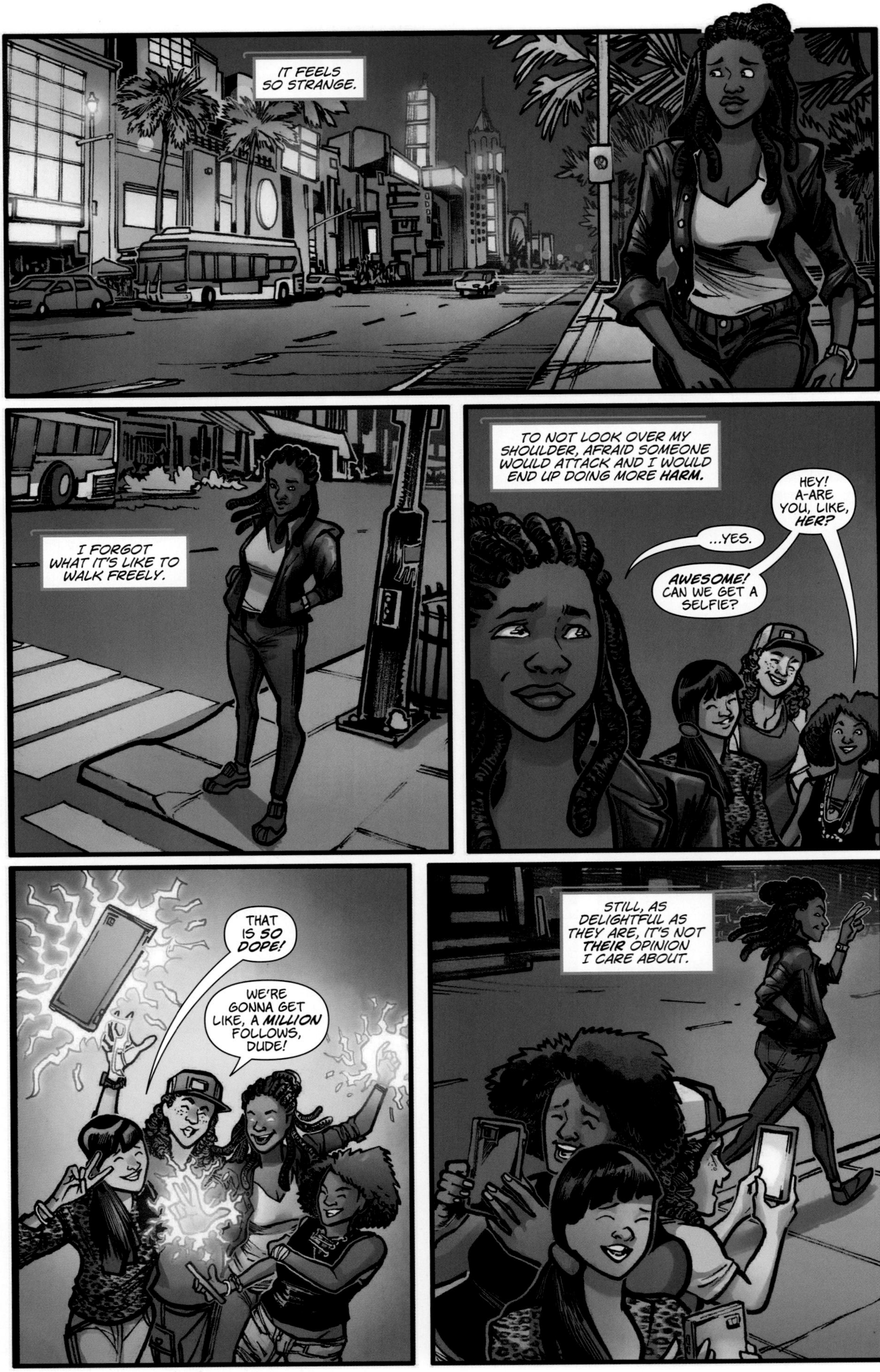
IT FEELS SO STRANGE.
I FORGOT WHAT IT'S LIKE TO WALK FREELY.
TO NOT LOOK OVER MY SHOULDER, AFRAID SOMEONE WOULD ATTACK AND I WOULD END UP DOING MORE HARM.
HEY! A-ARE YOU, LIKE, HER?
...YES.
AWESOME! CAN WE GET A SELFIE?
THAT IS SO DOPE!
WE'RE GONNA GET LIKE, A MILLION FOLLOWS, DUDE!
STILL, AS DELIGHTFUL AS THEY ARE, IT'S NOT THEIR OPINION I CARE ABOUT.

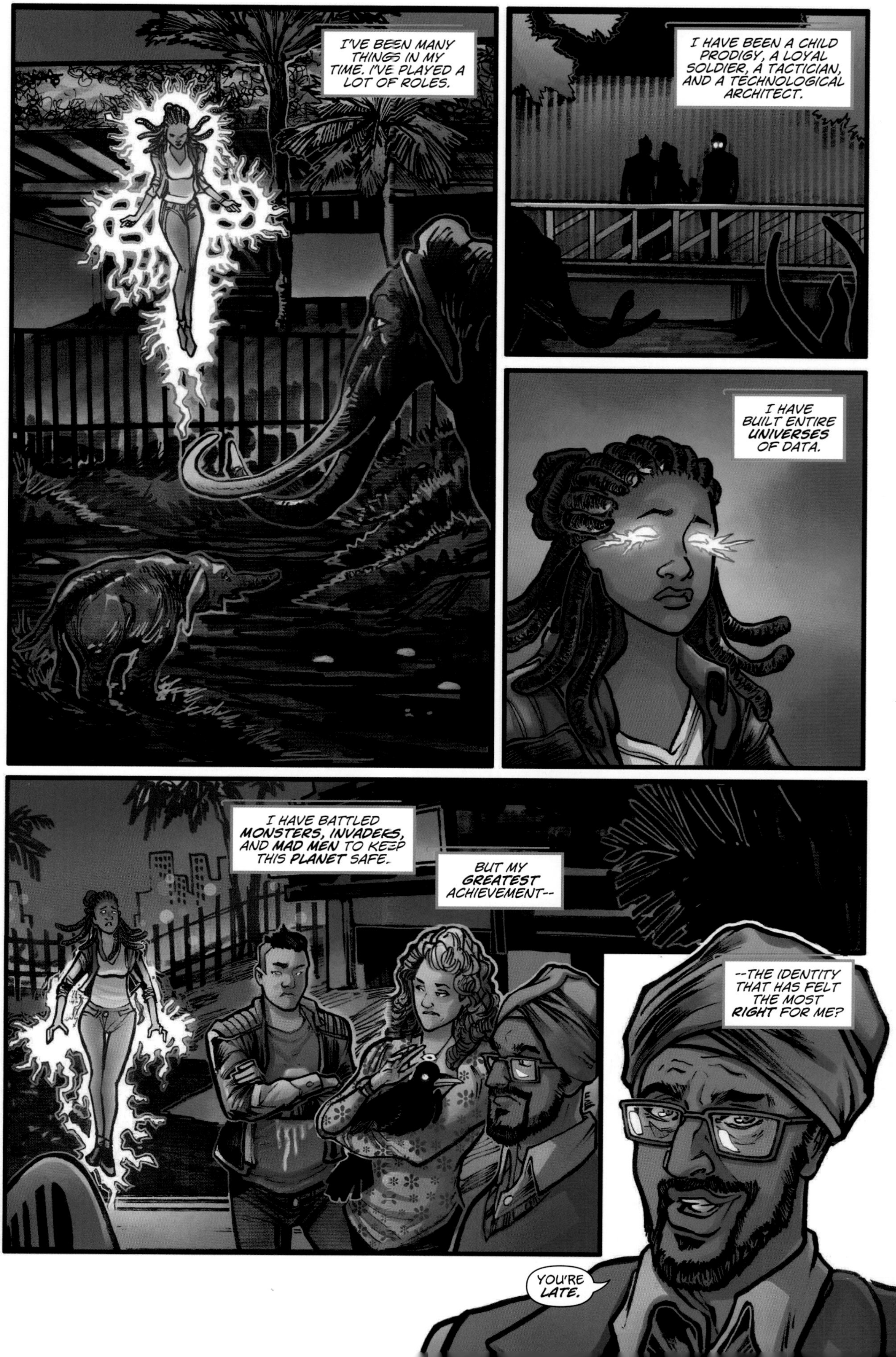
I'VE BEEN MANY THINGS IN MY TIME. I'VE PLAYED A LOT OF ROLES.
I HAVE BEEN A CHILD PRODIGY, A LOYAL SOLDIER, A TACTICIAN, AND A TECHNOLOGICAL ARCHITECT.
I HAVE BUILT ENTIRE **UNIVERSES** OF DATA.
I HAVE BATTLED **MONSTERS, INVADERS,** AND **MAD MEN** TO KEEP THIS **PLANET** SAFE.
BUT MY **GREATEST** ACHIEVEMENT--
--THE IDENTITY THAT HAS FELT THE MOST **RIGHT** FOR ME?
YOU'RE **LATE.**

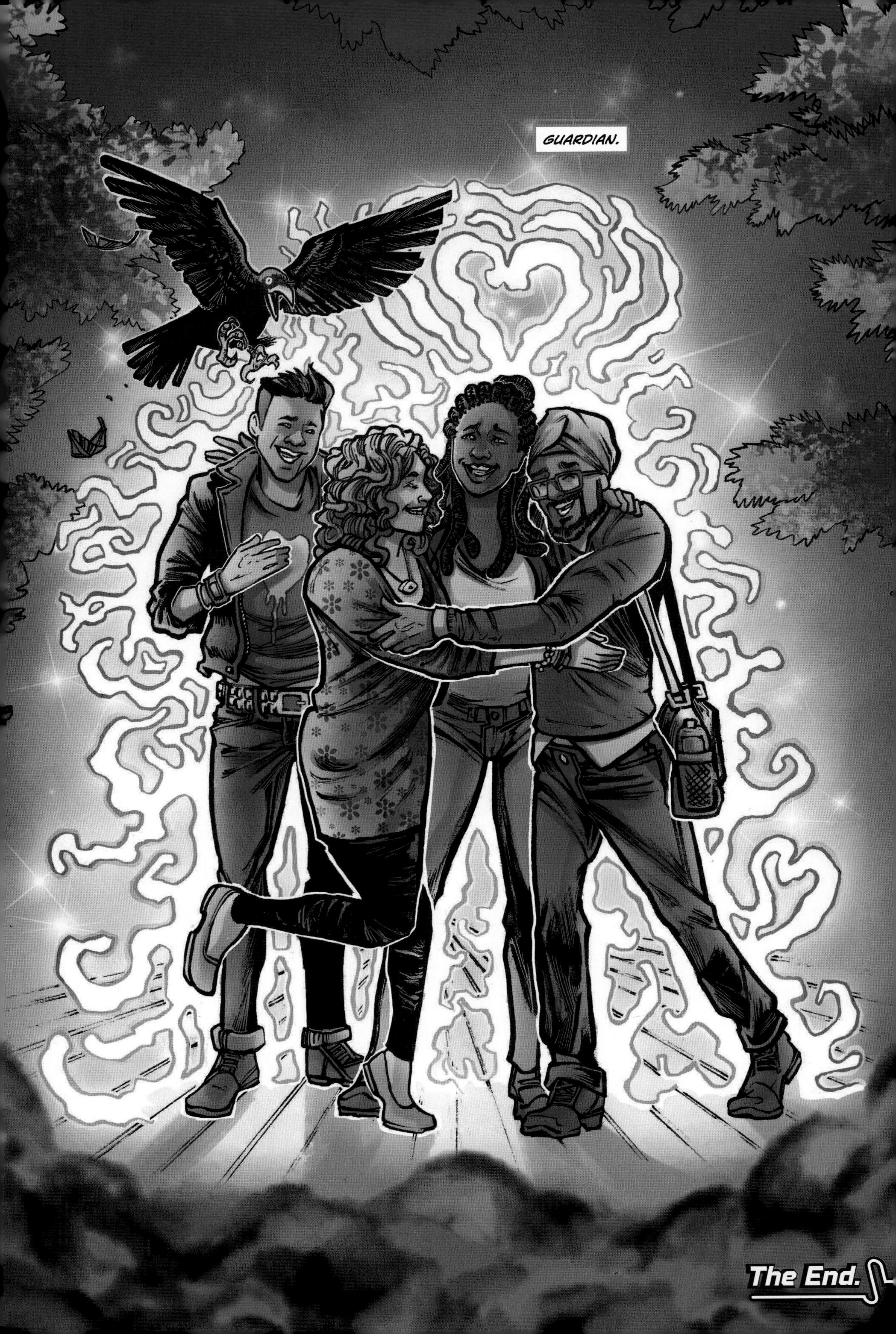
GUARDIAN.
The End.

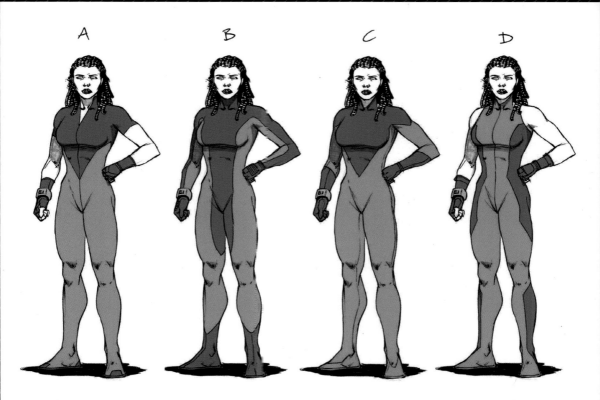

A   B   C   D

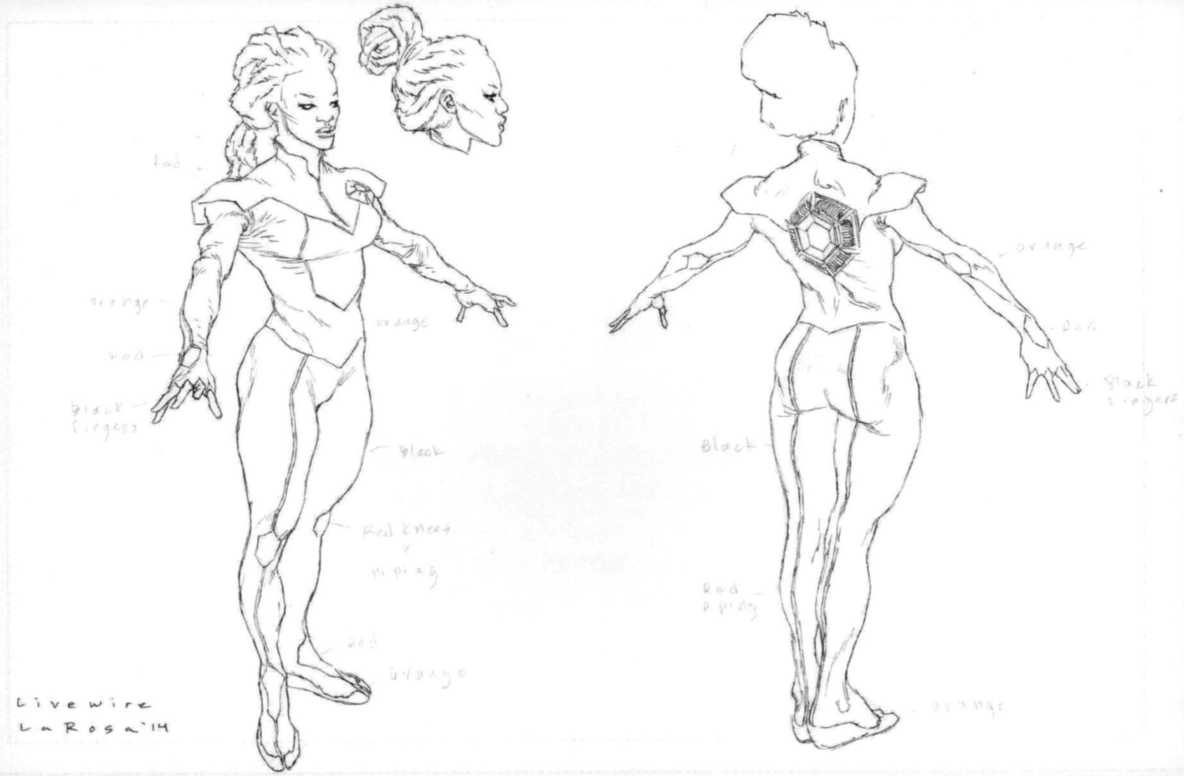
Red
orange
Red
Black fingers
orange
Black
Red knees & piping
Red
orange
Livewire
LaRosa '14
orange
Red
Black fingers
Black
Red piping
orange

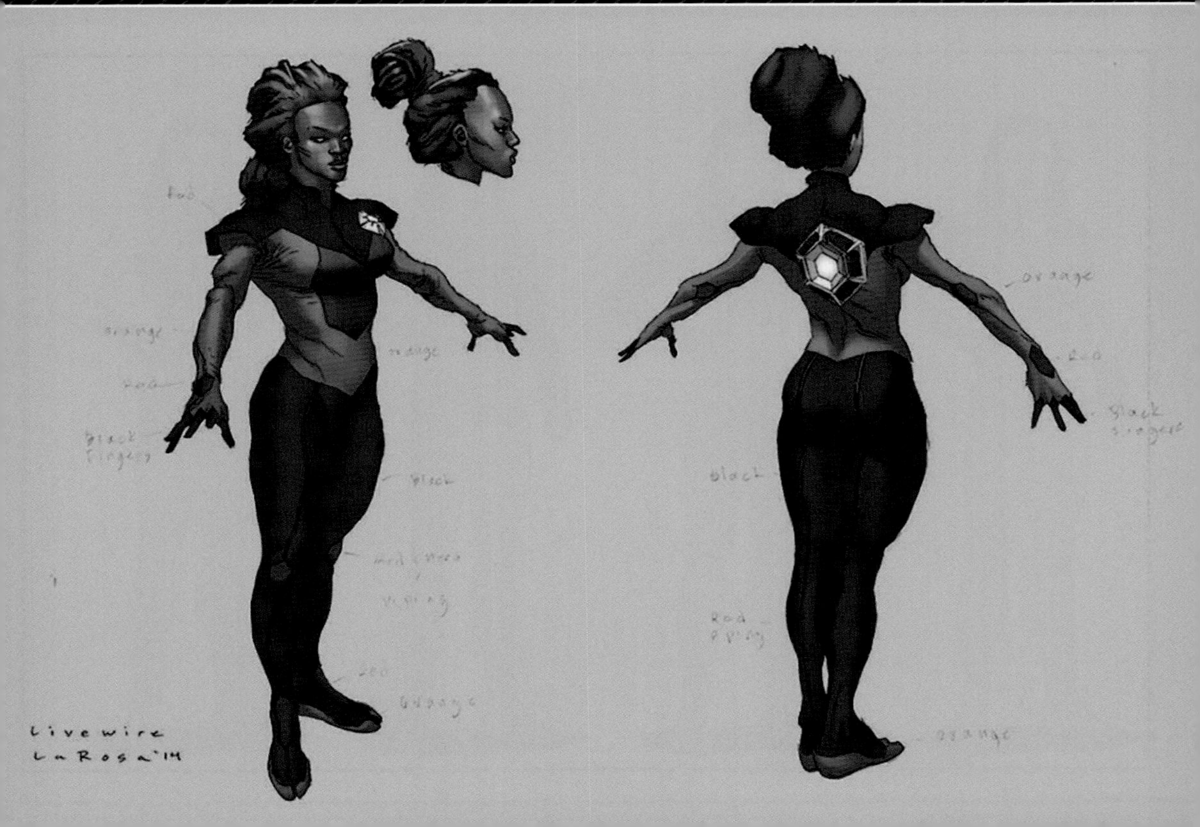
Red
orange
Red
Black fingers
orange
Black
Red knees & piping
Red
orange
Livewire
LaRosa '14
orange
Red
Black fingers
Black
Red piping
orange

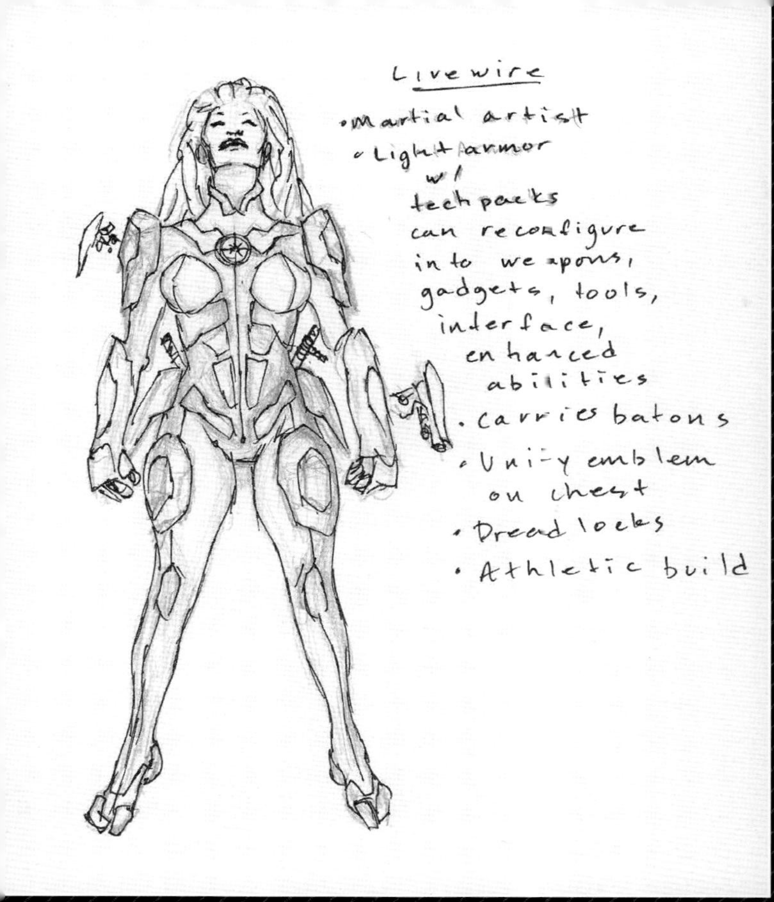
Livewire
• Martial artist
• Light armor w/ techpacks can reconfigure into weapons, gadgets, tools, interface, enhanced abilities
• carries batons
• Unity emblem on chest
• Dreadlocks
• Athletic build

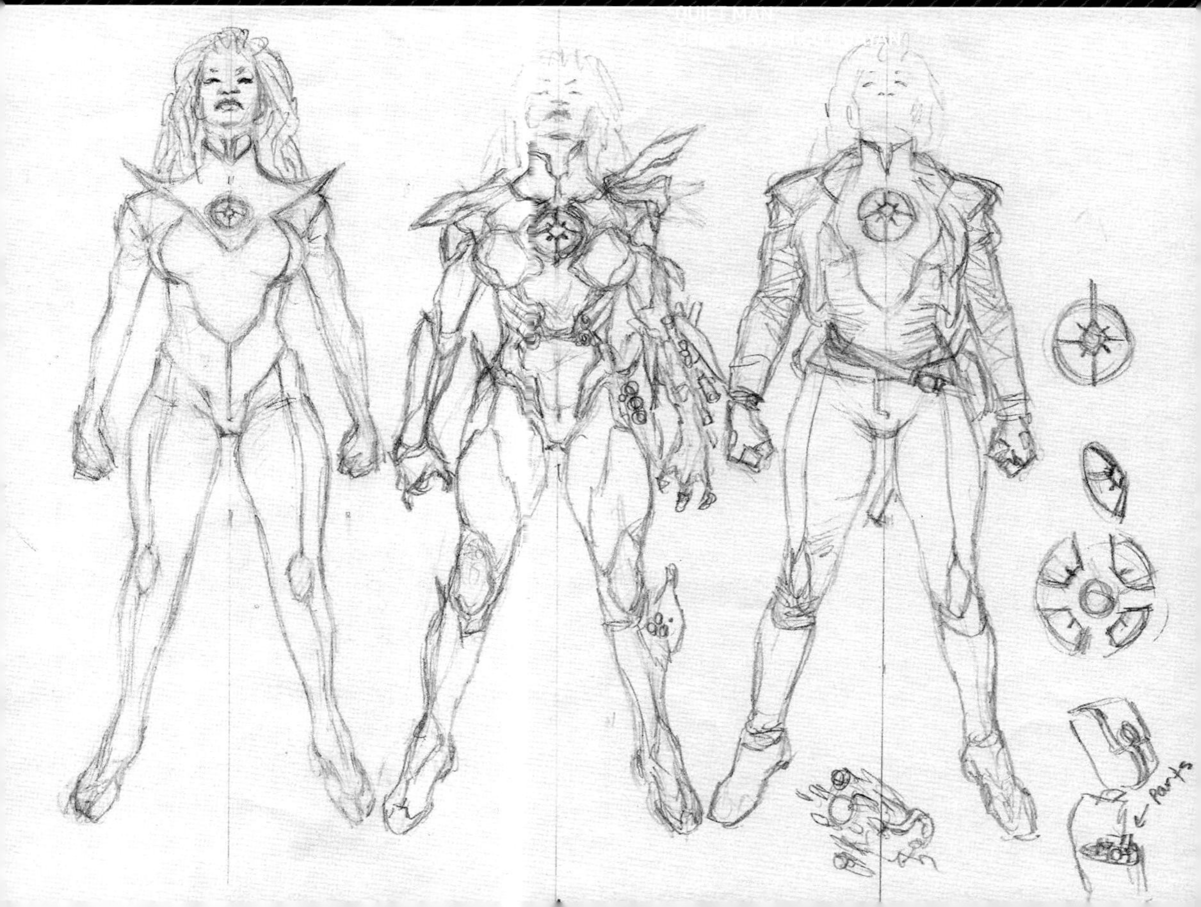
Parts

LIVEWIRE #1 COVER B
Art by HARVEY TOLIBAO

LIVEWIRE #2 COVER B
Art by MEGAN HUTCHISON

LIVEWIRE #3 COVER B (facing)
Art by KOI TURNBULL

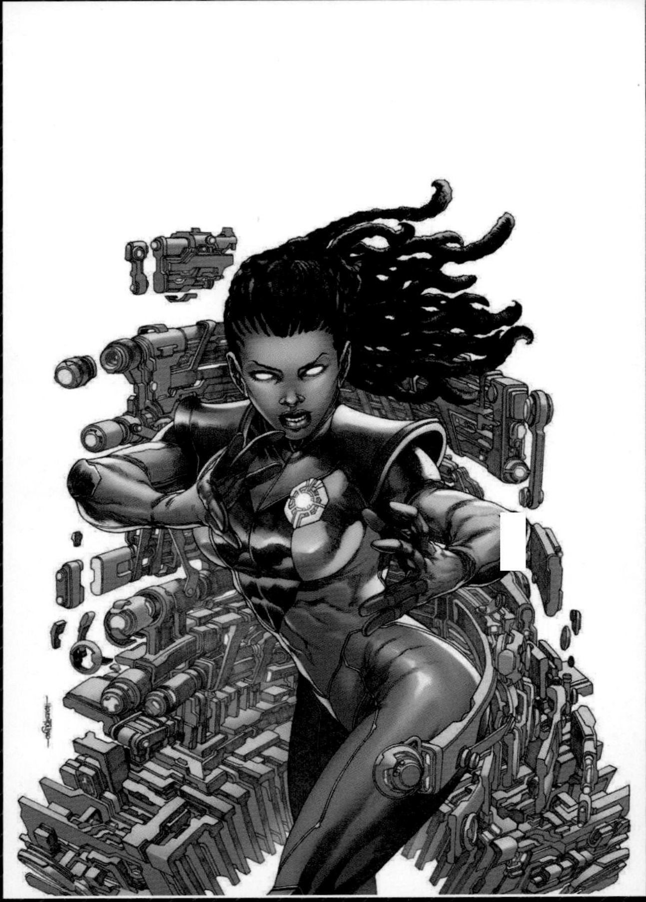

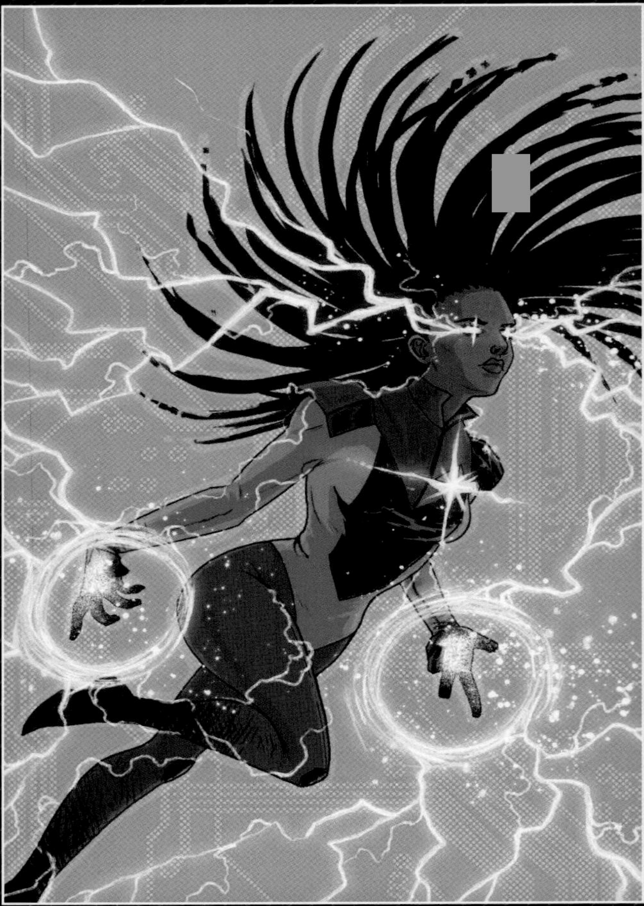

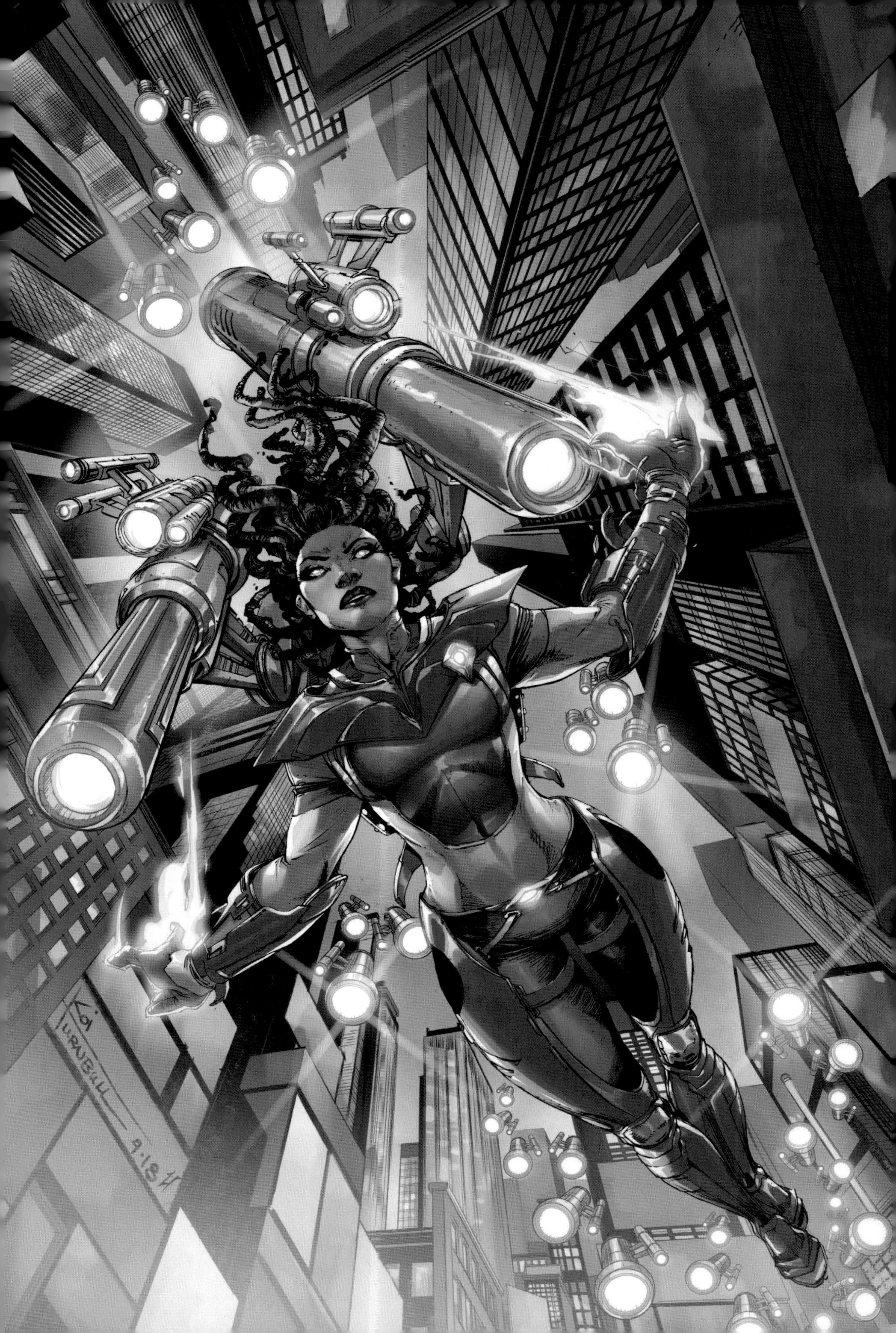

LIVEWIRE #3
PAGE EIGHT (five panels)

(Note: Dialogue and effects are often revised between the script and the final, lettered pages.)

The clouds that gathered before are dark and thick in the sky now.

PANEL 1: PAN has grabbed LIVEWIRE'S arm and is using it to draw her off balance!

   1 PAN: You like pointing fingers so much, but what about you?

PANEL 2: PAN is behind LIVEWIRE, holding onto one arm and kicking the backs of her knees.

   2 PAN: Harada offered the world progress and hope for a future.

   3 PAN: A future where psiots would be welcomed and respected.

PANEL 3: Tighter on them as PAN leans in close from behind, speaking into LIVEWIRE'S ear.

   4 PAN: All you seem to offer is chaos and fear.

PANEL 4: LIVEWIRE smashes the back of her head into PAN'S mouth!

   5 LIVEWIRE: He was a monster, Pan.

PANEL 5: PAN, bleeding lightly from their nose and mouth, has LIVEWIRE in a choke hold form behind.

   6 PAN: Pot calling the kettle, and all that.

   7 PAN: How many people died because you decided to shut off the country like a light?

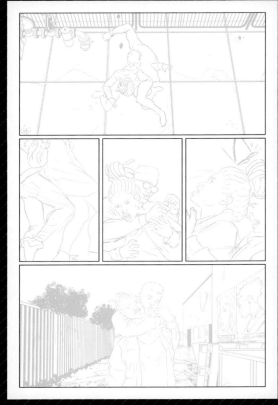

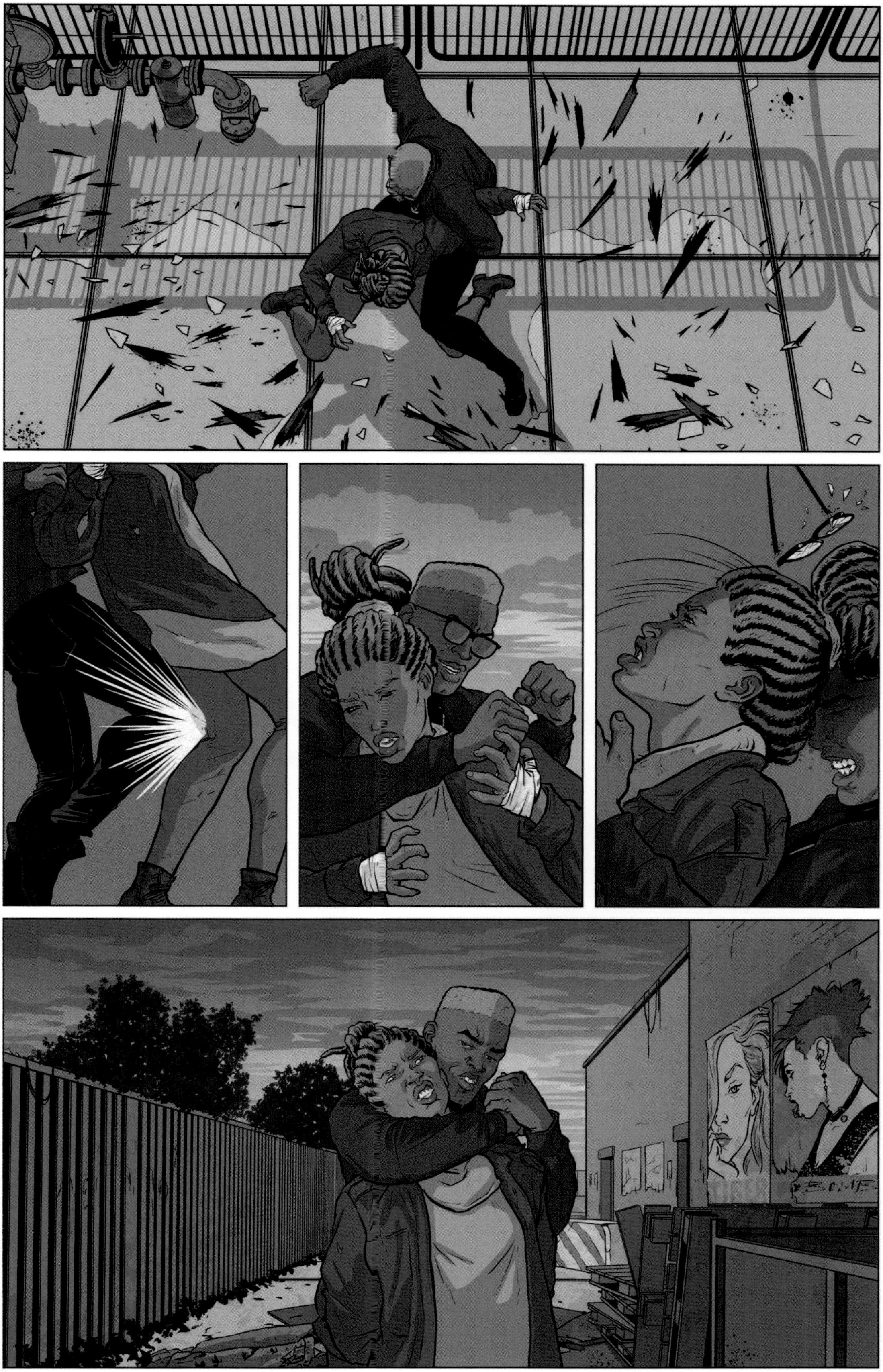

LIVEWIRE #3
PAGE NINE (six panels)

PANEL 1: LIVEWIRE flips PAN over her shoulder!

1 LIVEWIRE: They were hunting psiots –
hunting and killing children.

2 LIVEWIRE: I had no choice!

PANEL 2: PAN crouches, having landed a bit
like Spider-Man, one hand on the ground for
balance, and the other wiping at the blood on
their face.

3 PAN: I thought there were always
choices?

4 PAN: Gotta rise above, right?

PANEL 3: PAN rushes LIVEWIRE, hunting knife
out and ready to slash.

5 PAN: You lose all good guy cred when you
play god, Amanda.

PANEL 4: LIVEWIRE blocks the knife-blow by
blocking PAN'S forearm with both of hers, but
PAN'S plan was to hit their bare hand on her.

6 PAN: And I'm starting to forget what
exactly made you worthy of being his Right
Hand.

PANEL 5: PAN has LIVEWIRE by the throat. They
are beginning to use their powers on her. Just
gearing up though, not full on drawing.

7 PAN: Are you even curious how I found
you? You were so careful, and yet here I am
to ruin your day

8 LIVEWIRE: Hruk!

PANEL 6: Close on PAN'S face, their eyes
beginning to illuminate and change to the
colors of their power. They are smiling, and it
is VERY unsettling.

*I almost imagine them having the general
vibe of a viper about to strike, or like Kaa
from The Jungle Book as they hypnotize
Mogli. Not literally, but that vibe.*

9 PAN: Here, let me show you.

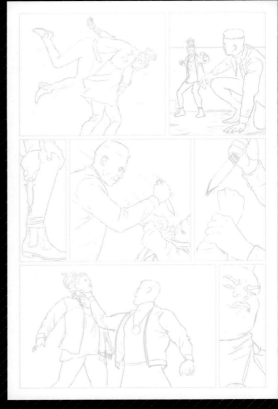

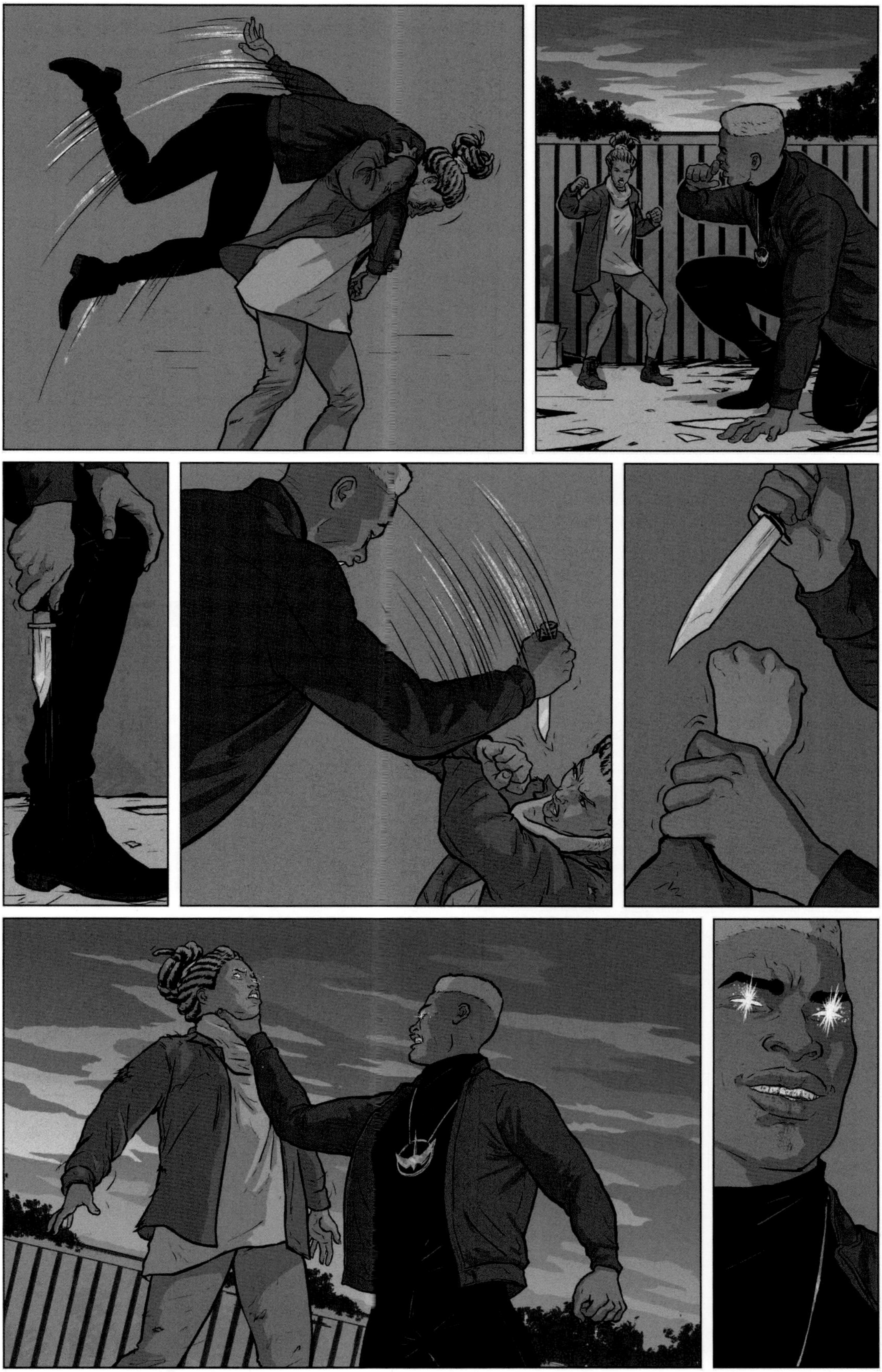

LIVEWIRE #3
PAGE TEN (five panels)

I am thinking that the flashbacks/images/ scenes we see because of Pan's powers should be linked to them somehow. Maybe through color scheme/tone, or maybe the borders reflect the power somehow?

The flashbacks are gonna be working their way backwards through time, as Pan sucks the energy and memories out of Amanda.

PANEL 1: It is beginning to drizzle. PAN begins to drain LIVEWIRE, forcing her to her knees again.

   1 PAN: My abilities, the ones that were deemed useless in the foundation?

PANEL 2: Pan flashback! LIVEWIRE fighting KYLE from the last issue.

   2 PAN (tailless word balloon): They evolved out here.

PANEL 3: Pan flashback! The surgery scene from the last issue, as ALEC is putting the HEX BUG into LIVEWIRE'S neck.

   3 PAN (tail-less word balloon): I've become something even Harada couldn't have dreamed of.

PANEL 4: Pan flashback! Slightly further back, to LIVEWIRE being dragged through the halls of the lab in the last issue.

   4 PAN (tailless word balloon): If he had known, he would never have chosen you over me to carry his legacy.

PANEL 5: Back in the present! LIVEWIRE breaks PAN'S hold! She is surprised and afraid, unsure of exactly what is happening to her.

   5 LIVEWIRE: W-what did you do to me?

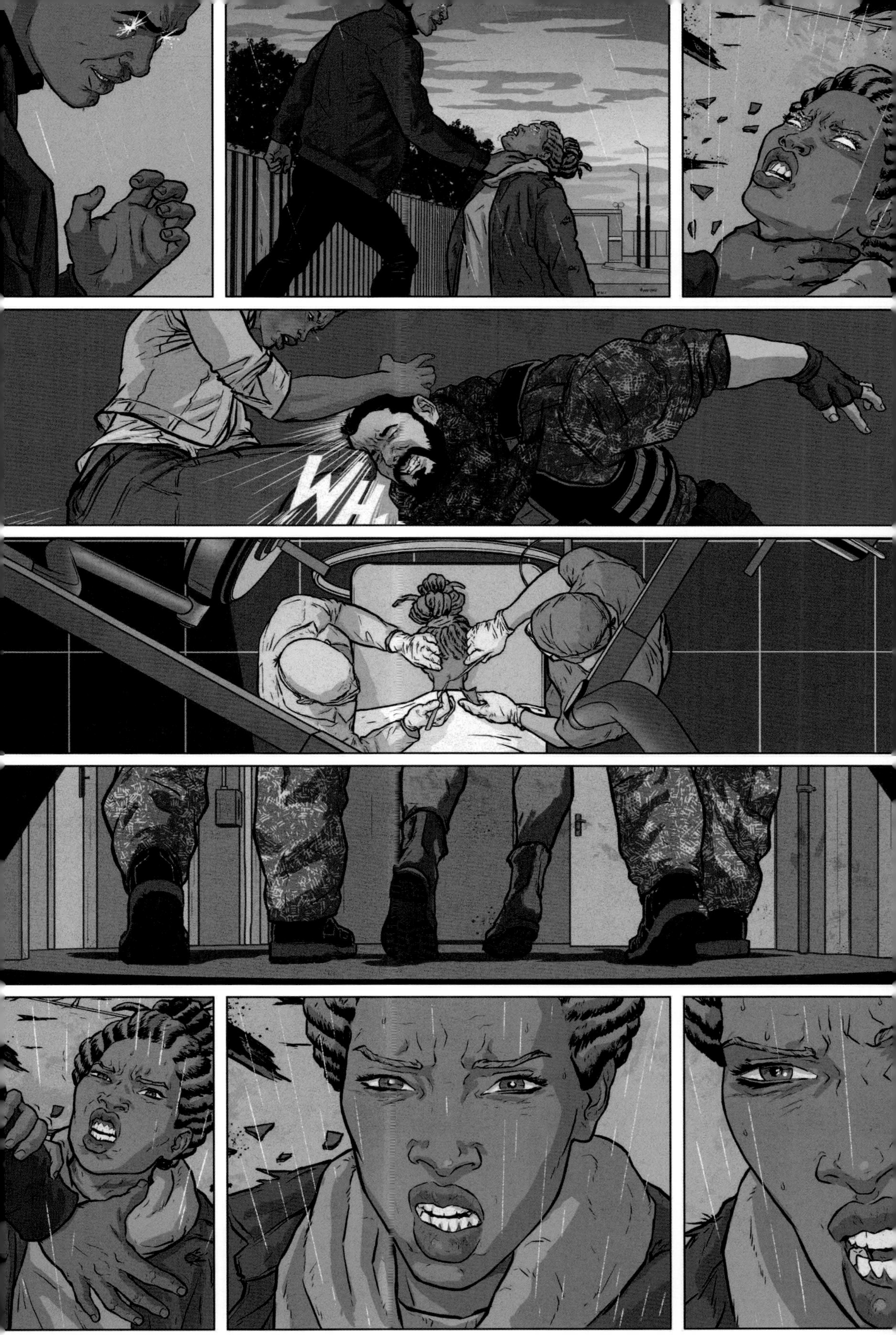
WH

LIVEWIRE #3
PAGE ELEVEN (six panels)

PANEL 1: PAN and LIVEWIRE stand, facing off, again. PAN is confident, body language aggressive, and LIVEWIRE is shrinking back.

   1 PAN: What should have been done from the get go.

PANEL 2: PAN un-holsters their gun.

   2 PAN: I've been contracted to take you out.

   3 PAN: But, and this is me being honest here, I would have gotten around to it eventually.

PANEL 3: LIVEWIRE takes a defensive stance, shard gone now so it is her fists up. She looks weakened, though, maybe favoring her side (the one that was hit by the car).

   4 LIVEWIRE: Why? I'm no threat to you.

   5 LIVEWIRE: All I want is for our people to be safe.

PANEL 4: PAN lays the gun down on the ground, looking at LIVEWIRE the whole time.

   6 PAN: No, what you want is to fit in. You're happy to let "our people" live in secret and squalor.

   7 PAN: That's the real difference between you and Harada.

PANEL 5: PAN cracks their neck with their hands, looking almost bored.

   8 PAN: He acknowledged that in order to achieve real and lasting peace and prosperity, there would have to be sacrifice.

   9 PAN: You like to pretend that every life you take is forced on you. But you are responsible for so much more death and destruction than him.

PANEL 6: PAN squares up, fists raised and ready for a fight.

   10 PAN: You're a liar and a coward.

   11 PAN: Although honestly, from an objective standpoint, what you did was impressive.

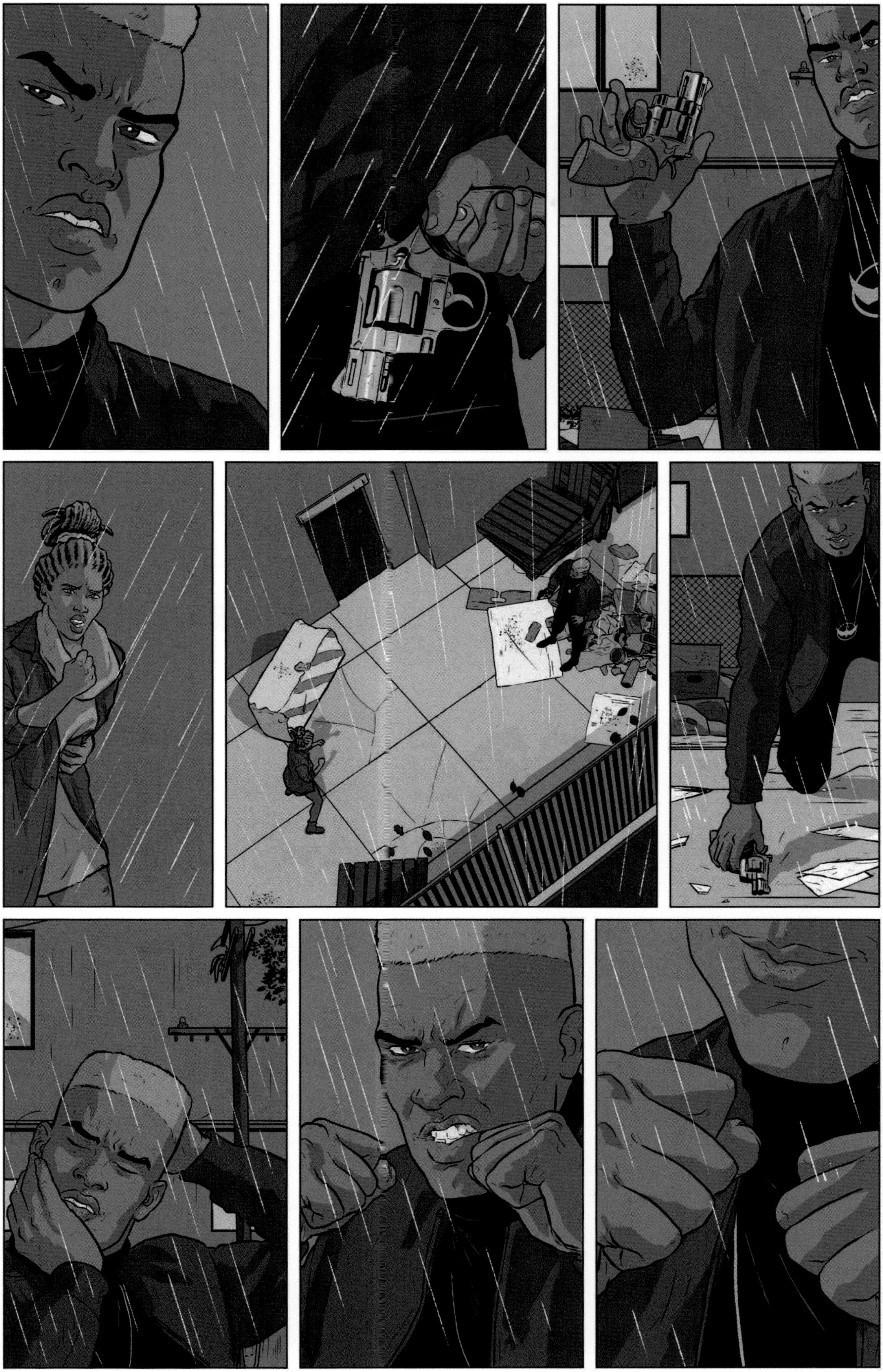

LIVEWIRE #3
PAGE TWELVE (five panels)

The drizzle has become a steady rain. This will be a lightning storm, though it doesn't have to flash here yet.

PANEL 1: LIVEWIRE and PAN clash, punching at each other.

    1 PAN: You've always been powerful, but I never thought you'd have the spine to declare war on the entire country.

PANEL 2: LIVEWIRE kicks at PAN, but they catch her leg.
No copy.

PANEL 3: PAN uses their hold on LIVEWIRE'S leg to flip her onto the ground!

    2 PAN: You're fooling yourself, though, trying to pretend it was all for the greater good.

PANEL 4: LIVEWIRE attempts to punch PAN.

    3 PAN: That sort of mental weakness? That's what makes you unworthy of the trust Harada put in you.

PANEL 5: Close on PAN catching LIVEWIRE'S fist in theirs, skin to skin contact.

    4 PAN: But I'll fix that. I'll show you what you really are.

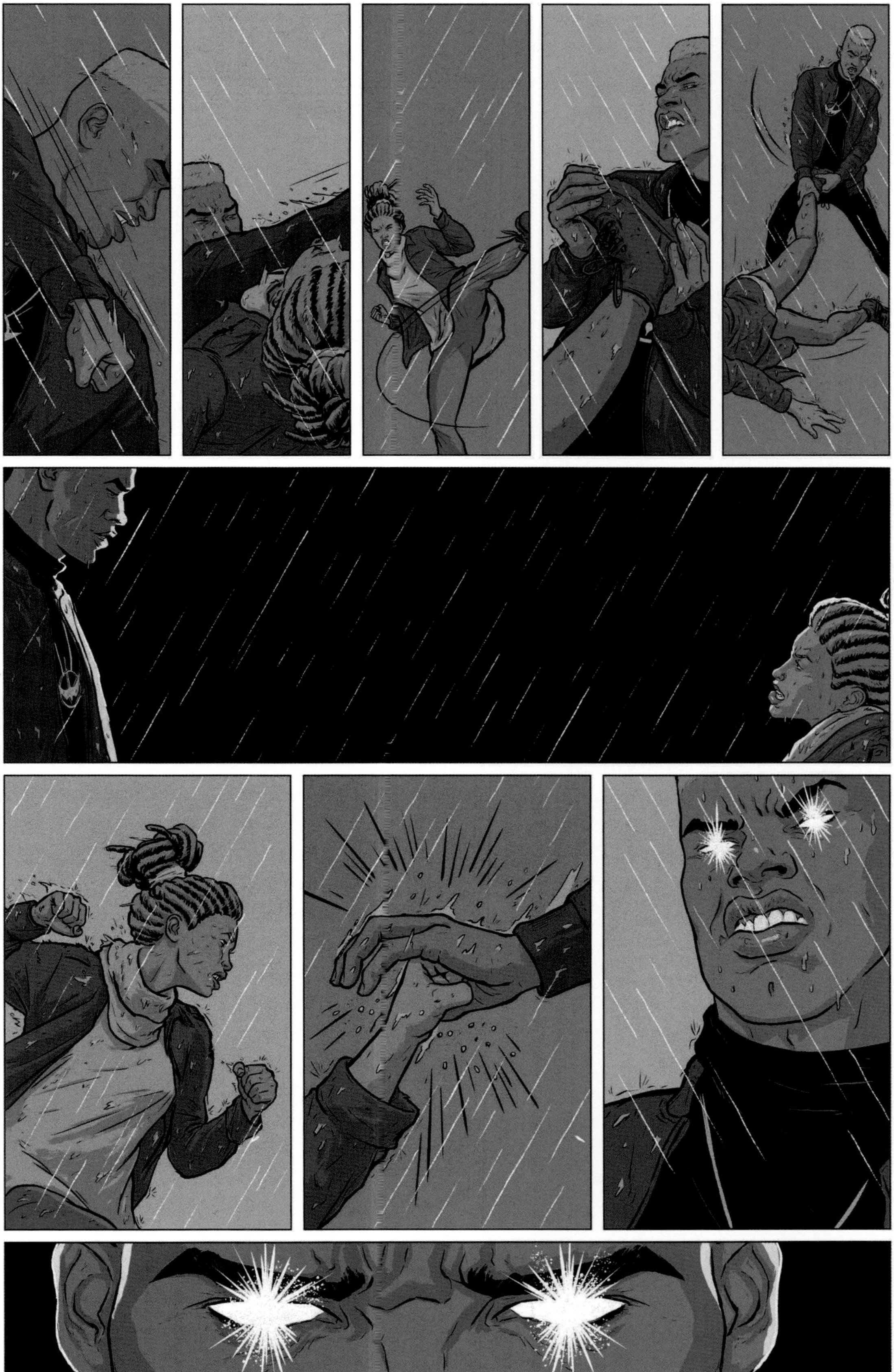

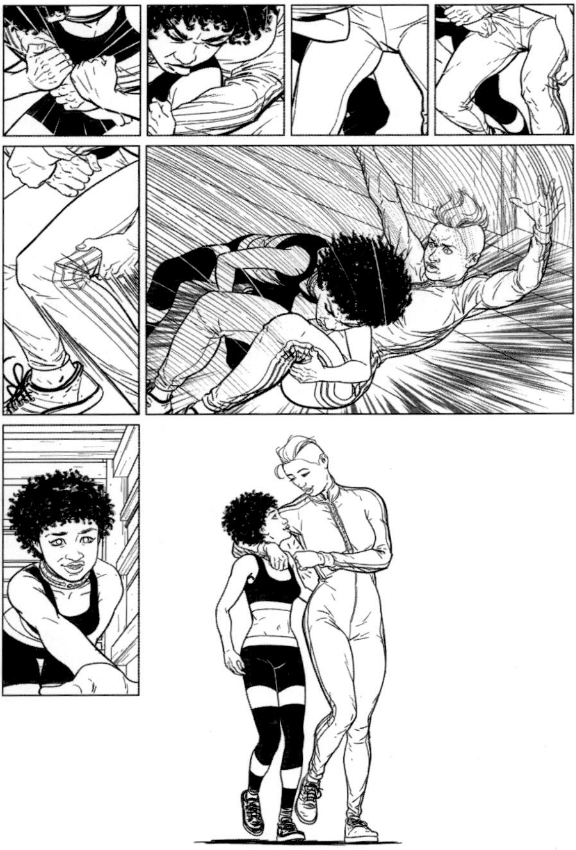

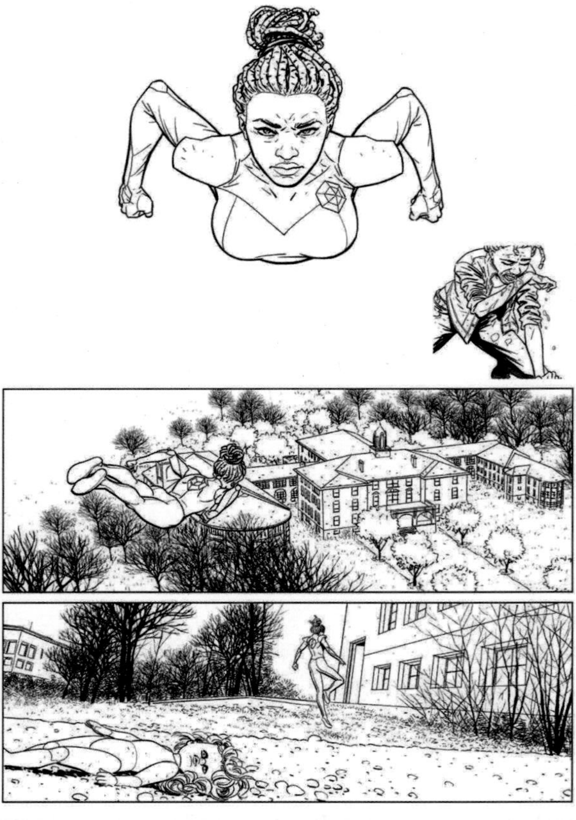

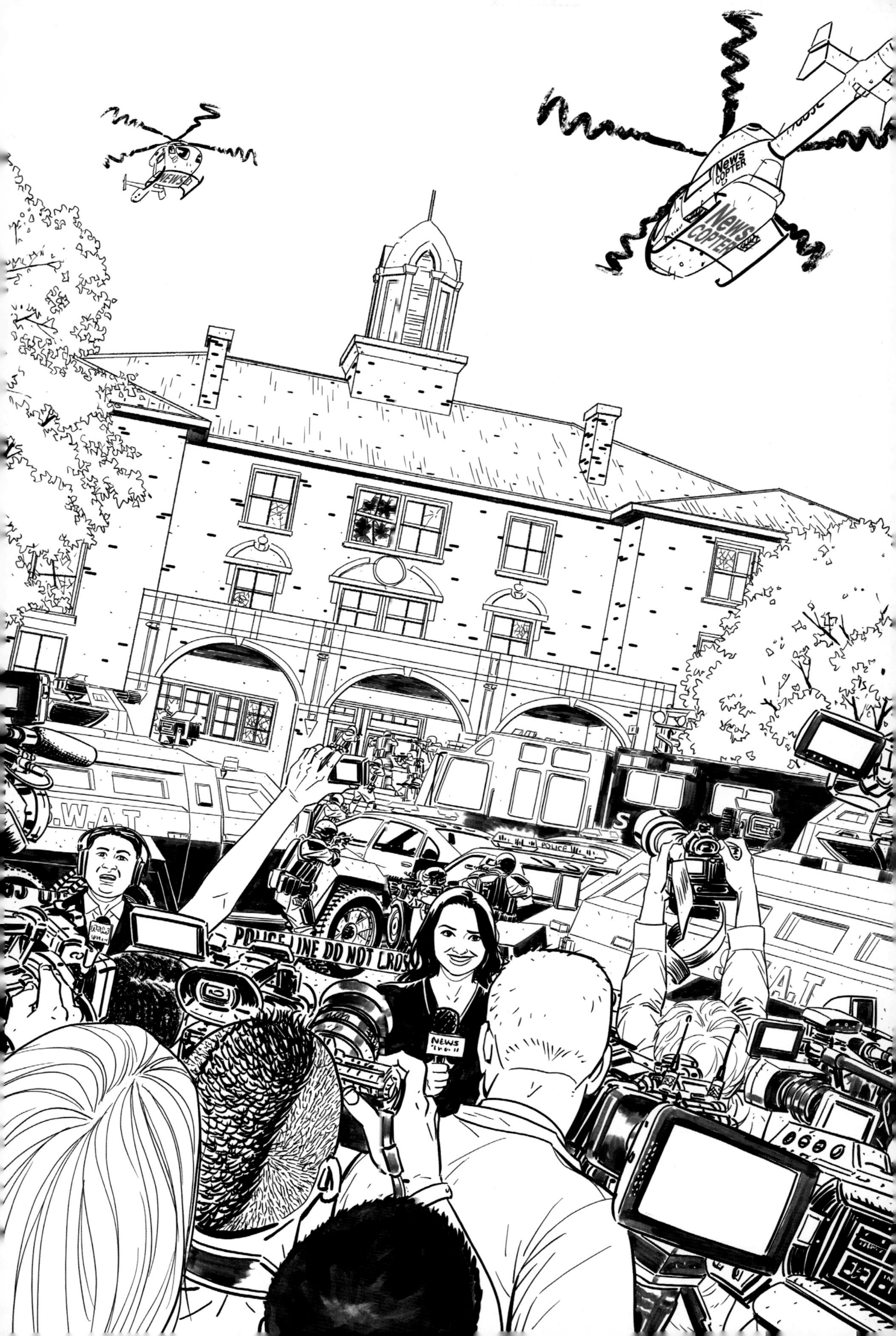
NEWS
News COPTER
News COPTER
S.W.A.T
POLICE
POLICE LINE DO NOT CROS
NEWS
S.W.A.T

19, and (facing) 20

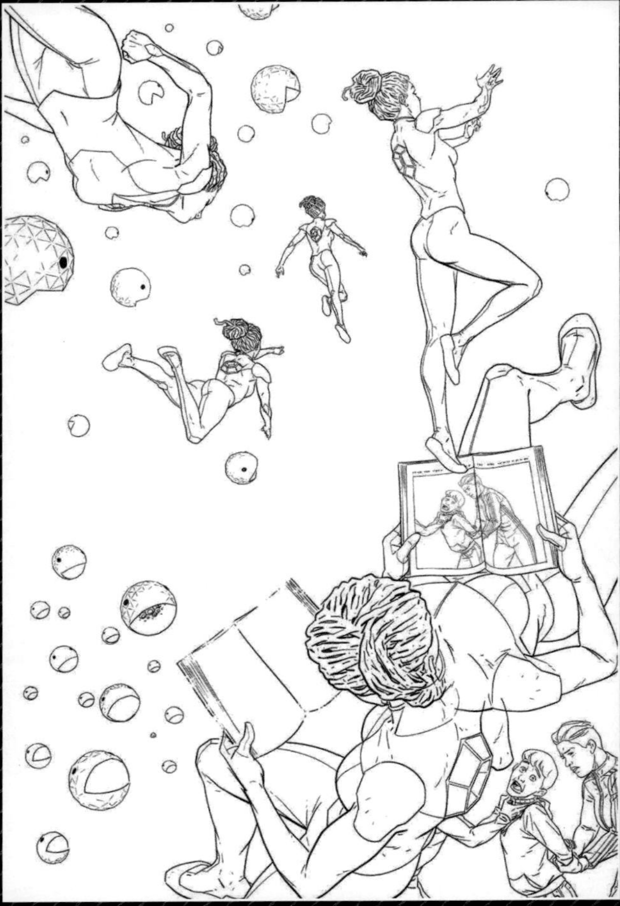

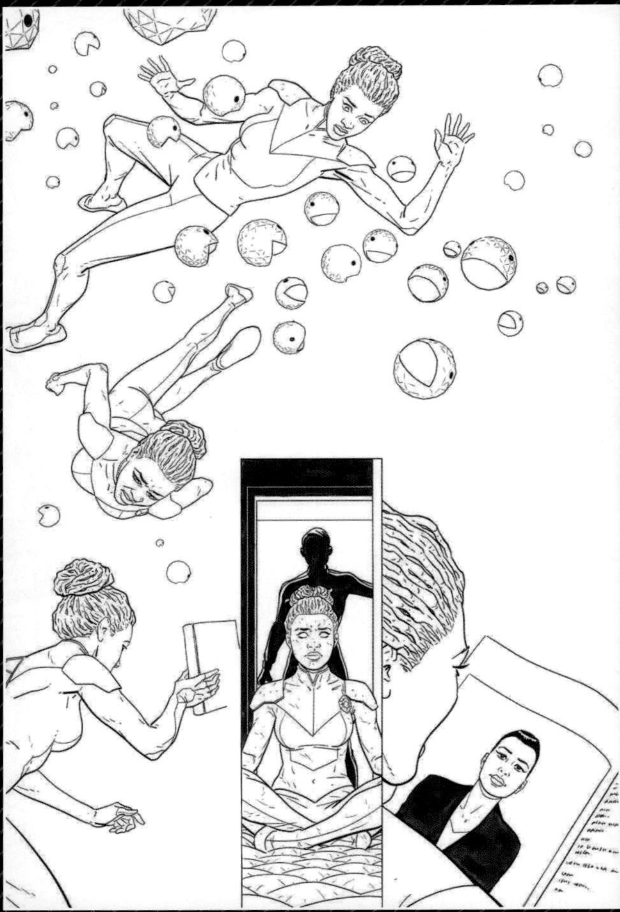

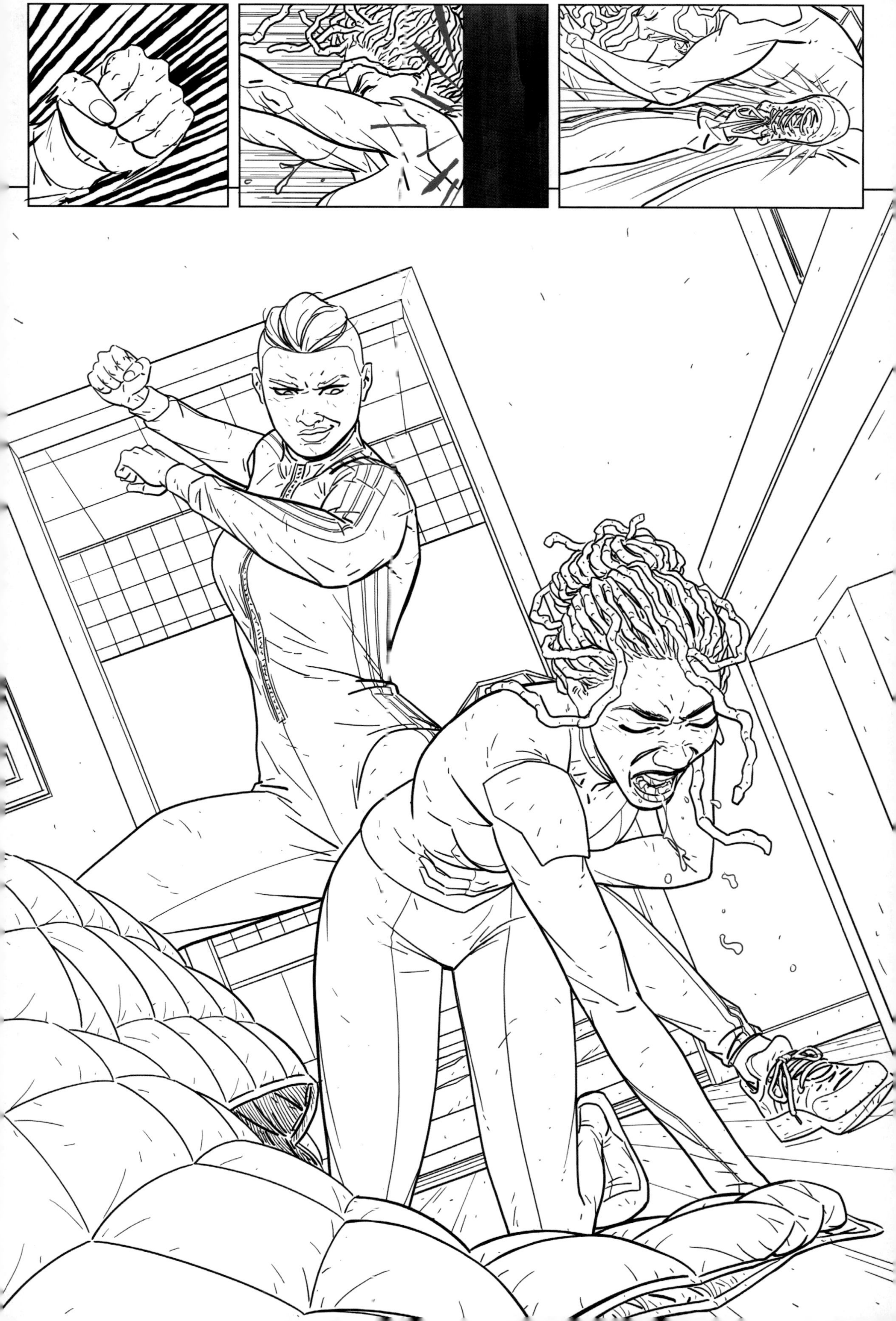

LIVEWIRE #7, pages 2, 3, and (facing) 4
Art by KANO

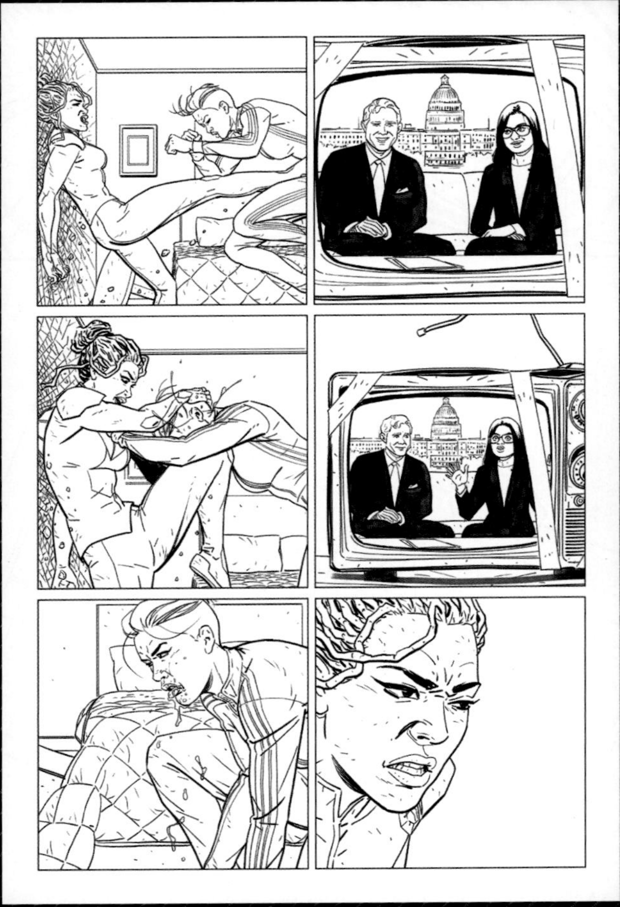

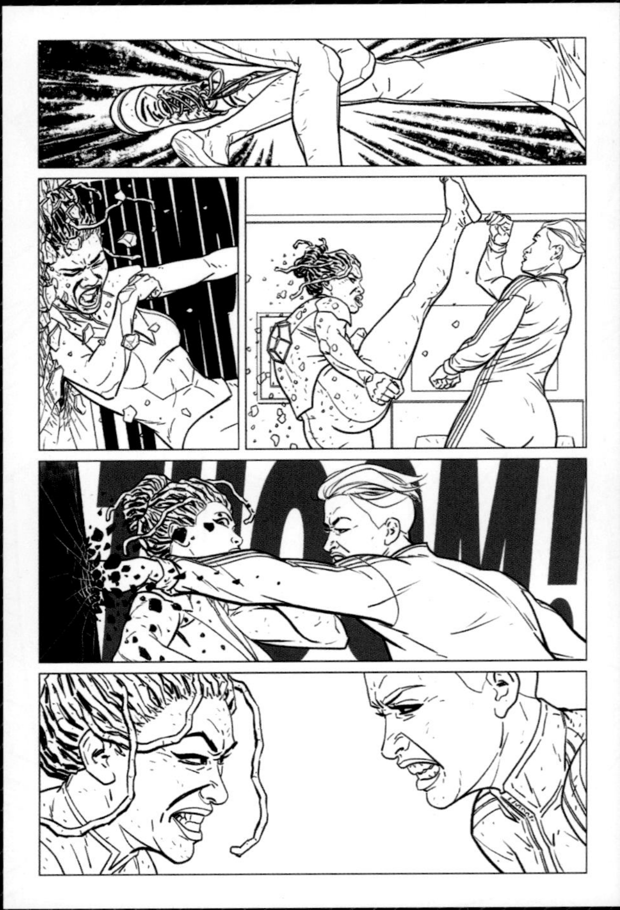

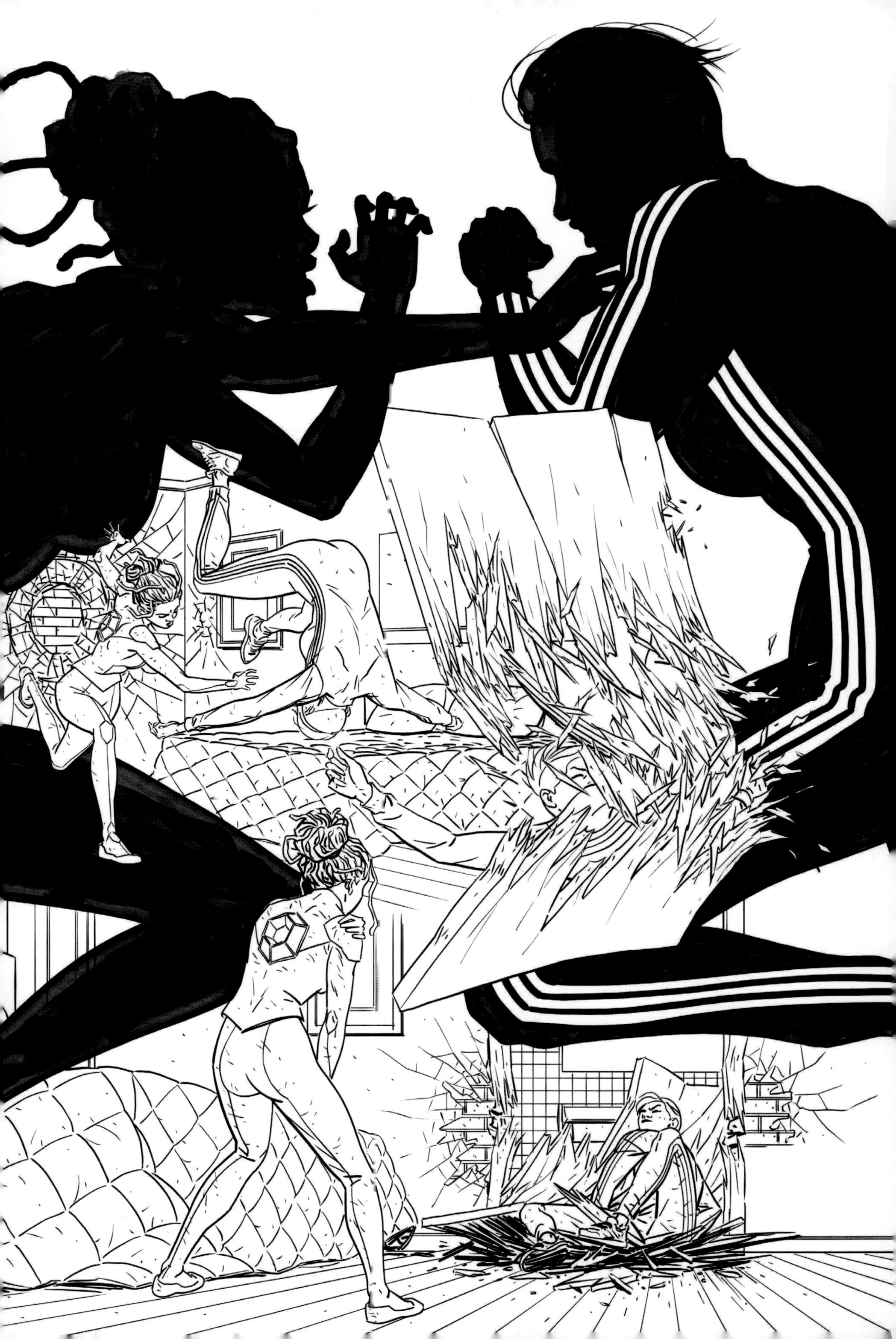

LIVEWIRE #9, pages 3 and 4
Art by TANA FORD

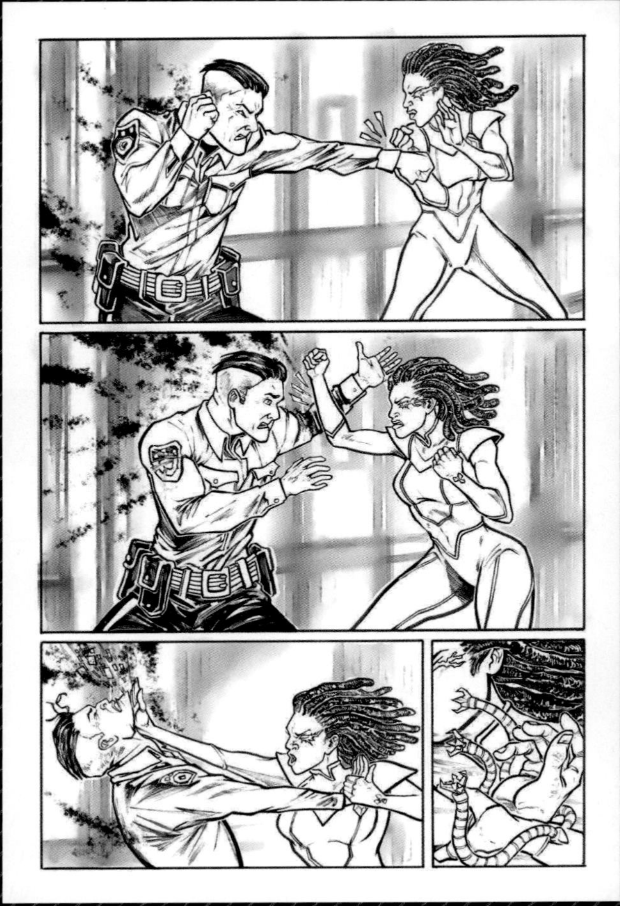

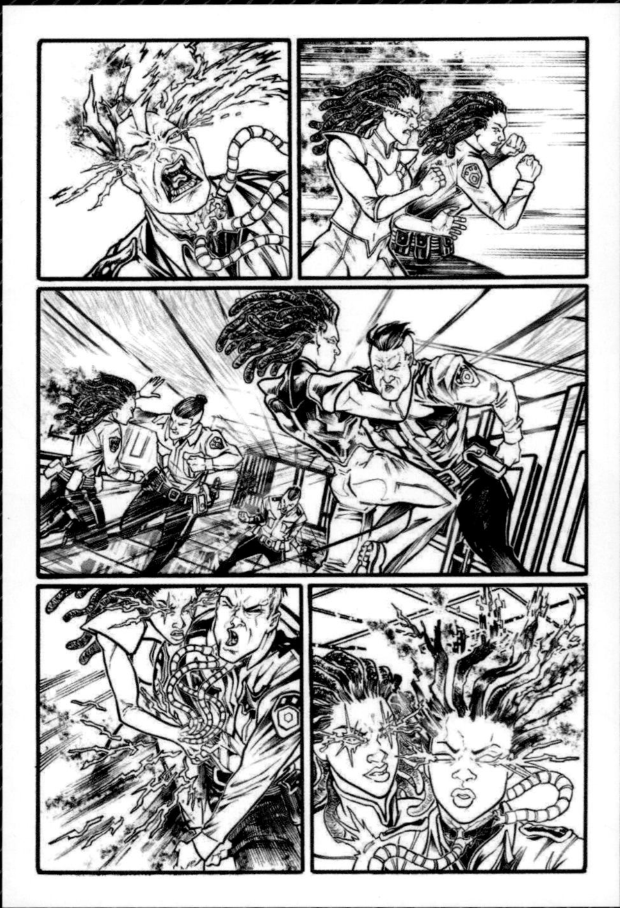

LIVEWIRE #9 FASHION VARIANT COVER (facing)
Art by KRIS ANKA

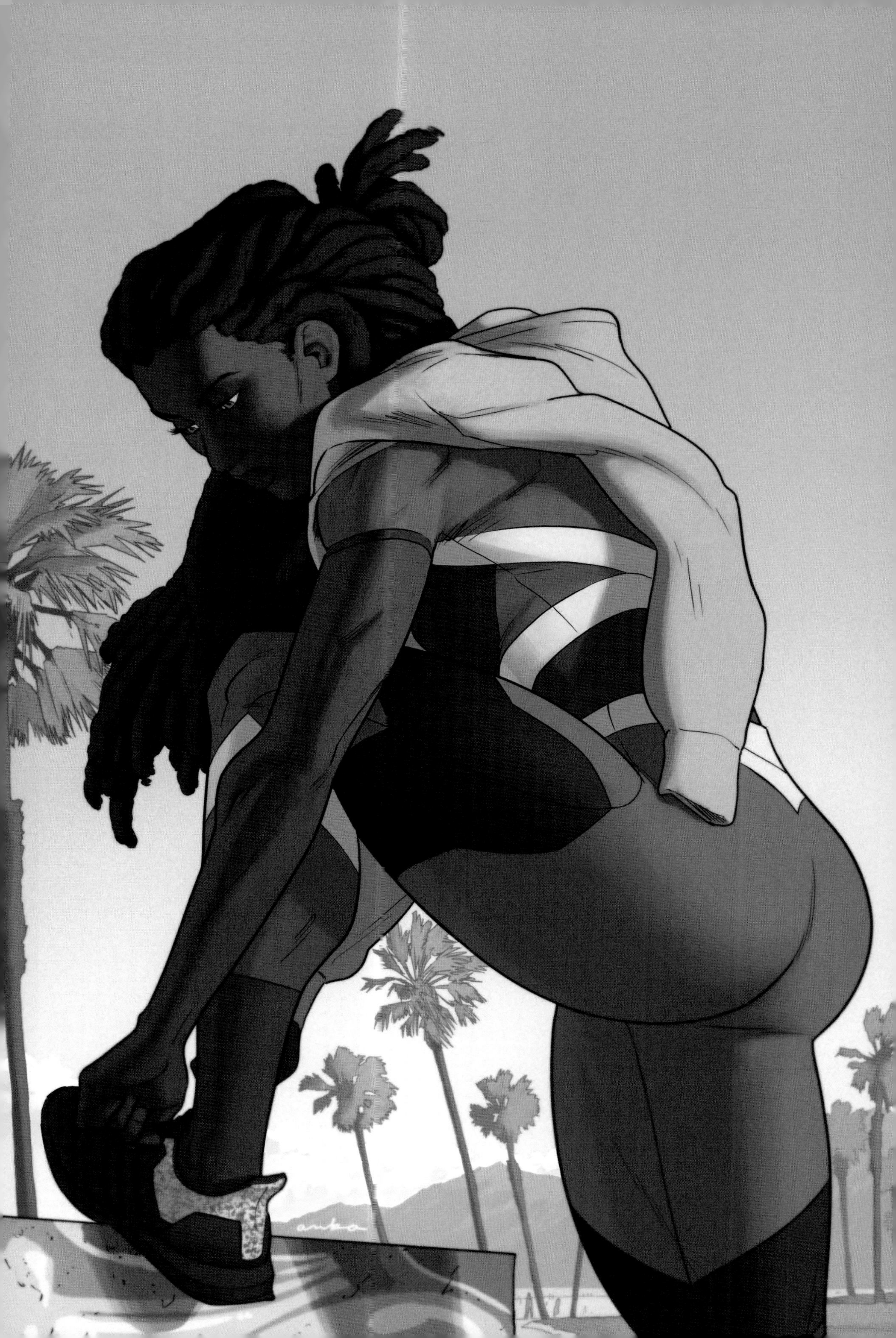

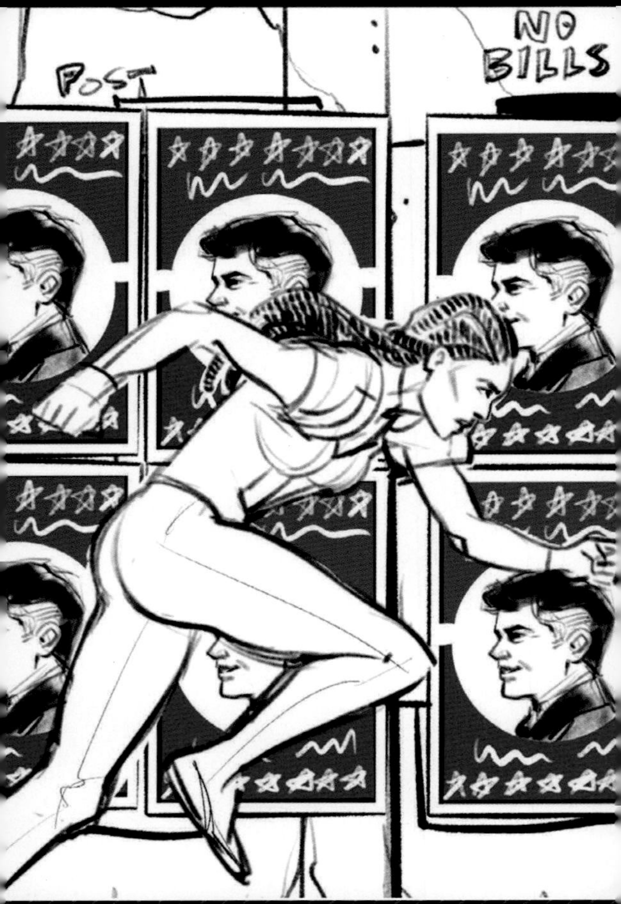
POST
NO BILLS
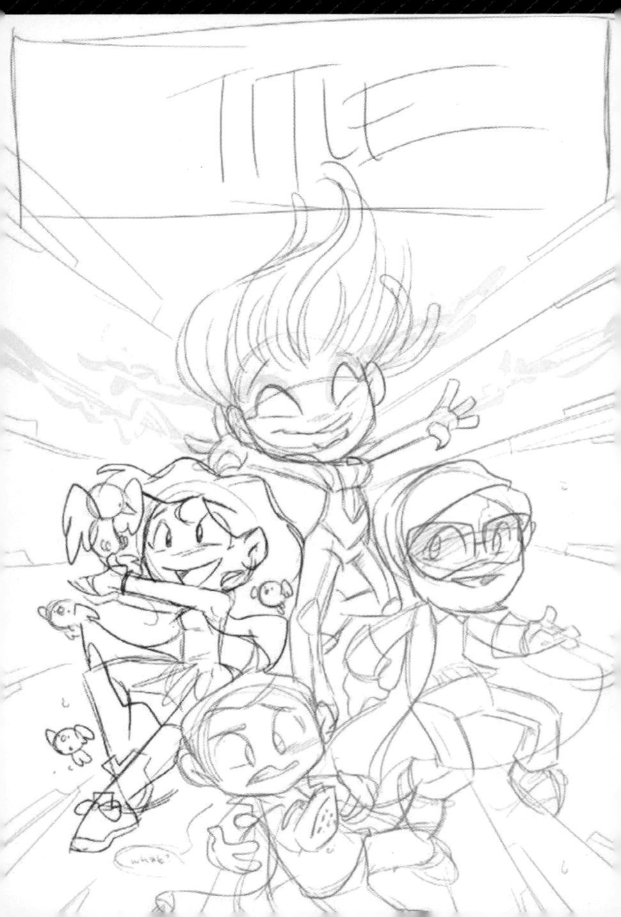
TITLE

LIVEWIRE — STREETWEAR
PRELIMINARY THUMBNAILS

IRENE KOH
APRIL 2019

(A) STOOP

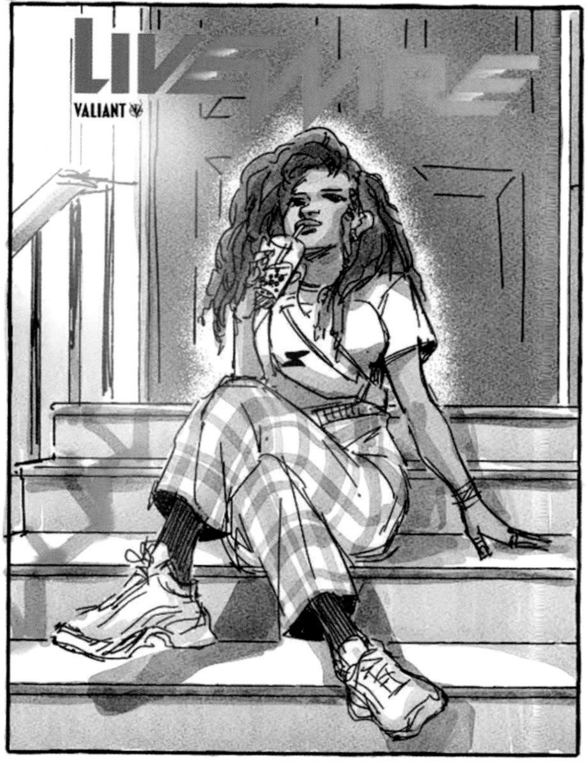
LIVEWIRE
VALIANT

(B) BACKLIT

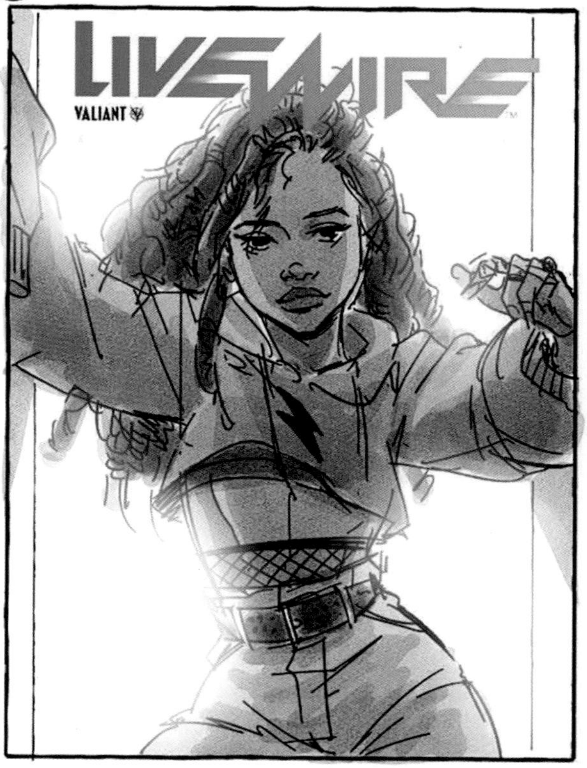
LIVEWIRE
VALIANT

(C) KNEEL

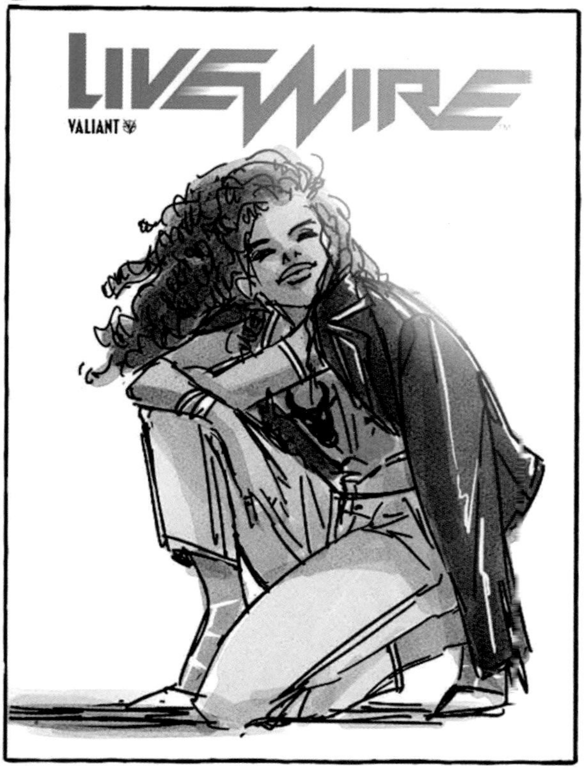
LIVEWIRE
VALIANT

(D) STREET

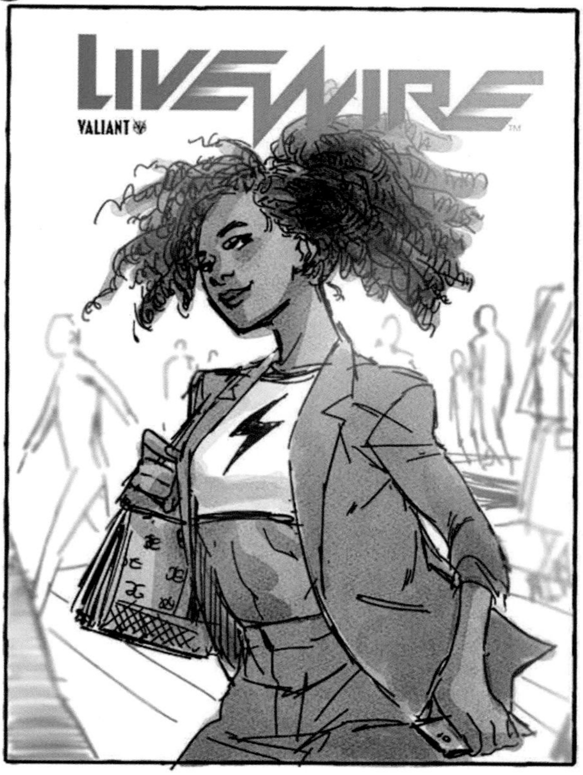
LIVEWIRE
VALIANT

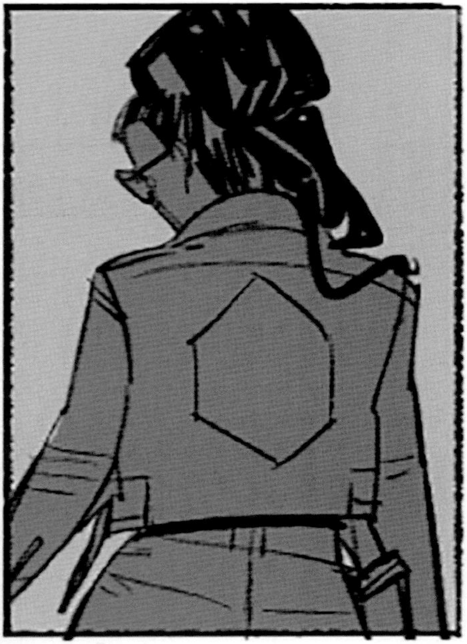

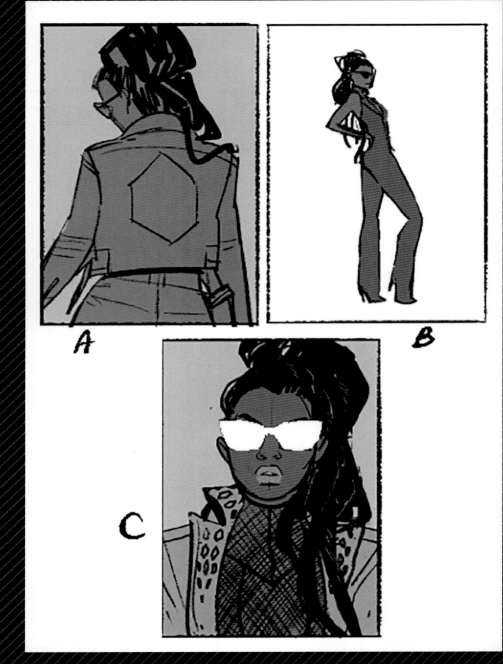

A

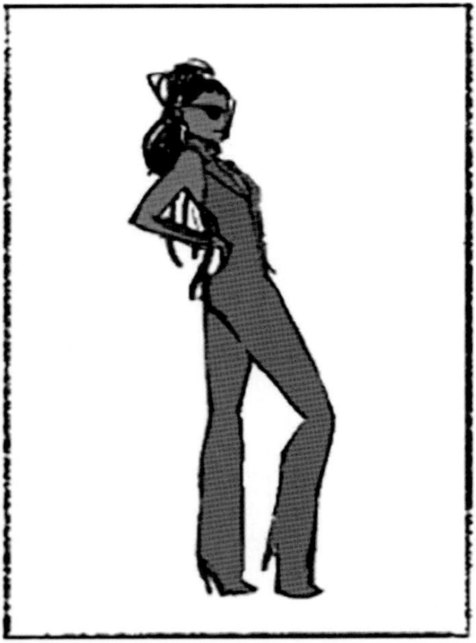

B

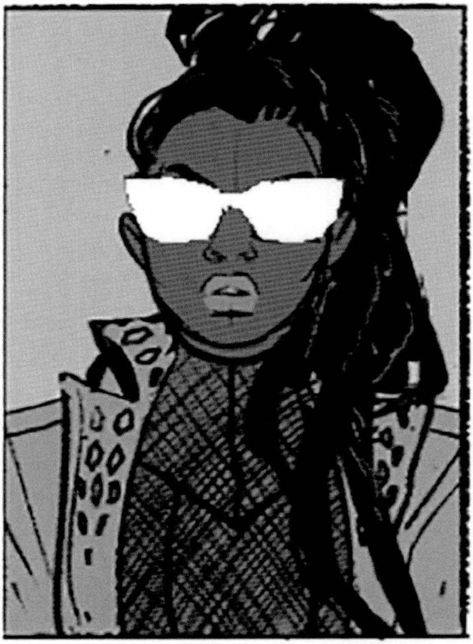

C

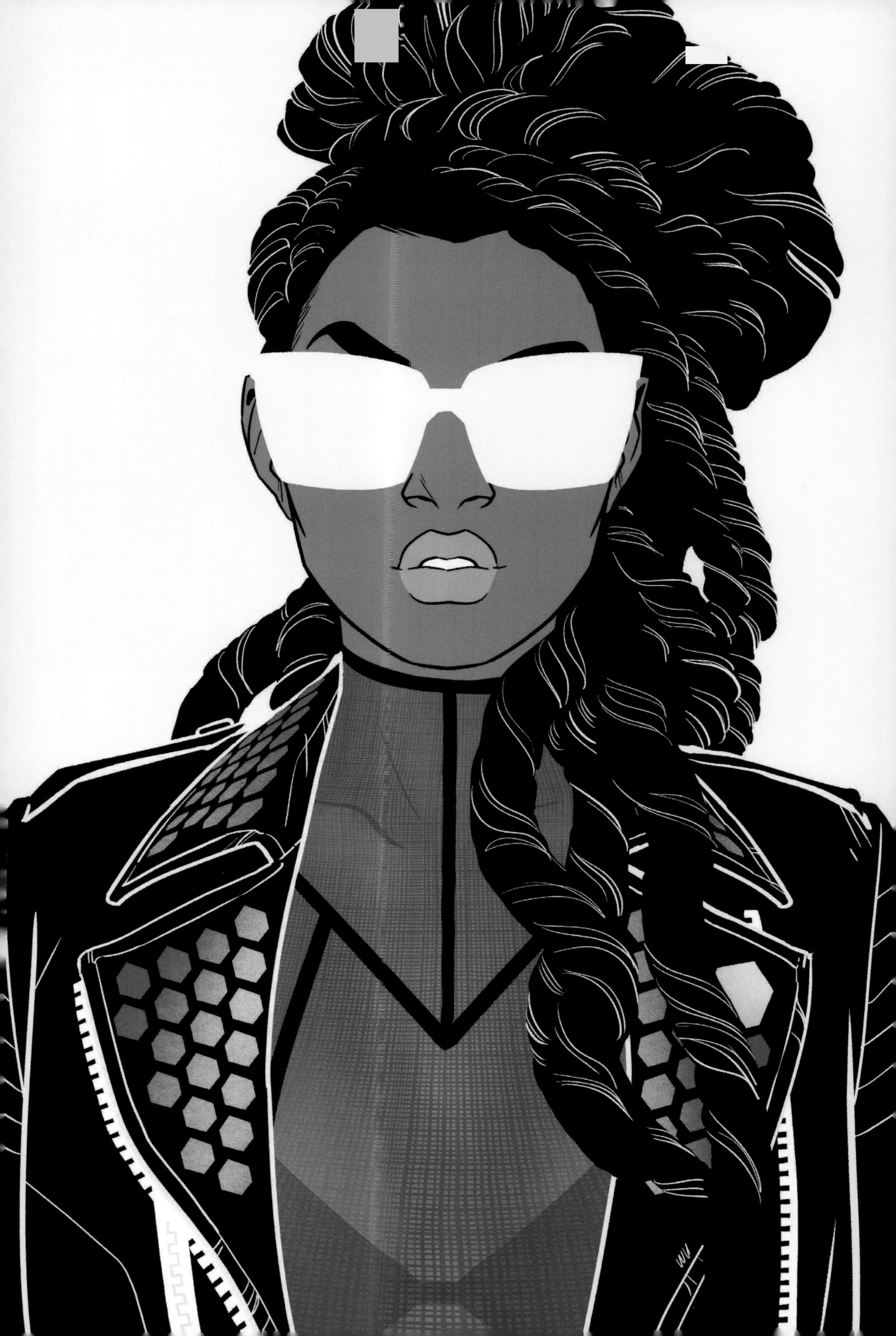

LIVEWIRE #9-12 FASHION VARIANT COVERS
Art by KRIS ANKA (#9), IRENE KOH (#10),
ANNIE WU (#11), and KEVIN WADA (#12)

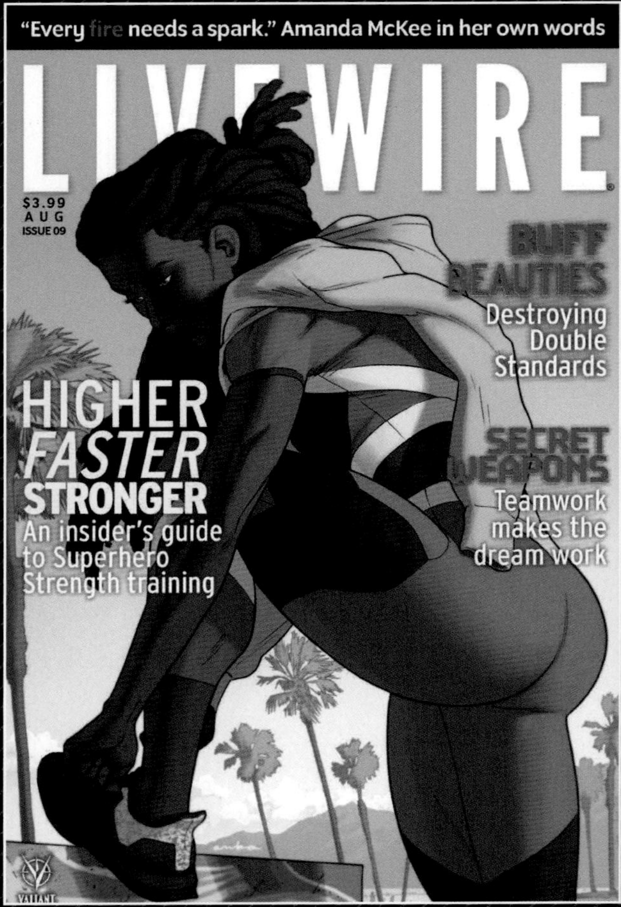
"Every fire needs a spark." Amanda McKee in her own words
LIVEWIRE
$3.99
AUG
ISSUE 09
BUFF BEAUTIES
Destroying Double Standards
HIGHER
FASTER
STRONGER
An insider's guide to Superhero Strength training
SECRET WEAPONS
Teamwork makes the dream work
VALIANT

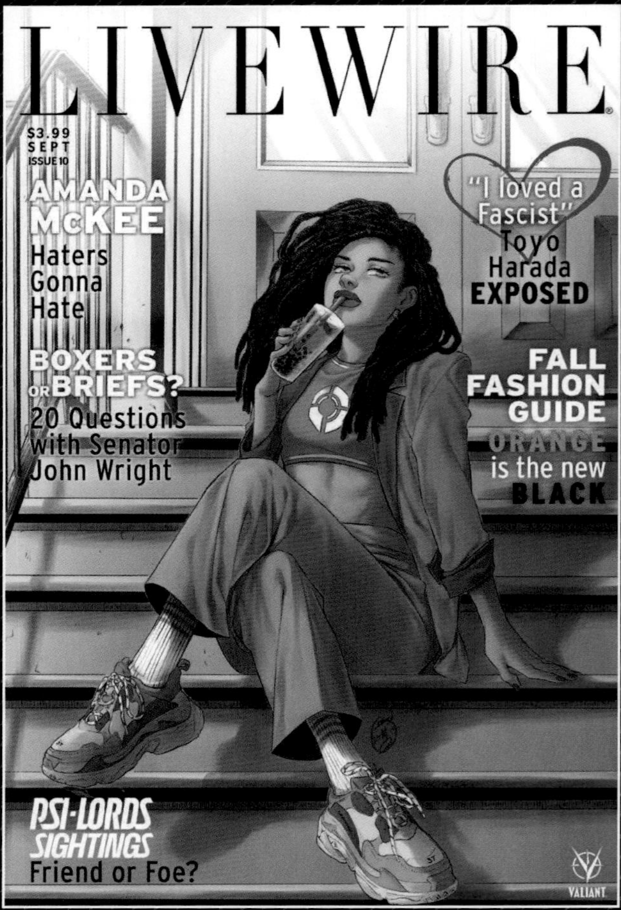
LIVEWIRE
$3.99
SEPT
ISSUE 10
AMANDA McKEE
Haters Gonna Hate
"I loved a Fascist"
Toyo Harada
EXPOSED
BOXERS OR BRIEFS?
20 Questions with Senator John Wright
FALL FASHION GUIDE
ORANGE is the new BLACK
PSI-LORDS SIGHTINGS
Friend or Foe?
VALIANT

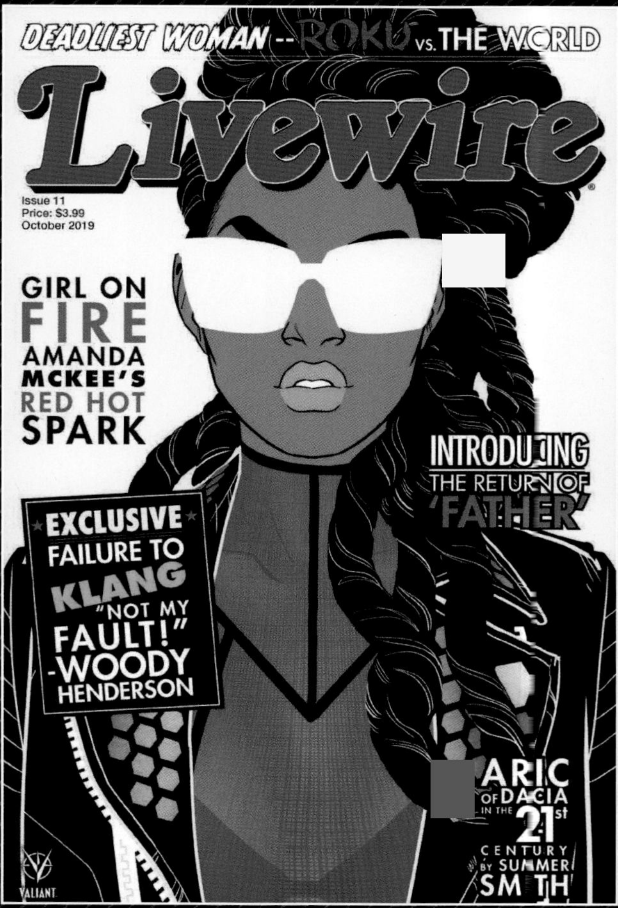
DEADLIEST WOMAN -- ROKU VS. THE WORLD
Livewire
Issue 11
Price: $3.99
October 2019
GIRL ON FIRE
AMANDA MCKEE'S RED HOT SPARK
INTRODUCING
THE RETURN OF 'FATHER'
EXCLUSIVE
FAILURE TO KLANG
"NOT MY FAULT!" -WOODY HENDERSON
ARIC OF DACIA IN THE 21st CENTURY
BY SUMMER SMITH
VALIANT

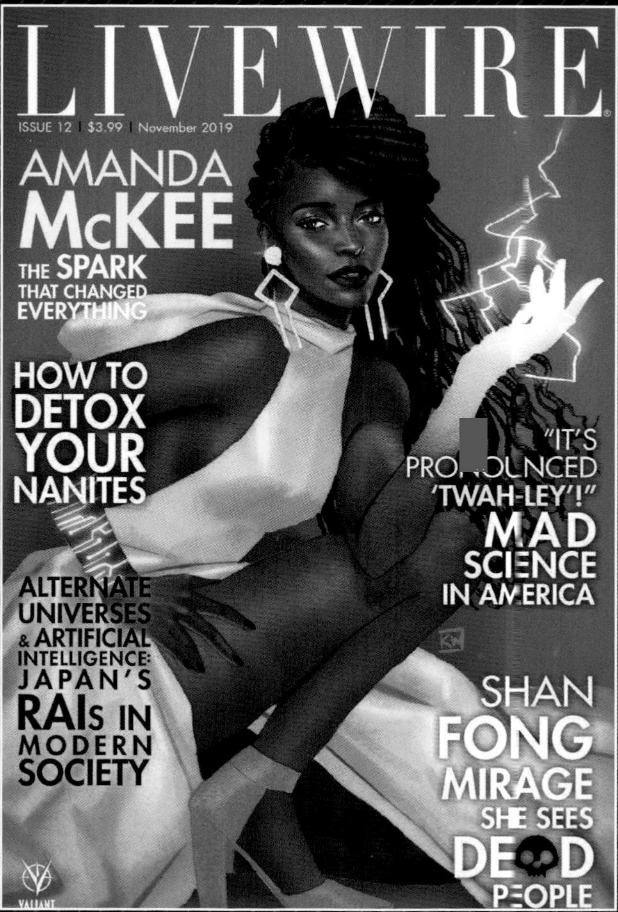
LIVEWIRE
ISSUE 12 | $3.99 | November 2019
AMANDA McKEE
THE SPARK THAT CHANGED EVERYTHING
HOW TO DETOX YOUR NANITES
"IT'S PRONOUNCED 'TWAH-LEY'!"
MAD SCIENCE IN AMERICA
ALTERNATE UNIVERSES & ARTIFICIAL INTELLIGENCE:
JAPAN'S RAIs IN MODERN SOCIETY
SHAN FONG
MIRAGE
SHE SEES DEAD PEOPLE
VALIANT

LIVEWIRE #12 FASHION VARIANT COVER
Thumbnail and final (page following) art by KEVIN WADA

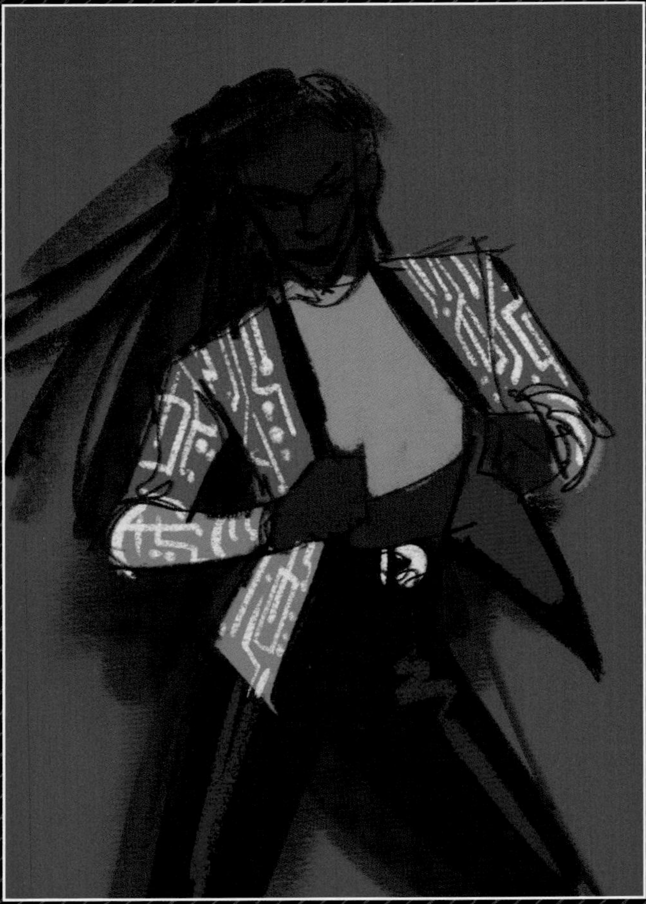

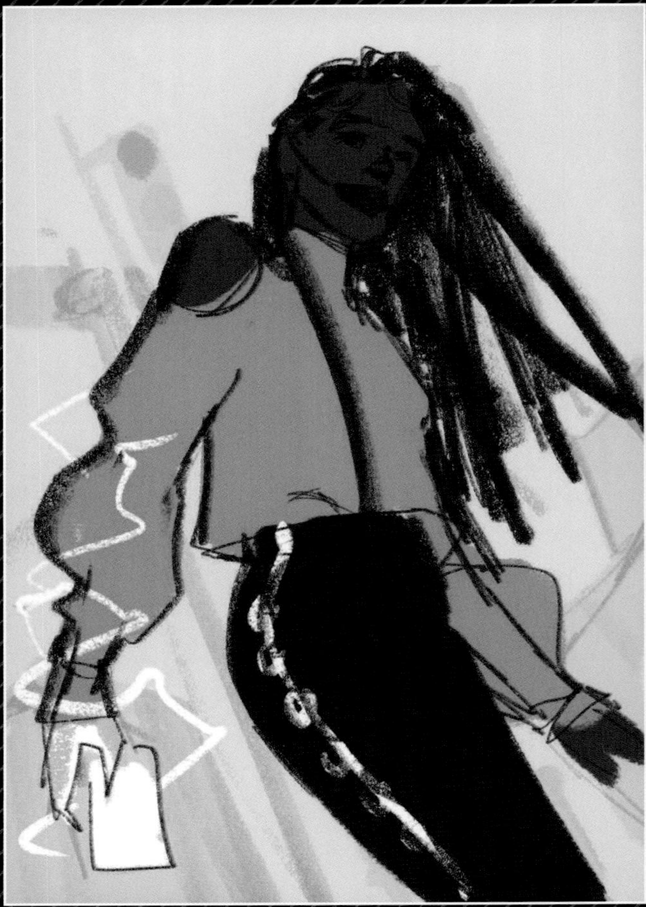

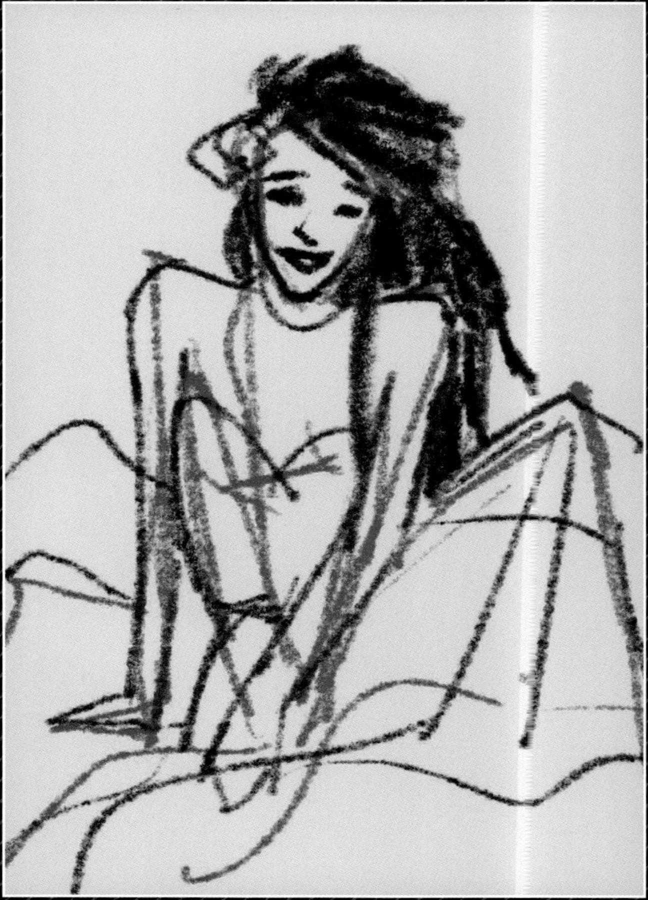

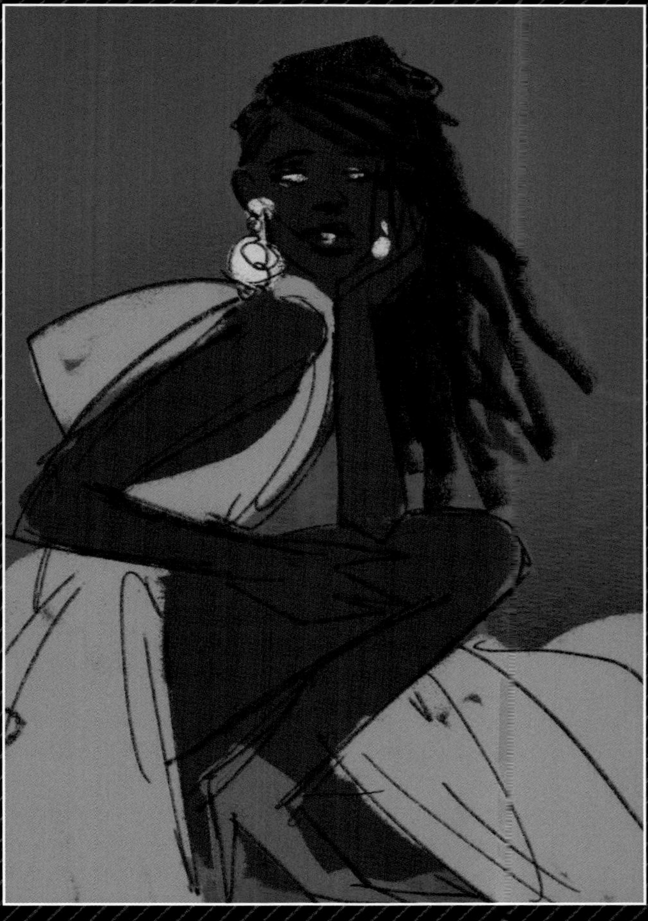

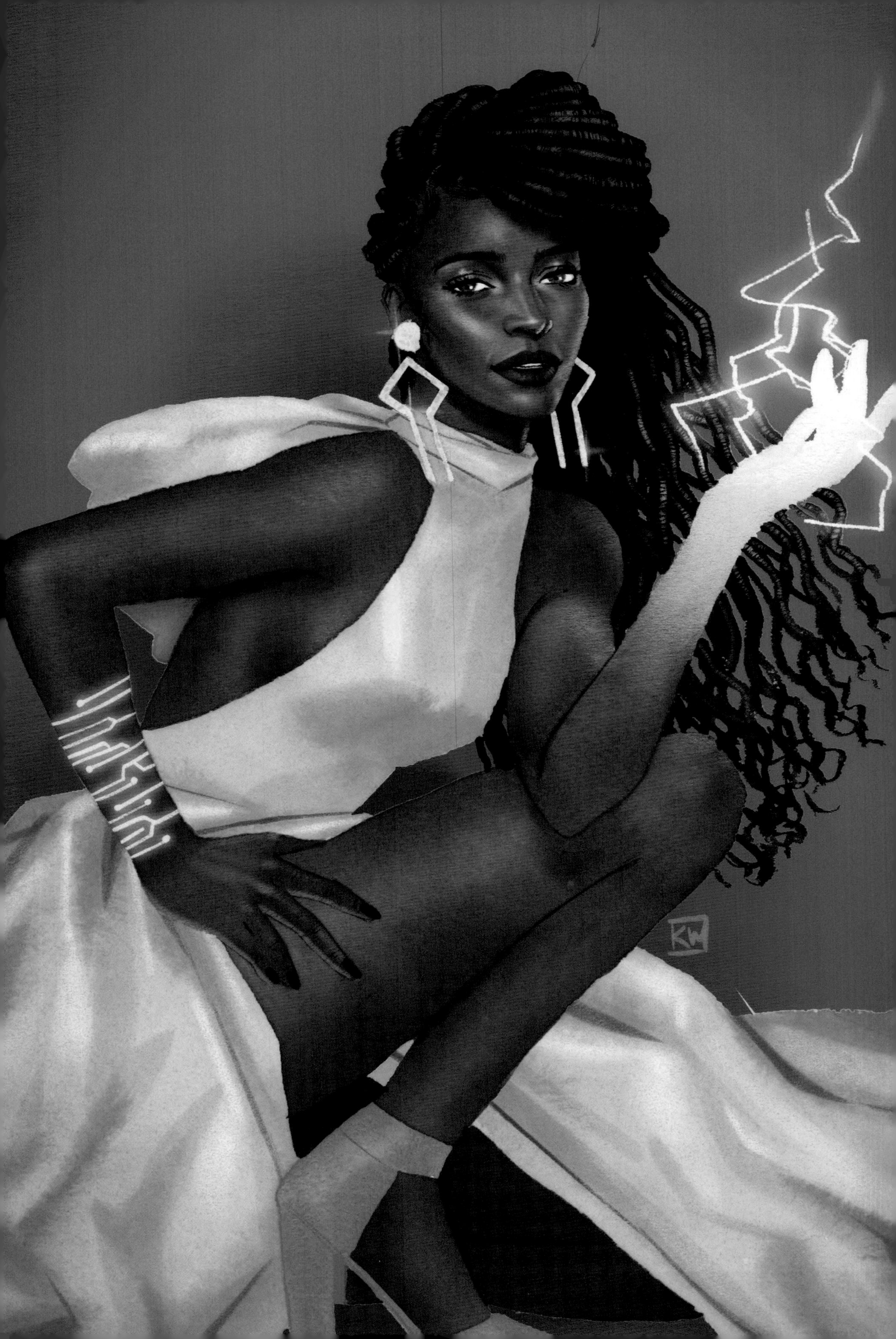